MW01169338

TOWNSEND PRESS
SUNDAY SCHOOL
COMMENTARY

International Bible Lessons

for Christian Teaching

1998-99

SEVENTY-EIGHTH EDITION

WRITER
Dr. William L. Banks

EDITOR
Rev. Ottie L. West

Published by
SUNDAY SCHOOL PUBLISHING BOARD
National Baptist Convention, U.S.A., Incorporated
Dr. E. L. Thomas, Executive Director

ACKNOWLEDGEMENTS

The publication of Christian literature is not an end in itself but is for the express purpose of providing enriching and educational materials for use among the various constituencies of the targeted community of readers. It is important that those who involve themselves in the process of production understand the task not in terms of the monetary rewards that accrue as a result of their labors, but develop self-concepts that embrace the consciousness of being God's instruments in the ministry of communication through the medium of the printed word. Hence, the participating persons in the total production process become that critical mass whose relationships to each other culminate in the finished product.

While we acknowledge the personal efforts of a coterie of individuals—writers, editors, typesetters, proofreaders, layout and technical personnel, as well as those in binding and mailing—the formation of a unity of purpose is not achieved by happenstance, but under the tutelage and motivation of a director whose devotion is contagious, and whose demand for quality is consistent with raising the standard beyond the norm to the level of excellence in a competitive world.

And so, we acknowledge the work of the Executive Director of the Sunday School Publishing Board, Dr. Earl L. Thomas, whose devotion has brought a new sense of purpose and dignity to the employees with the consciousness of concern in serving the needs of our constituencies. His business acumen has earned respect from the various vendors and providers of services with whom the Board interfaces, and most of all, our churches are assured that the timely delivery of their orders to serve their needs remains top priority.

Hence, all of the aforementioned persons constitute a consortium that extends grateful appreciation in acknowledging the commitment and contribution of Dr. Earl L. Thomas that undergirds this publication.

Ottie L. West
Editor in Chief

CYCLE OF 1998-2004
Arrangement of Quarters According to the
Church School Year, September through August

	1998-1999	1999-2000	2000-2001	2001-2002	2002-2003	2003-2004
Sep Oct Nov	God Calls a People to Faithful Living (Old Testament Survey) (13)	From Slavery to Conquest (Exodus, Leviticus, Numbers, Deuteronomy, Joshua) (13)	The Emerging Nation (Judges, 1, 2, Samuel [1 Chronicles], 1 Kings 1-11 [2 Chronicles 1-9]) (13)	Jesus' Ministry (Parables, Miracles Sermon on the Mount) (13)	Judgment and Exile (2 Kings 18-25 [2 Chronicles 29-36] Jeremiah, Lamentations, Ezekiel, Habakkuk, Zephaniah) (13)	Faith Faces the World (James, 1, 2, 2 Peter, 1, 2, 3, John, Jude) (13)
Dec Jan Feb	God Calls Anew in Jesus Christ (New Testament Survey) Christmas Sun. 12/20 (13)	Emmanuel: God With Us (Gospel of Matthew) Christmas Sun. 12/19 (13)	Good News of Jesus (Gospel of Luke) Christmas Sun. (12/24) (13)	Light for All People (Isaiah 9:1-7, 11:1-9; 40-66; Ruth, Jonah, Naham) Christmas Sun. 12/23 (13)	Portraits of Faith (Personalities in the New Testament) Christmas Sun. 12/22 (13)	A Child is Given (4) (Samuel, John the Baptist, Jesus [2]) Lessons from Life (9) (Esther, Job, Ecclesiastes, Song of Solomon) Christmas Sun. 12/21 (13)
Mar Apr May	That You May Believe (Gospel of John) Easter (4/4) (13)	Helping a Church Confront Crisis (1, 2, Corinthians) Easter (4/23) (13)	Continuing Jesus' Work (Acts) Easter (4/15) (13)	The Power of the Gospel (Romans, Galatians) Easter (3/31) (13)	Jesus: God's Power in Action (Gospel of Mark) Easter (4/20) (13)	Jesus Fulfills His Mission (6) (Passion Narratives) Living Expectantly (7) (1, 2 Thessalonians, Revelation) Easter (4/11)
Jun Jul Aug	Genesis: Beginnings (Genesis) (13)	New Life in Christ (Ephesians, Philippians, Colossians, Philemon) (13)	Division and Decline (1 Kings 1-17, [2 Chronicles 10-28], Isaiah 1-39, Amos, Hosea, Micah) (13)	Worship and Wisdom for Living (Psalms, Proverbs) (13)	God Restores a Remnant (Ezra, Nehemiah, Daniel, Joel, Obadiah, Haggai, Zechariah, Malachi) (14)	Hold Fast to the Faith (8) (Hebrews) Guidelines for the Church's Ministry (5) (1, 2 Timothy, Titus)

*Parenthetical numerals indicate number of sessions.

iv

PREFACE

The *Townsend Press Sunday School Commentary* on the International Sunday School Lessons is produced by the Sunday School Publishing Board of the National Baptist Convention, U.S.A., Inc. The contents herein are developed from curriculum guidelines by the Committee on the Uniform Series, Division of Education and Ministry, National Council of the Churches of Christ in the United States of America. Christian scholars and theologians who themselves affirm precepts, doctrines and positions of interpretation that are consistent with what we have come to believe use the subjects, selected texts and Biblical Content Emphases of the Uniform Series in the development, application and explanation of the historic faith that has been transmitted to us out of a rich heritage of worship and witness.

The format design of this Commentary consists of: The Unit Title, the general subject along with age-level topics, the Devotional Readings, the Scriptural Background pertaining to the lesson under consideration, the Printed Text with which the lesson is concerned, the objectives to be accomplished from the study of the lesson, the Topical Outline of the lesson, the Lesson Introduction intended to acclimate the reader to the context in which the lesson is discussed, Exposition and Application of the Scripture, and Special Features that address concerns indigenous to the experiences of our constituency with a Concluding Word that anticipates the Biblical Content Emphases, and the Home Daily Bible Readings designed to provide devotional continuity during the intervals of study.

The *Townsend Press Sunday School Commentary* is designed as an instructional aid for Christian Teachers, Sunday School Workers, Christian Educational Leaders, and others whose desire is to know more about God's Word. While our forte is the autonomy of the individual soul before God who is obliged to work out his/her own salvation, it is essential to recognize that the Truth contained in the Bible must be constantly related to the corporate experiences of the believing community that embraces those necessary correctives for those whose desire is to preserve the integrity of Biblical truth. Hence, the exposition and related materials presented in this Commentary have been derived from Biblical Texts that have been sanctioned within the community of faith that seek to grasp that which God has "said" and relate it to that which we "hear" or should understand as persons committed to do His Perfect will.

It goes without saying that where concepts and Scriptural texts do not lead themselves to meaningful comprehension by children, alternate passages of Scripture and content emphases are employed to assist them in their growth in spiritual understanding. As such, this Commentary is the centerpiece around which the age-level quarterlies are developed with the view to reach each person in his/her particular situation and bring/lead each toward a spiritual interaction with God's Word that will result in a transformed life.

It must be clearly understood that the historical situations with which we shall concern ourselves are not eclipsed by the past, but are in many ways consistent with the human situation of each generation. As we are created in the image of God, there is a structure of spiritual existence in the stride to study to show ourselves approved unto God. In this light, our study is not limited to the mere discovery of that which the Scriptures have to say, but also to the earnest desire to understand that which God has to say to us as we seek to become examples of His Word and will in the world.

INDEX OF PRINTED TEXT

The Printed Scriptural Texts used in the 1998-1999 Townsend Press Sunday School Commentary are arranged here in the order in which they appear in the Bible. Opposite each reference is the page number on which it appears in this Commentary Edition.

CONTENTS

Fall Quarter
God Calls a People to Faithful Living

Winter Quarter
God Calls Anew in Jesus Christ

Spring Quarter
That You May Believe

Summer Quarter
Genesis: Beginnings

FALL QUARTER

September, October, November 1998

GOD CALLS A PEOPLE TO FAITHFUL LIVING

General Introduction

During this quarter, the focus will be on a survey of the Old Testament with emphasis on pivotal events that give purpose and direction to the faith of Israel. Our study begins with the story of creation and traces the history of God's call to His people and their responses with both faithfulness and disobedience. Four units in this session recall that God created and saved this people; that they demonstrated faithfulness at times, but were disobedient at others; that they had prophets who warned them of the consequences of their disobedience; and that, finally, they drifted from God before eventually returning to Him.

Unit I, *"God Fashions a People,"* is a four lesson series that recounts the story of God's creative and saving acts beginning with the creation and concluding with the Children of Israel as inhabitants of the Promised Land.

Unit II, *"God Leads in Times of Change,"* highlights the response of the Children of Israel to God's action. Herein, it will be noted that despite the many and varied opportunities for Israel to live in a covenant relationship with God, the people elected to deport themselves in ways that alienated them from God, most graphically described as "sin." Their style of life consisted in alternating periods of faithfulness and disobedience as they failed to learn from the experiences of life. This in a sense verifies the statement that those who do not learn from history are doomed to repeat it.

Unit III, *"God Works Through People,"* consists of three sessions wherein is discussed the role of the prophets who warned the chosen people of their sins and the consequences that would ensue for their disobedience. The Prophets' messages of grace and judgment had their impact, but did not result in consistent fidelity of the people to God in spite of the assurance of God's dissatisfaction with their behavior. The concluding lesson in this unit examines Psalm 73 as an example of a confession of faith that had been tested under trying circumstances.

Unit IV, *"God Judges and Renews,"* discusses how the last-minute hope on the part of the people to be granted a reprieve is not realized, rather God exercises His judgment and they are sent back into slavery and foreign domination. Through it all, God does not abandon Israel, but in time, renews His covenant with them and restores the people as well as their worship.

As you assume the posture of personal interaction with individuals and events cited in these lessons, you will come to understand how there is an essential unity that binds faith and history as the one impacts and refines the other. It is important to remember that in a real sense, we share in the experiences of the biblical characters not only as beneficiaries of the blessings of God, but in our arrogance and disobedience. Through it all, God takes the initiative to bring us unto Himself in ways that are consistent with His will.

God is a God of purpose and plan who sets before humans His character as the guide for life. That which God expects is contained within His Word as we are grasped by the continuity of what God has done and what He will do as He works not only through the events of history, but also in the lives of those who are committed to His will. We shall see that God's judgment and discipline are both redemptive as they are conceived within the context of worship and praise. As we respond to God's call to faithfulness, we maximize our human potential as persons created in His image and likeness.

As you go forth in this quarter, there is high possibility that you will see yourself portrayed in ways that will deepen your self-understanding and bring you closer to that which God desires you to become. May you reap the fruits of your faithfulness.

God's Creation Marred by Sin

Unit 1—God Fashions a People
Children's Unit—Relating to God
Adult Topic—Humanity's Basic Problem

.....

Youth Topic—Sin! What's That?
Children's Topic—God Gives People Choices

.....

Devotional Reading—Romans 7:15-25a
Background Scripture—Genesis 3
Print—Genesis 3:1-13

• • • • • • • • • • •

PRINTED SCRIPTURE

Genesis 3:1-13 (KJV)

NOW the serpent was more subtil than any beast of the field which the LORD God had made. And he said unto the woman, Yea, hath God said, Ye shall not eat of every tree of the garden?

2 And the woman said unto the serpent, We may eat of the fruit of the trees of the garden:

3 But of the fruit of the tree which is in the midst of the garden, God hath said, Ye shall not eat of it, neither shall ye touch it, lest ye die.

4 And the serpent said unto the woman, Ye shall not surely die:

5 For God doth know that in the day ye eat thereof, then your eyes shall be opened, and ye shall be as gods, knowing good and evil.

6 And when the woman saw that the tree was good for food, and that it was pleasant to the eyes, and a tree to be desired to make one wise, she took of the fruit thereof, and did eat, and gave also unto her husband with her; and he did eat.

Genesis 3:1-13 (NRSV)

NOW THE serpent was more crafty than any other wild animal that the LORD God had made. He said to the woman, "Did God say, 'You shall not eat from any tree in the garden'?"

2 The woman said to the serpent, "We may eat of the fruit of the trees in the garden;

3 but God said, 'You shall not eat of the fruit of the tree that is in the middle of the garden, nor shall you touch it, or you shall die.' "

4 But the serpent said to the woman, "You will not die;

5 for God knows that when you eat of it your eyes will be opened, and you will be like God, knowing good and evil."

6 So when the woman saw that the tree was good for food, and that it was a delight to the eyes, and that the tree was to be desired to make one wise, she took of its fruit and ate; and she also gave some to her husband, who was with her, and he ate.

7 And the eyes of them both were opened, and they knew that they were naked; and they sewed fig leaves together, and made themselves aprons.

8 And they heard the voice of the LORD God walking in the garden in the cool of the day: and Adam and his wife hid themselves from the presence of the LORD God amongst the trees of the garden.

9 And the LORD God called unto Adam, and said unto him, Where art thou?

10 And he said, I heard thy voice in the garden, and I was afraid, because I was naked; and I hid myself.

11 And he said, Who told thee that thou wast naked? Hast thou eaten of the tree, whereof I commanded thee that thou shouldest not eat?

12 And the man said, The woman whom thou gavest to be with me, she gave me of the tree, and I did eat.

13 And the LORD God said unto the woman, What is this that thou hast done? And the woman said, The serpent beguiled me, and I did eat.

7 Then the eyes of both were opened, and they knew that they were naked; and they sewed fig leaves together and made loincloths for themselves.

8 They heard the sound of the LORD God walking in the garden at the time of the evening breeze, and the man and his wife hid themselves from the presence of the LORD God among the trees of the garden.

9 But the LORD God called to the man, and said to him, "Where are you?"

10 He said, "I heard the sound of you in the garden, and I was afraid, because I was naked; and I hid myself."

11 He said, "Who told you that you were naked? Have you eaten from the tree of which I commanded you not to eat?"

12 The man said, "The woman whom you gave to be with me, she gave me fruit from the tree, and I ate."

13 Then the LORD God said to the woman, "What is this that you have done?" The woman said, "The serpent tricked me, and I ate."

KEY VERSE

They heard the voice of the LORD God walking in the garden in the cool of the day: and Adam and his wife hid themselves from the presence of the LORD God amongst the trees of the garden.—Genesis 3:8

OBJECTIVES

After reading this lesson, the student should know that:
1. Humanity's basic problem is sin;
2. There is a malevolent, hateful creature called Satan who was instrumental in leading mankind in the initial disobedience to God's command; and,
3. As God sought the fallen Adam, so the Lord Jesus came to seek and to save the fallen children of Adam.

POINTS TO BE EMPHASIZED

Adult/Youth/Children
Key Verse: Genesis 3:8
Print: Genesis 3:1-13

—The serpent as tempter is introduced to the reader. (1)
—The woman told the serpent that God said the man and the woman were not to eat from the tree in the middle of the garden, for if they did so, they would die. (2-3)
—The woman found the forbidden fruit desirable, ate some of it, and gave some to the man to eat. (6)
—The eyes of the man and the woman were opened, so they made coverings to hide their nakedness. (7)
—The man and the woman hid themselves from the presence of God in the garden. (8)
—When confronted by God for their disobedience, the man and the woman began to blame others for their situation. (10-13)

(NOTE: Use KJV Scripture for Adults; NRSV Scripture for Youth and Children)

TOPICAL OUTLINE OF THE LESSON

I. Introduction
  A. Biblical Background
  B. A Literal Interpretation

II. Exposition and Application of the Scripture
  A. The Temptation (Genesis 3:1-5)
  B. The Fall (Genesis 3:6)
  C. The Conscience (Genesis 3:7)
  D. The Divine Inquest (Genesis 3:8-13)

III. Special Features
  A. Preserving Our Heritage
  B. A Concluding Word

I. Introduction

A. BIBLICAL BACKGROUND

We thought it best to say a word about Satan first, for we are mindful of the trick question, "Who created the devil?" The answer is: "No one. God created Lucifer who became the devil." Now when you read Genesis 3, you discover no specific mention is made of Satan. Yet, as we shall see, he is indeed behind the scenes. From the Old Testament, most of our information concerning the devil is garnered from Ezekiel 28:11-19, which describes the unfallen state of Satan; and from Isaiah 14:12-17, where we read of Lucifer's pride and fall. On the other hand, we learn from the New Testament that it is indeed Satan who speaks to Eve. The point is, there was a fall before the fall of man. It was the fall of Satan which occurred in the higher spiritual world, and involved angels who kept not their first estate (Jude 6; 2 Peter 2:4).

B. A LITERAL INTERPRETATION

Further explanation is due. Some scholars deny that the Genesis 3 account is historical. They say it is an allegory or symbolic representation. It is called a myth, a made-up story. It is therefore, we are told, not based on fact or reality, but is etiology— something invented to explain some religious belief. In our lesson, the purpose is to explain the origin of sin in mankind's experience. However, if there is no personal creature such as Satan, we are hard pressed to explain adequately the presence of evil in the world. If there were no individual human beings as Adam and Eve, then we cannot trust the Bible as the Word of a truthful God. Furthermore, the New Testament would be in error for assuming the historicity of the Genesis 3 account, if indeed it is but a myth. For example:

(1) Luke 3:38 traces Mary's genealogy back to Adam; (2) Paul speaks of death reigning from Adam to Moses (Romans 5:14). In the first man, Adam, all die (1 Corinthians 15:22, 45). See also 1 Timothy 2:13-14. The apostle very plainly states: "the serpent beguiled Eve" (2 Corinthians 11:3); and (3) Jude 14 also mentions Adam as an historical character. Our conclusion: We see nothing to be gained by denying the literal, historical Adam, Eve, and the serpent in Genesis 3. Further, beyond the question of the historical Adam, every human being replicates the experience of Adam and Eve in disobeying God—and this is a fact throughout the history of the human race.

II. Exposition and Application of the Scripture

A. THE TEMPTATION
(Genesis 3:1-5)

NOW the serpent was more subtil than any beast of the field which the LORD God had made. And he said unto the woman, Yea, hath God said, Ye shall not eat of every tree of the garden? And the woman said unto the serpent, We may eat of the fruit of the trees of the garden: But of the fruit of the tree which is in the midst of the garden, God hath said, Ye shall not eat of it, neither shall ye touch it, lest ye die. And the serpent said unto the woman, Ye shall not surely die: For God doth know that in the day ye eat thereof, then your eyes shall be opened, and ye shall be as gods, knowing good and evil.

Apparently, the serpent as originally created by God was not a reptile slithering or twisting on the ground, for later when cursed (Genesis 3:14), he is made to crawl upon his belly. The Hebrew word translated "serpent" is **nachash,** and there is the suggestion it has a root meaning to hiss. Some scholars say **nachash** means "shining one," but this may be due to the fact that the Hebrew word

nachash "is almost identical to the word for bronze or copper" *(Theological Word-book of the Old Testament).* This is interesting because the word Lucifer also means "shining one." No mention is made of the serpent in the first two chapters of Genesis, although we assume snakes were among the beasts Adam named in Genesis 2:19-20. Even so, his sudden appearance catches us off guard. The first description given concerns his subtlety; he was shrewd, prudent, clever, keen. Hear our Lord exhort the disciples, "be wise as serpents" (Matthew 10:16). In our lesson, the word "subtle" is used in a bad sense, and points to the serpent as a tool in Satan's hands, a beast that is crafty, deceitful.

The serpent's evil cleverness is seen in his approaching the woman first, rather than going first to Adam. His craftiness is also evident in the way he went about his deception. It does not appear that Eve was shocked that a beast should speak. We know that God caused a donkey to speak and save Balaam's life; now we see that Satan used a snake as his mouthpiece. Why Eve did not turn away from the creature is not known. Perhaps she was intrigued to hear its voice, surely not even knowing that a malevolent being, envious of mankind, and full of hatred, even existed. The devil was successful in his disguise, and deceived the first woman. What Eve did know, however, was that the Lord had commanded them not to eat of the tree of the knowledge of good and evil (Genesis 2:17).

Note Satan's immediate attack upon God's Word—"has God said?" Doubt and denial were introduced. The very question assumes that man is in a position to judge the Word of God. Furthermore, the question hints at an unfair strictness divinely imposed. "Surely God is holding back something from you," insinuated Satan. He thus cast suspicion upon God's goodness. And instead of turning away from the serpent, Eve fell for the bait, and engaged in dialogue with him. She listened to the creature instead of the Creator, and the suggested suspicion took root.

Eve admitted that God commanded them not to eat of the tree in the middle of the garden. But she added to the prohibition, "neither shall you touch it," thus betraying her own thoughts that God was unduly strict. However, it could be that "to touch" simply means to make it your own, another way of saying, consume. At this point, the Adversary told an awful lie: "You shall not surely die!" The doctrine of judgment is denied. Still today, people deny the facts of Hell and eternal punishment. They deny the inevitability of judgment; they preach their home-made brand of universalism. Satan went so far as to attribute God's threat of death as false, motivated by God's jealousy. This is an interesting accusation inasmuch as Satan is the one who is jealous and envious of human beings! The fact is, men do die! It is true that Adam and Eve did not immediately drop dead physically. But there was an immediate separation inwardly; and this eventually led to physical death. You see why the Lord Jesus called the devil "a murderer from the beginning" (John 8:44). Yea, "by one man's offense death reigned..." (Romans 5:17).

Finally, in verse 5, the serpent accused God of withholding good because He fears His creatures will achieve heights He has reserved for Himself. How ridiculous! Men cannot become God! God is! Always was, always shall be. Furthermore, Satan accused men of wanting the very thing he himself desires, for we hear him say, "I will be like the Most High!" (Isaiah 14:14). It is true that the word "Elohim" is plural and may be rendered "gods," but it is better translated here, "You shall be as God."

B. THE FALL
(Genesis 3:6)

And when the woman saw that the tree was good for food, and that it was pleasant to the eyes, and a tree to be desired to make one wise, she took of the fruit thereof, and did eat, and gave also unto her husband with her, and he did eat.

The Fall is a theological term for Adam's sin of disobeying God by eating the forbidden fruit in the Garden of Eden, and the consequent loss of innocence and grace by all of his descendants (*American Heritage Dictionary*). A very important aspect of what happened here is the place of the eye gaze! Eve saw that the tree was good for food. Her eyes led her into the first temptation, the lust of the flesh. Here was the appeal to the appetite. Her eyes led her then to consider the tree was pleasant to look upon. The pride of life is seen in the realization that the tree was desirable for acquiring wisdom. Altogether, we see the unfolding of 1 John 2:16: "For all that is in the world, the lust of the flesh, and the lust of the eyes, and the pride of life, is not of the Father, but is of the world." Eve saw. Lot lifted up his eyes, and beheld all the plain of Jordan, chose it, and soon found himself living in Sodom (Genesis 13:10). Samson saw a woman in Timnah, of the daughters of the hated Philistines, and sought her for his wife. At Gaza, he saw a prostitute, and went in unto her (Judges 14.1; 16.1)—and who knows what happened when he first saw Delilah! David saw Bathsheba, desired her, took her, and committed adultery (2 Samuel 11:2). The eye gaze is extremely important in the matter of temptation.

Again, see the steps of the Fall. Earlier, the seed was planted by Satan through doubting God's Word. Eve saw, she desired, she took, she ate. The last step involves getting Adam to sin. There is no such thing as a private sin, although we have heard people say, "I'm not hurting anybody but myself!" Sin blinds them to the fact of sin's nature to devour, to spread its slimy tentacles, to pollute everything it can. Every sin affects someone else! Eve offered the forbidden fruit to Adam, "and he did eat." Thus, both Adam and Eve sinned. However, Eve was deceived; she was fooled by Satan.

But Adam wilfully disobeyed. Paul brings this out in his discussion in 1 Timothy 2:14: "And Adam was not deceived, but the woman, being deceived, was in the transgression." Adam is held responsible because he was created first, and charged with the responsibility of leadership. And because of Adam's sin, the entire human race is affected: "Wherefore, as by one man sin entered into the world, and death by sin, and so death passed upon all men, for all have sinned" (Romans 5:12).

C. THE CONSCIENCE
(Genesis 3:7)

And the eyes of them both were opened, and they knew that they were naked; and they sewed fig leaves together, and made themselves aprons.

Satan was correct in stating, "Your eyes shall be opened" (verse 5). Opened eyes imply the ability to discern, to look into things otherwise not perceived. As usual, the devil's deceit involves "an inextricable tangle of truth and falsehood" (Leupold). Wisdom was acquired at the expense of suffering from the vainglory of life. The opening of the eyes here does not refer to physical eyes, but to the conscience, knowing good and evil.

We still try to hide or cover up the dirt we do with the fig leaves of good works. "Sin's proper fruit is shame" (Kidner). The first effect we notice is shame. They knew that they were naked, indicating a guilty conscience; so they sought to conceal their nakedness.

D. THE DIVINE INQUEST
(Genesis 3.8-13)

And they heard the voice of the LORD God walking in the garden in the cool of the day: and Adam and his wife hid themselves from the presence of the LORD God amongst the trees of the garden. And the LORD God called unto Adam, and said unto him, Where art thou? And he said, I heard thy voice in the garden, and I was afraid, because I was naked; and I hid myself. And he said, Who told thee that thou wast naked? Hast thou eaten of the tree, whereof I commanded thee that thou shouldest not eat? And the man said, The woman whom thou gavest to be with me, she gave me of the tree, and I did eat. And the LORD God said unto the woman, What is this that thou hast done? And the woman said, The serpent beguilded me, and I did eat.

At the time of the breeze of the day ("the cool of the day") means at the close of day. So it is evening time. Adam and Eve heard the Lord God walking in the garden and hid themselves from God's presence. Not really, for this is an impossibility. The God of the Bible is everywhere. His omnipresence is spelled out by David in Psalm 139:7-8: "Whither shall I go from thy Spirit? Or whither shall I flee from thy presence? If I ascend up into heaven, thou art there; if I make my bed in hell, behold, thou art there."

Their shame soon became fear. They no longer cherished communion with God. What is true of the fallen first parents is true of all their children. Instead of running to God, we run from Him. This is why in mercy He seeks us, for it is still true today that no man seeks after God (Romans 3:11). The initiative is God's, and so He called unto Adam. He did not call Eve first; Adam was interrogated first because the man had been put in charge. Why does God ask questions? Rest assured that it is not because He seeks information, or is ignorant. He knows all things: past, present and future. One purpose of the Divine Inquest is to give man the opportunity to confess, to come clean. God's first word then is a question calculated to help the sinner.

In closing our exposition, let's look at each of the four questions directed to Adam and Eve. Nothing is said to the devil, for his wicked motives are clear. Satan did what was expected of him. Calvin said: "The beast (the serpent) had no sense of sin, and the devil no hope of pardon." (1) "Where are you?" There is no reply, "Here am I," as from Abraham (Genesis 22:11), Moses (Exodus 3:4), Samuel (1 Samuel 3:4-8), Isaiah (6:8), or Ananias (Acts 9:10). Instead, Adam acknowledged that he heard the Lord's voice. He admitted his fear, basing that fear on being naked. He would have been more accurate to have based his fear on his disobedience. And he also admitted his attempt to hide from God; (2) Again to Adam: "Who told you that you were naked?" It appears that Adam was more concerned about his nakedness and shame than he was about his disobedience of God's plain command. God's question sought to stir up in Adam the sense of sin itself; (3) The cross-examination of Adam continues: "Have you eaten of the tree, whereof I told you not to eat?" At this juncture, Adam threw the blame directly upon Eve, and indirectly upon God who gave Eve to him; and, (4) The last question is directed to Eve: "What is this that you have done?" And Eve placed the blame directly upon the serpent: "He beguiled me, and I did eat." And yet, while shunting off the responsibility for her disobedience to the deceptive serpent, Eve indirectly charged the Creator for allowing the serpent to cross her path.

III. Special Features

A. PRESERVING OUR HERITAGE

Satan's attack on the Bible continues. Today God's Word is challenged by those who are devoted to other religions. As more and more Black Americans turn to other faiths, louder becomes the lie that Christianity is a White man's religion. The Scriptures repeatedly state that the God of the Bible is no respecter of persons or receiver of races. God so loved the world that He gave His only begotten Son, the Lord Jesus Christ, to die on the cross in our place. "Whosoever will" is still the all-inclusive clarion call!

Black Baptists need to maintain their reputation as "People of the Book." And remember that no other book or alleged sacred text can compare with the Bible. The Bible is composed of sixth-six books, written by forty different authors moved by the Holy Spirit. Three languages are involved (Hebrew, Aramaic and Greek). And the Bible was written on three continents (Africa, Asia and Europe) over a span of some 1,500 years. There are those who claim other writings as the heart of their belief, but Christians cast their lot with the Scriptures of the Canon.

There is no salvation apart from faith in Jesus Christ, for we are not saved by works of almsgiving, fasting, or praying. Furthermore, Jesus Christ is alive forevermore. Christ calls us to a life of love, not a religion of hatred and slavery based upon a lie" *(Hammond, Chalcedon Report, p. 23).*

B. A CONCLUDING WORD

Today's lesson is found in "the most tragic chapter in the Bible" Genesis, chapter three (Leupold). We are given the facts how sin and evil entered the world of mankind. By his own disobedience, man fell and dragged down with him his posterity. Fortunately, even as God sought Adam, even so the Son of Man has come to seek and to save that which was lost. Through faith in Christ's shed blood, the image of God, distorted and marred because of sin, is restored.

As we reflect upon the powerful message embedded within the experience of Adam and Eve in the Garden of Eden, it is not difficult to perceive ourselves portrayed therein. How often do we evade personal responsibility for our actions and blame others for our behavior? The truth about who we are is more insightful than history per se because it is through history that the truth about ourselves is revealed.

As the story goes, God, having placed humans in a perfect situation as symbolized by their residence in the Garden, gave to man and woman the freedom to act. Notice that their free moral choice is the prerequisite for responsible behavior. These persons' very first act was to test the nature of their God-given freedom, and in the process lost it. The point is that in real life, freedom is not actualized until it is tested, and once tested, the decisive moment becomes irrevocable. This is not only a word of caution for the very young alone, but words of advice for those of mature years. We are free to act or make decisions about our deportment within a given situation, but history itself points out the wisdom or folly of our ways. How else could Adam and Eve lose it all in the process of attempting to test God's Word rather than trust God's Word? It may be remembered that the child who trusts the parent's direction for life as it is understood within the context of the Bible has a better chance of growing up in the fear and admonition of the Lord than the child who must test and verify the validity of all advice. Notice that the desperate effort on the part of Adam and Eve to "pass the buck" did not eclipse personal responsibility. There is a difference between the reason for our action, and the responsibility for our action. As free persons, other individuals cannot "make" us do anything, we act out of desire or weakness, or we refuse to perform a given act out of our strength of character.

HOME DAILY BIBLE READINGS
Week of September 6, 1998
God's Creation Marred By Sin

Aug. 31 M. Genesis 3:1-7, The Serpent as Tempter
Sept. 1 T. Genesis 3:8-13, Disobedience Brings Fears
Sept. 2 W. Genesis 3:14-19, Disobedience Has Consequences
Sept. 3 T. Genesis 3:20-24, Expulsion from the Garden
Sept. 4 F. Romans 7:15-25a, Who Will Rescue Me...?
Sept. 5 S. Romans 8:1-11, No Condemnation...
Sept. 6 S. 1 Corinthians 15:12-22, Alive in Christ

Celebrate:
God Delivers a People from Slavery

Adult Topic—Freedom Is a Gift

.....

Youth Topic—Free at Last
Children's Topic—God Gives the People Freedom

.....

Devotional Reading—Psalm 105:37-45
Background Scripture—Exodus 2:23-25; 5:1-2; 11:1-8; 12:29-32; 15:1-2, 19-21
Print—Exodus 2:23-25; 5:1-2; 12:29-32; 15:1-2

● ● ● ● ● ● ● ● ● ● ●

PRINTED SCRIPTURE

Exodus 2:23-25; 5:1-2; 12:29-32; 15:1-2 (KJV)

23 And it came to pass in process of time, that the king of Egypt died: and the children of Israel sighed by reason of the bondage, and they cried, and their cry came up unto God by reason of the bondage.

24 And God heard their groaning, and God remembered his covenant with Abraham, with Isaac, and with Jacob.

25 And God looked upon the children of Israel, and God had respect unto them.

.....

AND afterward Moses and Aaron went in, and told Pharaoh, Thus saith the LORD God of Israel, Let my people go, that they may hold a feast unto me in the wilderness.

2 And Pharaoh said, Who is the LORD, that I should obey his voice to let Israel go? I know not the LORD, neither will I let Israel go.

Exodus 2:23-25; 5:1-2; 12:29-32; 15:1-2, (NRSV)

23 After a long time the king of Egypt died. The Israelites groaned under their slavery, and cried out. Out of the slavery their cry for help rose up to God.

24 God heard their groaning, and God remembered his covenant with Abraham, Isaac, and Jacob.

25 God looked upon the Israelites, and God took notice of them.

.....

AFTERWARD MOSES and Aaron went to Pharaoh and said, "Thus says the LORD, the God of Israel, 'Let my people go, so that they may celebrate a festival to me in the wilderness.'"

2 But Pharaoh said, "Who is the LORD, that I should heed him and let Israel go? I do not know the LORD, and I will not let Israel go."

29 And it came to pass, that at midnight the LORD smote all the firstborn in the land of Egypt, from the firstborn of Pharaoh that sat on his throne unto the firstborn of the captive that was in the dungeon; and all the firstborn of cattle.

30 And Pharaoh rose up in the night, he, and all his servants, and all the Egyptians; and there was a great cry in Egypt; for there was not a house where there was not one dead.

31 And he called for Moses and Aaron by night, and said, Rise up, and get you forth from among my people, both ye and the children of Israel; and go, serve the LORD, as ye have said.

32 Also take your flocks and your herds, as ye have said, and be gone; and bless me also.

.....

THEN sang Moses and the children of Israel this song unto the LORD, and spake, saying, I will sing unto the LORD, for he hath triumphed gloriously: the horse and his rider hath he thrown into the sea.

2 The LORD is my strength and song, and he is become my salvation: he is my God, and I will prepare him an habitation; my father's God, and I will exalt him.

.....

29 At midnight the LORD struck down all the firstborn in the land of Egypt, from the firstborn of Pharaoh who sat on his throne to the firstborn of the prisoner who was in the dungeon, and all the firstborn of the livestock.

30 Pharaoh arose in the night, he and all his officials and all the Egyptians; and there was a loud cry in Egypt, for there was not a house without someone dead.

31 Then he summoned Moses and Aaron in the night, and said, "Rise up, go away from my people, both you and the Israelites! Go, worship the LORD, as you said.

32 Take your flocks and your herds, as you said, and be gone. And bring a blessing on me too!"

.....

THEN MOSES and the Israelites sang this song to the LORD: "I will sing to the LORD: for he has triumphed gloriously; horse and rider he has thrown into the sea.

2 The LORD is my strength and my might, and he has become my salvation; this is my God, and I will praise him, my father's God, and I will exalt him.

KEY VERSE

And it came to pass in process of time, that the king of Egypt died: and the children of Israel sighed by reason of the bondage, and they cried, and their cry came up unto God by reason of the bondage. And God heard their groaning, and God remembered his covenant with Abraham, with Isaac; and with Jacob.—Exodus 2:23-24

OBJECTIVES

After reading this lesson, the student should be informed about:

1. The compassion of God for His Covenant people, Israel;
2. Judgment: How the God of the Bible deals with the hard-hearted; and,
3. The joy of deliverance

POINTS TO BE EMPHASIZED

Adult/Youth/Children
Key Verse: Exodus 2:23-24; Exodus 15:1 (Children)
Print: Exodus 2:23-25; 5:1-2; 12:29-32; 15:1-2

—The Israelites groaned under their Egyptian slavery. (2:23)

—God heard their cry, remembered the covenant, and took notice of the people. (2:24-25)

—Through Moses and Aaron, the Lord told Pharaoh to let the Children of Israel go into the wilderness to celebrate a festival to the Lord, but Pharaoh refused. (5:1-2)

—After the tenth plague, the death of the Egyptians' firstborn, Pharaoh told Moses and Aaron to take the Children of Israel and leave. (12:29-32)

—After the Lord delivered the Israelites at the Red Sea, Moses and the Israelites sang a song of praise to the Lord. (15:1-2)

(NOTE: Use KJV Scripture for Adults; NRSV Scripture for Youth and Children)

TOPICAL OUTLINE OF THE LESSON

I Introduction

A. A Perception of History
B. Biblical Background

II. Exposition and Application of the Scripture

A. God's Pity Upon Israel (Exodus 2:23-25)
B. Pharaoh's Contempt For Israel's God (Exodus 5:1-2)
C. God's Judgment Upon Egypt (Exodus 12:29-32)
D. Israel's Song of Redemption (Exodus 15:1-2)

III. Special Features

A. Preserving Our Heritage
B. A Concluding Word

I. Introduction

A. A PERCEPTION OF HISTORY

What occurred historically in today's lesson was predicted in Abram's day. God said to Abram: "Know of a surety that thy seed shall be a sojourner in a land that is not theirs, and shall serve them; and they shall afflict them four hundred years; and also that nation, whom they shall serve, will I judge; and afterward shall they come out with great substance" (Genesis 15:13-14). Incidentally, the 400 years in Genesis 15:13 refer to the time of harsh affliction; the 430 years mentioned in Exodus 12:40-41 refer to the total time of sojourning, the entire time spent in Egypt without settling down.

The Book of Exodus gives us the record of the fulfillment of this prediction. Now scholars are not sure of the date for the exodus event. This is partly because the word "Pharaoh" is an official title that was given to all of the Egyptian kings. One estimate has the beginning of the oppression of the Jews in Egypt occurring about 1550 B.C. This leaves the suggested date of 1447 B.C. for the Exodus, according to the Scofield Reference Bible; about 1491 B.C., according to the Pilgrim Bible for the Exodus. I repeat: scholars are not sure of the exact date of the Exodus.

B. BIBLICAL BACKGROUND

The English word "exodus" is derived from the Greek word, **exodos,** meaning going out; "ex" means out; "odos" means a way, road, so an exodos is an exit or departure. Our Lord spoke of His death at the Transfiguration scene (Luke 9:31) as a departure from life, or decease. Simon Peter also speaks of his exodos or demise in 2 Peter 1:15. The title Exodus was originally given to this book when the first five books (Pentateuch or Torah) were translated into Greek about 250 B.C. The translation of the other Old Testament books was completed during the next two centuries. Septuagint is the name given to the Greek translation of the Hebrew Old Testament.

Recall that the book of Genesis ends with the death of Joseph, and he was embalmed and put in a coffin in Egypt. In time, a new king arose in Egypt "who knew not Joseph" (Exodus 1:8). He was ignorant of the part Joseph played in the preservation of that nation. By this time, the Israelites had multiplied greatly. Their marvelous population increase was one of the things that inspired fear in the Egyptians.

II. Exposition and Application of the Scripture

A. GOD'S PITY UPON ISRAEL
(Exodus 2:23-25).

And it came to pass in process of time, that the king of Egypt died: and the children of Israel sighed by reason of the bondage, and they cried, and their

cry came up unto God by reason of the bondage. And God heard their groaning, and God remembered his covenant with Abraham, with Isaac, and with Jacob. And God looked upon the children of Israel, and God had respect unto them.

This section introduces the events of chapter three. The "process of time" or course of many days actually includes a generation, or some forty years. It is interesting that very little is said of the forty years Moses spent there in Midian after his flight from Egypt. We learn only that he married Zipporah, daughter of Reuel (also called Raguel, and Jethro), and had a son by her by the name of Gershom, and worked as a shepherd for his father-in-law. During those forty years, Egyptian anti-Semitism and the rigor of oppression was not relaxed or ameliorated, but steadily increased. God waited patiently in silence as the Jews cried by reason of their bondage. Jehovah had by no means forgotten or abandoned His people. He is never oblivious to the condition or plight of His own. And still today, no matter what happens to us as Christians, we must remember our Heavenly Father is concerned.

Note the strong verbs used with respect to God's feelings: He heard... remembered...looked...and knew their condition. When God "looks upon" His own children, rest assured it is more than a cursory glance or passive surveillance. When He looks, it means He is about to take action, about to interpose or intervene. God is never indifferent to the suffering of His own. He had made an unconditional covenant with Israel, and it was impossible for Him to abandon His chosen ones. He is a faithful, covenant-keeping, prayer-answering God!

B. PHARAOH'S CONTEMPT FOR ISRAEL'S GOD
(Exodus 5:1-2)

AND afterward Moses and Aaron went in, and told Pharaoh, Thus saith the LORD God of Israel, Let my people go, that they may hold a feast unto me in the wilderness. And Pharaoh said, Who is the LORD, that I should obey his voice to let Israel go? I know not the LORD, neither will I let Israel go.

Moved by His love for Israel, the Lord sent Moses and Aaron to stand before Pharaoh and demand the release of the Israelites. Pharaoh is told: "The Lord God of Israel says, 'Let My people go!'" To this demand, Pharaoh responds with contempt. True, he may have been ignorant of the name of the God of Israel, but his remark is with a sneer; there is sarcasm in his voice, as he said: "Who is the Lord...?" And so the Lord would make sure Pharaoh would find out who the Lord is in spite of the fact that Pharaoh claimed not to know Him.

Repeatedly we read: "You shall know that I am the Lord" (Exodus 7:17)... "that you may know that I am the Lord in the midst of the earth" (Exodus 8:22)... "that you may know that there is none like me in all the earth" (Exodus 9:14) "...that the Egyptians may know that I am the Lord" (Exodus 14:4). God used the plagues—turning river water into blood; sending swarms of flies upon the Egyptians, but withholding the plague in Goshen where the Jews lived; grievous hail, etc. These plagues were calculated to further harden Pharaoh's stubborn heart, moving him to refuse to let the Jews go and further harden his own heart.

C. GOD'S JUDGMENT UPON EGYPT
(Exodus 12:29-32)

And it came to pass, that at midnight the LORD smote all the firstborn in the land of Egypt, from the firstborn of Pharaoh that sat on his throne unto the firstborn of the captive that was in the dungeon; and all the firstborn of cattle. And Pharaoh rose up in the night, he, and all his servants; and all the Egyptians; and there was a great cry in Egypt; for there was not a house where there was not one dead. And he called for Moses and Aaron by night, and said, Rise up, and get you forth from among my people, both ye and the children of Israel; and go, serve the LORD, as ye have said. Also take your flocks and your herds, as ye have said, and be gone; and bless me also.

Here was the stroke that broke the Pharaoh's back—the midnight smiting of all the firstborn in the land of Egypt. Firstborn means the oldest son who was not yet a father himself. Otherwise, the firstborn of each generation would have died, and this probably would have included Pharaoh himself. In other words, if the father had been a firstborn child, and you were his firstborn son, then the father would not have been killed, but you would have died. As it was, there was not a house where there was not one dead. No stable was immune, for even the cattle were affected. You see, the animals you possess are an extension of you. So as you are affected, so are they.

The warning God made earlier (Exodus 4:23) was now fulfilled. Greatly distressed and grief-stricken, the king immediately called that very night for Moses and Aaron! They did not meet face to face, for you recall that Pharaoh had threatened, "in that day you see my face you shall die." And Moses had replied, "You have spoken well; I will see your face again no more" (Exodus 10:28-29).

This time the words "get you forth," "go out from among my people," ring forth with a finality that previous promises failed to deliver. "I will let the people go" was a promise made after the second strike, the plague of frogs. The compromise after the fourth plague was refused. After the seventh plague of hail and fire, the Pharaoh consented, "I will let you go and you shall stay no longer" (Exodus 9:28), but then changed his mind when the plagues ceased. Another time Pharaoh said, "Let the men go" (Exodus 10:7—but not the women), so the Lord sent the plague of locusts in the eighth stroke. In a final attempt to compromise, Pharaoh said, "Go, serve the Lord, but leave your livestock behind" (Exodus 10:24). This too Moses refused to do, and once again Pharaoh's heart was hardened. As foretold in Exodus 11:1, the killing of the firstborn would be the last blow, and Israel would finally be allowed to leave! But now at last, complete capitulation is seen in Pharaoh's request: "Leave! And bless me so that nothing else bad will happen!" And yet, with such extreme humility there was no contrition or change of heart (Exodus 14:5).

D. ISRAEL'S SONG OF REDEMPTION
(Exodus 15:1-2)

THEN sang Moses and the children of Israel this song unto the LORD, and

spake, saying, I will sing unto the LORD, for he hath triumphed gloriously: the horse and his rider hath he thrown into the sea. The LORD is my strength and song, and he is become my salvation: he is my God, and I will prepare him an habitation; my father's God, and I will exalt him.

At this point, the Israelites have left Egypt and have crossed the Red Sea dryshod. Israel was redeemed, set free (or ransom paid), a fact the nation would be reminded of many times (Deuteronomy 15:15). And as the psalmist said, "Let the redeemed of the Lord say so" (Psalm 107:2). One way of saying so is to sing—unto the Lord! It was only natural to praise God in thanksgiving for giving them victory over the Egyptian soldiers. Pharaoh's army was completely ruined, or as Paul Laurence Dunbar put it, "Pher'oh's ahmy wasn't wuth a ha'f a dime" (An Ante-Bellum Sermon).

A. C. Gaebelein (Moses) reminds us that the words "song" and "singing" are not found in the book of Genesis at all. According to Job 38:7, angels sang a song of creation, but the first singing recorded in the Bible is this song of redemption in the book of Exodus. Moses and the Israelites were filled with joy over their triumphant escape engineered by the power of God. The crossing of the Red Sea is celebrated as a great display of the power of God; Jehovah is superior to all earthly powers.

The proud army of the arrogant Pharaoh was destroyed, causing Moses to acclaim the Lord as his Strength, Song and Salvation. See then the Lord is the source of Moses' strength, the theme of his song and the origin of his salvation (deliverance). No wonder Moses and the children of Israel were filled with rejoicing! The words "I will prepare Him an habitation" are better rendered, "I will praise or thank Him."

The lesson closes with the Holy Spirit-led acknowledgment that Jehovah is God. In verse 2, the word translated "Lord" is in the Hebrew, YAH or JAH (see Psalm 68:4, King James Version). This contraction of Jehovah first occurs here in the Song of Moses. And of course, you see it often in the word, Hallelujah (praise ye the Lord). Surely salvation is of Jehovah God; it is not in ourselves. We Christians likewise have a song to sing, for Jesus Christ is our Strength, our Song, and our Salvation! And through His blood, we are saved from the penalty of sin which is death; by His power we are delivered from the bondage of sin, which is slavery! We too have victory in the Lord Jesus.

III. Special Features

A. PRESERVING OUR HERITAGE

In Exodus 12:31-36, when the Israelites were commanded to depart hastily from Egypt, they asked of "the Egyptians jewels of silver, and jewels of gold, and raiment." And the Egyptians gave unto the Jews all they needed, and were thus despoiled or plundered. You may want to see this as the collection of back wages for all of the toil and labor the Jews put in as slaves in Egypt. The idea of reparation for Black Americans is one that has popped up a number of times since

Emancipation (Note: the plural, reparations, has to do with payments made by a defeated country for the devastation of territory during war: *World Book Dictionary*). No doubt, the Egyptians were more than glad to see the Jews leave after all that had happened there—the misery, stench, pain, anguish, defeat of their gods and goddesses, horror and death!

Undoubtedly, there are those who would be delighted to see Blacks leave America. The story is told of a Black man at an airport begging for money. He went to a White man and said, "I need only a dollar more to go to Africa." The White man pulled out a five-dollar bill, gave it to the Black man, and said: "Here, take four more with you." But we are not so easily removed, for our roots go deep in this country—deeper, I dare say, than the majority of Whites now in America! Our sweat, blood, and tears have soaked American soil; our labor and gifts have erected monuments not easily or readily removed. And this land will remain our home until the Lord Jesus returns and translates us to a far better land—Heaven!

B. A CONCLUDING WORD

It still remains true that without the shedding of blood, there is no remission or forgiveness of sins. The death angel passed over those homes where the blood of the Passover lamb had been applied to the lintel and two side posts of the doors of their homes. Believers likewise are saved by the blood of the Lord Jesus Christ, the Lamb of God slain from the foundation of the world (Revelation 13:8). We thank God for delivering us from our Egypt, first by His blood, and then by His power. For we too were slaves to sin, self and Satan; and the Lord Jesus—superior to Moses (Hebrews 3:3)— redeemed us.

The bottom line is this: those who desire to please God in ways that are consistent with having been created in His image and likeness will view the commandments as more than negative prohibitions, but as appropriate behavior that results in positive goodness toward God and others. The contrast between "thou shalt not" and "thou shalt" is held in tension with each other. Obedience to God should not be conceived as merely restraints to personal deportment, but expressive of the spiritual tie between God and humans that the directives as expressed in the commandments were designed to achieve.

HOME DAILY BIBLE READINGS
Week of September 13, 1998
Celebrate: God Delivers a People from Slavery

Sept. 7	M.	Exodus 2:11-25, Israelites Enslaved
Sept. 8	T.	Exodus 3:1-12, Moses Called
Sept. 9	W.	Exodus 3:13-22, "I AM WHO I AM"
Sept. 10	T.	Exodus 4:27-5:9, Pharaoh Resists God
Sept. 11	F.	Exodus 6:1-9, God Repeats the Promise
Sept. 12	S.	Exodus 14:19-25, Free at Last!
Sept. 13	S.	Psalm 105:23-25, God Remembered the Holy Promise

What God Expects

Adult Topic—What Is the Law?

·····

Youth Topic—What's Expected of Me?
Children's Topic—God Wants Obedience

·····

Devotional Reading—Isaiah 49:1-6
Background Scripture—Deuteronomy 5:1-21
Print—Deuteronomy 5:6-14a, 16-21

•••••••••••••

PRINTED SCRIPTURE

Deuteronomy 5:6-14a, 16-21 (KJV)

6 I am the LORD thy God, which brought thee out of the land of Egypt, from the house of bondage.

7 Thou shalt have none other gods before me.

8 Thou shalt not make thee any graven image, or any likeness of any thing that is in heaven above, or that is in the earth beneath, or that is in the waters beneath the earth:

9 Thou shalt not bow down thyself unto them, nor serve them: for I the LORD thy God am a jealous God, visiting the iniquity of the fathers upon the children unto the third and fourth generation of them that hate me,

10 And shewing mercy unto thousands of them that love me and keep my commandments.

11 Thou shalt not take the name of the LORD thy God in vain: for the LORD will not hold him guiltless that taketh his name in vain.

12 Keep the sabbath day to sanctify it, as the LORD thy God hath

Deuteronomy 5:6-14a, 16-21 (NRSV)

6 I am the LORD your God, who brought you out of the land of Egypt, out of the house of slavery;

7 You shall have no other gods before me.

8 You shall not make for yourself an idol, whether in the form of anything that is in heaven above, or that is on the earth beneath, or that is in the water under the earth.

9 You shall not bow down to them or worship them; for I the LORD your God am a jealous God, punishing children for the iniquity of parents, to the third and fourth generation of those who reject me,

10 but showing steadfast love to the thousandth generation of those who love me and keep my commandments.

11 You shall not make wrongful use of the name of the LORD your God, for the LORD will not acquit anyone who misuses his name.

12 Observe the sabbath day and keep it holy, as the LORD your God

commanded thee.

13 Six days thou shalt labour, and do all thy work:

14 But the seventh day is the sabbath of the LORD thy God: in it thou shalt not do any work.

.....

16 Honour thy father and thy mother, as the LORD thy God hath commanded thee; that thy days may be prolonged, and that it may go well with thee, in the land which the LORD thy God giveth thee.

17 Thou shalt not kill.

18 Neither shalt thou commit adultery.

19 Neither shalt thou steal.

20 Neither shalt thou bear false witness against thy neighbour.

21 Neither shalt thou desire thy neighbour's wife, neither shalt thou covet thy neighbour's house, his field, or his manservant, or his maidservant, his ox, or his ass, or any thing that is thy neighbour's.

commanded you.

13 Six days you shall labor and do all your work.

14 But the seventh day is a sabbath to the LORD your God.

.....

16 Honor your father and your mother, as the LORD your God commanded you, so that your days may be long and that it may go well with you in the land that the LORD your God is giving you.

17 You shalt not murder.

18 Neither shall you commit adultery.

19 Neither shall you steal.

20 Neither shall you bear false witness against your neighbor.

21 Neither shall you covet your neighbor's wife. Neither shall you desire your neighbor's house, or field, or male or female slave, or ox, or donkey, or anything that belongs to your neighbor.

I am the LORD thy God, which brought thee out of the land of Egypt, from the house of bondage. Thou shalt have none other gods before me.— Deuteronomy 5:6-7

OBJECTIVES

After reading this lesson, the student should be informed about:

1. The fundamentals of the Law as expressed in the Ten Commandments; and,
2. The fact that the God of the Bible is concerned with the relationship of His people with Him and with others.

POINTS TO BE EMPHASIZED

Adult/Youth/Children
Key Verse: Deuteronomy 5:6-7; Deuteronomy 5:6 (Children)
Print: Deuteronomy 5:6-14a, 16-21

—The Israelites were to worship only the Lord God who brought them out of Egypt. (6-9)

—God promised steadfast love to those who keep the commandments. (10)

—God's name and the sabbath day were to be treated with reverence. (11-15)

—Israelites were to respect their parents. (16)

—The Israelites were not to murder, commit adultery, steal, bear false witness, or covet. (17-21)

(NOTE: Use KJV Scripture for Adults; NRSV for Youth and Children)

TOPICAL OUTLINE OF THE LESSON

I. Introduction
A. A Perception of History
B. Biblical Background

II. Exposition and Application of the Scripture
A. Commandments About Our Relationship with God
(Deuteronomy 5:6-14a)
B. Commandments About Our Relationship with Man
(Deuteronomy 5:16-21)

III. Special Features
A. Preserving Our Heritage
B. A Concluding Word

I. Introduction

A. A PERCEPTION OF HISTORY

Deuteros means second; nomos means law. Thus, the name Deuteronomy means literally, "Second Law." However, Deuteronomy is more than a Second Law; it is really a summary of the main points of the Law. Chapter 5 is more than a recapitulation of what is recorded in Exodus 20. We have here then not just a repetition of the law, but a restatement of the law intended for that new generation of Israelites born during the wilderness journey. Since they were soon to enter the Promised Land, they needed to know how to act. In other words, it was required that they know and obey the law! So in today's lesson, Moses stresses the importance of obeying God's Law given at Mount Sinai.

B. BIBLICAL BACKGROUND

By the early 1400s B.C., it is believed the book of Deuteronomy had been largely written. A review of Israel's history is made by Moses, telling of events already recorded in the book of Numbers. Deuteronomy opens with the Israelites encamped on the plain of Moab, just about to enter the Promised Land. This is a new generation. None of the soldiers who had left Egypt were allowed to enter, except Caleb and Joshua. And all of the people who left the land of Pharaoh some thirty-eight years earlier had died because of their disobedience. In chapter 2, after wanderings and continued fighting in the wilderness, including the defeat of Sihon the Amorite, who would not allow the Jews to pass through, the Israelites continued.

In chapter 3, God further delivered Og, the giant king of Bashan, into the hands of the children of Israel. Chapter 4 finds Moses rehearsing the greatness of the law, and exhorting the new generation to obedience. They are especially to obey the Ten Commandments which God wrote upon two tables of stone (Deuteronomy 4:13). This setting for the rehearsal of the law is seen in Deuteronomy 4:44-49.

II. Exposition and Application of the Scripture

A. COMMANDMENTS ABOUT OUR RELATIONSHIP WITH GOD
(Deuteronomy 5:6-14a)

I am the LORD thy God, which brought thee out of the land of Egypt, from the house of bondage. Thou shalt have none other gods before me. Thou shalt not make thee any graven image, or any likeness of any thing that is in heaven above, or that is in the earth beneath, or that is in the waters beneath the earth: Thou shalt not bow down thyself unto them, nor serve them: For I the LORD thy God am a jealous God, visiting the iniquity of the fathers upon the children unto the third and fourth generation of them that hate me, And shewing mercy unto thousands of them that love me and keep my commandments. Thou shalt not take the name of the LORD thy God in vain: for the LORD will not hold him guiltless that taketh his name in vain. Keep the sabbath day to sanctify it, as the LORD thy God hath commanded thee. Six days thou shalt labour, and do all thy work: But the seventh day is the sabbath of the LORD thy God: in it thou shalt not do any work.

It is interesting to know that man's relationship with God is dealt with first. The first four commandments have to do with man's association with Deity. A major principle involved is very plain: Only when we are right with God can we be right with each other. This is to say, the vertical comes before the horizontal. The two go together, but we argue for priority. We are reminded of 1 John 4:20: "If a man says, I love God, and hateth his brother, he is a liar; for he that loveth not his brother, whom he hath seen, how can he love God, whom he hath not seen?"

First Commandment: Deuteronomy 5:7 is the first Commandment in Exodus 20:3. Here is the forbidding of the worship of other gods. By their deliverance from Egypt, the Jews learned something of His holiness, His wholly otherness! For the plagues against the Egyptians were aimed at their gods and goddesses, and they were designed to destroy any confidence the Jews might have had in the phony deities worshiped by the Egyptians or other countries. The God of the Bible demands our undivided attention and affection. But so do the gods men serve so that idolatry becomes spiritual polygamy. We simply cannot serve two masters. Idolatry is treason. Idolatry is a contradiction of the purpose of our hearts—whether it is mother, wife, children, money, sex, education, Muhammad, sports, entertainment, etc. Jesus Christ alone is to rule and reign in our hearts.

Second Commandment: This commandment forbids the making of images (Deuteronomy 5:8-10). How strange that men should make their own gods. How dangerous, for they that make them shall be just like them (Psalm 115:8). God hates idolatry, the major sin of Israel, and warns of its far reaching consequences. Children who hate the Lord will suffer the same punishment as their unbelieving parents.

Third Commandment: Deuteronomy 20:11 (see Exodus 20:7). Here is one of those commandments often unthinkingly violated. Sometimes the violators are those who sing in our churches and repeat the Lord's name so many times in their renditions that it appears that they believe they will be heard for their much speaking! (Matthew 6:7). In addition to these violators, we have those guilty of a casual flippancy heard in calling God, "Somebody," as in the statement, "Somebody up there likes me," or the "Man Upstairs," or as one movie star called Him, "a livin' Doll." Surely, such familiarity with a Holy God violates the third commandment.

Fourth Commandment: In Exodus 20:8-11, the fourth commandment emphasizes that observance of the Sabbath is required by God's example. He labored six days, then rested on the seventh (Genesis 2:2). In Deuteronomy 5:12-15, the Jews are exhorted to be careful to give those who work for them a day of rest, remembering that Israel once suffered the evils of slavery. Thus, Deuteronomy stresses the social side of the fourth commandment. For humanitarian reasons, the Israelites were to give their dependents a day of rest.

Now this command to keep the Sabbath day holy has caused problems. We have Seventh-Day Adventists, Seventh-Day Baptists, etc., all seeking to make Jews out of themselves and others. Consider the facts against becoming a Sabbatarian (Saturday or Sabbath-day keeper): (1) From Adam to Moses there is no record of any Sabbath Commandment. There is not a shred of evidence prior to the giving of the Law at Mount Sinai that God ever commanded men to make a special observance of the Sabbath; (2) The penalty for Sabbath-breaking was death (Exodus 31:15). Who enforces this? You see, if you put yourself under a legal system, you must obey all of the laws (Galatians 3:10); (3) The commandment was given to Jews (Exodus 31:16-17), the children of Israel, as part of their covenant relationship with God. We are Gentiles; (4) Christians celebrate the first day of the week, Sunday, as resurrection day. This first day of the week celebration was repeatedly observed by the early saints; (5) Colossians 2:16-17 teaches that Christ is the fulfillment of all such observances. Read also Romans 14:5-7; and (6) It is interesting that in the New Testament, all of the Ten Commandments are repeated except one!—sabbath keeping!

B. COMMANDMENTS ABOUT OUR RELATIONSHIP WITH MAN
(Deuteronomy 5:16-21)

Honour thy father and thy mother, as the LORD thy God hath commanded thee; that thy days may be prolonged, and that it may go well with thee, in the land which the LORD thy God giveth thee. Thou shalt not kill. Neither shalt thou commit adultery. Neither shalt thou steal. Neither shalt thou bear false witness against thy neighbour. Neither shalt thou desire thy neighbour's wife, neither shalt thou covet thy neighbour's house, his field, or his manservant, or his maidservant, his ox, or his ass, or any thing that is thy neighbour's.

Fifth Commandment: This commandment in Deuteronomy 5:16 is the fifth in Exodus 20:12. It is a key to social stability. Without proper respect for parents, our society is in trouble. In Moses' day, the reward for obedience to this command was a long life in the Promised Land. The apostle Paul calls it the first commandment with promise. "Children, obey your parents in the Lord" (Ephesians 6:1-2) refers to the children being in the Lord; in other words, they are Christian children. Avoid the interpretation which would have the children obey only if the parents are Christians! How awful that Paul should later write of "murderers of fathers and murderers of mothers" (1 Timothy 1:9).

Sixth Commandment: Kill is better rendered, murder. There is a difference between the two. The essential element in murder is the inner attitude, as indeed, the real cause of all moral impurity is internal. Before outward violence is done, there is inward intention (Mark 7:21-22). Any man with hatred in his heart for another is a potential murderer. Should occasion arise, the hatred hidden in the heart will spring into action. Obviously, capital punishment justly administered is not murder, although some Christians do not agree. God established the death penalty, so we cannot say capital punishment is immoral. The God of the Bible is holy, therefore the principle of retributive justice is a divine principle, even as eternal punishment in Hell is! But how, when, and to whom it is applied is another matter! Finally, keep in mind that the murderer is in kinship with Satan (John 8:44; 1 John 3:12).

Seventh Commandment: Deuteronomy 5:18 is the seventh commandment in Exodus 20:14. To adulterate means to corrupt, deface, make impure. It is a sin of sexual impurity that is extremely destructive. It breaks hearts, destroys homes, ruins marriages, creates feelings of guilt and shame, and a sense of wrong-doing that makes for despondency. It corrodes, dopes the conscience, lessens the inner light, lowers spiritual life, dissipates energy, enslaves the adulterers, and makes them hate the Bible. It is also dangerous to life, for according to Proverbs 6:26-35, the irate husband (or wife, for that matter) may seek revenge.

Many things combine today to make adultery common and accepted: increased mobility, availability of hotels and motels; wars that break down morality, pornography, suggestive music and dances, indecent dress, alcohol and dope, Hollywood, legalized prostitution, easy divorce, dearth of judgment preaching, etc.

Eighth Commandment: This eighth commandment in Deuteronomy 5:19 (Exodus 20:15) needs to be heard! The apostle Paul exhorted saints to put off the old man of stealing and put on the new man of honest work and giving. Let the thief continue no longer stealing is what the tense suggests (Ephesians 4:28). The man who stole before his conversion is thus warned. Stealing includes all forms of getting something for nothing, something wrongfully: theft, cheating, embezzlement, fraud, looting, etc. These are days when we hear people attempting to justify stealing and looting, while crying exploitation and reparations. The Christian has no part in such. How sad that so many in our nation want so much so soon and so easily for doing so little.

Ninth Commandment: This ninth commandment in Deuteronomy 5:20 is found also in Exodus 20:16. It forbids malignant perjury, but is meant further to prohibit all sin in words against our neighbor. We are constantly warned not to injure the character and reputation of another person with our words. Study of the examples of false witnessing reveals this evil resulted in the death of Naboth (1 Kings 21:10-14), and of Stephen (Acts 6:8-15). Note, the false witnessing against our Lord (Mark 14:55-65); and in the life of Paul (Acts 25:1-12). As children of the true God whose Word is Truth, we are to speak the truth. Remember, the Church is the pillar and ground of the truth (1 Timothy 3:13). In a world of scam, flim-flam and sham, of hypocrisy, pretension, show, and make-believe, a witness to right living and good doctrine is much needed.

Tenth Commandment: In Deuteronomy 5:21 the word "desire" is the same word rendered "covet" in Exodus 20:17. The Hebrew word translated "covet" in Deuteronomy 5:21 means to desire for oneself. This commandment deals with inordinate, ungovernable, selfish desire. There is, of course, a legitimate possession of earthly goods. To see something we want and pray about it, and have the power and right to purchase it, is normal.

On the other hand, to see something which is not ours, and which we do not have the means or right to secure, and then to keep on wanting it with envy and unsatisfied desire brooding in our hearts leads us into scheming to secure what should not be ours—this is to covet. And hear this! "...whenever a Christian goes beyond what he has the means of paying—contracts a debt that he has no prospect of being able to repay—at that moment he is committing a covetous act" (Caldwell).

III. Special Features

A. PRESERVING OUR HERITAGE

The thought occurred: Are there any references to the Ten Commandments in the Hymns and spirituals we sing in our churches? If one of the Commandments had been: THOU SHALT NOT GAMBLE, our search would have been more successful. John Lovell states that for some reason the gambler is one of the easiest sinners to identify in spiritual songs. "Perhaps the slave observed the white gambler from afar and was impressed by his dazzling color and by the rapidity of his rise and fall" (p. 252 *Black Song*). Dice shooters were especially considered excellent models of evil.

Gamblers "may have been secretly admired by the creators of the song" (p. 376). In the spiritual, Dere's No Hidin' Place Down Dere, we sing: "Oh de sinner man he gambled an' fell: he wanted to go to hebben, but he had to go to hell" (Johnson & Johnson, pp. 75-76, *American Negro Spirituals*). There is one popular hymn in our churches that refers to the third commandment (Deuteronomy 5:11): It is "Yield Not to Temptation" (hymn number 28, *Gospel Pearls;* hymn number 577, *Baptist Standard Hymnal*). Do you recall these words: "Shun evil companions, Bad language disdain; God's name hold in rev'rence, Nor take it in vain"?

B. CONCLUDING WORD

Did you notice there are more negatives than positives in the Commandments? More "thou shalt NOTs" than "thou shalts"? This reflects upon our old nature, the adamic nature with which we are born, the old man in us (and equal opportunity, the old woman in the sisters!). Ask any parent: "How often do you have to tell your children, 'Don't do that! Stop that!' "? Though originally given to the nation of Israel, the Ten Commandments are relevant for all mankind throughout the ages. Furthermore, under the New Covenant, by faith in the shed blood of the Lord Jesus Christ, the Holy Spirit moves us and empowers us to live lives that are well pleasing to God. "The Ten Commandments are a landmark in human history, because they sum up in a few verses so much of what society and the individual need for a good, orderly, and productive life" (Cyrus H. Gordon).

As a consequence to the intercultural dimension of our multifaceted society, we have experienced a breakdown in those moral and spiritual values that once characterized human interactions. The psychosis that focuses attention on that which is good for the individual concerned has elevated personal preference in the minds of the permissive above that which we have long considered to be of ultimate value and significance. The old landmark that drew a line of demarcation between that which is right and that which is wrong must be reaffirmed as we return to the Bible as the guide for life and living. Personal moral discretion cannot be confused with divine direction; hence the church must ever proclaim that the wages of sin is death regardless of how society attempts to "rename" sin to make doing evil more acceptable in the eyes of those who do not embrace the Word of God as the very essence of life itself.

HOME DAILY BIBLE READINGS
Week of September 20, 1998
What God Expects

Sept. 14 M. Deuteronomy 5:1-10, No Other Side
Sept. 15 T. Deuteronomy 5:11-15, Observe the Sabbath Day and Keep It Holy
Sept. 16 W. Deuteronomy 5:16-21, Honor Your Mother and Father
Sept. 17 T. Deuteronomy 6:1-9, Recite Them to Your Children
Sept. 18 F. Deuteronomy 6:20-25, When Your Children Ask...
Sept. 19 S. Matthew 22:34-40, The Greatest Commandment
Sept. 20 S. Isaiah 49:1-6, A Light to the Nations

Remembering What God Has Done

Adult Topic—Building a Heritage
.....
Youth Topic—Meaningless Relics or Meaningful Treasures?
Children's Topic—God Wants People to Remember Him
....
Devotional Reading—Psalm 78:1-8
Background Scripture—Joshua 3:7—4:24
Print—Joshua 4:1-3, 8, 10-11, 20-24

• • • • • • • • • • • •

PRINTED SCRIPTURE

Joshua 4:1-3, 8, 10-11, 20-24 (KJV)

AND it came to pass, when all the people were clean passed over Jordan, that the LORD spake unto Joshua, saying,

2 Take you twelve men out of the people, out of every tribe a man,

3 And command ye them, saying, Take you hence out of the midst of Jordan, out of the place where the priests' feet stood firm, twelve stones, and ye shall carry them over with you, and leave them in the lodging place, where ye shall lodge this night.

.....

8 And the children of Israel did so as Joshua commanded, and took up twelve stones out of the midst of Jordan, as the LORD spake unto Joshua, according to the number of the tribes of the children of Israel, and carried them over with them unto the place where they lodged, and laid them down there.

.....

10 For the priests which bare the

Joshua 4:1-3, 8, 10-11, 20-24 (NRSV)

WHEN THE entire nation had finished crossing over the Jordan, the LORD said to Joshua:

2 "Select twleve men from the people, one from each tribe,

3 and command them, 'Take twleve stones from here out of the middle of the Jordan, from the place where the priests' feet stood, carry them over with you, and lay them down in the place where you camp tonight.'"

.....

8 The Israelites did as Joshua commanded. They took up twelve stones out of the middle of the Jordan, according to the number of the tribes of the Israelites, as the LORD told Joshua, carried them over with them to the place where they camped, and laid them down there.

.....

10 The priests who bore the ark

ark stood in the midst of Jordan, until every thing was finished that the LORD commanded Joshua to speak unto the people, according to all that Moses commanded Joshua: and the people hasted and passed over.

11 And it came to pass, when all the people were clean passed over, that the ark of the LORD passed over, and the priests, in the presence of the people.

.....

20 And those twelve stones, which they took out of Jordan, did Joshua pitch in Gilgal.

21 And he spake unto the children of Israel, saying, When your children shall ask their fathers in time to come, saying, What mean these stones?

22 Then ye shall let your children know, saying, Israel came over this Jordan on dry land.

23 For the LORD your God dried up the waters of Jordan from before you, until ye were passed over, as the LORD your God did to the Red sea, which he dried up from before us, until we were gone over:

24 That all the people of the earth might know the hand of the LORD, that it is mighty: that ye might fear the LORD your God for ever.

remained standing in the middle of the Jordan, until everything was finished that the LORD commanded Joshua to tell the people, according to all that Moses had commanded Joshua. The people crossed over in haste.

11 As soon as all the people had finished crossing over, the ark of the LORD, and the priests, crossed over in front of the people.

.....

20 Those twelve stones, which they had taken out of the Jordan, Joshua set up in Gilgal,

21 saying to the Israelites, "When your children ask their parents in time to come, 'What do these stones mean?'

22 then you shall let your children know, 'Israel crossed over the Jordan here on dry ground.'

23 For the LORD your God dried up the waters of the Jordan for you until you crossed over, as the LORD your God did to the Red Sea, which he dried up for us until we crossed over,

24 so that all the peoples of the earth may know that the hand of the LORD is mighty, and so that you may fear the LORD your God forever."

KEY VERSE

And he spake unto the children of Israel, saying, When your children shall ask their fathers in time to come, saying, What mean these stones? Then ye shall let your children know, saying, Israel came over this Jordan on dry land.—Joshua 4:21-22

OBJECTIVES

After reading this lesson, the student should be informed about:

1. The nature of the event God desired the Jews to commemorate;

2. God's purpose in having believers remember certain events or experiences in their lives; and,

3. The value of knowing how the God of history has worked in the lives of His people.

POINTS TO BE EMPHASIZED

Adult/Youth/Children
Key Verse: Joshua 4:21-22
Print: Joshua 4:1-3, 8, 10-11, 20-24

—Following the crossing of the Jordan River by the nation of Israel, God commanded Joshua to have twelve men choose stones from the river to create a memorial to commemorate this event. (4:1-3)

—The twelve men selected by Joshua did as he directed. (4:8-11)

—At Gilgal, Joshua set up the twelve stones taken from the river. (4:20)

—Joshua told the people to use their children's future questions about the stones as an opportunity to tell them how God enabled the Israelites to cross the Jordan into the promised land. (4:21-23)

—The purpose of the memorial was to exalt the Lord before all the peoples of the earth, and to encourage the Israelites to be faithful to the Lord. (4:24)

(NOTE: Use KJV Scripture for Adult; NRSV Scripture for Youth and Children)

TOPICAL OUTLINE OF THE LESSON

I. Introduction
  A. A Perception of History
  B. Biblical Background

II. Exposition and Application of the Scripture
  A. The Giving of the Command (Joshua 4:1-3)
  B. Obeying the Command (Joshua 4:8, 10-11)
  C. The Meaning of the Command (Joshua 4:20-24)

III. Special Features
  A. Preserving Our Heritage
  B. A Concluding Word

I. Introduction

A. A PERCEPTION OF HISTORY

The name Joshua is a contraction of Jehoshua, which means Jehovah is Salvation or Jehovah Saves. By contracting Jehoshua to Joshua, the "salvation" (or shua) is emphasized. In the New Testament, the name for Joshua in Greek is

Jesus. You may note in some copies of the King James Version of Hebrews 4:8 that the word Jesus is given instead of Joshua. The better translation there is Joshua.

At this point in the history of Israel Moses is dead, and Joshua is his successor as the leader of the nation. To Joshua is given the task of entering Palestine, and the preparation for and entry into Canaan is described in the first five chapters of the Book of Joshua. Upon assuming command, Joshua mobilized the people in order to go over to possess the land God gave them. Joshua's next step was to send out two men to spy out the land (chapter 2). In chapter 3, preparation is made to wage war as the means by which the Lord desired to drive out the pagan inhabitants of the land. Chapter 3 also records that the Jews cross the river Jordan dryshod.

B. BIBLICAL BACKGROUND

A word should be said here about memorials, or what Joshua called "a sign" among the Israelites (Joshua 4:6). Prior to the events cited in our lesson, Moses had instructed the Israelites (Deuteronomy 27:2) that they were to set up great stones and whitewash them with lime on the day they pass over the Jordan.

The word used here for "memorial" (**zikkaron,** Joshua 4:7) is a reminder, token, record; it brings something to mind or remembrance. As we shall see, the stones shall be reminders of how the Lord enabled the Israelites to enter the Promised Land. It was customary to pile up stones as rude monuments to honor God's revelation (Genesis 28:18, 35:14). For examples: Moses built twelve pillars at Mount Sinai as a sign of God's covenant (Exodus 24:4). Samuel erected a stone to commemorate his victory over the Philistines (1 Samuel 7:12). The name of this stone is Ebenezer, meaning, "Thus far the Lord has helped us." It may be noted that Ebenezer is a very popular name for our Baptist churches.

And so, here we find that Joshua set up a monument of stones to commemorate the passage over the Jordan (Joshua 4:3-9). Later, at Shechem, he set up a stone under an oak tree as a memorial of the covenant between God and His people (Joshua 24:26-27). The custom of setting up stones as memorials was an important part of the religious expression in Israel. It is suggested that the apostle Paul represented the Church as a pillar of testimony for the truth (1 Timothy 3:15), because God founded and raised the Church as a monument for that very purpose.

II. Exposition and Application of the Scripture

A. THE GIVING OF THE COMMAND
(Joshua 4:1-3)

AND it came to pass, when all the people were clean passed over Jordan, that the LORD spake unto Joshua, saying, Take you twelve men out of the people, out of every tribe a man, And command ye them, saying, Take you hence out of the midst of Jordan, out of the place where the priests' feet stood firm, twelve stones, and ye shall carry them over with you, and leave them in the lodging place, where ye shall lodge this night.

From Joshua chapter 3:14-17, we learn that the Israelites passed over the river Jordan. God performed the miracle for several reasons. First: simply to move the Jews further on into the Promised Land. Second: to magnify Joshua in the eyes of all the Israelites. They needed to know—to be reassured—that the Lord was with Joshua as He had been with Moses. In 4:14, we learn that because the Lord so exalted Joshua, that all Israel feared him "as they had feared Moses, all the days of his life." Third: the news of the event would soon spread and serve to further dishearten the Canaanites, and all whom the Lord had promised to drive out of the land.

Even while the river was in flood stage, swollen by melting snows, it came to pass that as soon as the feet of the priests bearing the ark of the Lord stepped into the river, the waters stood upon the waters! What a fantastic miracle! The waters rose up as one heap as far away as Adam, the city that is on the same side of the Jordan as Zarethan. And other streams south of Zarethan, feeding into the Jordan, were entirely cut off. Thus it appears that the waters may have been dammed up as far as fifteen or sixteen miles upstream from the area crossed by the Jews (Joshua 3:15-16). It is estimated that a stretch of twenty or thirty miles of the river bed was left dry.

And so, the priests stood firm on dry ground in the middle of the Jordan, and the people passed over opposite Jericho. Note that the ark of the covenant, the symbol of God's presence, was in front. The people followed, always keeping an eye on the ark. Thus their initial step of faith into the river came as they kept their eyes on the ark. Once past the priests, they could keep on going. It is still true today, that as we follow the Lord Jesus Christ, victory is assured. When He leads, no rivers are uncrossable!

The lesson proceeds to describe the steps Jehovah God took in order to commemorate the crossing. He commanded Joshua to take twelve men, one man from each tribe. Each man was to go back to where the priests were standing with the ark in the middle of the river, and take out a stone from the place where the feet of the priests stood firm. These stones were then to be carried out and left in a certain place.

B. OBEYING THE COMMAND
(Joshua 4:8, 10-11)

And the children of Israel did so as Joshua commanded, and took up twelve stones out of the midst of Jordan, as the LORD spake unto Joshua, according to the number of the tribes of the children of Israel, and carried them over with them unto the place where they lodged, and laid them down there. For the priests which bare the ark stood in the midst of Jordan, until every thing was finished that the LORD commanded Joshua to speak unto the people, according to all that Moses commanded Joshua: and the people hasted and passed over. And it came to pass, when all the people were clean passed over, that the ark of the LORD passed over, and the priests, in the presence of the people.

We see that in Joshua 4:2-3, Jehovah commanded Joshua. Then Joshua, repeating what the Lord told him, commanded the Israelites (4:4-7) who were appointed for the work. Now, we deal with the carrying out of these instructions. Each man passed over to where the ark of the Lord was in the middle of the Jordan, and put a stone on his shoulder, and carried it out of the river to a place where they lodged, and laid them there.

But now consider this: A second gathering of stones was made afterwards. Unless this is made clear, the entire story becomes confusing. In other words, a second memorial is made, according to Joshua 4:9. However, this second commemoration is not described in detail as is the first setting up of the stones (verses 1-8). So all we are told in 4:9 is that stones were also placed in the river itself, where the feet of the priests who bore the ark of the covenant stood.

The priests stood in their places until the twelve men, chosen earlier for the task (Joshua 3:12), had obtained the stones. The priests remained there until all the people had hastened across. All that God told Joshua to speak to the people, Joshua obeyed. All that Moses had commanded Joshua in his charge when Joshua was first called (Deuteronomy 31:7-8), Joshua obeyed. All was accomplished in the will of the Lord!

Once all the people had passed over, and the priests themselves came out of the midst of the river, then the waters of the river returned to their place, and overflowed all its banks as before (Joshua 4:15-18). The people hurried across, for the priests had been standing in the middle of the Jordan for a long time (4:10). Having to stand in one spot so long was physically exhausting; besides, the crossing had to take place in one day, and before nightfall. Furthermore, some scholars estimate that there were approximately two and a half million people crossing the Jordan!

C. THE MEANING OF THE COMMAND
(Joshua 4:20-24)

And those twelve stones, which they took out of Jordan, did Joshua pitch in Gilgal. And he spake unto the children of Israel, saying, When your children shall ask their fathers in time to come, saying, What mean these stones? Then ye shall let your children know, saying, Israel came over this Jordan on dry land. For the LORD your God dried up the waters of Jordan from before you, until ye were passed over, as the LORD your God did to the Red sea, which he dried up from before us, until we were gone over: That all the people of the earth might know the hand of the LORD, that it is mighty: that ye might fear the LORD your God for ever.

The ark was carried in first. This is because the ark represents the very Presence of God. It is God Himself who opened up the river. The waters stood still at the command of Jehovah, not at the behest of the priests, for they were but subordinate to the ark upon which the Almighty God Jehovah was enthroned.

We do well to remember, even today, that the Lord Jesus said: "Without me you can do nothing" (John 15:5). Recall that twelve stones were left in the midst of the river. The twelve men, one chosen from each tribe, thus representing all Israel, set the stones in the place where the feet of the priests stood bearing the ark of the covenant. When the waters returned, the stones were covered. This incident speaks of death to the old life style.

However, the memorial first initiated is the more important. It is described in Joshua 4:1-8. This time, each of the twelve men carried a stone from the river bed to the place called Gilgal, located perhaps some five miles from the bank of the Jordan, and several miles from the city of Jericho. It was here that the twelve-stone memorial was later set up. In contrast to the twelve stones left in the Jordan, and representing death to the old life, the twelve stones set up on dry ground represent the new life. Combined, the two sets of stones point us to the truth of the believer's death and the resurrection life with the Lord Jesus Christ.

In other words, the stones placed in the riverbed where the priests stood identify with Jesus Christ in death of the old. The stones taken out of the river, and placed on the west bank of the Jordan, identify with Christ in resurrection, the new creation. This is the answer to the question, "What mean these stones?" (Joshua 4:6, 21). They mean deliverance; they mean redemption; they mean witness; they mean victory. Even as God dried up the Red Sea and enabled the Jews to leave the land of Egypt, so now the world may once again see evidence of the mighty hand of the God of Israel.

III. Special Features

A. PRESERVING OUR HERITAGE

The Jordan River is very popular in our churches. This popularity is the result of the messages we preach and the music we sing. Who has not heard a Black preacher wax eloquent in his sermon on "The Swelling of the Jordan"? (Jeremiah 12:5); or, expound on Baptist beliefs concerning immersion because many people were baptized in the Jordan, including the Lord Jesus Christ? (Matthew 3:6, 13). How often the name of this river is mentioned at our funerals! And then, how popular is this name Jordan in the spirituals we sing! In the Negro Spirituals, Jordan represented the "dividing line between time and eternity, or between slave land and free land" (John Lovell, *Black Song,* p. 258).

Consider the following spirituals, and what they have to say about the Jordan River: Swing Low, Sweet Chariot: "I look'd over Jordan, an' what did I see, Comin' for to carry me home, A band of angels comin' after me, Comin' for to carry me home." Stan' Still Jordan: The title of this spiritual fits in well with our Sunday School lesson: "Jordan river, is chilly and cold, It will chilla my body, but not my soul." Deep River: "Deep river, my home is over Jordan, Deep river, Lord, I want to cross over into camp ground." Members, Don't Git Weary: "I'm gwine down to de ribbuh ob Jordan, When my work is done." Mary an' Martha Jes' Gone 'Long (To Ring Dem Charmin' Bells): "O, 'way over Jordan, Lord, 'Way over Jordan,

Lord, To ring dem charmin' bells." De Band o' Gideon: "Oh, de band o' Gideon over in Jordan." You Mus' Hab Dat True Religion: "Whar you gwine po' gambler whar you gwine, I say, I'm a gwine down to de ribbuh ob Jord'n, You can't cross dere." Roll, Jordan, Roll: "Roll Jordan, roll, I wanter go to heav'n when I die, To hear ol' Jordan roll." And finally, O, Wasn't Dat a Wide River?: "O, wasn't dat a wide river, dat river of Jordan, Lord, Wide river! Dere's one mo' river to cross. O, de river of Jordan is so wide, One mo' river to cross. I don't know how to get on de other side; One mo' river to cross." What an impression the Jordan River made in the lives of our slave foreparents! It is interesting that for many Blacks the crossing of the Jordan illustrates the passing of the Christian from physical life into eternity. And we hear prayers requesting the Lord Jesus to meet us down at the river of Jordan, and give us safe passage across. This idea also involves making the Promised Land a picture of Heaven. This is not an ideal interpretation of the crossing of the Jordan. It is better to see the symbolism as a picture of the believer going from the level of self-reliance to the level of relying on the Savior. The river of Jordan runs between the old life and the new life on earth. Which side of the river are you on? And finally on this issue, the Promised Land is not Heaven. Remember, many battles still had to be fought by Joshua and his army.

B. A CONCLUDING WORD

There are two sets of stones used for commemoration. The first set taken out of the river was placed on dry land. The second set remained in the river. Thus two sets of twelve stones bore witness to the fact that the entire nation, all twelve tribes (represented by the twelve men, one from each tribe), were in the wilderness together and by the hand of God, all entered the Promised Land.

The number two is a witness number. It is the Lord's desire that a difference be seen in the life we lived prior to crossing Jordan, and the life we live after the crossing. God's purpose was to remind the Israelites of their deliverance by His mighty hand, and at the same time be a witness to the world as well. Future generations of Jews would be reminded by the permanent monument of how God stopped the Jordan from flowing so that the Israelites could cross over on dry land.

HOME DAILY BIBLE READINGS
Week of September 27, 1998
Remembering What God Has Done

September 21 M. Joshua 3:7-13, Hear the Words of the Lord
September 22 T. Joshua 3:14—4:9, A Memorial Forever
September 23 W. Joshua 4:10-24, The Lord Exalted Joshua
September 24 T. Joshua 6:1-7, The Conquest of Jericho Begins
September 25 F. Joshua 6:12-25, The Walls Came Tumbling Down
September 26 S. Joshua 7:1-9, God's Covenant Transgressed

Cycle of Sin and Judgment

Unit II—God Leads in Times of Change
Children's Unit—God Provides Leaders
Adult Topic—Disobedience, Despair, Deliverance

.....

Youth Topic—Dead End Street
Children's Topic—Deborah Judges the People

.....

Devotional Reading—Psalm 78:17-32
Background Scripture—Judges 2
Print—Judges 2:11-20

• • • • • • • • • • •

PRINTED SCRIPTURE

Judges 2:11-20 (KJV)

11 And the children of Israel did evil in the sight of the LORD, and served Baalim:

12 And they forsook the LORD God of their fathers, which brought them out of the land of Egypt, and followed other gods, of the gods of the people that were round about them, and bowed themselves unto them, and provoked the LORD to anger.

13 And they forsook the LORD, and served Baal and Ashtaroth.

14 And the anger of the LORD was hot against Israel, and he delivered them into the hands of spoilers that spoiled them, and he sold them into the hands of their enemies round about, so that they could not any longer stand before their enemies.

15 Whithersoever they went out, the hand of the LORD was against them for evil, as the LORD had said, and as the LORD had sworn unto

Judges 2:11-20 (NRSV)

11 Then the Israelites did what was evil in the sight of the LORD and worshiped the Baals;

12 and they abandoned the LORD, the God of their ancestors, who had brought them out of the land of Egypt; they followed other gods, from among the gods of the peoples who were all around them, and bowed down to them; and they provoked the LORD to anger.

13 They abandoned the LORD, and worshiped Baal and the Astartes.

14 So the anger of the LORD was kindled against Israel, and he gave them over to plunderers who plundered them, and he sold them into the power of their enemies all around, so that they could no longer withstand their enemies.

15 Whenever they marched out, the hand of the LORD was against them to bring misfortune, as the LORD had warned them and

them: and they were greatly distressed.

16 Nevertheless the LORD raised up judges, which delivered them out of the hand of those that spoiled them.

17 And yet they would not hearken unto their judges, but they went a whoring after other gods, and bowed themselves unto them: they turned quickly out of the way which their fathers walked in, obeying the commandments of the LORD; but they did not so.

18 And when the LORD raised them up judges, then the LORD was with the judge, and delivered them out of the hand of their enemies all the days of the judge: for it repented the LORD because of their groanings by reason of them that oppressed them and vexed them.

19 And it came to pass, when the judge was dead, that they returned, and corrupted themselves more than their fathers, in following other gods to serve them, and to bow down unto them, they ceased not from their own doings, nor from their stubborn way.

20 And the anger of the LORD was hot against Israel.

sworn to them; and they were in great distress.

16 Then the LORD raised up judges, who delivered them out of the power of those who plundered them.

17 Yet they did not listen even to their judges; for they lusted after other gods and bowed down to them. They soon turned aside from the way in which their ancestors had walked, who had obeyed the commandments of the LORD; they did not follow their example.

18 Whenever the LORD raised up judges for them, the LORD was with the judge, and he delivered them from the hand of their enemies all the days of the judge; for the LORD would be moved to pity by their groaning because of those who persecuted and oppressed them.

19 But whenever the judge died, they would relapse and behave worse than their ancestors, following other gods, worshiping them and bowing down to them. They would not drop any of their practices or their stubborn ways.

20 So the anger of the LORD was kindled against Israel.

KEY VERSE

Nevertheless the LORD raised up judges, which delivered them out of the hand of those that spoiled them. And yet they would not hearken unto their judges, but they went a whoring after other gods, and bowed themselves unto them: they turned quickly out of the way which their fathers walked in, obeying the commandments of the LORD, but they did not so.— Judges 2:16-17

OBJECTIVES

After reading this lesson, the student should be informed about:

1. The destructiveness of idolatry;
2. The love of God shown by His repeated deliverance of His people; and,
3. The sovereignty of God demonstrated by His use of evildoers as instruments of judgment.

POINTS TO BE EMPHASIZED

Adult/Youth

Key Verse: Judges 2:16-17

Print: Judges 2:11-20

—Because the Israelites turned from the Lord to worship other gods, the Lord gave them over to plunderers who caused them great distress. (11-15)

—God raised up judges—or deliverers—to lead the people out of their oppressive situations. (16, 18)

—After the people were delivered, they would not listen to their judges, but turned again to other gods. (17)

—Again, the Lord, moved with pity because of His people's suffering, raised up judges and worked through them to help His people. (18)

—After the death of each judge, the people would revert to idolatry, the Lord would be angered, and the cycle of disobedience and oppression would begin again. (19-20a)

—Israel did not complete the task of driving out the foreigners from the land of promise and God used those foreign people as an instrument of judgment on the sinful nation of Israel. (22-23).

Children

Key Verse: Psalm 9:9

Print: Judges 2:16, 18; 4:1-16

—God raised up judges—or deliverers—to lead the people out of their oppressive situations. (2:16, 18)

—Israel did what was evil in God's sight and God sold them into the hand of King Jabin of Canaan. (4:1-2)

—The Israelites cried to the Lord for help because of King Jabin's cruelty. (4:3)

—Deborah, a prophetess, judged the people from the hill country of Ephraim. (4:4-5)

—Deborah made a plan to draw Sisera, the general of Jabin's army, into battle. (4:6-7)

—Deborah instructed Barak to engage Sisera in battle because the Lord was going to give him a victory. (4:14-16)

(NOTE: Use KJV Scripture for Adults; NRSV Scripture for Youth and Children)

TOPICAL OUTLINE OF THE LESSON

I. Introduction
A. A Perception of History
B. Biblical Background

II. Exposition and Application of the Scripture
A. Israel's Sin (Judges 2:11-13)
B. Idolatry's Result (Judges 2:14-15)
C. God's Deliverance (Judges 2:16-18)
D. God's Anger (Judges 2:19-20)

III. Special Features
A. Preserving Our Heritage
B. A Concluding Word

I. Introduction

A. A PERCEPTION OF HISTORY

At this moment in the history of Israel, Joshua is dead (Judges 2:8). The nation is left without capable spiritual and military leadership such as Joshua had provided, although the God of Joshua was still present. Conquest is one thing, settlement is another. The Jews were in the land, and occupied the strategic sites. The various tribes had been assigned their portions. However, their work of conquest was far from finished; they had to constantly defend the territory they had seized.

We as Christians are saved, but we must wear the whole armor of God and constantly defend ourselves from a world that seeks to take away our day of worship, plagiarize our music, "Hollywoodize" our Bible, steal away our young people's allegiance, and desecrate and destroy our church property. So it was that the Israelites needed to maintain vigil against any encroachments into the land God had given them.

The old generation that had served under Joshua, and those who outlived Joshua—all who had experienced the great things the Lord had done for the nation—they too all died. The new generation that arose was wicked, for it knew not the Lord (Judges 2:10), nor what Jehovah had done for Israel. And it was not long before idolatry ruled the day. Failure to subdue and drive out the enemy nations is one of the factors contributing to Israel's lapse again into idolatry.

Throughout our entire study of the Old Testament, we see that idolatry is the major sin that caused the downfall of Israel. Failure to comprehend the role that idol worship played will make it impossible to accurately and adequately interpret the Scriptures. One word that is basic then in this lesson is "idolatry." Inherent in the human heart is the desire to express religious conception in visible forms. Originally, idolatry meant the worship of idols, the worship of a statue or image of a god or spirit. Idolatry then is the worship of false gods by means of idols. Among the Old Testament Jews, idolatry came to mean any worship of false gods by whatever means. Finally, for the Israelite, it came to mean the worship of Jehovah through visible symbols.

In the book of Romans, the apostle Paul describes man's spiritual decline. In the beginning, men knew God (Romans 1:21). Adam and Eve had been taught by God how to worship the Lord; and they in turn taught their children. These descendants took that knowledge with them, but mixed it with falsehood, giving rise to idolatry. In time, men glorified Him not, but became ungrateful. Ingratitude is seen as one of the first steps into idolatry. It was not long before men sought to exchange God's incorruptible glory for the image of corruptible man. Note the downward trend of the objects of worship: God, man, birds, four-footed beasts, you name it and men have worshiped it. Thus in the New Testament, idolatry is seen as: (1) giving to any creature that honor or devotion which belongs to God alone, and (2) giving to our human desires precedence over the will of God.

B. BIBLICAL BACKGROUND

A number of different gods and goddesses are mentioned in this lesson, and it is important to know something about them. Baalim are mentioned in Judges 2:11. The singular is Baal, the plural is Baalim. You see the plural ending (im) in such words as seraphim, and cherubim (Do not sing "cherubims" in the hymn, Holy, Holy, Holy, for the Hebrew "im" is the plural).

Baal means master, lord, possessor, owner, proprietor. When the Jews settled in Canaan, they discovered the local Baalim were looked upon as individual lords of the land. Thus, to worship Baal meant to abandon the lordship of the true God. Baal is not a proper name, but the title of the chief god of the Canaanite tribes. Whatever god was worshiped by a community, that god was ordinarily spoken of as the "Baal." Thus sometimes the plural, Baalim, signifies the multitude of local deities. And in our lesson, the singular, Baal, may stand for the entire genus of false gods. Thus, Baalim is also a general term used to designate all false deities, or what are called, "other gods."

Baal was considered a fertility god, believed to bring productivity to crops, animals, and human beings. He is also depicted in carvings as holding a lightning bolt in his hand, signifying he is the god of fire. However, he never responded to Elijah's challenge (1 Kings 18:29). As the chief god of Canaan's vegetation, he was worshiped to ensure good harvests or productivity. Now, the female counterpart to Baal is Ashtoreth (Judges 2:13). As Baalim is the plural of Baal, so Ashtaroth is the plural of Ashtoreth. She was the goddess of love and fertility. Often the worship of this goddess included bizarre sexual practices. Ashtoreth came to be regarded as the consort of Baal; thus there were as many Ashtoreths or (Ashtaroth) as there were Baals (or Baalim).

II. Exposition and Application of the Scripture

A. ISRAEL'S SIN
(Judges 2:11-13)

And the children of Israel did evil in the sight of the LORD, and served Baalim: And they forsook the LORD God of their fathers, which brought them out of the land of Egypt, and followed other gods, of the gods of the people that were round about them, and bowed themselves unto them, and provoked the LORD to anger. And they forsook the LORD, and served Baal and Ashtaroth.

This generation of Israelites did not know the Lord, but the Lord knew them. They had not seen or experienced the wonderful deeds of God. They had heard of the God of Israel, but the words went in one ear and out the other. It is easy to have truth in the head with nothing in the heart and an idol in the hand. Their behavior—idolatry, serving Baal—was seen by the Lord. In fact, this refrain is repeated seven times in the Book of Judges: "And the children of Israel did evil in the sight of the Lord" (Judges 2:11; 3:7, 12; 4:1; 6:1; 10:6; 13:1). The word translated "evil" combines the deed with its consequences, and signifies breaking up or ruin.

"It is a breach of harmony, a breaking up of what is good and desirable in man and in society" (Girdlestone, p. 80). Those people who consider sin relative should know that what really counts is what God says. If in His sight a thing is wrong, it is wrong, no matter what men assert. His judgment "stands as a moral absolute" (Theological Wordbook of the Old Testament, 2:854).

Thus the words "in His sight" highlight God's evaluation of a deed. Idolatry is seen as the rejection of God, a violation of the very first of the Ten Commandments. Serving Baalim is an abandonment of the Lord. God and Baalim cannot be served by the same person at the same time. Our Lord warned: "No man can serve two masters; for either he will hate the one, and love the other, or else he will hold to the one, and despise the other" (Matthew 6:24). We see there is no vacuum in the human heart. It is "either or." The man who claims to be an atheist practices the religion of atheism. A man who claims to be an agnostic practices agnosticism. And likewise, the man who swears that he has no need for religion has No-Need-For-Religion as his religion.

We see both a forsaking and a forgetting here with respect to the nature of idolatry. "They forsook...they forsook..." (Judges 2:12-13). Idolatry is an abandonment, desertion, leaving, departure. Imagine deserting the God who brought them out of the land of Egypt. Deliverance from Egypt is the most frequently mentioned miracle in the Old Testament. God's manifold purpose in repeatedly reminding the Jews of the Exodus is a terrific study in itself. Dozens of verses throughout the Old Testament drum home how God redeemed Israel. Awareness of where we as believers were when Christ found us is to be the motivation for a life style that pleases Him. An example is Deuteronomy 15:15, the favorite verse of John Newton ("Amazing Grace"): "And thou shalt remember that thou wast a slave in the land of Egypt, and the Lord thy God redeemed thee...."

B. IDOLATRY'S RESULT
(Judges 2:14-15)

And the anger of the LORD was hot against Israel, and he delivered them into the hands of spoilers that spoiled them, and he sold them into the hands of their enemies round about, so that they could not any longer stand before their enemies. Withersoever they went out, the hand of the LORD was against them for evil, as the LORD had said, and as the LORD had sworn unto them: and they were greatly distressed.

Is it any wonder that the Lord was provoked to anger? The Hebrew word used for "provoked" means to stir up the heart to a heated condition. His anger is described as "hot" (Judges 2:14). Applied to God, we learn that human beings can cause God's heart pain, heat, and grief in different degrees of intensity *(Theological Wordbook of the Old Testament,* 1:451). Thus, Israel's idolatry deeply vexed God. And the nation stood warned that when the Lord is continuously and deeply provoked, He removes the object of vexation. God's decision not to drive out the enemy nations which remained in the land is one expression of divine anger. Israel would not lose the land God promised, but neither would the heathen Canaanites be dispossessed altogether. In Judges 2:14, we see that the Lord used the enemies of Israel to punish Israel. In His wrath, He delivered the Jews into the hands of the plunderers, and Israel could no longer stand before their enemies. Sin pays! Indeed, the wages of sin is death (Romans 6:23). Disobedience to God's Word pays off in misery, slavery, sickness and death. Israel discovered this truth, for in Judges 2:15 we see some of the results of idolatry.

C. GOD'S DELIVERANCE
(Judges 2:16-18)

Nevertheless the LORD raised up judges which delivered them out of the hand of those that spoiled them. And yet, they would not hearken unto their judges, but they went a whoring after other gods, and bowed themselves unto them: they turned quickly out of the way which their fathers walked in, obeying the commandments of the LORD; but they did not so. And when the LORD raised them up judges, then the LORD was with the judge, and delivered them out of the hand of their enemies all the days of the judge: for it repented the LORD because of their groanings by reason of them that oppressed them and vexed them.

This section opens with a great word, "nevertheless." It is a word of grace. In spite of Israel's folly and deserved punishment for her idolatry, the Lord answered the prayers of the penitent. Oppression served to bring the Jews to the point of repentance. In contrition they cried out, and the Lord, hearing their lament, raised up leaders for them. From these leaders the book gets its name, Judges. The Hebrew word **shaphat** (see it in the name, Jehoshaphat, God is Judge) generally speaks of the administration of justice. "Judge" here is not used in a judicial or court way to describe one who decides another man's destiny. Rather, the noun **"shaphat"** is administrative, pointing to the manner in which man's affairs are handled. We see these judges then as saviors or deliverers, raised up by God. Their purpose was to bring Israel back to God. They were military leaders, not simply jurists or magistrates or legal scholars. They were ordinary tribesmen, people of humble birth.

Unfaithfulness to God is called "whoring" or playing the part of a prostitute. This is strong language, for idolatry is spiritual in nature. Such a representation is made because Israel was married to Jehovah and lived in a covenant relationship with Him. Idolatry was a breach of that covenant. Furthermore, the immoral ceremonies involved in idolatry were altogether contrary to and incompatible with the holiness demanded by the God of Israel. Upon hearing the groanings of affliction, God "repented." To say the Lord changed His mind is what theologians call anthropomorphism, literally, "man-form." It is the language of accommodation, the use of words describing man, but applied to God. To us it seems the Lord changes His mind, but of course, He knows all along what is and shall be.

D. GOD'S ANGER
(Judges 2:19-20a)

And it came to pass, when the judge was dead, that they returned, and corrupted themselves more than their fathers, in following other gods to serve them, and to bow down unto them; they ceased not from their own doings, nor from their stubborn way. And the anger of the LORD was hot against Israel.

As long as the judge was alive, the Jews prospered. Their national security was a reality, for they lived in obedience to the will of the Lord. But when the judge died, the Jews returned to their idolatry. Their corrupting, destructive relapse gave evidence of their stubborn, stiff-necked wills, all the more heightening the grace of God and the need for divine intervention.

III. Special Features

A. PRESERVING OUR HERITAGE

A Sovereign God moved on the hearts of men and used them to bring an end to American slavery. Slowly but surely, the external signs of segregation have crumbled. Many doors have opened to us. But we must remember that Jim Crow is basically a spiritual bird, and unless the Lord fights our battles, the racist heart remains. Today's lesson then is a reminder to Black American Christians that life is a spiritual battle, and only through God in Christ are we really free. Once truly delivered, we must not lapse into the practice of idolatry, especially serving that idol which would exalt skin and violate the teaching that in God's Presence, no flesh should glory (1 Corinthians 1:29). In a larger sense, we cannot allow our victories to become the god whom we worship. Each day is a battle to win or lose, and our trust must be placed in God rather than our success.

B. A CONCLUDING WORD

In some respects, the Book of Judges is considered a pivotal book in the Old Testament. It covers the time from Joshua's death to Samuel's birth, some 325 years. Because it reveals the folly of the human heart, it is a discouraging book to read. But then again, we are encouraged by God's "NEVERTHELESS;" His patience, His love and mercy. No other book in the Bible demonstrates as sharply the contrast between the utter failure of Israel and the persistent grace of the Lord.

God raised up rulers to defend the Israelites, save them from their oppressors, indoctrinate them, and keep them walking in the straight path of obedience. Their ministry, however, had no lasting effect upon the nation. Israel repeatedly fell into idolatry, defeat, penitence, deliverance, rest, and again, idolatry (Rebellion, Retribution, Repentance, Rest, Rebellion). This was the history of the nation following the death of Joshua.

In short, we see victory and defeat, victory and defeat in a constantly repetitive pattern. How is it then in your life? Is it also in-and-out, up-and-down? True, the old nature is still in us. However, the indwelling Holy Spirit is in us also. God grant that this lesson will impress our hearts to live what is called "the victorious life." One key to such a life is: Let there be no known, unconfessed sins in our life. And, watch the company we keep. Christ alone gives us victory over the cycle of sin and judgment.

One of the tragedies that is inherent within the human situation is that many times we conceive of God as One who rescues from trouble and disaster, while we fail to express our gratitude in faithful obedience in response to His protective care. Under the conditions of existence, could it be that God allows the difficult days and weary nights—even long periods of untoward circumstances—to overtake us so that we come to realize our continuous need for Him, rather than follow personal preferences when all is well from a human point of view? In a real sense, we have come to that state wherein delivery from trouble is the mainstay of our spirituality as contrasted to fidelity to God as a deliberate choice in the midst of our common existence.

HOME DAILY BIBLE READINGS
Week of October 4, 1998
Cycle of Sin and Judgment

Sept.	28	M.	Judges 2:1-10, The Risk of Forgetfulness
Sept.	29	T.	Judges 2:11-23, A Recurring Pattern Emerges
Sept.	30	W.	Judges 6:1-10, The Cycle Continues
Oct.	1	T.	Judges 13:2-12, The Saga of Samson
Oct.	2	F.	Judges 16:18-31, Samson's Twenty Years Ends
Oct.	3	S.	Hosea 8:1-10, Sow the Wind...Reap the Whirlwind
Oct.	4	S.	Galatians 6:1-10, You Reap Whatever You Sow

Townsend Press Commentary

From Judges to Kings

Adult Topic—Demanding One's Own Way

.....

Youth Topic—Like Everybody Else
Children's Topic—Samuel Is Asked to Appoint a King

.....

Devotional Reading—1 Peter 2:13-17
Background Scripture—1 Samuel 7:15—8:22
Print—1 Samuel 7:15—8:9, 19-22

• • • • • • • • • • •

PRINTED SCRIPTURE

1 Samuel 7:15—8:9, 19-22 (KJV)

15 And Samuel judged Israel all the days of his life.

16 And he went from year to year in circuit to Bethel, and Gilgal, and Mizpeh, and judged Israel in all those places.

17 And his return was to Ramah; for there was his house; and there he judged Israel; and there he built an altar unto the LORD.

.....

AND it came to pass, when Samuel was old, that he made his sons judges over Israel.

2 Now the name of his firstborn was Joel; and the name of his second, Abiah: they were judges in Beersheba.

3 And his sons walked not in his ways, but turned aside after lucre, and took bribes, and perverted judgment.

4 Then all the elders of Israel gathered themselves together, and came to Samuel unto Ramah.

5 And said unto him, Behold,

1 Samuel 7:15—8:9, 19-22 (NRSV)

15 Samuel judged Israel all the days of his life.

16 He went on a circuit year by year to Bethel, Gilgal, and Mizpah; and he judged Israel in all these places.

17 Then he would come back to Ramah, for his home was there; he administered justice there to Israel, and built there an altar to the LORD.

.....

WHEN SAMUEL became old, he made his sons judges over Israel.

2 The name of his firstborn son was Joel, and the name of his second, Abijah; they were judges in Beersheba.

3 Yet his sons did not follow in his ways, but turned aside after gain; they took bribes and perverted justice.

4 Then all the elders of Israel gathered together and came to Samuel at Ramah,

5 and said to him, "You are old

thou art old, and thy sons walk not in thy ways: now make us a king to judge us like all the nations.

6 but the thing displeased Samuel, when they said, Give us a king to judge us. And Samuel prayed unto the LORD.

7 And the LORD said unto Samuel, Hearken unto the voice of the people in all that they say unto thee: for they have not rejected thee, but they have rejected me, that I should not reign over them.

8 According to all the works which they have done since the day that I brought them up out of Egypt even unto this day, wherewith they have forsaken me, and served other gods, so do they also unto thee.

9 Now therefore hearken unto their voice: howbeit yet protest solemnly unto them, and shew them the manner of the king that shall reign over them.

.....

19 Nevertheless the people refused to obey the voice of Samuel; and they said, Nay; but we will have a king over us;

20 That we also may be like all the nations; and that our king may judge us, and go out before us, and fight our battles.

21 And Samuel heard all the words of the people, and he rehearsed them in the ears of the LORD.

22 And the LORD said to Samuel, Hearken unto their voice, and make them a king. And Samuel said unto the men of Israel, Go ye every man unto his city.

and your sons do not follow in your ways; appoint for us, then, a king to govern us, like other nations."

6 But the thing displeased Samuel when they said, "Give us a king to govern us." Samuel prayed to the LORD,

7 and the LORD said to Samuel, "Listen to the voice of the people in all that they say to you; for they have not rejected you, but they have rejected me from being king over them.

8 Just as they have done to me, from the day I brought them up out of Egypt to this day, forsaking me and serving other gods, so also they are doing to you.

9 Now then, listen to their voice; only—you shall solemnly warn them, and show them the ways of the king who shall reign over them."

.....

19 But the people refused to listen to the voice of Samuel; they said, "No! but we are determined to have a king over us,

20 so that we also may be like other nations, and that our king may govern us and go out before us and fight our battles."

21 When Samuel had heard all the words of the people, he repeated them in the ears of the LORD.

22 The LORD said to Samuel, "Listen to their voice and set a king over them." Samuel then said to the people of Israel, "Each of you return home."

KEY VERSE

And the LORD said to Samuel, Hearken unto their voice, and make them a king.—1 Samuel 8:22a

OBJECTIVES

After reading this lesson, the student should be informed about:

1. The steps taken in Israel's transformation into a monarchy;
2. The danger of following others and neglecting God's leadership; and,
3. A Sovereign God uses man's evil will to accomplish God's plan.

POINTS TO BE EMPHASIZED

Adult/Youth/Children
Key Verse: 1 Samuel 8:22a; Acts 5:19 (Children)
Print: 1 Samuel 7:15—8:9, 19-22

—Samuel served Israel faithfully as a judge, traveling a regular circuit from his home in Ramah. (7:15-17)
—In his old age, Samuel appointed his sons judges, but they took bribes and perverted justice. (8:1-3)
—The elders pointed out the sons' shortcomings and asked Samuel to appoint a king to govern them like other nations. (8:4-5)
—Samuel felt rejected; but the Lord told Samuel that the people were rejecting the Lord, not Samuel. (8:6-9)
—Samuel warned the people of abuses they would suffer under a king, but they ignored his warning. (8:19-21)
—The Lord told Samuel to grant the request for a king. (8:22)

(NOTE: Use KJV Scripture for Adult; NRSV Scripture for Youth and Children)

TOPICAL OUTLINE OF THE LESSON

I. Introduction

A. A Perception of History
B. Biblical Background

II. Exposition and Application of the Scripture

A. Summary of Samuel's Duties (1 Samuel 7:15-17)
B. Israel's Demand (1 Samuel 8:1-5)
C. God's Displeasure (1 Samuel 8:6-9)
D. Israel's Determination (1 Samuel 8:19-22)

III. Special Features

A. Preserving Our Heritage
B. A Concluding Word

I. Introduction

A. A PERCEPTION OF HISTORY

Samuel's ministry covered an important part of Israel's history and his role in the development of the Old Testament kingdom of God. We thrill at the story of Samuel's birth to a wonderful woman of prayer by the name of Hannah (Her name is derived from Johanna or John, and means "grace"). Every Mother's Day we are tempted to preach again of this woman who prayed for a son, and said in essence: "Lord, give me, that I may give You." And then when blessed by God, she gave the boy to the Lord, "to appear before the Lord, and there abide forever" (1 Samuel 1:22, 28).

In Samuel's life, we have an illustration of the fact that God indeed deals with young people (1 Samuel 3). Samuel grew up to be used of the Lord to bridge the transition period of leadership by divinely chosen judges to the choice of leadership by a divinely chosen king. Through Samuel, the Lord rebuilt a social and religious unity within Israel, and such was his influence that all Israel "knew Samuel was established to be a prophet of the Lord" (1 Samuel 3:20). Samuel was Jehovah's representative to finish the work of the Judges. He stands as one of the greatest reformers in the history of the nation. He was not a mere warrior like his predecessors who judged, but through prayer, integrity, self-sacrifice, faith and intercession was blessed by God to deliver the children of Israel out of the hand of the Philistines, and into revival. Kirkpatrick wrote that Samuel was: "The last representative of the old Judges, the first of the regular succession of Prophets, the inaugurator of the new monarchy." And as such, Samuel "occupied the most trying of all positions, to stand between the Old and the New, and to mediate successfully between them" *(Cambridge Bible Commentary)*.

B. BIBLICAL BACKGROUND

Prior to the events of today's lesson, the Philistines, who at the time ruled over Israel, had captured the ark of God, having defeated the Israelites at Ebenezer, and having slain Hophni and Phinehas, the two sons of Eli. Loss of the ark signified that God's glory had departed from the nation (1 Samuel 4:21-22). When the Philistines took the ark, they brought it from Ebenezer to Ashdod, and placed it into the house of Dagon, their god. Jehovah humiliated the statue of Dagon, and afflicted the Philistines with tumors. This led to the decision to return the ark to the Jews. And so after seven months, the ark was returned.

The men of Kirjath Jearim came and took the ark of the Lord, and brought it into Abinadab's house. There it remained some twenty years. At this point Samuel admonished all the house of Israel to straighten out their lives spiritually and morally. He exhorted them to return to the Lord with all their hearts; put away their idol gods, prepare their hearts to serve the Lord only, "and He will deliver you from the hand of the Philistines" (1 Samuel 7:3). The Jews obeyed, and when they gathered together at Mizpah, they worshiped, fasted, confessed, prayed— and Samuel judged. However, their actions stirred up the Philistines. Satan hates to see revival. And the Philistines went up against Israel to subdue them further. The Israelites pleaded with Samuel to pray for them, that Jehovah would save them out of the hands of the foe. Samuel prayed and offered a sacrifice to Jehovah, and as he did so, the Lord thundered (roared with His voice; sent that noise which results from the discharge of lightning) upon the approaching Philistines, confused them, and gave the Jews the victory over them.

It was at this point that Samuel took a stone and set it up between Mizpah and Shen, and called its name Ebenezer, which means, "Thus far the Lord has helped us." Thus the Philistines were beaten, and they did not invade Israel's territory anymore. "And the hand of the Lord was against the Philistines all the days of Samuel" (1 Samuel 7:13). The cities the Philistines had captured were returned to Israel, and there was peace between Israel and the Amorites.

II. Exposition and Application of the Scripture

A. SUMMARY OF SAMUEL'S DUTIES
(1 Samuel 7:15-17)

And Samuel judged Israel all the days of his life. And he went from year to year in circuit to Bethel, and Gilgal, and Mizpeh, and judged Israel in all those places. And his return was to Ramah; for there was his house; and there he judged Israel; and there he built an altar unto the LORD.

From the death of Eli to this juncture, Samuel had labored as a prophet among the people. God had favored him in this capacity to bring about revival, and conversion to the Lord. His prophetic labors are generally described in 1 Samuel 3:19-21. Now with the calling of the Israelites to Mizpah, and the triumph over the Philistines at Ebenezer that had come through his prayers, Samuel became judge. Having assumed the office of governing the entire nation, his office as judge is dated from this point on: "Samuel judged Israel all the days of his life" (1 Samuel 7:15).

Samuel was a remarkable man! Almost single-handedly, he was responsible for re-educating the Jews in the laws of the Lord. See him then as prophet, judge, priest, Levite and ruler. It was his custom to travel from year to year from his home at Ramah (his father's home) to the various well-known sanctuaries of the famous cities of Bethel, Gilgal, and Mizpah. The spelling for one of the cities on the circuit varies: Mizpah, or Mizpeh. The name means "watchtower," and was used for a number of different cities in Bible lands. There were also several Gilgals. Scholars are not sure which one is meant here. As for the altar at Ramah, there is a violation of the law. According to Deuteronomy 12:5, 13, God was to select the places where His name would dwell, where burnt offerings would be sacrificed. Because of the need for revival, and for unification of the nation, it has been suggested that building the altar at Ramah was better than having no sacrifices at all. Another suggestion is that acceptance of the altar as the place of sacrifice for Jehovah was occasioned by the public disorder of the times, and the destruction of both the Tabernacle and its altar. At any rate, whatever the reason for the deviation from the law, we see Samuel voluntarily performing the functions of an itinerant judge. He administered justice, settled controversies, and carried out all the duties as judge or administrator.

B. ISRAEL'S DEMAND
(1 Samuel 8:1-5)

AND it came to pass, when Samuel was old, that he made his sons judges over Israel. Now the name of his firstborn was Joel; and the name of his second, Abiah: they were judges in Beersheba. And his sons walked not in his ways, but turned aside after lucre, and took bribes, and perverted judgment. Then all the elders of Israel gathered themselves together, and came to Samuel unto Ramah, And said unto him, Behold, thou art old, and thy sons walk not in thy ways: now make us a king to judge us like all the nations.

We come now to one of the most important events in the life of Israel. With the end of chapter 7, the era of the judges terminates. Samuel was now up in age. He was the father of two sons, Joel and Abijah. Joel is called Vashni in 1 Chronicles 6:28. Samuel made them judges in Beersheba. Many young men had been trained in his school of the prophets, but it is only natural that he would desire his own sons to assist him, and eventually take over as leaders of Israel. However, they were shameful disappointments to him. "Sons of the best of judges had perverted judgment" (B.C. Chapman, *Parallel Bible Commentary*, P. 546).

Samuel's sons failed to follow their father's example. In this, they were like the sons of Eli (1 Samuel 2:12, 22; 4:11). Samuel's sons set their hearts upon money, and took bribes, and perverted justice. The King James Version uses the word, "lucre," a word used often in our sermons concerning gambling, when it is suggested that there are members of our churches who "stand in long lottery lines lusting after lucky lucre." The love of money ever remains a root of every evil. In other words, there is nothing some men won't do for money (1 Timothy 6:10). Two factors furnish the elders of Israel with the opportunity to approach Samuel and demand that a king be crowned to rule over them like all the other nations have: (1) the old age of Samuel, and (2) the corruption of his sons. The demand is in keeping with the prophecy God foretold through His servant Moses in Deuteronomy 17:14-15.

C. GOD'S DISPLEASURE
(1 Samuel 8:6-9)

But the thing displeased Samuel, when they said, Give us a king to judge us. And Samuel prayed unto the LORD. And the LORD said unto Samuel, Hearken unto the voice of the people in all that they say unto thee: for they have not rejected thee, but they have rejected me, that I should not reign over them. According to all the works which they have done since the day that I brought them up out of Egypt even unto this day, wherewith they have forsaken me, and served other gods, so do they also unto thee. Now therefore hearken unto their voice: howbeit yet protest solemnly unto them, and shew them the manner of the king that shall reign over them.

This demand displeased Samuel. After all, he had given a lifetime of service to Israel, and now to be told that old age and maladministration of justice called for the establishment of a monarchy, a new form of government! He had spent a lifetime teaching Israel that God was their King, and now this demand for a human king! So we are not surprised that Samuel was displeased. One thing that Samuel did that speaks to our hearts is this: He prayed unto the Lord. How many of us take our "dislikes" to the Lord? Or do we keep them inside of us, "unspoken," and let them fester, grow and gnaw at our souls? Learn a lesson not only from Samuel, but from David in the Psalms, and from Jeremiah. When something displeases us, irks us, angers us, we should tell the Lord about it. Confess it, and request that the Holy Spirit help change attitudes, dispositions and values in our quest to become more like the Lord Jesus Christ.

God answered Samuel's prayer and gave this twofold response: First of all, "Heed the voice of the people, when they demand, 'Give us a king to judge us!'" Second: "Their demand is not that they have rejected you, but they have rejected Me!" The Hebrew word translated "rejected" means, "scorned, belittled." In the Greek Old Testament, called the Septuagint, a verb is used meaning, "to make light of." Give them what they ask for, says the Lord. He knew their determination not to have it any other way. Indeed, Israel had shown rebellion from the day the Lord delivered them from Egypt centuries earlier. "So heed their voice, Samuel, but protest solemnly. Warn them of the kind of king who shall reign over them." Samuel obeyed, and what he has to say in 1 Samuel 7:10-18 is touched upon in Deuteronomy 17:14-20. What God had warned Israel against through Moses is predicted to actually happen. As Israel had failed before in Moses' day, so they would fail again for idolatry is the issue, not monarchy vs. theocracy.

D. ISRAEL'S DETERMINATION
(1 Samuel 8:19-22)

Nevertheless the people refused to obey the voice of Samuel; and they said, Nay; but we will have a king over us; That we also may be like all the nations; and that our king may judge us, and go out before us, and fight our battles. And Samuel heard all the words of the people, and he rehearsed them in the ears of the LORD. And the LORD said to Samuel, Hearken unto their voice, and make them a king. And Samuel said unto the men of Israel, Go ye every man unto his city.

In spite of the warnings, the people turned a deaf ear to Samuel's voice: "We will—we want (NIV)—there shall be (NASB)—we will have a king over us!" And for the second time the words "like all the nations" are spoken (1 Samuel 8:5, 20). Are we Christians fearful of being ostracized, counted as peculiar, oddballs, religious fanatics? Or worse, called narrow-minded if we don't join the crowd? Christ would remind us that the road to destruction is broad (Matthew 7:13-14); Paul would remind us that we are not to conform to this world-age (Romans 12.2). James (4:4) would remind us that friendship of the world is enmity with God. Does the fear of being "different" move us to water down our doctrine, and give in to shackling habits just to be "accepted," or "sociable"?

"They have kings, we want a king. Their king judges; we want a king to judge us. Their kings fight their battles; we want a king to fight our battles, too!" And so Samuel heard all these words, took them and rehearsed them in the ears of the Lord. This means he reported them; the word "rehearse" means to "harrow over again." Picture a farmer harrowing again a plot of ground before planting. This indicates Samuel's concern. And once again, the Lord Jehovah calms Samuel with the order: "Heed their voice; do as they say; make them a king."

III. Special Features

A. PRESERVING OUR HERITAGE

The part the people played in making such momentous decisions leads us to think of our denomination. Black Baptists pride themselves on congregational polity or democracy. Freedom to elect leaders was not a freedom enjoyed by other nations of antiquity. Had the Israelites thought of this? They could never be like the heathen nations. For even in the establishment of a monarchy, it was still God's intention that Israel be holy, not like other countries. Unfortunately, the Jews did not want to be different; conformity was their desire. The doctrine of separation should remain strong in our churches. We ought to have no desire to be like people who reject Jesus Christ. We are called upon to be sanctified, set apart, in the world but not of the world. We are salt that preserves, salt that slows up corruption; we are lights in a world draped in darkness.

True freedom is to be a slave of the Lord Jesus Christ. Of all people, Black American Christians want to preserve their freedom, and especially be mindful of our belief in separation of church and state. We must remember that majority rule is not always majority right. Our strength lies in the congregation (or Convention, Association, Conference, etc.) or local assembly that is led by the Holy Spirit. When this happens, our majority rule is Holy Spirit rule; any other rule is a rejection of the Lordship of Jesus Christ. As democratization of the church becomes the order of the day, and spirituality declines, may it not be said of Black Baptists that God "gave them their request, but sent leanness unto their soul" (Psalm 106:15).

B. A CONCLUDING WORD

How often we ask of God those things which are not best for us! Yes, even Christians, people cleansed by the blood of the Lord Jesus, get out of God's will, and make demands of God that are not pleasing to Him. At times, the Lord allows His own to have their way! For in His wisdom, He uses our self-will and the subsequent sad experiences and disastrous results to teach us lessons evidently we have no desire to learn at all. Israel's bad experiences during the period of Judges were blamed on their political constitution. So they desired a king to lead them, to fight their wars, to triumph over their enemies—just as the heathen nations also were ruled by monarchs. Their motives and reasons were wrong. It did not dawn upon them that their evil behavior, especially their idolatry, was the principal cause of their misfortunes. Apostasy was the root cause of their adversity. Nonetheless, God acquiesced to their demand, but not without warning of the consequences. Determined to have their own way, they persisted in their demand. And so it was. Some of us look back at various experiences in our lives, and recall how determined we were to do as we pleased. Thank God, by His grace, He looked beyond our faults, saw our needs, and supplied them from His riches in glory in Christ Jesus; and somehow, God made all things work together for our good!

In a larger sense, the propensity to embrace those patterns which may be popular at the moment is often contrasted with the personal piety and fidelity that should characterize us as Christians. As did the people of Israel, depending upon the circumstances in the case, we attempt to solve problems as we perceive them and in the process make matters worse in preference to a course of action based upon a careful analysis of the situation before taking impulsive actions. We see this indicated in many churches that structure their services of worship around that which will attract the most attendees and calculate the "success" of their ministry on the number who join the church at any given point in time. In point of fact, there are those who tread likely over the more serious issues of morality and spirituality because should they take a strong stand against moral evils they believe that many persons will be turned away from the church. The Christ has called Christians to "come out from among them and be ye separated" and further that we "are in the world but not of the world." The church is not a society whose purpose and aim is to win friends and influence people, but a saved community of those who are committed to Jesus Christ. While that which is secular has an affinity with those who are in the world, the church can ill afford to lose its identity by adopting those standards of the world that are problematic when it comes to the essence of the Christian faith. As those who find their identity in the shed blood of Jesus Christ, the role of those who suffer persecution and ostracism for their uncompromising loyalty and fidelity must be understood as an essential embodiment of their faith.

HOME DAILY BIBLE READINGS
Week of October 11, 1998
From Judges to Kings

Oct.	5	M.	1 Samuel 1:3-11,	Hannah Prays for a Male Child
Oct.	6	T.	1 Samuel 1:21-28,	Hannah Did As She Promised
Oct.	7	W.	1 Samuel 3:1-10,	Speak, for Your Servant Is Listening
Oct.	8	T.	1 Samuel 7:15-8:9,	Samuel Administered Justice
Oct.	9	F.	1 Samuel 8:10-22,	Samuel Listened to the People and God
Oct.	10	S.	1 Timothy 2:1-7,	Pray for Kings
Oct.	11	S.	1 Samuel 11:5-15,	Saul Made Israel's First King

Jeroboam's Sin

Adult Topic—Anything to Keep Power
.....
Youth Topic—Less than Best
Children's Topic—The People Reject King Rehoboam
.....
Devotional Reading—Matthew 27:15-26
Background Scripture—1 Kings 12
Print—1 Kings 12:20, 25-33

• • • • • • • • • • •

PRINTED SCRIPTURE

1 Kings 12:20, 25-33 (KJV)

20 And it came to pass, when all Israel heard that Jeroboam was come again, that they sent and called him unto the congregation, and made him king over all Israel: there was none that followed the house of David, but the tribe of Judah only.

.....

25 Then Jeroboam built Shechem in mount Ephraim, and dwelt therein; and went out from thence, and built Penuel.

26 And Jeroboam said in his heart, Now shall the kingdom return to the house of David:

27 If this people go up to do sacrifice in the house of the LORD at Jerusalem, then shall the heart of this people turn again unto their lord, even unto Rehoboam king of Judah, and they shall kill me, and go again to Rehoboam king of Judah.

28 Whereupon the king took counsel, and made two calves of

1 Kings 12:20, 25-33 (NRSV)

20 When all Israel heard that Jeroboam had returned, they sent and called him to the assembly and made him king over all Israel. There was no one who followed the house of David, except the tribe of Judah alone.

.....

25 Then Jeroboam built Shechem in the hill country of Ephraim, and resided there; he went out from there and built Penuel.

26 Then Jeroboam said to himself, "Now the kingdom may well revert to the house of David.

27 If this people continues to go up to offer sacrifices in the house of the LORD at Jerusalem, the heart of this people will turn again to their master, King Rehoboam of Judah; they will kill me and return to King Rehoboam of Judah."

28 So the king took counsel, and made two calves of gold. He said to the people, "You have gone up

gold, and said unto them, It is too much for you to go up to Jerusalem: behold thy gods, O Israel, which brought thee up out of the land of Egypt.

29 And he set the one in Bethel, and the other put he in Dan.

30 And this thing became a sin: for the people went to worship before the one, even unto Dan.

31 And he made an house of high places, and made priests of the lowest of the people, which were not of the sons of Levi.

32 And Jeroboam ordained a feast in the eighth month, on the fifteenth day of the month, like unto the feast that is in Judah, and he offered upon the altar. So did he in Bethel, sacrificing unto the calves that he had made: and he placed in Bethel the priests of the high places which he had made.

33 So he offered upon the altar which he had made in Bethel the fifteenth day of the eighth month, even in the month which he had devised of his own heart; and ordained a feast unto the children of Israel: and he offered upon the altar, and burnt incense.

to Jerusalem long enough. Here are your gods, O Israel, who brought you up out of the land of Egypt."

29 He set one in Bethel, and the other he put in Dan.

30 And this thing became a sin, for the people went to worship before the one at Bethel and before the other as far as Dan.

31 He also made houses on high places, and appointed priests from among all the people, who were not Levites.

32 Jeroboam appointed a festival on the fifteenth day of the eighth month like the festival that was in Judah, and he offered sacrifices on the altar; so he did in Bethel, sacrificing to the calves that he had made. And he placed in Bethel the priests of the high places that he had made.

33 He went up to the altar that he had made in Bethel on the fifteenth day in the eighth month, in the month that he alone had devised; he appointed a festival for the people of Israel, and he went up to the altar to offer incense.

 KEY VERSE

Whereupon the king took counsel, and made two calves of gold, and said unto them, It is too much for you to go up to Jerusalem: behold thy gods, O Israel, which brought thee up out of the land of Egypt.—1 Kings 12:28

OBJECTIVES

After reading this lesson, the student should be informed about:

1. Why the nation of Israel divided;
2. Israel's besetting sin, idolatry; and,
3. The character and deeds of king Jeroboam.

POINTS TO BE EMPHASIZED

Adult/Youth
Key Verse: 1 Kings 12:28
Print: 1 Kings 12:20, 25-33

—All the tribes except Judah and Benjamin made Jeroboam their king after Solomon's death. (20-21)
—Jeroboam built up Shechem and Penuel to consolidate his power, but he worried that his kingdom might revert to "the house of David." (25-26)
—To keep the people from visiting Jerusalem to worship God, Jeroboam made two calves of gold and encouraged people to worship before them. (27-29)
—The people sinned by worshiping before the golden calves. (30)
—Jeroboam also sinned by establishing new sites for worship, appointing new priests, and declaring a new festival. (31-33)

Children
Key Verse: Proverbs 8:33
Print: 1 Kings 12:1-11, 15-16

—Rehoboam went to Shechem to be made king of Israel. (1)
—The people of Israel asked Rehoboam to lighten their heavy yoke in exchange for service to him. (3-4)
—Rehoboam sought out the advice of older men who advised him to be kind to the people. (6-7)
—Rehoboam disregarded the advice of the older men and turned to the younger men who advised him to add to the people's already heavy yoke. (8-11)
—When Israel saw that Rehoboam was not going to lighten their yoke, they chose not to serve him and went to their tents. (15-16)

(NOTE: Use KJV Scripture for Adult; NRSV Scripture for Youth and Children)

TOPICAL OUTLINE OF THE LESSON

I. Introduction
   A. A Perception of History
   B. Biblical Background

II. Exposition and Application of the Scripture
   A. Jeroboam's Coronation (1 Kings 12:20)
   B. Jeroboam's Fears (1 Kings 12:25-27)
   C. Jeroboam's Idolatry (1 Kings 12:28-30)
   D. Jeroboam's Sinful Changes (1 Kings 12:31-33)

III. Special Features
   A. Preserving Our Heritage
   B. A Concluding Word

I. Introduction

A. A PERCEPTION OF HISTORY

Our lesson is found in what is appropriately called the Books of the Kings, for they contain the record of the main events and characteristics of the reigns of the kings of Israel and Judah. Originally, 1 and 2 Kings were one book. Jewish tradition gives Jeremiah the prophet as the human author. Beginning with the history of the last days of David, and his death, 1 Kings relates the attempted plot and failure of Adonijah to become king. Amnon had been killed earlier by Absalom; and Absalom had been slain by Joab (2 Samuel 13:28; 18:14), so that at this point Adonijah was the oldest living son of David. There is no mention of number three son, Chileab; we assume he also was dead.

Actually, the first major narrative of 1 Kings covers the reign of Solomon (2:12-11:43), with an extended account of the building of the Temple under his rule. It was God's plan that Solomon should follow David as king. While Solomon was still a young boy, his father David told him this; and it was also publicly proclaimed (1 Chronicles 22:1-19; 28:1-8). The plots and fratricides which occurred were used by Jehovah to accomplish God's plan; the Lord would allow nothing to thwart His desire or decree for Solomon to reign.

It is during the rule of Solomon that we see the seeds sown leading to the eventual division of the nation. The beginning of Solomon's downfall was his disobedience to God's law against mixed marriages, marriages with the Canaanites. Jehovah had warned the Jews not to intermarry with the heathen women of the land lest Israel become involved in idolatry (Exodus 34:16). The command to be separate is repeated in Deuteronomy 7:3-4: "Neither shalt thou make marriages with them...for they will turn away thy son from following me, that they may serve other gods...." What God predicted is exactly what happened. Solomon's foreign wives turned him from the Lord. Imagine having seven hundred wives, and three hundred concubines! No wonder his heart was turned away from the Lord (1 Kings 11:3). We are told that Solomon "loved many strange women" (1 Kings 11.1). But whether sexual lust or political maneuverings (marrying the daughters of kings), or a combination of these and other factors, Solomon's relationship with them brought about a deterioration of his relationship with the Lord God Jehovah. "And the Lord was angry with Solomon, because his heart was turned from the Lord God of Israel, which had appeared unto him twice," chastening him about his disobedience. God stirred up enemies against Solomon, intending to bring the king into confession and repentance, but to no avail. Hadad the Edomite, and Rezon the son of Eliadah were stirred up (Hebrew: raised up) by God as adversaries to Solomon. Among the adversaries was also a man by the name of Jeroboam—a mighty man of valor.

B. BIBLICAL BACKGROUND

Jeroboam is brought to our attention during the reign of Solomon. The king was impressed with Jeroboam's diligence, and made him the officer in charge of the labor force of the house of Joseph. It came to pass that the prophet Ahijah prophesied to Jeroboam that God would tear the kingdom out of Solomon's hand and give ten tribes to Jeroboam. However, it would not take place under Solomon, but under the rule of Solomon's son. Unfortunately, Jeroboam could not wait for the Lord to give him the kingdom, but in unbelief attempted to usurp power in his own strength. Solomon then sought to kill Jeroboam, who then fled into Egypt. After forty years of rule over the nation, the monarch Solomon died and was buried in Jerusalem, the city of David his father. In his place, Rehoboam reigned. It is interesting that with all of the wives Solomon had, we might assume he fathered many sons; however, Rehoboam is the only son of Solomon mentioned in the Bible! At this point Jeroboam returned, and, along with other citizens, delivered an ultimatum to king Rehoboam to lighten up on the taxes imposed upon the people. Rehoboam refused, and set the stage for the fulfillment of God's prophecy, given through Ahijah, with respect to Jeroboam.

II. Exposition and Application of the Scripture

A. JEROBOAM'S CORONATION
(1 Kings 12:20)

And it came to pass, when all Israel heard that Jeroboam was come again, that they sent and called him unto the congregation, and made him king over all Israel: there was none that followed the house of David, but the tribe of Judah only.

When the Jews saw that king Rehoboam had no intention of lightening the heavy yoke, they rebelled. "And upon hearing of the return of Jeroboam, they sent for him and made him king over the ten tribes of Israel." The history of the divided kingdom begins here and continues right through the book of 2 Kings. Note that Israel here refers to the northern ten tribes; Israel is sometimes referred to as "Ephraim." Unfortunately, as history reveals, all the kings of the northern kingdom were wicked. On the other hand, the southern kingdom, made up of the tribe of Judah (and the very small tribe of Benjamin), was ruled by Rehoboam; and some of the kings of Judah turned out to be men of faith. Whereas the north had a succession of nine different dynasties (rulers from different families or lines), the southern kingdom had only one dynasty. All of its kings were descendants of David; and so the tribe of Judah followed the house of David.

Now here is the first wrong step made by Jeroboam the Ephraimite. True, God had predicted Jeroboam's rule, and had ordained Jeroboam's success as a punishment for Solomon's idolatry, and for Rehoboam's disobedience and imprudence. Yet Jeroboam was essentially guilty of rebellion against the Lord's anointed, and participation in the conspiracy of the tribes against Judah. How mysterious are the ways of the Lord! God's promise of the throne to Jeroboam did not warrant Jeroboam's rebellion and usurpation! A Sovereign God uses whatever He pleases to accomplish His purposes. Understand then this first part of our exposition; Jeroboam was promptly crowned king of Israel, the northern ten tribes.

B. JEROBOAM'S FEARS
(1 Kings 12:25-27)

Then Jeroboam built Shechem in mount Ephraim, and dwelt therein; and went out from thence, and built Penuel. And Jeroboam said in his heart, Now shall the kingdom return to the house of David: If this people go up to do sacrifice in the House of the LORD at Jerusalem, then shall the heart of this people turn again unto their lord, even unto Rehoboam king of Judah, and they shall kill me, and go again to Rehoboam king of Judah.

Rehoboam wanted to declare war, and fight to bring the kingdom together again. But the Lord warned him not to do so. "This thing is from Me," said Jehovah (1 Kings 12:24). And so Rehoboam obeyed and disbanded his army of 180,000 chosen warriors. Since God had decreed the schism, He saw to it that bloodshed was avoided. In the meantime, Jeroboam's fears led him to commit a second grievous sin. He reasoned that if the people continued to worship and do sacrifice at Jerusalem, then the heart of the people would turn again to Rehoboam, and the people would kill Jeroboam and once again support Rehoboam. So Jeroboam changed the place of sacrifice. He built Shechem or Sichem, (Genesis 12:6), a place of great importance, and made it his capital from the very beginning of his rule.

Once Jerusalem had been established as the place for the Lord's worship, any setting up of another place was of necessity idolatrous and divisive. According to law, all Israel was to make the pilgrimage to Jerusalem to worship the Lord three times a year (Exodus 23:17; Leviticus 23). Jeroboam felt such a trip would jeopardize his hold upon the people, and so he took steps to prevent the use of Jerusalem for worship. After choosing Shechem for his capital, he also built Penuel, which means, "The Face of God." It is also called Peniel (Genesis 32:30).

C. JEROBOAM'S IDOLATRY
(1 Kings 12:28-30)

Whereupon the king took counsel, and made two calves of gold, and said unto them, It is too much for you to go up to Jerusalem: behold thy gods, O Israel, which brought thee up out of the land of Egypt. And he set the one in Bethel, and the other put he in Dan. And this thing became a sin: for the people went to worship before the one, even unto Dan.

Here we see Jeroboam's third sinful act: He sought to establish his own brand of religion, an unlawful worship. Note that he took counsel, or asked advice, a case of the blind advising the blind, for evidently approval was given to make two golden calves to represent Jehovah. Once again, we see Jeroboam's plan to make it unnecessary to travel to Jerusalem. It is believed that the calves were not made of solid pure gold, but like the golden calf fashioned by Aaron for the Jews at Mount Sinai was made of a kernel of wood, then covered with gold plate. The words "behold thy gods, O Israel, which brought thee up out of the land of Egypt" take us back to Exodus 32 in which we hear Aaron say: "These be thy gods, O Israel, which brought thee up out of the land of Egypt." Here was an appeal that informed the Israelites that what Jeroboam sought to establish was no new religion, but one which their fathers had used in the desert centuries earlier, and led by no less a person than Aaron!

Jeroboam then set one calf in Bethel, and the other in Dan. "This thing became a sin" because it violated the fundamental Old Testament law which prohibited the use of images and symbols in the worship of Jehovah (Exodus 20:4: the Second Commandment). This was in addition to the fact that the Lord had not left it up to the people to determine where God was to be worshiped. Deuteronomy 12:5 teaches the one place was to be chosen by God.

D. JEROBOAM'S SINFUL CHANGES
(1 Kings 12:31-33)

And he made an house of high places, and made priests of the lowest of the people, which were not of the sons of Levi. And Jeroboam ordained a feast in the eighth month, on the fifteenth day of the month, like unto the feast that is in Judah, and he offered upon the altar. So did he in Bethel, sacrificing unto the calves that he had made: and he placed in Bethel the priests of the high places which he had made. So he offered upon the altar which he had made in Bethel the fifteenth day of the eighth month, even in the month which he had devised of his own heart; and ordained a feast unto the children of Israel: and he offered upon the altar, and burnt incense.

Another step of spiritual declension and apostasy was taken. Jeroboam brought non-Levites into the priesthood. "No man takes this honor unto himself, but he that is called of God, as was Aaron" (Hebrews 5:4). Jeroboam did the calling here, not God. He placed the men he chose where he wanted them to be (2 Chronicles 11:15). The law of Moses specifically states that no one except men from the tribe of Levi should attend holy ordinances (Exodus 28:1; Numbers 16:40). Finally, Jeroboam took one more step calculated to weaken the religious and political ties between the tribes. He went so far as to change not only the symbols of worship, the places of worship, and the priesthood—but now, the scheduled feasts were changed. According to the law in Leviticus 23, the Jews were to celebrate the seventh month: (1) The first day was The Feast of Trumpets; (2) the tenth day, The Day of Atonement; and (3) the fifteenth day, The Feast of Tabernacles.

It was this latter day that Jeroboam sought to annul by scheduling a comparable feast on the fifteenth day of the eighth month. By making the celebration as elaborate as possible, with all the ritual and pomp at his command, Jeroboam sought to make the feasts at Jerusalem less attractive, hoping that eventually the pilgrimages there would cease. He attempted to make the break with Judah final and complete not only by political isolation, but also by his blatant redefinition of the manner and place of worship. As such, he translated the promise of God into the language of personal gratification. This is always danger involved when the concept of God is re-conceived to accommodate personal advancement and gratification.

III. Special Features

A. PRESERVING OUR HERITAGE

Some Black religious leaders and church members impress us that we too have fallen into the same trap that enmeshed Jeroboam, namely, worshiping God the way we want to, rather than His way. This is the same terrible mistake Cain made at the very beginning of man's history, so that what Jeroboam did was nothing new. And man-made religion still exists today. What we see in some church assemblies is a lack of dedication, an ignorance of the Bible, an appeal to the old nature, the love of entertainment, the excitement of the novel and different, and the influence of the world-system, all combining to produce a worship service that dishonors and displeases God.

Dare I mention the "Come-As-You-Are" invitations which emphasize the point that God looks at our hearts, and not our clothing. First Samuel 16:7 is often taken out of context, and we fail to accept the fact that the Lord is concerned with our outside apparel (1 Peter 3:3-5; Romans 2:2; Deuteronomy 22:5). All such may be the efforts of sincere church members—even as Jeroboam was sincere—but it may well be that as is written of Jeroboam, so may it be said of us: "This thing has become a sin!"

B. A CONCLUDING WORD

Jeroboam was guilty of setting up a false religion, for we learn from the Bible that man does not know how to worship God. We must be taught. But when we refuse to accept the divine indoctrination, then we go about seeking to establish our own brand of worship. This is why it is necessary for us to study and know the Bible; ignorance of God's Word, and therefore of His will, leaves us vulnerable to the many cults and false religions extant today. Finally, we see that all too often, the people in roles of leadership in man-made religions are spiritually deficient, lacking in holiness. In summary: Baptists who remain "People of the Book" protect themselves from all such heresies and apostasies. Students of the Bible do not fall for the half-truths as proclaimed by popular religion.

HOME DAILY BIBLE READINGS
Week of October 18, 1998
Jeroboam's Sin

Oct. 12	M.	1 Kings 11:26-35, Jeroboam Succumbs to Temptation
Oct. 13	T.	1 Kings 1136-43, Jeroboam Flees to Egypt
Oct. 14	W.	1 Kings 12:1-19, Rehoboam's Rejects the Advice of the Elders
Oct. 15	T.	1 Kings 12:20-33, Rehoboam's Downfall; Jeroboam's Sin
Oct. 16	F.	1 Kings 13:1-10, Jeroboam's Sin Had Consequences
Oct. 17	S.	1 Kings 13:33-14:10a, More Consequences of Jeroboam's Sin
Oct. 18	S.	2 Kings 14:10b-20, Jeroboam's Son Dies

The Work of Prophets

Unit III. God Works Through People

Children's Unit—God Works Through People
Adult Topic —Healing in Unexpected Ways

.....

Youth Topic—Just Wash!
Children's Topic—A Young Slave Girl Helps Naaman

.....

Devotional Reading—2 Samuel 12:1-15
Background Scripture—2 Kings 5:1-19
Print—2 Kings 5:2-6, 9-14

• • • • • • • • • • •

PRINTED SCRIPTURE

2 Kings 5:2-6, 9-14 (KJV)

2 And the Syrians had gone out by companies, and had brought away captive out of the land of Israel a little maid; and she waited on Naaman's wife.

3 And she said unto her mistress, Would God my lord were with the prophet that is in Samaria! for he would recover him of his leprosy.

4 And one went in, and told his lord, saying, Thus and thus said the maid that is of the land of Israel.

5 And the king of Syria said, Go to, go, and I will send a letter unto the king of Israel. And he departed, and took with him ten talents of silver, and six thousand pieces of gold, and ten changes of raiment.

6 And he brought the letter to the king of Israel, saying, Now when this letter is come unto thee, behold, I have therewith sent Naaman my servant to thee, that thou mayest recover him of his leprosy.

2 Kings 5:2-6, 9-14 (NRSV)

2 Now the Arameans on one of their raids had taken a young girl captive from the land of Israel, and she served Naaman's wife.

3 She said to her mistress, "If only my lord were with the prophet who is in Samaria! He would cure him of his leprosy."

4 So Naaman went in and told his lord just what the girl from the land of Israel had said.

5 And the king of Aram said, "Go then, and I will send along a letter to the king of Israel." He went, taking with him ten talents of silver, six thousand shekels of gold, and ten sets of garments.

6 He brought the letter to the king of Israel, which read, "When this letter reaches you, know that I have sent to you my servant Naaman, that you may cure him of his leprosy."

9 So Naaman came with his horses and with his chariot, and stood at the door of the house of Elisha.

10 And Elisha sent a messenger unto him, saying, Go and wash in Jordan seven times, and thy flesh shall come again to thee, and thou shalt be clean.

11 But Naaman was wroth, and went away, and said, Behold, I thought, He will surely come out to me, and stand, and call on the name of the Lord his God, and strike his hand over the place, and recover the leper.

12 Are not Abana and Pharpar, rivers of Damascus, better than all the waters of Israel? may I not wash in them, and be clean? So he turned and went away in a rage.

13 And his servants came near, and spake unto him, and said, My father, if the prophet had bid thee do some great thing, wouldest thou not have done it? how much rather then, when he saith to thee, Wash, and be clean?

14 Then went he down, and dipped himself seven times in Jordan, according to the saying of the man of God: and his flesh came again like unto the flesh of a little child, and he was clean.

9 So Naaman came with his horses and chariots, and halted at the entrance of Elisha's house.

10 Elisha sent a messenger to him, saying, "Go, wash in the Jordan seven times, and your flesh shall be restored and you shall be clean."

11 But Naaman became angry and went away, saying, "I thought that for me he would surely come out, and stand and call on the name of the LORD his God, and would wave his hand over the spot, and cure the leprosy!

12 Are not Abana and Pharpar, the rivers of Damascus, better than all the waters of Israel? Could I not wash in them, and be clean?" He turned and went away in a rage.

13 But his servants approached and said to him, "Father, if the prophet had commanded you to do something difficult, would you not have done it? How much more, when all he said to you was, 'Wash, and be clean'?"

14 So he went down and immersed himself seven times in the Jordan, according to the word of the man of God; his flesh was restored like the flesh of a young boy, and he was clean.

KEY VERSE Let him come to me, and he shall know that there is a prophet in Israel.—2 Kings 5:8b

OBJECTIVES

After reading this lesson, the student should be informed about:

1. The pride of Naaman, commander of the army of the king of Syria;

2. The faith and attitude of a little Jewish slave girl;
3. The power of the God of Elisha; and,
4. The need for all human beings to wash and be clean!

POINTS TO BE EMPHASIZED

Adult/Youth/Children
Key Verse: 2 Kings 5:8b; Acts 10:34 (Children)
Print: 2 Kings 5:2-6, 9-14

—Naaman, commander in chief of the army of Aram, suffered from leprosy. (1)

—A young Israelite slave girl told Naaman's wife that a prophet of Israel could cure Naaman. (2-3)

—With a letter of explanation from his king, plus many riches, Naaman went to the Israelite king. (4-6)

—The king of Israel was troubled by Naaman's visit, but Elisha told the king to send Naaman to him. (8)

—When Naaman reached Elisha's house, the prophet sent a messenger to tell Naaman to wash in the Jordan seven times. (9-11)

—Naaman was enraged by the prophet's attitude toward him, but he finally washed in the river, was healed, and praised the God of Israel. (5:11-14)

(NOTE: Use KJV Scripture for Adults; NRSV Scripture for Youth and Children)

TOPICAL OUTLINE OF THE LESSON

I. Introduction

A. A Perception of History
B. Biblical Background

II. Exposition and Application of the Scripture

A. A Slave Girl's Recommendation (2 Kings 5:2-3)
B. A Syrian King's Response (2 Kings 5:4-6)
C. A Seer's Response (2 Kings 5:9-10)
D. A Soldier's Reaction (2 Kings 5:11-14)

III. Special Features

A. Preserving Our Heritage
B. A Concluding Word

I. Introduction

A. A PERCEPTION OF HISTORY

The prophet Elijah was walking and talking with Elisha when suddenly there appeared a chariot of fire, and horses of fire, and separated them. And Elijah went up by a whirlwind into heaven (2 Kings 2:11). Elijah's mantle fell upon Elisha, and from this point on, we deal with the ministry of Elisha. At this time, Jehoshaphat ruled in Judah, and Jehoram became the king of Israel (the northern kingdom). When the king of Moab rebelled against the king of Israel, a pact was formed between Israel and Judah in order to fight Moab. To the combination of Jehoshaphat and Jehoram was added the king of Edom, and the trio went to fight Moab. During the campaign, they ran out of water, and became fearful that the Lord had called the three kings together in order to deliver them into the hand of Moab. However, a servant of king Jehoram pointed out that the prophet Elisha lived in the area. So, Jehoram and Jehoshaphat went down to visit Elisha. The prophet rebuked Jehoram, but had respect for the presence of Jehoshaphat. Consequently, even as Elisha predicted, the Moabites were defeated and made to return to their own land.

B. BIBLICAL BACKGROUND

We are impressed with the miracles performed by the prophets of God during this period in the life of the divided nation. Miracles are the extraordinary works of God—extraordinary to us. They transcend the ordinary powers of nature. A miracle is defined as a wonderful happening that is beyond the known laws of nature; it is an event that appears unexplainable by the laws of nature, and so is held to be supernatural in origin or an act of God *(World Book Dictionary; American Heritage Dictionary)*. Wrought as manifestations of God, they are evidences of His character and will. God used miracles in times of crisis to display His glory and power as He judged sin and delivered His own people. Miracles were wrought by God for the deliverance of the Israelites from Egypt. Miracles were wrought in the era of Joshua and the Judges. Miracles wrought by God through the prophet Elijah also revealed the will and power of God.

And now in our lesson, during a time of apostasy in both Judah and Israel, we find the Lord performing miracles through His servants. Elijah's preaching ministry was backed up by Holy Spirit power enabling him for the task. He predicted drought, and it came to pass. Fed by the poor widow of Zarephath, he blessed her with a cruse of oil and barrel of meal that never ran out. He raised the dead boy of this same woman. He called down fire from heaven to burn up the sacrifice in the contest with the phony prophets of Baal at Mount Carmel. This brings us to the prophet Elisha. With the mantle of the translated Elijah, he struck the waters of the Jordan, and the river split, allowing Elisha to cross over dry shod. He cast salt into the spring of the waters in Jericho, and healing the waters, made them potable. By his curse, she-bears came out of the woods and wounded the children who had insulted him and thereby insulted God. He predicted the defeat of the Moabites. He caused the oil in the pot of the poor widow to multiply so that she could sell oil, pay her debt, and live. To the barren Shunnamite woman prediction was made that she would become a mother. Later, when the child took sick and died, God used Elisha to revive the boy and return him alive to his mother.

At a meeting of the sons of the prophets, a pot of soup was found to be poisoned; there was "death in the pot." Elisha cast some meal into the pot and the food was safe to eat. Again, God used the prophet to feed many people with some barley and corn, for the Lord multiplied the provision. This brings us to the miracle of the cleansing of the leper, Naaman, a man described as great and honorable in the eyes of the king, his master, and a mighty man of valor. It is here that Elisha's public ministry begins.

II. Exposition and Application of the Scripture

A. A SLAVE GIRL'S RECOMMENDATION
(2 Kings 5:2-3)

And the Syrians had gone out by companies, and had brought away captive out of the land of Israel a little maid; and she waited on Naaman's wife. And she said unto her mistress, Would God my lord were with the prophet that is in Samaria! for he would recover him of his leprosy.

Naaman, commander of the Syrian army, had leprosy. In Israel, leprosy was considered an uncleanness, and therefore affected one's spiritual relationship with God, the priests, and the community. In Syria, the disease caused only physical problems. Naaman was able physically to carry out the duties required of him as a solider. Evidently, as a leper, he won no further military victories. Naturally, the king of Syria would be genuinely concerned about losing such military expertise. But understand that in Syria, lepers were not social outcasts as they were in Israel (Leviticus, chapters 13 and 14). They were not excluded from holding public office.

It is interesting to note also that Naaman had been an instrument in the hands of the Lord. Jehovah used this warrior to give "deliverance unto Syria." This expression (verse 1) teaches us that the God of the Bible is Sovereign, for even the victories heathen nations have in battle are decreed by God. Surely, the powers that be are ordained of God (Romans 13:1). On one of their raiding expeditions in Israel, the Syrians captured a little Jewish girl and brought her back to Syria. As God would have it, she became the servant of Naaman's wife, a woman evidently solicitous in her desire for her husband's well-being. But we are more impressed with the unnamed little maid. She had been torn away from her homeland, from her loved ones and family. But she did not give way to sorrow and despair. Instead, she placed herself into the family life of Naaman and his wife.

How God enables us to remain faithful even in adverse circumstances. She was of little importance in the eyes of the world—a female, a slave girl, a captive, and in the demonism of anti-Semitism, a Jew! But, God used her. Slavery had not deprived her of her faith. Indeed, the story of Naaman's cleansing hinges on the part she played. She said to her mistress: "If only my master were with the prophet who is in Samaria! For he would heal him of his leprosy!" What a remarkable statement! How did she know what Elisha could or would do? When the Lord Jesus preached and taught in the synagogue at Nazareth, He said: "And many lepers were in Israel in the time of Elisha, the prophet; and none of them was cleansed, but only Naaman, the Syrian" (Luke 4:27).

In other words, Elisha had not cleansed anyone of leprosy there in Israel! So the maid had no proof of an actual cure of leprosy. But her faith moved her to suggest that Naaman could be healed. She believed the true and living God existed in Israel; and He is able to heal. One writer (W. W. White) likened the young girl's recommendation of Elisha to Naaman's wife as an excellent illustration of a word "fitly spoken which is like apples of gold in baskets (settings or pictures) of silver" (Proverbs 25:11).

B. A SYRIAN KING'S REPORT
(2 Kings 5:4-6)

And one went in, and told his lord, saying, Thus and thus said the maid that is of the land of Israel. And the king of Syria said, Go to, go, and I will send a letter unto the king of Israel. And he departed, and took with him ten talents of silver, and six thousand pieces of gold, and ten changes of raiment. And he brought the letter to the king of Israel, saying, Now when this letter is come unto thee, behold, I have therewith sent Naaman my servant to thee, that thou mayest recover him of his leprosy.

Someone informed the king of Syria what the Israelite maid had said. The king is not named, but it appears that he is Ben-Hadad (2 Kings 8:17). Neither is the name of the king of Israel given, but it is believed that he is Joram (Jehoram). The description of what takes place between these two monarchs gives an interesting picture of international customs of that time. The king of Syria believed Israel's king could get "his prophet" (attached to the court) to heal Naaman. And so, he wrote a letter. In addition to the letter sent by Syria's king, the messenger carried with him rich presents quite in keeping with Naaman's lofty position. Ten thousand talents of silver, and six thousand shekels of gold, and ten changes of raiment were brought along. The words "talents" and "shekels" refer primarily to weights, although the shekel came to be both weight and coin. However, because of the changes in purchasing power at different periods of time, it is not possible to ascertain the exact value of these precious metals.

And so, the letter was brought to the king of Israel. In the letter, the king of Syria informed the king of Israel that Naaman his servant accompanied the report, and they expected his servant Naaman to be healed of his leprosy. When the king of Israel received the report, he went to pieces! He was convinced that it was Ben-Hadad's intention to start a war with him. "Who does he think I am? Does he think I am omnipotent, like God?"

It was well known that leprosy was a terrible disease. And it appears that in Naaman's case, his malady would be fatal in time. The concern displayed by the Jewish maid, by Naaman's wife, and the promptness of the king of Syria in sending Naaman to Samaria, convince us of the seriousness of the type of leprosy that Naaman had.

C. A SEER'S RESPONSE
(2 Kings 5:9-10)

So Naaman came with his horses and with his chariot, and stood at the door of the house of Elisha. And Elisha sent a messenger unto him, saying, Go and wash in Jordan seven times, and thy flesh shall come again to thee, and thou shalt be clean.

Naaman came with his retinue and stood at the door of Elisha's house, but there was no prophet standing outside to greet him. Instead, Elisha sent a messenger out to where Naaman stood with his horses and with his chariot, and the servant said: "Wash and be clean!" God knew the proud heart of Naaman, and led Elisha to do nothing that would lead Naaman to think some hocus-pocus or magic was involved. He needed to see that the healing would be purely by the grace of God. Naaman needed to learn that the cure was not due to any magic touch of the prophet Elisha, but to Jehovah working through Elisha. Furthermore, by remaining inside, Elisha emphasized the point that neither wealth nor position could purchase cleansing. The power to heal comes from God; and it is a gift.

D. A SOLDIER'S REACTION
(2 Kings 5:11-14)

But Naaman was wroth, and went away, and said, Behold, I thought, He will surely come out to me, and stand, and call on the name of the LORD his God, and strike his hand over the place, and recover the leper. Are not Abana and Pharpar, rivers of Damascus, better than all the waters of Israel? may I not wash in them, and be clean? So he turned and went away in a rage. And his servants came near, and spake unto him, and said, My father, if the prophet had bid thee do some great thing, wouldest thou not have done it? how much rather then, when he saith to thee, Wash, and be clean? Then went he down, and dipped himself seven times in Jordan, according to the saying of the man of God: and his flesh came again like unto the flesh of a little child, and he was clean.

Elisha was not the kind of exorcist Naaman expected; he looked for something more sensational and spectacular! Enraged at what he considered an improper reception, he went away. He had thought the prophet would surely come out to him, stand there and call on the name of the Lord his God, wave his hands over his afflicted body, and cure the leprosy. He was furious! Why the rivers of Abana and Pharpar, in Damascus, were superior to all the waters of Israel. He asked this question, "May I not wash in them, and be clean?" Well, no, not really. For it is not left up to us to decide or prescribe how to be cleansed.

Fortunately, Naaman's servants prevailed upon him to not compare the muddy waters of Israelite Jordan with the pure, cool streams of the Damascan oases. He was persuaded to do the easy thing, for if the prophet had demanded something difficult to do, Naaman would have tried it. So why not this easy thing? Why not do what he says, "Wash and be clean"? And so, addressed by his servants with the title of respect and affection, "My father," Naaman agreed. He came so close to losing a blessing through pride! Naaman went down from Samaria to the Jordan and like any good Baptist would have done, he dipped, yea, he dipped in the Jordan seven times. Thus, he was a perfect Baptist! (Please do not seek to establish a new denomination, The Seven Dipped Baptists!!!). God wanted him to do it seven times to convince him the healing was the work of God. His flesh became sound, like the skin of a little boy. Thus God's perfect power to perfectly heal was perfectly demonstrated through Elisha, the servant of a Perfect God.

III. Special Features

A. PRESERVING OUR HERITAGE

It is true that certain Americans have looked down their noses at Black American Churches, and have despised the simple faith in Christ that we profess. What such sophisticated religionists fail to realize is that the conservatism of our Black Baptist churches is the very heart-beat of Christianity in the United States. May we never forget that we are in "the Wash and Be Clean" business. Pressure is always upon us to get so involved in other matters, to get off on a tangent, miss the target, be sidetracked and get into some other business. Recall after the Resurrection that Simon Peter announced to the other disciples, "I'm going fishing!" (John 21:3).

Our task is to fish for men, women, boys and girls. We are to win the lost and edify the saved. Only when the Church is about its biblical business, that task laid down for us in the Bible, only then are we a beacon light in a lost world of darkness. Only then are we salt preserving and slowing down the fast corruption all about us. Only when we stick to the "Wash and Be Clean" task are we a hospital for souls sick with sin. Only then can we boldly tell political leaders that righteousness exalts a nation, but sin is a reproach to any people. The world needs to know that like Elisha, Black Baptists are in the "Wash and Be Clean" business. However, our cleansing agent is not the river of Jordan, but the blood of the Lamb of God. For, there is power in the blood!

B. A CONCLUDING WORD

Leprosy is a type or symbol of sin. Naaman's affliction therefore gives us a picture of man at his best—but still a sinner. Naaman was not down and out, but up and out. He held an exalted position in the government; people bowed before him; he was respected, honored, adulated—but still a sinner. He was "up" in the sense of possessing great power, prestige, position, influence and renown.

D. L. Moody said that Naaman had two diseases—pride and leprosy. Both needed curing, but the besetting sin was his pride. He would have to swallow his pride in order to lose his leprosy. For God resists the proud, but gives grace to the humble. Without humility, no man can be saved. He must believe that he is a sinner, a leper, unclean in God's sight. Our message is that only the blood of Jesus Christ cleanses from sin. Men, women, boys and girls everywhere need to hear the message: Wash and Be Clean! Thank God for the Christian Church as we continue to point people to the crimson tide of Calvary!

When we take into full consideration the situation in which Naaman found himself, it is not difficult for us to perceive in his actions characteristics that are similar to our own. In a period wherein miracle medicine is the first option of choice, there are those who neglect the simple rules of good health that would circumvent the onslaught of incurable diseases. The simple things of life are many times deferred because our claim to greatness takes precedence over the fundamentals of behavior that assure our well being. Naaman had another problem with which we can identify—his status within society had become in his own mind inconsistent with humility and obedience to a simple command. The Bible is insightful at this point as it states categorically that "all have sinned and have fallen short of the glory of God." Should we keep this description of the human situation in mind, then there should not be that arrogance which is associated with the feeling that we are better than others. Humility motivates us to do whatever is necessary to become the kind of persons that God requires us to be. How often do we refuse to follow good and constructive advice simply because it did not come from the right persons or individuals with status and clout within society. As persons created in the image of God, we must come to believe that God can use both persons and events as the means by which He communicates His Word to us. The biblical injunction that "a little child shall lead them" is most appropriate in this situation, and it should not be alien to our understanding of God's discretion to use whomever He wills to actualize His plan and purpose in the world.

HOME DAILY BIBLE READINGS
Week of October 25, 1998
The Work of Prophets

Oct. 19	M.	2 Kings 5:1-19, Elisha Cures Naaman's Leprosy
Oct. 20	T.	2 Kings 2:9-14, Elisha Dons Elijah's Mantle
Oct. 21	W.	2 Kings 2:15-22, Elisha Purifies Jericho's Water Supply
Oct. 22	T.	2 Kings 3:9-20, Elisha Encounters King Jehoshaphat
Oct. 23	F.	2 Kings 4:1-7, Elisha Performs Another Miracle
Oct. 24	S.	2 Kings 4:8-17, A Shunammite Woman Has a Son
Oct. 25	S.	2 Kings 4:38-44, Elisha Performs More Miracles

Courage to Speak for God

Adult Topic—Courage to Speak for God

·····

Youth Topic—Measure Up!
Children's Topic—Amos, Preacher for God

·····

Devotional Reading—Acts 4:13-22
Background Scripture—Amos 6—7
Print—Amos 6:1; 7:7-15

● ● ● ● ● ● ● ● ● ● ●

PRINTED SCRIPTURE

Amos 6:1; 7:7-15 (KJV)

WOE to them that are at ease in Zion, and trust in the mountain of Samaria, which are named chief of the nations, to whom the house of Israel came!

·····

7 Thus he shewed me: and, behold the Lord stood upon a wall made by a plumbline, with a plumbline in his hand.

8 And the LORD said unto me, Amos, what seest thou? And I said, A plumbline. Then said the LORD, Behold, I will set a plumbline in the midst of my people Israel: I will not again pass by them any more:

9 And the high places of Isaac shall be desolate, and the sanctuaries of Israel shall be laid waste; and I will rise against the house of Jeroboam with the sword.

10 Then Amaziah the priest of Bethel sent to Jeroboam king of Israel, saying, Amos hath conspired against thee in the midst of the

Amos 6:1; 7:7-15 (NRSV)

ALAS FOR those who are at ease in Zion, and for those who feel secure on Mount Samaria, the notables of the first of the nations, to whom the house of Israel resorts!

·····

7 This is what he showed me: the Lord was standing beside a wall built with a plumb line, with a plumb line in his hand.

8 And the LORD said to me, "Amos, what do you see?" and I said, "A plumb line." Then the Lord said, "See, I am setting a plumb line in the midst of my people Israel; I will never again pass them by;

9 the high places of Isaac shall be made desolate, and the sanctuaries of Israel shall be laid waste, and I will rise against the house of Jeroboam with the sword."

10 Then Amaziah, the priest of Bethel, sent to King Jeroboam of Israel, saying, "Amos has conspired against you in the very center of the

house of Israel: the land is not able to bear all his words.

11 For thus Amos saith, Jeroboam shall die by the sword; and Israel shall surely be led away captive out of their own land.

12 Also Amaziah said unto Amos, O thou seer, go, flee thee away into the land of Judah, and there eat bread, and prophesy there:

13 But prophesy not again any more at Bethel: for it is the king's chapel, and it is the king's court.

14 Then answered Amos, and said to Amaziah, I was no prophet, neither was I a prophet's son; but I was an herdman, and a gatherer of sycamore fruit:

15 And the LORD took me as I followed the flock, and the LORD said unto me, Go, prophesy unto my people Israel.

house of Israel; the land is not able to bear all his words.

11 For thus Amos has said, 'Jeroboam shall die by the sword, and Israel must go into exile away from his land.' "

12 And Amaziah said to Amos, "O seer, go, flee away to the land of Judah, earn your bread there, and prophesy there;

13 but never again prophesy at Bethel, for it is the king's sanctuary, and it is a temple of the kingdom."

14 Then Amos answered Amaziah, "I am no prophet, nor a prophet's son; but I am a herdsman, and a dresser of sycamore trees,

15 and the LORD took me from following the flock, and the LORD said to me, 'Go, prophesy to my people Israel.' "

KEY VERSE

Then answered Amos, and said to Amaziah, I was no prophet, neither was I a prophet's son; but I was an herdman, and a gatherer of sycamore fruit: And the LORD took me as I followed the flock, and the LORD said unto me, Go, prophesy unto my people Israel.—Amos 7:14-15

OBJECTIVES

After reading this lesson, the student should be informed about:

1. The danger of believers having a love of luxury and a false sense of security;
2. The awareness that the God of the Bible is a Righteous Judge; and,
3. The fact that phony religion is often a major adversary of the truth.

POINTS TO BE EMPHASIZED

Adult/Youth/Children
Key Verse: Amos 7:14-15; Acts 5:29 (Children)
Print: Amos 6:1, 7:7-15

—Amos warned those who were at ease in Zion and those who felt secure on Mount Samaria. (6:1)

—Amos had a vision in which the Lord promised to devastate the religious areas of Israel and the house of Jeroboam II. (7:7-9)

—Amaziah the priest told Jeroboam II that Amos had conspired against the king. (7:10-11)

—Amaziah told Amos to flee to Judah and prophesy there, but never again to prophesy at Bethel because it was the king's sanctuary. (7:12-13)

—Amos testified that God had called him to prophesy to Israel. (7:14-15)

(NOTE: Use KJV Scripture for Adults; NRSV Scripture for Youth and Children)

TOPICAL OUTLINE OF THE LESSON

I. Introduction

A. A Perception of History

B. Biblical Background

II. Exposition and Application of the Scripture

A. Resting in False Security (Amos 6:1; 7:7-9)

B. Reviled by a False Priest (Amos 7:10-13)

C. Repudiation of False Accusations (Amos 7:14-15)

III. Special Features

A. Preserving Our Heritage

B. A Concluding Word

I. Introduction

A. A PERCEPTION OF HISTORY

The theme of the Book of Amos is the Judgment on Sin, a mission voiced by God when He said, "You only have I known of all the families of the earth; therefore I will punish you for all your iniquities" (Amos 3:2). At the time of his ministry (c. 760 B.C.) in the Northern Kingdom, Israel was outwardly prosperous, but inwardly corrupt. At the height of its power and prosperity, Israel was shackled by idolatry. We learn that when a nation is not right with God, it does not treat its people right. Oppression, injustice, and mistreatment of its citizens are commonplace. When the vertical is not right, it is impossible for the horizontal to be right. Contempt for God easily leads to shameless immorality. "Social justice is inseparable from true piety" (Scofield Reference Bible). Amos was used by Jehovah to expose the sins of the nation, and to exhort Israel with these famous words: "Let justice run down like waters, and righteousness like a mighty stream" (Amos 5:24).

B. BIBLICAL BACKGROUND

Amos made it known that because of sin, God's judgment is inevitable. He then deliberately exposed the sins of Israel, and told what Jehovah intended to do about them. Just as the Lord judged the surrounding nations, so He will judge His own people. Israel's sins are many; yet, Jehovah pleads with the nation to return to Him and be blessed. "Seek Me and live...Seek the Lord and live...seek good and not evil, that you may live" (Amos 5:4, 6, 14). But the people were hard of heart, and stiff of neck. In spite of adversity used by the Lord as a corrective measure—drought, pestilence, warfare, famine—the Jews remained recalcitrant and unrepentant. "Yet have ye not returned unto Me, saith the Lord" (Amos 4:11). Our lesson today expands on the evils committed by the nation, and warns through the vision of the plumb line of the consequences of continued rebellion against the will of the Lord God.

II. Exposition and Application of the Scripture

A. RESTING IN FALSE SECURITY
(Amos 6:1; 7:7-9)

WOE to them that are at ease in Zion, and trust in the mountain of Samaria, which are named chief of the nations, to whom the house of Israel came! Thus he shewed me: and, behold, the Lord stood upon a wall made by a plumbline, with a plumbline in his hand. And the LORD said unto me, Amos, what seest thou? And I said, A plumbline. Then said the Lord, Behold, I will set a plumbline in the midst of my people Israel: I will not again pass by them any more: And the high places of Isaac shall be desolate, and the sanctuaries of Israel shall be laid waste; and I will rise against the house of Jeroboam with the sword.

Mention of both Zion and Samaria indicates that both Judah and Israel are under the spotlight. Although the prophet's message is directed primarily to Israel (the North), both suffer the same sin-sickness and lack of spiritual sensitivity. Both Judah and Israel were in bad shape. They despised the law of the Lord, disobeyed His commandments. The nation was in apostasy. Lip-service was paid to the Lord, but the people lived as they pleased. And all kinds of gods were worshiped—gods of fertility (soil and sex), gods of the heavenly hosts (sun, moon and stars).

The righteous were sold for silver, and the poor for a pair of shoes. The meek were turned aside as the poor were oppressed. Father and son had sex with the same woman. They even told the prophets to stop preaching. Their life of luxury showed their disregard for the poverty-stricken in their society. The needy were cursed. They afflicted the just, took bribes, turned aside the poor in the gate. Is it any wonder Amos preached, "Woe to them who are at ease in Zion?" Pettingill said, "Nothing in the wide world is so hateful to God as religion when used as a cover for corruption." The Jews blindly believed that ritual satisfied God; however, their ceremony was not designed to please God, but to please self. They went through the motions, or as we say in our churches, their worship was but "a form and fashion."

The Hebrew word rendered "ease" (**shaanan**) means also to be at peace, secure, with the collateral idea of being careless, wanton, arrogant (Brown, Driver, Briggs). The language vividly designates those who, while in a position of privilege and blessing, are indifferent and blind to the needs of those less fortunate. Such language may well be used of local assemblies who spend enormous amounts of money on trips, excursions, gowns, and "institutionalization"—but their missions budget is negligible. They are self-centered. There is no evangelism thrust, no fervent desire to win souls to a saving knowledge of the Lord Jesus Christ. The Jews felt that even if judgment came, the mountains which surrounded them would protect them. Amos 6:1 also teaches that the godless leaders are taken to task for their extravagant lifestyles of luxury and self-indulgence. They lived in ease at the expense of the poor whom they exploited.

Next, we see that it is Jehovah's intention to break up this false sense of security. He must judge evil. But first He warned Israel in a series of visions. The first two visions are of calamity in the realm of nature—grasshoppers and fire (Amos 7:1-3, 4-6). But in the third vision, instead of natural disasters, politics and religion are the issues. "The high places (or hilltop shrines) of Isaac (a synonym for Israel) shall be desolate, and the sanctuaries of Israel shall be laid waste. I will rise with the sword against the house of Jeroboam" (v. 9). In this third vision, we see Jehovah standing upon a wall made by a plumbline, and with a plumbline in His hand. Originally, Israel had been built with vertical rectitude, but the nation failed to maintain the standard, primarily because of idolatry. The worship of false gods made the wall unstable, fit only to be toppled! "Amos, what do you see?" God does not ask questions because He does not know the answer. He is omniscient. Here the question was asked in order to follow up the answer with an explanation of the symbol.

And so Amos replied: "A plumbline." Then the Lord said, "Behold, I will set a plumbline in the midst of My people, Israel; I will not again pass by them any more." His patience had run out. Judgment now is inevitable. A plumbline or plummet is a string or line with a weight fastened to one end. The weight, called a plumb bob, keeps the line straight up and down. It is used by bricklayers and stone masons as vertical guides in building walls. Plumbum is the Latin word for lead (see also the word, Plumber). The force of gravity pulls things down to the earth. If we entered the very heart of the earth, there would be no such force and thus no weight. And the further away we get from the earth, the lesser the pull becomes. But understand, it is this pull that gives the plumbline its straightness (cf. 2 Kings 21:13).

In today's lesson, God is His own "straightness." He does not change His standard. In essence, He is unchangeable, immutable in His attributes, consciousness and will. He is perfect, a concept we imperfect human beings find incomprehensible. There is no variation in His character, power, plans, purposes or promises, love or mercy. Nor in His justice, for we read in Isaiah 28:17: "Also I will make justice the measuring line, and righteousness the plummet."

Righteousness means "that which is straight." In order to determine what is straight, we need a perfect standard by which to judge. Without standards, life would be chaotic. For the Christian church, the Bible is the plumbline. It reveals man's lost condition and at the same time shows God's method of salvation through faith in the shed blood of Jesus Christ. Every rule of measurement manufactured by man is temporary, and belongs to that scheme of things which is passing away. The plumbline of God revealed this to Israel in the day of Amos, and reveals it still to us today.

B. REVILED BY A FALSE PRIEST
(Amos 7:10-13)

Then Amaziah the priest of Bethel sent to Jeroboam king of Israel, saying, Amos hath conspired against thee in the midst of the house of Israel: the land is not able to bear all his words. For thus Amos saith, Jeroboam shall die by the sword, and Israel shall surely be led away captive out of their own land. Also Amaziah said unto Amos, O thou seer, go, flee thee away into the land of Judah, and there eat bread, and prophesy there.

Having announced the absolute uprightness of God's judgment through the plumbline vision, and warned that Jehovah would no longer "pass by them," or spare them, Amos also included judgment against the house of Jeroboam. At this point, Amaziah the idolatrous priest of Bethel, of whom little is known apart from the context, informed Jeroboam that Amos had conspired against the king. Indeed, Amos had preached that the dynasty of the reigning royal family would be overthrown, the Israelitish monarchy destroyed, and that Israel would be led away in captivity.

When Amaziah heard the bold attack upon his employer, Jeroboam, he did not bother to investigate. Instead, he sought to defend the signer of his paycheck! Evidently, Amaziah's manipulation of the prophet's message did not impress Jeroboam, for it appears that the king took no immediate action. So then, failing to get a sympathetic ear from the king, Amaziah made a personal attack. With a sneer, Amaziah called Amos a seer (one who sees, one who has visions).

"Flee to the land of Judah—go back south where you came from!" And then, to show he believed that Amos was not only a professional prophet, one preaching for a living, but an insincere one at that, Amaziah said, "There eat bread, and there prophesy!" (v. 12). He then called upon Amos to leave Bethel (the house of God), leave the country. "Don't preach here where the king has set up the main worship center! Don't come here and prophesy against the king!" Amaziah thus implied that Amos preached primarily for money. This accusation came from the lips of the king's priest, one who himself was a hireling!

C. REPUDIATION OF FALSE ACCUSATIONS
(Amos 7:14-15)

Then answered Amos, and said to Amaziah, I was no prophet, neither was I a prophet's son; but I was an herdman, and a gatherer of sycamore fruit:

And the LORD took me as I followed the flock, and the LORD said unto me, Go, prophesy unto my people Israel.

As mentioned earlier, king Jeroboam did not regard the remarks reported to him as dangerous to his rule, and so he took no action against the troublesome prophet. However, Amos was led to defend himself, to repudiate the insinuations and charges made by the phony priest, Amaziah. "I am not a prophet by profession, I am not a member of any prophetic guild," Amos said. In those days, there were schools of the prophets where young men were trained to instruct the nation. Those who attended were called "sons of prophets," so that biological parenthood is not meant by the expression.

"I did not seek this position," answered Amos. It was by a sovereign act of God that he was called to proclaim God's Word. It never entered his mind to become a prophet, or as some men have done, "to select the ministry as a profession." At the time of his calling, Amos was a herdsman of a peculiar breed of desert sheep. The word means shepherd, sheep raiser, sheep dealer, sheep tender, sheep breeder (NKJV). In addition, Amos was a gatherer or tender of sycamore fruit, or dresser of sycamore trees (RSV), or a gatherer of wild figs (Ironside); one who plucks mulberry-figs *(Keil & Delitzsch)*.

As Amos followed his flock, Jehovah spoke to him, and commanded him to "Go, prophesy to My people, Israel." Obviously, Amaziah placed himself in direct opposition to Jehovah by telling Amos not to prophesy! No wonder the apostate priest and his family came to such a dreadful end (Amos 7:17).

Finally, this observation: God uses busy people. Moses was busy tending the flock of Jethro his father-in-law when the Angel of the Lord spoke to him from the burning bush that was not consumed, and commissioned him (Exodus 3:1-2). Gideon threshed wheat in the wine press when the Angel of the Lord appeared to him, and commissioned him (Judges (6:11, 14). David was keeping the sheep, when Samuel ordered Jesse to send for him (1 Samuel 16:11). Simon Peter and his brother Andrew were casting a fishing net into the sea when the Lord Jesus commanded, "Follow Me, and I will make you fishers of men" (Matthew 4:18-19). James and John were in the boat with their father, Zebedee, mending their nets. Our Lord called them also (Matthew 4:21). Matthew (Levi) was sitting at the tax office table when Christ bade him, "Follow Me" (Mark 2:14). Even Saul who became Paul was busy—persecuting Christians—when the Lord apprehended him on the road to Damascus (Acts 9:1-6). And so it was, that Amos also was among the busy ones whom God called into service.

III. Special Features

A. PRESERVING OUR HERITAGE

For many decades, one of the strengths of the Black Church has been its high concept of a "calling." Although we sometimes joke about the matter, even suggesting that some preachers "were not sent, but just went," the matter of calling still remains an important part of our church life. To be called of God into the Christian ministry has long been considered an act of God that bestows upon man the highest of privileges. We have heard preachers of our race assert they would rather be a preacher than be the president, and that their calling was above that of any other position man might hold.

Unfortunately, immorality chips away at this ideal. Abuse and misuse of office likewise undermine our regard for the ministry. And when those claiming to be called fail to preach the unsearchable riches of Jesus Christ, the ministry is disparaged. Furthermore, political expediency has sought to oppose the truth preached from faithful pulpits. Ask the prophet Elijah (1 Kings 18:17), or inquire of Jeremiah (37:13-15). Ask the disciples (John 11:48-50), or Paul (Acts 17:6-7). Yea, ask our Lord Himself (John 19:12). But in spite of all attempts to undermine the prophetic ministry, the truth is: God still calls whom He will into the ministry. And this concept of a divine call helps to strengthen the spiritual life of our local congregation, as well as the spiritual life of the nation.

B. A CONCLUDING WORD

The task of Amos was not pleasant. But God had called him to prophesy, and in obedience, he responded. His message is one of doom and gloom, and yet ends with the promise of the final restoration of the nation Israel during the Millennium or Kingdom age. His message was totally unacceptable to the people, especially to the wealthy, and the political and religious leaders. Because the nation was out of the will of Jehovah, the inhabitants could not help but manifest bad relationships with each other. Amos pleaded with them to return to Jehovah, repent, consider the cause of the poor, do what is right. Jesus Christ speaks to our hearts today. As the blessed recipients of His finished work on Calvary, we are to express our gratitude for salvation in ways that demonstrate the love of God, and His desire for justice and righteousness.

HOME DAILY BIBLE READINGS
Week of November 1, 1998
Courage to Speak for God

Oct. 26 M. Amos 1:1-8, Amos Speaks for God
Oct. 27 T. Amos 2:4-8, Both Judah and Israel have Transgressed God's Laws
Oct. 28 W. Amos 6:1-7, Amos Condemns Those at Ease in Zion
Oct. 29 T. Amos 6:8-14, You Have Turned Justice Into Poison
Oct. 30 F. Amos 7:1-9, I Am Setting A Plumb Line in Israel
Oct. 31 S. Amos 7:10-17, Flee Away to the Land of Judah...
Nov.   1 S. Luke 16:19-31, Jesus Condemns Waste and Indifference

Writers of Songs

Adult Topic—The Songs We Sing

.....

Youth Topic—Sing Blues—Sing Hope
Children's Topic—A Song of Praise

.....

Devotional Reading—Psalm 27:1-14
Background Scripture—Psalm 73
Print—Psalm 73:1-3, 12, 13, 16-18, 21-26

· · · · · · · · · · · ·

PRINTED SCRIPTURE

Psalm 73:1-3, 12-13, 16-18, 21-26 (KJV)

TRULY God is good to Israel, even to such as are of a clean heart.

2 But as for me, my feet were almost gone; my steps had well nigh slipped.

3 For I was envious at the foolish, when I saw the prosperity of the wicked.

.....

12 Behold, these are the ungodly, who prosper in the world; they increase in riches.

13 Verily I have cleansed my heart in vain, and washed my hands in innocency.

.....

16 When I thought to know this, it was too painful for me;

17 Until I went into the sanctuary of God; then understood I their end.

18 Surely thou didst set them in slippery places: thou castedst them down into destruction.

.....

Psalm 73:1-3, 12-13, 16-18, 21-26 (NRSV)

TRULY GOD is good to the upright, to those who are pure in heart.

2 But as for me, my feet had almost stumbled; my steps had nearly slipped.

3 For I was envious of the arrogant; I saw the prosperity of the wicked.

.....

12 Such are the wicked; always at ease, they increase in riches.

13 All in vain I have kept my heart clean and washed my hands in innocence.

.....

16 But when I thought how to understand this, it seemed to me a wearisome task,

17 until I went into the sanctuary of God; then I perceived their end.

18 Truly you set them in slippery places; you make them fall to ruin.

.....

21 Thus my heart was grieved, and I was pricked in my reins.

22 So foolish was I, and ignorant: I was as a beast before thee.

23 Nevertheless I am continually with thee: thou hast holden me by my right hand.

24 Thou shalt guide me with thy counsel, and afterward receive me to glory.

25 Whom have I in heaven but thee? and there is none upon earth that I desire beside thee.

26 My flesh and my heart faileth: but God is the strength of my heart, and my portion for ever.

21 When my soul was embittered, when I was pricked in heart,

22 I was stupid and ignorant; I was like a brute beast toward you.

23 Nevertheless I am continually with you; you hold my right hand.

24 You guide me with your counsel, and afterward you will receive me with honor.

25 Whom have I in heaven but you? And there is nothing on earth that I desire other than you.

26 My flesh and my heart may fail, but God is the strength of my heart and my portion forever.

KEY VERSE

But it is good for me to draw near to God: I have put my trust in the Lord GOD, that I may declare all thy works.—Psalm 73:28

OBJECTIVES

After reading this lesson, the student should be informed about:

1. God's purpose in allowing the wicked to prosper;
2. Overcoming the temptation to lose faith; and,
3. The value of basking in the presence of the Lord.

POINTS TO BE EMPHASIZED

Adult/Youth/Children
Key Verse: Psalm 73:28; 73:26 (Children)
Print: Psalm 73:1-3, 12, 13, 16-18, 21-26

—The psalmist declared that God is good to the upright and the pure in heart. (1)
—The psalmist, however, had nearly lost faith in God, seeing the prosperity of evildoers. (2-3)
—The psalmist had trouble understanding until he went to the sanctuary; then he perceived that God causes the fall of the wicked. (16-18)
—The psalmist recognized the foolishness of his complaints and rejoiced in the sense of God's presence. (21-24)
—The psalmist desired nothing but God, and God gave the psalmist strength. (25-26)

(NOTE: Use KJV Scripture for Adult; NRSV Scripture for Youth and Children)

I. Introduction

A. A PERCEPTION OF HISTORY

The first psalm attributed to Asaph is Psalm 50. Today's lesson is the second Psalm ascribed to him; the next eleven consecutive Psalms (74-83) also bear his name. Some scholars believe that David was the author of these Psalms, and that he dedicated them to Asaph, one of his chief musicians and eminent singers. However, in 2 Chronicles 29:30, we read: "Moreover, Hezekiah, the king, and the prince commanded the Levites to sing praise unto the Lord with the words of David, and of Asaph, the seer." Furthermore, in Nehemiah 12:46, David and Asaph are named together as joint authors of "songs of praise and thanksgiving unto God." We hold to the belief that Asaph, one of the leading choristers of David's time, is the human author of Psalm 73, a Psalm depicting God as a Righteous Judge ruling over mankind in spite of the prosperity of the wicked. Asaph was blessed to have four sons who were also singers in the Temple (1 Chronicles 25:1-2; Ezra 2:41).

B. BIBLICAL BACKGROUND

The subject of the prosperity of the wicked and the suffering of the righteous presents an age-old problem not easily answered. For man's thoughts and ways are not those of the God of the Bible. From the very beginning, this problem of the righteous suffering is evident. We see it in the murder of righteous Abel by his evil brother, Cain. We see it in the cruel treatment of Joseph by his brothers. Take for example, Job. He was a good man, blameless and upright. He feared God and shunned evil. And yet within a brief span of time, he lost his seven sons and three daughters when the home of the oldest son collapsed and fell upon them. Job's oxen and donkeys were stolen; fire burned up his sheep; camels were taken; and nearly all of his servants were killed. Then Job suffered painful boils from the bottom of his feet to the top of his head. Why was he exposed to such catastrophe? God sought to broaden Job's capacity for divine fellowship. Indeed, at the very heart of the matter is the fact that He who knew no sin was made sin for us, that we might become the righteousness of God in Him (2 Corinthians 5:21). Christ, the Righteous One, suffered for us, in our place, and died in our stead. And to this day, there are wicked unbelievers who prosper, and there are righteous believers who suffer.

II. Exposition and Application of the Scripture

A. THE PROBLEM OF THE PROSPERITY OF THE WICKED
   (Psalm 73:1-3)

TRULY God is good to Israel, even to such as are of a clean heart. But as for me, my feet were almost gone; my steps had well nigh slipped. For I was envious at the foolish, when I saw the prosperity of the wicked.

Asaph asserts that God is good to Israel. The Hebrew word translated "truly" may be rendered: now, verily, only, after all; it is probably best translated, "surely." The writer expresses confidence in his conclusion that God has been nothing else but good to His own, to the true Israel. Christians likewise confidently conclude that God is good "all the time!" He makes all things work together for the well-being of those who love Him, those called according to His plan and purpose (Romans 8:28). What a wonderful attitude to have—even when we do not understand what is happening in our lives, and find adversity difficult to bear—to be able to say: "Surely, God is good!"

But now having stated that he has no doubt in his mind concerning the goodness of the Lord, Asaph confesses there was a time when he almost turned away from trusting God. When the mind is not right, the feet go astray, the steps become slippery. What was the reason for his faith coming so close to failing? It was because he saw the prosperity of the wicked. The word translated "prosperity" here is shalom or peace, completeness, integrity, wholeness. Within this context, it suggests the wicked are more than adequately compensated; they have more than enough goods; they possess a complete amount of money (although undoubtedly wishing they had more).

The word for wicked **(rasha)** refers to the tossing and confusion in which the wicked live (Girdlestone p. 81). They are like "the troubled sea when it cannot rest, whose waters cast up mire and dirt; there is no peace, saith my God, to the wicked" (Isaiah 57:20, 21). How strange this sounds: "the prosperity of the wicked" becomes "the peace of those who have no peace"—"the riches of the restless!" The word for "wicked" then "betrays the inner disharmony and unrest of a man" *(Theological Wordbook of the O. T., 2:863).*

It is dangerous to keep our eyes on evildoers. When we dwell on how well off the wicked are, it adversely affects us spiritually. For one thing, we become envious, jealous; we see, we want. But note; Asaph calls these prosperous evildoers "foolish." Here the Hebrew word **(halal)** means "boastful: denoting an arrogance "a blustering presumption" (Kirkpatrick). Proud of their "success" and possessions, they show their arrogance towards those less "successful" than themselves. Their attitude shouts: "Money will buy whatever I want or need!" This same Hebrew word rendered "foolish" or "boastful," means madness, insanity, thus describing the minds of the wicked wealthy *(Theological Wordbook of the Old Testament* 1:218-219). When we focus attention on the lifestyles of the unrighteous, we jeopardize our own behavior. We strive to have what they have, drive ourselves into terrible debt, and limit our usefulness to Christ. Asaph would advise: fix your eyes on Christ, and find in Him your all in all.

B. THE DILEMMA OF THE RIGHTEOUS
(Psalm 73:12-13)

Behold, these are the ungodly, who prosper in the world; they increase in riches. Verily I have cleansed my heart in vain, and washed my hands in innocency.

The following story points out the dilemma in part. A Sunday School teacher had just related to a class of boys the story of the rich man (Dives is a Latin word meaning rich) and Lazarus (Luke 16:19-31). Afterwards the teacher inquired: "Now which would you rather be, the rich man or Lazarus?" There was silence for a few moments, then one boy finally answered: "I'd like to be the rich man while I'm living, and Lazarus when I die."

At this point, Asaph briefly describes the ones who caused his dilemma. They are the ungodly (rendered "wicked" in v. 3). Asaph pleads, "Look at what's happening to them! The rich are getting richer. They are healthy; their bills are paid; their consciences (cauterized) don't bother them. They are at ease, living in luxury. It isn't fair I live a good, honest, respectable life, spend hours reading my Bible, stay in prayer, and yet I'm in serious need." Is Asaph's lifestyle all in vain? Does it not pay to live a clean life in a dirty age? Asaph expresses doubts and misgivings and asks, "What value is holiness?" A cleansed heart speaks of pure thoughts; hands washed in innocence speaks of good deeds. But what good is such integrity of heart and uprightness of deeds? Asaph feels the good life is not rewarded by evidence of Divine approval.

It seems that Divine approval fell on the bad guys. And so Asaph expresses his doubts and perplexity concerning the endeavor to live a life pleasing to God. Have you ever expressed similar feelings to the Lord? Or do you keep your thoughts in your mind and not talk them out? Take a cue from Asaph: confess, tell the Lord exactly how you feel. If you too are puzzled by the lack of punishment of the wicked, tell the Lord. Keep in mind that every experience we have in life is for a purpose, and the Lord desires to use them all to draw us closer to Jesus Christ. Whatever the dilemma, the perplexity, the seeming contradiction—confess it, for "a smothered grief is hard to endure" (Spurgeon).

C. THE ANSWER OF THE LORD
(Psalm 73:16-18)

When I thought to know this, it was too painful for me; Until I went into the sanctuary of God; then understood I their end. Surely thou didst set them in slippery places: thou castedst them down into destruction.

Asaph is so disturbed by this question of the prosperity of the wicked and the distress of the righteous that he calls it painful (laborious, a toil, burdensome). The question was too weighty for his weak powers (Barnes). You see then his dilemma. It was not until Asaph went into the sanctuary of God that he understood the final destiny of the prosperous wicked. The sanctuary represents God's Presence; it is the place where the Lord manifests Himself, where He reveals His power and glory.

Rather than see a literal sanctuary here, consider that Asaph turned to God Himself. It is not the literal temple in Jerusalem, but that heart place, that heavenly place in which we enter by faith and commune with the Lord. Only here, in fellowship with Jehovah, was Asaph's problem solved. And, he understood what the end of the wealthy wicked would be. The Bible often speaks of the "end." This particular Hebrew word rendered "end" means afterpart, latter part, future. Your end is your future. The future of the blameless man is peace; the future of the wicked shall be cut off (Psalm 37:37-38). The end of the immoral woman is bitter as wormwood (Proverbs 5:4). There is a way that seems right to a man, but the end thereof are the ways of death (Proverbs 14:12). Concerning the gambler, Jeremiah 17:11 states that the ill-gotten gain will leave the gambler in the midst of his days, "and at his end he will be a fool."

What is the end or future of the prosperous wicked? Two things are said in verse 18. First, God sets them in slippery places. This speaks of their precarious existence. In the original language, the word for "slippery" means slick, smooth (flattery). One is likely to fall on slippery places. Wicked men walk on glass or ice or a smooth polished floor. Second, God casts them down into destruction. This is Divine judgment, ruin; it may be a reference to Hell. They shall slip and fall down never again to rise, but shall remain in the dust like a fallen wall in utter ruin. Their transitory prosperity is nothingness in God's sight. Whatever their end, it is in terrible antithesis with their long-continued prosperity. Ask the rich man in Luke 16:19-31.

D. THE SOLUTION FOR THE BELIEVER
(Psalm 73:21-26)

Thus my heart was grieved, and I was pricked in my reins. So foolish was I, and ignorant: I was as a beast before thee. Nevertheless I am continually with thee: thou hast holden me by my right hand. Thou shalt guide me with thy counsel, and afterward receive me to glory. Whom have I in heaven but thee? and there is none upon earth that I desire beside thee. My flesh and my heart faileth: but God is the strength of my heart, and my portion for ever.

Upon reviewing his inner struggle, Asaph realized his folly, and remonstrated with himself for having such treacherous thoughts. A grievous heart is a sour heart; it is an embittered soul made so by what Asaph considered as the inconsistency between innocence and affliction. The "reins" (KJV) are the kidneys. According to Hebrew psychology, they are the seat of the deepest emotions. And God alone knows our "inward parts." In Revelation 2:23, the Greek word for "Reins" is **nephros.** So Asaph complains that he was vexed in his mind (pained in his kidneys!) because of his foolish impatience.

Indeed, he acted brutish like a beast before Jehovah—like a stupid animal without knowledge, unable to fathom what it all meant. The word for "beast" is **behemoth,** a Hebrew word taken into English (transliterated). It may refer to the hippopotamus (river horse) as in Job 40:15. In short, Asaph declared that it was dumb to become bitter over what appeared to be the prosperity of the ungodly. He acted more like an animal than a human being. What counts in life is a personal relationship with God. We as Christians have this through faith in the shed blood of the Lord Jesus Christ.

Asaph acknowledged that throughout his experiences of envy, doubt, bitterness, brooding and shortsightedness, the Lord held on to his right hand. Victory over his doubts is the result of God's counsel and strength. Here is the very reality of life—communion with God. It is through the continuous Presence of the Lord, who is always ready and willing to advise and strengthen, that ultimately Asaph is brought to experience personal honor and glory in this present life. No one but God could do this! Whether Asaph is in heaven or on earth, God alone is his only delight. Fanny Crosby took these words and wrote: "Thou the spring of all my comfort, More than life to me, Whom have I on earth beside Thee? Whom in heav'n but Thee? Savior, Savior, Hear my humble cry; While on others Thou art calling, do not pass me by."

In the Bible, the heart includes the entire inner person: will, motives, feelings, affections, desire, aims, principles, thoughts, intellect. The flesh, of course, is the body. So Asaph informs us of the failure of his total being. To fail means to be spent, used up, come to an end, be finished, exhausted, or waste away as fading grass, a vanishing cloud, or the fleeting days of life. Asaph points to a decline in physical and mental powers. Within the context dealing with the problem of the prosperity of the wicked, flesh and heart may also include all that we possess, all our power. These too may fail. However, there is someone who does not, cannot, fail. He is God, the strength of our heart. The word "strength" here is in the Hebrew, "rock," a symbol of strength and unchangeableness. God is the Rock (Deuteronomy 32:4), the support and defense of His own people. For us, Jesus Christ is a Rock, our Strength: "On Christ the Solid Rock I stand." Conscious of our weaknesses, we receive strength from the Rock. Conscious of our bent to wander, we are stabilized by the Rock that remains steadfast. A second reason we are not unduly concerned about the failure of heart and flesh is because God is our portion forever. He is our eternal possession. Since God Himself is without beginning or ending, so shall our portion be. We need not envy folks whose portion in life is all of this world. Once again, we hear from Fanny J. Crosby:

"Thou my everlasting portion, More than friend or life to me; all along my pilgrim journey, Savior, let me walk with Thee. Close to Thee, close to Thee."

III. Special Features

A. PRESERVING OUR HERITAGE

Some years ago, the Nielsen Media Research reported that Black households watch 48 percent more TV than "other groups." And among Blacks, women watch the most TV. What effect does this have on us? Soap operas usually portray wealthy people, with their beautiful homes, automobiles, clothing, etc. What is observed creates a desire to possess. Judging from the lifestyles portrayed on the screen, or actually lived by the actors, wickedness is commonplace. Unfortunately, some other performers and superathletes whom we adulate and see as role models also live immoral lives. Asaph would warn us: "For I was envious of the foolish, when I saw the prosperity of the wicked" (Psalm 73:30). Watch what you watch!

B. A CONCLUDING WORD

Modern-day prosperity prophets teach that since God is rich and God is in you, therefore, you should not be poor. They say that poverty signifies a lack of faith. Over the centuries, the matter of material wealth has remained an issue for the church. We have come a long way from Simon Peter's statement: "Silver and gold have I none, but, such as I have, give I thee. In the name of Jesus Christ of Nazareth, rise up and walk" (Acts 3:6). In our desire for silver and gold, we have lost the desire for spiritual power that enables men to break the congenital fetters of sin and leap into the freedom of Christ. Asaph would have us refuse to allow the lifestyles of the wicked to adversely affect our growth in Christlikeness. The psalmist would have us learn to be content with whatever we have; avoid envy and covetousness, and above all, to desire only Him who promised, "I will never leave thee, nor forsake thee" (Hebrews 13:5).

HOME DAILY BIBLE READINGS
Week of November 8, 1998
Writers of Songs

Nov. 2 M. Psalm 73:1-14, My Feet Had Almost Stumbled
Nov. 3 T. Psalm 73:15-20, I Went into the Sanctuary of God
Nov. 4 W. Psalm 73:21-28, I Was Stupid and Ignorant
Nov. 5 T. Psalm 27:1-14, Reassurance Is Found in Worship
Nov. 6 F. Psalm 37:1-13, The Fate of the Wicked
Nov. 7 S. Psalm 26:1-12, Integrity Is Affirmed
Nov. 8 S. Psalm 121:1-8, The Lord Is Our Protector

False Hopes and Judgment

Unit IV. God Judges and Renews
Children's Unit—The People's Response to God
Adult Topic—False Hopes

.....

Youth Topic—No Quick Fix!
Children's Topic—Learn to Obey God

.....

Devotional Reading—Joshua 24:14-28
Background Scripture—Jeremiah 19; 21:1-10
Print—Jeremiah 19:1-4, 10-11; 21:1-2, 8-10

• • • • • • • • • • •

PRINTED SCRIPTURE

Jeremiah 19:1-4, 10-11; 21:1-2, 8-10 (KJV)

THUS saith the LORD, Go and get a potter's earthen bottle, and take of the ancients of the people, and of the ancients of the priests;

2 And go forth unto the valley of the son of Hinnom, which is by the entry of the east gate, and proclaim there the words that I shall tell thee,

3 And say, Hear ye the word of the LORD, O kings of Judah, and inhabitants of Jerusalem; Thus saith the LORD of hosts, the God of Israel; Behold, I will bring evil upon this place, the which whosoever heareth, his ears shall tingle.

4 Because they have forsaken me, and have estranged this place, and have burned incense in it unto other gods, whom neither they nor their fathers have known nor the kings of Judah, and have filled this place with the blood of innocents;

.....

Jeremiah 19:1-4, 10-11; 21:1-2, 8-10 (NRSV)

THUS SAID the LORD: Go and buy a potter's earthenware jug. Take with you some of the elders of the people and some of the senior priests,

2 and go out to the valley of the son of Hinnom at the entry of the Potsherd Gate, and proclaim there the words that I tell you.

3 You shall say: Hear the word of the LORD, O kings of Judah and inhabitants of Jerusalem. Thus says the LORD of hosts, the God of Israel: I am going to bring such disaster upon this place that the ears of everyone who hears of it will tingle.

4 Because the people have forsaken me, and have profaned this place by making offerings in it to other gods whom neither they nor their ancestors nor the kings of Judah have known; and because they have filled this place with the blood of the innocent,

.....

10 Then shalt thou break the bottle in the sight of the men that go with thee,

11 And shalt say unto them, Thus saith the LORD of hosts; Even so will I break this people and this city, as one breaketh a potter's vessel, that cannot be made whole again: and they shall bury them in Tophet, till there be no place to bury.

.....

THE word which came unto Jeremiah from the LORD, when king Zedekiah sent unto him Pashur the son of Melchiah, and Zephaniah the son of Maaseiah the priest, saying,

2 Enquire, I pray thee, of the LORD for us; for Nebuchadrezzar king of Babylon maketh war against us; if so be that the LORD will deal with us according to all his wondrous works, that he may go up from us.

.....

8 And unto this people thou shalt say, Thus saith the LORD; Behold, I set before you the way of life, and the way of death.

9 He that abideth in this city shall die by the sword, and by the famine, and by the pestilence: but he that goeth out, and falleth to the Chaldeans that besiege you, he shall live, and his life shall be unto him for a prey.

10 For I have set my face against this city for evil, and not for good, saith the LORD: it shall be given into the hand of the king of Babylon, and he shall burn it with fire.

10 Then you shall break the jug in the sight of those who go with you,

11 and shall say to them: Thus says the LORD of hosts: So will I break this people and this city, as one breaks a potter's vessel, so that it can never be mended. In Topheth they shall bury until there is no more room to bury.

.....

THIS IS the word that came to Jeremiah from the LORD, when King Zedekiah sent to him Pashhur son of Malchiah and the priest Zephaniah son of Maaseiah, saying,

2 "Please inquire of the LORD on our behalf, for King Nebuchadrezzar of Babylon is making war against us; perhaps the LORD will perform a wonderful deed for us, as he has often done, and will make him withdraw from us."

.....

8 And to this people you shall say: Thus says the LORD: See, I am setting before you the way of life and the way of death.

9 Those who stay in this city shall die by the sword, by famine, and by pestilence; but those who go out and surrender to the Chaldeans who are besieging you shall live and shall have their lives as a prize of war.

10 For I have set my face against this city for evil and not for good, says the LORD: it shall be given into the hands of the king of Babylon, and he shall burn it with fire.

KEY VERSE

And unto this people thou shalt say, Thus saith the LORD; Behold, I set before you the way of life, and the way of death.—Jeremiah 21:8

OBJECTIVES

After reading this lesson, the student should be informed about:

1. The significance of the impossibility of mending a broken bottle;
2. The reason behind God's threat of judgment upon Judah;
3. How God gives us the choice between the way of life and the way of death; and,
4. How that God is committed to His people, but that God must affirm His righteous judgment when they disobey.

POINTS TO BE EMPHASIZED

Adult/Youth

Key Verse: Jeremiah 21:8

Print: Jeremiah 19:1-4, 10-11, 21:1-2, 8-10

—The Lord told Jeremiah to buy a jug, take it with him to the Potsherd Gate, and speak the words of the Lord to the leaders of the people of Judah. (19:1-2)

—Jeremiah told the people that because of their sins, God was going to bring terrible disaster upon them. (19:3-4)

—Jeremiah broke the jug and told the people that God would break them in the same manner. (19:10-11)

—The king's representatives asked Jeremiah if the Lord would deliver Judah from the army of the king of Babylon. (21:1-2)

—Jeremiah advised the people of Jerusalem that if they remained in the city they would die, but if they surrendered they would live. (21:8-9)

—Jeremiah said that God would deliver Jerusalem to the king of Babylon, who would destroy it by fire. (21:10)

Children

Key Verse: Jeremiah 22:3

Print: Jeremiah 22:1-9

—The Lord told Jeremiah to go to the house of the king of Judah and to speak His Word there to all of the people who lived there. (22:1-2)

—The Lord said for the people to act with justice and righteousness, to do no wrong or violence, and to shed no innocent blood. (22:3)

—The Lord warned the people that should they fail to obey Him, they would be destroyed. (22:5)

—The Lord promised to destroy the kingdom of Judah for disobedience, even though the Lord continued to love the people.

—The Lord said that when other nations questioned Israel, they would recall that they had broken their covenant. (22:8-9)

(NOTE: Use KJV Scripture for Adult; NRSV Scripture for Youth and Children)

I. Introduction

A. A Perception of History
B. Biblical Background

II. Exposition and Application of the Scripture

A. The Prophet's Proclamation (Jeremiah 19:1-4)
B. The Broken Bottle (Jeremiah 19:10-11)
C. The Royal Request (Jeremiah 21:1-2)
D. Surrender and Survive (Jeremiah 21:8-10)

III. Special Features

A. Preserving Our Heritage
B. A Concluding Word

I. Introduction

A. A PERCEPTION OF HISTORY

God called and ordained Jeremiah to be a prophet even before he came out of his mother's womb (Jeremiah 1:5). One wonders what the abortionists think of Jeremiah's divine prenatal call and commission? He actually began to preach when he was a young priest of Anathoth, and was led by the Lord to boldly proclaim the impending doom of the southern kingdom, Judah. For nearly fifty years, Jeremiah was God's spokesman to Judah. His message was of course unwelcome, for his sermons were of judgment. Repeatedly, he called the people to repentance, but his pleas were rejected. He warned the nation against neglecting Jehovah, and cautioned the people about the awful consequences of breaking God's covenant. For all of his reproofs, advice, exhortations and warnings, Jeremiah himself was persecuted even by members of his own family, as well as by the phony priests, unscrupulous political leaders and the soldiers. He was plotted against, falsely accused, beaten, put in stocks, imprisoned—and eventually, after being forced to go to Egypt was murdered there.

It is impossible to study the Book of Jeremiah without becoming deeply aware of how enmeshed the personal experiences of the prophet are with the history of the nation. This is one of the reasons you will find more about the personal life and character of Jeremiah than of any of the other Old Testament writing prophets. His faithfulness to his God, and his compassion for the people, in spite of their mistreatment of him, commend Jeremiah to our hearts. He indeed well represents some characteristics of our Lord and Savior, Jesus Christ. And though warning and divine judgment are the main issues of his writings, his love for the people—an expression of God's love for Judah—impresses our hearts as well. As we shall see, the lesson is found in the earlier days of his ministry in chapter 19; and then, in his later prophecies in chapter 21.

B. BIBLICAL BACKGROUND

Jeremiah's task was to preach judgment against Judah. Led of the Lord, he often used object lessons or parables to illustrate Judah's judgment and destruction. For example: (1) The linen girdle or belt became marred and disintegrated, thus symbolizing that though Jehovah once wore Israel as an ornament, the nation was now so corrupt that it was useless to Him, and had to be rejected (Jeremiah 13:4); (2) the drought God sent was a sign of His judgment, (chapters 14 and 15); (3) the prophet was ordered to remain unmarried (chapters 16-17:18). By not allowing Jeremiah to marry, the Lord showed the eminent disruption of Judah's entire social life. Celibacy in Israel at this time was highly unusual. This prohibition also indicated that the nation's children would reap the harvest of their sin; and (4) the potter, (chapters 18 and 19), is one who fashions clay; he may form pots, bottles, idol statues, etc. Here the prophet observed how a piece of clay, marred or corrupted in the potter's hand, was refashioned by the craftsman into another vessel of whatever sort he desired. In this object lesson of the Potter, the Lord illustrates to the nation His power to take a ruined vessel (Israel) and remake it into a useful vessel. God deals sovereignly with us, but not arbitrarily. As Israel was clay in His hands, so are we. As the potter takes into account the nature of the clay, so the Lord takes into account our nature; and He acts and works accordingly (see Romans 9:20-24). These then are the four object lessons used in chapters 13 through 19. In our lesson for today, the use of the broken vessel is studied.

II. Exposition and Application of the Scripture

A. THE PROPHET'S PROCLAMATION
(Jeremiah 19:1-4)

THUS saith the LORD, Go and get a potter's earthen bottle, and take of the ancients of the people, and of the ancients of the priests; And go forth unto the valley of the son of Hinnom, which is by the entry of the east gate, and proclaim there the words that I shall tell thee, and say, Hear ye the word of the LORD, O kings of Judah, and inhabitants of Jerusalem; Thus saith the LORD of hosts, the God of Israel; Behold, I will bring evil upon this place, the which whosoever heareth, his ears shall tingle. Because they have forsaken me, and have estranged this place, and have burned incense in it unto other gods, whom neither they nor their fathers have known, nor the kings of Judah, and have filled this place with the blood of innocents.

Just looking at the words, "thus saith (says) the Lord," reminds us once again of the nature of the Bible. If what is attributed to God never really happened, then the very basis of Christianity will crumble, for the Bible would be judged untrue inasmuch as it states, "God says." If God did not say what the Bible asserts He said, then the Bible is not worth the paper it is printed on. But God did speak, and Jeremiah took God at His word, for when Jehovah commanded Jeremiah to go and get a potter's earthen bottle or flask, he obeyed. Since mankind is the work of God's hand, God also is described as a Potter. Having secured the bottle, the prophet's next step was to take out some of the ancients or elders with him to the Valley of the Son of Hinnom, which is by the entry of the Potsherd Gate. The "ancients" are the aged, the elders, the senior citizens.

They are the "bearded ones," for the Hebrew word translated "ancients" is derived from a word meaning "beard." As used here by Jeremiah, the elders are the ruling body of the city, the governors. They met at the gate of the city, settled citizen disputes, made property agreements and other negotiations, adjudicated murder and other cases brought before them. And so Jeremiah obeyed, and took the elders with him. They were to literally, physically witness what he preached and performed. They proceeded to the Valley of the Son of Hinnom which is by the entry of the Potsherd Gate. There Jeremiah was commanded to preach the words that the Lord would tell him. Jonah (3:2) likewise was told to preach only that which the Lord bade him preach. This is still good advice for all preachers; preach only that which God commands.

We live in an age in which society tends to dictate to the preacher, and social pressures and modern theological trends seek to obscure the fact that God calls men into the ministry, equips them, and bids them preach His Word. Jeremiah was not to preach what Jeremiah wanted, but what Jehovah desired and demanded.

In the New Testament, the Apostle Peter wrote: "If any man speak, let him speak as the oracles of God" (1 Peter 4:11). John the Baptist said, "He whom God hath sent speaketh the words of God" (John 3:34). Obedience to God's Word is stressed also in the preaching ministries of Moses, and the disciples, and in the ministry of every prophet who said, "thus saith the Lord." The Apostle Paul predicted the time would come when people would dictate to the minister what they wanted to hear. The time would come, he said, when men would not endure sound solid instruction, but after their own desires would collect teachers and preachers who would tickle their itching ears (2 Timothy 4:3). Ministers of the Gospel need to hear anew God's voice saying "Preach the words that I shall tell thee."

So great is the coming evil upon Jerusalem that those who hear about it shall suffer tingling (quivering, vibrating as cymbals) ears. Once again, idolatry is named as the reason for their judgment. Idolatry is described as: (1) forsaking God; (2) making the place of worship an alien place—this is to say, by disowning Jerusalem, sanctified by God as His abode; (3) burning incense (symbolizes ascending prayer) in God's place to idol gods; and (4) filling this same place with the blood of innocents. This point may be interpreted as the judicial murder or bloody persecution of the godly (Keil and Delitzsch); or seen as offering children in sacrifice to Moloch, burning them to death.

B. THE BROKEN BOTTLE
(Jeremiah 19:10-11)

Then shalt thou break the bottle in the sight of the men that go with thee, And shalt say unto them, Thus saith the LORD of hosts; Even so will I break this people and this city, as one breaketh a potter's vessel, that cannot be made whole again: and they shall bury them in Tophet, till there be no place to bury.

In the sight of the elders who went with him as witnesses, Jeremiah acted out this parable by going out to the city dump and smashing the clay water decanter or flask. And he preached that God said: "Just as I shattered this vessel, even so will I break this people and this city." Here is a picture of the inevitability of the coming judgment. Just as the pieces cannot be put together again, so Israel's doom cannot be avoided. Broken bottles are simply thrown away! Earlier verses (Jeremiah 19:5-9), though not part of our printed lesson, reveal the judgment includes death by the sword; unburied bodies, eaten by vultures and jackals; plagues, cannibalism.

Tophet, in the Valley of the Son of Hinnom, just south of Jerusalem, is mentioned several times in this chapter: verses 2, 6, 11-14. This was the place where children were burned alive to appease the god, Moloch (2 Chronicles 28:3). When King Josiah abolished this heinous practice (2 Kings 23:10), the valley became a city dump. Continuous fires destroyed the refuse from Jerusalem. This is why Gehinnom became a type of Hell (Gehenna in the New Testament). There are those who are quick to point out the origin of this particular word for Hell, but miss the spiritual nature of that invisible place God prepared for the Devil and his angels. No one is presently in Gehenna, the Lake of Fire.

C. THE ROYAL REQUEST
(Jeremiah 21:1-2)

THE word which came unto Jeremiah from the LORD, when king Zedekiah sent unto him Pashur the son of Melchiah, and Zephaniah the son of Maaseiah the priest, saying, Enquire, I pray thee, of the LORD for us; for Nebuchadrezzar king of Babylon maketh war against us; if so be that the LORD will deal with us according to all his wondrous works, that he may go up from us.

Zedekiah, king of Judah, is much stirred about the fate of his country. So he asks Pashur and Zephaniah to inquire of Jeremiah. This Zephaniah is the son of Maaseiah the priest; he is not the prophet Zephaniah, the son of Cushi. This Pashur is the son of Machijah, and is not the same Pashur, son of Immer in Jeremiah 20:1. The latter was a wicked man who beat Jeremiah and put the prophet in stocks. The Pashur of our lesson was sent to request that Jeremiah intercede to God for the nation: "Please inquire of the Lord for us." Nebuchadnezzar was on the move, conquering, and king Zedekiah desired that Jehovah intervene and save them. Note the different spelling for the king of Babylon. Nebo was the name of a Chaldean (Babylonian) god. Nebuchadnezzar and Nebuchadrezzar are the same person; he is one of the most prominent and important heathen kings of the Old Testament. Jeremiah's spelling (21:20) is closer to the Babylonian form of the name. Nebuchadnezzar may be the Aramaic translation of the Babylonian.

D. SURRENDER AND SURVIVE
(Jeremiah 21:8-10)

And unto this people thou shalt say, Thus saith the LORD; Behold, I set before you the way of life, and the way of death. He that abideth in this city shall die by the sword, and by the famine, and by the pestilence: but he that goeth out, and falleth to the Chaldeans that besiege you, he shall live, and his life shall be unto him for a prey. For I have set my face against this city for evil, and not for good, saith the LORD: it shall be given into the hand of the king of Babylon, and he shall burn it with fire.

Following the instructions of the Lord, Jeremiah set before king Zedekiah the way of life and the way of death. Simply put: obey and live; disobey and die. But listen to the terms! "Do NOT fight Nebuchadrezzar! If you stay and fight, you will die by the sword, by the famine, and by the pestilence. If you go out and surrender (fall to: KJV; defect: NKJV) to the Chaldeans, your life will be spared." Resistance will ruin you; war will waste you; but surrender saves! Jeremiah repeatedly prescribed this (see 27:11ff; 38:2, 17ff). What Jeremiah advised was of the Lord, for God's prediction of the devastation of Jerusalem as punishment for sins was irrevocable.

God promises: "your life shall be unto him for a prey" (Jeremiah 21:9; 38:2; 39:18). This is an interesting expression. It means that if you surrender to the Chaldeans, your life shall be unto you for a prize. I will give your life to you as booty (NASB), as a snatched up prize of war (Amplified); I will protect you wherever you go, as your reward (LB); I will protect you from death (CEV); but wherever you go, I will let you escape with your life (NIV). The lesson closes with unchanging condemnation. God's face is set (determined) against Jerusalem for evil. Panim, literally faces, is always plural, probably because the face is composed of a number of features (nose, eyes, lips, mouth, jaw, etc.). Jerusalem shall indeed be delivered up to the king of Babylon, and he shall destroy it by fire.

III. Special Features

A. PRESERVING OUR HERITAGE

Several things come to mind when we think of Jeremiah and Christian Black Americans. First of all, there is the expression, "I am black" in Jeremiah 8:21. Unfortunately, some people interpret this to mean Jeremiah was a Black man. However, as the context suggests, the phrase is an expression of sadness. Jeremiah had the "blacks," as we today have the "blues." He was in mourning, just as we are accustomed today to wear black clothing to show bereavement. In short, the word for "black" here does not refer to the color of Jeremiah's skin or to his race.

Second, in the search for "Blacks in the Bible," Ebed-melech, the Ethiopian ("burnt-face") eunuch in the service of King Zedekiah (Jeremiah 38:12) is cited. He saved Jeremiah from death in a miry dungeon, and did so at the risk of losing his own life at the hands of the mob. God promised Ebed-melech (lit. servant of the king) his life would be spared in the fall and destruction of Jerusalem (Jeremiah 39:15-18). A third matter is Jeremiah 8:22: "Is there no balm in Gilead...." Jeremiah sees the sin of the nation as a sickness. Its malady could not be treated by medicines or physicians. The only One who can heal the nation is the Lord Himself. Gilead's balsam, an odoriferous resin extracted from certain trees, was famous as a medicine. Jeremiah refers figuratively to its medicinal properties as an application to wounds and as a sedation (ISBE; Jeremiah 46:11; 51.8). It is interesting that somehow the slaves recognized that while the literal balm could not help Israel, there is a Balm that makes the wounded whole, and heals the sin-sick soul—the Lord Jesus Christ! (Hymn #158 - *Gospel Pearls*). He is the Holy Spirit who revives our souls; He is the Lord Jesus our Friend, who loves us and died for all. How marvelous that Black slaves should be helped so much by a "weeping prophet"!

B. A CONCLUDING WORD

Jeremiah was mandated by God to demonstrate His message to the people. Should the evil that was so much a part of the religious and political life of Judah have rendered them unable to "hear the Word of the Lord" perhaps they could "see" and understand. The rhetorical question, "can the Ethiopian change his skin, or the leopard his spots" has nothing to do with race, but references the total inability of the people to rectify their situation based upon their own ingenuity and creative endeavors. The point is that salvation must come from a higher source than those strategies that are part of the human situation. But as in so many cases, we as humans insist upon attaching ourselves to those indices of hope that are contrived by flawed imagination and rely on those visible idols of gratification that pacify for the moment. We need to affirm that our real hope lies in God that is actualized when we commit to do His will. Hope is not hope unless it is God-based.

HOME DAILY BIBLE READINGS
Week of November 15, 1998
False Hopes and Judgment

Nov. 9 M. Jeremiah 18:1-11, I Went Down to the Potter's House...
Nov. 10 T. Jeremiah 19:1-9, I Will Bring Disaster on This Place
Nov. 11 W. Jeremiah 19:10-15, I Will Break This People and Their City
Nov. 12 T. Jeremiah 20:1-6, Jeremiah Is Placed in Stocks
Nov. 13 F. Jeremiah 20:7-18, Jeremiah's Complaint
Nov. 14 S. Jeremiah 21:1-10, I Myself Will Fight Against You
Nov. 15 S. Jeremiah 22:1-9, They Abandoned the Covenant of the Lord God

God's Vision for Exiles

Adult Topic—Envisioning a Future

.....

Youth Topic—Dry Bones Live!
Children's Topic—Listen to God's Promises

.....

Devotional Reading—Jeremiah 29:4-14
Background Scripture—Ezekiel 37
Print—Ezekiel 37:1-11a, 25a, 26-27

• • • • • • • • • • • •

PRINTED SCRIPTURE

Ezekiel 37:1-11a, 25a, 26-27 (KJV)

THE hand of the LORD was upon me, and carried me out in the spirit of the LORD, and set me down in the midst of the valley which was full of bones,

2 And caused me to pass by them round about: and, behold, there were very many in the open valley; and, lo, they were very dry.

3 And he said unto me, Son of man, can these bones live? And I answered, O Lord GOD, thou knowest.

4 Again he said unto me, Prophesy upon these bones, and say unto them, O ye dry bones, hear the word of the LORD.

5 Thus saith the Lord GOD unto these bones; Behold, I will cause breath to enter into you, and ye shall live:

6 And I will lay sinews upon you, and will bring up flesh upon you, and cover you with skin, and put breath in you, and ye shall live; and ye shall know that I am the LORD.

7 so I prophesied as I was com-

Ezekiel 37:1-11a, 25a, 26-27 (NRSV)

THE HAND of the LORD came upon me, and he brought me out by the spirit of the LORD and set me down in the middle of a valley; it was full of bones.

2 He led me all around them; there were very many lying in the valley, and they were very dry.

3 He said to me, "Mortal, can these bones live?" I answered. "O Lord GOD, you know."

4 Then he said to me, "Prophesy to these bones, and say to them: O dry bones, hear the word of the LORD.

5 Thus says the Lord GOD to these bones: I will cause breath to enter you, and you shall live.

6 I will lay sinews on you, and will cause flesh to come upon you, and cover you with skin, and put breath in you, and you shall live; and you shall know that I am the LORD."

7 So I prophesied as I had been commanded; and as I prophesied,

manded: and as I prophesied, there was a noise, and behold a shaking, and the bones came together, bone to his bone.

8 And when I beheld, lo, the sinews and the flesh came up upon them, and the skin covered them above: but there was no breath in them.

9 Then said he unto me, Prophesy unto the wind, prophesy, son of man, and say to the wind, Thus saith the Lord GOD; come from the four winds, O breath, and breathe upon these slain, that they may live.

10 So I prophesied as he commanded me, and the breath came into them, and they lived, and stood up upon their feet, an exceeding great army.

11 Then he said unto me, Son of man, these bones are the whole house of Israel:

.....

25 And they shall dwell in the land that I have given unto Jacob my servant, wherein your fathers have dwelt.

.....

26 Moreover I will make a covenant of peace with them; it shall be an everlasting covenant with them: and I will place them, and multiply them, and will set my sanctuary in the midst of them for evermore.

27 My tabernacle also shall be with them: yea, I will be their God, and they shall be my people.

suddenly there was a noise, a rattling, and the bones came together, bone to its bone.

8 I looked, and there were sinews on them, and flesh had come upon them, and skin had covered them; but there was no breath in them.

9 Then he said to me, "Prophesy to the breath, prophesy, mortal, and say to the breath: Thus says the Lord GOD: Come from the four winds, O breath, and breathe upon these slain, that they may live."

10 I prophesied as he commanded me, and the breath came into them, and they lived, and stood on their feet, a vast multitude.

11 Then he said to me, "Mortal, these bones are the whole house of Israel."

.....

25 They shall live in the land that I gave to my servant Jacob, in which your ancestors lived.

.....

26 I will make a covenant of peace with them; it shall be an everlasting covenant with them; and I will bless them and multiply them, and will set my sanctuary among them forevermore.

27 My dwelling place shall be with them; and I will be their God, and they shall be my people.

KEY VERSE

My tabernacle also shall be with them: yea, I will be their God, and they shall be my people.—Ezekiel 37:27

OBJECTIVES

After reading this lesson, the student should be informed about:

1. The place of Israel in the interpretation of the "dry bones" vision;
2. God's promise to restore the nation of Israel; and,
3. The significance of God's new covenant with Israel.

POINTS TO BE EMPHASIZED

Adult/Youth
Key Verse: Ezekiel 37:27
Print: Ezekiel 37:1-11a, 25a, 26-27

—Ezekiel was carried away by the spirit of the Lord to a valley of dry bones and asked if he believed the bones could become people again. (1-3)

—The Lord told the prophet to prophesy to the bones that God would restore them to life. (4-6)

—Ezekiel prophesied as the Lord commanded; the bones knit together, and they became covered with flesh and skin. (7-8)

—Ezekiel again prophesied as the Lord commanded; and breath came into the multitude, causing them to live. (9-10)

—The Lord said these bones were the house of Israel, devoid of hope. (11)

—God promised that the people would return to their own land, live in peace under their own rulers, and be the people of God. (25-27)

Children
Key Verse: Ezekiel 37:27
Print: Ezekiel 37:21-28

—God promised to gather the people of Israel from among the nations of the world and bring them home to their own land and make one nation. (21-22)

—The Lord promised to be their God and to save them from their wrongdoings. (23)

—The Lord promised that David would rule the nation and the people would obey. (24-25)

—The Lord promised to make a covenant of peace with Israel and to put His temple among them forever. (26-28)

(NOTE: Use KJV Scripture for Adult; NRSV Scripture for Youth and Children)

I. Introduction

A. A PERCEPTION OF HISTORY

Usually, the study of the prophets has the Exile or Captivity as the focal point. Thus, the prophets are grouped around this great historical event in the life of Israel. For example: If we set the date of the Captivity at 586 B.C., we find the following men served before the Exile: Joel, Jonah, Amos, Hosea, Micah, Isaiah, Nahum, Zephaniah, Habakkuk, and Jeremiah. They are called Pre-Exilic prophets. During the Exile, we have Daniel, Ezekiel, and Obadiah. And after the Exile, Haggai, Zechariah and Malachi served. They are called Post-Exilic prophets. As you see, our lesson deals with Ezekiel, one of the Exilic prophets.

One purpose of Ezekiel's ministry to the "whole house of Israel" was to have them keep in mind why they had been brought to their present low level—captives in a foreign land! He particularly speaks of their sins in chapters 8-33. Evidently, Captivity did not change the heart of Israel. Sins committed before the Captivity flourished still among the captives in Babylon, so that the Old Testament record of man's utter failure continued. The sins of Ezekiel's day include: bloodshed, bribery, child sacrifice, covenant-breaking, disobedience to parents, extortion, false prophets, idolatry (they copied these abominations from the heathen nations), oppression, profane priests, Sabbath-breaking, and violence.

B. BIBLICAL BACKGROUND

Our lesson is found in the midst of prophecies dealing with restoration. Remember, the Jewish exiles were carried away to Babylon; thus, the appropriateness of preaching restoration. Ezekiel sought to sustain the faith of the exiles by predicting their restoration. Jehovah had not reneged on His covenant obligations. Israel's oppressors would eventually be defeated, and the glory of the nation restored.

At least five major themes are found in the Book of Ezekiel: (1) The majesty of God. This glory of the Lord is described in the first vision, that of the Cherubim Chariot, in chapter one; (2) the apostasy or falling away of Israel with the resultant chastisement and warnings of judgments on Jerusalem, chapters 4-24; (3) future judgments upon the Gentile (heathen) nations, chapters 25-32; (4) the restoration of Israel, chapters 34-39. According to the Bible, Israel shall take possession of all the land God promised to the nation. As for its population, presently approximately 25 percent of all the Jews in the world are in Palestine. Today's lesson (chapter 37) sheds some light on this issue; and, (5) The final consummation of the kingdom of peace is realized during the Millennial age when the Prince of Peace reigns in Jerusalem, chapters 40-48.

II. Exposition and Application of the Scripture

A. THE QUESTION ABOUT THE DRY BONES
(Ezekiel 37:1-3)

THE hand of the LORD was upon me, and carried me out in the spirit of the LORD, and set me down in the midst of the valley which was full of bones, and caused me to pass by them round about: and, behold, there were very many in the open valley; and lo, they were very dry. And he said unto me, Son of man, can these bones live? And I answered, O Lord GOD, thou knowest.

God had earlier announced the restoration of the nation: "For I will take you from among the nations, and gather you out of all countries, and will bring you into your own land" (Ezekiel 36:24). Now in chapter 37, how this restoration is accomplished is given in vision and symbolism. Two thoughts concerning Ezekiel's experience may be noted: (1) He did not actually travel anywhere, but saw the valley in a vision, or (2) He was actually, literally removed by the Holy Spirit and placed in the valley where he could receive the vision. I am in favor of this latter interpretation.

In a similar way, in Ezekiel 3:22, when the hand of the Lord was upon Ezekiel there, in obedience to God's command, the prophet arose and went out into the plain. This suggests actual, physical action, and not merely a vision or trance. We are taught then that Ezekiel was impelled or carried bodily by the Holy Spirit to the place described. This interpretation is aided by the words, "the hand of the Lord was upon me." What need would there be of God's hand coming upon Ezekiel if there was no physical transition? Taken from his own home by God's supernatural intervention, the prophet was set down in the midst of the valley that was full of human bones. He was then made to pass by them all around, and he discovered there were very many bones and they were disjointed, bleached, scattered (not in a pile), and extremely dry. The scene was reminiscent of an army slain in battle. Ezekiel was given a clear view, and then walked among the bones in order to ascertain the possibility of their resuscitation.

God then said to Ezekiel: "Son of man, can these bones live?" Note the title "son of man" is used of Ezekiel about ninety times by God. It first occurs in Ezekiel 2:1. It is a common Semitic way of emphasizing humanity (just as Son of God stresses deity). "Son of Man" is also the title the Lord Jesus used about eighty times in the Gospels concerning Himself. It is clearly a Messianic title, chosen by our Lord in order to get the Jews' minds away from the prophetic idea of a conquering Messiah. It is believed that Christ took the phrase "Son of Man" from Daniel 7:13. He did so in order to teach the Jews that although He came in humility this time, the next time He would come in great glory and power. Thus Jesus used the title to emphasize: (1) His earthly ministry; (2) prediction of His Passion (suffering during the period following the Last Supper and including the Crucifixion); (3) His Second Coming to earth.

In Revelation 7:14, when one of the elders inquired, "Who are these arrayed in white robes, and where did they come from?" John said: "Sir, you know." This is a rhetorical style that places emphasis on the all knowing dimension of the character of God rather than the assessment of human knowledge. Questions that are raised by God can only be answered by God. Obviously, the question was for Ezekiel's benefit, not to provide God with any information. His answer showed that Ezekiel recognized from the human standpoint the impossibility of making dead bones live! From Ezekiel's point of view, it was hopeless. But by saying, "Lord, You know," the prophet indicated it would take superhuman power to revive such bones. And so by not giving a direct "yes" or "no" answer, Ezekiel reverently replied, "Lord, You know."

B. THE ANSWER CONCERNING THE DRY BONES
(Ezekiel 37:4-6)

Again he said unto me, Prophesy upon these bones, and say unto them, O ye dry bones, hear the word of the LORD. Thus saith the Lord GOD unto these bones; Behold, I will cause breath to enter into you, and ye shall live: And I will lay sinews upon you, and will bring up flesh upon you, and cover you with skin, and put breath in you, and ye shall live; and ye shall know that I am the LORD.

The English word "prophesy" has Greek roots, and means literally, "to speak forth, speak out." Much has been written about the Hebrew word **"naba,"** to prophesy **(nabi,** prophet). The derivation of nabi is a matter of controversy *(Theological Wordbook of the OT:* 2:544), but we settle for the essential idea of an "authorized spokesman." Ezekiel is authorized by God to speak to the dry bones, and command them to hear the word of the Lord. The promise is made that God will cause breath to enter into the bones and they shall live. "Breath" in verses 5, 6, 8, 9, 10; "Spirit" in verses 1, 14; and "wind" in verse 9—all are renderings of the same Hebrew word, ruach.

Wherever you have one word in the original language with several meanings, you will have to let the context help you decide which meaning is correct or best for any given verse. There are some interpretations that fail to do this, and consequently come up with such false doctrines as "soul-sleep," and "annihilationism." And so the question in verse 3 is answered. Jehovah has the power to do whatever He pleases, and to fulfill whatever He promises. His word is powerful.

C. THE RESTORATION OF THE DRY BONES
(Ezekiel 37:7-10)

So I prophesied as I was commanded: and as I prophesied, there was a noise, and behold a shaking, and the bones came together, bone to his bone. And when I beheld, lo, the sinews and the flesh came up upon them, and the skin covered them above: but there was no breath in them. Then said he unto me, Prophesy unto the wind, prophesy, son of man, and say to the wind, Thus saith the Lord GOD; Come from the four winds, O breath, and breathe upon these slain, that they may live. So I prophesied as he commanded me, and the breath came into them, and they lived, and stood up upon their feet, an exceeding great army.

Ezekiel did as he was told. As he spoke, there came a loud rumbling noise, and a rattling, shaking or trembling like an earthquake. There is no mention of a trumpet blast or the voice of the archangel, or the voice of the Son of God (1 Thessalonians 4:16; John 5:25) which will be instrumental in the resurrection of the dead. So do not take the scene here for the first or second resurrection! Besides, our resurrection does not depend upon a preacher's prophesying. Furthermore, the bodily resurrection of the believer is instantaneous, not piece meal— bone to bone, sinews, flesh, etc.

The bones came together, and the sinews and flesh came upon the bones, but there still was no breath in them. So once again God spoke to Ezekiel, and commanded, "Prophesy to the breath (RSV, NKJV, NIV, NASB; only the KJV has "wind" here, Ezekiel 37:9), and say to the breath...." Wind itself does not bring life into dead bodies. What matters is the breath of life itself, not a symbol of the breath of life. There is that divine breath of life in every creature, for the Creator holds the breath of every living creature in His hands (Job 12:10; Psalm 104:29).

D. THE INTERPRETATION OF THE DRY BONES
(Ezekiel 37:11a, 25a, 26-27)

And they shall dwell in the land that I have given unto Jacob my servant, wherein your fathers have dwelt; Moreover I will make a covenant of peace with them; it shall be an everlasting covenant with them: and I will place them, and multiply them, and will set my sanctuary in the midst of them for evermore. My tabernacle also shall be with them: yea, I will be their God, and they shall be my people.

Verse 11 is a key verse for our understanding of the vision. The bones are the whole house of Israel living at the time of the restoration. The dry bones that come to life speak of the national resurrection of Israel. It deals with the nation, not with individuals. Jews presently scattered all over the world have no breath in them, having rejected the Lord Jesus as Messiah. The word "graves" used in Ezekiel 37:12-13 refers to the various nations in which the Jewish people reside. And although regathered (pulled out of their graves) in unbelief, the declaration of Israel as an independent State, May 14, 1948 shows the possibility of the fulfillment of Ezekiel's prophecy. Coming from the "four winds" means Jews are regathered from the four corners of the earth. The full regathering, restoration and regeneration through faith in the shed blood of Jesus Christ remains a viable possibility for Israel. In that day, God promises, He will do a number of things confirming His relationship with Israel. He will establish a covenant of peace. In the Bible, a covenant with God is more than an agreement. The Lord initiates the covenant **(berith),** and sets the terms. The covenant may be conditional or unconditional. In our lesson, the new covenant is unconditional; this means the Lord is going to fulfill it, and it is not left up to men to fulfill any obligation or requirement. It is to be an eternal covenant. Furthermore, the Lord will place the Jews and cause them to multiply; He will set His sanctuary in their midst for evermore; and His tabernacle (presence) will be above them protecting them.

This everlasting covenant of peace is none other than the new covenant in Jeremiah 31:31-34. Grounded in God's grace, it will be in operation at the return of the Lord Jesus Christ to the earth to rule, not only over regathered and restored Israel, but over the entire earth. Christ will be the God of Israel; and Israel shall be His people.

III. Special Features

A. PRESERVING OUR HERITAGE

Growing up as a boy, I heard the name of Ezekiel mentioned in both song and sermon. As for the Spirituals, we sang about Ezekiel, "the interpreter of life through wheels and dry bones" (Lovell, John; *Black Song*, p. 259). In the Spiritual, "Zekiel Saw de Wheel," we learn that "de big wheel run by faith, little wheel run by de grace of God" (Ezekiel 1:16). As for sermons, the topic, "I Sat Where They Sat" (Ezekiel 3; 15) has been popular with our ministers. And of course, sermons on "Dry Bones" were often heard.

Unfortunately, little of anything was said about the nation of Israel. Today's lesson serves as a reminder that the bones "are the whole house of Israel" (Ezekiel 37:11a). Without acceptance of this fact, the vision cannot be understood. And we will remain in the condition of one minister who took a text from Ezekiel, then announced to his waiting congregation: "Brothers and Sisters, this morning I intend to explain the unexplainable, find out the indefinable, ponder over the imponderable, and unscrew the inscrutable."

We repeat: the phrase "Dry Bones" does not speak of physical resurrection of the dead, but deals with the revival and restoration of the spiritual life of the nation of Israel. It is impossible to be a good Bible student without an adequate grasp of the place of Israel in God's Plan of the Ages. Furthermore, recognition of the role this nation plays in the scheme of our Sovereign Lord helps to combat the rising anti-Semitism among American Blacks—an anti-Semitism increasing as a result of the influence of Islamic and pseudo-Islamic organizations in our country.

B. A CONCLUDING WORD

The Jews in Exile were naturally despondent. Their distress greatly increased at the news that Jerusalem had fallen. You see, Ezekiel had been taken to Babylon between the first and last deportations of Judah (2 Kings 24:11-16). And these early captives had given up hope for any future blessings as a nation. Hear them cry in Ezekiel 37:11b: "Our bones are dried, and our hope is lost, and we ourselves are cut off." These are the words of despair and despondency.

But Ezekiel was led of the Lord to preach that Israel would not remain in the state of a bunch of dead bones. And so our lesson is one of hope and encouragement to the Jews who feared national annihilation. What God had announced in chapter 36, He showed to Ezekiel in a remarkable vision in chapter 37. The God of the Bible still speaks to our hearts. As Christians, we too have moments of gloom, and fail to obey the command to rejoice! Then the Holy Spirit comes and dispels our sorrows and our pessimism, points us to the empty tomb, and reminds us that God is our Father and we are His children. As members of the Church, we have a future that is more glorious than any earthly Israel can ever have!

HOME DAILY BIBLE READINGS
Week of November 22, 1998
God's Vision for Exiles

Nov.	16	M.	Ezekiel 3:22-27, The Spirit Entered into Me
Nov.	17	T.	Ezekiel 8:1-13, The Spirit Lifted Me Up
Nov.	18	W.	Ezekiel 37:1-14, Can These Bones Live?
Nov.	19	T.	Ezekiel 37:15-23, I Will Make Them One Nation
Nov.	20	F.	Ezekiel 37:24-28, My Servant David Shall Be Their King
Nov.	21	S.	Ezekiel 40:1-4, In Visions of God
Nov.	22	S.	Ezekiel 43:1-9, The Glory of the Lord Filled the Temple

Renewal and Worship

Adult Topic—Renewal and Worship

·····

Youth Topic—Let's Party!
Children's Topic—Worship God

·····

Devotional Reading—Galatians 3:23-29
Background Scripture—Nehemiah 8—9
Print—Nehemiah 8:13—9:3

· · · · · · · · · · ·

PRINTED SCRIPTURE

Nehemiah 8:13-9:3 (KJV)

13 And on the second day were gathered together the chief of the fathers of all the people, the priests, and the Levites, unto Ezra the scribe, even to understand the words of the law.

14 And they found written in the law which the LORD had commanded by Moses, that the children of Israel should dwell in booths in the feast of the seventh month:

15 And that they should publish and proclaim in all their cities, and in Jerusalem, saying, Go forth unto the mount, and fetch olive branches, and pine branches, and myrtle branches, and palm branches, and branches of thick trees, to make booths, as it is written.

16 So the people went forth, and brought them, and made themselves booths, every one upon the roof of his house, and in their courts, and in the courts of the house of God, and in the street of the water gate, and in the street of the gate of Ephraim.

Nehemiah 8:13—9:3 (NRSV)

13 On the second day the heads of ancestral houses of all the people, with the priests and the Levites, came together to the scribe Ezra in order to study the words of the law.

14 And they found it written in the law, which the LORD had commanded by Moses, that the people of Israel should live in booths during the festival of the seventh month,

15 and that they should publish and proclaim in all their towns and in Jerusalem as follows, "Go out to the hills and bring branches of olive, wild olive, myrtle, palm, and other leafy trees to make booths, as it is written."

16 So the people went out and brought them, and made booths for themselves, each on the roofs of their houses, and in their courts and in the courts of the house of God, and in the square at the Water Gate and in the square at the Gate of Ephraim.

17 And all the congregation of them that were come again out of the captivity made booths, and sat under the booths: for since the days of Jeshua the son of Nun unto that day had not the children of Israel done so. And there was very great gladness.

18 Also day by day, from the first day unto the last day, he read in the book of the law of God. And they kept the feast seven days; and on the eighth day was a solemn assembly, according unto the manner.

.....

NOW in the twenty and fourth day of this month the children of Israel were assembled with fasting, and with sackclothes, and earth upon them.

2 And the seed of Israel separated themselves from all strangers, and stood and confessed their sins, and the iniquities of their fathers.

3 And they stood up in their place, and read in the book of the law of the LORD their God one fourth part of the day; and another fourth part they confessed, and worshipped the LORD their God.

17 And all the assembly of those who had returned from the captivity made booths and lived in them; for from the days of Jeshua son of Nun to that day the people of Israel had not done so. And there was very great rejoicing.

18 And day by day, from the first day to the last day, he read from the book of the law of God. They kept the festival seven days; and on the eighth day there was a solemn assembly, according to the ordinance.

.....

NOW ON the twenty-fourth day of this month the people of Israel were assembled with fasting and in sackcloth, and with earth on their heads.

2 Then those of Israelite descent separated themselves from all foreigners, and stood and confessed their sins and the iniquities of their ancestors.

3 They stood up in their place and read from the book of the law of the LORD their God for a fourth part of the day, and for another fourth they made confession and worshiped the LORD their God.

KEY VERSE

Thou, even thou, art LORD alone, thou hast made heaven, the heaven of heavens, with all their host, the earth, and all things that are therein, the seas, and all that is therein, and thou preservest them all; and the host of heaven worshippeth thee.— Nehemiah 9:6

OBJECTIVES

After reading this lesson, the student should be informed about:

1. The importance of knowing the Word of God and obeying it;
2. The significance of the Feast of Tabernacles;
3. Different modes of worship practiced by the Israelites; and,
4. The great importance of public reading of the Scriptures.

Adult/Youth/Children
Key Verse: Nehemiah 9:6; Nehemiah 9:5 (Children)
Print: Nehemiah 8:13—9:3

—While studying the law with Ezra, the Jewish leaders discovered the laws concerning the festival of booths. (8:13-14)
—All the people who had returned from captivity brought in branches and made booths on the roofs of their houses, which they had not done since the time of Jeshua. (8:16-17)
—The people lived in the booths and celebrated the festival for seven days, and each day Ezra read from the book of the law of God. (8:18)
—On the twenty-fourth day of the month, the people gathered to fast and repent. (9:1)
—Setting themselves apart from foreigners, the people studied the law, made confession, and worshiped the Lord their God. (9:2-3)
—During the time of confession, Ezra declared the Lord to be the maker of heaven, earth, and the seas, and to be the giver of life. (9:6)

(NOTE: Use KJV Scripture for Adult; NRSV Scripture for Children and Youth)

TOPICAL OUTLINE OF THE LESSON

I. Introduction

A. A Perception of History
B. Biblical Background

II. Exposition and Application of the Scripture

A. Discovery of God's Word (Nehemiah 8:13-15)
B. Joy of Obeying God's Word (Nehemiah 8:16-18)
C. Public Acknowledgment of God's Word (Nehemiah 9:1-3)

III. Special Features

A. Preserving Our Heritage
B. A Concluding Word

I. Introduction

A. A PERCEPTION OF HISTORY

The historical setting of today's lesson finds Babylon conquered by Cyrus of Persia in 539 B.C. Many Jews who had been in captivity returned to their homeland, after paying taxes and promising loyalty to Cyrus. Because the policies set up by Cyrus were followed by his successors, Ahasuerus and Artaxerxes, both Ezra and Nehemiah were allowed to return home. In the year 444 B.C., Nehemiah, whose name means Jehovah Consoles, Jehovah Comforts, led a group of Babylonian Jews to Jerusalem to rebuild the walls and set up a government there. At this time, Artaxerxes ruled.

Earlier, the Temple had been rebuilt as recorded by Ezra; however, the city walls were still broken down. The continued ruin was primarily because of the laziness of the people. A threefold division of the Book of Nehemiah includes: (1) Survey and preparatory work on the walls of Jerusalem, chapters 1 and 2; (2) building the walls, chapters 3-6; and, (3) preparation for the Great Revival under Ezra, chapters 7-13.

B. BIBLICAL BACKGROUND

As the work of building the walls of the city of Jerusalem was finished, there was now a recognition that what was accomplished was by the grace and providence of God. There was a desire to hear from God's Word. Ezra, who was both scribe and priest, was asked to bring the book of the law of Moses. Ezra did so, and with great reverence, the people stood for half a day—from the morning until midday—listening to the reading of the Word of God.

The Levites helped the people to understand what was written, for the Books of the Law were written in Hebrew, and translation was necessary. While in captivity, the Jews used Aramaic, the Syrian language used by the Babylonians and Persians. Consequently, very few of the people knew Hebrew, therefore, translators were provided (Nehemiah 8:7).

The people wept when they heard the words of the Law, for they were convicted of having neglected the Word of God. Now they took the Word seriously, but Nehemiah then encouraged them not to mourn, not to weep. Biblical mourning involved emotion, usually expressed audibly. The word for weep means to shed tears, and gives us the picture of less emotion expressed. When the returned exiles heard the Law read to them, they realized how far short they had fallen, and had to be reminded by Nehemiah that a holy day was not for mourning, and that genuine repentance could lead to joy. It is at this point that we read a verse that is often heard in our Black churches: "The joy of the Lord is your strength" (Nehemiah 8:10). Their sadness was turned to joy.

II. Exposition and Application of the Scriptures

A. DISCOVERY OF GOD'S WORD
(Nehemiah 8:13-15)

And on the second day were gathered together the chief of the fathers of all the people, the priests, and the Levites, unto Ezra the scribe, even to understand the words of the law. And they found written in the law which the LORD had commanded by Moses, that the children of Israel should dwell in booths in the feast of the seventh month: And that they should publish and

proclaim in all their cities, and in Jerusalem, saying, Go forth unto the mount, and fetch olive branches, and pine branches, and myrtle branches, and palm branches, and branches of thick trees, to make booths, as it is written.

Our opening verse lists the participants in the lesson. First mentioned is the chief of the fathers of all the people. "Chief" (KJV) is rendered "heads" (RSV, NKJV)— "the heads of all the families" (NIV). Second: the priests; third: the Levites, men of the tribe of Levi; they were assistants to the Temple priests. On the second day, they gathered unto Ezra, the scribe (scholar and guardian of the Law; professional student of the Law). The first day had been spent reading and hearing the Law. Now their purpose was to understand the words of the Law, for they felt they needed further instruction and exposition of the Law.

Bible study should always excite Christians, for the Holy Spirit stirs up within us the desire for more intimate understanding of God's will and Word. The more we learn about the Lord Jesus Christ, the more we love Him. Furthermore, they were to publish (announce) and proclaim throughout the country what kinds of tree branches were to be collected and used (palm, willows: Leviticus 23:40); olive, pine, myrtle, palm trees (Nehemiah 8:15).

B. JOY OF OBEYING GOD'S WORD
(Nehemiah 8:16-18)

So the people went forth, and brougth them, and made themselves booths, every one upon the roof of his house, and in their courts, and in the courts of the house of God, and in the street of the water gate, and in the street of the gate of Ephraim. And all the congregation of them that were come again out of the captivity made booths, and sat under the booths: for since the days of Jeshua the son of Nun unto that day had not the children of Israel done so. And there was very great gladness. Also day by day, from the first day unto the last day, he read in the book of the law of God. And they kept the feast seven days; and on the eighth day was a solemn assembly, according unto the manner.

The people obeyed. They went forth, brought the branches and made themselves booths on the tops of their houses, or in the courts of the Temple. Those who did not live in Jerusalem probably built their booths in the streets or open places. And, they sat under the booths. While the Jews had celebrated this feast in the years past, they had not observed the entire service; that is to say, one thing the entire congregation did not do was to dwell in the booths.

Note, there was great gladness; this was the result of obedience. Gladness is joy; it may be expressed in singing, leaping, a loud cry; it is mirth, rejoicing. A study of the verses using the word "gladness" (simchah) reveals that in the Old Testament, religion is seen as touching the deepest springs of emotion, often finding outward expression in such actions as leaping, shouting and singing (ISBE). Repeatedly, we see joy and gladness as the natural outcome of fellowship with the Lord. God gives us gladness through His loving kindness, salvation, laws, judgments, and His words of comfort. The service of the Lord elicits a gladness in the hearts of those who love Him. Deuteronomy 16:15 states: "The solemn Feast of Tabernacles is kept seven days, because the Lord thy God shall bless thee in all thine increase, and in all the works of thine hands; therefore thou shalt surely rejoice." In the New Testament, the element of joy and gladness is even more prominent.

Finally, in this section of the lesson, we see again the emphasis upon reading from the book of the Law of God. First of all, it was read daily. How often do we read the Bible? Or the question may be asked, how much time is spent reading the Scriptures in our churches—morning services or at other times? Public reading of the Bible in our schools has been eliminated, but we still have the right to read the Bible at home and in church.

The word "read" in the Old Testament is often used in the sense of reading aloud to others. You see this done by Moses (Exodus 24:7) and by Ezra in our lesson (Nehemiah 8:3, 18) with respect to the public reading of God's Law or of prophecy. The reading of the Scriptures should not be perfunctory, just going through the motions, but prayerful, devotional, and in a studious manner. In this way, as we listen to the Word, read, meditate and memorize it, we give the indwelling Holy Spirit something to work with as He works on and in us.

C. PUBLIC ACKNOWLEDGMENT OF GOD'S WORD
(Nehemiah 9:1-3)

Now in the twenty and fourth day of this month the children of Israel were assembled with fasting, and with sackclothes, and earth upon them. And the seed of Israel separated themselves from all strangers, and stood and confessed their sins, and the iniquities of their fathers. And they stood up in their place, and read in the book of the law of the LORD their God one fourth part of the day; and another fourth part they confessed, and worshipped the LORD their God.

On the 24th day of this seventh month, the children of Israel met together to worship. The mood of joy and gladness is set aside in order to publicly acknowledge before God their sins and their sorrow for their sins. Several categories combine to help in this description of worship. First: There is an assembling, a coming together. Unfortunately, there are those today who feel the public meeting is not for them. They prefer staying home and listening to the radio and television preachers. "I can worship God at home just as well," they say. But the writer of Hebrews exhorts us not to forsake "the assembling of ourselves together, as the manner of some is" (Hebrews 10:25).

Second: There is fasting. This act of self-denial or "affliction of soul or self" was originally a natural expression of grief. Fasting became the customary way of demonstrating to others an inner emotion of sorrow. It soon became a recognized way of seeking God's favor and protection, and thus became associated with confession of sin, and as proof of sorrow or repentance for sin. How strange, too, that both fasting and feasting are used as religious acts!

Third: The wearing of sackcloth. This was a rough cloth of camel's hair or goat's hair, hemp, cotton, or flax that was worn as a symbol of mourning or penitence. Fourth: Earth was put upon their heads! This signified humility and deep mourning, heaviness of heart. The word **"humus"** which means earth is the root of the word for "humble." Fifth: There was also the element of separation. The Jews voluntarily separated themselves from all the foreigners and their heathen customs.

According to the Law of Moses, the Jews were not to mix or marry with the surrounding nations. This had been forgotten over the years, and reading the Law brought it back to their remembrance. God had warned the Israelites repeatedly about the need for separation from idol worshipers (Exodus 23:23-33; Deuteronomy 7:1-6). Unequal yokes (2 Corinthians 6:14) always produce evil results. It is ironic that today, some Christians are so busy staying separated from other Christians that they lack discernment to see their close relationship with the world!

Sixth: Confession. In the New Testament, this is **"homologeo,"** and it means to speak the same, to say the same thing about our sin that God says! Avoid generalizing, avoid euphemisms, and attempts to sugar-coat evil. In our private prayers, tell it like it is! Where confession is made, the Lord willingly forgives. Still today it is true for all genuine Christians, "If we confess (say what God says about our sins), He is faithful and just to forgive us our sins, and to cleanse us from all unrighteousness" (1 John 1:9). "Confession is the road to revival" (MacDonald). Seventh: The reading of the Law. Once again, we cannot overemphasize the reading and hearing of God's Word in worship.

Some of the other things—fasting, wearing sackcloth, casting dirt upon the head—we may not want to do, but the reading of the Word is essential. Nehemiah's people spent a fourth part of the day listening to the reading of Scripture. Remember, the day is twelve hours, and the night is twelve hours in the Bible (John 11:9). So the fourth part equals three hours. That's how long they stood and listened to the reading of the Book of the Law of the Lord, their God. And, another three hours of confession followed as they worshiped Jehovah (see Nehemiah 9:4-37).

III. Special Features

A. PRESERVING OUR HERITAGE

Are Baptists still "People of the Book?" Today's lesson drives home the importance of reading the Scriptures, especially publicly. In Nehemiah's day and earlier times, there was no printing press, and so scrolls made of leather or papyrus (or bark or clay tablets) were precious. But today we have no excuse. There are Bibles in practically every home, even if only as a piece of furniture.

May today's lesson impress our hearts to have more public reading of the Bible in all of our services. Paul told Timothy: "Till I come, give attendance to reading..." (1 Timothy 4:13). "Faith comes by hearing, and hearing by the word of

God" (Romans 10:17). Concerning the Book of Revelation, John said: "Blessed is he that readeth, and they that hear the words of this prophecy..." (Revelation 1:3). May our hearts be encouraged to bring our Bibles to church and to prayer meetings. Some churches I have visited have few if any Bibles in the pews. And some do not use the Scriptural readings in the back of their hymnals (few hymnals also!). Let's remain "People of the Book," and thank God we don't have to stand for half a day, or even for three hours!

B. A CONCLUDING WORD

We have seen the important part played by the public reading of the Scriptures in the worship services of the Israelites under Nehemiah. There is a close connection between the reading of the Law and confession and worship. Here are three things we who are Christians ought to be engaged in every day of our lives as we worship the Lord Jesus Christ in spirit and in truth. And of course, we ought always to pray. We recognize that we do not know how to worship God on our own. We must be taught. This is one reason He has given us the Bible. His Word is profitable for reproof and correction. This is why it is beneficial spiritually to start the day with reading the Word. Surely, we are not to live by bread alone, but by every word that proceeds out of the mouth of God. And, for the Word made flesh, Jesus Christ, our hearts rejoice.

HOME DAILY BIBLE READINGS
Week of November 29, 1998
Renewal and Worship

Nov. 23 M. Nehemiah 8:1-12, All the People Gathered
Nov. 24 T. Nehemiah 8:13-18, To Study Words of the Law
Nov. 25 W. Nehemiah 9:1-5, They Confessed Their Sins
Nov. 26 T. Nehemiah 9:6-15, You are the Lord!
Nov. 27 F. Nehemiah 9:16-25, You are Ready to Forgive, Gracious and Merciful
Nov. 28 S. Nehemiah 9:26-37, You have Been Just
Nov. 29 S. Psalm 122:1-9, Peace Be Within Your Walls

WINTER QUARTER

December, 1998, January, February 1999

GOD CALLS ANEW IN JESUS CHRIST

General Introduction

The survey of the New Testament during this quarter will complement our study of the Old Testament's survey that we have just completed. The theme is consistent in both the Old and New Testaments in that God takes the initiative to fashion a people whose mission was to bring about the kingdom of God, and the advent of the Christ places this mandate as the top priority for all those who are redeemed by His blood as participants in His work of reconciliation.

Unit I, *"The Good News of Jesus Christ,"* calls attention to the basic gospel story including the birth, life, death and resurrection of Jesus, and the nature of Christ's presence in the world today.

Unit II, *"Good News for Daily Living,"* is a presentation of four important teachings of Jesus regarding love, greed, true greatness, and forgiveness. While these have been persistent throughout human history, Jesus holds them in sharp contrast with the way in which His followers must distinguish themselves as believers in the world.

Unit III, *"Good News for Changing Times,"* is a discussion of how the faithful should live according to the teachings of Jesus in a world that does not embrace the message of the gospel. The experiences of the first-century Christians gives us insight into the faith that enabled them to face internal strife, expansion, and change as they engaged in the mission of reconciling the world to Christ.

It will be noted that the lessons for the children generally follow those for the youth and adults, except that session two is based on another Scripture passage to allow for a more adequate development of the theme leading to the Christmas story. In addition, a different portion of the background Scripture is used for the printed passage.

We shall see in the progression of the study of the life of Jesus as the Christ the struggle that the disciples encountered when they attempted to understand his birth, life, death and resurrection in terms of their significance for the human race. In an effort to really comprehend the initiative of God that is embodied in the person of the Christ, the disciples appropriated types or symbols of this anticipatory event that were embedded within the historic faith of Israel and conceived them as having been fulfilled in the advent of the Christ. The problem for them was not just simply to understand Jesus as the Christ, but to live lives consistent with that understanding. The struggle to embrace the message was exacerbated by the influx of Gentiles into the church who even though converted to the faith in many instances understood it relative to their pagan roots. We shall see how Paul devoted himself to refining the faith as the complete death of the old person and the birth of the new creation in Christ.

As we apply the gospel of the transforming power of the grace of God as depicted in the life of Jesus as the Christ, we would do well to remind ourselves that being in Christ is not a posture to be taken lightly or adopted and understood in terms of our own prejudices and preferences in style of life. We must come to understand that God in Christ makes all things new and this includes all of those forms of behavior that stand in contradiction to the transforming power of the redemptive blood of Jesus Christ. As such, being Christian is not just simply holding a set of beliefs as important as they may be, but the proof of the power lies in that sincere and dedicated life that is indicative of the life of God in us. May we go forth in commitment to His will as we execute the Great Commission to reconcile the world unto God.

Who Is This?

Unit I. The Good News of Jesus Christ
Children's Unit—Good News About Jesus
Adult Topic—Who Is Jesus to You?

.....

Youth Topic—Who Am I?
Children's Topic—Who Is Jesus?

.....

Devotional Reading—Isaiah 11:1-10
Background Scripture—Hebrews 1:1-4; Matthew 16:13-26
Print—Hebrews 1:1-4; Matthew 16:13-23

• • • • • • • • • • •

PRINTED SCRIPTURE

Hebrews 1:1-4; Matthew 16:13-23 (KJV)

GOD, who at sundry times and in divers manners spake in time past unto the fathers by the prophets,

2 Hath in these last days spoken unto us by his Son, whom he hath appointed heir of all things, by whom also he made the worlds;

3 Who being the brightness of his glory, and the express image of his person, and upholding all things by the word of his power, when he had by himself purged our sins, sat down on the right hand of the Majesty on high;

4 Being made so much better than the angels, as he hath by inheritance obtained a more excellent name than they.

.....

13 When Jesus came into the coasts of Caesarea Philippi, he asked his disciples, saying, Whom do men say that I the Son of man am?

14 And they said, Some say that

Hebrews 1:1-4; Matthew 16:13-23 (NRSV)

LONG AGO God spoke to our ancestors in many and various ways by the prophets,

2 but in these last days he has spoken to us by a Son, whom he appointed heir of all things, through whom he also created the worlds.

3 He is the reflection of God's glory and the exact imprint of God's very being, and he sustains all things by his powerful word. When he had made purification for sins, he sat down at the right hand of the Majesty on high,

4 having become as much superior to angels as the name he has inherited is more excellent than theirs.

.....

13 Now when Jesus came into the district of Caesarea Philippi, he asked his disciples, "Who do people say that the Son of Man is?"

14 And they said, "Some say John

thou art John the Baptist: some, Elias; and others, Jeremias, or one of the prophets.

15 He saith unto them, But whom say ye that I am?

16 And Simon Peter answered and said, Thou art the Christ, the Son of the living God.

17 And Jesus answered and said unto him, Blessed art thou, Simon Barjona: for flesh and blood hath not revealed it unto thee, but my Father which is in heaven.

18 And I say also unto thee, That thou art Peter, and upon this rock I will build my church; and the gates of hell shall not prevail against it.

19 And I will give unto thee the keys of the kingdom of heaven: and whatsoever thou shalt bind on earth shall be bound in heaven: and whatsoever thou shalt loose on earth shall be loosed in heaven.

20 Then charged he his disciples that they should tell no man that he was Jesus the Christ.

21 From that time forth began Jesus to shew unto his disciples, how that he must go unto Jerusalem, and suffer many things of the elders and chief priests and scribes, and be killed, and be raised again the third day.

22 Then Peter took him, and began to rebuke him, saying, Be it far from thee, Lord: this shall not be unto thee.

23 But he turned, and said unto Peter, Get thee behind me, Satan: thou art an offence unto me: for thou savourest not the things that be of God, but those that be of men.

the Baptist, but others Elijah, and still others Jeremiah or one of the prophets."

15 He said to them, "But who do you say that I am?"

16 Simon Peter answered, "You are the Messiah, the Son of the living God."

17 And Jesus answered him, "Blessed are you, Simon son of Jonah! For flesh and blood has not revealed this to you, but my Father in heaven.

18 And I tell you, you are Peter, and on this rock I will build my church, and the gates of Hades will not prevail against it.

19 I will give you the keys of the kingdom of heaven, and whatever you bind on earth will be bound in heaven, and whatever you loose on earth will be loosed in heaven."

20 Then he sternly ordered the disciples not to tell anyone that he was the Messiah.

21 From that time on, Jesus began to show his disciples that he must go to Jerusalem and undergo great suffering at the hands of the elders and chief priests and scribes, and be killed, and on the third day be raised.

22 And Peter took him aside and began to rebuke him, saying, "God forbid it, Lord! This must never happen to you."

23 But he turned and said to Peter, "Get behind me, Satan! You are a stumbling block to me; for you are setting your mind not on divine things but on human things."

 **KEY VERSE** And Simon Peter answered and said, Thou art the Christ, the Son of the living God.—Matthew 16:16

OBJECTIVES

After reading this lesson, the student should be informed about:

1. The superiority of God's Son, the Lord Jesus Christ;
2. The finished work of Christ who is the last word from God;
3. The significance of Simon Peter's confession of Christ; and,
4. Simon Peter's reaction to the prediction of the death of Christ.

POINTS TO BE EMPHASIZED

Adult/Youth/Children
Key Verse: Matthew 16:16
Print: Hebrews 1:1-4; Matthew 16:13-23

—God has spoken many times and in many ways; in the latter days, God has spoken through a Son. (Hebrews 1:1-2)
—The Son, the reflection of God's glory and the sustainer of all things, has made purification for sins and is superior to angels. (3-4)
—When Jesus asked His disciples who the people said He was, they reported John the Baptist, Elijah, Jeremiah, or one of the prophets. (Matthew 16:13-14)
—Jesus then asked them who they thought He was; Simon Peter answered, "You are the Messiah, the Son of the Living God." (15-16)
—Jesus said Peter was blessed because his revelation came from God and therefore on this rock Jesus would build His church. (17-20)
—As Jesus began to foretell His crucifixion and resurrection, Peter protested and was firmly rebuked. (21-23)

(NOTE Use KJV Scripture for Adults; NRSV Scripture for Youth and Children)

TOPICAL OUTLINE OF THE LESSON

I. Introduction

A. Questions Concerning the Identity of Christ
B. Biblical Background

II. Exposition and Application of the Scripture

A. Spoken in the Son (Hebrews 1:1-4)
B. Confession of Christ (Matthew 16:13-17)
C. Characteristics of the Church (Matthew 18-20)
D. Prediction and Protest (Matthew 16:21-23)

III. Special Features

A. Preserving Our Heritage
B. A Concluding Word

I. Introduction

A. QUESTIONS CONCERNING THE IDENTITY OF CHRIST

Throughout the Bible we find the question, "Who are you?" This question first occurs in Genesis 27:32 when blind Isaac asked Jacob, "Who are you?" And Jacob replied, "I am your son, your firstborn, Esau." A second example of deceit is seen when Joshua inquired of the Hivites, "Who are you, and where do you come from?" (Joshua 9:8). They too lied, claiming to be from a distant land. Boaz was startled to find at midnight a woman lying at his feet, and he said, "Who are you?" (Ruth 3:9). It was Ruth.

Now our concern is with the Lord Jesus Christ. Some men thought John the Baptist was the Messiah, and inquired, "Who are you?" (John 1:19, 22). Perhaps the first time this question is recorded of the Lord is when the Pharisees asked, "Who is this who speaks blasphemies?" The Lord said to the paralytic, "Man, your sins are forgiven you" (Luke 5:21). A second record of question is Luke 7:49: "Who is this who even forgives sins?"

Third: When Herod heard of all Christ had done, he said, "Who is this of whom I hear such things?" (Luke 9:7). A fourth example of record is John 8:25, when the Pharisees inquired: "Who are you?" Fifth: When our Lord entered Jerusalem, all the city was moved, saying, "Who is this?" (Matthew 21:10). Sixth: When Christ predicted, "The Son of Man must be lifted up," the religious leaders responded: "Who is this Son of Man?" (John 12:34). Seventh: Finally, from the Gospel of John we read that after the resurrection, the Lord bade the disciples to eat breakfast, but none of them dared ask Him, "Who are You" (John 21:12), for they knew it was the Lord. Surely we should add Saul's (Paul's) question! See him on the road to Damascus when suddenly interrupted from carrying out his evil purpose. A voice said, "Saul, Saul, why are you persecuting me?" And he said, "Who are You, Lord?" (Acts 9:5). He soon found out. Suppose you are asked, "Who is Jesus Christ?" What would your answer be? Do you know who He is?

B. BIBLICAL BACKGROUND

The theme of the Book of Hebrews is the Superiority of Jesus Christ. We learn that He is better than the prophets, angels, Moses, Joshua, the priests of Aaron, and His blood a better sacrifice than all the blood of animals shed through the centuries. As the poet (Isaac Watts) has said:

> "Not all the blood of beasts, on Jewish altars slain,
> Could give the guilty conscience peace, Or wash away the stain.
> But Christ, the heav'nly Lamb, Take all our sins away.
> A sacrifice of nobler name, And richer blood than they."

Hebrews is not an easy book to study. One of the key issues to remember is, to paraphrase the late Dr. Donald Grey Barnhouse, "The Book of Hebrews was written to the Hebrews to get the Hebrews to stop being Hebrews." Remember, you have two different audiences, both profess but not all possess. To the mere professor, there is the exhortation to genuinely accept the Lord Jesus as Messiah; to the possessor, there is the encouragement to continue in Christ. As for the Matthew Scripture, we see a continuation of events leading to Calvary. The miracles performed, the doctrines taught, parables used, the humiliation by the religious leaders—all were calculated to draw our Lord closer to His predetermined goal, Calvary. In Matthew chapter 16, the Pharisees and the Sadducees are indeed roughly dealt with. Christ rebuked them for their sign-seeking mentality, calling them hypocrites, and members of a wicked and adulterous generation. He then warned His own followers to beware of "the leaven of the Pharisees and of the Sadducees," that is to say, of their false doctrine. It is at this point, having arrived at the boarders of Caesarea Philippi, our Lord asked: "Who do men say that I, the Son of Man, am?"

II. Exposition and Application of the Scripture

A. SPOKEN IN THE SON
(Hebrews 1:1-4)

GOD, who at sundry times and in divers manners spake in time past unto the fathers by the prophets, Hath in these last days spoken unto us by his Son, whom he hath appointed heir of all things, by whom also he made the worlds; Who being the brightness of his glory, and the express image of his person, and upholding all things by the word of his power, when he had by himself purged our sins, sat down on the right hand of the Majesty on high; Being made so much better than the angels, as he hath by inheritance obtained a more excellent name than they.

We are not told who is the human author of Hebrews. And there is no opening salutation as in the Church Letters. However, these early verses in our lesson strike the keynote for the entire Epistle. Immediately, we learn that Deity is not speechless. God spoke at sundry times. The word is sundry and not Sunday! It means in many ways or portions, in fragmentary fashion. God did not drop the whole book on man at one time. Progression is to be seen.

God also spoke in divers or varied manners and methods. He used His voice as a rainbow, Melchizedek, angels, dreams and visions, burning bush, plagues, donkey, ravens, a great fish, symbols, furniture, pillar of fire and cloud, earthquakes, worms, men and women (prophets), etc. The Hebrews had received the oracles of God, and the Lord used the prophets or messengers as His spokesmen. The author moves from time past to last days. He moves from the fact that God spoke unto the fathers to the fact that He spoke unto us; he moves from speaking by the prophets to speaking by His Son. Indeed, God has spoken Son-wise (literally, in Son). This means that Jesus Christ is the last word from God, and that any and all other claims are false. Jesus as the Christ is the last prophet of God. No one supercedes Christ. Now consider this Person, Jesus Christ. See His sevenfold (perfect) superiority over the prophets. First of all, He was appointed heir to all things. This speaks of His Lordship and dominion. The matter of appointment concerns His Incarnation, and His reward for His voluntary humiliation here on earth. Second: He is Creator; He made the worlds (John 1:3; Colossians 1:16, 17). He is the Source, Origin or Beginning of all creation, contrary to the views of those who hold on erroneous interpretation of Revelation 3:14, and attempt to make Jesus Christ a creature. No, He is the Creator!

Third: He is the brightness, effulgence, irradiation of God's glory; He is the invisible "outshining" of God's glory. This is because He is genuine, absolute Deity. Fourth: Christ is the express image of God's Person. The Greek word rendered "express" has given us the English word, "character." It is derived from a verb meaning to engrave. Our Lord then is the impression, reproduction, representation of God's real being. And of course, only God can perfectly thus represent God (John 1:18; Philippians 2:6).

Fifth: He upholds the universe by His Word. The verb translated "upholding" means to carry, support. Christ preserves and governs the entire world. What a mighty God we serve! Sixth: He dealt with the filthiness of our sin. The tense of the verb denotes a finished work; literally, "having purged" indicates the cleansing is finished, once for all, and He Himself did it. Seventh: He sat down; this is called His session. The right hand symbolizes the place of honor, power. He is settled. His redemptive work is finished, and cannot be undone! Furthermore, what He did—purging us—nobody else could do. How wonderfully well this section of Hebrews answers the question, "Who is this?"

B. CONFESSION OF CHRIST
(Matthew 16:13-17)

When Jesus came into the coasts of Caesarea Philippi, he asked his disciples, saying, Whom do men say that I the Son of man am? And they said Some say that thou art John the Baptist: some, Elias; and others, Jeremias, or one of the prophets. He saith unto them, But whom say ye that I am? And Simon Peter answered and said, Thou art the Christ, the Son of the living God. And Jesus answered and said unto him, Blessed art thou, Simon Barjona: for flesh and blood hath not revealed it unto thee, but my Father which is in heaven.

The lesson returns now to the days of our Lord's flesh, His ministry on earth. We find Him in the region of Caesarea Philippi, about 25 miles north of the Sea of Galilee. At this point He asked the disciples, "Who do men say that I, the Son of Man, am?" "Son of Man" is a Messianic title Christ consistently used of Himself; it stresses His humanity. He was the representative Man. The disciples mentioned several names: (1) John the Baptist. Recall John recently had been beheaded. (2) Elijah, who had been translated and was expected to return preceding the Day of the Lord. (3) Jeremiah, who according to the Apocrypha ("hidden," writings not accepted as canon) was expected to appear and restore the ark he is said to have hidden. (4) One of the prophets (Matthew 21:11).

What men were saying about Him indicated they did not really know who He was. Upon hearing these various names, the Lord inquired of the disciples, "But who do you (first in the Greek for emphasis) say that I am?" Simon Peter answered and said: "You are the Christ (Messiah), the Son of the living God." Making Christ known is the work of the Holy Spirit, and Simon was blessed by God to answer as he did. What he expressed was not revealed to him by "flesh and blood." This latter phrase emphasizes man's frailty and ignorance. Thus Simon's response did not come out of a "logical conviction based upon outward facts acting upon his mind" (ISBE). What Peter said was revealed to him by God.

C. CHARACTERISTICS OF THE CHURCH
(Matthew 16:18-20)

And I say also unto thee, That thou art Peter, and upon this rock I will build my church; and the gates of hell shall not prevail against it. And I will give unto thee the keys of the kingdom of heaven: and whatsoever thou shalt bind on earth shall be bound in heaven: and whatsoever thou shalt loose on earth shall be loosed in heaven. Then charged he his disciples that they should tell no man that he was Jesus the Christ.

Here we have the first mention of the word, church, **ekklesia.** "Ek" means out; the "klesia" comes from the verb to call (kaleo). So literally, the church is the "called-out," the assembly of God's people. Historically, the church did not come into existence until the day of Pentecost (Acts 2), but Christ spoke of the future: "I will build My church." Now our definition of the church makes it absurd to even suggest the church was founded upon a man—and Simon Peter at that!

The word **petros** is masculine and has no definite article; while the word **"petra"** has a feminine ending and a definite article. This suggests a literal translation: "But also I say to you, that you are Peter, a little pebble, and upon this the big Rock, I will build My church." That Rock is Christ (1 Corinthians 10:4). Simon had just confessed the Deity and Messiahship of our Lord, and now Christ points to the truth of Peter's confession. Invariably, we explain the "the gates of Hell" as the forces of evil. It is true that wickedness shall not utterly destroy the true church. Throughout the centuries, wicked emperors, tyrants, dictators, and evil religionists have attempted to annihilate the church, but they all have failed. But now see the word translated "hell" (Hades) also means the unseen. Combined with the word "gates," where the elders sat to judge, give counsel, and deliberate, the phrase suggests the plots, schemes, plans, stratagems, and machinations of invisible evil foes. The idea of unseen councils reminds us that we wrestle not against flesh and blood, but against spiritual wickedness in high places (Ephesians 6:12). All of the errors, heresies, false ideologies of phony brethren have failed and will fail—this is the promise of the Word of God, the Word made Flesh. Recognize here also that our Lord predicted His triumph over death. He stated that Death will never overcome the church. See then in Matthew 16:18 a prediction of triumph, a prediction of resurrection and indestructibility.

D. PREDICTION AND PROTEST
(Matthew 16:21-23)

From that time forth began Jesus to shew unto his disciples, how that he must go unto Jerusalem, and suffer many things of the elders and chief

priests and scribes, and be killed, and be raised again the third day. Then Peter took him, and began to rebuke him, saying, Be it far from thee, Lord: this shall not be unto thee. But he turned, and said unto Peter, Get thee behind me, Satan: thou art an offence unto me: for thou savourest not the things that be of God, but those that be of men.

Now it must not be thought that Simon Peter was given the authority to admit men to heaven. Keys of course represent power to open and shut, but here they symbolize an authority exercised on earth. Two interpretations which appeal to us are: (1) the apostles (not just Simon Peter; cf. Matthew 18:18) had the authority to discipline believers. See this in the case of Ananias and Sapphira (Acts 5:1-11). (2) The apostles had the ability to announce what God has bound or loosed in heaven already.

This section closes with the Lord's commandment that His disciples not disclose the fact that He was the Messiah. Christ did not want the crowds to attempt to crown Him, for the turmoil created would serve only to have the Roman soldiers come and crush the rebellious Jews. After the resurrection would be the appropriate time! From this point on, the Lord began to show the disciples that His redemptive work was yet to be completed. Recall that at the first cleansing of the Temple He said, "Destroy this temple, and in three days I will raise it up" (John 2:19). He told Nicodemus, "so must the Son of Man be lifted up" (John 3:14). But here in Matthew 16:21, His Passion plans are made plain. Note how simply put are the things which must occur: (1) He must go to Jerusalem (2) He must suffer many things from the religious leaders (the Sanhedrin) (3) be killed, and (4) be raised again on the third day. This was shocking news to the disciples who had missed altogether previously veiled references to Christ's goal. And Simon Peter, doubtless revealing the minds of the other disciples, immediately and impetuously as usual, sought to dissuade the Lord from carrying out His purpose. Simon said: "In no way shall this be!" The double negative (this shall not happen to you) is emphatic in Greek. The Lord replied, "Get behind Me, Satan!" (cf. Matthew 4:10). Taken from the Hebrew, Satan means adversary. "You are an offense (skandalon: trap, snare) to Me, for you are not mindful of the things of God, but the things of man." How quickly we fall from the mountain top (vs. 16) to the valley (vs. 22)!

III. Special Features

A. PRESERVING OUR HERITAGE

Black Americans are confronted increasingly with the pull of anti-Christian elements. Athletic superstars have become Muslims; Black parents give their children Arabic-sounding names. There are those who with pseudo-Islamic doctrines take advantage of every opportunity to exalt themselves as savior of Black America. Pressure is put on Blacks in prison to join other faiths. And so it goes. And not only here in America, but in sub-Saharan Africa as well. But today's lesson brings to our attention the extremely sharp differences between other religions and Christianity; and the biggest difference has to do with the Person of Jesus Christ. Just who is He? The Bible states that God has in these last days spoken to us in His Son (Son-wise: Hebrews 1:2). The Bible states that God has in these last days spoken to us in His Son. I have deliberately repeated this verse to drive home to our hearts the contradiction between biblical Christianity and those who seek to distort its message. One other point: the settlement of the sin issue: men are not saved by works (fasting, giving alms, praying, trips to holy places). The Bible teaches that Christ once-for-all purged away our sins by the shedding of His blood. Then, He sat down at the right hand of the Majesty on high.

B. A CONCLUDING WORD

We sing in our churches, "Everybody Ought to Know Who Jesus Is." How true! For the most important thing in life is to give the correct answer to the question concerning the Lord Jesus Christ. The pharaoh of Egypt said, in a voice mixed with arrogance and sarcasm, "Who is the Lord...I do not know the Lord, nor will I let Israel go" (Exodus 5:2). Another person in trouble is the one who professes to know who Christ is, but who hears the Lord say, "I never knew you; depart from Me..." (Matthew 7:23).

We learn from today's lesson that Jesus Christ is the last word from God, superior to the prophets; He is the Christ, the Son of the living God, Builder and Protector of His Church. He is the One who predicted and fulfilled His death, burial, and resurrection. Let all who have been cleansed by the blood of the Lord Jesus Christ rejoice that they understand and know Him (Jeremiah 9:24).

Who Jesus is embraces more than an academic question derived from the study of His historicity, but a personal inquiry that grows out of the need to find meaning and significance in life relative to one's ultimate destiny. We come to know Him for ourselves and we verify to others that we know Him by the life that we live. Hence, the knowledge of Jesus Christ has to do with the process of salvation as we seek to establish the appropriate relationship with God as it is depicted in a ministry that is totally committed to His will.

HOME DAILY BIBLE READINGS
Week of December 6, 1998
Who Is This?

Nov. 30 M. Isaiah 7:10-17, She Shall Name Him Immanuel
Dec. 1 T. Isaiah 9:1-7, A Child Has Been Born to Us
Dec. 2 W. Isaiah 11:1-10, A Vision of Peace
Dec. 3 T. Isaiah 53:1-12, He Was Wounded for Our Transgressions
Dec. 4 F. Isaiah 60:1-7, Arise, Shine; for Your Light Has Come
Dec. 5 S. Hebrews 1:1-4, God Has Spoken By a Son
Dec. 6 S. Matthew 16:13-26, You Are the Messiah!

Good News: Spoken and Written

Adult Topic—Reporting the Good News

.....

Youth Topic—Reporting the Good News
Children's Topic—Jesus Is Coming

.....

Devotional Reading—Colossians 1:15-20
Background Scripture—Luke 1:1-4; 1 Corinthians 15:1-4; 1 John 1:1-4
Print—Luke 1:1-4; 1 Corinthians 15:1-4; 1 John 1:1-4

• • • • • • • • • • •

PRINTED SCRIPTURE

Luke 1:1-4; 1 Corinthians 15:1-4; 1 John 1:1-4 (KJV)

FORASMUCH as many have taken in hand to set forth in order a declaration of those things which are most surely believed among us,

2 Even as they delivered them unto us, which from the beginning were eyewitnesses, and ministers of the word;

3 It seemed good to me also, having had perfect understanding of all things from the very first, to write unto thee in order, most excellent Theophilus,

4 That thou mightest know the certainty of those things, wherein thou hast been instructed.

.....

MOREOVER, brethren, I declare unto you the gospel which I preached unto you, which also ye have received, and wherein ye stand;

2 By which also ye are saved, if ye keep in memory what I preached unto you, unless ye have believed

Luke 1:1-4; 1 Corinthians 15:1-4; 1 John 1:1-4 (NRSV)

SINCE MANY have undertaken to set down an orderly account of the events that have been fulfilled among us,

2 just as they were handed on to us by those who from the beginning were eyewitnesses and servants of the word,

3 I too decided, after investigating everything carefully from the very first, to write an orderly account for you, most excellent Theophilus,

4 so that you may know the truth concerning the things about which you have been instructed.

.....

NOW I would remind you, brothers and sisters, of the good news that I proclaimed to you, which you in turn received, in which also you stand,

2 through which also you are being saved, if you hold firmly to the message that I proclaimed to you—

in vain.

3 For I delivered unto you first of all that which I also received, how that Christ died for our sins according to the scriptures;

4 And that he was buried, and that he rose again the third day according to the scriptures.

.....

THAT which was from the beginning, which we have heard, which we have seen with our eyes, which we have looked upon, and our hands have handled, of the Word of life;

2 (For the life was manifested, and we have seen it, and bear witness, and shew unto you that eternal life, which was with the Father, and was manifested unto us;)

3 That which we have seen and heard declare we unto you, that ye also may have fellowship with us: and truly our fellowship is with the Father, and with his Son Jesus Christ.

4 And these things write we unto you, that your joy may be full.

unless you have come to believe in vain.

3 For I handed on to you as of first importance what I in turn had received: that Christ died for our sins in accordance with the scriptures,

4 and that he was buried, and that he was raised on the third day in accordance with the scriptures.

.....

WE DECLARE to you what was from the beginning, what we have heard, what we have seen with our eyes, what we have looked at and touched with our hands, concerning the word of life—

2 this life was revealed, and we have seen it and testify to it, and declare to you the eternal life that was with the Father and was revealed to us—

3 we declare to you what we have seen and heard so that you also may have fellowship with us; and truly our fellowship is with the Father and with his Son Jesus Christ.

4 We are writing these things so that our joy may be complete.

 KEY VERSE

That which we have seen and heard declare we unto you, that ye also may have fellowship with us: and truly our fellowship is with the Father, and with his Son Jesus Christ.—1 John 1:3

OBJECTIVES

After reading this lesson, the student should understand that:

1. Luke wrote his Gospel informed by eye-witnesses, confirmed by other written accounts, and superintended by the Holy Spirit;
2. Paul's information was received by him from the resurrected Savior, and confirmed by the salvation of those who believed;
3. John wrote about that which he personally had heard, seen, look at and touched; and,
4. Overall, the accounts are true, factual, trustworthy—the Word of God!

POINTS TO BE EMPHASIZED

Adult/Youth
Key Verse: 1 John 1:3
Print: Luke 1:1-4; 1 Corinthians 15:1-4; 1 John 1:1-4

—Luke's orderly account of the life of Jesus was compiled from eyewitness accounts in order that the truth might be known. (Luke 1:1-4)
—Paul reminded the Corinthians to hold on to the good news that he had received from Christ and proclaimed to them. (1 Corinthians 15:1-3a)
—The good news that Paul taught is that Christ died for sins, was buried, and was raised on the third day. (3b-4)
—John testified to the eternal life that was with the Father and was revealed. (1 John 1:1-2)
—John wrote his testimony so that the readers may have true fellowship with the Father and with His Son Jesus Christ. (3-4)

Children
Key Verse: Luke 1:31
Print: Luke 1:26-35

—The angel Gabriel was sent by God to a virgin named Mary in a town called Nazareth. (26-27)
—The angel told Mary that she was favored by God and that the Lord was with her. (28)
—Because she was perplexed, the angel told Mary not to be afraid. (29-30)
—Mary was told that she would become pregnant, have a Son, and was to name Him Jesus. (31)
—Jesus would be great and will reign as king over His people. (32)
—Jesus would be holy because He is the Son of God. (35)

(NOTE: Use KJV Scripture for Adults; NRSV Scripture for Youth and Children)

TOPICAL OUTLINE OF THE LESSON

I. Introduction

A. The Doctrine of Verbal Inspiration
B. Biblical Background

II. Exposition and Application of the Scripture

A. Eyewitnesses of the Good News (Luke 1:1-4)
B. Evidence of the Good News (1 Corinthians 15:1-4)
C. Eternity and the Good News (1 John 1:1-4)

III. Special Features

A. Preserving Our Heritage
B. A Concluding Word

I. Introduction

A. THE DOCTRINE OF VERBAL INSPIRATION

Because the lesson deals with the spoken and written Word of God, it is essential that we briefly study the doctrine of Verbal Inspiration. Verbal means words; we believe that each word in the original manuscripts was breathed out by God. This truth completely does away with the subjective theories: (1) that the Bible contains God's Word, or (2) that the Bible becomes God's Word. Verbal Inspiration teaches that the Bible is the Word of God. Just as it is impossible for a man to read another man's mind, so it is impossible for man to read God's mind. God must reveal His mind to us (1 Corinthians 2:11). This sharing of God's mind is called Revelation. Thus the Bible is not a man-inspired book, but holy men of old spoke as they were moved or borne along by the Holy Spirit (2 Peter 1:20, 21). The words were God-breathed. And though men were permitted to exercise their own personalities and literary talents, they wrote under the control of the Holy Spirit.

Admittedly, this is a mystery. Even as God the Son became Man, and is the God-Man, so the Bible is the Word of God, written by men (1 Thessalonians 2:13). Do not reject the doctrine because you do not understand how it could be. Thank God that He has given us Good News that can be trusted!

B. BIBLICAL BACKGROUND

Luke was a doctor (Colossians 4:14), a Gentile convert, and companion of Paul (2 Timothy 4:11). He is also the human author of the Book of Acts. One of the things that corroborates our definition of the doctrine of Verbal Inspiration is the fact that the Gospel of Luke and the Book of Acts contain so many medical terms, and show such an interest in disease and healing. God did not violate Luke's intellect and training while superintending the writing of the Scripture.

Paul's background is adequately covered in Acts 9:1-31; 2 Corinthians 11:22-30. As for the Letter to the saints at Corinth, we have an Epistle directed to a church with a major problem of holding the wrong concept of true wisdom. People who think they know and really do not know, live badly. Chapter 15 is the great chapter on the physical, bodily resurrection of Jesus Christ. Our lesson deals with the truth of Christ's rising from the dead, and the fact of a living Savior was taught, preached, and proven by eyewitnesses, among whom is included Paul, for he met Christ on the road to Damascus.

John, of course, is the apostle, the author of the Gospel of John, the three Epistles, and the Book of Revelation. In his Gospel the Deity of Christ is stressed; in the Book of Revelation, judgment is emphasized. In his First Epistle, the aged one shows that his theme on fellowship is important because the Word of life still lives. And so all three men wrote as they were moved by the Holy Spirit, and their accounts, based on eyewitnesses, on oral tradition, and written documents, are true. As John says: "These things are written that believers may know the certainty of their salvation" (1 John 5:13).

II. Exposition and Application of the Scripture

A. EYEWITNESSES OF THE GOOD NEWS
(Luke 1:1-4)

FORASMUCH as many have taken in hand to set forth in order a declaration of those things which are most surely believed among us, Even as they delivered them unto us, which from the beginning were eyewitnesses, and ministers of the word; It seemed good to me also, having had perfect understanding of all things from the very first, to write unto thee in order, most excellent Theophilus, That thou mightest know the certainty of those things, wherein thou hast been instructed.

If we accept the punctuation of the King James Version, the four verses in the lesson constitute one sentence, making it all the more difficult for us to break down the historian's statement. He is evidently concerned with producing a concise summary, a factual narrative of "those things which have been fulfilled among us." He does not identify the "so many" who have taken in hand already the task of telling the story of things taken for granted that are true. Some scholars doubt Matthew and Mark were the authors Luke had in mind, but it is not known for certain. Doubtless, there were written records and other oral tradition behind the synoptic Gospels, but the Lord allowed them to vanish. We need not concern ourselves today with some so-called "Lost Books of the Gospel," or "The Boyhood Days of Jesus Christ."

Luke does not disparage the attempts of others to draw up a narrative or rearrange the facts contained in the oral gospel. However, he wants it known that what he has done was performed with great care. He used what was delivered to him. The apostle Paul also employed this word "deliver" with respect to the contents of the Gospel orally transmitted (1 Corinthians 11:23; 15:3). Some material was received from eyewitnesses **(autoptai,** literally, self-eye; thus, seeing with one's own eyes). These were people who had seen the resurrected Lord in person, and because of their allegiance to Him, became ministers (servants, attendants, assistants) of the Word. Luke makes no claim for himself to have been an eyewitness. But he does claim that what he had been told step by step was affirmed, "from the very first," or as the Greek word **(anothen)** also may be rendered, "from above." This revelation from heaven is the basis for his "perfect understanding." In short, we realize why and how Luke wrote the Gospel in an orderly fashion.

Theophilus, to whom Luke wrote, is mentioned twice: here in Luke 1:3 and Acts 1:1. The name literally means God-Lover or Lover of God. Some scholars also suggest that "lover of God" refers to anyone who indeed loves the Lord, since it is not known whether Theophilus was a real person. We prefer to believe he was a personal friend of Luke. A Gentile Christian, Theophilus was a man of some prominence, since Luke calls him, "most excellent," **(kratiste),** a Greek word that means mightiest, noblest, strongest, best, most illustrious. It points to a high official rank (Acts 23:26; 26:25). However, because it is not used in

Acts 1:1, it may have been simply an expression of friendship (Thayer). This section of the lesson closes with the assurance Theophilus is to know for certain the truth of the instructions (literally, oral teaching; we have derived the word "catechized" from the Greek word translated "instructed" here).

B. EVIDENCE OF THE GOOD NEWS
(1 Corinthians 15:1-4)

MOREOVER, brethren, I declare unto you the gospel which I preached unto you, which also ye have received, and wherein ye stand; By which also ye are saved, if ye keep in memory what I preached unto you, unless ye have believed in vain. For I delivered unto you first of all that which I also received, how that Christ died for our sins according to the scriptures; And that he was buried, and that he rose again the third day according to the scriptures.

There is a hint of slight rebuke or reproach here, as if surprised that it should be necessary to declare anew or make known again to them the Gospel in its fullness. Four things are said here about the Gospel. First: It was preached. Paul said, "It is the Good News which I 'Goodnewsed' to you, the evangel which I evangelized to you." Second: It was received; it was accepted by the Corinthians. Third: The saints at Corinth stood in it. This signifies a being or existing within the scope of the Gospel; remaining firm, steady, unshaken and steadfast in the News of God's grace. Fourth: They were being saved by this Gospel. Salvation may be seen as past, present and future. In speaking here of salvation as a continuous process, the apostle considers that daily growing and becoming more like the Lord Jesus Christ.

Paul then said, "If you do not hold fast the word I preached to you, especially that word concerning the resurrection, then nothing has been gained; you have believed in vain." You see how essential it is to believe in the physical resurrection of Jesus Christ. Failure to hold on to this doctrine means that whatever else you believe is in vain. Evidently, there were at Corinth those who did not believe in the resurrection of the material body. They thought it unnecessary. Indeed, to the philosophical mind it was obnoxious. Whereas most of the people did believe in a life hereafter, they could not conceive of a physical resurrection. Denial of the resurrection means a loss of the key to the incarnation; it means a plunge into hopelessness, despair and ignorance. In verse 3, the words "first of all" do not refer to priority in time, but to importance of the subject. The fact that Jesus Christ died for our sins is of the utmost importance; it is a vital part of the true Gospel of peace (Romans 10:9). Here is the point emphasized in our lesson. Paul did not manufacture this Good News; it was no figment of his imagination. He delivered that which he had received. We may render this: "I gave over to you that which I heard and took hold of in my mind."

Note the words, "according to the scriptures" refer to the Old Testament. This means that the mention of the death of the Messiah is to be found in the Old Testament. Where? Psalm 21:1; Isaiah 53. The words "according to the scriptures" also teach us that His death was no accident, no unforeseen event, not something that sneaked up on God. It was predetermined, foreordained, for the Lamb of God was slain from the foundation of the world (Revelation 13:8). The second point of the Gospel message is: Christ was buried. This is made very plain in all four of the Gospels. The third point: He rose from the grave. Use of the perfect passive tense (He has been raised) suggests at least two things. One: passive voice indicates Someone else raised Him (God the Father). That He raised Himself is taught elsewhere (John 10:17-18), but overwhelmingly the Scriptures point to God the Father raising His Son. Two: the perfect tense points to abiding results or consequences. In other words, He was raised and remains raised and shall always so remain. He will never die again!

C. ETERNITY AND THE GOOD NEWS
(1 John 1:1-4)

That which was from the beginning, which we have heard, which we have seen with our eyes, which we have looked upon, and our hands have handled, of the Word of life; (For the life was manifested, and we have seen it, and bear witness, and shew unto you that eternal life, which was with the Father, and was manifested unto us;) That which we have seen and heard declare we unto you, that ye also may have fellowship with us: and truly our fellowship is with the Father, and with his Son Jesus Christ. And these things write we unto you, that your joy may be full.

The human author is not identified, but we have no doubt First John is a personal letter written by old man John, the apostle. Customarily, the author introduced himself in his greeting, but this is not done here. Now understand that the main verb in this portion of our lesson is not found until verse 3; it is the word, declare. It is preceded by five clauses: (1) "That which was from the beginning." The beginning of what? Some scholars say the beginning of time, or the creation, or the Gospel. Others suggest it is the same as Genesis 1:1 and John 1:1, teaching the eternal preexistence of Jesus Christ. (2) "which we have heard" (3) "which we have seen" (4) "which we have looked upon," and (5) "our hands have handled." The word for "handle" means to grope or feel after in order to find, to examine closely.

This is the One we declare! The apostles heard, saw, beheld and handled the Person who is the Logos of Life. Logos means message, mind, life, word. We express ourselves with words. A word is an idea or concept expressed through a combination of sounds or letters. Without the idea or concept behind it, the medium would be meaningless. Logos implies not only the spoken word, but implies the intelligence behind the idea. The invisible thought is made visible by the spoken word.

How could the disciples hear, see, handle the Word of Life? Well, the Word became flesh, that's how! They could witness that which they saw and heard. And in order to proclaim fellowship and joy, they must have received a commission from Christ. If others are to join this fellowship, they must be told the Good News. Things seen and heard must be declared. Good News too good to keep must be proclaimed that others might enjoy fellowship with you. Remember then: Fellowship with other Christians is centered around fellowship with God the Father and His Son. Fellowship with God means to love what He loves—righteousness; and to hate what He hates—sin!

III. Special Features

A. PRESERVING OUR HERITAGE

We often hear today attacks made upon the Bible as "the White Man's book." However, the Book itself makes no such claim. Nor is Christianity "the White Man's religion." If it were solely his, it would not bode him well, considering his wars, attempted genocide and holocaust of the Jewish people, exploitation, crime syndicates, dope cartels, and racism. Today's lesson causes us to marvel at the writing of the Scriptures. As much as Black Americans appreciate oral tradition, we have learned to value even more highly the written message.

God's use of Luke, Paul and John, and others, preserved the Bible from any inaccuracies inherent in oral transmission. And we have a Book we can live by. What the God of the Bible has spoken, caused to be written and preserved, translated and disseminated, is indeed Good News. Its message transcends culture and race. The Good News is for all people, for all sinned (past tense) and are falling short (present tense) of God's glory.

B. A CONCLUDING WORD

Note that although three different writers are involved, Christ is central. Each—Luke, Paul, John—has something unique to say about the Lord, yet each gives the assurance that what is said is fact, and that the Lord Jesus rose from the dead to live forevermore. Preaching the resurrection is always a part of the Good News! Today's lesson strengthens our confidence in what the Bible has to say about Jesus Christ. Superintended by the Holy Spirit of Truth, the writers took advantage of oral tradition, of their own eyewitnessing and that of others, of written accounts, and arranged events in the order they were led. Thank God for the spoken and written Good News!

HOME DAILY BIBLE READINGS
Week of December 13, 1998
Good News: Spoken and Written

Dec. 7 M. Luke 1:1-4, An Orderly Account
Dec. 8 T.   1 Corinthians 15:1-4, The Good News Paul Proclaimed
Dec. 9 W. 1 John 1:1-4, What We Have Seen and Heard...
Dec. 10 T.   1 John 2:15-29, Those Who Do God's Will
Dec. 11 F.   1 John 3:1-10, We Are Children of God
Dec. 12 S.   1 John 3:11-24, We Should Love One Another
Dec. 13 S.   1 John 4:13-21, God Is Love

The Birth of Jesus

Adult Topic—Beyond Christmas Wrappings

.....

Youth Topic—A New Beginning
Children's Topic—Jesus Is Born

.....

Devotional Reading—Isaiah 9:2-7
Background Scripture—Luke 2:1-20
Print—Luke 2:1-17

• • • • • • • • • • •

PRINTED SCRIPTURE

Luke 2:1-17 (KJV)

AND it came to pass in those days, that there went out a decree from Caesar Augustus, that all the world should be taxed.

2 (And this taxing was first made when Cyrenius was governor of Syria.)

3 And all went to be taxed, every one into his own city.

4 And Joseph also went up from Galilee, out of the city of Nazareth, into Judaea, unto the city of David, which is called Bethlehem; (because he was of the house and lineage of David:)

5 To be taxed with Mary his espoused wife, being great with child.

6 And so it was, that, while they were there, the days were accomplished that she should be delivered.

7 And she brought forth her firstborn son, and wrapped him in swaddling clothes, and laid him in a manger; because there was no room for them in the inn.

8 And there were in the same country shepherds abiding in the field, keeping watch over their flock

Luke 2:1-17 (NRSV)

IN THOSE days a decree went out from Emperor Augustus that all the world should be registered.

2 This was the first registration and was taken while Quirinius was governor of Syria.

3 All went to their own towns to be registered.

4 Joseph also went from the town of Nazareth in Galilee to Judea, to the city of David called Bethlehem, because he was descended from the house and family of David.

5 He went to be registered with Mary, to whom he was engaged and who was expecting a child.

6 While they were there, the time came for her to deliver her child.

7 And she gave birth to her firstborn son and wrapped him in bands of cloth, and laid him in a manger, because there was no place for them in the inn.

8 In that region there were shepherds living in the fields, keeping watch over their flock by night.

by night.

9 And, lo, the angel of the Lord came upon them, and the glory of the Lord shone round about them: and they were sore afraid.

10 And the angel said unto them, Fear not: for, behold, I bring you good tidings of great joy, which shall be to all people.

11 For unto you is born this day in the city of David a Saviour, which is Christ the Lord.

12 And this shall be a sign unto you; Ye shall find the babe wrapped in swaddling clothes, lying in a manger.

13 And suddenly there was with the angel a multitude of the heavenly host praising God, and saying,

14 Glory to God in the highest, and on earth peace, good will toward men.

15 And it came to pass, as the angels were gone away from them into heaven, the shepherds said one to another, Let us now go even unto Bethlehem, and see this thing which is come to pass, which the Lord hath made known unto us.

16 And they came with haste, and found Mary, and Joseph, and the babe lying in a manger.

17 And when they had seen it, they made known abroad the saying which was told them concerning this child.

9 Then an angel of the Lord stood before them, and the glory of the Lord shone around them, and they were terrified.

10 But the angel said to them, "Do not be afraid; for see—I am bringing you good news of great joy for all the people:

11 to you is born this day in the city of David a Savior, who is the Messiah, the Lord.

12 This will be a sign for you: you will find a child wrapped in bands of cloth and lying in a manger."

13 And suddenly there was with the angel a multitude of the heavenly host, praising God and saying,

14 "Glory to God in the highest heaven, and on earth peace among those whom he favors!"

15 When the angels had left them and gone into heaven, the shepherds said to one another, "Let us go now to Bethlehem and see this thing that has taken place, which the Lord has made known to us."

16 So they went with haste and found Mary and Joseph, and the child lying in the manger.

17 When they saw this, they made known what had been told them about this child.

 KEY VERSE

For unto you is born this day in the city of David a Saviour, which is Christ the Lord.—Luke 2:11

OBJECTIVES

After reading this lesson, the student should be more aware of:

1. The Scriptures predicting the birth of Jesus Christ;
2. The historical setting of His birth;
3. The angelic announcement of His birth; and,
4. The visit and report of the shepherds concerning His birth.

POINTS TO BE EMPHASIZED

Adult/Youth/Children
Key Verse: Luke 2:11
Print: Luke 2:1-17

—Augustus decreed that all the world should go to their own towns to be registered. (1-3)
—Joseph and Mary went to Bethlehem to register because Joseph was from the house and family of David. (4)
—In Bethlehem, Mary gave birth to her firstborn Son and laid Him in a manger because no space was available at the inn. (6-7)
—An angel from the Lord announced to shepherds that the Messiah had been born in the city of David. (8-12)
—A heavenly host praised God. (13-14)
—The shepherds hurried to Bethlehem, found the child, and reported the message of the angel. (15-17)

(**NOTE:** Use KJV Scripture for Adults; NRSV Scripture for Youth and Children)

TOPICAL OUTLINE OF THE LESSON

I. Introduction

A. Historical Background
B. Biblical Background

II. Exposition and Application of the Scripture

A. Register at Rome (Luke 2:1-5)
B. Birth in Bethlehem (Luke 2:6-7)
C. Announcement By An Angel (Luke 2:8-14)
D. Seen By Shepherds (Luke 2:15-17)

III. Special Features

A. Preserving Our Heritage
B. A Concluding Word

I. Introduction

A. HISTORICAL BACKGROUND

For many years, the Gospel of Luke had been attacked by certain scholars who considered erroneous some statements made by the author. Luke is the only one of the Gospel writers who mentions the decree from Caesar Augustus, and assigns the rule of Quirinius, governor of Syria, as the time of the registration. Apparently, the facts are these: Although Caesar Augustus was the grandnephew of Julius Caesar, he was adopted as his son. After his great uncle Julius Caesar was murdered, young Octavian took the name Galius Julius Caesar Octavianus in 44 B.C.

He ruled in what is called a triumvirate (a group of three men jointly governing a realm) which included Mark Anthony and Aemilius Lepidus. A few years after Anthony (and Cleopatra) committed suicide, and Lepidus had been forced to retire, Octavian formally restored the republican government. At this time, the Senate bestowed upon him the name Augustus (which means the Exalted). He ruled more than forty years (27 B.C. to A.D. 14) as the first Roman Emperor. It was during his reign that Christ was born, that God the Son became a human being.

Now Syria was the most important of all the Roman provinces, and Quirinius (Cyrenius) was governor there, but served in several capacities at different times. An earlier census may have been set in motion in Rome about 8 B.C., while Quirinius was the military governor of Syria. Of course, it would take several years to complete such a registration. Suffice it to say that archaeological discoveries have helped confirm Luke's record. Thank God for the corroboration, but how much better to take God at His Word anyhow! After all, He is the Lord of History!

B. BIBLICAL BACKGROUND

The birth of the Messiah (Christ, the Anointed One) had been long predicted, but the time and place were God's prerogative. When things were just right—what Paul calls "the fullness of the time"—God sent forth His Son, the Lord Jesus (Galatians 4:4-5). The political situation was one of peace. Geographically, He was born exactly where God's Word predicted He would be. The economic scene was good, for roads had been built, piracy on the high seas curbed, commerce improved. Socially, it was a time of unrest, approximately six million slaves existed in the Roman Empire. Intellectually, it was not an illiterate age. "One could speak Greek and be understood almost anywhere" (A. T. Robertson). The religious scene found Judaism a failure, its religious leaders self-righteous; and paganism satisfied no one (Ephesians 2:12). Morally, it was an age of corruption and widespread immorality (see Paul's description of his day, Romans 1:22-32). The Lord Jesus was born at a ripe moment, the psychological moment of the world's clock. Circumstances and conditions were just right; the world was divinely prepared for the coming of Jesus Christ and the spread of the Gospel. Biblically, we hear the promise of the seed of the woman (Genesis 3:15). We hear the prophecy of Genesis 49:10: "The scepter shall not depart from Judah, nor a lawgiver from between his feet, until Shiloh come." The prophecy of Isaiah 7:14 is heard: "Behold, the virgin shall conceive, and bear a son, and shall call his name Immanuel." See also Isaiah 49:1-7. In Isaiah 9:6 we read, "For unto us a child is born, unto us a son is given." In Micah 5:2, the place of His birth is plainly spelled out as Bethlehem Ephrathah!

II. Exposition and Application of the Scripture

A. REGISTER AT ROME
(Luke 2:1-5)

AND it came to pass in those days, that there went out a decree from Caesar Augustus, that all the world should be taxed. (And this taxing was first made when Cyrenius was governor of Syria.) And all went to be taxed, every one into his own city. And Joseph also went up from Galilee, out of the city of Nazareth, into Judaea, unto the city of David, which is called Bethlehem; (because he was of the house and lineage of David:) To be taxed with Mary his espoused wife, being great with child.

The Greek word for "decree" is **dogma.** It means an opinion, a judgment, doctrine, ordinance or decree. Often today when someone is called dogmatic, it is implied that he or she is overbearing, opinionated. In our lesson, the dogma is an imperial order issued by Caesar Augustus, first Roman Emperor. It was an order to register the whole world. In the original language, the word rendered "taxed" or "taxation" literally means to write off, to copy. Here it is to "enter in the public records the names of men, their property and income, to enroll" (Thayer). And so the names, profession, fortunes and families were copied down (ICC). This periodical census or enrollment would serve as a basis for taxation. You can imagine that the gathering of such statistics was disliked by the people. The Jews were exempt from military service, so that the enrollment was not for that purpose among them. Today in Israel, military service is compulsory for men and unmarried women after reaching the age of eighteen. Men are drafted for three years, women for two—unless they can prove military service violates their religious beliefs.

The word for world **(oikoumene)** means the inhabited world. Two other words for world are **kosmos** (world-system) and **aion** (world-age). Unfortunately, these three original different words are translated the same—world. The Romans regarded their Empire as the world; anything beyond their borders was barbaric. We are told that this enrollment was the first made, and although some scholars disputed the accuracy of verse two, later archaeological discoveries have helped to confirm the record.

Now in this census, men, women, and children were obliged to be enrolled. For the Romans enrollment took place at their residence, wherever they lived, not necessarily at the place of their birth. But for the Jews, the census was based upon place of extraction or family origin, place of birth. So each man returned to the city of his ancestors, the place where family records were maintained. The Romans allowed the Jews to follow the Jewish custom, under the Jewish king Herod. This is why Joseph had to leave Nazareth where he lived, and return to Bethlehem. Naturally, Mary accompanied him on the sixty-five mile trip. Bethlehem means House of Bread; it is one of the oldest towns in Palestine. In ancient times, it was called Ephrath or Ephratah (fruitful), Genesis 35:16. Located about six miles from Jerusalem, it is also called the City of David. This is because David was born there (1 Samuel 17:12, 58), and Joseph was from the house and lineage of David.

While Caesar Augustus may have felt that he was in charge, demonstrating his supremacy as Emperor, the truth is, he was just one more actor on God's stage. The decree of Augustus and the registration of Quirinius were but events used by the Lord to fulfill God's word (Micah 5:2). Thus at the time decreed by God, the decree of Augustus was put into operation. The God of the Bible is always on time!

Finally, in this section of the lesson, note that the pregnant Mary (Mariam in Greek) is called Joseph's "espoused wife" (verse 5). She was the "having been promised in marriage one." In the Jewish sense, she was virtually married. The vows of marriage had been made publicly; the betrothal had been consummated. Jewish law held engagement as binding as marriage. And so Joseph had every right to travel to Bethlehem taking Mary with him. See even in the timing of the pregnancy the hand of God.

B. BIRTH IN BETHLEHEM
(Luke 2:6-7)

And so it was, that, while they were there, the days were accomplished that she should be delivered, And she brought forth her firstborn son, and wrapped him in swaddling clothes, and laid him in a manger; because there was no room for them in the inn.

While there in Bethlehem, Mary felt labor pangs. And she brought forth her firstborn Son. The term "firstborn" may be used of an only child, and scholars are reluctant to suggest the expression implies there were other children. In other words, "firstborn" does not help us decide one way or the other. However, we do have other Scriptures which teach Mary and Joseph did have other children (Matthew 12:46-50; 13:55-56; John 2:12; 1 Corinthians 9:5; Galatian 1:19). The Roman Catholic concept of what is called the perpetual virginity of Mary is not biblical.

The Baby Jesus was wrapped in Swaddling clothes; these were long bands of cloth like those used to wrap the bodies of the dead. Someone has interpreted this to intimate He was born to die, even as later the wise men brought gifts of myrrh (Matthew 2:11). The manger was a cattle feeding trough, or perhaps the stable (Arndt and Gingrich). Because of the census crowds no rooms were vacant;

inhospitality is not implied. And the word translated "inn" is literally, "a place where burdens are loosed and let down for a rest." Tradition says it was a cave in the side of the hill behind the inn. Whatever the manger and the inn were, one thing is sure. Here was the God-man who left Heaven's glory to be born in poverty and loneliness. He was rich, yet for our sakes He became poor, that we through His poverty might be rich (2 Corinthians 8:9).

C. ANNOUNCEMENT BY AN ANGEL
(Luke 2:8-14)

And there were in the same country shepherds abiding in the field, keeping watch over their flock by night. And, lo, the angel of the Lord came upon them, and the glory of the Lord shone round about them: and they were sore afraid. And the angel said unto them, Fear not: for, behold, I bring you good tidings of great joy, which shall be to all people. For unto you is born this day in the city of David a Saviour, which is Christ the Lord. And this shall be a sign unto you; Ye shall find the babe wrapped in swaddling clothes, lying in a manger. And suddenly there was with the angel a multitude of the heavenly host praising God, and saying, Glory to God in the highest, and on earth peace, good will toward men.

Scholars vary in their opinions concerning December as the birth month of our Lord. We are reminded that the tradition that the Lord Jesus was born December 25 is not older than the fourth century. Furthermore, we are told that this time of year may have been chosen in order to have a church festival coincide with the pagan Saturnalia celebration that honored Saturn, the Roman harvest god, and began on December 17, lasting for seven days. The truth is, we are not sure of the year, month, or day when the Lord Jesus was born. We would suggest that had the record clearly stated the exact day and month, we would have done with it exactly what has been done with the 25th of December, Christmas! The shepherds were minding their own business, taking turns guarding their sheep by night. Suddenly, as out of nowhere, the bright glory of the Lord shone round about them. This glory speaks of the **Shekinah,** a word not found in the Bible; it means "that which dwells." There are however allusions to it. See it in that light greater than the brightness of the sun which appeared at Paul's conversion experience (Acts 26:13). Isaiah spoke of it (Isaiah 6:1-3; 60:2); it filled the inner sanctuary of the house (1 Kings 8:10). And read of it in Matthew 17:5; Romans 9:4. As always, such glory is a token of God's very presence or that of His emissaries. In verse 14 of our lesson, the same word for glory is used in the expression, "Glory to God in the highest."

Now naturally the shepherds were scared stiff. But God in mercy commanded, "Do not continue to be afraid!" How many times has the Lord exhorted saints not to fear! Look at the record. Abram: Fear not: I am your shield, and your exceeding great reward. Moses: Do not fear Og, king of Bashan; for I have delivered him into your hand. Joshua: Fear not, neither be dismayed. Gideon: Peace be unto you; fear not; you shall not die. Daniel: Fear not...Your words were heard, and I am come for your words. Zacharias: Fear not, for your prayer is heard; and your wife Elisabeth shall bear you a son, and you shall call his name John. Mary: Fear not; for you have found favor with God. Paul: Fear not, you must be brought before Caesar. John: He laid His right hand upon me and said, "Fear not; I am the first and the last." The Gospel is intended to eliminate fears. God has not called the Christian to fear. To think that God so loved us and became a Babe in Bethlehem in order to die a Sin-Bearer at Calvary! Such love—perfect love—casts out fear and enables the believer to obey the divine command, "Fear not!"

Note the angel said, "I bring you good tidings." Here are five English words to translate the one word in the original (euaggelizomai). Here was great news calculated to bring great joy!—a joy born of the Holy Spirit and based upon a Person, Jesus Christ, not on the possession of things. And here is Good News for everybody! In verse 11, we have an interesting title: "a Savior, who is Christ the Lord." The combination "Christ the Lord" is found in the New Testament only here. Savior or Deliverer is expressed by the name, Jesus (Matthew 1:21). Christ is Greek, Messiah is Hebrew, for the Anointed One. And Lord points to God manifest in the flesh. Alford sees this title as pertaining to the Hebrew Jehovah. The two signs (wrapped in swaddling cloth, and lying in a manger) would prove the truth of the announcement of the angel.

Finally, the angel's announcement is closed with a multitude of the heavenly host, praising God, and saying, "Glory to God in the highest, and on earth peace, good will toward men." Peace is wholeness, completeness, soundness, integrity. Perhaps a better translation of Luke 2:14 is: "On earth peace among men with whom he is pleased" (NASB). Or: "Peace on earth for all those pleasing Him" (LB). Or: "On earth peace among men of good will" (JBP). Or: "On earth his peace for men on whom his favor rests" (NEB, NIV). And just who are the men with whom God is pleased? These are those who believe in the Lord Jesus Christ. None else need apply for this peace, for whoever denies Jesus Christ does not know the truth; without truth, there is no real freedom. And no peace.

D. SEEN BY SHEPHERDS
(Luke 2:15-17)

And it came to pass, as the angels were gone away from them into heaven, the shepherds said one to another, Let us now go even unto Bethlehem, and see this thing which is come to pass, which the Lord hath made known unto us. And they came with haste, and found Mary, and Joseph, and the babe lying in a manger. And when they had seen it, they made known abroad the saying which was told them concerning this child.

The angel had done his part, now it was up to the shepherds to make the message known. But first they had to go to Bethlehem to see what the Lord had revealed unto them. And so with haste they went, and found Mary, and Joseph, and the babe lying in a manger. Their acceptance of the angel's message was rewarded by discovering the reality of the proclamation, "unto you is born this day...a Savior."

III. Special Features

A. PRESERVING OUR HERITAGE

Because of the oft-repeated falsehood that Christianity is the White Man's religion, we seize every opportunity to show the Bible teaches otherwise. Here in the message of the angel to the shepherds is proof once again of the universality of the Gospel of Jesus Christ. It is true that "all the people" in verse 10 has first reference to Israel, but the appeal goes to the other nations through Israel, just as God uses Black Americans to witness to and lead White Americans to Christ. We are further encouraged by the fact that the Lord came first to the poor, to lowly shepherds with their "mean occupation." The glad tidings are for everyone. May it be ours to spread the Good News to everyone—God the Son became a human being in order that He might die, be buried, and rise again to live forevermore.

B. A CONCLUDING WORD

The glad message of this lesson has been told throughout the centuries. And still today, the world is filled with fighting, poverty, murder, famine, racism—a lack of peace! Without Christ there is no peace, can be no peace! From Bethlehem it was not long before His path led to Calvary. There He made peace by His own blood (Ephesians 2:15). As a result, all believers have peace with God, and there is available to us the peace of God. And we too join the heavenly host in praise of the God who so loved us that He sent His only begotten Son into the world over nineteen centuries ago!

Our praise of Jesus as the Christ must be more than an outward show, but rather an authentic life that attests to the fact that we are participant within the redemptive work of God that is manifested in the Christ. While we celebrate His birth with great joy, the seriousness of God's initiative is seen in the death of Jesus on the cross, for without the shedding of blood there is no remission of sin. We honor God when we embrace the salvific work of Christ not only as final and effective, but that initiative of God that reveals to us the seriousness of His love that we are called to imitate.

HOME DAILY BIBLE READINGS
Week of December 20, 1998
The Birth of Jesus

Dec. 14 M. Luke 1:5-17,   John's Birth Foretold
Dec. 15 T. Luke 1:24-38, Gabriel Visits Mary
Dec. 16 W. Luke 1:39-55, My Spirit Rejoices in God My Savior
Dec. 17 T. Luke 1:57-66, The Hand of the Lord Was With Him
Dec. 18 F. Luke 1:67-80, The Child Grew and Became Strong in Spirit
Dec. 19 S. Luke 2:1-7, Joseph Went from Nazareth to Bethlehem
Dec. 20 S. Luke 2:8-20, Good News of a Great Joy

Christ's Presence Continues

Adult Topic—Promise of Power

.....

Youth Topic—Finding Encouragement
Children's Topic—Jesus Is With Us

.....

Devotional Reading—John 16:1-11
Background Scripture—Luke 24:13-53
Print—Luke 24:36-53

PRINTED SCRIPTURE

Luke 24:36-53 (KJV)

36 And as they thus spake, Jesus himself stood in the midst of them, and saith unto them, Peace be unto you.

37 But they were terrified and affrighted, and supposed that they had seen a spirit.

38 And he said unto them, Why are ye troubled? and why do thoughts arise in your hearts?

39 Behold my hands and my feet, that it is I myself: handle me, and see; for a spirit hath not flesh and bones, as ye see me have.

40 And when he had thus spoken, he shewed them his hands and his feet.

41 And while they yet believed not for joy, and wondered, he said unto them, Have ye here any meat?

42 And they gave him a piece of a broiled fish, and of an honeycomb.

43 And he took it, and did eat before them.

44 And he said unto them, These are the words which I spake unto

Luke 24:36-53 (NRSV)

36 While they were talking about this, Jesus himself stood among them and said to them, "Peace be with you."

37 They were startled and terrified, and thought that they were seeing a ghost.

38 He said to them, "Why are you frightened, and why do doubts arise in your hearts?

39 Look at my hands and my feet; see that it is I myself. Touch me and see; for a ghost does not have flesh and bones as you see that I have."

40 And when he had said this, he showed them his hands and his feet.

41 While in their joy they were disbelieving and still wondering, he said to them, "Have you anything here to eat?"

42 They gave him a piece of broiled fish,

43 and he took it and ate it in their presence.

you, while I was yet with you, that all things must be fulfilled, which were written in the law of Moses, and in the prophets, and in the psalms, concerning me.

45 Then opened he their understanding, that they might understand the scriptures.

46 And said unto them, Thus it is written, and thus it behoved Christ to suffer, and to rise from the dead the third day:

47 And that repentance and remission of sins should be preached in his name among all nations, beginning at Jerusalem.

48 And ye are witnesses of these things.

49 And, behold, I send the promise of my Father upon you: but tarry ye in the city of Jerusalem, until ye be endued with power from on high.

50 And he led them out as far as to Bethany, and he lifted up his hands, and blessed them.

51 And it came to pass, while he blessed them, he was parted from them, and carried up into heaven.

52 And they worshipped him, and returned to Jerusalem with great joy:

53 And were continually in the temple, praising and blessing God. Amen.

44 Then he said to them, "These are my words that I spoke to you while I was still with you—that everything written about me in the law of Moses, the prophets, and the psalms must be fulfilled."

45 Then he opened their minds to understand the scriptures,

46 and he said to them, "Thus it is written, that the Messiah is to suffer and to rise from the dead on the third day,

47 and that repentance and forgiveness of sins is to be proclaimed in his name to all nations, beginning from Jerusalem.

48 You are witnesses of these things.

49 And see, I am sending upon you what my Father promised; so stay here in the city until you have been clothed with power from on high."

50 Then he led them out as far as Bethany, and lifting up his hands, he blessed them.

51 While he was blessing them, he withdrew from them and was carried up into heaven.

52 And they worshiped him, and returned to Jerusalem with great joy;

53 and they were continually in the temple blessing God.

KEY VERSE

And, behold, I send the promise of my Father upon you: but tarry ye in the city Jerusalem, until ye be endued with power from on high.—Luke 24:49

OBJECTIVES

After reading this lesson, the student should know more about:

1. The nature of the Lord's resurrected body;
2. The necessity of fulfilling God's predictive Word;
3. A fuller concept of the Great Commission; and,
4. The Ascension of our Lord.

POINTS TO BE EMPHASIZED

Adult/Youth
Key Verse: Luke 24:49
Print: Luke 24:36-53

—While the disciples were talking about the resurrection appearances, the risen Jesus stood among them saying, "Peace be with you." (36)
—Jesus spoke to the frightened disciples, showed them His hands and feet, and invited them to touch Him. (37-40)
—While they were still disbelieving, Jesus asked for something to eat and ate some broiled fish. (41-43)
—Jesus reminded the disciples that He had told them that the Scriptures about Him must be fulfilled. (44)
—Jesus opened their minds so that they could understand and proclaim the good news when they received power from on high. (45-49)
—While Jesus was blessing the disciples, He was carried up into heaven after which they worshiped Him and continually blessed God in the temple. (50-53)

Children
Key Verse: Luke 24:15
Print: Luke 24:13-20, 28-35

—As two of the disciples walked from Jerusalem to Emmaus, Jesus joined them and asked what they were discussing. (13-17)
—Cleopas asked Jesus if He were the only person in the city who had not heard about the events that had taken place. (18)
—To the question, "What things?" they told about the crucifixion and Jesus interpreted to them the things concerning Himself in the Scriptures. (19-20)
—The disciples urged Jesus to stay with them when it appeared that He was about to depart. (28-29a)
—The disciples recognized Jesus as He broke bread at the supper meal. (29b-32)
—The disciples returned to Jerusalem to tell the other disciples that Jesus was alive. (33-35)

(NOTE: Use KJV Scripture for Adults; NRSV Scripture for Youth and Children)

I. Introduction

A. SCRIPTURES CONSTITUTING THE GREAT COMMISSION

So often when we hear the word "Great Commission," we think only of Matthew 28:19-20. But there are other passages which are a part of the command to spread the Gospel, and because our lesson contains one such passage (Luke 24:46, 47), we thought it helpful to mention briefly all of the verses in the Commission. First of all, we note that the pronouncements are all after the resurrection. Second, though there are differences of opinion about the correctness of the order, I have sought to put the verses in their proper chronological order. Thus John 20:21 is put first, for we believe it was spoken on the very day of resurrection: "Peace be unto you; as my Father hath sent me, even so send I you." The second post-resurrection appearance to the disciples as a group is recorded in Mark 16:15, 16: "Go ye into all the world, and preach the gospel to every creature. He that believeth and is baptized shall be saved; but he that believeth not shall be damned." The third passage is the longest and best known, Matthew 28:19, 20: "Go ye, therefore, and teach all nations, baptizing them in the name of the Father, and of the Son, and of the Holy Spirit, teaching them to observe all things whatsoever I have commanded you; and, lo, I am with you always, even unto the end of the age."

The fourth Scripture is the one in our lesson, Luke 24:46, 47. The fifth and final verse is Acts 1:8: "But ye shall receive power, after the Holy Spirit is come upon you; and ye shall be witnesses unto me both in Jerusalem, and in all Judea, and in Samaria, and unto the uttermost part of the earth." In summary: These five passages constitute what is called the Great Commission. These are the words of the resurrected Lord Jesus Christ commanding His followers to spread the Good News! Thus any study of His continuing Presence in the world of necessity includes the order to proclaim the fact of His resurrection to all people without distinction or prejudice. For the God of the Bible desires that all men be saved; He is not willing that any should perish.

B. BIBLICAL BACKGROUND

Here we concern ourselves with our Lord's resurrection appearances. It is believed He manifested Himself at least ten times before His Ascension. Only believers saw Him in these final appearances; and it is held that only believers will see Him when He returns in the clouds to snatch up (rapture) the Church. According to the record, He was seen by: (1) Mary Magdalene (2) the women returning from the tomb (3) Simon Peter (4) The Emmaus disciples (4) the disciples, except for Thomas (6) the disciples, Thomas present (7) seven disciples beside the Sea of Galilee, who went back to the fishing business (8) the eleven apostles plus more than 500 brethren (9) James, the half-brother of our Lord, and (10) those present at His ascension from the Mount of Olives. We believe the appearance made in Luke 24:46, 47 fits best in the time slot just before the Ascension described in Acts 1. Remember that the exact interval between our Lord's resurrection and ascension is forty days. Each time He presented, manifested, or showed Himself, the "appearing," or "letting Himself be seen" was going on at the same time. In other words, He was not constantly being seen the entire forty days, but at times during the forty days. So that not all of the appearances were made in one day. He had free access to heaven and earth during that period, and moved back and forth at will to indicate to His followers that He did not intend to continue in the same way as in the days prior to His death and resurrection.

II. Exposition and Application of the Scripture

A. A POST-RESURRECTION APPEARANCE
(Luke 24:36-43)

And as they thus spake, Jesus himself stood in the midst of them, and saith unto them, Peace be unto you. But they were terrified and affrighted, and supposed that they had seen a spirit. And he said unto them, Why are ye troubled? and why do thoughts arise in your hearts? Behold my hands and my feet, that it is I myself: handle me, and see; for a spirit hath not flesh and bones, as ye see me have. And when he had thus spoken, he shewed them his hands and his feet. And while they yet believed not for joy, and wondered, he said unto them, Have ye here any meat? And they gave him a piece of a broiled fish, and of an honeycomb. And he took it, and did eat before them.

Here we find that even as the Eleven and others were gathered together talking about the Lord's appearance to the women, and to Simon Peter—behold, the Lord Jesus Himself stood in their midst! Transcending the laws of matter as we know them, He had the ability to appear and disappear at will, and to travel at the speed of thought. And although they were talking about Him, sharing testimonies, they were not expecting Him. Evidently, they were not yet completely convinced of the promise He had made to them.

"Peace be unto you" were His greeting words. Luke used two words to describe their emotions: "terrified" comes from a verb meaning to agitate with fear, startle, alarm; "frightened" is the general term to fear (we have derived from it the word, phobia). From their shocked perspective they were gazing upon a spirit. The Bible throughout denies the ability of spirits of the dead to return to this world and communicate with us. Of late, we have heard much of the people who claimed to have died, and then came to life again. Even if they had died, being revived is not the same as being resurrected. Those who claim they were brought back from the dead came back with the same old body they had before. They look the same, perhaps worse! Same eyeglasses, same teeth, same arthritis. Jesus Christ is the only person with a resurrected, glorified body! And so the Lord proceeded immediately to disabuse their minds of such an idea. "Why are ye troubled?" The Greek verb used would prompt us to ask, "Why are you so shook up?" He knew of course what they were thinking, yet questioned: "Why do thoughts arise in your hearts?" What's the reason for the dialogue (Greek: **dialogismos);** the deliberation, the inward reasoning? And to prove His corporeality, He commanded: "Behold my hands and my feet, that it is I myself; handle me, and see; for a spirit hath not flesh and bones, as ye see me have" (Luke 24:39). Having invited them to behold, He showed them His hands and feet with their wounds in order to satisfy them, to prove to them His identity. The scars would tie Him in with the man they saw crucified. See all the only New Testament biblical evidence for believing our Lord's feet as well as His hands were nailed to the cross. Of course, Psalm 22:16 states, "They pierced my hands and my feet."

The command to "handle" is a verb that means to touch, feel (about for), grope after. This would convince them of the reality of the appearance. Handling Him would prove His corporeity, tangibility, substantiality, His natural, physical existence. Touching and eating with them proved the reality of His body. He was not a ghost, spirit, phantom, apparition or hallucination, for a ghost is not tangible. As far as we know, ghosts do not eat. Here we learn that the glorified body may eat if it so desires. "Have you any food here?" He asked. So they gave Him a piece of a broiled fish and some honeycomb (that still contained honey). And He took it and ate in their presence. Simon Peter mentioned this later in Acts 10:41. We do not suggest that He ate because He needed to, but because He wanted to, and it helped convince the disciples of His materiality.

Some scholars say our glorified bodies will have nothing to do with wounds or with food. However, we believe the scars on the Lamb of God are eternally permanent, and the price paid for our redemption displayed for ever. Note at this appearance to the Eleven and others, He does not say, "for a spirit has not flesh and blood." Flesh and blood cannot inherit the kingdom of God; nor does corruption inherit incorruption (1 Corinthians 15:50). Some believe His resurrection body had no blood in it. And that when we receive bodies like His, there will be within our bodies not blood, but a new life principle. There are others who feel no reference is made to the composition of His resurrection body. But we do learn from other Scriptures about our future bodies. From Philippians 3:21, we learn that our present lowly bodies will one day be transformed and thus conformed to Christ's body. We do not know fully what this means, but whatever it takes for us to live in Heaven, that is what will happen. Our new bodies will be unlike those of any ever known before. Not even Adam originally had this kind of body. Former mortals will have put on immortality. Those who died with faith in Christ, and whose bodies were placed in the grave to corrupt, will put on incorruption. As His body shines as the sun in divine glory, our bodies will shine as the stars in created glory. Peter, James and John got a glimpse of that glory at the Mount of Transfiguration (Matthew 17:2). Paul had that glory to shine upon him when he met the risen Christ on the road to Damascus (Acts 9:3).

But basically, we will have to wait and see. Some things, however, are sure. When the trumpet sounds we shall be changed. There is life after death! And glorious it will be. We shall see Him as He is, and seeing Him we shall be changed and made like Him (1 John 3:2). We will recognize and be recognized. There will be no eyeglasses; false teeth; braces, slings or halters; no girdles, pacemakers, flu shots, etc. There will be no more sickness; no more aches and pains; no more need to dial 911; no more ambulances or hospitals. And no more Death!

B. OPENING UP THE SCRIPTURES
(Luke 24:44-48)

And he said unto them, These are the words which I spake unto you, while I was yet with you, that all things must be fulfilled, which were written in the law of Moses, and in the prophets, and in the psalms, concerning me. Then opened he their understanding, that they might understand the scriptures. And said unto them, Thus it is written, and thus it behoved Christ to suffer, and to rise from the dead the third day: And that repentance and remission of sins should be preached in his name among all nations, beginning at Jerusalem. And ye are witnesses of these things.

In verse 44, we have phrases which correspond to the main threefold division of the Old Testament as seen in the Jewish canon of Scripture: the Law, the Prophets, and the Writing. The Law of Moses is the Pentateuch (five scrolls) or Torah; the Prophets include some of the historical books; and the Psalms include the poetic books. In short, our Lord claimed the Old Testament concerned Him, referred to Him. Surely, the seed of the woman, the I AM THAT I AM, the Suffering Servant, the typology of Jonah, the Holy One Who would see no corruption, etc.—all these point to Christ. And all that was written of Him must be fulfilled. The disciples must be made to understand this.

At this point, Christ opened their understanding (mind: the intellectual faculty). Three times in this chapter this particular verb rendered "opened" is used. In Luke 24:31, the eyes of the two Emmaus disciples were opened. In verse 32, the disciples rejoiced because the Lord had opened the Scriptures to them. And now in our lesson, in verse 45, He opened their understanding of the Scriptures. Here is a verb that means to open thoroughly (what had been closed), to open by dividing or drawing asunder. In short, He explained, expounded the sense of the Scriptures; He opened minds and caused men to understand. Jesus Christ is the God Who Opens Things! He showed by the Old Testament that it was predicted He would suffer (Psalm 22:1-21; Isaiah 53:1-10) and rise from the dead the third day (Jonah 1:17; Psalm 16:10; Hosea 6:2).

The Lord continued and taught that repentance (a complete change of mind or heart) and remission (sending away, riddance, forgiveness) of all sins should be preached. He not only instructed the disciples what to preach, but also how (in His name); to whom (all the nations), from where (beginning from Jerusalem). "You," said Christ, "are witnesses-preachers!" Testify what you have seen and learned!

C. THE ASCENSION
(Luke 24:49-53)

And, behold, I send the promise of my Father upon you: but tarry ye in the city of Jerusalem, until ye be endued with power from on high. And he led them out as far as to Bethany, and he lifted up his hands, and blessed them. And it came to pass, while he blessed them, he was parted from them, and carried up into heaven. And they worshipped him, and returned to Jerusalem with great joy: And were continually in the temple, praising and blessing God. Amen.

Our Lord's ascension or return to heaven took place forty days after His resurrection. Only believers were present, as we noted earlier. Upon them He sent the promise of God the Father. The Holy Spirit was indeed promised (John 14:16, 17;15:26; Isaiah 44:3). The disciples were to remain in the city of Jerusalem until endued with divine power. Only in this way would they be able to carry out the terms of the Great Commission. Christians need to be reminded constantly that the Lord's work is to be done the Lord's way, and in the Lord's power and according to His time schedule. This is seen in verse 49. Of course, reference is to the Holy Spirit soon to come (on the day of Pentecost) and live in the bodies of all who have been cleansed by the blood of Jesus Christ. The Lord then led them out as far as Bethany, then with uplifted hands, blessed them. He was carried up into heaven on a cloud, to be seated at the right hand of God the Father (Acts 2:33; Hebrews 1:3), making intercession for us (Romans 8:34). Note the disciples worshiped Him—not because Jehovah authorized Him to receive worship, but because Jesus Christ is God, the eternal, omnipotent Creator of the universe, our Lord and Savior. May we also be ready and willing to wait on Him with praise, blessing and great joy. For we have an ascended Savior who blesses a believing people with all spiritual blessings. Because we serve a risen Savior, we must understand blessings from His point of view. Within the context of His love and care, even the tragic experiences of life that we so often encounter may prove in the long run to be blessings in disguise.

III. Special Features

A. PRESERVING OUR HERITAGE

It may well be that a combination of racism and lack of solid Bible teaching is partly responsible for what is termed Black America's inclination to cultism. Within our large cities the membership of the Watchtower Society is overwhelmingly Black. Many cults and "isms" teach a "spiritual resurrection" of Christ. "Jehovah's Witnesses" teach Christ was not raised in flesh, but with spiritual body. Christian Science tells us that the resurrection is spiritualization of thought. Armstrongism states Christ's body disappeared, and Christ was raised as a divine spirit being. And Mr. Moon's Unification Church informs us that even in the spirit world after His resurrection, Christ lives as a spirit man with His disciples. On the other hand, Islam gets around this entire matter. According to the Koran, Jesus Christ did not die on the cross, but someone who looked like Him was mistakenly placed there. And Allah took Jesus Christ up to heaven! Thank God for every Black church that believes in the physical, bodily resurrection of the Lord Jesus Christ.

B. A CONCLUDING WORD

Yes, Christ's Presence continues, and we commemorate the resurrection of Jesus Christ every Sunday! The historical evidence of His continued Presence is overwhelming. Though He had been crucified and buried, He rose from the grave to be seen by human eyes, touched with human hands, and heard by human ears. Do not then attempt to spiritualize the resurrection. Indeed, the word "resurrection" can be used only with respect to the body. "If Christ be not raised...ye are yet in your sins" (1 Corinthians 15:17). Apart from the raising up of the Son of God, there can be no salvation. The physical, bodily resurrection of Christ is proof that what He accomplished has been accepted by God the Father. You and I, and all who trust Him, now have a full and complete salvation.

HOME DAILY BIBLE READINGS
Week of December 27, 1998
Christ's Presence Continues

Dec. 21 M. Luke 24:13-27, Jesus Himself Came Near
Dec. 22 T. Luke 24:28-35, Stay With Us; It Is Almost Evening
Dec. 23 W. Luke 24:36-43, Peace Be With You
Dec. 24 T. Luke 24:44-53, Everything Must Be Fulfilled
Dec. 25 F. John 14:15-24, I Will Not Leave You Orphaned
Dec. 26 S. John 14:25-31, The Holy Spirit Promised
Dec. 27 S. John 16:12-28, Jesus Speaks in Riddles

People of Love

Unit II. Good News for Daily Living
Children's Unit—Helps for Daily Living - Part I
Adult Topic—Love One Another

.....

Youth Topic—What Is Important?
Children's Topic—Love Others

.....

Devotional Reading—1 John 4:7-12
Background Scripture—Mark 12:28-34; Luke 6:27-36; John 13:31-35
Print—Mark 12:28-34; Luke 6:27-31; John 13:34-35

● ● ● ● ● ● ● ● ● ● ● ●

PRINTED SCRIPTURE

Mark 12:28-34; Luke 6:27-31; John 13:34-35 (KJV)

28 And one of the scribes came, and having heard them reasoning together, and perceiving that he had answered them well, asked him, Which is the first commandment of all?

29 And Jesus answered him, The first of all the commandments is, Hear, O Israel; The Lord our God is one Lord:

30 And thou shalt love the Lord thy God with all thy heart, and with all thy soul, and with all thy mind, and with all thy strength: this is the first commandment.

31 And the second is like, namely this, Thou shalt love thy neighbour as thyself. There is none other commandment greater than these.

32 And the scribe said unto him, Well, Master, thou hast said the truth: for there is one God; and there is none other but he:

33 And to love him with all the

Mark 12:28-34; Luke 6:27-31; John 13:34-35 (NRSV)

28 One of the scribes came near and heard them disputing with one another, and seeing that he answered them well, he asked him, "Which commandment is the first of all?"

29 Jesus answered, "The first is, 'Hear, O Israel: the Lord our God, the Lord is one;

30 you shall love the Lord your God with all your heart, and with all your soul, and with all your mind, and with all your strength.'

31 The second is this, 'You shall love your neighbor as yourself.' There is no other commandment greater than these."

32 Then the scribe said to him, "You are right, Teacher; you have truly said that 'he is one, and besides him there is no other';

33 and 'to love him with all the

heart, and with all the understanding, and with all the soul, and with all the strength, and to love his neighbour as himself, is more than all whole burnt offerings and sacrifices.

34 And when Jesus saw that he answered discreetly, he said unto him, Thou art not far from the kingdom of God. And no man after that durst ask him any question.

.....

27 But I say unto you which hear, Love your enemies, do good to them which hate you,

28 Bless them that curse you, and pray for them which despitefully use you.

29 And unto him that smiteth thee on the one cheek offer also the other; and him that taketh away thy cloke forbid not to take thy coat also.

30 Give to every man that asketh of thee; and of him that taketh away thy goods ask them not again.

31 And as ye would that men should do to you, do ye also to them likewise.

.....

34 A new commandment I give unto you, That ye love one another; as I have loved you, that ye also love one another.

35 By this shall all men know that ye are my disciples, if ye have love one to another.

heart, and with all the understanding, and with all the strength', and 'to love one's neighbor as oneself,'—this is much more important than all whole burnt offerings and sacrifices."

34 When Jesus saw that he answered wisely, he said to him, "You are not far from the kingdom of God." After that no one dared to ask him any question.

.....

27 "But I say to you that listen, Love your enemies, do good to those who hate you,

28 bless those who curse you, pray for those who abuse you.

29 If anyone strikes you on the cheek, offer the other also; and from anyone who takes away your coat do not withhold even your shirt.

30 Give to everyone who begs from you; and if anyone takes away your goods, do not ask for them again.

31 Do to others as you would have them do to you."

.....

34 "I give you a new commandment, that you love one another. Just as I have loved you, you also should love one another.

35 By this everyone will know that you are my disciples, if you have love for one another."

By this shall all men know that ye are my disciples, if ye have love one to another.—John 13:35

OBJECTIVES

After reading this lesson, the student should better understand:

1. The meaning and place of love in God's program;
2. The biblical order of loving God, loving believers, loving unbelievers; and,
3. The fact that love is the Christian badge of discipleship.

POINTS TO BE EMPHASIZED

Adult/Youth/Children

Key Verse: John 13:35; Mark 12:31 (Children)

Print: Mark 12:28-34; Luke 6:27-31; John 13:34-35

—In the midst of an argument, Jesus was asked which is the first commandment. (Mark 12:28)

—Jesus said that the most important commandment is to love God and the second is to love your neighbor. (29-31)

—The Scribe praised Jesus' answer and Jesus responded "You are not far from the kingdom." (32-34)

—Jesus gave guidelines for relating to others in difficult situations. (Luke 6:27-31)

—Jesus gave a new commandment that identifies love as the mark of discipleship. (John 13:34-35)

(NOTE: Use KJV Scripture for Adults; NRSV Scripture for Youth and Children)

TOPICAL OUTLINE OF THE LESSON

I. Introduction

A. Words For Love
B. Biblical Background

II. Exposition and Application of the Scripture

A. Love God (Mark 12:28-30)
B. Love Your Neighbor (Mark 12:31-34)
C. Love Your Enemies (Luke 6:27-31)
D. Love Fellow Believers (John 13:34-35)

III. Special Features

A. Preserving Our Heritage
B. A Concluding Word

I. Introduction

A. WORDS FOR LOVE

There are at least three Greek words for love, but only the two that are used in the New Testament concern us. **Eros,** from which we have derived the word "erotic" is not used. In Greek Mythology, Eros was the god of love; the Romans called him Cupid. Today the word "Erotic" has to do with sexual passion. In short, the element of sex is very strong in this Greek word for love.

On the other hand, **philos** and **agape** are used throughout the New Testament. First, consider **philos,** the noun; **phileo,** the verb. Thayer's Greek Lexicon, and Trech's Synonyms of the New Testament are very helpful here. **Philos** as a prefix is seen in such English words as Philip, Philadelphia, Philanthropy, etc. **Phileo** means to be fond of, friendly to someone. It is a love of lesser degree than **agape.** It is more instinctive, implies more passion, feelings, natural spontaneous affections. We are never told to **phileo** God. Incidentally, the verb also means to kiss (Judas: Matthew 26:48).

In comparison, the verb **agapao** means to love deeply; it is used of divine love, never of sexual love. It is seen as purposeful, a more reasoning attachment, involving the will or intellect. Notions of respect and reverence are continually implied in the use of the noun, **agape.** For further study, read John 21:15-17, and see how the conversation between the Lord and Simon Peter evolved. Twice the Lord used **agapao** in asking Peter, "Simon, do you love me?" Twice Simon answered, using **phileo,** "Lord, you know I love you." The third time the Lord used **phileo** when He inquired, "Simon, do you love me?" And once again, Peter answered, using **phileo,** "Lord, you know that I love you." Now in our lesson only the verb **agapao** is used!

B. BIBLICAL BACKGROUND

As best as can be determined from a Harmony of the Gospels, the passage from Luke chapter 6 was uttered first, in fact, early in our Lord's ministry, and was a part of the Beatitudes and the Sermon on the Mount (cf. Matthew 5:43-48). The passage in our lesson taken from Mark chapter 12 occurred during the Passion Week. As usual, what He taught antagonized the religious leaders, for He answered them well, indeed, as One having authority. In this chapter, Mark records the parable of the Vineyard Owner, and tells how the leaders were moved to attempt to kill Christ. In this same chapter, our Lord took on the Herodians and answered them; confronted the Sadducees, answered them; and then, as part of our lesson, answered the Pharisees. After these confrontations we are told: "No man after that dared to ask Him any question" (Mark 12:34).

Events in John chapter 13 took place a little later in that same Passion Week. In this chapter, the Lord predicted His betrayal. Indeed, Satan entered Judas, and the traitor left the group to effectuate his wicked plans. It was our Lord's announcement that He was going away (John 13:33) that troubled the disciples' hearts (John 14:1). And so we see the varied background for this lesson on love, given by the Lover of our souls, Jesus Christ.

II. Exposition and Application of the Scripture

A. LOVE GOD
(Mark 12:28-30)

And one of the scribes came, and having heard them reasoning together, and perceiving that he had answered them well, asked him, Which is the first commandment of all? And Jesus answered him, The first of all the commandments is, Hear, O Israel; The Lord our God is one Lord: And thou shalt love the Lord thy God with all thy heart, and with all thy soul, and with all thy mind, and with all thy strength: this is the first commandment.

The scribe was a man "learned in the Mosaic law and in the sacred writings, an interpreter, teacher" (Thayer). **Gramma** (not grandmother!) is a Greek word meaning a letter, that which has been written. See it in such words as cablegram, telegram, diagram. So a **grammateus** is a clerk, scribe, especially a public scribe, secretary, recorder. He explained the meaning of the sacred oracles. Skilled in the law, scribes were needed to solve difficult questions. It is said that they had divided the whole law into 613 precepts (248 things to do, and 365 things not to do)! They concerned themselves with matters like Sabbath observance, sacrifices, what to wear, circumcision, what to eat, etc. You see why they are often mentioned with the other religious leaders, the Pharisees, and the Sadducees.

Now this particular scribe in our lesson, who probably was also a Pharisee, is not named. But having heard and approved of our Lord's answer to the Sadducees, he felt led to ask Christ, "Which is the first commandment of all?" This is to say, which commandment is first in importance? He was impressed by our Lord's adroit and skillful handling of the trumped up story put forth by the Sadducees (Mark 12:18-23). And it appears that this scribe was not like the questioners in Matthew 22:15 who sought to entangle the Lord in His talk. Sometimes, we encounter people who ask questions in order to: (1) test (2) trip up (3) argue (4) answer themselves to show their knowledge (5) fulfill a genuine desire for knowledge. This scribe appears to be an honest, sincere questioner, without any ulterior motive. The Lord's answer goes back to Deuteronomy 6:4-5, to what is called the Shema (from the Hebrew verb meaning, to hear). "Hear, O Israel: The Lord our God is one Lord: And thou shalt love the Lord thy God with all thine heart, and with all thy soul, and with all thy might." This Jewish statement of faith uses the words heart, soul, and might. In our lesson, Mark 12:30, it is heart, soul, mind, and strength. In Luke 10:27, it is heart, soul, strength, and mind. In Matthew 22:37, it is heart, soul and mind. "There is no difference in substance" (Lenski).

We see the heart is placed first, for the heart is the very center of personality. The soul is the seat of affections, desires, emotions or feelings, and the will; it is the life that animates the body. The mind is the reason, with its thoughts and convictions. Note the word "whole" or "all" is used in each aspect of man's makeup. This is because God does not want just a piece of us, but the entire being, the whole person, all of man's powers and capacities. In other words, the Shema speaks of God's desire that we love Him to the uttermost degree, our full potential (by His enablement). God is to have the number one place in our lives! No other love is to rival our love for the Lord—who loved us first. This is why such strong language is used by our Savior in His statement: "If any man come to me, and hate not his father, and mother, and wife, and children, and brethren, and sisters, yea, and his own life also, he cannot be my disciples" (Luke 14:26). Whatever affection we have for others, it is hatred compared to what we should have for Jesus Christ!

B. LOVE YOUR NEIGHBOR
   (Mark 12:31-34)

And the second is like, namely this, Thou shalt love thy neighbour as thyself. There is none other commandment greater than these. And the scribe said unto him, Well, Master, thou hast said the truth: for there is one God; and there is none other but he: And to love him with all the heart, and with all the understanding, and with all the soul, and with all the strength, and to love his neighbour as himself, is more than all whole burnt offerings and sacrifices. And when Jesus saw that he answered discreetly, he said unto him, Thou art not far from the kingdom of God. And no man after that durst ask him any question.

First, love God. Now second, love your neighbor as yourself. This is true life. Those who selfishly live only for themselves are really not living; they are only existing. Here our Lord brings in Leviticus 19:18: "Thou shalt not avenge, nor bear any grudge against the children of thy people, but thou shalt love thy neighbor as thyself: I am the Lord." So we are to love God MORE than ourselves, and love our neighbors AS ourselves. Keep in mind that within the context the neighbors are, first of all, fellow Jews ("the children of thy people"). The word translated neighbor means one who dwells nigh, or near. It also means friend. In the Old Testament and Hebrew concepts, the neighbor is a member of the Hebrew race and commonwealth. Christ expanded it to mean any other person, regardless of race or religion, with whom we live or even chance to meet. Upon hearing these words, the scribe acknowledge the truth spoken by the Teacher, and he repeats with approval what the Lord had said. He adds, however, a statement that modern day church goers also need to hear: Loving God and loving others is a package deal, and is more important than rites and ceremonies. The ethical is superior to the ritual. If the heart is not right, ceremonial observances are futile.

All too often our society praises the philanthropy, but is not interested in motives, or with inward personal holiness. The scribe's response is commendable, and so the Lord said, "You are not far from the kingdom of God." You see, kingdom folks do not try to fool God, or deceive their fellow men by relying upon external form and fashion. This man had answered discreetly: wisely (NIV, RSV), with thoughtfulness (JBP), sensibly (NEB), prudently (Thayer), intelligently (NASB). The word so rendered is found in the New Testament only here (Mark 12:34). After this, there were no more attempts to ensnare Christ with theological conundrums, leading questions or legal traps.

C. LOVE YOUR ENEMIES
(Luke 6:27-31)

But I say unto you which hear, Love your enemies, do good to them which hate you, Bless them that curse you, and pray for them which despitefully use you. And unto him that smiteth thee on the one cheek offer also the other; and him that taketh away thy cloke forbid not to take thy coat also. Give to every man that asketh of thee; and of him that taketh away thy goods ask them not again. And as ye would that men should do to you, do ye also to them likewise.

Our theme, People of Love, goes now to the Gospel of Luke. And immediately, we are faced with a teaching that would eliminate revenge. Here we are encouraged to do just the opposite of what comes naturally; we are commanded to love our enemies! In English, the word "enemy" has Latin roots, **inimical,** literally, one who is not a friend. The Greek word speaks of one who is odious, hated, hateful, hostile. We are to do good to all such! Luke uses a present tense command, meaning do good and keep on doing or practicing doing good to such personal enemies.

Here our Lord goes beyond our neighbors and extends the command to love to cover the entire round of active life. This love is to manifest itself: (1) in blessing others. Here the word for "eulogy" is used; it means to speak well of, praise. We are to speak well of those who curse or condemn us; and ask God's blessing on them; (2) we are to pray for those who insult, revile, abuse, or falsely accuse us; (3) we are to suffer personal indignity, and not give way to anger or seek physical retaliation; (4) in suffering personal loss of property, do not clamor to get it back. The basic principle here is: Keep On Showing Love! Do not put any limits on love when you are personally mistreated. Let this principle dictate your reaction to abuse. With this in mind, listen to what Lenski says: "Christ never told me not to restrain the murderer's hand, not to check the thief and robber, not to oppose the tyrant, or to foster shiftlessness, dishonesty, and greed by my gifts" (Luke, p. 365). Read also Romans 12:17-21.

Finally, in this section, verse 31 defines Christian Love. Here is what is often called "The Golden Rule." It is only partly true to say that Buddha, Confucius, Socrates, and others prior to Christ, also taught this same rule. Their statements stressed the negative only; positive action is not suggested by them. Selfishness was their motivation, not the good of the other person. This tremendous difference should be remembered. Christ's command is spiritual, and He requires that believers actively help those who are categorized as "enemies."

D. LOVE FELLOW BELIEVERS
(John 13:34-35)

A new commandment I give unto you, That ye love one another; as I have loved you, that ye also love one another. By this shall all men know that ye are my disciples, if ye have love one to another.

The lesson closes with this word of our Lord from the Gospel of John. What

He commands is not "new" **(neos)** in the sense of "Brand new," never having been commanded before. No. This "new" **(kainos)** means different in quality. Centuries earlier, Moses had been moved to write in Leviticus 19:18, "thou shalt love thy neighbor as thyself." What is new is this: It is a love based on Jesus Christ. It is for His sake. Here is a brotherhood based on a relationship with Jesus Christ—a new relationship for men and women. A love based on His love for us—"as I have loved you," He said—founded on the new thing soon to take place at Calvary. New, because it was not established upon who was a member of the commonwealth of Israel, or who was a Jew! But who is a Christian!

New, because it was founded upon such love as the world had never seen before—the love of Him who would shed His own blood for the unlovely. New, by virtue of the fact that the Holy Spirit would for the first time soon make the bodies of all believers His temple, and thus enable the saints to manifest such love. New, because it is superior to the old; love your enemies is superior to love your neighbors.

The believer's love for all other believers is indeed proof of being disciples of Christ. And God wants the world to know that there are to be no secret disciples here! We are commanded: "Owe no man anything, but to love one another; for he that loveth another hath fulfilled the law" (Romans 13:8). Saints are exhorted, "walk in love, as Christ also hath loved us" (Ephesians 5:2). How does all of this stack up in our time of splits and schisms? Church court cases? Saints suing saints? What a goal the lesson sets before us! Not a cross worn around the neck. Not an automobile bumper sticker exhorting: Honk If You Love Jesus! But genuine, Holy Spirit, Christ ordained, agape love for other Christians. Here is a Divine Imperative that dispels ignorance while demonstrating a definite identification!

III. Special Features

A. PRESERVING OUR HERITAGE

With all of our faults and failures, what would it be like if it were not for the love genuine Black Christians have shown in their lives? A love that prays for White church-bombers. A love that has never officially denied White Christians the opportunity to enter and worship with us. What but our love for Christ has kept down the degree of retaliatory violence that would occur because of the evil racism practiced by certain Americans?

Who can evaluate how the love that does exist in our Black churches has helped us as a people—has unified us, strengthened us, preserved our lives? First mentioned as a part of the fruit of the Holy Spirit, which is Christlikeness, is love. But what of the joy and peace we possess? God grant that we continue to sing with meaning, "Oh, How I Love Jesus," and let that love show itself in every aspect of our lives.

B. A CONCLUDING WORD

Chronologically, we place the Scriptures for our lesson in this order: Luke chapter 6; Mark chapter 12, and John chapter 13. Topically, we would place this matter of love in the following order: (1) Love God, who first loved us (2) Love other Christians (3) then let that love overflow and affect the lives of unbelievers. This is the biblical order. We cannot love (agape love) other human beings if we do not love God. The vertical comes first, and if it is right, it will prove beneficial to the horizontal.

But first in the horizontal level are other believers. Sometimes church folks seem to skip over this second category, but failure to love the brethren is a serious matter (1 John 3:14). You can rest assured that where there is little genuine love among church members, there is very little, if any, evangelism, and still less missions activity! Remember then the biblical order: Love God, love other Christians, love unbelievers. For it is the desire of the God of the Bible for all who claim cleansing in the blood of Christ to be a People of Love.

HOME DAILY BIBLE READINGS
Week of January 3, 1999
People of Love

Dec. 28 M. Mark 12:28-34, Which Commandment First of All?
Dec. 29 T. Luke 6:27-36, Love Your Enemies
Dec. 30 W. John 13:31-35, Evidence of Discipleship
Dec. 31 T. Ephesians 3:14-19, Rooted and Grounded in Love
Jan. 1 F. Romans 13:1-10, Love Fulfills the Law
Jan. 2 S. 1 Corinthians 8:1-6, Love Builds Up
Jan. 3 S. 1 John 4:7-12, God Abides in Those Who Love

Kingdom Priorities

Adult Topic—First Things First

.....

Youth Topic—What Is Enough?
Children's Topic—Serve God

.....

Devotional Reading—Habakkuk 3:17-19
Background Scripture—Luke 12:13-34
Print—Luke 12:13-21

• • • • • • • • • • •

PRINTED SCRIPTURE

Luke 12:13-21 (KJV)

13 And one of the company said unto him, Master, speak to my brother, that he divide the inheritance with me.

14 And he said unto him, Man, who made me a judge or a divider over you?

15 And he said unto them, Take heed, and beware of covetousness: for a man's life consisteth not in the abundance of the things which he possesseth.

16 And he spake a parable unto them, saying, The ground of a certain rich man brought forth plentifully:

17 And he thought within himself, saying, What shall I do, because I have no room where to bestow my fruits?

18 And he said, This will I do: I will pull down my barns, and build greater; and there will I bestow all my fruits and my goods.

19 And I will say to my soul, Soul, thou hast much goods laid up for

Luke 12:13-21 (NRSV)

13 Someone in the crowd said to him, "Teacher, tell my brother to divide the family inheritance with me."

14 But he said to him, "Friend, who set me to be a judge or arbitrator over you?"

15 And he said to them, "Take care! Be on your guard against all kinds of greed; for one's life does not consist in the abundance of possessions."

16 Then he told them a parable: "The land of a rich man produced abundantly.

17 And he thought to himself, 'What should I do, for I have no place to store my crops?'

18 Then he said, 'I will do this: I will pull down my barns and build larger ones, and there I will store all my grain and my goods.

19 And I will say to my soul, 'Soul, you have ample goods laid up for

many years; take thine ease, eat, drink, and be merry.

20 But God said unto him, Thou fool, this night thy soul shall be required of thee: then whose shall those things be, which thou hast provided?

21 So is he that layeth up treasure for himself, and is not rich toward God.

many years; relax, eat, drink, be merry.'

20 But God said to him, 'You fool! This very night your life is being demanded of you. And the things you have prepared, whose will they be?'

21 So it is with those who store up treasures for themselves but are not rich toward God."

KEY VERSE

And he said unto them, Take heed, and beware of covetousness: for a man's life consisteth not in the abundance of the things which he possesseth.—Luke 12:15

OBJECTIVES

After reading this lesson, the student should be fully aware that:

1. Life is more than material possessions;
2. It is foolish to put all of our eggs in the "here-and-now" basket;
3. Covetousness is indeed idolatry; and,
4. True life is doing God's will, not our wills.

POINTS TO BE EMPHASIZED

Adult/Youth/Children
Key Verse: Luke 12:15
Print: Luke 12:13-21

—Jesus was asked to settle a dispute about an inheritance, but refused to get involved. (13-14)
—Jesus warned against greed and taught that life is more than having possessions. (15)
—Jesus then told a parable of a rich man who had no place to store his abundant crops. (16-17)
—The farmer decided to build larger barns to store his grain and live secure in his success. (18-19)
—Jesus taught that God judged the man as a fool and would do likewise to those who give priority to storing up treasures for themselves. (20-21)

(NOTE: Use KJV Scripture for Adults; NRSV Scripture for Youth and Children)

I. Introduction

A. THE DANGER OF COVETOUSNESS

The Bible has much to say about covetousness. In the Old Testament, one word rendered "covetousness" means to desire; it is used in the last of the Ten Commandments (Exodus 20:17). In Psalm 10:3, the word employed signifies to gain dishonestly; it is the most frequently found of the Hebrew words translated "covetousness."

In the New Testament, one word for "covet" suggests to fix the mind on. Paul used it in his farewell address to the Ephesian elders: "I have coveted no man's silver, or gold, or apparel" (Acts 20:33). In 1 Timothy 6:10, a word meaning "to extend the arms for" is employed. There is another word for covetousness which means silver lover (lover of silver). It is found in Luke 16:14 and describes the Pharisees (cf. 2 Timothy 3:2). Interestingly, in the well known verse, "for the love of money is the root of all evil," the phrase "love of money' is literally, "silver lover." Thus, we might say that covetousness is a root of all evil. Finally, in the New Testament, in 1 Corinthians 5:10-11, the apostle's verb to covet is one who wishes more, or as one writer put it, has "the itch for more." This is the word found in our lesson for today (Luke 12:15).

In summary, when our minds' desire becomes so fixed that we extend our arms out to dishonestly get hold of that which does not belong to us, and our wish for more moves us to fall in love with money—we are covetous! All such is idolatry (Ephesians 5:5; Colossians 3:5). No wonder folks who practice covetousness and extortion shall not inherit the kingdom of God (1 Corinthians 6:10).

B. BIBLICAL BACKGROUND

Keep in mind that the Bible does not condemn the wealthy simply because they are wealthy. God is concerned not only with how we obtain riches, and what is done with our material possessions, but also our attitude toward wealth. Riches are not necessarily evil. It does not take long for the Bible student to ascertain that Abraham was a man of great affluence. "And Abram was very rich in cattle, in silver, and in gold" (Genesis 13:2). Of Isaac it is said: "He had possession of flocks, and possession of herds, and great store of servants: and the Philistines envied him" (Genesis 26:14).

Jacob "had much cattle, and maidservants, and menservants, and camels, and donkeys" (Genesis 30:1). We read of Job's prosperity also, and that he "was the greatest of all the men of the east" (Job 1:3). And don't leave out David or Solomon! Joseph of Arimathea was also a rich man (Matthew 27:57). Prosperity is not condemned by the Word of God. Yea, He has given us all things richly to enjoy (1 Timothy 6:17).

However, we are constantly warned of the perils of wealth, and we find it difficult to accept present-day emphasis in some religious circles made by prosperity prophets and wealth wizards. The Bible cautions: (1) The wealthy may be inclined to forget God, and leave Him out of their lives (Deuteronomy 8:13-14); (2) Set their hearts on riches and become greedy (Psalm 62:10); (3) Make haste to become rich and compromise their integrity (Proverbs 28:20); (4) Succumb to the powerful temptations to "play God" and to dominate the poor (1 Timothy 6:9). James 2:2-4 also points this out. These then are some of the dangers inherent in being wealthy.

II. Exposition and Application of the Scripture

A. ASSUMPTIONS THAT ARE FALSE
(Luke 12:13-15)

And one of the company said unto him, Master, speak to my brother, that he divide the inheritance with me. And he said unto him, Man, who made me a judge or a divider over you? And he said unto them, Take heed, and beware of covetousness: for a man's life consisteth not in the abundance of the things which he possesseth.

An unnamed materialist, called an "incongruous fool" by Lindsay (Cambridge), asked the Lord Jesus to intervene in a family money squabble. "Master (Teacher), speak to my brother, that he divide the inheritance with me." In Deuteronomy 21:17, the younger received one-third, the elder, two-thirds. Nothing more is said, as if he assumed the Lord would indeed take his side of the argument. What the facts were in this case are unknown. What we sense is, however, the man was not concerned with justice at all. He simply wanted to get his hands on some money, or rather, some more money!

Now the Lord saw through this man's attempt to use Him for his own personal convenience and covetousness. Some people are like that; they seek to use you for their own personal gain. They may attempt to flatter you or butter you up; or cajole, frighten, threaten; or make promises. But Christ had not come into the world to handle such affairs (John 18:36). And He said, "Man, who made Me a judge or divider over you?"

Use of the word "man" shows a stern tone, expresses indignation and rebuke (Lindsay); it is a word of solemn reproof (Alford). Our Lord could see through the man's greedy heart and covetous spirit. It is important to point out that **what** a man **is** is more important than what a man **has.** It is false to think otherwise, for covetousness is a lie that would incline us to believe that happiness is found only in things. But man was not so made by God that material goods should fully satisfy the human heart; our life consists of God, not of goods. To assume goods will not rust, break down, become obsolete, go out of style, malfunction, be stolen, or eaten by moths, decrease in value because of inflation, is a false assumption. And now in order for us to see better the covetousness of the human heart, and to realize that all kinds of covetousness are to be avoided, the Lord told a parable. As you know, paraballo means to throw alongside of, or cast before, it is to put one thing by the side of another for the sake of comparison or illustration. In this parable, peculiar to Luke, we learn about the errors of the Rich Fool.

B. NEGLECT OF THE FUTURE
(Luke 12:16-19)

And he spake a parable unto them, saying, The ground of a certain rich man brought forth plentifully: And he thought within himself, saying, What shall I do, because I have no room where to bestow my fruits? And he said, This will I do: I will pull down my barns, and build greater; and there will I bestow all my fruits and my goods. And I will say to my soul, Soul, thou hast much goods laid up for many years: take thine ease, eat, drink, and be merry.

This man was a successful farmer. We are not told how many acres of farmland he owned, nor whether he purchased the ground or inherited it. Furthermore, there is no indication he was oppressive or employed migrant workers illegally, or used and abused sharecroppers. Nor did he remove landmarks, or attempt to get the government to subsidize any crops, or keep prices up by burning grain, pouring dye on potatoes or killing hogs. The ground was cultivated, plowed land; it was fertile, and brought forth plentifully. Found only here in the New Testament, the word translated "brought forth plentifully" has given us the English word, "euphoria," literally, well-bearing, easy to bear. All of this may sound like the farmer did not have too much to do with the productivity or fertility of the soil. Remember, the Lord Jesus said: "For He makes His sun to rise on the evil and on the good, and sendeth rain on the just and on the unjust" (Matthew 5:45). Perhaps this man used good farming methods. He knew about rotating crops, the proper use of fertilizer, control of insects, or even owned one of those machines which suck off or vacuum the bugs off of the crop without having to use an insecticide. So he had good modern equipment.

It is evident also that he was not lazy, but had initiative, get-up-and-go, progressive ideas. Give him credit for being a successful farmer, blessed by God with productive soil, with know-how, abundant sunshine and sufficient rain, and energy to work hard. The fact then that he was rich is not held against him. It is no crime to be rich. However, it was God's blessing upon this farmer and his land. It was the providence of the Creator shown to the creature. This man's mistake was to forget God and concentrate on his goods. Though a good farmer, he failed to thank God for the abundance of his crops and for all his wealth. At this point, we see how false it is to assume that things can satisfy the human soul, for he was led also to think he was the very center of life.

Two things support our contention here. First, note his selfishness. Eleven times he used the personal pronouns **"I"** and **"my"** (Read Luke 12:17-19). "What shall **I** do—**I** have no place to store **my** crops—this will **I** do—**I** will pull down **my** barns—**I** will bestow all **my** crops and **my** goods—**I** will say to **my** soul—take thine ease!" What self-centeredness! What egocentricity! Self-will was substituted for God's will. His selfishness blinded and deceived him so that he thought more highly of himself than he ought to have thought. He assumed that the abundance was calculated to be used for him alone.

Second, his selfishness moved him to assume there was no one else in the world who mattered. Surely, there were empty barns of farmers less fortunate than he, but he did not see them. There were empty cupboards of widows and orphans, but he did not see them. There were empty plates of the poor and the beggars, the street persons, but he did not see them. There were the mouths of hungry babies, but he did not see them. He saw only himself. And sad to say, this man's ancestors and relatives still lived.

Selfishness blinds people to long-range sight. He was reasoning (dialoguing) with himself, but could see no further than self. His "I wills" were more immediate than eternal. It never entered his mind that the abundance of crops might not last, or that he himself might die. If death can separate us from our possessions, do we really own them? One of the things about being a Christian is the emphasis upon the future. Belief in the shed blood of Calvary guarantees our future. When the future is properly accented, we enjoy the here and now. But a man who puts all of his eggs in the "here-and-now" basket makes a grave mistake. He robs himself of present blessings and future rewards.

C. CONDEMNED A FOOL
(Luke 12:20-21)

But God said unto him, Thou fool, this night thy soul shall be required of thee: then whose shall those things be, which thou hast provided? So is he that layeth up treasure for himself, and is not rich toward God.

There are all kinds of fools in the Bible. Various Hebrew words refer to the fool as boaster, self-confident, empty, thickheaded, one who despises wisdom and discipline, mocks at guilt, is quarrelsome, licentious, useless to instruct. In the New Testament, we find several Greek words translated "fool" or "foolish." They have such meanings as thoughtless, unwise, useless. In Luke 12:20, the word **aphron** for fool means witless, heedless, senseless, stupid. Literally, it is "without mind." We would say he was not "clothed in his right mind."

The fool here is one without reason, reflection or intelligence. Here is a word for "fool" used by Christ of the Pharisees who were so interested in making the outside of the cup clean, while inwardly they themselves were full of corruption (Luke 11:40). The apostle Paul used it to describe folks who question the physical, bodily resurrection of Christ (1 Corinthians 15:36).

And so it was that abruptly, suddenly challenged to give an account of his life, this man was found sadly wanting. For him, what you have was more important than what you are. From him, there came no thanks to God for material blessings. He thought only of himself, "me, myself and I," and not of others. He assumed material things could perfectly satisfy an immaterial soul. This was foolish. As Vance Havner said, "God does not give the soul a vacation; He gives it a vocation."

And so it was that very night, a time of judgment, the Lord suddenly reproved him (Proverbs 29:1). God never wastes time. Soon after this farmer comforted himself with his own plans, God discomfited him with the divine plan. "Thou fool!"—you who are devoid of sense, without mind or reason, without reflection or intelligence—this is strong language. To be called a fool may or may not mean anything. It depends upon who calls us a fool. If another fool calls us a fool, we may not pay him any attention. But if God calls us a fool, we had better pay attention. Unless, of course, we are fools for Christ (1 Corinthians 4:10). Only then would we be good farmers, bringing forth good fruit, with true assumptions, facing a glorious future. It may well be that some of us see ourselves in this parable. The Lord Jesus Christ, the Wisdom of God, comes to us and says, "don't be a fool! True wealth is found only in Me."

III. Special Features

A. PRESERVING OUR HERITAGE

One of the dangers a deprived, segregated and exploited people face is what may be called a "jack-in-the-box" response. In other words, when kept down for a long time, and the restraints are relaxed, we spring up suddenly, often without organization, discipline, or purpose. In poverty for a long time, and then suddenly faced with opportunity to improve our material possessions, covetousness may breed and grow.

Material prosperity does not go well with everybody. In Deuteronomy 32:15, we read: "Jeshurun (a poetical name for Israel) grew fat, and kicked. Thou art become fat, thou art grown thick, thou art covered with fatness; then he forsook God who made him, and lightly esteemed the Rock of his salvation." The Black middle class has grown tremendously, but spirituality appears to have gone downhill. All of us want our slice of the American pie, but some of us seem not to consider God in our lives.

We have come a long ways from singing, "Give me Jesus, give me Jesus, You may have all dis worl', give me Jesus." For that matter what about Kenneth Morris' selection:

"I don't possess houses or lands, fine clothes or jewelry,
Sorrows and cares in this old world my lot seems to be,
But I have a Christ who paid the price way back on Calv'ry,
And Christ is all, all and all this world to me.

Christ is all, He's ev'rything to me,
Christ is all, He rules the land and sea,
Christ is all, without Him nothing could be,
Christ is all, all and all this world to me."

B. A CONCLUDING WORD

Some Christians appear unhappy, distressed, greatly perturbed that they do not own all of the material goods of life they desire. Without these "things," they have no peace and rancor fills their hearts. How sad! They have fallen for the lie that covetousness has created. The writer in Hebrews exhorts: "Let your manner of life be without covetousness, and be content with such things as ye have; for He hath said, I will never leave thee, nor forsake thee" (Hebrews 13:5). Satisfaction is to be found in the Lord Jesus Christ, who bought us with His own blood, owns us, and has promised to be with us always (Matthew 28:20).

HOME DAILY BIBLE READINGS
Week of January 10, 1999
Kingdom Priorities

Jan. 4 M. Luke 12:13-21, Be on Guard Against All Kinds of Greed
Jan. 5 T. Luke 12:22-34, Do Not Worry About Your Life
Jan. 6 W. Proverbs 1:8-19, Greed Takes Away Life
Jan. 7 T. Ecclesiastes 5:1-10, Money Alone Does Not Satisfy
Jan. 8 F. Jeremiah 17:5-11, Amassing Wealth Unjustly Is Hazardous!
Jan. 9 S. Micah 2:1-5, Beware the Sin of Covetousness!
Jan. 10 S. James 5:1-6, Greed is Self-Defeating

Reversing the World's Standard

Adult Topic— Greatness in Service

.....

Youth Topic—What Is Real Leadership?
Children's Topic—Help Others

.....

Devotional Reading—Galatians 5:13-15
Background Scripture—Matthew 18:1-4; 20:17-28
Print—Matthew 18:1-4; 20:17-28

PRINTED SCRIPTURE

Matthew 18:1-4; 20:17-28 (KJV)

AT the same time came the disciples unto Jesus, saying, Who is the greatest in the kingdom of heaven?

2 And Jesus called a little child unto him, and set him in the midst of them,

3 And said, Verily I say unto you, Except ye be converted, and become as little children, ye shall not enter into the kingdom of heaven.

4 Whosoever therefore shall humble himself as this little child, the same is greatest in the kingdom of heaven.

.....

17 And Jesus going up to Jerusalem took the twelve disciples apart in the way, and said unto them,

18 Behold, we go up to Jerusalem; and the Son of man shall be betrayed unto the chief priests and unto the scribes, and they shall condemn him to death,

19 And shall deliver him to the Gentiles to mock, and to scourge,

Matthew 18:1-4; 20:17-28 (NRSV)

AT THAT time the disciples came to Jesus and asked, "Who is the greatest in the kingdom of heaven?"

2 He called a child, whom he put among them,

3 and said, "Truly I tell you, unless you change and become like children, you will never enter the kingdom of heaven.

4 Whoever becomes humble like this child is the greatest in the kingdom of heaven."

.....

17 While Jesus was going up to Jerusalem, he took the twelve disciples aside by themselves, and said to them on the way,

18 "See, we are going up to Jerusalem, and the Son of Man will be handed over to the chief priests and scribes, and they will condemn him to death;

19 then they will hand him over to the Gentiles to be mocked and

and to crucify him: and the third day he shall rise again.

20 Then came to him the mother of Zebedee's children with her sons, worshipping him, and desiring a certain thing of him.

21 And he said unto her, What wilt thou? She saith unto him, Grant that these my two sons may sit, the one on thy right hand, and the other on the left, in thy kingdom.

22 But Jesus answered and said, Ye know not what ye ask. Are ye able to drink of the cup that I shall drink of, and to be baptized with the baptism that I am baptized with? They say unto him, We are able.

23 And he saith unto them, Ye shall drink indeed of my cup, and be baptized with the baptism that I am baptized with: but to sit on my right hand, and on my left, is not mine to give, but it shall be given to them for whom it is prepared of my Father.

24 And when the ten heard it, they were moved with indignation against the two brethren.

25 But Jesus called them unto him, and said, Ye know that the princes of the Gentiles exercise dominion over them, and they that are great exercise authority upon them.

26 But it shall not be so among you: but whosoever will be great among you, let him be your minister;

27 And whosoever will be chief among you, let him be your servant:

28 Even as the Son of man came not to be ministered unto, but to minister, and to give his life a ransom for many.

flogged and crucified; and on the third day he will be raised."

20 Then the mother of the sons of Zebedee came to him with her sons, and kneeling before him, she asked a favor of him.

21 And he said to her, "What do you want?" She said to him, "Declare that these two sons of mine will sit, one at your right hand and one at your left, in your kingdom."

22 But Jesus answered, "You do not know what you are asking. Are you able to drink the cup that I am about to drink?" They said to him, "We are able."

23 He said to them, "You will indeed drink my cup, but to sit at my right hand and at my left, this is not mine to grant, but it is for those for whom it has been prepared by my Father."

24 When the ten heard it, they were angry with the two brothers.

25 But Jesus called them to him and said, "You know that the rulers of the Gentiles lord it over them, and their great ones are tyrants over them.

26 It will not be so among you; but whoever wishes to be great among you must be your servant,

27 and whoever wishes to be first among you must be your slave;

28 just as the Son of Man came not to be served but to serve, and to give his life a ransom for many."

KEY VERSE

But it shall not be among you: but whosoever will be great among you, let him be your minister.—Matthew 20:26

OBJECTIVES

After reading this lesson, the student should better understand:

1. The meaning of childlike faith;
2. The events of Passion Week;
3. What true greatness really is; and,
4. Why the Son of Man came into the world.

POINTS TO BE EMPHASIZED

Adult/Youth/Children
Key Verse: Matthew 20:26
Print: Matthew 18:1-4; 20:17-28

—When the disciples asked Jesus who would be the greatest in the kingdom, He showed them a child and challenged them to develop childlike humility. (18:1-4)

—While journeying to Jerusalem, Jesus reminded His disciples that He would be crucified and raised again. (20:17-19)

—When the mother of James and John asked that her sons be given positions of honor and power in Jesus' kingdom, Jesus asked them if they were able to share in His suffering. (22a)

—Though James and John said they were able, Jesus said that special positions were granted only by His Father. (22b-23)

—The other disciples were angry with James and John because of their mother's request. (20:24)

—Jesus explained that the values of His kingdom would be radically different from the values of worldly kingdoms. (25-28)

(NOTE: Use KJV Scripture for Adults; NRSV Scripture for Youth and Children)

TOPICAL OUTLINE OF THE LESSON

I. Introduction

A. Some Worldly Standards
B. Biblical Background

II. Exposition and Application of the Scripture

A. The Necessity for Childlike Faith (Matthew 18:1-4)
B. Christ Predicts His Death and Resurrection (Matthew 20:17-19)
C. Response to a Mother's Request (Matthew 20:20-24)
D. Purpose of the Son of Man (Matthew 20:25-28)

III. Special Features

A. Preserving Our Heritage
B. A Concluding Word

I. Introduction

A. SOME WORLDLY STANDARDS

The world-system or **kosmos** has a number of criteria which are at odds with what the Bible teaches. We propose to consider just a few of them in the hope that as Christians, we shall see in an even better way that friendship with the world is enmity with God (James 4:4). For one thing, the world-system loves its own (John 15:19), so we should not be surprised at the world's hostility toward those who are not of the world. "Marvel not, my brethren, if the world hate you" (1 John 3:13). We learn, secondly, that the world hates Christ and therefore hates Christians. Only through faith in the shed blood of Jesus Christ is this horrible attitude of the individual unbeliever changed. A third standard of the world is its despising of humility. The pride of life is the way of the world-system (1 John 2:16). Humility is considered a weakness to the carnal minded. A fourth characteristic of the kosmos is its love of works versus its derogation of grace. It is an inherent trait of men to desire to do something in order to win God's approval or merit heaven.

And so today's lesson delves further into the matter of reversing the world's standard, especially in matters of honor, esteem, position, and greatness. The world would, if it could, change the key verse of our lesson (Matthew 20:26), and make it read: "If you want to be great don't act like a servant, show them who's boss!" You can see then the opposition to the believer's emphasis on loving God, not loving the world, stressing humbleness, and thanking God for His grace whereby we are saved through faith, and not of works (Ephesians 2:8-9).

B. BIBLICAL BACKGROUND

Perhaps a brief study of the relationship of the disciples with one another will help in better understanding our lesson. Several things may be noted. The disciples were unaware that Judas had been stealing money all along. John 12:6 uses an imperfect tense, indicating Judas "bore" or was helping himself to what was put in the money bag. Not only were they ignorant of the nature of a fellow disciple, but despite the times the Lord predicted His sufferings, they did not take to heart what He foretold. After the resurrection, they remembered.

Another issue, as we learn from today's lesson, is the fact of their disgruntlement concerning their positions. From Mark's Gospel, we learn that they had disputed among themselves who should be the greatest (Mark 9:34). They remained silent when the Lord inquired about their argument. Luke calls it "a strife among them" (Luke 22:24, literally, "love of contention"). It was at this point that Matthew's Gospel picks up the story that constitutes part of today's lesson. On an earlier occasion, Peter, James and John had been selected to be with the Lord there on the Mount of Transfiguration (Matthew 17:1). The other disciples were well aware of this inner circle. See Peter, James and John at the healing of the daughter of the synagogue ruler (Mark 5:37); see them again in the Garden of Gethsemane (Matthew 26:37). It could be that the prominence given them kindled the discussion about greatness. The point is, there was commotion, a stirring among them.

Things have not changed over the centuries. Some of us are still overly concerned about our positions in the various conventions, associations, conferences, and in the various clubs and auxiliaries of our local assemblies. We still need to learn, "Whoever wishes to be great among you must be your servant" (Matthew 20:26).

II. Exposition and Application of the Scripture

A. THE NECESSITY FOR CHILDLIKE FAITH
(Matthew 18:1-4)

AT the same time came the disciples unto Jesus, saying, Who is the greatest in the kingdom of heaven? And Jesus called a little child unto him, and set him in the midst of them, And said, Verily I say unto you, Except ye be converted, and become as little children, ye shall not enter into the kingdom of heaven. Whosoever therefore shall humble himself as this little child, the same is greatest in the kingdom of heaven.

Before the question that is asked in Matthew 18:1, there was a dispute among the disciples, according to Mark (9:34). Christ knew, of course, what was on their minds even before the question was broached. They were at first reluctant to tell the Lord about their argument, but finally the question came out. And the Lord interrupted their discussion with this revolutionary idea: "If anyone wants to be first, he shall be last of all, and servant of all." You and I probably would have rebuked them immediately for asking such a question. But the Lord does not. For, there is inherent in the question an element of faith. So He sought to transfer their concept of greatness from the applause of men to the approval of God.

He then proceeded to illustrate His principle. He placed a little child in their midst. Some commentators suggest it could have been a member of Peter's family. Christ told them: "You must be converted, and become as little children." The word for "converted" **(strepho)** means "turned." To turn one's self from one's course of conduct is to change one's mind (Thayer). In their case, it was to turn away from their path of selfish, ambitious rivalry, turn around and go in the opposite direction! For the path they were on could lead to pride, jealousy, and hatred, and eventually disrupt the band of disciples. What Christ commanded could be accomplished by the power of divine grace.

This child represented humility. In Judaism, the child had practically no public status, no influence at all. It owned nothing, and depended on others to supply its needs. A child cannot lend to a man's prestige or advance a man's career. But in making the child an object lesson, our Lord not only showed the importance of children, but demonstrated the believer's need for childlike simplicity. In coming to Christ when called, the child exhibited a trusting confidence, a ready submissiveness, a natural humbleness, an absence of pretentiousness. Likewise, the subjects of the Kingdom of Heaven are to manifest meekness and gentleness.

This passage (Matthew 18:1-6,10,14) is often used to teach parents and god-parents at Baby Blessings or Baby Dedication services that the Lord Jesus Christ loves children. Believing parents are encouraged to bring their babies to the Lord from the very beginning, and bathe them in prayer. See then the need for child-like faith in order to enter into the kingdom of heaven. The new birth is required (John 3:3ff), and for the new creature there is to be no concern for status or position. What counts is being "in Christ."

B. CHRIST PREDICTS HIS DEATH AND RESURRECTION
(Matthew 20:17-19)

And Jesus going up to Jerusalem took the twelve disciples apart in the way, and said unto them, Behold, we go up to Jerusalem; and the Son of man shall be betrayed unto the chief priests and unto the scribes, and they shall condemn him to death, and shall deliver him to the Gentiles to mock, and to scourge, and to crucify him: and the third day he shall rise again.

The lesson switches now to chapter 20 of Matthew. Note first of all that Christ again calls Himself the Son of Man. This was the designation He habitually used of Himself. It is clearly a Messianic title, taken we believe from Daniel 7:13. Use of this title teaches that He who came in humility—a representative Man—shall come again, but in power and great glory. In short, Son of Man emphasizes Christ's earthly ministry, the prediction of His Passion, and His return as King of all the earth.

And here for the third time the Lord predicts His Passion, His Sufferings. In His first prediction, (Matthew 16:21), the general statement is made that He must suffer much. In the second prediction, (Matthew 17:22), mention is made of betrayal. But here in Matthew 20:19, reference is made of mocking (which includes spitting on Him, Mark 10:34), crucifixion, scourging—all new details of His much suffering. Betrayed and condemned by Jews, He is beaten and cruci-fied by Gentiles. Use of the word "crucify" makes Matthew the only evangelist using this word in our Lord's predictions of His death. And for the first time, He indicates the part played by the Gentiles. The Jewish Sanhedrin had no author-ity to execute capital punishment, and so, after condemning Christ to die, would have to turn Him over to the Roman governor Pilate and to the Gentile soldiers under his command.

C. RESPONSE TO A MOTHER'S REQUEST
(Matthew 20:20-24)

Then came to him the mother of Zebedee's children with her sons, worship-ping him, and desiring a certain thing of him. And he said unto her, What wilt thou? She saith unto him, Grant that these my two sons may sit, the one on thy right hand, and the other on the left, in thy kingdom. But Jesus answered and said, Ye know not what ye ask. Are ye able to drink of the cup that I shall drink of, and to be baptized with the baptism that I am baptized with? They say unto him, We are able. And he saith unto them, Ye shall drink

indeed of my cup, and be baptized with the baptism that I am baptized with: but to sit on my right hand, and on my left, is not mine to give, but it shall be given to them for whom it is prepared of my Father. And when the ten heard it, they were moved with indignation against the two brethren.

This next episode further impresses us that the predictions of suffering and death made little headway in the lives of the disciples. They had not understood before or now in this third attempt to enlighten them. For in whatever time it took between verses 19 and 20, the mother of Zebedee's children came to Him, bringing her sons with her. We presume the father, Zebedee, was deceased. Mark (10:35) has James and John making the request, but from Matthew, we see they do so through their mother, Salome, and then later they join in the conversation.

Salome, we believe, is the sister of Mary the mother of our Lord, and she came worshiping Him, and desiring a certain thing of Him. He knew of course what she would request, but said to her, "What wilt thou?" ("what is it you desire?"). She replied: "command that these, my two sons, may sit, the one on thy right hand, and the other on the left, in thy kingdom." Here was a bold request born of faith that the Lord was indeed the Messiah, and His kingdom a reality.

But she, like the disciples, had missed the predicted intervening stage of suffering. They had in mind the setting up of His earthly kingdom in the not too distant future (indeed, "immediately," Luke 19:11). They thought of a crown but not of a cross, of glory but not suffering, of a throne but not an altar. They thus had no concept of the cup—the emblem of both good and bad, of joy and sorrow, in Hebrew speech. In Psalm 23:5, it is a good cup, a cup of blessings. In Psalm 11:6, the cup of the wicked contains snares, fire, brimstone, and an horrible tempest. In Matthew 20:22-23, it is indeed the cup of sorrow, the symbol of His sufferings. This cup contained mocking, scourging or whipping, beating, slapping, spitting, cursing, beard-plucking, pain and death! More than these, all our sins were there, and He who knew no sin would become sin!

Ignorant of what they asked, and confident of their ability to drink of the cup, the sons of thunder (Boanerges, Mark 3:17), the name given James and John, reply that they are able to drink of His cup and be baptized with His baptism. Alford sees the cup representing the inner, spiritual bitterness; and the baptism representing the outward persecution and testing. Christ could not command what they desired; God the Father would handle that. But, He predicted the sons of Zebedee shall indeed drink a bitter cup.

James was put to death with the sword (Acts 12:2), the first disciple to die for Christ. John lived a long life full of trouble, and was exiled on the isle of Patmos (Revelation 1:9). Naturally, when the other disciples heard about the request, they were moved with indignation (grieved, pained), greatly provoked! This demonstrates that they too had their minds set on holding positions of rank in an earthly kingdom. They themselves wanted what James and John wanted, and so they resented anyone attempting to put his bid in before the rest of them. How often do we follow the Christ for ulterior motives only to find that true commitment to Him demands our all, even the emptying of ourselves in order to be filled with His love.

D. PURPOSE OF THE SON OF MAN
(Matthew 20:25-28)

But Jesus called them unto him, and said, Ye know that the princes of the Gentiles exercise dominion over them, and they that are great exercise authority upon them. But it shall not be so among you: but whosoever will be great among you, let him be your minister; And whosoever will be chief among you, let him be your servant: Even as the Son of man came not to be ministered unto, but to minister, and to give his life a ransom for many.

In this final section of the lesson, we see three things Christ taught the disciples. First of all, the Kingdom of Heaven is not patterned after Gentile rule. Gentiles think of greatness in terms of domination, ruling, mastery, wielding power. This was not to be the method used by the disciples. They were not to "lord it over" others. Note the warning to pastors not to "lord it over" those whom God allots them: 1 Peter 5:3.

Second, true greatness, spiritual greatness, involves doing the work of a servant or minister **(diakonos)** in verse 26, and being chosen as chief which involves being a servant **(doulos)** or bond-slave in verse 27. Third: Jesus Christ Himself is the Model Servant. He came not to be served, but to serve **(diakoneo),** to minister. He came to give His life (soul) a ransom for many. We call this substitutionary, "in the stead of." The One who died was a ransom for the many. A ransom is a price paid for the deliverance of captives, for the release or loosing of those held in bondage. The price paid was His life, the shedding of His blood for us, in our place. His life was the cost of our redemption. See Him then as the Perfect Example of the lowly Servant. God became a Man in order to serve and to give!

III. Special Features

A. PRESERVING OUR HERITAGE

How does this lesson strike you—a descendant of slave foreparents? Do you still remember reading about the brutality, the breaking up of families, the exploitation, rape, enforced illiteracy, dehumanization, "deculturization," and murder of yesteryear? And now Jesus Christ comes along and demands that we be good, honest servants **(douloi),** and faithful ministers **(diakonoi).**

In a society that seeks to demean people of color, despise, look down their noses at, consider intellectually inferior—what are your thoughts about being humble? Does the attitude of the White majority destroy any desires of Blacks to be humble? Our lesson teaches that humility in serving others is the key to greatness in the kingdom of heaven.

Black believers must remember that Black unbelievers are still part of the world-system! One key to accepting this reversal of the world's standard is to keep our eyes on the Lord Jesus Christ. What He commands, He empowers to do. And though our position displeases those who are not Christians, let us follow Him who loved us and gave Himself for us.

B. A CONCLUDING WORD

To emphasize Christian character is automatically to go against the world's grain. And yet, this is the very issue with which we deal—the greatness of personal character shown by a life of service to others. The world appears unconcerned about the internal. A person who excels in the external is applauded and richly remunerated. He or she may be a scoundrel, an alcoholic, embezzler, etc., but considered great because of his or her position in society. There is no real positional greatness without inner character greatness. "It's better to be listed among the saints than among the stars" (MacDonald).

True ministry involves the desire to be great in the eyes of the Lord. To hear Him say, "well done!" is worth more than the accolades of men. Spiritual ambition is to serve wherever the Lord wants and to do whatever He directs. Thank God for the new birth that causes us to realize our personal inadequacy, but enables us to become more than adequate in Jesus Christ. We have found true freedom as slaves of the Lord Jesus Christ!

It is tragic indeed that we live in a society wherein we desire to be in control not only of the activities that characterize the daily routine of our lives, but our own final destiny as persons. This is not a new phenomenon within the human experience, but endemic to the very nature of our existence. We see this attitude displayed within the experience in the Garden of Eden when Adam and Eve elected to live according to their own rules by rejecting the explicit command of God in Whose image they were created and by Whose will they were to live. The permissive behavior that has characterized our culture is in blatant contradiction to the way in which the servants of God should live. The use of the word "slave" may not be one by which we desire to identify ourselves because of all of the historic evils associated with it. However, in the biblical sense of the word, slave means total and complete surrender to the will of the Master and that is what being Christian is all about. We have already proven that we self-destruct when we allow our own will to rule. Only as slaves to Christ are we really and fully free. And, those whom the Son makes free are truly liberated from all of that which condemns us to the bondage of the forces with which our strength is not equal.

HOME DAILY BIBLE READINGS
Week of January 17, 1999
The World Upside Down

Jan. 11 M. Matthew 18:1-4, A Child Among Them
Jan. 12 T. Matthew 20:17-28, Not to be Served, But to Serve
Jan. 13 W. John 13:1-5, I Have Set You an Example
Jan. 14 T. Romans 15:1-6, The Strong Ought to Help the Weak
Jan. 15 F. Genesis 32:3-12, I Am Not Worthy
Jan. 16 S. Proverbs 15:25-33, Humility Goes Before Honor
Jan. 17 S. Isaiah 57:15-21, Humble in Spirit

Forgiving Each Other

Adult Topic—Forgiving Each Other

.....

Youth Topic—What Is the Limit?
Children's Topic—Forgive Others

.....

Devotional Reading—Psalm 103:6-14
Background Scripture—Matthew 18:6-35
Print—Matthew 18:21-35

• • • • • • • • • • •

PRINTED SCRIPTURE

Matthew 18:21-35 (KJV)

21 Then came Peter to him, and said, Lord, how oft shall my brother sin against me, and I forgive him? till seven times?

22 Jesus saith unto him, I say not unto thee, Until seven times: but, Until seventy times seven.

23 Therefore is the kingdom of heaven likened unto a certain king, which would take account of his servants.

24 And when he had begun to reckon, one was brought unto him, which owed him ten thousand talents.

25 But forasmuch as he had not to pay, his lord commanded him to be sold, and his wife, and children, and all that he had, and payment to be made.

26 The servant therefore fell down, and worshipped him, saying, Lord, have patience with me, and I will pay thee all.

27 Then the lord of that servant

Matthew 18:21-35 (NRSV)

21 Then Peter came and said to him, "Lord, if another member of the church sins against me, how often should I forgive? As many as seven times?"

22 Jesus said to him, "Not seven times, but, I tell you, seventy-seven times.

23 "For this reason the kingdom of heaven may be compared to a king who wished to settle accounts with his slaves.

24 When he began the reckoning, one who owed him ten thousand talents was brought to him;

25 and, as he could not pay, his lord ordered him to be sold, together with his wife and children and all his possessions, and payment to be made.

26 So the slave fell on his knees before him, saying, 'Have patience with me, and I will pay you everything.'

27 And out of pity for him, the

was moved with compassion, and loosed him, and forgave him the debt.

28 But the same servant went out, and found one of his fellow-servants, which owed him an hundred pence: and he laid hands on him, and took him by the throat, saying, Pay me that thou owest.

29 And his fellowservant fell down at his feet, and besought him, saying, Have patience with me, and I will pay thee all.

30 And he would not: but went and cast him into prison, till he should pay the debt.

31 So when his fellowservants saw what was done, they were very sorry, and came and told unto their lord all that was done.

32 Then his lord, after that he had called him, said unto him, O thou wicked servant, I forgave thee all that debt, because thou desiredst me:

33 Shouldest not thou also have had compassion on thy fellowservant, even as I had pity on thee?

34 And his lord was wroth, and delivered him to the tormentors, till he should pay all that was due unto him.

35 So likewise shall my heavenly Father do also unto you, if ye from your hearts forgive not every one his brother their trespasses.

lord of that slave released him and forgave him the debt.

28 But that same slave, as he went out, came upon one of his fellow slaves who owed him a hundred denarii, and seizing him by the throat, he said, 'Pay what you owe.'

29 Then his fellow slave fell down and pleaded with him, 'Have patience with me, and I will pay you.'

30 But he refused; then he went and threw him into prison until he would pay the debt.

31 When his fellow slaves saw what had happened, they were greatly distressed, and they went and reported to their lord all that had taken place.

32 Then his lord summoned him and said to him, 'You wicked slave! I forgave you all that debt because you pleaded with me.

33 Should you not have had mercy on your fellow slave, as I had mercy on you?'

34 And in anger his lord handed him over to be tortured until he would pay his entire debt.

35 So my heavenly Father will also do to every one of you, if you do not forgive your brother or sister from your heart."

KEY VERSE

For if ye forgive men their trespasses, your heavenly Father will also forgive you: But if ye forgive not men their trespasses, neither will your Father forgive your trespasses.—Matthew 6:14-15

OBJECTIVES

After reading this lesson, the student will be better informed about:

1. The meaning of forgiveness;
2. The unsurpassed forgiveness bestowed by God; and,
3. The Christian's obligation to forgive others.

POINTS TO BE EMPHASIZED

Adult/Youth/Children
Key Verse: Matthew 6:14-15; Matthew 18:21-22 (Children)
Print: Matthew 18:21-35

—When Peter offered to forgive another church member seven times, Jesus told him to forgive seventy-seven times. (Matthew 18:21-22)
—Jesus used a parable to compare the kingdom of heaven to a king settling accounts with his slaves. (23)
—A slave who owed ten thousand talents asked for more time to pay and was forgiven his debt. (24-27)
—The forgiven slave later attacked and had imprisoned a fellow slave who failed to pay him a small debt. (28-30)
—When the king learned from the other slaves what the wicked slave had done, the king had him tortured until he paid his entire debt. (31-34)
—Jesus challenged His hearers to forgive others. (35)

TOPICAL OUTLINE OF THE LESSON

I. Introduction

A. Forgiveness: A Word Study
B. Biblical Background

II. Exposition and Application of the Scripture

A. The Savior's Answer (Matthew 18:21-22)
B. The Settling of an Account (Matthew 18:23-27)
C. The Servant's Attitude (Matthew 18:28-34)
D. The Savior's Admonition (Matthew 18:35)

III. Special Features

A. Preserving Our Heritage
B. A Concluding Word

I. Introduction

A. FORGIVENESS: A WORD STUDY

Forgiveness is one of those words you take for granted that you can define. You believe you know its meaning, then you discover you do not. We found there are at least three different Hebrew words, and at least three different Greek words translated "forgive" in the KJV of the Bible. In the Old Testament, the words **kaphar** and **salach** are used only in reference to God's forgiveness. "To err is human, to forgive, divine" (Alexander Pope).

Kaphar means to cover or shelter, and speaks of God's merciful disposition to cover the sinner (Psalm 78:38). **Salach** is the Hebrew word most often used; it means to send away or let go (2 Chronicles 7:14). The third Hebrew word is **nasa,** signifying to lift up, carry, take away. "The transition from the vicarious bearing of sin to the idea of pardon is very natural" (Girdlestone, Synonyms of the Old Testament, p.137). **Nasa** is used in the Divine sense, but also for human forgiveness ("pardon": 1 Samuel 15:25). Israel did not esteem forgiveness of enemies as a virtue. The Imprecatory (cursing) Psalm shows this, i.e., Psalm 69:22-28.

In the New Testament, one Greek word, **apoluo,** denotes to let go, dismiss, loose from, undo (Luke 6:37). A second word employed in the New Testament for forgiveness is **charizomai,** which means to show oneself gracious, kind, benevolent, and thus to grant forgiveness, pardon (Colossians 2:13, 3:13). A third Greek word **aphiemi,** indicates to send off, send away, thus to remit or let go a debt, by not demanding it, to forgive. It is used in our lesson for today (Matthew 18:21, 27, 32, 25). **"Aphesis** is the standing word by which forgiveness, or remission of sin, is expressed in the New Testament" (Trench, *Synonyms of the New Testament.* p. 114). In summary, to forgive means to cover, send away, let go, pardon, loose from, release, be gracious, and remit as a debt. You can see why it is said: "Forgiveness was not a pagan virtue" (ISBE).

B. BIBLICAL BACKGROUND

Our lesson begins with the words, "Then came Peter to Him" (Matthew 18:21). This suggests that the preceding verses (Matthew 18:15-20) are the origin or cause of Simon's inquiry. The Lord had taught what procedure to use with respect to discipline and forgiveness of personal injury of members of the assembly. Christ's explanation concerning offenders, and the offended saint's willingness to forgive, moved Peter to wonder just how far this forgiveness should extend for repeated or continuous offenses.

Our Lord had taught that when it comes to a personal offense, the following administrative steps should be taken: (1) forgive him with heartfelt forgiveness (2) go tell the offender personally (3) if he will not listen, take one or two others with you (4) if he still neglects to listen, take it to the church assembly (5) if still there is no repentance and confession or apology, let him be disciplined. Simon probably desired to follow the rules; concerned about the limit of his obligation to forgive, he came to the Lord.

II. Exposition and Application of the Scripture

A. THE SAVIOR'S ANSWER
(Matthew 18:21-22)

Then came Peter to him, and said, Lord, how oft shall my brother sin against me, and I forgive him? till seven times? Jesus saith unto him, I say not unto thee, Until seven times: but, Until seventy times seven.

Simon Peter may have spoken what the other disciples thought. The Lord had just dealt with forgiveness on a personal level, and how the entire assembly is affected by the personal relationships of its members. According to the Rabbinical (persons authorized to interpret Jewish law; Rabbis) rule, three times and no more was the extent of forgiveness. In the fourteen references to forgiveness in the teachings of the Rabbis, men were exhorted to forgive once, twice, but no more than three times. They justified this by their interpretation of Amos 1:3: "Thus saith the Lord: For three transgressions of Damascus, and for four, I will not turn away its punishment...."

Probably meaning to be generous, Simon Peter went beyond the Rabbinical measure, suggesting seven times, perhaps with Proverbs 24:16 in mind: "For a just man falleth seven times, and riseth up again...." But what may have seemed progress to Simon Peter was derailed by the Lord. With emphatic denial, Christ answered, "No I tell you, not till seven times, but until seventy times seven!"

This is not to be interpreted literally to mean forgiving 490 times! He sets no numerical standard. Actually, it is a prescription for that which is continuous, infinite, everlasting, indefinite. Alford sees a reference to Genesis 4:24. It is best to see our Lord teaching that we are to forgive all wrongs personally perpetrated against us. The seventy times seven is equivalent to always, and is put this way to contrast with Simon's limiting "seven." Furthermore, we want to avoid what appears to be a retaliatory listing of offenses. Unlimited forgiveness is the idea.

B. THE SETTLING OF AN ACCOUNT
(Matthew 18:23-27)

Therefore is the kingdom of heaven likened unto a certain king, which would take account of his servants. And when he had begun to reckon, one was brought unto him, which owed him ten thousand talents. But forasmuch as he had not to pay, his lord commanded him to be sold, and his wife, and children, and all that he had, and payment to be made. The servant therefore fell down, and worshipped him, saying, Lord, have patience with me, and I will pay thee all. Then the lord of that servant was moved with compassion, and loosed him, and forgave him the debt.

At this juncture, Christ tells the parable of the Unforgiving Servant to illustrate His teaching concerning unlimited forgiveness. Parables are but illustrations, and are not to be pushed in every detail. This warning needs to be often repeated because preachers and Sunday school teachers sometimes forget the principle the parable illustrates, and they expand the parable to the point that it no longer serves as "something thrown alongside of" **(paraballo)** for the sake of comparison.

In the kingdom of heaven unlimited forgiveness is the law. The kingdom is likened unto a certain king who desired to settle accounts with his servants. "This is the first of the parables in which God appears as King. We are the servants with whom He takes account" (Trench, *Parables,* p. 152). Auditing quickly revealed one of the servants owed the king ten thousand talents. It is obvious that to owe such an amount points to the high ranking of the servant, a man highly trusted. He may have been a chief officer, or administrator of the royal treasury. Rather than attempt to find out what a talent represents, we conclude the amount involved was a tremendous sum. For we agree that "exact calculations are idle or pedantic" *(Expositor's),* for the values of talents varied at different times. They were of different metallic content (gold, silver). Whatever the worth of a talent, the total amount was beyond the official's ever dreaming of paying back. It was an insurmountable debt, equivalent to millions of dollars in our present society.

Now, the servant was brought to the king. He never would have come on his own. No one seeks God! This man had nothing with which to pay back the money he had stolen; he had no Swiss bank account. Who knows how he had squandered the stolen funds? It was the custom in those days to sell the wife and children into slavery to help pay debts. Among the Jews, under Moses, however, this law had been softened by the year of Jubilee in which slaves were set free. But in this parable, Oriental despotism is more harsh, and the man and his family are commanded to be sold. They are considered to be no more than property or chattel.

At this point, the servant fell down on his knees and face, kissed the feet of his lord, and begged for more time. What he promised to do was impossible to fulfill, but in the anguish and fear of the moment, the heart will say anything! "Give me time, have patience with me, and I will pay it back!" We emphasize the ridiculous aspect of this promise in order to show the immensity of his debt. It is essential to understand that he could not repay what he owed, no matter what he promised. We are to see in this servant our own total bankruptcy before God. Indeed, with us, only one sin would be impossible to pay for; think of all the evils we commit in a lifetime—sins of commission and omission, of thought and deed. Well, in mercy and great compassion, the king decided the best course of action was to loose him, and forgive him the debt. And so he did.

C. THE SERVANT'S ATTITUDE
(Matthew 18:28-34)

But the same servant went out, and found one of his fellowservants, which owed him an hundred pence: and he laid hands on him, and took him by the throat, saying, Pay me that thou owest. And his fellowservant fell down at his feet, and besought him, saying, Have patience with me, and I will pay thee all. And he would not: but went and cast him into prison, till he should

pay the debt. So when his fellowservants saw what was done, they were very sorry, and came and told unto their lord all that was done. Then his lord, after that he had called him, said unto him, O thou wicked servant, I forgave thee all that debt, because thou desiredst me: Shouldest not thou also have had compassion on thy fellowservant, even as I had pity on thee? And his lord was wroth, and delivered him to the tormentors, till he should pay all that was due unto him.

Now having been forgiven of such a great debt, this servant showed how rotten he really was. Instead of expressing gratitude to God for the pity shown him by the king, this servant went out and found a fellow servant who owed him some money. Strange, isn't it? that the forgiveness shown him did not change his heart. After all, he did not have to remain in jail, but was freed; his debt was totally wiped out; and evidently he remained in his official position. Now that's mercy! But in no way was his character improved. He found a fellow servant who owed him an hundred denarii (small silver coins).

Note the comparison between the talent and the denarius; compared to the talent, the denarius was an insignificant amount. It is like comparing a copper penny with a thousand dollar bill, not to mention the amounts of one hundred denarii to ten thousand talents. We see how little we sin against each other, but how much we sin against God. How trifling our transgressions against each other, how vast our transgressions against God! Seizing the man by the throat, he throttled him without mercy, and demanded: "Pay me what you owe me!" Was the sum too small to be announced?

The fellow servant fell at the man's feet, begged him saying: "Have patience with me, and I will pay thee all." In the original language, the words the first servant spoke to the king (v. 26) are the same words this fellow servant spoke (v. 29), except the word "all" is omitted in the former. One wonders what went through the mind of the man who heard the same words he had spoken to the king. Evidently, there was no remembrance of the similarity of pleas, for he ignored the fellow servant's cry for mercy, and cast him into prison till he should pay the debt. How it would be possible to pay off a debt while in prison is not mentioned.

News travels fast. When the other workers heard and saw what happened, they were grieved. Their sorrow was not so much based on sympathy as it was upon annoyance at the merciless behavior of the one who had obtained mercy. And so, they came and told the king what had transpired. The lord of the servants called in the unforgiving man, and said, "O thou wicked servant!" Dishonesty with the money could be overlooked, but the inhumanity shown could not. It is no wonder the king called him "wicked." The Greek word used **(poneros)** speaks of the active working out of evil; the positive activity of evil. This evil is not content unless it corrupts others (Proverbs 4:16). It refers to one with an evil nature. The king charged him with ingratitude and cruelty, because having received mercy, he showed no mercy.

Whereas the other servants showed sorrow, the king expressed anger **(orge).**

He was wroth—internally stirred to anger, provoked, agitated. The Greek language has another word for anger (thumos) which signifies a sudden burst, a flare-up, a boiling up and soon subsiding again (Thayer). However, the word used here to describe the king's anger denotes an indignation which has arisen gradually, and become more settled. We would call it "the slow burn." It is "an abiding and settled habit of mind with the purpose of revenge" (Trench, *Synonyms*). And so, the king delivered the unforgiving servant into the hands of the tormentors (KJV), torturers (NKJV, NASB), to the jailers (RSV), to the jailers to be tortured (NIV). The original word used here is defined as "one who elicits the truth by the use of the rack, an inquisitor," used of a jailer in Matthew 18:34 because the business of torturing was also assigned to him (Thayer). James 2:13 states: "For he shall have judgment without mercy, that hath shown no mercy...." Now the torment till he should pay all that was due unto the king is not a reference to what is called Purgatory, although the Roman Catholic Church has made use of this verse (and Matthew 5:26) to support their teaching. There is no such intermediate place of suffering for believers to have their failings atoned for in order to be admitted to heaven! Jesus Christ has purged all of our sins already, and the genuine Christian upon death is considered to be with the Lord. As harsh as Matthew 18:34 sounds, we would agree with Trench (*Parables,* p. 165) that the proverbial phrase signifies the offender shall taste of the extreme rigor of the law, and shall experience justice without mercy (cf. *Scofield Bible* note on Matthew 18:34).

D. THE SAVIOR'S ADMONITION
(Matthew 18:35)

So likewise shall my heavenly Father do also unto you, if ye from your hearts forgive not every one his brother their trespasses.

Here our Lord ties the parable together. Even if we could pay for the sins committed against other human beings, the amount paid would be absolutely insignificant compared to that owed God for our sins against Him. Our Heavenly Father hates mercilessness! Our forgiveness of one another is not to be a sham, phony, lip service, but thoroughgoing, real, genuine, unreserved, unlimited, the definite inclination of the heart. May we take this admonition, this warning to heart, and act accordingly.

II. Special Features

A. PRESERVING OUR HERITAGE

When Christians are deeply involved in the life of the local assembly, there is an extraordinary degree of personal fellowship, exchange of thought, feelings, and communication. Naturally, in such relationships, in such dealings within a congregation, there are many opportunities for hard feelings, misunderstandings, or what is called, implosion (the act or action of bringing to or as if to a center). This is especially true in the life of Black American Christians. Church life means more to us, it appears, than it means to the average White American Christian. It is imperative therefore that we Saints of Color obey the imperative, "Be kind to one another, tenderhearted, forgiving one another, as God in Christ forgave you" (Ephesians 4:32, RSV).

B. A CONCLUDING WORD

The thought occurred that there is little happening in the world today that would encourage us to exercise a spirit of forgiveness. Our newspapers are full of evidence of violence, racism, crime; the movies and television shows, even the language we hear—all manifest scenarios of revenge, vengeance, retaliation, "getting even," payback, etc. This Sunday school lesson is definitely out of kilter, out of line, incongruous with the times! And yet, what the Lord requires of us, He empowers us to do. May we ever remember that the God of mercy who has forgiven us an astronomical number of sins against Him commands that we in mercy forgive those who trespass against us—not just seven times, but seventy times seven!

In a larger sense, forgiveness is not only the spiritually correct thing to do, but the failure to forgive can impact our interpersonal relationships with those persons against whom we hold no grudge. Whereas we are made of one blood to dwell upon the face of the earth, oneness means the free interplay of emotions and feelings as we interact within the arena of social involvement. The failure to forgive becomes a self-imposed limitation to our human interactions and cuts us off from the very persons to whom we belong. As such, the unforgiving spirit circumvents the development of our full potential as humans who are obliged to live in community with each other. If the failure to forgive alienates us from those to whom we belong, how much more are we separated from the God Who loves us and Whose forgiveness of us is predicated upon our capacity to forgive others? We fail to understand the seriousness of the need to be forgiven if we have the inability to demonstrate a forgiving attitude toward others.

HOME DAILY BIBLE READINGS
Week of January 24, 1999
Forgiving Each Other

Jan. 18 M. Matthew 18:6-14, No Stumbling Blocks!
Jan. 19 T. Matthew 18:15-20, Dealing With Church Members
Jan. 20 W. Matthew 18:21-35, How Often Must I Forgive?
Jan. 21 T. Galatians 6:1-5, Restore Transgressors!
Jan. 22 F. Ephesians 4:25-32, Be Kind...Tenderhearted, Forgiving
Jan. 23 S. Psalm 103:6-14, God Forgives; So Should We
Jan. 24 S. Hebrews 10:11-25, I Will Remember...Their Sins No More

The Gospel Has No Boundaries

Adult Topic—Good News for Everyone

....

Youth Topic—All Are Welcome
Children's Topic—Tell Others About Jesus

.....

Devotional Reading—Psalm 96:1-13
Background Scripture—Acts 17:16-34
Print—Acts 17:22-34

• • • • • • • • • • • •

PRINTED SCRIPTURE

Acts 17:22-34 (KJV)

22 Then Paul stood in the midst of Mars' hill, and said, Ye men of Athens, I perceive that in all things ye are too superstitious.

23 For as I passed by, and beheld your devotions, I found an altar with this inscription, TO THE UNKNOWN GOD. Whom therefore ye ignorantly worship, him declare I unto you.

24 God that made the world and all things therein, seeing that he is Lord of heaven and earth, dwelleth not in temples made with hands;

25 Neither is worshipped with men's hands, as though he needed any thing, seeing he giveth to all life, and breath, and all things;

26 And hath made of one blood all nations of men for to dwell on all the face of the earth, and hath determined the times before appointed, and the bounds of their habitation;

27 That they should seek the Lord, if haply they might feel after

Acts 17:22-34 (NRSV)

22 Then Paul stood in front of the Areopagus and said, "Athenians, I see how extremely religious you are in every way.

23 For as I went through the city and looked carefully at the objects of your worship, I found among them an altar with the inscription, 'To an unknown god.' What therefore you worship as unknown, this I proclaim to you.

24 The God who made the world and everything in it, he who is Lord of heaven and earth, does not live in shrines made by human hands,

25 nor is he served by human hands, as though he needed anything, since he himself gives to all mortals life and breath and all things.

26 From one ancestor he made all nations to inhabit the whole earth, and he allotted the times of their existence and the boundaries of the places where they would live,

him, and find him, though he be not far from every one of us:

28 For in him we live, and move, and have our being; as certain also of your own poets have said, For we are also his offspring.

29 Forasmuch then as we are the offspring of God, we ought not to think that the Godhead is like unto gold, or silver, or stone, graven by art and man's device.

30 And the times of this ignorance God winked at; but now commandeth all men every where to repent:

31 Because he hath appointed a day, in the which he will judge the world in righteousness by that man whom he hath ordained; whereof he hath given assurance unto all men, in that he hath raised him from the dead.

32 And when they heard of the resurrection of the dead, some mocked: and others said, We will hear thee again of this matter.

33 So Paul departed from among them.

34 Howbeit certain men clave unto him, and believed: among the which was Dionysius the Areopagite, and a woman named Damaris, and others with them.

27 so that they would search for God and perhaps grope for him and find him—though indeed he is not far from each one of us.

28 For 'In him we live and move and have our being'; as even some of your own poets have said, 'For we too are his offspring.'

29 Since we are God's offspring, we ought not to think that the deity is like gold, or silver, or stone, an image formed by the art and imagination of mortals.

30 While God has overlooked the times of human ignorance, now he commands all people everywhere to repent,

31 because he has fixed a day on which he will have the world judged in righteousness by a man whom he has appointed, and of this he has given assurance to all by raising him from the dead."

32 When they heard of the resurrection of the dead, some scoffed; but others said, "We will hear you again about this."

33 At that point Paul left them.

34 But some of them joined him and became believers, including Dionysius the Areopagite and a woman named Damaris, and others with them.

KEY VERSE

And the times of this ignorance God winked at; but now commandeth all men every where to repent: Because he hath appointed a day, in the which he will judge the world in righteousness by that man whom he hath ordained; whereof he hath given assurance unto all men, in that he hath raised him from the dead.—Acts 17:30-31

OBJECTIVES

After reading this lesson, the student should have a better understanding of:

1. Two philosophies existing in Paul's day in Athens;
2. The place of God the Creator in religion;
3. The role played by the resurrection of Jesus Christ; and,
4. The guarantee of coming judgment.

POINTS TO BE EMPHASIZED

Adult/Youth/Children

Key Verse: Acts 17:30-31; Acts 17:30 (Children)
Print: Acts 17:22-34

—Paul stood before the Areogpagus and told the Athenians that he had observed how religious they were, that they even had an altar to an unknown god, and that Paul would tell them about that god. (22-23)

—This unknown God, Paul said, made the world and does not live in shrines made by human hands nor does he need to be served by human hands. (24-25)

—Paul declared that God made all nationalities and determined the times and places of their existence so they would search for God. (26-27)

—God commanded all people to repent because he has fixed a day on which Christ will come to judge the world. (28-31)

—Paul stated that because we are God's offspring, we ought not to think of God as a material image. (29)

—Some listeners scoffed at Paul's words about Jesus' resurrection, others asked to hear more on the matter, and still others believe. (32-34)

(NOTE: Use KJV Scripture for Adults; NRSV Scripture for Youth and Children)

TOPICAL OUTLINE OF THE LESSON

I. Introduction

    A. Glossary of Terms
    B. Biblical Background

II. Exposition and Application of the Scripture

    A. The Religious Taught (Acts 17:22-23)
    B. The Creator Described (Acts 17-24-29)
    C. The Judgment Guaranteed (Acts 17:30-31)
    D. The Resurrection Mocked (Acts 17:32-34)

III. Special Features

    A. Preserving Our Heritage
    B. A Concluding Word

I. Introduction

A. A GLOSSARY OF TERMS

In order to better understand this lesson, it is necessary to study the names of certain philosophical groups and individuals named in the Book of Acts. Areopagus Ares was the god of war in Greek mythology; **pagos** means a hill. And since Mars was the Roman god resembling Ares, we have the translation, Mars' Hill. So see the Areopagus as a place, a rocky height in the city of Athens. Because this was the meeting place of the members of the highest court of Athens, it was called the Areopagus. The court saw to it that laws in force were observed and executed by the properly constituted authorities.

Damaris is the name of a female Christian of Athens, converted under Paul's preaching. She probably was not the wife of Dionysius; it is more likely her name was singled out to indicate some personal or social distinction. Dionysius was one of the few Athenians converted by Paul. We know nothing more about him (Acts 17:34).

Epicureans: Followers of Epicurus (C. 341 B.C. to 270 B.C.), a philosopher born in Samos, an island of Greece. They believed the chief aim of life was happiness or pleasure (primarily of the mind, rather than pleasures of the body). "Pleasure means the absence of pain in the body and trouble in the soul." Evil is defined as that which gives pain. Death is the end of all things: "Eat, drink, and be merry, for tomorrow we die!"

Stocis: a school of Greek philosophy founded at Athens about 294 B.C. by Zeno (c. 336-264 B.C.), a native of a Greek colony in Cyprus. The name was derived from the painted porch at Athens, where the founders of the school first lectured (**stoa** means porch or portico). They believed unruffled peace of mind could be attained by uniting the individual with the divine principle of the universe. Some believed that at death the soul is absorbed again into that from which it sprang. They were pantheists, identifying Deity with the various forces and workings of nature: that is to say, God and the universe are the same. You can easily see why these groups resisted Paul's gospel (Acts 17:32).

B. BIBLICAL BACKGROUND

In chapter 17, we find the apostle Paul and company on their Second Missionary Journey (Acts 15:36-18:22). After the harrowing experience in Philippi, Paul visited Thessalonica, and founded a church there. A riot was started in that city by the Jews, and Paul and Silas were forced to leave undercover by night to Berea. However, the Jews followed the Christians there too, stirred up the people, and once again Paul had to flee. While Silas and Timothy remained there at Berea, Paul was brought to Athens.

Our lesson begins here, as Paul waited for Silas and Timothy to come to Athens. As the apostle traveled through the city, and observed that the populace was totally given over to idolatry, his spirit was provoked. He could not restrain himself, and so disputed with the Jews and other religious persons that he met daily in the **agora** (marketplace), "the most frequented part of a city or village" (Thayer). Two of the groups he met were philosophers of the Epicureans and of the Stocis. In Acts 17:18, they called Paul a "Babbler" (KJV, NKJV, RSV, NIV). Study of the word **(spermologos)** proves very interesting. Literally, the word means "seed-picker."

The paraphrasers and translators have had a field day with this word; for example: ignorant showoff (TEV); he's a dreamer (LB); whatever does the fellow mean with his scraps of learning (Moffatt); what is this blabber with his scrap-picked learning trying to say (Amplified); this idle babbler—one who makes his living by picking up scraps (NASB); what is this cock sparrow trying to say? (JBP); what can this charlatan be trying to say (NEB); what would this seed-picker say (Lenski). Goodspeed called him a ragpicker (incorrect, says Lenski).

All of this suggests that we have a bit of Athenian slang applied to a man picking up an idea here and there and passing these ideas on without a real knowledge of their meaning. What he says amounts to nothing!!! Their curiosity was piqued, and as the Lord would have it, the door was opened for Paul to preach "strange things" to their ears. Preach Jesus Christ, crucified, buried, risen, and coming again—and hear what the worldly philosophers have to say about you!

II. Exposition and Application of the Scripture

A. THE RELIGIOUS TAUGHT
   (Acts 17:22-23)

Then Paul stood in the midst of Mars' hill, and said, Ye men of Athens, I preceive that in all things ye are too superstitious. For as I passed by, and beheld your devotions, I found an altar with this inscription, TO THE UNKNOWN GOD. Whom therefore ye ignorantly worship, him declare I unto you.

Our lesson begins with Paul standing in the midst of the members of the Areopagus. Emphasis is not on the place, but on the identification of those present—the Areopagites! As mentioned earlier in the lesson, Mars' Hill is the same word translated "Areopagus" (verse 19). And so, there in the midst of the council, Paul boldly said to the Gentile philosophers: "Men of Athens! I perceive that in all things you are very religious."

The KJV says, "ye are too superstitious." Literally, the long Greek word **(deisidaimonesterous)** rendered "superstitious" means "fearing the deities." Used in a bad sense, it means superstitious, a Latin term meaning "a standing over something in amazement and awe." Thus in this sense, it means excessive fear, a worship based on fear or ignorance. This is the point of view of the KJV, but it appears unlikely that Paul would immediately attack the Athenians this way. We prefer then the good sense of the word—a reverencing god, pious, religious. The word may mean: (1) "a pious attitude towards the gods," i.e., "religion," or (2) "excessive fear of them" (Kittel: 2:20, TDNT). As used here in Acts 17:22,

Paul points to their piety. He continued: "Wherever I looked, I saw evidence of your religiousness. I observed accurately, again and again; I surveyed (considered well) the objects of your worship, as I passed by." As Paul walked about the city, he saw the numerous statues, idols and temples of the Athenians. It is said there were more idol statues in Athens than there were men! Paul even found an altar with the engraving: TO THE UNKNOWN GOD. Evidently the zealous citizens of Athens had no desire to leave out any god.

The apostle went on to say that there was indeed One whom they did not know, and he would declare Him to them! Their confession of ignorance was recognized by Paul as proof of an unsatisfied hunger in their hearts, a real yearning for a deeper knowledge of Deity. By this inscription, we see the Athenians believed in the existence of God, but were ignorant of Him.

B. THE CREATOR DESCRIBED
   (Acts 17:24-29)

God that made the world and all things therein, seeing that he is Lord of heaven and earth, dwelleth not in temples made with hands; Neither is worshipped with men's hands, as though he needed any thing, seeing he giveth to all life, and breath, and all things; And hath made of one blood all nations of men for to dwell on all the face of the earth, and hath determined the times before appointed, and the bounds of their habitation; That they should seek the Lord, if haply they might feel after him, and find him, though he be not far from every one of us: For in him we live, and move, and have our being; as certain also of your own poets have said, For we are also his offspring. Forasmuch then as we are the offspring of God, we ought not to think that the Godhead is like unto gold, or silver, or stone, graven by art and man's device.

Paul's first step was to talk about God the Creator. The One unknown to the Athenians was known to Paul. They were religious, but lost. God the Creator was not known to them. Here indeed was a good place for Paul to begin. Even today, missionaries tell us that it is a good procedure to begin to teach pagans about the Creator. Perhaps this is one of the reasons Satan uses the theory of Evolution so extensively. Evolution seeks to undermine the Biblical concept of creation, and thus do away with the Creator, and any responsibility to Him. It comes to mind also, that with so much said in the Bible about God the Creator, we seldom hear sermons on this great theme preached in our churches. We know, of course, that "the earth is the LORD'S, and the fulness thereof; the world, and they that dwell therein" (Psalm 24:1). We know that "all things were made by Him; and without Him was not any thing made that was made" (John 1:3). We know that "all things were created by Him, and for Him: and He is before all things, and by Him all things consist" (Colossians 1:16-17).

Paul's point is: if God is Creator, why would He need men to erect a temple for Him to live in? "The heaven and heaven of heavens cannot contain" God (1 Kings 8:27). "The heaven is my throne, and the earth is my footstool: where is the house that ye build unto me? and where is the place of my rest?" (Isaiah 66:1;

Acts 7:48-50). Not only does the Creator not reside in man-made temples, but neither is He worshiped with the hands of men. Indeed, what shall we humans give God? All we have was given to us (1 Corinthians 4:7). He is not poor. Every beast of the forest is His, and the cattle upon a thousand hills. The fowls of the air, the animals in the field, the fish in the sea—all are His.

The silver and the gold are His (Psalm 50:8-15; Haggai 2:8). Furthermore, even the breath that all creatures breathe is the gift of God. If He takes away our breath, we die (Psalm 104:29). In His hand is the soul of every living thing, and the breath of all mankind (Job 12:10). God the Creator made of one—one man, one piece of dirt, one blood (Though not in the best manuscripts)—all nations of men to dwell on this earth. During the time of Black Slavery in the United States, there arose a theory called POLYGENESIS, the idea that God made not just one Adam and then one Eve, but made many human beings all at the same time, scattered all over the world. This theory was invented by White racists so that they could make some human beings (?) inherently inferior to themselves! We have more to say about Acts 17:26 in the Special Features section.

In Acts 17:27, the apostle quotes from the writings of one of the Gentile poets named Epimenides of Crete: "For in him we live and move and have our being." Titus 1:12 also contains a quote from Epimenides. From other writers, Aratus of Cilicia, and the Greek Stoic, Cleanthes (c. 300-232 B.C.) come the words, "For we are also his offspring." Paul shows that from their own poets there existed: (1) a concept of a Creator who needed nothing that men could give, and (2) the fact that the Creator is the source of all life. The Creator's goodness demonstrated in the world should lead men to seek God (Romans 1:20). And as the offspring (geons means race) of God, we are more than gold or silver statues, or figures carved out of wood, or sculpted from stone. If He created us, is He not then greater than we are? Shall the creature then create the Creator? What folly that men should desire to make God in man's own image!

C. THE JUDGMENT GUARANTEED
(Acts 17:30-31)

And the times of this ignorance God winked at; but now commandeth all men every where to repent: Because he hath appointed a day, in the which he will judge the world in righteousness by that man whom he hath ordained; whereof he hath given assurance unto all men, in that he hath raised him from the dead.

A merciful God has "winked at," overlooked, passed over sins committed in former times. In other words, men were not immediately struck down for the evils committed. But now Christ has come, and all men everywhere are commanded to repent—change their minds with respect to sin, to God, to self. Such repentance is more than sorrow for sin, more than sorry they did wrong, more than sorry they were caught. True repentance (Matthew 21:28-29) is needed before coming to the Lord in genuine, believing faith. No one can believe with the heart without a thorough repentance or change of mind and attitude.

Men ought to repent now, for God the Father who raised His Son from the dead has appointed a day when He will judge the world in righteousness. This judgment will take place by and through Jesus Christ. How do we know there will be such a judgment? By the fact the Father has raised the Judge from the dead. In other words, just as sure as Jesus Christ is alive, there will be a judgment of the world in righteousness. Repent now! and be cleared of all charges. Repent now! and escape the judgment which is sure to come. Repent now! is the urgent message of redemption.

D. THE RESURRECTION MOCKED
(Acts 17:32-34).

And when they heard of the resurrection of the dead, some mocked: and others said, We will hear thee again of this matter. So Paul departed from among them. Howbeit certain men clave unto him, and believed: among the which was Dionysius the Areopagite, and a woman named Damaris, and others with them.

When the philosophers heard of the resurrection of the dead, some of them mocked (Jested, jeered, derided, scoffed). This was not the first or last time the resurrection was denied or ridiculed. The Sadducees said there was no resurrection (Matthew 22:23-33). In First Corinthians 15, Paul answered those who sought to refute the resurrection. And in Second Timothy 2:17-18, Hymenaeus and Philetus "erred, saying that the resurrection" was past already.

Others of Paul's audience were desirous of further discussion, and dismissed Paul with their promise to hear him again on this matter. And so, the apostle left them. In spite of the rejection of the gospel by the majority present, there were some converts, including Dionysius, the Areopagite, and Damaris, and others. God's Word has no boundaries; it accomplishes its purpose.

III. Special Features

A. PRESERVING OUR HERITAGE

Acts 17:26 is a verse that has been much maligned by segregationists. The first part of the verse teaches that if we trace our roots back as far as we can go, we run smack dab into Adam. We have a common ancestry; the unity of the human race is taught here. From the second half of this Scripture, we learn that God has allotted to each nation both time and place of their existence. Yet, some racists would use this verse to forbid interracial marriage, or any integration whatever. It actually teaches that the Creator is in charge of determining what people of what country shall occupy what land when!

The God of the Bible puts people wherever He wants them! (Deuteronomy 32:8). Reduce the racists' argument to absurdity, and all of the White Americans would return to Europe, the recent influx of Orientals would return to Asia; and all Black Americans would return to Africa. This latter step would make certain

Whites happy, but if they are incarcerated in Europe, a Black-free America would do them no good. Only the native American would be here in the land of the free and the home of the brave.

B. A CONCLUDING WORD

Some scholars believe Paul's intellectual approach was the cause for so little fruit. They say Paul tried to be philosophical instead of preaching the simple gospel, and consequently only "certain men joined him, and believed" (Acts 17:34). This really is not a valid criticism; this was no "wrong approach." Paul's main emphasis was the physical, bodily resurrection of Jesus Christ. But this message was most unpalatable to the philosophers. It was the truth that turned them away, not Paul's "philosophical preaching."

While philosophical preaching has its place within the Christian community, we must look at it for what it is. Philosophy is an intellectual endeavor whose function is to purify the faith from all of those ideas that are in contradiction to the basic tenets of beliefs and to hold at bay ideas that are in fact a corruption of that which the Christ proclaimed. The church is in need of theologians who can stand shoulder to shoulder with those intellectuals who believe that the mind can grasp the totality of reality. But persons who are lost cannot be won to the Christ by the power of the mind alone as total corruption is the essence of the human predicament. While by searching we cannot by find God, it is in searching that God finds us regardless of our personal and communal condition as long as there is the sensitivity which affirms that apart from Jesus Christ the privation of the soul is constant and persistent. We need theologians and religious philosophers to stand as watchmen on the wall whose task it is to serve as guardians of the faith.

From the standpoint of winning persons for Christ, there is no substitute for that exemplary life that proclaims to the world that the death and resurrection of Jesus as the Christ has changed forever the way one looks at the world as well as at himself or herself. We can learn well from Paul's experience through his own words. After the Mars' Hill fiasco, Paul determined to know nothing among them but Jesus Christ and Him crucified. To accept the fact that Jesus Christ died for us is to embrace the full reality that we must "live for Him."

HOME DAILY BIBLE READINGS
Week of January 31, 1999
The Gospel Has No Boundaries

Jan. 25 M. Acts 17:16-34, God...Commands All People Everywhere to Repent
Jan. 26 T. Acts 10:1-8, Cornelius Is Instructed By an Angel
Jan. 27 W. Acts 10:9-16, Peter's Vision
Jan. 28 T. Acts 10:17-23a, Peter Welcomes the People From Cornelius
Jan. 29 F. Acts 10:23b-33, No One is Profane or Unclean
Jan. 30 S. Acts 10:34-48, God Shows No Partiality
Jan. 31 S. Romans 1:8-17, Salvation Is for Everyone

Civic Responsibility

Children's Unit III. Helps for Daily Living—Part 2
Adult Topic—Showing Honor, Living Honorably
.....
Youth Topic—Being Good Citizens
Children's Topic— Obey the Law
.....
Devotional Reading—Psalm 15:1-5
Background Scripture—Romans 12:9-13:14
Print—Romans 13

PRINTED SCRIPTURE

Romans 13 (KJV)

LET every soul be subject unto the higher powers. For there is no power but of God: the powers that be are ordained of God.

2 Whosoever therefore resisteth the power, resisteth the ordinance of God: and they that resist shall receive to themselves damnation.

3 For rulers are not a terror to good works, but to the evil. Wilt thou then not be afraid of the power? do that which is good, and thou shalt have praise of the same:

4 For he is the minister of God to thee for good. But if thou do that which is evil, be afraid; for he beareth not the sword in vain: for he is the minister of God, a revenger to execute wrath upon him that doeth evil.

5 Wherefore ye must needs be subject, not only for wrath, but also for conscience sake.

6 For for this cause pay ye tribute also: for they are God's minis-

Romans 13 (NRSV)

LET EVERY person be subject to the governing authorities; for there is no authority except from God, and those authorities that exist have been instituted by God.

2 Therefore whoever resists authority resists what God has appointed, and those who resist will incur judgment.

3 For rulers are not a terror to good conduct, but to bad. Do you wish to have no fear of the authority? Then do what is good, and you will receive its approval;

4 for it is God's servant for your good. But if you do what is wrong, you should be afraid, for the authority does not bear the sword in vain! It is the servant of God to execute wrath on the wrongdoer.

5 Therefore one must be subject, not only because of wrath but also because of conscience.

6 For the same reason you also pay taxes, for the authorities are

ters, attending continually upon this very thing.

7 Render therefore to all their dues: tribute to whom tribute is due; custom to whom custom; fear to whom fear; honour to whom honour.

8 Owe no man any thing, but to love one another: for he that loveth another hath fulfilled the law.

9 For this, Thou shalt not commit adultery, Thou shalt not kill, Thou shalt not steal, Thou shalt not bear false witness, Thou shalt not covet; and if there be any other commandment, it is briefly comprehended in this saying, namely, Thou shalt love thy neighbour as thyself.

10 Love worketh no ill to his neighbour: therefore love is the fulfilling of the law.

11 And that, knowing the time, that now it is high time to awake out of sleep: for now is our salvation nearer than when we believed.

12 The night is far spent, the day is at hand: let us therefore cast off the works of darkness, and let us put on the armour of light.

13 Let us walk honestly, as in the day; not in rioting and drunkenness, not in chambering and wantonness, not in strife and envying.

14 But put ye on the Lord Jesus Christ, and make not provision for the flesh, to fulfil the lusts thereof.

God's servants, busy with this very thing.

7 Pay to all what is due them—taxes to whom taxes are due, revenue to whom revenue is due, respect to whom respect is due, honor to whom honor is due.

8 Owe no one anything, except to love one another; for the one who loves another has fulfilled the law.

9 The commandments, "You shall not commit adultery; You shall not murder; You shall not steal; You shall not covet"; and any other commandment, are summed up in this word, "Love your neighbor as yourself."

10 Love does no wrong to a neighbor; therefore, love is the fulfilling of the law.

11 Besides this, you know what time it is, how it is now the moment for you to wake from sleep. For salvation is nearer to us now than when we became believers;

12 the night is far gone, the day is near. Let us then lay aside the works of darkness and put on the armor of light;

13 let us live honorably as in the day, not in reveling and drunkenness, not in debauchery and licentiousness, not in quarreling and jealousy.

14 Instead, put on the Lord Jesus Christ, and make no provision for the flesh, to gratify its desires.

KEY VERSE

LET every soul be subject unto the higher powers. For there is no power but of God: the powers that be are ordained of God.—Romans 13:1

OBJECTIVES

After reading this lesson, the student should know that:

1. Orderly government is the will of God;
2. Christians are to be good citizens;
3. The law of love is to prevail; and,
4. We are to live a clean life in a dirty age.

POINTS TO BE EMPHASIZED

Adult/Youth/Children
Key Verse: Romans 13:1
Print: Romans 13

—Paul stated that Christians should be subject to governing authorities instituted by God, and God will judge those who resist these authorities. (Romans 13:1-2)
—God appointed authorities to exist for the good of society, so those who do good have no reason to fear. (3-4)
—Because of both conscience and the fear of punishment, Christians are called to pay taxes and revenue and to give respect and honor to whom such are due. (5-7)
—Every believer is responsible to love other people, for loving others fulfills all laws related to human relationships. (8-10)
—Out of a sense of urgency, Paul exhorted believers to live honorably and put on Christ rather than revel in sin and gratify fleshly desires. (13:11-14)

(NOTE: Use KJV Scripture for Adults; NRSV Scripture for Youth and Children)

TOPICAL OUTLINE OF THE LESSON

I. Introduction

A. Doctrinal Versus Practical
B. Biblical Background

II. Exposition and Application of the Scripture

A. Rulers Commissioned (Romans 13:1-4)
B. Responsibilities of Citizens (Romans 13:5-7)
C. Relationships With Christians (Romans 13:8-10)
D. Righteous Conduct (Romans 13:11-14)

III. Special Features

A. Preserving Our Heritage
B. A Concluding Word

I. Introduction

A. DOCTRINAL VERSUS PRACTICAL

At this point, we seek only to bring to your attention that in general, the Epistle that Paul was moved by the Holy Spirit to write is divided into two basic sections, the Doctrinal and the Practical. The Doctrinal always comes first, and such matters as the resurrection, grace, the Sovereignty of God, the second coming, the concept of the Church, the nature and purpose of the law, salvation, justification, sanctification, glorification, man's ruin in sin, the significance of the ordinances, etc. are some of the basic doctrines taught in the first sections of the Church Letters.

Now following such doctrinal messages, we find the Scriptures dealing with practical matters as master-slave relationship, citizenship, church behavior, family life, husbands and wives, raising children, paying taxes (Romans 13:7), church service, expressing love, stewardship, inner peace, exhortations to moral living, prayer, the ministry, deacons, etc.

Always maintain this order—doctrine, then deeds. Knowing what to do (Practice), without knowing why we do it (Doctrine) leads to fanaticism, zeal without knowledge, working without the proper spiritual motivation. Today's lesson is found in the Book of Romans, and the practical section begins with chapter twelve. Chapter thirteen continues the emphasis on Christianity in practice, and deals with such pragmatic matters as government, capital punishment, taxes, love of neighbor, and personal ethics.

B. BIBLICAL BACKGROUND

Note that the beginning of chapter 12 of Romans uses the word, "therefore." This refers to all that precedes; it points to the doctrines of justification, sanctification, and election. Transition is made from these doctrines to concern with the Christian's relationship with other Christians, and with those who are not Christians, people who are outside of the ark of safety, outside of the family of God. The life of faith is now in view.

Then from the more personal matters of chapter twelve, the apostle passes to what is called "political ethics." The bridge between chapter twelve and chapter thirteen is a natural one. As Paul dealt with the injustices and personal wrongs believers suffer at the hands of personal, wicked individuals, so Christians may suffer at the hands of unscrupulous judges or government officials, or may not receive just treatment from them when they plead their case and cause.

II. Exposition and Application of the Scripture

A. RULERS COMMISSIONED
(Romans 13:1-4)

LET every soul be subject unto the higher powers. For there is no power but

of God: the powers that be are ordained of God. Whosoever therefore resisteth the power, resisteth the ordinance of God: and they that resist shall receive to themselves damnation. For rulers are not a terror to good works, but to the evil. Wilt thou then not be afraid of the power? do that which is good, and thou shalt have praise of the same: For he is the minister of God to thee for good. But if thou do that which is evil, be afraid; for he beareth not the sword in vain: for he is the minister of God, a revenger to execute wrath upon him that doeth evil.

It sometimes escapes our attention that government authorities are commissioned by God. "To commission" is defined as the act of committing or giving authority to carry out a particular task or duty, or granting or entrusting certain powers or authority. This is exactly what God does—He entrusts men with authority to rule others. Whether we live in a democracy, monarchy, or dictatorship, those in office are ordained by God. He is the One who sets up and takes down, installs and deposes.

In the use of the word "soul" in Romans 13:1, we recognize that the soul represents the person, and specifically, the Christian, for the Letter is addressed to "all that be in Rome, beloved of God, called saints" (Romans 1:7). The command "be subject to" speaks of habit; continually, habitually, consistently subordinate yourself, obey the higher powers. Use of the verb "be subject to" is stronger than "obey." It denotes voluntary self subjection; literally, it is to place or put under.

The verb "be subject to" is used throughout the New Testament. It speaks of (1) subjection to the prophet's spirit (2) subjection of the woman who would speak in tongues, and creates confusion in the church (3) subjection to fellow Christians who labor in the gospel (4) subjection to the righteousness of God (5) subjection of the twelve-year-old boy Jesus to Joseph and His mother (6) subjection of the evil spirits unto the disciples through the name of Jesus Christ (7) subjection of all things under the feet of the Lord Jesus Christ (8) subjection of all Christians to the concern for one another (9) subjection of the wife to the husband (10) subjection of servants to their own masters (11) subjection of the future inhabited world to saints (12) and subjection to our Heavenly Father. Obviously, one huge element in life is this matter of subjection.

Some people rebel against it and make themselves miserable. They are mavericks who talk about freedom, independence, doing their own thing, self-expression, and their rights. But their failure to submit first of all to God means that in truth they are not really free. You see why Paul exhorts Christians to habitually subordinate themselves to the higher powers, that is, human authorities, officials, governments.

We discover that the words "be subject unto," "ordained," and "resisteth" the power, all have the same root. Literally, we would translate: "Whoever does not place himself under the authorities placed by God, but places himself against the authority, withstands the God-placed rule, and for such withstanding he shall receive condemnation." It is clear that the punishment meted out to those who resist the government is sanctioned by God. It is God's will that those who withstand authority should be punished by authority. Why? Because God instituted government. He wants men to be governed. Anarchy is not of God. The Lord ordained that civil government promote good and prevent evil.

To this end, government is certainly beneficial. So the believer is to obey because it is God's purpose that magistrates keep order. This is, of course, the legitimate design of government, and for the most part it works this way. Make it a habit of obeying the authority, and rather than be frightened, you will have praise. At least, ideally, you will be protected and unmolested as a law-abiding citizen. The sword wielded by the minister **(diakonos)** is seen as a symbol of the power of the authorities to punish evildoers. God uses the magistrate as the avenger who brings His wrath against the evildoer; and he does not bear the sword without purpose or in vain.

B. RESPONSIBILITIES OF CITIZENS
   (Romans 13:5-7)

Wherefore ye must needs be subject, not only for wrath, but also for conscience sake. For for this cause pay ye tribute also: for they are God's ministers, attending continually upon this very thing. Render therefore to all their dues: tribute to whom tribute is due; custom to whom custom; fear to whom fear; honour to whom honour.

Because of the truths stated in verses 1-4, there is a two-fold moral necessity for saints to be submissive: (1) the wrath of God. The fear of punishment is a useful fear; it has its place in the regulation of behavior, in the matter of morals. (2) the sake of the conscience. There is an intrinsic obligation, an inner sense which obligates us to God, a desire to maintain a good conscience.

Paying taxes is one proof of submission to the government. It also shows a willingness to share in the cost of running a society of law and order. The tax-gatherers are called ministers (public servants) of God, inasmuch as they are officers of the government, and government has been ordained of God. The Lord who commissioned and gave to them the authority to restrain evil and punish evildoers also gave them the right to demand subsidy from the citizenry in order to carry out their operations. Romans 13:7 points out our responsibilities as Christian citizens. We are to render to all what is due them. Four things are categorized: (1) Tribute to whom tribute is due. The same word for "tribute" is mentioned once in verse 6, and twice in verse 7; it means taxes. (2) Custom to whom custom: Here the Greek word translated "custom," means end, close, final lot, finish. It is a toll, or indirect tax on goods. (3) Fear to whom fear means respect, a conscientious desire not to displease those in authority. (4) Honor to whom honor. Here the word "honor" means respect for the office. It is the "Tim" of Timothy. Saints should remember that it is God's will for us to never speak disrespectfully of our president, governor, mayor, et al (Exodus 22:28; Acts 23:5). It is true, of course, that a very wicked person may hold high office, but we are to respect the office by showing respect to the one who holds the office. This does not mean that we approve of and endorse the behavior. In our society, we can vote the person out of office and replace him or her with one whose deportment restores respect for the office concerned.

C. RELATIONSHIPS WITH CHRISTIANS
(Romans 13:8-10)

Owe no man any thing, but to love one another: for he that loveth another hath fulfilled the law. For this, Thou shalt not commit adultery, Thou shalt not kill, Thou shalt not steal, Thou shalt not bear false witness, Thou shalt not covet; and if there be any other commandment, it is briefly comprehended in this saying, namely, Thou shalt love thy neighbour as thyself. Love worketh no ill to his neighbour: therefore love is the fulfilling of the law.

While it is true that the Epistle is directed to the saints of Rome, the words "no man" include all men, whether believers or unbelievers. If we owe money to non-Christians and do not pay them, we paint a poor picture of Christ and give cause for criticism. On the other hand, if we owe other believers some money, and do not pay, we paint a poor picture of Christian brotherhood. In fact, we are self-destructive at this point. If we mistreat those who belong in the same body with us, we then mistreat ourselves.

We should not push the interpretation of "owe no man anything" to mean prohibiting contracting legal debts such as mortgages and business loans. Undoubtedly, some of us would be wise to cut up most of our credit cards, and adopt a policy of saving for what we want or feel we need, and then paying cash for it. God may use this Scripture, however, to stop us from getting into arrears, contracting debts for stuff we really do not need; borrowing money for products that depreciate in value as soon as we purchase them, and bringing to mind that the borrower is a slave to the lender (Proverbs 22:7). But, the debt of love never ends. We pay by loving, but our debt remains. Love is inexhaustible. The more it is paid, the more we owe, for the practice of love makes the principle of love deeper and deeper, and more active. A. T. Robertson said: "The debt can never be paid off, but we should keep the interest paid up." Keep ever in mind that it is not doing the law that is the fullness of the law, but love is the fulfilling of the law. What the law seeks is exhibited by the one who loves.

In Romans 13:9, we have singled out five of the Ten Commandments. Paul wants to show that keeping these particular statutes of the Decalogue sums up the command to love. Adultery, murder, stealing, false witness, and coveting are forbidden. And, any other commandment that might be mentioned are all boiled down to this point: Love your neighbor as yourself. Love not only does not harm, but it does good! By acting in love, we fulfill what the law requires concerning our relationship with others.

D. RIGHTEOUS CONDUCT
(Romans 13:11-14)

And that, knowing the time, that now it is high time to awake out of sleep: for now is our salvation nearer than when we believed. The night is far spent, the day is at hand: let us therefore cast off the works of darkness, and let us put on the armour of light. Let us walk honestly, as in the day; not in

rioting and drunkenness, not in chambering and wantonness, not in strife and envying. But put ye on the Lord Jesus Christ, and make not provision for the flesh, to fulfil the lusts thereof.

In many of our churches, the covenant we read at the Communion service mentions "walking circumspectly." With eyes wide open, we see that it is no time to be asleep spiritually. Moral inattention and apathy are deplored. Believers should know what is happening in society. Paul warns against sluggishness in good works. We are exhorted to arouse ourselves from the slumber of do-nothing. Why? Because the coming of Jesus Christ is imminent. No prophecy remains to be fulfilled before He can return to snatch up all who are cleansed in His blood. We are exhorted to alertness and watchfulness because we are nearer the end of the Christian race and battle than when we first believed.

Because of the approaching blessedness of the next life, we are stimulated by the signs of the times to live the life that pleases God. As one would take off a suit or dress, so we are to rid ourselves of the works of darkness: dishonesty, reveling (partying), drunkenness, immorality, wantonness, strife, envying, etc. We are to put on the armor of light, the protective covering of holiness; we are to put on Jesus Christ, and let Him live His life in us.

III. Special Features

A. PRESERVING OUR HERITAGE

Here is a topic that will enliven discussion in the class: Capital Punishment. Because the death penalty has been used so long in our country in an unjust manner, many Blacks have problems with Capital Punishment. Our task as Christians, however, is to determine what the Bible teaches. The Bible is the Word of God; and His Word is truth. Our desire as Black Baptist Bible Believers is to see to it that whatever laws we have should be justly applied. The following Scriptures should be studied: Genesis 9:6; Exodus 20:13 (where the word is "murder," not "kill").

In the Pentateuch, you will find that a Holy God told Israel that lives should be taken for the following offenses: adultery, bestiality, cursing parents, incest, witchcraft, unchastity, rape, idolatry, blasphemy, homosexuality, sabbath-breaking, and murder (see Exodus 21:17; 22:18-19; Leviticus 20:9-17, 24:16; Numbers 15:32-36; Deuteronomy 13:6-10; 22:21,25). No one claims today that people should be put to death for all of these evils, but we seek to establish the principle that a Holy God does not decree that which is immoral. Romans 13:1-4 gives us a good basis for talking about the matter. Do not fear prayerfully dealing with the issue in your class (Luke 23:40-41; Acts 25:11; Ecclesiastes 8:11).

B. A CONCLUDING WORD

In this practical section of the Book of Romans, all who have been justified by faith in the Lord Jesus Christ are obligated to be subject to those in authority.

This obligation does not seem to fit too well with many Americans. Perhaps in a democracy (people rule), it is difficult for its citizens to imagine that the powers that be are ordained of God.

As long as government remains in its God-ordained realm and role, we are exhorted to obey. We are to submit ourselves "to every ordinance of man for the Lord's sake" (1 Peter 2:13-14).

We are to render unto Caesar what belongs to Caesar (Matthew 22:21). However, remember Caesar does not control our spirits. He steps out of his role when he attempts to tell us when and where to pray, whom to worship, what to believe. Although our position in Christ is that we are citizens of heaven (Philippians 3:20), we still have the responsibility to behave as good earthly citizens. We pay our taxes, respect authority, obey the rules, live clean (1 Peter 4:15-16). And through it all, we love, and thereby fulfill what the law demands in this area of life.

HOME DAILY BIBLE READINGS
Week of February 7, 1999
Civic Responsibility

Feb. 1 M. Romans 12:9-21, Hate What Is Evil; Hold Fast the Good
Feb. 2 T. Romans 13:1-7, Be Subject to the Governing Authorities
Feb. 3 W. Romans 13:8-14, Love Does No Wrong to a Neighbor
Feb. 4 T. Psalm 15:1-15, Walking Blamelessly
Feb. 5 F. 1 Peter 2:11-17, Accept the Authority of Every Human Institution
Feb. 6 S. 2 Peter 1:2-11, Everything Needed for Life and Godliness
Feb. 7 S. Romans 12:1-8, A Living Sacrifice...Spiritual Worship

Caring Community

Adult Topic—Sharing Community

.....

Youth Topic—Sharing Community
Children's Topic—Care for Others

.....

Devotional Reading—1 Corinthians 12:14-27
Background Scripture—1 Corinthians 11:17-34
Print—1 Corinthians 11:20-34

• • • • • • • • • • •

SCRIPTURE PRINT

1 Corinthians 11:20-34 (KJV)

20 When ye come together therefore into one place, this is not to eat the Lord's supper.

21 For in eating every one taketh before other his own supper: and one is hungry, and another is drunken.

22 What? have ye not houses to eat and to drink in? or despise ye the church of God, and shame them that have not? What shall I say to you? shall I praise you in this? I praise you not.

23 For I have received of the Lord that which also I delivered unto you, That the Lord Jesus the same night in which he was betrayed took bread:

24 And when he had given thanks, he brake it, and said, Take, eat: this is my body, which is broken for you: this do in remembrance of me.

25 After the same manner also he took the cup, when he had supped, saying, This cup is the new testa-

1 Corinthians 11:20-34 (NRSV)

20 When you come together, it is not really to eat the Lord's supper.

21 For when the time comes to eat, each of you goes ahead with your own supper, and one goes hungry and another becomes drunk.

22 What! Do you not have homes to eat and drink in? Or do you show contempt for the church of God and humiliate those who have nothing? What should I say to you? Should I commend you? In this matter I do not commend you!

23 For I received from the Lord what I also handed on to you, that the Lord Jesus on the night when he was betrayed took a loaf of bread,

24 and when he had given thanks, he broke it and said, "This is my body that is for you. Do this in remembrance of me."

25 In the same way he took the cup also, after supper, saying, "This cup is the new covenant in my blood. Do this, as often as you drink it, in

ment in my blood: this do ye, as oft as ye drink it, in remembrance of me.

26 For as often as ye eat this bread, and drink this cup, ye do shew the Lord's death till he come.

27 Wherefore whosoever shall eat this bread, and drink this cup of the Lord, unworthily, shall be guilty of the body and blood of the Lord.

28 But let a man examine himself, and so let him eat of that bread, and drink of that cup.

29 For he that eateth and drinketh unworthily, eateth and drinketh damnation to himself, not discerning the Lord's body.

30 For this cause many are weak and sickly among you, and many sleep.

31 For if we would judge ourselves, we should not be judged.

32 But when we are judged, we are chastened of the Lord, that we should not be condemned with the world.

33 Wherefore, my brethren, when ye come together to eat, tarry one for another.

34 And if any man hunger, let him eat at home; that ye come not together unto condemnation. And the rest will I set in order when I come.

remembrance of me."

26 For as often as you eat this bread and drink the cup, you proclaim the Lord's death until he comes.

27 Whoever, therefore, eats the bread or drinks the cup of the Lord in an unworthy manner will be answerable for the body and blood of the Lord.

28 Examine yourselves, and only then eat of the bread and drink of the cup.

29 For all who eat and drink without discerning the body, eat and drink judgment against themselves.

30 For this reason many of you are weak and ill, and some have died.

31 But if we judged ourselves, we would not be judged.

32 But when we are judged by the Lord, we are disciplined so that we may not be condemned along with the world.

33 So then, my brothers and sisters, when you come together to eat, wait for one another.

34 If you are hungry, eat at home, so that when you come together, it will not be for your condemnation. About the other things I will give instructions when I come.

 KEY VERSE

But let a man examine himself, and so let him eat of that bread, and drink of that cup. For he that eateth and drinketh unworthily, eateth and drinketh damnation to himself, not discerning the Lord's body.—1 Corinthians 11:28-29

OBJECTIVES

After reading this lesson, the student will have a better appreciation of:

1. The relationship Christians have with one another;
2. The significance and seriousness of properly celebrating the Lord's Supper;
3. The possibility of being chastened by the Lord; and,
4. The fact that God desires discipline and order in the church.

POINTS TO BE EMPHASIZED

Adult/Youth/Children
Key Verse: 1 Corinthians 11:28-29; Ephesians 4:32 (Children)
Print: 1 Corinthians 11:20-34; 1 Corinthians 11:17-22, 28-29 (Children)

—Paul chastised believers who discriminated against others in observing the Lord's Supper. (1 Corinthians 11:20-22)
—Paul recalled Jesus' own words to His disciples during the supper on the night He was betrayed. (23-25)
—Paul claimed that eating the bread and drinking the cup proclaims the Lord's death until He comes again. (26)
—Because the Lord judges those who eat the bread and drink the cup in an unworthy manner, Paul warned that believers should examine themselves and be sure they are paying attention to the Lord's body in the experience. (27-32)
—When Christian brothers and sisters gather to observe the Lord's Supper, they should wait for one another, having satisfied their hunger at home. (33-34)

(NOTE: Use KJV Scripture for Adults; NRSV Scripture for Youth and Children)

TOPICAL OUTLINE OF THE LESSON

I. Introduction

A. The Lord's Supper
B. Biblical Background

II. Exposition and Application of the Scripture

A. Conduct Is Reproved (1 Corinthians 11:20-22)
B. Christ Instructs (1 Corinthians 11:23-26)
C. Christians Are Warned (1 Corinthians 11:27-30)
D. Condemnation Is Withheld (1 Corinthians 11:31-34)

III. Special Features

A. Preserving Our Heritage
B. A Concluding Word

I. Introduction

A. THE LORD'S SUPPER

Satan has been very clever stirring up strife over the two ordinances, Baptism and Communion. Take for example our differences with the Roman Catholic Church. It speaks of Sacraments. But, we Baptists avoid this term because of its sacerdotal (priesthood) implication. New Testament believers hold that all Christians are priests. One of the worst errors is the teaching that in the mass the bread actually becomes our Lord's body, the wine actually becomes His blood. The truth is, they are only symbols.

Christ died once for all. He is not hanging on a cross. Crucifixes are out of place in Baptist churches. Some Protestant groups celebrate the Lord's Supper every Sunday; a few, only twice a year. There are some who prefer to spiritualize the ordinances altogether. How sad, the very thing intended to bring us together is used to separate us. Perhaps just knowing this will help us to be more concerned about our love for all others who love the Lord Jesus Christ.

B. BIBLICAL BACKGROUND

The early church celebrated what was called an agape or love feast. This was a social meal of a rather general character eaten in common with other believers. It was a time of fellowship, a repast shared in a spirit of love. Acts 2:42, 46 and Jude 12 make reference to such a meal. Here was food prepared not only to satisfy hunger, but also to give expression to the sense of Christian brotherhood (ISBE).

The excesses of which some of the saints were guilty indicate that full meals were served, not just bread and wine. So keep in mind the agape or love feast came first, and then at the end of the meal, the Lord Jesus was remembered with the bread and fruit of the vine. Unfortunately, some of the people were so stuffed, and some drunk, that they could not possibly please Christ in their attempt to celebrate the Lord's Supper.

II. Exposition and Application of the Scripture

A. CONDUCT IS REPROVED
(1 Corinthians 11:20-22)

When ye come together therefore into one place, this is not to eat the Lord's supper. For in eating every one taketh before other his own supper: and one is hungry, and another is drunken. What? have ye not houses to eat and to drink in? or despise ye the church of God, and shame them that have not? What shall I say to you? shall I praise you in this? I praise you not.

The divisions and heresies or parties at Corinth were not based upon doctrinal differences. It was more a matter of economic status and personal tastes. However, regardless of the root cause, the party spirit led to misbehavior at the love feasts and thence at the Lord's Supper. This was the practical outcome of their divisive spirit. In fact, said Paul, they really did not assemble to eat the Lord's Supper. This was not their basic intention, their real motive. And this accusation was especially directed to the wealthier Christians. They were to be rebuked because they came to the love feasts and immediately separated themselves.

Coming early, they would take the choice seats, and without waiting for the others would begin to eat. From their point of view, the meal was a private, personal affair. In this way they denied the spirit of Christian fellowship which was intended by the love feasts. The poor saints came late, after working all day; they came hungry. Instead of being welcomed and fed, they were ignored, neglected, and made to suffer by the selfish greed of the wealthier Christians. And worse, while the poor remained hungry, the gluttonous became drunk. You can see why the apostle rebuked them and insisted that they had not come to partake of the Lord's Supper.

Indignant, Paul asked: "What? Have ye not houses to eat and to drink in?" If their main purpose was to eat, drink, and make pigs of themselves, why didn't they stay at home and do that? This is not to suggest that Paul approved of drunkenness and gluttony if practiced at home. Two things were evident in their conduct: (1) They despised the church of God, (2) They shamed their poor fellow saints. Now to despise the church of God is to be ignorant of the fact that it is His church. The assembly was composed of God's people; it was His church. Their failure to share with the other saints signified they held a low concept of the church. The English word "despise" has Latin roots meaning to look down upon; the Greek word so translated, means literally to think down. If you think down, you will look down. Such thinking down does not remain a passive matter; the contempt felt in the mind is actively displayed and demonstrated in harmful action. Some of the professed Christians at Corinth did not properly esteem the value of the church, they had no concept of true Christian fellowship. The result? They treated the church in a disrespectful manner. It remains true today that men and women show that they despise the church by their attempts to undermine authority. We must be ever mindful that we all belong to the family of God. We have one Father, God: and only by our faith in the shed blood of Jesus Christ have we been given the authority to become the children of God.

The second consequence of their misbehavior was the humiliation of the poor saints. The have-nots—those who had neither food nor houses to eat in—were humiliated as they watched their gluttonous and besotted richer brethren. The poor saints had come hungry and expected to receive from the wealthy. Many, perhaps, had come expecting a blessing from the Christian fellowship and the mutual edification. They were disappointed. Under such conditions of strife, and with such a bad spirit as was manifested, it was impossible to discern the solemnity of the Lord's Supper. How could they? There can never be a proper spirit of fellowship in an assembly where some saints make other saints feel ashamed, sorry, humiliated, inferior, or class conscious by virtue of differences in race, skin-color, education, personality, or economic status. The church of God is not a private social club established for a select chosen few. It is for all who believe in Jesus Christ. And so the apostle bluntly announced that what he had to say was not praise, but rebuke. The Lord's Supper was intended to symbolize the great love of God the Father who sacrificed His Son, the Lord Jesus, for us. The conduct of some at Corinth made it impossible to properly discern the Lord's Supper.

B. CHRIST INSTRUCTS
(1 Corinthians 11:23-26)

For I have received of the Lord that which also I delivered unto you, That the Lord Jesus the same night in which he was betrayed took bread: And when he had given thanks, be brake it, and said, Take, eat: this is my body, which is broken for you: this do in remembrance of me. After the same manner also he took the cup, when he had supped, saying, This cup is the new testament in my blood: this do ye, as oft as ye drink it, in remembrance of me. For as often as ye eat this bread, and drink this cup, ye do shew the Lord's death till he come.

Paul had spoken to them before about the Lord's Supper, but evidently the message did not register. "I delivered unto you" is past tense; he had instructed them earlier in this matter. Now, because of the abuse, he was moved to repeat his instructions. But it is not really his instructions, for what he spoke had been told to him. He had received his information, not from the other apostles, but from the Lord Jesus Christ Himself. When or where this special revelation occurred, we do not know. There are, of course, instances of special revelation to Paul during the course of his ministry. The gospel he preached was not after man; therefore he was not obligated to please men. He said: "For I neither received it of man, neither was I taught it, but by the revelation of Jesus Christ" (Galatians 1:12). Having received direct revelation, he now claimed direct authority. The saints at Corinth had to be impressed that this memorial, this celebration of the Lord's Supper was not a man-made thing, conceived in the minds of men. This was Christ Himself; and therefore sacred and solemn. Indeed, its solemnity is heightened by the fact that Christ instituted it the same night He was betrayed. Interestingly, the words "He was being betrayed" come from the same Greek word rendered, "I delivered to you" (1 Corinthians 11:23). The Lord and the disciples had gathered to observe the Passover supper, a commemoration of the Jews' great deliverance from slavery in Egypt. Judas, of course, was present at this Passover Supper. But after the dipping of the cup he immediately went out, and it was night (John 13:30). That left only believers present, at which time our Lord instituted this memorial.

Consider now the words, "This is My body." The bread was not His actual, physical body. He was at that time alive, not dead, present with the disciples. The bread represents or symbolizes His body. This is a legitimate grammatical interpretation. For example: When Christ said, "I am the door" (John 10:9), we would not take it to mean he was a piece of wood or a metal gate. Take note of the words, "as oft as ye drink...For as often as ye eat this bread and drink this cup...." It is made crystal clear that there is no set number or frequency when saints should observe the Lord's Supper—whether every day, every week, once a month, twice a year, etc. Most Black Baptists celebrate the Lord's Supper once a month, though different churches observe it on different Sundays in the month.

The Communion is also a time of remembrance, the word occurs twice in verses 24 and 25. This symbolic memorial looks two ways; backward to Calvary over 1900 years ago, and forward to a future time, the hour of which is unknown to man. The words "till He come" indicate that the Lord's Supper is a reminder of the Second Coming of Christ. It bears a two-fold witness: one to His death, and another to His return (1 Thessalonians 4:16,17). Either way, His death, or His coming, we are reminded of Him, we feel His presence with us. This is the purpose of Holy Communion.

C. CHRISTIANS ARE WARNED
   (1 Corinthians 11:27-30)

Wherefore whosoever shall eat this bread, and drink this cup of the Lord, unworthily, shall be guilty of the body and blood of the Lord. But let a man examine himself, and so let him eat of that bread, and drink of that cup. For he that eateth and drinketh unworthily, eateth and drinketh damnation to himself, not discerning the Lord's body. For this cause many are weak and sickly among you, and many sleep.

There is a difference between the words, unworthy and unworthily. All of us are unworthy of taking the Lord's Supper. This is why salvation is free, the gift of God; this Supper which memorializes God's gift finds us all unworthy sinners saved by grace. Unworthily is an adverb modifying the verbs "eat" and "drink." Unworthily refers to the manner in which we partake of the Supper. Reference is NOT made to the character of the communicant. Emphasis is upon the way and manner we take the communion. It is not the saint's character, but his or her conduct. Some of the saints at Corinth had demonstrated a carelessness and indifference toward the Lord's table, indicating they had lost sight of its spiritual significance.

Each Christian is to stop and think; we are not to come to the Lord's Supper in outward manner of levity, glibness, gum-chewing, indifference, flippancy, and irreverence. We are to examine ourselves (prove, test our attitudes with an eye to approval); we are to recognize the communion's solemnity, appreciate its meaning. And THEN EAT. There is never any worthwhile excuse for not eating the Supper.

A careless, irreverent attitude may lead to chastisement. The failure to discern the Lord's body, and then to regard His death with indifference, are acts of dishonor. God visited the saints at Corinth with weakness of body, sickness and physical death. Never forget that. Divine chastisement includes premature physical death. This does not mean eternal condemnation; the believer's salvation is secure, but it does mean the early physical death of the believer may be an act of chastisement. It is dangerous for the saint to get out of the will of God; and getting out of His will, displeasing Him includes approaching the Lord's table in an irreverent, unworthy manner.

D. CONDEMNATION IS WITHHELD
(1 Corinthians 11:31-34).

For if we would judge ourselves, we should not be judged. But when we are judged, we are chastened of the Lord, that we should not be condemned with the world. Wherefore, my brethren, when ye come together to eat, tarry one for another. And if any man hunger, let him eat at home; that ye come not together unto condemnation. And the rest will I set in order when I come.

The doctrine of eternal security of the believer does not mean license to live in immorality. And we do have God's Word that there is no condemnation (John 3;18; 5:24; 6:37; Romans 8:1, 39). But Paul does point out in this last section of our lesson the fact of divine chastisement and the possibility of escaping it. Self-examination is insisted upon. We are exhorted to keep an eye on our motives, our reasoning, our thoughts and attitudes. Then, when we detect sin—and such discernment comes by the Holy Spirit—we are to confess it. Confession is the clue to avoiding chastening (1 John 1:9). The word translated "chastened" (1 Corinthians 11:32) means properly to train children; that is, in the sense of bring up, instruct, educate. Now obviously, chastening teaches; it is a schooling process. And since we are the children of God through faith in Jesus Christ, this becomes a family affair (Proverbs 3:11.12; Hebrews 12:7-11). There are many factors involved in this matter of discipline. And we are to be concerned with judging the sin in our own personal lives.

If we fail to do this, the Lord will have to do it for us. He will seek to bring us to our senses, correct us, restore the fellowship, mold us into the image of His Son that we might be partakers of His holiness. And whatever the discipline or chastisement, it is calculated to prevent our being condemned with the world. Paul wanted the Corinthian saints to judge their own behavior, confess and forsake their gluttony, selfishness, and divisiveness. Surely, the failure to think of others is worthy of condemnation; and the lesson warns us that we come not together unto condemnation. The point is, said Paul, the Lord wants us to conduct church services in a decent and orderly manner. There are other things to be straightened out, he said, "And I will attend to them when I come."

III. Special Features

A. PRESERVING OUR HERITAGE
Decades ago, the communion service was something special in our churches. Whatever Sunday it was held—whether the first or third, or whenever—the pastor was sure to be there. It was part of an unwritten law that the pastor would be present on Communion Sunday. Then too, the service was separate, either at

3:30 in the afternoon, or later in the evening. Today, in many of our churches, the Lord's Supper is commemorated immediately following the morning worship. One other thing comes to mind: the singing, the testimonies, the prayers! What rejoicing and excitement we experienced in the Lord! We're busy these days—too busy. And the competition from television, sports, recreation, jobs, etc. all help to erase the old way! Thank God for those Black churches which still make a big fuss over the Lord's Supper! More power to you.

B. A CONCLUDING WORD

Every believer is a member of the body of Christ. As we properly discern that body at the Lord's table, let us also properly deal with the members of that body, our brothers and sisters in Christ. May our attitude and behavior at the Lord's Supper reflect our relationship with one another—to the praise and glory of the Lord Jesus Christ, till He comes again.

As one of the two basic ordinances of the Baptist Church, the service of communion or the Lord's Supper cannot be taken as just an appendage to the order of worship. In reality, it is a re-enactment of the Last Supper that Jesus had with His disciples in which He proclaimed an inseparable connection between the broken bread and the wine with His death on the cross. The bread was broken as His body would be broken, and the wine was poured our in a similar manner that His blood would be shed during the crucifixion. The Lord's Supper observance recalls this experience as an act of redemption whereby those who participate in it understand that Jesus died not for Himself, but for those whose alienation from God would become reconciled by accepting His sacrifice on Calvary as the atoning act whereby their sins are forgiven.

The observance of the Lord's Supper not only points backward to the moment of sacrifice, but also forward to that day when the redeemed shall celebrate the complete triumph over sin and evil with Jesus Christ in the Kingdom of Heaven. As no limitation is placed on how often those who believe should celebrate this two dimensional aspect of the service itself, the focus is on the individual participant to exclude himself or herself if the right attitude of heart and mind does not accompany that participation.

HOME DAILY BIBLE READINGS
Week of February 14, 1999
Caring Community

Feb.   8 M.   1 Corinthians 11:17-22, For the Better, Not for Worse
Feb.   9 T.   1 Corinthians 11:23-24, Do This in Remembrance of Me
Feb. 10 W   Exodus 12:1-13, Origin of the Passover
Feb. 11 T.   Exodus 12:14-28, A Day of Remembrance
Feb. 12 F.   Exodus 12:43-51, The Passover for the Whole Congregation of Israel
Feb. 13 S.   Exodus 13:1-16, Remember This Day
Feb. 14 S.   1 Corinthians 12:14-27, One Body, Many Members

Reconciling the World to Christ

Adult Topic—Reconciling the World

.....

Youth Topic—Making Peace
Children's Topic—Live for Jesus

.....

Devotional Reading—1 Peter 2:18-25
Background Scripture— 2 Corinthians 5:11-21
Print—2 Corinthians 5:11-21

• • • • • • • • • • •

PRINTED SCRIPTURE

2 Corinthians 5:11-21 (KJV)

11 Knowing therefore the terror of the Lord, we persuade men; but we are made manifest unto God; and I trust also are made manifest in your consciences.

12 For we commend not ourselves again unto you, but give you occasion to glory on our behalf, that ye may have somewhat to answer them which glory in appearance, and not in heart.

13 For whether we be beside ourselves, it is to God: or whether we be sober, it is for your cause.

14 For the love of Christ constraineth us; because we thus judge, that if one died for all, then were all dead:

15 And that he died for all, that they which live should not henceforth live unto themselves, but unto him which died for them, and rose again.

16 Wherefore henceforth know we no man after the flesh: yea, though we have known Christ after

2 Corinthians 5:11-21 (NRSV)

11 Therefore, knowing the fear of the Lord, we try to persuade others; but we ourselves are well known to God, and I hope that we are also well known to your consciences.

12 We are not commending ourselves to you again, but giving you an opportunity to boast about us, so that you may be able to answer those who boast in outward appearance and not in the heart.

13 For if we are beside ourselves, it is for God; if we are in our right mind, it is for you.

14 For the love of Christ urges us on, because we are convinced that one has died for all; therefore all have died.

15 And he died for all, so that those who live might live no longer for themselves, but for him who died and was raised for them.

16 From now on, therefore, we regard no one from a human point of view; even though we once knew Christ from a human point of view,

the flesh, yet now henceforth know we him no more.

17 Therefore if any man be in Christ, he is a new creature: old things are passed away; behold, all things are become new.

18 And all things are of God, who hath reconciled us to himself by Jesus Christ, and hath given to us the ministry of reconciliation;

19 To wit, that God was in Christ, reconciling the world unto himself, not imputing their trespasses unto them; and hath committed unto us the word of reconciliation.

20 Now then we are ambassadors for Christ, as though God did beseech you by us: we pray you in Christ's stead, be ye reconciled to God.

21 For he hath made him to be sin for us, who knew no sin; that we might be made the righteousness of God in him.

we know him no longer in that way.

17 So if anyone is in Christ, there is a new creation: everything old has passed away; see, everything has become new!

18 All this is from God, who reconciled us to himself through Christ, and has given us the ministry of reconciliation;

19 that is, in Christ God was reconciling the world to himself, not counting their trespasses against them, and entrusting the message of reconciliation to us.

20 So we are ambassadors for Christ, since God is making his appeal through us; we entreat you on behalf of Christ, be reconciled to God.

21 For our sake he made him to be sin who knew no sin, so that in him we might become the righteousness of God.

KEY VERSE

To wit, that God was in Christ, reconciling the world unto himself, not imputing their trespasses unto them; and hath committed unto us the word of reconciliation.—2 Corinthians 5:19

OBJECTIVES

After reading this lesson, the student should be informed about:

1. What it means to be an ambassador for Christ;
2. The Doctrine of Reconciliation;
3. What constitutes a new creature in Christ; and,
4. How Christ's love constrains us.

POINTS TO BE EMPHASIZED
Adult/Youth/Children
Key Verse: 2 Corinthians 5:19; 2 Corinthians 5:15 (Children)
Print: 2 Corinthians 5:11-21

—Paul said he feared God and sought to persuade others, knowing that God knew him and hoping that the Corinthians knew him also. (11)

—Paul, who desired only to please God, was not commending himself to the Corinthians; but he was helping them to answer people who boasted in outward appearance. (12-13)

—Paul identified Christ's love and death as that which urged him to live for Christ, who died and was raised for all. (14-15)

—Paul no longer viewed any one, not even Christ, from a human point of view, because if anyone is in Christ, everything has become new. (16-17)

—Paul said that believers are to be ambassadors for Christ, reconciled to Him in whom we become the righteousness of God. (20-21)

(NOTE: Use KJV Scripture for Adults; NRSV Scripture for Youth and Children)

TOPICAL OUTLINE OF THE LESSON

I. Introduction

A. Ambassadors for Christ
B. Biblical Background

II. Exposition and Application of the Scripture

A. Reaching Others: Our Motive (2 Corinthians 5:11-13)
B. Reconciliation: Our Ministry (2 Corinthians 5:14-19)
C. Responsibility: Our Message (2 Corinthians 5:20-21)

III. Special Features

A. Preserving Our Heritage
B. A Concluding Word

I. Introduction

A. AMBASSADORS FOR CHRIST

The study of the meaning of the word "ambassador" is essential to our understanding of the ministry of reconciliation. An ambassador is an official representative of a sovereign state or nation as an authorized or appointed messenger. The task of an ambassador is one of honor and responsibility. He or she must represent the nation's point of view, assert its rights, yet seek to create a spirit of harmony in dealing with others.

In the Old Testament, there are three Hebrew words translated "ambassador" in our King James Version of the Bible. The first word is found in 2 Chronicles 32:31 and is derived from a word meaning to scorn, scoff, sneer. We see the idea of twisting the mouth in trying to pronounce a foreign language. From the idea of treating as a scorner or foreigner, eventually came the translation, "interpreter"

(Genesis 42:23). A second Hebrew word translated "ambassador" is found in Joshua 9:4. The Gibeonites pretended that they were envoys (ambassadors) from a far country, and therefore were not stumbling-blocks to Israel's advance. This word appears to come from a root meaning "to fashion, form, delineate," leading perhaps to the concept of representation. The third and most common Hebrew word sometimes translated "ambassador" is the "malach" we have in Malachi, which means, "my messenger." In Zechariah 1:12-13, this word is also rendered "angel."

Now in the New Testament there is only one Greek word that is translated "ambassador." It is derived from a verb which means to be a senior, elder, more advanced in years. It is **"presbuteros,"** from which we get the words "presbyter" and "Presbyterian." Because the elder is put first in rank, honor and dignity, the senior man acts as representative or spokesman. In his prayer in Ephesians 6:20, Paul called himself an "ambassador in bonds." An ambassador of what? In bonds for what? The Gospel! We are God's agents, deputies, elders, envoys, evangels, interpreters, messengers, mouthpieces, preachers, prophets, representatives, spokesmen, teachers, translators, and servant-slaves. In short, we are Ambassadors for Christ!

B. BIBLICAL BACKGROUND

We understand that Paul's main purpose for writing Second Corinthians, as he was led by the Holy Spirit, was to defend his authority as an apostle. This Epistle is thus called an apologetic. The Greek word **"apologia"** means verbal defense, speech in defense *(Thayer)*. The evidence Paul gives concerning his sincerity in serving the Savior is overwhelming. And so, in the first seven chapters of Second Corinthians, we have Paul's exposition of the Christian ministry of which he was a part.

His work had been blessed by God: souls saved, lives changed, saints edified. His ministry had been an honest one, and he had preached Christ, not self. Furthermore, he had suffered as a minister of the Gospel. What a far cry from the soft living brand of American Christianity! Paul had worked hard at the task given him by the Lord. He labored boldly, triumphantly, honestly, in afflictions, as a true minister of the Gospel of Christ. While false teachers at Corinth sought to undermine Paul's work by questioning his authority, and calling him insincere, untrustworthy, Paul was not to be hindered or intimidated. They sought to recruit others to despise him and his companions, but all their schemes failed. Paul still was able to sing, "Look where He brought me from!"

II. Exposition and Application of the Scripture

A. REACHING OTHERS: OUR MOTIVE
(2 Corinthians 5:11-13)

Knowing therefore the terror of the Lord, we persuade men; but we are made manifest unto God; and I trust also are made manifest in your consciences. For we commend not ourselves again unto you, but give you

occasion to glory on our behalf, that ye may have somewhat to answer them which glory in appearance, and not in heart. For whether we be beside ourselves, it is to God: or whether we be sober, it is for your cause.

Paul sought to persuade men and women, to induce them to believe *(Thayer)*. One motive for such persuasion was the knowledge of the fear of the Lord. The King James Version says "terror," but "phobos" is better translated "fear." Paul had in mind that deep, reverential awe. He had just mentioned (2 Corinthians 5:10) the fact that all Christians will be judged for the deeds done in their bodies. So emphasis is not on trying to scare the unsaved into heaven, but to encourage believers to remember the time will come when they will stand before Jesus Christ, the Judge.

Furthermore, Paul sought to convince the saints that he was a minister with integrity. But of course, some folks will never be convinced that we are real, so the main thing is to be right with the Lord, for He alone knows our hearts, our inner minds. Indeed, we are open books in the eyes of God, although Paul desired that the Corinthians likewise would see that he was genuine. The apostle said, "I am not bragging. I am not reading off my resume, or listing my credentials to try to prove anything to you. I simply desire to authenticate my integrity." Some folks like a big outside show, and rejoice in their membership in their mutual admiration societies.

But all too often there is nothing on the inside—no integrity, no honesty, no character, no sincerity. They boast (glory) in externals. To those who may have considered Paul a fanatic or mad, Paul stated: "If I am crazy (Acts 26:24), it's unto the Lord. If I appear out of my head, it's because I'm doing what the Lord told me to do! If I am in my right mind, it is unto the Lord." There may have been those who felt Paul was too laid back, too unassuming to be effective. Either way, it was for their good, their edification. The world looks at the believer who is sold out to the Lord, and considers him or her unbalanced (a nice way of putting it!). William MacDonald calls the fully consecrated, "irregulars in His army." Indeed, the Captain of our Salvation was likewise considered beside Himself, eccentric (Mark 3:21).

B. RECONCILIATION: OUR MINISTRY
(2 Corinthians 5:14-19)

For the love of Christ constraineth us; because we thus judge, that if one died for all, then were all dead: And that he died for all, that they which live should not henceforth live unto themselves, but unto him which died for them, and rose again. Wherefore henceforth know we no man after the flesh: yea, though we have known Christ after the flesh, yet now henceforth know we him no more. Therefore if any man be in Christ, he is a new creature: old things are passed away; behold, all things are become new. And all things are of God, who hath reconciled us to himself by Jesus Christ, and hath given to us the ministry of reconciliation; To wit, that God was in Christ, reconciling the world unto himself, not imputing their trespasses unto them; and hath committed unto us the word of reconciliation.

The love of Christ here is not our love for Him, but His love for us. He showed that love by dying on the cross for us— loving us when we were unloving, when we were unlovely. This love constrains us. It controls us (RSV, *LB*, NASB, Moffatt); we are ruled by it (TEV); it compels *(NKJV, NIV)*; it leaves us no choice *(NEB)*; it is the very spring of our actions *(JBP)*. The verb, "sunecho" means to hold together. But here the idea of urge on, impel, control is seen. Alford states that "a better word could not be found than constrains." Paul felt that the love of Jesus Christ held him in such a strong grip that it only was a compelling force that kept him going crazy, but controlled everything he did. This totality is seen in the figure of death.

For if Jesus Christ died for all of us, then we all died. Totally depraved natures can not do any good that pleases God. So, He died for all of us. If one died the death that belonged to all of us, then all died in and with Him. Believers are seen by God the Father as having died with Christ on the cross (Romans 6:6). By faith, we are to reckon ourselves dead to the old life of sin and selfishness (Romans 6:11). We are to live for Him.

Now the reason He died for all is that all of us who believe in Him should no longer live for ourselves, but for Him. Here is where some Christians live so miserably. They have not yet come to the realization that they died to sin and self, and are to live only in the Savior. At this point, Paul refers to the idea of judging men in a worldly, carnal way. Indeed, carnal ideas are no longer to control us. With the love of Christ in our hearts, we look at people in a different light. Motives, customs, purposes which before our conversion controlled or influenced the way we thought of others no longer rules. The way Paul thought of Jesus Christ changed. Prior to his conversion, Paul considered Jesus Christ to be a false Messiah! But now that estimate has changed drastically.

Thus (wherefore, therefore) to be in Christ —connected with, in intimate union with—means we are new creatures. This truth concerning our position in Christ is important! There are two main words for "new" in the Greek. One word, **neos,** emphasizes time. We speak of something being "brand new." The word used twice in 2 Corinthians 5:17 is **"kainos,"** which stresses quality and is concerned with differences. The adamic nature is passing away, though still in us. But eventually, everything that is of Adam will move off the scene. Old things—the junk we used to do, the attitudes and values we used to hold— pass away once for all. A decisive break with the old life took place the very moment we were saved. Whatever is of Christ will abide; the newly created, Christ-centered things will remain for all eternity. Indeed, things have become new. We put on the new man (Ephesians 4:24); we shall have new names (Revelation 2:17); we shall sing a new song (Revelation 14:3). We are changed creatures because of what God in Christ has wrought in us. See then what He has done!

Well, for one thing, He has given us the ministry of telling sinners that they may be reconciled to God, that God "was in Christ reconciling the world unto Himself, not imputing (counting, reckoning, accounting) their trespasses unto them." This does not mean that everybody in the world will be saved, but that their estate before God is changed. By reason of Christ's death, the necessity of condemnation is removed. Before this, there was no way out; now there is open a way for man's salvation. God, on His part, had disposed of all that which made such peace impossible. We call this Reconciliation. The Greek word so translated means to be thoroughly or completely changed. The basic idea is that a change has been wrought from some position or relationship formerly held. It has to do with the establishment of harmonious relations where before there had been estrangement and hostility. Reconciliation, then, is the overcoming of that estrangement; it is the bringing into agreement. Theologians are in agreement with the action described by the word "reconciliation," but they are not in agreement with the roles played by man and God.

Some believe that only man is reconciled and never God. They claim that God Himself is not affected because God is immutable, unchangeable. The idea of a complete change, they say, cannot be applied to Him. Other scholars say the range or scope of the term immutable should include only those things moral, only the ethical aspects of God's character, not His dealings or methods of dealing with men, nor His relationship with men. Some believe that reconciliation should be seen as a two-sided affair, like the two sides of a single coin. The God-ward aspect should certainly be included and we can say that God Himself is reconciled. This means that in the face of Jesus Christ, God put away everything that on His side meant estrangement and separation. He accomplished this through the death of Christ. Seen primarily from the man-ward point of view, it means that through Christ, man the sinner is changed thoroughly in God's sight—from hatred of God to love, from aversion to trust, from rejection to acceptance.

C. RESPONSIBILITY: OUR MESSAGE
(2 Corinthians 5:20-21)

Now then we are ambassadors for Christ, as though God did beseech you by us: we pray you in Christ's stead, be ye reconciled to God. For he hath made him to be sin for us, who knew no sin; that we might be made the righteousness of God in him.

We have the responsibility of representing Christ in this world. We call upon men to demonstrate a changed life through faith in the shed blood of Jesus Christ. Here then is the main business of the church member: Witness! Jesus Christ is the not-having-known-sin One (at any time). There is certainly ample proof of His holiness. However, our sins were placed on Him (not in Him); and He was made sin (not a Sinner) for us. Here is the very heart of the Gospel. This wonderful thing was done that we might become, once and for all, the righteousness of God in Christ. By this act, God demonstrated His intense hatred of sin, and His love for you and for me.

III. Special Features

A. PRESERVING OUR HERITAGE

Second Corinthians 5:16: "...henceforth know we no man after the flesh" is a good verse for Black American Christians to remember. This Scripture informs us that the death, burial and resurrection of the Lord Jesus Christ helped Paul to eliminate the way in which he judged others. The way we should view other people is this: They are folks for whom Jesus Christ shed His blood. What would happen in the United States if all Christians did this? See then what Paul teaches here. As Saul, he knew some things about Jesus Christ, he knew what others said about Him. That's why he persecuted the church (and thereby persecuted Christ, Acts 9:4). After his conversion experience with the risen Christ—salvation made a difference—Saul, who became Paul, had a different view of the Lord, and a different view of all mankind. If Christ died for all, then all needed to be saved. And if all still need to be saved, then all are still on the same level. There are no distinctions that amount to anything. Nationality, race, skin color, education, etc. mean nothing so far as one's relationship with God is concerned. Herein is one reason Black Christians need not feel inferior to anyone. When we have spiritual insight, we are not so readily caught up with man's self-centeredness (whether Afrocentric or Eurocentric). When life is Christocentric, then we are on the right track!

B. A CONCLUDING WORD

Though it is contrary to the rules of international law, sometimes an ambassador is mistreated. When David sent messengers to comfort Hanun in the death of his father, Hanun was advised by the princes of Ammon that these Israelite messengers or ambassadors were spies (2 Samuel 10:4). Consequently, they had half of their beards shaved off, and they were sent away with their garments cut off in the middle, at their hips—humiliated! Shall we not expect to be shamefully maltreated by the world which despises Him who sent us, and whom we represent? Even so, we are never relieved of our responsibilities as Christians. We may become prisoners, but we are still ambassadors for Christ. Satan may seek to shackle our efforts, but let us be faithful to our calling until Christ comes again. This ought to be the great desire of every child of God. The Good News is that there is now no barrier; the way is now open to receive the forgiveness of God.

HOME DAILY BIBLE READINGS
Week of February 21, 1999
Reconciling the World to Christ

Feb. 15 M. 2 Corinthians 5:11-15, The Love of Christ Urges Us On
Feb. 16 T. 2 Corinthians 5:16-21, There is A New Creation!
Feb. 17 W. Romans 5:18—6:4, Justification and Life for All
Feb. 18 T. Romans 6:5-11, Alive to God in Christ Jesus
Feb. 19 F. Romans 6:12-23, God's Gift Is Eternal Life
Feb. 20 S. Romans 7:1-13, Instructed by Law; Saved by Grace
Feb. 21 S. Romans 7:14-25a, Thanks Be to God!

Confident Hope

Adult Topic—Confident Hope

•••••

Youth Topic—Finding Hope

Children's Topic— Trust in the Lord

•••••

Devotional Reading—1 Peter 1:3-9

Background Scripture—Titus 2:11-14; Hebrews 12:18-29;
Revelation 1:14-20; 11:15-19

Print—Titus 2:11-14; Hebrews 12:26-29; Revelation 1:17-20; 11:15

• • • • • • • • • • • •

PRINTED TEXT

Titus 2:11-14; Hebrews 12:26-29;
Revelation 1:17-20; 11:15 (KJV)

11 For the grace of God that bringeth salvation hath appeared to all men,

12 Teaching us that, denying ungodliness and worldly lusts, we should live soberly, righteously, and godly, in this present world;

13 Looking for that blessed hope, and the glorious appearing of the great God and our Saviour Jesus Christ;

14 Who gave himself for us, that he might redeem us from all iniquity, and purify unto himself a peculiar people, zealous of good works.

•••••

26 Whose voice then shook the earth: but now he hath promised, saying, Yet once more I shake not the earth only, but also heaven.

27 And this word, Yet once more, signifieth the removing of those things that are shaken, as of things

Titus 2:11-14; Hebrews 12:26-29;
Revelation 1:17-20; 11:15 (NRSV)

11 For the grace of God has appeared, bringing salvation to all,

12 training us to renounce impiety and worldly passions, and in the present age to live lives that are self-controlled, upright, and godly,

13 while we wait for the blessed hope and the manifestation of the glory of our great God and Savior, Jesus Christ.

14 He it is who gave himself for us that he might redeem us from all iniquity and purify for himself a people of his own who are zealous for good deeds.

•••••

26 At that time his voice shook the earth; but now he has promised, "Yet once more I will shake not only the earth but also the heaven."

27 This phrase, "Yet once more," indicates the removal of what is shaken--that is, created things--so

that are made, that those things which cannot be shaken may remain.

28 Wherefore we receiving a kingdom which cannot be moved, let us have grace, whereby we may serve God acceptably with reverence and godly fear:

29 For our God is a consuming fire.

.....

17 And when I saw him, I fell at his feet as dead. And he laid his right hand upon me, saying unto me, Fear not; I am the first and the last:

18 I am he that liveth, and was dead; and, behold, I am alive for evermore, Amen; and have the keys of hell and of death.

19 Write the things which thou hast seen, and the things which are, and the things which shall be hereafter;

20 The mystery of the seven stars which thou sawest in my right hand, and the seven golden candlesticks. The seven stars are the angels of the seven churches: and the seven candlesticks which thou sawest are the seven churches.

.....

15 And the seventh angel sounded; and there were great voices in heaven, saying, The kingdoms of this world are become the kingdoms of our Lord, and of his Christ; and he shall reign for ever and ever.

that what cannot be shaken may remain.

28 Therefore, since we are receiving a kingdom that cannot be shaken, let us give thanks, by which we offer to God an acceptable worship with reverence and awe;

29 for indeed our God is a consuming fire.

.....

17 When I saw him, I fell at his feet as though dead. But he placed his right hand on me, saying, "Do not be afraid; I am the first and the last,

18 and the living one. I was dead, and see, I am alive forever and ever; and I have the keys of Death and of Hades.

19 Now write what you have seen, what is, and what is to take place after this.

20 As for the mystery of the seven stars that you saw in my right hand, and the seven golden lampstands: the seven stars are the angels of the seven churches, and the seven lampstands are the seven churches."

.....

15 Then the seventh angel blew his trumpet, and there were loud voices in heaven, saying, "The kingdom of the world has become the kingdom of our Lord and of his Messiah, and he will reign forever and ever."

KEY VERSE

Looking for that blessed hope, and the glorious appearing of the great God and our Saviour Jesus Christ.—Titus 2:13

OBJECTIVES

After reading this lesson, the student should know more about:

1. The Biblical Hope: its definition;
2. The Blessed Hope: the return of Christ;
3. The Boundary of Hope: an unshakable kingdom; and,
4. The Basis of Hope: Christ, Lord of the Churches.

POINTS TO BE EMPHASIZED

Adult/Youth/Children
Key Verse: Titus 2:13
Print: Titus 2:11-14; Hebrews 12:26-29; Revelation 1:17-20; 11:15

—God brings salvation to all and trains believers to renounce impiety and to live godly lives while awaiting the blessed hope and manifestation of the glory of Christ. (Titus 2:11-13)
—Christ gave Himself for us that He might redeem believers from iniquity and purify a people of His own who are zealous for good deeds. (14)
—The writer encouraged acceptable worship and awe for God, who once shook the earth with His voice and now offers an unshakable kingdom. (Hebrews 12:26-29)
—John told of a vision in which the Son of Man declared that He is the first and the last, the living one who holds the keys to Death and Hades. (Revelation 1:17-18)
—The Son of Man told John to write what he had seen and revealed to John the mystery of the seven stars and the seven lampstands. (Revelation 1:19-20)
—The seventh angel blew a trumpet and loud voices in heaven proclaimed the eternal kingdom of God. (Revelation 11:15)

(NOTE: Use KJV Scripture for Adults; NRSV Scripture for Youth and Children)

TOPICAL OUTLINE OF THE LESSON

I. Introduction

A. Biblical Hope Defined
B. Biblical Background

II. Exposition and Application of the Scripture

A. The Coming (Titus 2:11-14)
B. The Consuming (Hebrews 12:26-29)
C. The Church (Revelation 1:17-20)
D. The Celebration (Revelation 11:15)

III. Special Features

A. Preserving Our Heritage
B. A Concluding Word

I. Introduction

A. BIBLICAL HOPE DEFINED

As we hear the word "hope" employed in everyday language in the street, it contains a large element of uncertainty, a wishfulness, a desire for something against the odds, a pessimistic expectation of fulfillment. Ask a man, "If you should drop dead right now, would you go to heaven?", and the answer comes, "Well...I hope so!" This means he is not sure. There is expectation, but he lacks assurance. On the other hand, Biblical hope is absolute confidence; it is that on which we rely. In fact, "trust" and "faith" are often given as translations of the same word rendered "hope." Keep this in mind. Hope in the Bible is no perhaps, maybe, "iffy," peradventure, "climbing up the rough side of the mountain, if I can just make it in" matter. There is no element of chance or unforeseen misfortune showing up and causing good to change into bad, or a blessing turned into a tragedy. Indeed, hope is simply faith directed toward the future *(ISBE);* it is expectation directed toward that which is good *(Chafer).* Hope is the expectation of good, whereas fear is the expectation of evil. Hope is trust with reference to the future. Yea, hope is the belief that what is desired is obtainable. Hope is a long patient waiting; it is the "straining of the mind in a certain direction in an expectant attitude" *(Girdlestone).*

B. BIBLICAL BACKGROUND

Two basic things are said in the Bible about hope. First: Unbelievers have no real hope. The hypocrite's hope (confidence) shall be cut off, and perish. The hope of the wicked "is to breathe their last" *(RSV; NASB). NIV* states: "their hope will become a dying gasp" (Job 8:13; 11:20). Proverbs 11:7 agrees: "The hope of unjust men perishes." The New Testament continues this negative portrayal of the unbeliever's hope. Paul teaches us the folly of the unregenerate's hope: He sorrows at funerals as if he has no well-founded trust in a future after death (1 Thessalonians 4:13). Without Christ, the unbeliever is an atheist (literally, without God) in the world, and has no hope (Ephesians 2:12).

Second: Believers have a wonderful hope. For example: "The hope of the righteous shall be gladness...The righteous has hope in his death...Our hope is laid up for us in heaven...we are saved by hope" (Proverbs 10:28; 14:32; Colossians 1:5; Romans 8:24). Our hope is an anchor of the soul (Hebrews 6:19); an helmet of salvation (1 Thessalonians 5:8). Christ in us, the hope of glory (Colossians 1:27). Thank God for the Christian's hope.

II. Exposition and Application of the Scripture

A. THE COMING
(Titus 2:11-14)

For the grace of God that bringeth salvation hath appeared to all men,

teaching us that, denying ungodliness and worldly lusts, we should live soberly, righteously, and godly, in this present world; looking for that blessed hope, and the glorious appearing of the great God and our Saviour Jesus Christ; Who gave himself for us, that he might redeem us from all iniquity, and purify unto himself a peculiar people, zealous of good works.

God's grace is the unearned, unmerited, undeserved favor or kindness of God. It is the expression of an infinite, incomprehensible love for fallen mankind. We deserve Hell, but are made citizens of Heaven. This grace which appeared once for all brings salvation, and reference is made to the Incarnation and work at Calvary by Jesus Christ (Titus 3:4), and all the blessings of redemption. Soterios (soteriology, the study of salvation) means safety, deliverance, rescue. In the Old Testament, it was rescue from enemies, deliverance from captivity, safety from war, traps, defeat, etc. In the New Testament, emphasis is more spiritual (but does not exclude the physical). Salvation has to do with death, hell, and separation from God which is the penalty of sin.

When this salvation suddenly appeared in the world, it showed itself to all classes of people--to aged men (verse 2), aged women (verse 3), young women (verse 4), young men (verse 6), and slaves (verse 9). As Christians, they would in turn affect the entire world. Thus, no one need despair. After we became believers, this same grace became our instructor. There we learn the important lessons about the unprofitableness of the flesh. We learn sober living, refusing to follow anything that is unworthy of God. Daily grace trains us to renounce dirty living and encourages us to live a clean life. It is said that some Christians get on board the Salvation Train at Justification, sleep through Sanctification and expect to wake up in Glorification! To motivate us, the blessed hope of the return of the Lord is put to us. Compared to dying on the cross for our sins, our most dedicated service appears trivial indeed.

Note that in verse 13, the phrase "great God and our Savior" refers to one Person. The word "and" may be rendered "also" (Ephesians 4:11, "pastors and teachers" refers to the pastor who is also a teacher). It is interesting that in Titus 2:13, Jesus Christ is our Savior, and in Titus 3:4, we read of the "Kindness and love of God, our Savior." We conclude that Christ is God, for there is only one Savior! Jehovah said in Isaiah: "I am the Lord, and beside me there is no savior...there is no God else beside me, a just God and a Savior; there is none beside me" (43:11; 45:21). In Hosea 13:4, the Lord said: "...for there is no savior beside me." Thank God for Him who gave Himself to redeem us from every lawless deed. He gave Himself for us to cleanse us for Himself as His own special people (peculiar means private property, literally, "wealth in cattle"), zealous to do good works.

B. THE CONSUMING
(Hebrews 12:26-29)

Whose voice then shook the earth: but now he hath promised, saying, Yet once more I shake not the earth only, but also heaven. And this word, Yet once more, signifieth the removing of those things that are shaken, as of things that are made, that those things which cannot be shaken may remain. Wherefore we receiving a kingdom which cannot be moved, let us have grace, whereby we may serve God acceptably with reverence and godly fear: For our God is a consuming fire.

Unbelief says NO to God, but do not be fooled. If at Sinai people refused God, do not think that because now we stress grace we can refuse God and escape with impunity. The Lord shook up things at Sinai, but that was just a foretaste of the shaking to come. Shaking shows instability and temporariness. Shaking Sinai showed Sinai was not the final stopping place. When God finishes shaking both earth and heaven, only that which is permanent remains. Fire, of course, is the final form of judgment. Therefore, do not get tied up with that which can be shaken loose; rather, build your hopes on things eternal.

C. THE CHURCH
(Revelation 1:17-20)

And when I saw him, I fell at his feet as dead. And he laid his right hand upon me, saying unto me, Fear not: I am the first and the last: I am he that liveth, and was dead; and, behold, I am alive for evermore, Amen; and have the keys of hell and of death. Write the things which thou hast seen, and the things which are, and the things which shall be hereafter; the mystery of the seven stars which thou sawest in my right hand, and the seven golden candlesticks. The seven stars are the angels of the seven churches: and the seven candlesticks which thou sawest are the seven churches.

The lesson deals with John's vision of the glorified Christ. Overwhelmed by the glory and majesty of our Lord, John sank to the ground--finite being who encountered the Infinite--overcome with awe, a sinner in the Presence of a Holy God. Throughout the Gospels, accounts are given of men and women who fell at the feet of Christ and worshiped Him. Not once did He forbid them. Not once did He say, "Don't do that! Worship God and Him only." Not once did He reject their worship.

Our Lord placed His right hand (authority) upon John and comforted him with these words: "Do not continue (**phobou,** present imperative) to be afraid." Throughout God's Word, we hear the refrain, Fear not! It has been necessary because since the Fall of Adam, men have experienced fear. Lot was afraid to dwell in Zoar; Jacob was afraid of Esau; Joseph's brothers were fearful that Joseph might seek revenge; the Israelites were afraid of the pursuing Egyptians; David fled from Saul; and the disciples were afraid of the storm and awoke the sleeping Lord Jesus. Men and women without Christ cannot obey such a command. Only those who fear God are today told by God, "Fear not." Humans are born to fear. If we do not fear God, if we show no reverence, no awe to Him, we will soon fear the gods of our own making. Any man who does not fear the true and living God opens himself up to the fears and phobias of all that is false and unreal, as well as fearing that which is true and real. When these fears run out, man begins to fear fear itself. He becomes afraid of being afraid. We emphasize this matter because hope is the expectation of good; but, fear is the expectation of evil.

Now the Lord proceeded to identify Himself with a five-fold statement. After all, He is the very center of the Revelation, its Author and Subject. The statement, "I am the first and the last," is similar to, "I am Alpha and Omega." The word "last" is **"eschatos"** in Greek, and has given us the word, Eschatology, the study of Last Things. This title expresses the eternality of Jesus Christ. Next, we see that He is the "Living One." His life is inherent, self-contained; He lives continually. We do not have to worry about Him dying again. Third, we see that He was dead, literally, He became dead, or passed into a state of death.

Fourth: He said, "I am alive for evermore. Amen." The incarnate Son of God who suffered abject death triumphed over death to live unto the ages of the ages! Fifth: He has the keys of Hades and of Death. A key is the means of control, especially of entry or possession. It is thus a symbol of authority and power. Hades is the Greek word comparable to the Hebrew word, **Sheol.** It means the unseen place, and the souls of dead unbelievers are presently there. Later, they will be given bodies and cast into Ghana or the Lake of Fire. How unfortunate that some people do not believe in a literal place called Hell. Logically, one would think that they also deny that Heaven is a literal place! Hell must be a place if the Lord Jesus has a key to it. Deliverance from fear is found in Christ: (1) By realizing who He is, the First and the Last, (2) By realizing His victory over death, (3) By realizing that He alone controls the future, the keys are in His hands.

In verse 19, John is commanded to write what is one of the most important verses in the Book of Revelation. It is a key to the proper interpretation of the entire Book. Most conservative scholars hold that we have here a three-fold outline of the Revelation. First: The things which John had seen include the vision of the glory of the resurrected Christ described in verses 12-18, the Christ who rules and dominates the entire Revelation. It is the Revelation of Jesus Christ-- by Him and about Him! Second: The things which are: We believe that chapters two and three, dealing with the Seven Churches, constitute the period designated by the words, "the things which are." Seven churches are chosen to teach us the nature of the moral character of the entire Church Age. Third: The things which shall be (hereafter) are the things described in chapters 4 to 22. And it will be seen that once again Israel takes the spotlight of world history.

We encounter for the first time in the Book of Revelation the word "mystery," something hidden, secret, unknown, and which would remain undiscovered by man if God Himself did not reveal it. If God did not explain to us the meaning of the seven stars and the seven golden lampstands, we would never find out on our own. Remember, the word for angel means messenger. The angels here are human beings, pastors. Calling them "stars" indicates they have a high official place. Pastors are held in the right hand of Him who is the Lord of the Church, and He stands in the middle of the churches with authority, power and the right to examine both preachers and church. May we see anew the vision of Christ which John saw, and may our hope likewise be renewed.

D. THE CELEBRATION
(Revelation 11:15)

And the seventh angel sounded; and there were great voices in heaven, saying, The kingdoms of this world are become the kingdoms of our Lord, and of his Christ; and he shall reign for ever and ever.

If any one word sums up the book of Revelation, it is the word, "Judgment." Remember, the true Church will be raptured or snatched from the earth before the Tribulation starts. First, the seven seal judgments, one after another. Then out of the seventh seal judgment come the seven trumpet judgments, one after another. And eventually, out of the seventh trumpet judgment, the seven bowl (vial) judgments will commence. Our lesson is the last or seventh trumpet judgment. We read that the seventh angel sounded or blew a trumpet. The loudness of the blast suggests severity of public judgment. We are not told whose voices were heard--whether the voices of cherubim, angels, living creatures, or the saints in glory with God. In this terrific symphony of majestic words are heard one of the grandest statements in the Bible concerning the Lord Jesus: "The kingdom of this world is become the kingdom of our Lord, and of His Christ, and He shall reign forever and ever."

This is anticipative! or what scholars call proleptic (interpretation by the prophet of future events). Celebration of divine conquest of the world takes place as if conquest has been achieved already (compare Ezekiel 21:26-27; Daniel 2:44; and Zechariah 14:). Do not spiritualize this prophecy; take it literally, that the earthly kingdom will pass into the hands of the Lord Jesus Christ. And the jubilant note of the great voices in heaven is in anticipation of the certain establishment of God's kingdom on earth.

Satan's power is snatched away from him. The process began at Calvary when the penalty for sin was paid and Christ shed His blood for us. This text is part of the process of the destruction of evil's earthly powers and the end of the Devil's usurpation. Whatever happens from this point on, the fact is that never again will the kingdom of this world come under the control of wicked men or of the Devil.

III. Special Features

A. PRESERVING OUR HERITAGE

It may well be that we have not seen the last of church bombers and arsonists, and other agents of destruction. Our confidence may be shattered even by our own acts of self-destruction. This is all the more reason that we need to depend upon the Word of God. The Bible assures us that He who is Lord of the Church offers an unshakable kingdom, an eternal kingdom, and is coming back again. Our blessed hope is a purifying hope--a confident hope. And, rest assured that Jesus Christ keeps His Word. One line in a hymn that is sung in many of our churches fits well today's lesson: "Build your hopes on things eternal, Hold to

God's unchanging hand" *(Baptist Standard Hymnal, #298)*. This is our challenge for all the days ahead!

B. A CONCLUDING WORD

The Second Coming of the Lord Jesus Christ is the great hope of the church. Some Christians have other hopes, such as the conversion of the world and worldwide revival. There are those who believe that it is up to them to make the world a better place in which to live! However, Titus 2:13 emphasizes our "looking for the blessed hope and the appearing of the glory of our great God and Savior, Christ Jesus. 1 Peter 1:3 praises God for causing us "to be born again to a living hope through the resurrection of Jesus Christ from the dead." And 1 John 3:2f states that "every one who has this hope fixed on Him purifies himself, even as He is pure." You can see that our Confident Hope is composed of a Blessed Hope, a Living Hope, and a Purifying Hope. May the God of all hope be praised!

The certainty of the return of Christ should intensify the desire to live as if His return was immanent, rather than lull one into that mental state whereby he or she feels that "death bed salvation will suffice." Those who are saved are defined by having that quality of character that is undergirded by integrity. To love God with all of one's mind, heart, soul and strength not only is indicative of the fact that the total personality, inclusive of every dimension of one's being, is under the mandate and direction of God, but that one lives as if he or she were in the very presence of God. Anticipation is not a technique of delay, but the bringing into the present that which is in fact a future reality. The very character of God as eternal eliminates the time deferential between past, present and future, and as such, those who would imitate God as revealed in Jesus as the Christ must dare to live in that which may be called the "eternal now." The challenge may be too great for those who desire to "do their own thing" as long as they desire and hope that the return of the Christ will not catch them unaware. Those who really and truly affirm belief in the Second Coming of the Christ live in the present moment as if He has already returned. The difference is between "getting ready" and "being ready." What is your attitude or demeanor?

HOME DAILY BIBLE READINGS
Week of February 28, 1999
Confident Hope

Feb.	22	M.	Titus 2:11-14, The Blessed Hope
Feb.	23	T.	Hebrews 12:18-29, What Cannot Be Shaken Remains
Feb.	24	W.	Revelation 1:12-20, Do Not Be Afraid
Feb.	25	T.	Revelation 11:15-19, He Will Reign Forever and Ever
Feb.	26	F.	1 Peter 1:3-9, A Living Hope
Feb.	27	S.	Ephesians 1:15-23, The Hope to Which God Has Called Us
Feb.	28	S.	Revelation 21:1-8, A New Heaven and a New Earth

SPRING QUARTER

March, April, May 1999

THAT YOU MAY BELIEVE

General Introduction

The gospel of John was written for the expressed purpose of convincing persons that Jesus is the Christ and that those who come to believe in Him would have eternal life. Using John's gospel as the basis for our study for the quarter, we shall survey the teachings relative to the mission and the message of the Word who became flesh and lived among us.

Unit I, *"Jesus' Coming Called for Faith,"* consists of four sessions about the call for a response of faith from those who heard the message of Jesus. Beginning with the prologue of the gospel and the statement of the purpose of the book, we shall assess the witness of John the Baptist as he attests that Jesus is the Son of God. After summarizing the encounter that Jesus had with Nicodemus, the discussion will focus on the experience of Jesus with the woman at the well in Samaria, wherein deep insight into the meaning of true worship will claim our attention.

Unit II, *"Jesus Raised to Life,"* comprises two sessions associated with Easter. The first lesson in this unit will deal with the crucifixion and resurrection of Jesus, while the following session examines Jesus' resurrection appearances to the disciples, especially to Thomas who moves from initial doubt to the affirmation of Jesus Christ as "My Lord and my God."

Unit III, *"Jesus Declared God's Message,"* will be discussed in three sessions. In the first lesson, we shall deal with Jesus' teaching on the bread of life, one of the symbols He employs to illustrate His power and deity. Lesson two focuses on Jesus' identification of Himself as the light of the world and what He taught the Pharisees about the truth that sets people free. The final lesson in this unit deals with the Jewish religious leaders' rejection of Jesus pursuant to what He taught regarding His approaching death.

Unit IV, *"Jesus Prepared His Followers,"* directs attention to the intensive effort on the part of Jesus to prepare the disciples for His death and resurrection and the resources that God would provide for their subsequent role in His kingdom. The first lesson in this session depicts Jesus teaching about the meaning of being a servant through an object lesson, during which He washed the disciples' feet. The next lesson examines instructions Jesus made to His disciples regarding the necessity of their living close to Him as illustrated by the relationship of a vine to its branches. After summarizing Jesus' promise about the coming of the

Holy Spirit, the final lesson in this unit concentrates on Jesus' prayer for Himself, for the disciples who were with Him at the time, and for all future believers who would embrace the faith through the proclamation of the gospel.

The children's course for this quarter has been developed as one unit entitled "Learning About Jesus." The lessons will focus on the life and teachings of Jesus during His earthly ministry.

As we engage in dialogue, it will become apparent that the ideas with which our lessons deal are those which place great strain upon the mind but warm our hearts. Who can conceive of the fact that God who is wholly other than the creatures whom He has made would Himself become one with us in the person of Jesus Christ? Such initiative on the part of God antedates the creation itself in that the salvation of humans is embodied in the Lamb who was slain from the foundation of the earth. While this idea may be discussed with great enthusiasm, it can best be understood through active acceptance of and participation in the salvific work of the Christ that bridges the estrangement between God and man and effects reconciliation. This vertical dimension that relates humans to God in a most significant way must be held in constant tension with that horizontal bond with our brothers and sisters as we learned from the preceding discussions.

As with any study, that which we derive from it is contingent upon our personal historicity that is inclusive of the cumulative effect of our total experiences. In our day with the impact of the media in all its forms and formats, the advent of a highly mobile society that is multicultural both in ideas and principles of behavior, the international conglomerates with orientation toward profits rather than people, as well as all of the other aspects of a world in conflict, it is significant that the quarter concludes with the study of Jesus' death and the meaning of His resurrection. Herein there is hope that as we fully embrace that which is implied in the experience, we shall come to understand ourselves and our world in ways that motivate us to become transformers rather than conformers; to direct the destiny thereof, instead of becoming victims of blind fate.

May we go forth with faith.

The Word Became Flesh

Unit 1—Jesus' Coming Called for Faith

Children's Unit—Learning About Jesus
Adult Topic—Believe and Live!

.....

Youth Topic—God's Word and Me
Children's Topic—John Tells About Jesus

.....

Devotional Reading—Psalm 33:1-9
Background Scripture—John 1:1-18; 20:30-31
Print—John 1:1-18; 20:30-31

PRINTED SCRIPTURE

John 1:1-18; 20:30-31 (KJV)

IN the beginning was the Word, and the Word was with God, and the Word was God.

2 The same was in the beginning with God.

3 All things were made by him; and without him was not any thing made that was made.

4 In him was life; and the life was the light of men.

5 And the light shineth in darkness; and the darkness comprehended it not.

6 There was a man sent from God, whose name was John.

7 The same came for a witness, to bear witness of the Light, that all men through him might believe.

8 He was not that Light, but was sent to bear witness of that Light.

9 That was the true Light, which lighteth every man that cometh into the world.

10 He was in the world, and the

John 1:1-18; 20:30-31 (NRSV)

In the beginning was the Word, and the Word was with God, and the Word was God.

2 He was in the beginning with God.

3 All things came into being through him, and without him not one thing came into being. What has come into being

4 in him was life, and the life was the light of all people.

5 The light shines in the darkness, and the darkness did not overcome it.

6 There was a man sent from God, whose name was John.

7 He came as a witness to testify to the light, so that all might believe through him.

8 He himself was not the light, but he came to testify to the light.

9 The true light, which enlightens everyone, was coming into the world.

world was made by him, and the world knew him not.

11 He came unto his own, and his own received him not.

12 But as many as received him, to them gave he power to become the sons of God, even to them that believe on his name:

13 Which were born, not of blood, nor of the will of the flesh, nor of the will of man, but of God.

14 And the Word was made flesh, and dwelt among us, (and we beheld his glory, the glory as of the only begotten of the Father,) full of grace and truth.

15 John bare witness of him, and cried, saying, This was he of whom I spake, He that cometh after me is preferred before me: for he was before me.

16 And of his fulness have all we received, and grace for grace.

17 For the law was given by Moses, but grace and truth came by Jesus Christ.

18 No man hath seen God at any time; the only begotten Son, which is in the bosom of the Father, he hath declared him.

.....

30 And many other signs truly did Jesus in the presence of his disciples, which are not written in this book:

31 But these are written, that ye might believe that Jesus is the Christ, the Son of God; and that believing ye might have life through his name.

10 He was in the world, and the world came into being through him; yet the world did not know him.

11 He came to what was his own, and his own people did not accept him.

12 But to all who received him, who believed in his name, he gave power to become children of God,

13 who were born, not of blood or of the will of the flesh or of the will of man, but of God.

14 And the Word became flesh and lived among us, and we have seen his glory, the glory as of a father's only son, full of grace and truth.

15 (John testified to him and cried out, "This was he of whom I said, 'He who comes after me ranks ahead of me because he was before me.' ")

16 From his fullness we have all received, grace upon grace.

17 The law indeed was given through Moses; grace and truth came through Jesus Christ.

18 No one has ever seen God. It is God the only Son, who is close to the Father's heart, who has made him known.

.....

30 Now Jesus did many other signs in the presence of his disciples, which are not written in this book.

31 But these are written so that you may come to believe that Jesus is the Messiah, the Son of God, and that through believing you may have life in his name.

KEY VERSE

And the Word was made flesh, and dwelt among us, (and we beheld his glory, the glory as of the only begotten of the Father,) full of grace and truth.—John 1:14

OBJECTIVES

After reading this lesson, the student should understand better the doctrines of:

1. The Deity of Jesus Christ;
2. The Incarnation of Jesus Christ;
3. The Creation Work of Jesus Christ; and,
4. The Written Word of Jesus Christ.

POINTS TO BE EMPHASIZED

Adult/Youth
Key Verse: John 1:14
Print: John 1:1-18; 20:30-31

—The Word existed with God in the beginning and was God. (1:1-2)
—The Word created everything, bringing life that is the light to all people; and darkness cannot extinguish the light. (1:3-5)
—God sent John to bear witness to the true light who was entering the world. (1:6-9)
—The light came to His own world and to His own people; and though many rejected Him, those who received Him became God's children. (1:10-13)
—The Word became human, full of grace and truth, and made God known. (1:14-18)
—John selected events from the life of Jesus and recorded them so that people might believe in Him and might have life in His name. (20:30-31)

Children
Key Verse: John 1:12
Print: John 1:6-9, 21-34

—God sent John to witness to the light that was coming into the world.
—John said he was not the Messiah but the one sent to prepare the way for the Lord.
—John said he was baptizing with water but one greater than he would come and baptize with the Holy Spirit.
—When John saw Jesus coming he said, "Here is the Lamb of God who takes away the sins of the world."
—John testified that Jesus is the Son of God, because he saw the Holy Spirit come as a dove and remain on Jesus.
—When the priests and Levites sent some Jews from Jerusalem to find out who John really was, he told them that he was not Elijah or even a prophet, but that the Messiah of whom he spoke was among them.

(NOTE: Use KJV Scripture for Adults; NRSV Scripture for Youth and Children)

I. Introduction

A. THE SIGNIFICANCE OF THE WORD "THEOS"

The Greek word **theos** means God. You see it in such words as theology, pantheon, Theodore, etc. Biblical Christianity teaches that the One true and living God exists as Father, Son, and Holy Spirit at the same time. We use the word "Trinity" to express what we believe the Bible teaches here. There are religious groups that do not affirm the trinitarian concept of God's self revelation. While the word **theos** refers to the concept of the deity, it is not potent when biblical theology employs it to identify the God of Israel's historic faith whose manifestation came to full fruition in Jesus as the Christ. When used in reference to "other gods," the citation is to deny the reality of their existence. Walter Martin suggests that they make a big fuss over this one verse "because of the surprise effect derived from the show of pseudo-scholarship in the use of a familiar text."

B. BIBLICAL BACKGROUND

Since this entire quarter will center upon John's Gospel, it is appropriate to consider the following. We hold to the traditional view that the human author of this Gospel is the fisherman of Galilee, John the Apostle, brother of James. "He can hardly have been other than John the Son of Zebedee" (Tenney: Matthew 4:21). He also wrote the Epistles of John and the Revelation. Dates for this Gospel vary, but we shall settle for 90 AD, which suggests that it may have been the last of the Gospels to be written.

As we shall see in later lessons, John, along with Peter and James, belonged to the inner circle of the disciples. Led by the Holy Spirit, John chose to give us some of the great signs and messages of our Lord. In so doing, he emphasizes the Deity of Christ. Finally, included in today's lesson is the very purpose of this Gospel—"that ye might believe that Jesus is the Christ, the Son of God; and that believing ye might have life through His name" (John 20:31).

II. Exposition and Application of the Scripture

A. THE WORD MADE FLESH
(John 1:1-5, 14)

IN the beginning was the Word, and the Word was with God, and the Word was God. The same was in the beginning with God. All things were made by him; and without him was not any thing made that was made. In him was life; and the life was the light of men. And the light shineth in darkness; and the darkness comprehended it not. And the Word was made flesh, and dwelt among us, (and we beheld his glory, the glory as of the only begotten of the Father,) full of grace and truth.

Here we learn the foundational truth of Biblical Christianity: God the Son became a Human Being. "The Thesis of the Gospel is that Jesus Christ is the Revealer of God" (Bernard, ICC). The words "in the beginning" take our minds immediately to Genesis 1:1, "In the beginning God...." Perhaps the parallel is intentional, but John goes back before creation. Moses in Genesis points to that moment when time began, and the first creative act of God happened, but John looks back into eternity before there was time.

We express ourselves with words. By combining sounds or letters, we express ideas. Of course, without the idea behind the words, speech is meaningless. Logos or Word implies not only the spoken word, but the thought expressed by the spoken word. "It is the spoken word as expressive of thought" (Plummer). Logos then implies the intelligence behind the idea, the idea itself, and its expression. In other words, the invisible thought is made visible by the spoken word. Note that "in the beginning was the Word" or Logos. This implies pre-existence, for the Word is eternal. "The Word was with God" implies association. The Word was on a level with, or in communication with God. This speaks of a living, intelligent, active personality. "The Word was God" points to His Deity.

Jesus Christ is also Creator. Along with God the Father, and God the Holy Spirit, God the Son also took part in creation. He made all things! (Ephesians 3:9). And for Him were all things created (Colossians 1:16). Yea, He is the Source or Origin of the Creation of God (Revelation 3:14). How blasphemous are the efforts of those who seek to make Jesus Christ a creature—an angel (Michael)! Furthermore, Jesus Christ is the source of life. Indeed, "life" is a key word in John's Gospel. But not only is He the Life-Giver, He is also the Light-Giver. He came from Heaven to light up this dark, sinful world, for He is the Light of the World (John 8:12; 9:5).

Because sin plunged the world into darkness, and darkened even the minds of men, Christ came to be the light of men. However, the darkness did not comprehend it. **Katalambano** is not an easy Greek verb to translate. It means to appropriate, to lay hold of so as make one's own. The sentence could be rendered, "The darkness has not understood" the light (NIV). Or "did not grasp it" or comprehend it, or lay hold of it with the mind. Another meaning is the darkness did not overpower, quench or put out the light. Thus, the darkness was unable to overcome the light. This would mean that man's hatred and rejection of the light still did not stop the light from shining. "Or perhaps John intended to include both meanings here, and some such translation as master would suggest this" (Arndt and Gingrich), an expression true on more than one level (Morris).

Verse 14 is our basis for what is called the Incarnation, for there we learn that the Word became flesh. This was God's method of revealing Himself to man. This coming into the world was preplanned; it was no spur of the moment, whimsical, capricious, sudden flash of an idea or brainstorm on God's part. He did nothing unrighteous, although there are men who believe flesh is intrinsically evil and therefore a holy God cannot have dealing with flesh. But, "God sending His own Son, in the likeness of sinful flesh and for sin, condemned sin in the flesh" (Romans 8:3). There is nothing unholy about the Incarnation. The God-Man is Grace personified; He is Truth revealed.

B. THE WITNESS OF JOHN THE BAPTIST
(John 1:6-8; 15-18)

There was a man sent from God, whose name was John. The same came for a witness, to bear witness of the Light, that all men through him might believe. He was not that Light, but was sent to bear witness of that Light. John bare witness of him, and cried, saying, This was he of whom I spake, He that cometh after me is preferred before me: for he was before me. And of his fulness have all we received, and grace for grace. For the law was given of Moses, but grace and truth came by Jesus Christ. No man hath seen God at any time; the only begotten Son, which is in the bosom of the Father, he hath declared him.

Note that we deal here with John the Baptist, not John the apostle, the author of this Gospel. The man sent from God is John the Baptist (John 1:29-34). He came as a forerunner of the Lord Jesus. It was his task to witness Christ, and to bear witness of the Light. He did this by preaching repentance and by baptizing those who professed belief. John pointed men to the Lord Jesus, not to himself. The last recorded words John spoke in this Gospel are: "He (Christ) must increase, but I must decrease" (John 3:30).

As a forerunner, John told men about Jesus Christ before our Lord entered His public ministry. Though John was born some six months before our Lord, yet Christ was before John, for Christ existed from all eternity. God's abundant grace was showered upon all in undeserved kindness or grace. God gave the law (the first five books of the Old Testament) to Moses for the Jewish people. No one could perfectly keep the law system based on Scripture. Therefore, no one could be saved by it. By supplying all the needs—grace and truth—of His people, He has shown His superiority over Moses and the Law. At this point, we have the climax of the whole Prologue (verses 1-18 form a preface or summary of all that follows), and we want to spend more time studying verse 18 in our Concluding Word.

C. THE WORLD'S LIGHT
(John 1:9-13)

That was the true Light, which lighteth every man that cometh into the world. He was in the world, and the world was made by him, and the world knew him not. He came unto his own, and his own received him not. But as many as received him, to them gave he power to become the sons of God, even to them that believe on his name: Which were born, not of blood, nor of the will of the flesh, nor of the will of man, but of God.

Jesus Christ is the true Light that comes into the world. Note the King James Version makes it appear the word "cometh" modifies "every man." But emphasis is not upon "every man that comes into the world," but upon "the light that comes into the world." Revised Standard Version: "The true light that enlightens every man was coming into the world" (also New International Version). The New American Standard Bible: "There was the true light which, coming into the world, enlightens every man."

He resides in the world He made, yet the world did not come to know Him or recognize Him. This knowledge is more than intellectual. It means to know intimately, to be in a good relationship with, to know and love as a friend. "He came home" to His own, His own things, and His own people rejected Him. His own inheritance includes the land, city, temple, people (the Jews) who should have bowed before Him, but resisted and refused to do so. Verse 11 sums up the Gospel story. Not only His neighbors, but members of His own family at first rejected Him. He came to His homeland and His homefolks rejected Him.

Authority to become a child of God must be given by God. The Bible does not teach the Universal Fatherhood of God or the Universal Brotherhood of Man. God is not the Father of all men; and all men are not brothers. God is the Creator of all men; seen from a purely physical, creational or creaturely level, all men are the offspring of God (Acts 17:28, 29). However, the New Testament emphasis is upon a spiritual relationship. No man has the right (authority, power) to call God, Father, unless he has first accepted the shed blood of Jesus Christ. Only those born again, born of God, have this right—not those born of mere human parents, or of man's weak physical body, or of man's volition! "Nothing human, however great or excellent, can bring about the birth of which he speaks" (Morris).

D. THE WRITER'S PURPOSE
(John 20:30-31)

And many other signs truly did Jesus in the presence of his disciples, which are not written in this book: But these are written, that ye might believe that Jesus is the Christ, the Son of God; and that believing ye might have life through his name.

Here we have the purpose and scope of John's Gospel. We learn that not everything the Lord did is recorded by John. Although all the "signs" Christ did were seen by His disciples, all were not recorded by them. It is notable that nothing is said about the "signs" of cleansing lepers or casting out demons in John's Gospel! John selected as he felt led; indeed, the Holy Spirit picked out what He wanted, that which would best suit His purpose. In short, although John had more to say, it was not God's purpose (through John) to write a full narrative of our Lord's earthly ministry.

But what has been written has a grand purpose. Notice the use of the perfect tense in the Greek, **gegraptai,** it has been written. This suggests that what he wrote still stands; it was written in time past but with present results. John's evangelistic thrust had a two-fold goal. First, that his readers believe that Jesus is the true Christ (Messiah). Second, that they believe He is the Son of the living God. These are the two basic beliefs. The Gift of eternal life (and available abundant life) is for all who believe in Him as He is (in His name).

III. Special Features

A. PRESERVING OUR HERITAGE

There are Black American Christians who sometimes appear to be more concerned with race than with grace, and with skin than with sin. This is to say, wrong is wrong no matter who does it, and we must not excuse wrongdoing because of some mistaken idea of racial unity. The Black skin of an unbeliever is not enough to make him my brother. By the same token, the White skin of a believer should not cause me to mistreat him. If he loves Jesus Christ, he is my brother. Authority to be called the children of God is not based on race, but is the gift of God, and founded on His authority alone (John 1:12-13). One other point: Inasmuch as some cults in our country are based on race, encouraged by White racism—it is necessary that we remember the God of the Bible sovereignly chose to become a Jew. The word that became flesh took on the seed of Abraham; after the flesh He became a Jew. Therefore any cult group which rejects Christ (John 1:11) or preaches hatred of Jewish people is an abomination. And Black Christians should be more discerning about their associations.

B. A CONCLUDING WORD

Our last word comes from John 1:18. No one has ever seen God in His fullness, completeness, essence, or the totality of His being. It is simply impossible. First of all, God is a Spirit (John 4:24), and as such has no bodily form. Second, God is omnipresent; that is, He is everywhere present at the same time. It is thus impossible for any human being to see God as He is essentially. We are in one place at one time.

Third: God is holy and we are sinners. We could not stand the sight of Him. To look upon God would be instant death. He dwells "in the light which no man can approach unto; whom no man hath seen, nor can see" (1 Timothy 6:16). This is why there are theophanies (God appearances) in the Old Testament; God appearing in the form of men or angels. Men like Abraham, Jacob, Moses, Gideon, Manoah and others had experiences with God who thus appeared to them. From their point of view, they met God face to face, however obscure and at a distance. But the truth remains: God in His naked majesty and essential being and glory, God as Father, Son and Holy Spirit—never at any time has been seen by the eyes of mortal men.

Now the second part of John 1:18 speaks of the only begotten of God who is in the bosom of the Father (New American Standard Bible). You see the King James Version has "the only begotten Son." The New International Version has: "No one has ever seen God, but God the One and Only, who is at the Father's side, has made him known." Manuscript differences are involved here. The student is advised that this part of the text emphasizes the kindred tie, the intimacy involved in the Godhead so that the Son could say, "I and My Father are one" (John 10:30). To be in one's bosom means to share or communicate secrets. Third: The Lord Jesus declared the Father. The Greek verb used has given us the English word, "exegeted." Christ exegeted God; that is, He unfolded in teaching, declared, explained, interpreted, described, reported, expounded, revealed, elucidated, analyzed Him. In other words, the invisible God was made visible in Jesus Christ. He made God known; He gave a full revelation, a perfect exegesis. Without Christ, man would wallow in ignorance concerning the true nature of God. By his own wisdom, man could never discover who God is (Matthew 11:27). How grateful we are that God the Son became Flesh!

The Mission of John the Baptist serves as a living example of how the person who is committed to Christ should be. His ability to preach the gospel in a manner that attracted persons of high society, as well as those who stood on the outer edges of the social arena, had gained for John popularity that had not been witnessed for over four hundred years among the people of Israel. John was able to convince those who were acutely aware of their sinful condition to accept baptism as the outward sign that they desired to begin to live a new life, and He was bold enough to confront those who believed that they were righteous to re-examine their faith and evaluate it on the basis of that which God required.

HOME DAILY BIBLE READINGS
Week of March 7, 1999
The Word Became Flesh

Mar. 1	M.	John 1:1-5, In the Beginning Was the Word
Mar. 2	T.	John 1:6-9, The Witness of John the Baptizer
Mar. 3	W.	Mark 1:1-15, John Baptizes Jesus
Mar. 4	T.	John 1:10-13, To All Who Received Him
Mar. 5	F.	Acts 16:25-34, Believe on the Lord Jesus
Mar. 6	S.	John 1:14-18, The Word Became Flesh and Lived Among Us
Mar. 7	S.	Ephesians 1:3-14, Before the Foundations of the World

The Witness of John the Baptist

Adult Topic—Bearing Witness

.....

Youth Topic—Pointing the Way
Children's Topic—Jesus Calls Disciples

.....

Devotional Reading—Ephesians 4:25—5:2
Background Scripture—John 1:19-42
Print—John 1:19-34

• • • • • • • • • • • •

PRINTED SCRIPTURE

John 1:19-34 (KJV)

19 And this is the record of John, when the Jews sent priests and Levites from Jerusalem to ask him, Who art thou?

20 And he confessed, and denied not; but confessed, I am not the Christ.

21 And they asked him, What then? Art thou Elias? And he saith, I am not. Art thou that prophet? And he answered, No.

22 Then said they unto him, Who art thou? that we may give an answer to them that sent us. What sayest thou of thyself?

23 He said, I am the voice of one crying in the wilderness, Make straight the way of the Lord, as said the prophet Esaias.

24 And they which were sent were of the Pharisees.

25 And they asked him, and said unto him, Why baptizest thou then, if thou be not that Christ, nor Elias, neither that prophet?

26 John answered them, saying,

John 1:19-34 (NRSV)

19 This is the testimony given by John when the Jews sent priests and Levites from Jerusalem to ask him, "Who are you?"

20 He confessed and did not deny it, but confessed, "I am not the Messiah."

21 And they asked him, "What then? Are you Elijah?" He said, "I am not." "Are you the prophet?" He answered, "No."

22 Then they said to him, "Who are you? Let us have an answer for those who sent us. What do you say about yourself?"

23 He said, "I am the voice of one crying out in the wilderness, 'Make straight the way of the Lord.'" as the prophet Isaiah said.

24 Now they had been sent from the Pharisees.

25 They asked him, "Why then are you baptizing if you are neither the Messiah, nor Elijah, nor the prophet?"

26 John answered them, "I

I baptize with water: but there standeth one among you, whom ye know not;

27 He it is, who coming after me is preferred before me, whose shoe's latchet I am not worthy to unloose.

28 These things were done in Bethabara beyond Jordan, where John was baptizing.

29 The next day John seeth Jesus coming unto him, and saith, Behold the Lamb of God, which taketh away the sin of the world.

30 This is he of whom I said, After me cometh a man which is preferred before me: for he was before me.

31 And I knew him not: but that he should be made manifest to Israel, therefore am I come baptizing with water.

32 And John bare record, saying, I saw the Spirit descending from heaven like a dove, and it abode upon him.

33 And I knew him not: but he that sent me to baptize with water, the same said unto me, Upon whom thou shalt see the Spirit descending, and remaining on him, the same is he which baptizeth with the Holy Ghost.

34 And I saw, and bare record that this is the Son of God.

baptize with water. Among you stands one whom you do not know,

27 the one who is coming after me; I am not worthy to untie the thong of his sandal."

28 This took place in Bethany across the Jordan where John was baptizing.

29 The next day he saw Jesus coming toward him and declared, "Here is the Lamb of God who takes away the sin of the world!

30 This is he of whom I said, 'After me comes a man who ranks ahead of me because he was before me.'

31 I myself did not know him; but I came baptizing with water for this reason, that he might be revealed to Israel."

32 And John testified, "I saw the Spirit descending from heaven like a dove, and it remained on him.

33 I myself did not know him, but the one who sent me to baptize with water said to me, 'He on whom you see the Spirit descend and remain is the one who baptizes with the Holy Spirit.'

34 And I myself have seen and have testified that this is the Son of God."

KEY VERSE

The next day John seeth Jesus coming unto him, and saith, Behold the Lamb of God, which taketh away the sin of the world.—John 1:29

OBJECTIVES

After reading this lesson, the student should appreciate more:

1. The character, commission, and personality of John the Baptist;
2. The role played by John the Baptist in the life of Israel; and,
3. The role played by John the Baptist in the life of the Lord Jesus Christ.

POINTS TO BE EMPHASIZED

Adult/Youth
Key Verse—John 1:29
Print—John 1:19-34

—When questioned by the Jewish leaders, John the Baptist testified that he was not the Messiah. (19-20)
—John the Baptist identified himself as one crying in the wilderness admonishing people to prepare the way of the Lord. (21-23)
—When asked by the Jewish leaders why he baptized, John the Baptist responded that one greater than he, but unknown to them, would come from among them. (24-27)
—John the Baptist identified Jesus as the Lamb of God who takes away the sin of the world. (29)
—John baptized with water so that Jesus might be revealed to Israel. (31)
—John the Baptist testified that Jesus is God's Son, because he saw the Holy Spirit come as a dove and remain on Jesus. (32-34)

Children
Key Verse—John 1:43
Print—John 1:35-50

—John identified Jesus as the Lamb of God. (35-36)
—Two of John's disciples followed Jesus. (37)
—Andrew told Peter they had found the Messiah. (38-41)
—Andrew brought Peter to Jesus and Jesus identified him. (42)
—Jesus invited Philip to follow Him.(43-44)
—Philip brought Nathanael to Jesus. (45-50)

(NOTE: Use KJV Scripture for Adults; NRSV Scripture for Youth and Children)

TOPICAL OUTLINE OF THE LESSON

I. Introduction

A. The Meaning of the Term, "The Jews"
B. Biblical Background

II. Exposition and Application of the Scripture

A. Question and Response, Part I (John 1:19-23)
B. Question and Response, Part II (John 1:24-28)
C. John's Witness, Part I (John 1:29-31)
D. John's Witness, Part II (John 1:32-34)

III. Special Features

A. Preserving Our Heritage
B. A Concluding Word

I. Introduction

A. THE MEANING OF THE TERM, "THE JEWS"

In order to better understand the interrogation of John the Baptist, it is necessary to study the use of the phrase, "the Jews," used in John 1:19. In recent years, the New Testament has again come under attack and has been labeled anti-Semitic, primarily, of course, by Jewish religious leaders. One major criticism has been the use of this expression, "the Jews." Originally, "the Jews" designated the tribes of Judah and Benjamin, but after the Captivity it denoted all Israelites.

John uses the term more than seventy times, compared to only five times in the Synoptic Gospels (Matthew, Mark and Luke). Does this mean John was an anti-Semite? By no means. John, himself was a Jew, as was the Lord Jesus after the flesh. This fact alone would suggest that no genuine Christian has any business being anti-Jewish! The meaning of Ioudaioi (Jews) is in part determined by the context or setting of the word. If John was led by the Holy Spirit to use the phrase "the Jews," we cannot really criticize the writer. He wrote as he was moved by God's Spirit—the Holy Spirit!

Investigation reveals that "the Jews" refers in a general sense to the nation. However, there is with the phrase an air of hostility. It refers to those religious leaders and their followers who were "deeply imbued with national sentiment, intensely conservative in religious matters, bigoted and intolerant in their pride of race" (Bernard, ICC). Thus, "the Jews" would be like saying, "the enemies of Christ." Basically, it means the leaders of the nation—the Pharisees, Sadducees, Scribes, the priests—the members of the Sanhedrin. See then "the Jews" as reference to that community of leaders who deeply opposed the Lord Jesus Christ. And, of course, see John's Gospel as pre-eminently the story of the rejection of the Lord Jesus by these leaders of religious thought in Jerusalem. He came unto His own—"the Jews"—and they received Him not.

B. BIBLICAL BACKGROUND

All four of the Gospels introduce the ministry of the Lord Jesus with accounts of the role of John the Baptist. In Matthew chapter 3, Mark 1:1-11; Luke 1:5-17, 57-66; 3:1-20, Matthew deals with the preaching, personal appearance, and baptizing ministry of John the Baptist. Mark likewise describes John's ministry. Luke gives us the most information. He tells of the birth and parents of John the Baptist, as well as of his ministry and imprisonment. His murder is described by Matthew 14:1-14; Mark 6:14-29, and Luke 9:7-9. John's Gospel says nothing about the demise of the Baptist (except to mention he was not yet cast into prison, John 3:24). The Gospel of John apparently takes for granted the general history of John the Baptist, and emphasizes not so much the Baptist's life as it stresses the testimony given to the Lord Jesus as the Messiah and Son of God.

II. Exposition and Application of the Scripture

A. QUESTION AND RESPONSE, PART I
(John 1:19-23)

And this is the record of John, when the Jews sent priests and Levites from Jerusalem to ask him, Who art thou? And he confessed, and denied not; but confessed, I am not the Christ. And they asked him, What then? Art thou Elias? And he saith, I am not. Art thou that prophet? And he answered, No. Then said they unto him, Who art thou? that we may give an answer to them that sent us. What sayest thou of thyself? He said, I am the voice of one crying in the wilderness, Make straight the way of the Lord, as said the prophet Esaias.

We see immediately the influence of John the Baptist, for the Jews sent a detachment of common priests (not high priests) and Levites—men who did the menial work, and who served as Temple police—to inquire of John. For, John's strong preaching and baptizing had stirred up the people! Indeed, it is said, "Then went out to him Jerusalem, and all Judea, and all the region round about Jordan, and were baptized of him in Jordan, confessing their sins" (Matthew 3:5-6).

We are introduced to the record or witness **(Marturia: martyr)** of John at the very height of his ministry. Those commissioned (sent, appointed) asked the question: "Who are you?" The Greek is literally, "You, who are you?" The committee is not really concerned about his name, or parentage—they knew those. But John knew what they were after. And so he answered with a positive, a negative, and a positive. This was typical of his style as he sought to impress with the seriousness of his reply. To confess **(homologeo)** is to speak the same thing (as God says). So that very emphatically, John the Baptist denies he is the Christ (Messiah), or Anointed One of God. "I—I am not the Christ."

"Are you Elijah?" John said, "No I am not." It was believed that Elijah would return to earth to prepare the way of the Messiah (Malachi 4:5). On one occasion the Lord said to the multitude, "If you will receive it, this is Elijah, who was to come" (Matthew 11:14). In other words, accept Christ and John the Baptist will be your Elijah. And so, while not actually Elijah, yet he served in function as Elijah (Matthew 17:11-13). Zacharias, the father of John, had been told that his son would go "before him in the spirit and power of Elijah" (Luke 1:17). Historically speaking, the return of the Old Testament prophet Elijah remains in the future, for it is believed he will be one of the two witnesses of the Tribulation era (Revelation 11:3). And, so John denied that he was the Christ or Elijah.

"Are you that prophet?" We read in Deuteronomy 18:15: "The Lord thy God will raise up unto thee a Prophet from the midst of thee, of thy brethren, like unto me; unto him ye shall hearken" (cf. verses 18-19). In four places in John's Gospel, allusion is made to "that Prophet." We find it twice in our lesson (verses 21 and 25); then in John 6:14, where after the five thousand men (plus women and children) were fed with five barley loaves and two small fishes, those (Galileans) who had witnessed the miracle the Lord performed, said, "This is of a truth that prophet that should come into the world."

Then in John 7:40, after the Lord prophesied of the Holy Spirit's coming, some of the multitude, upon hearing what the Lord said (John 7:37-38), remarked: "Of a truth this is the Prophet," But others said, "This is the Christ." Note the emphasis in John 6:14 on Christ's performance, but in John 7:40, upon what He said. What is recorded here in 7:40 and in 1:21, 25, indicates that many of the Jews did not see in the Prophet the Messiah. In their minds they were two different persons. In their minds, this Prophet would precede the Messiah! However, in his second sermon, Simon Peter applied Deuteronomy 18:15 to Christ (Acts 3:22). This interpretation was thereafter adapted by the Christian Church. Stephen likewise preached that Jesus Christ is the Prophet of whom Moses spoke (Acts 7:37).

And so, John was asked, "Are you that prophet?" To this John simply said, "No." Once again, he is pressed to tell them who he claims to be, for they are not satisfied with his denials or negatives. The question came (verse 22), "Who are you? We need to know so we can inform our superiors who sent us. What do you have to say about yourself?" John replied, quoting from Isaiah 40:3, that he was but a voice crying in the wilderness. We have here a picture of Israel represented by the wilderness, a dry waste, barren and fruitless, pathless desert land. Such is the language describing Israel's spiritual condition. What is needed to turn such a desert into a land of blooming roses and beauty is Christ the Word. Only the repentance of which John preached prepared the coming of their King. For John the Baptist, the only thing that counted in life was his testimony to the Messiah. That was the work God had given him. John is not to be seen; he is only to be heard.

B. QUESTION AND RESPONSE, PART II
(John 1:24-28)

And they which were sent were of the Pharisees. And they asked him, and said unto him, Why baptizest thou then, if thou be not that Christ, nor Elias, neither that prophet? John answered them, saying, I baptize with water: but there standeth one among you, whom ye know not; He it is, who coming after me is preferred before me, whose shoe's latchet I am not worthy to unloose. These things were done in Bethabara beyond Jordan, where John was baptizing.

The interrogation by the delegates sent by the Pharisees continued. "If you are not that Christ, nor Elijah, neither that Prophet, why then are you baptizing?" The Jews practiced baptism because it symbolized removing pollution contacted in the Gentile world; it was then a symbolic ceremony of purification. The Pharisees regarded John's practice of baptizing as a claim to authority. John replied that what he was doing was nothing compared with what the Messiah would do. "You see me baptizing with water, but you don't even know the One who stands among you, and who is greater than I. His cleansing is far beyond what I or any other man can provide."

What John did then was only a sign; what Christ did was the real thing—namely, a cleansing by the power of the Holy Spirit. Water baptism is but an outward symbol of an inward change. For John, baptism was not an end in itself. His purpose was to point men to Christ—One whose shoe latchet John considered himself unworthy to unloose, unworthy to be His servant. When an honored guest entered a house, it was the task of the servant to unfasten the thong or strap of the shoe (or sandal), and remove the shoes. He would then wash the feet of the guest, and cleanse the shoes. John felt unworthy even to do this for the Lord Jesus.

C. JOHN'S WITNESS, PART I
(John 1:29-31)

The next day John seeth Jesus coming unto him, and saith, Behold the Lamb of God, which taketh away the sin of the world. This is he of whom I said, After me cometh a man which is preferred before me: for he was before me. And I knew him not: but that he should be made manifest to Israel, therefore am I come baptizing with water.

At this point, a new situation is introduced. Whereas John had based his ministry on the fact of sin and the need for repentance, now we see the ministry of Christ concerned with the removal of sin. Upon seeing the Lord Jesus coming, John uttered one of the most important sayings in the New Testament: "Behold the Lamb of God, who takes away the sin of the world."

This is also a rather difficult verse to interpret. First of all, what Lamb did John the Baptist have in mind? As popular as the title is today, the name "the Lamb of God" is found only here (John 1:29, 36). To whom then did John refer? Who was the Lamb? Was it a reference to the Passover Lamb which had been killed to save the Jews from God's judgment of death? You recall that on the night the Israelites left Egypt, a lamb without blemish was slain and its blood applied to the two side posts and on the upper door posts of the houses. God promised: "When I see the blood, I will pass over you" (Exodus 12:3-13). Another suggestion is that reference is made to Isaiah 53:6-7 and the Suffering Servant of the Lord. A third idea is that it signifies the blood of all the lambs in all Old Testament rituals! One thing is sure, the Lamb connotes sacrifice, and the fact that blood is to be shed. We missed the mark (sinned)—the mark set by God—in thought, deed, and the corrupt nature within us. And since the wages of sin is death, Christ died for us in our place—yea, He took away our sin!

In his commentary on the Gospel of John, Leon Morris offers some nine ideas about this Lamb. He concludes that John purposely used an expression which "cannot be confined to any one view," but alludes to the very general concept of sacrifice. We believe this is the best interpretation of the wonderful announcement: "Behold the Lamb of God, who takes away the sin of the world!"

Verse 30 repeats for the most part verse 15. Timewise, the ministry of John preceded that of our Lord. However, He who comes later is He who actually existed before. John was born some six months before the Lord Jesus, but actually

Jesus Christ pre-existed from all eternity. So, He is superior to John. In other words, John's successor preceded him. When John says, "I knew Him not," he means he did not know He was the Messiah. John had been looking for the Christ, not knowing really who He was. And so the statements, "I knew Him not," twice said (verses 31, 33), do not mean John had never seen the Lord before. After all, they were cousins, and more than likely well acquainted. But this is not to say he recognized his Cousin to be the Christ. He did not know Him in His divine greatness.

D. JOHN'S WITNESS, PART II
(John 1:32-34)

And John bare record, saying, I saw the Spirit descending from heaven like a dove, and it abode upon him. And I knew him not: but he that sent me to baptize with water, the same said unto me, Upon whom thou shalt see the Spirit descending, and remaining on him, the same is he which baptizeth with the Holy Ghost. And I saw, and bare record that this is the Son of God.

When the Lord came to be baptized, it was at that point John recognized who He was, for the Holy Spirit descending from heaven like a dove, and remaining on Him, was the sign that assured John of Christ's identity. Three times John mentions he baptizes with water (verses 26, 31, 33), but the One upon whom the Spirit descended baptizes with the Holy Spirit. John's testimony was an eyewitness account. The King James Version states, "I bore witness" (v. 34); the Greek tense used (perfect) gives us "I have witnessed." It was as if the vision was still before him, as if he still saw it. His testimony was continuing up to the very time of speaking that "this is the Son of God."

III. Special Features

A. PRESERVING OUR HERITAGE

All the talk about John the Baptist was relished in the church circles of my early childhood. In those days, I heard it often said that John the Baptist organized the first Baptist Church in Jerusalem. We never took this seriously, but we took pride in being called Baptists; and we appreciated all the more this one who came crying in the wilderness! Though some Black Protestant groups are growing more rapidly in the United States than Black Baptists, we still represent the largest denomination among Black American Christians. May we continue to support our Foreign Mission Board in letting the world know that Jesus Christ "is the lamb of God who takes away the sin of the world." And may our churches ever maintain the zeal that John the Baptist demonstrated in exalting the Lord Jesus Christ as the Son of God.

B. A CONCLUDING WORD

The baptism of our Lord is often used to illustrate the concept of the Trinity.

What John saw was indeed one of the reasons he could be so sure about what he said concerning the Lord Jesus. Note, this event is recorded in Matthew 3:13-17; Mark 1:9-11; and Luke 3:21-22. The baptism story is a fitting climax to the purpose of John the Baptist, namely, to exalt Jesus Christ. See then in John's splendid testimony these facts:

(1) Christ as the Lamb of God had the mission of redemption; (2) as Baptizer with the Holy Spirit, He would find the Church; and (3) as Son of God, He was worthy of our adoration and obedience (E.F. Harrison, *Wycliffe Bible Commentary*). Those who deny that One God of the Bible exists as Father, Son and Holy Spirit are hard pressed to deny this teaching as it is demonstrated at our Lord's baptism. The voice from heaven was that of God the Father. He called the Lord Jesus His beloved Son in whom He was well pleased. And the Spirit of God descended like a dove, and lighted upon the Lord. Surely John the Baptist fulfilled his calling—to witness a good witness of Jesus Christ.

The mission of John the Baptist serves as a living example of how the person who is committed to Christ should be. His ability to preach the gospel in a manner that attracted persons of high society, as well as those who stood on the outer edges of the social arena, had gained popularity that had not been witnessed for over four hundred years among the people of Israel. John was able to convince those who were acutely aware of their sinful condition to accept baptism as the outward sign that they desired to begin to live a new life, and He was bold enough to confront those who believed that they were righteous to re-examine their faith and evaluate it on the basis of that which God required. Through it all, his popularity did not inflate his ego to the extent that he forgot to remember his true role within the process of salvation. He was only an instrument in the hand of the Divine whose task it was to begin building the kingdom of God rather than construct monuments that would endear him with posterity. He knew that as the people accepted the message about the Christ, he would diminish both in popularity and importance and that only the Christ would stand forth as that word which each person would embrace with saving power. May our teaching and preaching reveal the Christ, not spotlight the self.

HOME DAILY BIBLE READINGS
Week of March 14, 1999
The Witness of John the Baptist

Mar. 8 M. John 1:19-23, John's Testimony
Mar. 9 T. John 1:24-28, I Baptize With Water
Mar. 10 W. John 1:29-34, Here Is the Lamb of God
Mar. 11 T. John 1:35-42, What Are You Looking for?
Mar. 12 F. John 3:22-36, Jesus Commends John
Mar. 13 S. Luke 7:18-28, Jesus Must Increase
Mar. 14 S. Mark 6:14-29, John Is Beheaded

Nicodemus Visits Jesus

Adult Topic—Seeking Answers for Life's Questions

.....

Youth Topic—Seeking Help for Life's Questions
Children's Topic—Nicodemus Visits Jesus

.....

Devotional Reading—1 Corinthians 15:17-22
Background Scripture—John 3:1-21
Print—John 3:1-17

• • • • • • • • • • •

PRINTED SCRIPTURE

John 3:1-17 (KJV)

THERE was a man of the Pharisees, named Nicodemus, a ruler of the Jews:

2 The same came to Jesus by night, and said unto him, Rabbi, we know that thou art a teacher come from God: for no man can do these miracles that thou doest, except God be with him.

3 Jesus answered and said unto him, Verily, verily, I say unto thee, Except a man be born again, he cannot see the kingdom of God.

4 Nicodemus saith unto him, How can a man be born when he is old? can he enter the second time into his mother's womb, and be born?

5 Jesus answered, Verily, verily, I say unto thee, Except a man be born of water and of the Spirit, he cannot enter into the kingdom of God.

6 That which is born of the flesh is flesh; and that which is born of the Spirit is spirit.

7 Marvel not that I said unto

John 3:1-17 (NRSV)

NOW THERE was a Pharisee named Nicodemus, a leader of the Jews.

2 He came to Jesus by night and said to him, "Rabbi, we know that you are a teacher who has come from God; for no one can do these signs that you do apart from the presence of God."

3 Jesus answered him, "Very truly, I tell you, no one can see the kingdom of God without being born from above."

4 Nicodemus said to him, "How can anyone be born after having grown old? Can one enter a second time into the mother's womb and be born?"

5 Jesus answered, "Very truly, I tell you, no one can enter the kingdom of God without being born of water and Spirit.

6 What is born of the flesh is flesh, and what is born of the Spirit is spirit.

7 Do not be astonished that I said to you, 'You must be born from

thee, Ye must be born again.

8 The wind bloweth where it listeth, and thou hearest the sound thereof, but canst not tell whence it cometh, and whither it goeth: so is every one that is born of the Spirit.

9 Nicodemus answered and said unto him, How can these things be?

10 Jesus answered and said unto him, Art thou a master of Israel, and knowest not these things?

11 Verily, verily, I say unto thee, We speak that we do know, and testify that we have seen; and ye receive not our witness.

12 If I have told you earthly things, and ye believe not, how shall ye believe, if I tell you of heavenly things?

13 And no man hath ascended up to heaven, but he that came down from heaven, even the Son of man which is in heaven.

14 And as Moses lifted up the serpent in the wilderness, even so must the Son of man be lifted up:

15 That whosoever believeth in him should not perish, but have eternal life.

16 For God so loved the world, that he gave his only begotten Son, that whosoever believeth in him should not perish, but have everlasting life.

17 For God sent not his Son into the world to condemn the world; but that the world through him might be saved.

above.'

8 The wind blows where is chooses, and you hear the sound of it, but you do not know where it comes from or where it goes. So it is with everyone who is born of the Spirit."

9 Nicodemus said to him, "How can these things be?"

10 Jesus answered him, "Are you a teacher of Israel, and yet you do not understand these things?

11 Very truly, I tell you, we speak of what we know and testify to what we have seen; yet you do not receive our testimony.

12 If I have told you about earthly things and you do not believe, how can you believe if I tell you about heavenly things?

13 No one has ascended into heaven except the one who descended from heaven, the Son of Man.

14 And just as Moses lifted up the serpent in the wilderness, so must the Son of Man be lifted up,

15 that whoever believes in him may have eternal life.

16 For God so loved the world that he gave his only Son, so that everyone who believes in him may not perish but may have eternal life.

17 Indeed, God did not send the Son into the world to condemn the world, but in order that the world might be saved through him."

KEY VERSE

For God sent not his son into the world to condemn the world; but that the world through him might be saved.—John 3:17

OBJECTIVES

After reading this lesson, the student will have more knowledge of:

1. The doctrine and necessity of Regeneration;
2. The character of Nicodemus;
3. The mysterious nature of conversion; and,
4. The greatness of the love of God.

POINTS TO BE EMPHASIZED

Adult/Youth/Children
Print: John 3:1-17; John 3:1-10, 16-21 (Children)
Key Verse: John 3:17; John 3:16 (Children)

—A religious leader named Nicodemus came to Jesus by night and acknowledged Jesus as a teacher who came from God. (1-2)

—Jesus told Nicodemus that a person must be born from above to see God's kingdom. (3)

—Nicodemus, not understanding that Jesus spoke of a spiritual birth, wondered how an adult could experience physical birth. (4)

—Jesus said a person must be born of water and Spirit to enter God's kingdom and used the wind, as metaphor, to explain the Spirit's activity. (5-8)

—In response to Nicodemus' question Jesus identified Himself as the Son of Man who would be lifted up so that whoever would believe in Him would have eternal life. (9-15)

—God's great love for people caused God to send His Son not to condemn the world but that people who believe in Him might have eternal life. (16-17)

(NOTE: Use KJV Scripture for Adults; NRSV Scripture for Youth and Children)

TOPICAL OUTLINE OF THE LESSON

I. Introduction

A. The Doctrine of Regeneration
B. Biblical Background

II. Exposition and Application of the Scripture

A. Nicodemus Visits at Night (John 3:1-2)
B. The Necessity and Nature of the New Birth (John 3:3-8)
C. What Nicodemus Needed to Know (John 3:9-13)
D. The Love Gift of God (John 3:14-17)

III. Special Features

A. Preserving Our Heritage
B. A Concluding Word

I. Introduction

A. THE DOCTRINE OF REGENERATION

The word "regeneration" is found only twice in the King James Version of the New Testament. **Paliggenesia** is used in Matthew 19:28 as a re-creation or renewing of the order of things on the earth during the Millennium (the 1,000 years when Christ will rule on earth with a rod of iron). Maybe better for our study is Titus 3:5, where Paul speaks of God who "saved us, by the washing of regeneration, and renewing of the Holy Spirit." This is the cleansing which is a new birth. From today's lesson, we consider John 3:1-6, especially verse 3, and the words, "born again." The Greek word here is **anothen,** which also means "from above." It is interesting that we often hear church members talk about "born again Christians!" Are there any other kinds of Christians? No, we are either born again or we are not born again; we are either Christians or we are not Christians. The word "regeneration" speaks of a creative act of God wherein the divine nature is imparted to the human being who accepts the Lord Jesus Christ as Savior. It is a radical change of heart. Regeneration is God's gift of "a new nature and a new life that is like Him and wants to please Him" *(Pilgrim Bible).*

B. BIBLICAL BACKGROUND

Nicodemus is mentioned only in the Gospel of John (3:1, 4, 9; 7:50; 19:39). **Nike** in Greek means victory, conquest. Does this bring to mind the appeal of the name of the footwear of some athletes? **Demos** means people. Combined, the name Nicodemus means "Conqueror of the people." It was a common name among both Jews and Gentiles (Arndt and Gingrich, *Lexicon).* Little is known about this main character of today's lesson. Apparently as a Pharisee, he was a member of the Sanhedrin, for the Lord called him, "a teacher of Israel" (John 3:10). Look briefly at the three chapters in which Nicodemus is mentioned. First, in chapter 3, the thing stressed is his interview with the Lord. Evidently, there is an element of faith, however faint or incomplete, that moved him to visit Christ.

Second, in chapter 7, Nicodemus vindicated or defended the Lord, pointing out to his fellow Pharisees that in all fairness, according to their laws, a man is not judged before he is heard and his deeds made known. Third, in chapter 19, he boldly assisted Joseph of Arimathea in the embalmment of the body of the crucified Savior. Note that in each section, mention is made of the fact that Nicodemus was the one "who came to Jesus by night." Thus, attention is drawn to what is variously described by the commentators as: "his fear of the Jews and excommunication" (John 12:42); "desire not to offend his colleagues in that prestigious body, the Sanhedrin"; his "natural timidity"; his "reluctant faith"; his being a "a cautious politician," or his "unwillingness to compromise his position as a Pharisee." I don't think he should be painted as a coward. Each step shows growth in a heart made inquisitive by the Holy Spirit, with an increasing boldness to no longer accept being a "secret follower."

II. Exposition and Application of the Scripture

A. NICODEMUS VISITS AT NIGHT
(John 3:1-2)

THERE was a man of the Pharisees, named Nicodemus, a ruler of the Jews: The same came to Jesus by night, and said unto him, Rabbi, we know that thou art a teacher come from God: for no man can do these miracles that thou doest, except God be with him.

Nicodemus was a Pharisee, a religious separatist. As a member of the body of leaders called the Sanhedrin, he enjoyed a position of influence at the top level of political and religious life in Israel. He came by night obviously to avoid letting his colleagues know he had visited the One they had rejected, One who had not been accepted by the majority of the people. There certainly was no need to compromise his position, for it appears that Nicodemus had a genuine desire to know the truth. Whatever his motive for his approach, the Lord Jesus received him graciously. Nicodemus began his personal talk with the Lord by acknowledging that he and others (John 2:23) were convinced by the miracles He had performed, that He was indeed a teacher come from God. Note Nicodemus addressed Him as Rabbi (literally, "my Great One"); it was used much like we might say, "Sir," today. Perhaps, too, there was a dissatisfaction with the manner in which his colleagues had treated the Man called Jesus. Some of us readily believe the negative things our co-workers, peers, and schoolmates say about others! Nicodemus wanted to see for himself. In his mind, there was the possibility that this might be the Messiah!

B. THE NECESSITY AND NATURE OF THE NEW BIRTH
(John 3:3-8)

Jesus answered and said unto him, Verily, verily, I say unto thee, Except a man be born again, he cannot see the kingdom of God. Nicodemus saith unto him, How can a man be born when he is old? can he enter the second time into his mother's womb, and be born? Jesus answered, Verily, verily, I say unto thee, Except a man be born of water and of the Spirit, he cannot enter into the kingdom of God. That which is born of the flesh is flesh; and that which is born of the Spirit is spirit. Marvel not that I said unto thee, Ye must be born again. The wind bloweth where it listeth, and thou hearest the sound thereof, but canst not tell whence it cometh, and whither it goeth: so is every one that is born of the Spirit.

Our Lord's answer indicates that He knew what was in the heart of Nicodemus; He knew what the man needed. The words rendered "verily, verily" are literally, "amen, amen," and draw our attention to the importance of what is about to be said. "Amen" points to the assurance of the truth to be given. Here is the tremendous concept of being "born again." We come into this world with corrupt, fallen, sinful natures—no matter how cute we may have been as babies. We are born with a human nature that is evil (Psalm 51:5). Failure to accept this biblical truth concerning the make-up of man leaves one with a woefully inadequate explanation for the evil that is in this world. What is required, said Christ, is a new nature. Without it, we cannot see the kingdom of God; we cannot see the universal rule of the sovereign God. To the Jewish mind of that day, the kingdom of God included future prosperity and peace promised to Israel, as announced by the prophets.

Now, one of the things that impresses us is the fact that a man like Nicodemus is told that he must be born from above, born afresh, born anew, born again. Imagine telling a religious Jew like Nicodemus that he must be changed or reborn! So much for entering the kingdom by keeping the law or by our "good deeds!" What is needed is a radical change of heart (Ezekiel 36:26-28). Here was Nicodemus, a fine example of a conscientious Jew, faithful, religious, high up in Judaism, irreproachable in character—but needing to be born again! What a shocking answer to all who seek to enter a spiritual kingdom by their own fleshly efforts—fasting, "witnessing for Jehovah," giving alms, a trip to Mecca, praying five times a day, etc. Not even our family trees or genealogies or "roots" help us here. Being physically related to Abraham means nothing without an inner change. Nicodemus did not understand and inquired, "How can an old man be born again?" The way Nicodemus puts the question shows that he knew the Lord did not mean a second physical birth.

This is seen in the rendering from the *New American Standard Bible:* "He cannot enter a second time into his mother's womb and be born, can he?" (John 3:4). Once again, the Lord calls for alert hearing with the words, "amen, amen." With divine authority, he assured Nicodemus that except a man be born of water and Spirit, he cannot enter into God's kingdom. The word translated "and" here may be rendered "even." This means the words, "water" and "Spirit" are used synonymously, so that unless one is born of water, even (the) Spirit, he cannot enter God's kingdom. Without the aid of the Holy Spirit, a man can neither see nor enter the kingdom of God.

In John 5:28, the command "marvel not" means "do not continue to wonder at the fact that the time is coming when all the dead in the graves shall hear the voice of Jesus Christ and be resurrected." In 1 John 3:13, we read: "Marvel not," this is to say, "do not continue to be astonished that the world hates genuine Christians."

In our lesson, John 3:7, the "marvel not" means, "do not be astonished that a man must be born again." Regeneration is a mystery. We do not know the source or origin of the wind; we don't know what direction it will take at any given moment. We see what the wind does; we hear it howling. But we cannot make any predictions concerning its activities. Note the word for wind is **pneuma,** the same word for Spirit. He is incomprehensible in His operations in the new birth; the new birth is inexplicable. So do not remain amazed. Elsewhere in the Bible, we read of the Holy Spirit symbolized not only by water and wind, but also by fire and oil, symbols which further support our inability to "pigeon-hole" the Holy Spirit.

C. WHAT NICODEMUS NEEDED TO KNOW
(John 3:9-13)

Nicodemus answered and said unto him, How can these things be? Jesus answered and said unto him, Art thou a master of Israel, and knowest not these things? Verily, verily, I say unto thee, We speak that we do know, and testify that we have seen; and ye receive not our witness. If I have told you earthly things, and ye believe not, how shall ye believe, if I tell you of heavenly things? And no man hath ascended up to heaven, but he that came down from heaven, even the Son of man which is in heaven.

Because Nicodemus could not understand this teaching, he inquired: "How can this be?" thus admitting the possibility, but baffled by the manner of fulfillment. "Are you the authorized (or, well known) teacher of the Israel of God?" Note the definite article, "the" is used to indicate that Nicodemus was indeed well known. "And you do not understand these things?" "These things" are believed to be the various manifestations of the Holy Spirit in the life of man; and also include faith, repentance, baptism, etc. Within our context, it appears that Nicodemus should have known that no one is able to enter God's kingdom in his own strength or righteousness.

What Christ has to say is not debatable. He does not speak based on hearsay, but speaks what He knows. And yet, the Jews reject His witness of these things! He spoke of things which men could readily see were true on earth. If these are rejected, how will they receive heavenly things? Nobody here on earth went up to Heaven to get information and bring it down to men. Enoch and Elijah went up, of course, but never came back down to inform us. Only the Lord Jesus Christ made the trip. He who was already up there (at home), came down with perfect knowledge to reveal a Perfect God to imperfect men. In other words, no one else has the authority so to speak. And, no one else has first-hand knowledge. Only God who became a Man possesses such knowledge.

D. THE LOVE GIFT OF GOD
(John 3:14-17)

And as Moses lifted up the serpent in the wilderness, even so must the Son of man be lifted up: That whosoever believeth in him should not perish, but have eternal life. For God so loved the world, that he gave his only begotten Son, that whosoever believeth in him should not perish, but have everlasting life. For God sent not his Son into the world to condemn the world; but that the world through him might be saved.

How then is the Son of Man to disseminate this knowledge? To answer this, our Lord directs attention to the incident that occurred in the wilderness as recorded in Numbers 21:4-9. Discouraged and impatient because of their wandering, the Israelites complained against God. In punishment, the Lord sent fiery serpents among the people and many died. When those surviving cried out unto the Lord in repentance, Jehovah told Moses to make a serpent of brass and put it on a pole. The snake symbolized sin; the brass stood for judgment. We see a picture of the fact that we were bitten by the viper of sin; and eternal death is the penalty. The pole then was lifted up as a symbol of the cross of Christ, and just a look at the serpent on the pole resulted in being saved alive physically. It was the look of faith! We are saved by looking to Him in faith. Thank God that Moses did not hide the pole and the brass serpent, or admit only certain people among the Israelites to look upon it. Rather, the pole was lifted upon for all to see, to look and to be saved! So must the Son of Man be lifted up on the cross (John 12:32). We thus have here an emphatic statement of the purpose for the death of Jesus Christ. Failure to believe that Christ died for our sins means separation from God forever—and such separation is Hell.

III. Special Features

A. PRESERVING OUR HERITAGE

One of the best arguments against the erroneous contention that Biblical Christianity is the White Man's religion is the universality of the Gospel presented in today's lesson. We see that all men must be born again, which suggests that all men were born in sin. Whether a law keeper like Nicodemus, or an ignorant savage—neither can see nor enter the kingdom of God. On the other hand, all who are born of the Spirit are those born from above. Whosoever believes shall not perish. God so loved the world that He gave His only begotten Son, that whosoever believes should not perish, but have everlasting life. Such words as all, whosoever and world clearly point out the universal appeal of the Gospel of the Lord Jesus Christ.

B. A CONCLUDING WORD

We would agree with those scholars who believe that the words of Christ end with verse 15, but that John speaks again, beginning with verse 16 (red letters notwithstanding). John 3:16 is said to be, "The Gospel in a nutshell." Martin Luther called it, "The Miniature Bible." Here, it is believed, is the most quoted verse in the Bible; certainly, it is the most familiar text in the Scriptures. And, it satisfies the longings of our hearts. Thank God for His Gift!

HOME DAILY BIBLE READINGS
Week of March 21, 1999
Nicodemus Visits Jesus

Mar. 15 M. John 3:1-10, Nicodemus Came to Jesus
Mar. 16 T.   John 3:11-21, God So Loved the World
Mar. 17 W. John 7:45-52, Nicodemus Takes a Stand
Mar. 18 T.   John 19:38-42, Joseph and Nicodemus Claim Jesus' Body
Mar. 19 F.   Matthew 19:16-22, A Contrasting Response to Jesus
Mar. 20 S.   Acts 24:22-27, Another Contrasting Response
Mar. 21 S.   Psalm 91:1-16, God Cares for All

A Woman Brings Her Village to Jesus

Adult Topic—Choose Life

.....

Youth Topic—Close Encounters
Children's Topic—Jesus and the Woman at the Well

.....

Devotional Reading—Revelation 7:13-17
Background Scripture—John 4:1-42
Print—John 4:7, 9-15, 28-30, 39-40

• • • • • • • • • • • •

PRINTED SCRIPTURE

John 4:7, 9-15, 28-30, 39-40 (KJV)

7 There cometh a woman of Samaria to draw water: Jesus saith unto her, Give me to drink.

.....

9 Then saith the woman of Samaria unto him, How is it that thou, being a Jew, askest drink of me, which am a woman of Samaria? for the Jews have no dealings with the Samaritans.

10 Jesus answered and said unto her, If thou knewest the gift of God, and who it is that saith to thee, Give me to drink; thou wouldest have asked of him, and he would have given thee living water.

11 The woman saith unto him, Sir, thou hast nothing to draw with, and the well is deep: from whence then hast thou that living water?

12 Art thou greater than our father Jacob, which gave us the well, and drank thereof himself, and his children, and his cattle?

13 Jesus answered and said unto her, Whosoever drinketh of

John 4:7, 9-15, 28-30, 39-40 (NRSV)

7 A Samaritan woman came to draw water, and Jesus said to her, "Give me a drink."

.....

9 The Samaritan woman said to him, "How is it that you, a Jew, ask a drink of me, a woman of Samaria?" (Jews do not share things in common with Samaritans.)

10 Jesus answered her, "If you knew the gift of God, and who it is that is saying to you, 'Give me a drink,' you would have asked him, and he would have given you living water."

11 The woman said to him, "Sir, you have no bucket, and the well is deep. Where do you get that living water?

12 Are you greater than our ancestor Jacob, who gave us the well, and with his sons and his flocks drank from it?"

13 Jesus said to her, "Everyone who drinks of this water will be

this water shall thirst again:

14 But whosoever drinketh of the water that I shall give him shall never thirst; but the water that I shall give him shall be in him a well of water springing up into everlasting life.

15 The woman saith unto him, Sir, give me this water, that I thirst not, neither come hither to draw.

.....

28 The woman then left her waterpot, and went her way into the city, and saith to the men,

29 Come, see a man, which told me all things that ever I did: is not this the Christ?

30 Then they went out of the city, and came unto him.

.....

39 And many of the Samaritans of that city believed on him for the saying of the woman, which testified, He told me all that ever I did.

40 So when the Samaritans were come unto him, they besought him that he would tarry with them: and he abode there two days.

thirsty again,

14 but those who drink of the water that I will give them will never be thirsty. The water that I will give will become in them a spring of water gushing up to eternal life."

15 The woman said to him, "Sir, give me this water, so that I may never be thirsty or have to keep coming here to draw water."

.....

28 Then the woman left her water jar and went back to the city. She said to the people,

29 "Come and see a man who told me everything I have ever done! He cannot be the Messiah, can he?"

30 They left the city and were on their way to him.

.....

39 Many Samaritans from that city believed in him because of the woman's testimony, "He told me everything I have ever done."

40 So when the Samaritans came to him, they asked him to stay with them; and he stayed there two days.

KEY VERSE

But whosoever drinketh of the water that I shall give him shall never thirst; but the water that I shall give him shall be in him a well of water springing up into everlasting life.—John 4:14

OBJECTIVES

After reading this lesson, the student will be aware that:

1. Racial prejudice is nothing new;
2. True salvation is for all people;
3. Only Christ can satisfy the thirsty soul; and,
4. Christians are obligated to be witnesses.

POINTS TO BE EMPHASIZED

Adult/Youth/Children
Key Verse: John 4:14; John 4:39 (Children)
Print: John 4:7, 9-15, 28-30, 39-40; John 4:7-15, 28-30, 39-42 (Children)

—When Jesus asked a Samaritan woman for a drink of water, she wondered why a Jew would make such a request of a Samaritan. (7-9)

—Jesus told her that if she knew the gift of God and who was asking her for a drink, she would have asked for and received living water. (10)

—When Jesus said the water He gives will satisfy thirst forever, the woman asked to receive such water. (13-15)

—The woman returned to the city and urged the people to go out to see a prophet who had told her everything she had ever done. (28-30)

—As a result of the woman's testimony and meeting Jesus in person, many from the city believed Jesus to be the Savior of the world. (39-42)

(NOTE: Use KJV Scripture for Adults; NRSV Scripture for Youth and Children)

TOPICAL OUTLINE OF THE LESSON

I. Introduction

A. The Samaritans
B. Biblical Background

II. Exposition and Application of the Scripture

A. The Woman at the Well (John 4:7, 9)
B. The Well of Water (John 4:10-15)
C. The Witnessing Word (John 4:28-30)
D. The Winning Word (John 4:39-40)

III. Special Features

A. Preserving Our Heritage
B. A Concluding Word

I. Introduction

A. THE SAMARITANS

After the fall of Samaria in 722 B.C., many of the chief men—the influential, the wealthy, the priests—were taken away captive by the Assyrians. The cities were then repopulated with foreigners. Intermarriage took place between the surviving Jews and those aliens imported into the land. While the population remained mostly Israelite, the intermixture followed "their own gods." (Read 2 Kings 17:24-41.) In time, they began to worship only Jehovah.

When the Samaritans sought to make common cause with the Jews returning from Babylon, they were refused. This caused a rift which by the time of Nehemiah could not be repaired. Thus, it was that the Jews who remained in Palestine intermarried with the heathen who were imported. Their descendants were considered "half-breeds" and not full-blooded Jews; and they were called Samaritans. The Samaritans then set up their own worship, claiming to be the true Israelites. Their authority was the Torah or Pentateuch (five books: Genesis, Exodus, Leviticus, Numbers, Deuteronomy). They looked for the coming of a prophet like Moses; claimed descent from Jacob, and adopted Mount Gerizim as their official place of worship. As time went on, hatred between the Jews and the Samaritans increased. Note the insulting expression used against Christ by the Pharisees: "Say we not well that thou art a Samaritan, and hast a demon?" (John 8:48). Realize then, that the hatred and disdain of the Jews for the Samaritans was based more upon historical and racial aspects than upon any basic differences in religion.

B. BIBLICAL BACKGROUND

Here we would like to make a brief exposition of John 4:1-6. The Pharisees had heard that the Lord was making and baptizing more disciples than John. It appears that the religious leaders sought to use the growing popularity of the One called Jesus (and the decline of John the Baptist) to cast reproach upon the entire movement of Jesus and John. Perhaps it was in their minds to stir up strife between the disciples of John and those of the Lord. Understand, however, that as the Pharisees resented the ministry of John the Baptist, they would resent much more the ministry of the more popular Jesus Christ.

We are quickly reminded that the Lord Himself actually baptized no one. But His disciples did, and as was customary, the teacher was held responsible for what his disciples did. Those baptized by the disciples were then considered Christ's followers or disciples. Christ did not want anyone to later claim that His baptism at the hands of the Master was a superior baptism. You can see why the apostle Paul also had to make it known that he had been called not to be a baptizer, but to be a preacher of the Gospel of the shed blood of Jesus Christ (1 Corinthians 1:14-17). Note that our Lord left Judea, and departed again into Galilee, and by so doing prevented the Pharisees from having any success in their efforts to cause a split between John's followers and those following the Lord Jesus. By stating that the Savior "must" go through Samaria, a divine compulsion is suggested. So more than the desire to reach Galilee by the most direct route is the compulsion to serve and to save those in Samaria. This divine necessity or what I call the "mustness" or "oughtness" of Jesus Christ makes an interesting study. As a young lad, He knew that He must be about His Father's business (Luke 2:49). He said that He must preach the kingdom of God to other cities (Luke 4:43). On another occasion He stated, "I must work the works of Him that sent Me while it is day" (John 9:4).

"Other sheep I have, which are not of this fold: them also I must bring" (John 10:16). To Zacchaeus, He said: "I must abide at your house" (Luke 19:5). By far, most of the Scriptures point out that He must be lifted up (John 3:14), and must suffer many things (Matthew 16:21; Mark 8:31, 9:12; Luke 9:22, 17:25, 22:37). See then in today's lesson that divine compulsion, necessity, obligation, duty to go through Samaria!

The Master reached a city in Samaria called Sychar. Some scholars believe this is another name for Shechem. Not too far from the city was a parcel of ground that centuries earlier Jacob had bought and given to Joseph (Genesis 33:19, 48:22); and then was buried there (Joshua 24:32). Jacob's well (or spring or fountain) was there, and our Lord, being wearied, sat down by the well. We see the physical limitations of Christ; truly Man, He was wearied with the journey and heat. He paused to rest about noon, the sixth hour. Though perfect God and perfect Man, He grew tired. He was experiencing the same physical restrictions or limitations we humans know. And yet, there was a grand purpose in His fatigue—a desire to reach lost souls even in Samaria.

II. Exposition and Application of the Scripture

A. THE WOMAN AT THE WELL
(John 4:7, 9)

There cometh a woman of Samaria to draw water: Jesus saith unto her, Give me to drink. Then saith the woman of Samaria unto him, How is it that thou, being a Jew, askest drink of me, which am a woman of Samaria? for the Jews have no dealings with the Samaritans.

For the Jew, the day began at 6 a.m., so the sixth hour would be about noon. We are not told why at this hour a woman of Samaria should come to draw water from the well. Conjectures are, based upon what we later learn (John 4:16-18), that she was a social outcast, living in open adultery. Usually, women went early in the morning to the well, and they would not go alone, but accompanied. So it would appear that this woman had been ostracized or shunned by the others. Simply put, she chose the time and the place to avoid any confrontation with the other women. The Lord said to her, "Give Me to drink." His disciples had gone to the city to purchase food. So He spoke first, for otherwise she never would have initiated a conversation. This request surprised her. "What? You are a Jew, and you ask me for a drink—me, a Samaritan!" (Moffatt). No clue is given as to how she knew He was a Jew. Perhaps by His clothing, or by His speech (Matthew 26:73) or dialect; or even by His features.

The request was altogether unexpected, for as John writes, "The Jews have no dealings with the Samaritans." The word translated "dealings" is found in the New Testament only here in John 4:9. "To use with" appears to be the proper meaning of the word rendered, "dealings" (Morris), so that one interpretation means a Jew would not drink out of the same cup with a Samaritan (or a Gentile), lest he be ceremonially defiled. So "dealings" refers here to the common use of food and drink utensils. Hostility and antagonism between Jews and Samaritans were well known, dating from the return of the Jews from the Captivity.

B. THE WELL OF WATER

(John 4:10-15)

Jesus answered and said unto her, If thou knewest the gift of God, and who it is that saith to thee, Give me to drink; thou wouldest have asked of him, and he would have given thee living water. The woman saith unto him, Sir, thou hast nothing to draw with, and the well is deep: from whence then hast thou that living water? Art thou greater than our father Jacob, which gave us the well, and drank thereof himself, and his children, and his cattle? Jesus answered and said unto her, Whosoever drinketh of this water shall thirst again: But whosoever drinketh of the water that I shall give him shall never thirst; but the water that I shall give him shall be in him a well of water springing up into everlasting life. The woman saith unto him, Sir, give me this water, that I thirst not, neither come hither to draw.

Immediately, the Lord took the conversation to a higher level by mention of God's gift. From the letters of Paul, we are led to interpret the gift of God as eternal life through Jesus Christ (Romans 6:23; Ephesians 2:8), or make the gift Jesus Christ Himself. However, the better interpretation is to see the living water as the free gift. Of course, the only One who can give the gift is the One sent from God, Jesus Christ. Just as water satisfies thirst, so salvation satisfies the sinner's needs. Living water is flowing water, as in a stream or river, and here signifies the new life which the Lord gives to the believer. As the water He offered is life, so the drinking is faith.

This living water symbolizes the Holy Spirit (John 7:37-39), and proceeds from Jesus Christ who sends the Holy Spirit. We repeat: The gift here is not the Lord Jesus; it is the free gift of the Holy Spirit Himself. He is the Gift, the living water, given by Christ. As water is an absolute necessity of life, so the life our Lord offers is a vital necessity. In His desire to reach the heart and soul of the Samaritan woman, He implied that He is the Source and Spring of living waters which refresh the soul and assuage or quench spiritual thirst. He told her this because sin blinds us to the exact nature of our need. We feel the need; something is missing in life. Sin pushes us in all directions and ways to attempt to satisfy the thirst, and we become even thirstier!

But now her reply shows her mind was still on the physical water. Christ did not speak of ordinary drinking water. She still did not understand this. From her perspective, this living water is at the deepest part of the well, and He has nothing with which to draw it up. Indeed, if He can draw it up, then He is greater than Jacob, whom the Samaritans claimed was their father. Christ had then to teach her the difference between the literal water and the living water. The literal water keeps us coming back. We thirst, we drink; we thirst, we drink. Thus, all the wells in the world would not satisfy man's spiritual thirst. Nothing material in this life is able to permanently satisfy the thirsty soul.

Christ replied: "Whosoever shall have drunk of the water I give him shall thirst no more forever." He or she needs to drink only once. The tense of the verb points to a once-for-all act of drinking which removes forever such thirst. Water from Christ keeps on bubbling, constantly overflowing, and keeping us alive spiritually. Still the Samaritan thought on the physical level. Her concern was centered on her own personal convenience, and not having to come all the way out to Jacob's well every day to fetch water.

C. THE WITNESSING WORD
(John 4:28-30)

The woman then left her waterpot, and went her way into the city, and saith to the men, Come, see a man, which told me all things that ever I did: is not this the Christ? Then they went out of the city, and came unto him.

In the verses omitted from today's lesson, the woman is reminded of her sad moral condition. She had had five husbands, and was at the time living with a man to whom she was not married. The impression made upon her caused her to automatically think of the Messiah. So the Lord said simply: "I that speak unto thee am He" (John 4:26). The disciples approached, and marveled to see the Master talking with the woman. She then left and returned to the city. She left behind her water pot—that pot that symbolized all the things of life we use in our attempt to satisfy our soul's yearning. "She abandoned the bringing of water for the bringing of men" (Morris). "Come, see a man, who told me all things that ever I did. Is not this the Christ?" (John 4:29). Here was a simple, direct, forthright witness and testimony: Come and see! And the men were impressed to return to the well with her.

D. THE WINNING WORD
(John 4:39-40)

And many of the Samaritans of this city believed on him for the saying of the woman, which testified, He told me all that ever I did. So when the Samaritans were come unto him, they besought him that he would tarry with them: and he abode there two days.

Her excitement sparked them. This woman who first saw a Jew, then a prophet, then the Messiah—this woman whose life was a wreck—was used by the Lord to win others to Christ. For, many of the Samaritans of that city believed on Him. Their faith was the result of the woman's testimony and invitation, "Come see a man!" How interesting that these first converts at Samaria were won without any visible miracles or signs, they were changed by the winning word of the woman who reported what Christ had said to her. Is there a message here that we too should preach what God has said, and that our sermons and Sunday school lessons should be Christ centered? Finally, their faith is shown by their invitation to Him to remain with them. And, He abode there two days.

III. Special Features

A. PRESERVING OUR HERITAGE

The relationship between the Jews and the Samaritans intrigues us because of our own situation in the United States. Black American Christians have experienced also what it means to be despised. This story of the Samaritan woman points out that hatreds and animosities between groups are nothing new. Sometimes, the differences are political, or racial, or tribal, or nationalistic, economic, educational, religious, etc. Pride takes these molehill distinctions and makes mountains out of them. As a result, we invent demeaning epithets, derogatory descriptions; we mistreat, injure, torture and even murder.

The Samaritan woman at the well needed to realize she was dealing with the Creator who has no respect of faces or races. And still today, there are professed Christians who have not learned this; they have not allowed the Holy Spirit to raise their sights above their petty concepts of superiority and inferiority based upon race and skin color, or so-called culture gaps. Biblical Christianity transcends the barriers of race. Soul winning is no respecter of race, rank or religion. Christ's love rises above Jew-Samaritan and Jew-Gentile differences. Why not above Black-White differences for those claiming the same Heavenly Father, and proclaiming the same Gospel of the same shed blood?

B. A CONCLUDING WORD

The words "come see a man" loom large in our thinking at this point. We first hear a similar invitation in John 1:39, when the Lord spoke to the two disciples of John the Baptist. They had been following the Lord, and when He inquired, "What seek ye?", they asked Him where He was staying. The Lord responded, "come and see." This was His call to them to become disciples. In John 1:46, we have Philip's response to Nathanael's question, "Can any good thing come out of Nazareth?"

Nathanael simply could not imagine the Christ would come out of such a small, despised, insignificant place like Nazareth. But Philip did not debate with Nathanael. There was no prolonged argument. Instead, all he said was, "Come and see." This brings us to the Samaritan woman who likewise used this simple formula, "Come, see..." (John 4:29). She had been impressed profoundly by the Lord's knowledge of her private life, and included this fact in her witnessing: He "told me all things that ever I did." Bernard (ICC) calls this the "exaggerated language of an uneducated woman," but the results speak for themselves. Her testimony was more than effective!

HOME DAILY BIBLE READINGS
Week of March 28, 1999
A Woman Brings Her Village to Jesus

Mar. 22 M. John 4:1-6, Jesus Went Through Samaria
Mar. 23 T. John 4:7-15, Jesus' Encounter With a Samaritan Woman
Mar. 24 W. John 4:16-26, I Am the Messiah
Mar. 25 T. John 4:27-42, Jesus' Disciples Were Astonished
Mar. 26 F. Matthew 10:37-42, Even a Cup of Cold Water
Mar. 27 S. Revelation 22:16-21, Take the Water of Life as a Gift
Mar. 28 S. Mark 11:1-11, Jesus Rides into Jerusalem

Jesus Crucified and Resurrected (Easter)

Unit II. Jesus Raised to Life
Adult Topic—From Death to Life
.....

Youth Topic—From Death to Life
Children's Topic—Jesus Lives
.....

Devotional Reading—Acts 2:32-39
Background Scripture—John 18—20:18
Print—John 19:16-18, 28-30; 20:11-18

• • • • • • • • • • •

PRINTED SCRIPTURE

John 19:16-18, 28-30; 20:11-18 (KJV)

16 Then delivered he him therefore unto them to be crucified. And they took Jesus, and led him away.

17 And he bearing his cross went forth into a place called the place of a skull, which is called in the Hebrew Golgotha:

18 Where they crucified him, and two other with him, on either side one, and Jesus in the midst.

.....

28 After this, Jesus knowing that all things were now accomplished, that the scripture might be fulfilled, saith, I thirst.

29 Now there was set a vessel full of vinegar: and they filled a sponge with vinegar, and put it upon hyssop, and put it to his mouth.

30 When Jesus therefore had received the vinegar, he said, It is finished: and he bowed his head, and gave up the ghost.

.....

John 19:16-18, 28-30, 20:11-18 (NRSV)

16 Then he handed him over to them to be crucified. So they took Jesus;

17 and carrying the cross by himself, he went out to what is called The Place of the Skull, which in Hebrew is called Golgotha.

18 There they crucified him, and with him two others, one on either side, with Jesus between them.

.....

28 After this, when Jesus knew that all was now finished, he said (in order to fulfill the scripture), "I am thirsty."

29 A jar full of sour wine was standing there. So they put a sponge full of the wine on a branch of hyssop and held it to his mouth.

30 When Jesus had received the wine, he said, "It is finished." Then he bowed his head and gave up his spirit.

.....

11 But Mary stood without at the sepulchre weeping: and as she wept, she stooped down, and looked into the sepulchre,

12 And seeth two angels in white sitting, the one at the head, and the other at the feet, where the body of Jesus had lain.

13 And they say unto her, Woman, why weepest thou? She saith unto them, Because they have taken away my Lord, and I know not where they have laid him.

14 And when she had thus said, she turned herself back, and saw Jesus standing, and knew not that it was Jesus.

15 Jesus saith unto her, Woman, why weepest thou? whom seekest thou? She, supposing him to be the gardener, saith unto him, Sir, if thou have borne him hence, tell me where thou hast laid him, and I will take him away.

16 Jesus saith unto her, Mary. She turned herself, and saith unto him, Rabboni; which is to say, Master.

17 Jesus saith unto her, Touch me not; for I am not yet ascended to my Father: but go to my brethren, and say unto them, I ascend unto my Father, and your Father; and to my God, and your God.

18 Mary Magdalene came and told the disciples that she had seen the Lord, and that he had spoken these things unto her.

11 But Mary stood weeping outside the tomb. As she wept, she bent over to look into the tomb;

12 and she saw two angels in white, sitting where the body of Jesus had been lying, one at the head and the other at the feet.

13 They said to her, "Woman, why are you weeping?" She said to them, "They have taken away my Lord, and I do not know where they have laid him."

14 When she had said this, she turned around and saw Jesus standing there, but she did not know that it was Jesus.

15 Jesus said to her, "Woman, why are you weeping? Whom are you looking for?" Supposing him to be the gardener, she said to him, "Sir, if you have carried him away, tell me where you have laid him, and I will take him away."

16 Jesus said to her, "Mary!" She turned and said to him in Hebrew, "Rabbouni!" (which means Teacher).

17 Jesus said to her, "Do not hold on to me, because I have not yet ascended to the Father. But go to my brothers and say to them, 'I am ascending to my Father and your Father, to my God and your God.'"

18 Mary Magdalene went and announced to the disciples, "I have seen the Lord"; and she told them that he had said these things to her.

KEY VERSE

And he saith unto them, Be not affrighted: Ye seek Jesus of Nazareth, which was crucified: he is risen; he is not here: behold the place where they laid him.—Mark 16:6

OBJECTIVES

After reading this lesson, the student should be informed about:

1. The events that took place at the Crucifixion of our Lord;
2. Two of the Seven Last Words spoken on the cross;
3. The Resurrection of Jesus Christ; and,
4. Our Lord's appearance to Mary Magdalene.

POINTS TO BE EMPHASIZED

Adult/Youth

Key Verse: Mark 16:6

Print: John 19:16-18, 18-30; 20:11-18

—Pilate delivered Jesus over to the authorities to be crucified. (16)

—Jesus carried His own cross to Golgotha where He was crucified between two others. (19:17-18)

—Jesus asked for drink to fulfill the Scripture; and then saying, "It is finished" He gave up His spirit. (19:28-30)

—Mary stood outside the sepulchre weeping as she stooped to look inside. (11)

—When the angels asked Mary why she was weeping, she told them Jesus' body was gone and she did not knew where it was. (20:12-15)

—Jesus asked Mary why she was weeping, but she did not recognize Him until He called her by name. (20:16-17)

—Mary told the disciples she had seen the Lord. (20:18)

Children

Key Verse: Luke 24:5

Print: John 19:16-18, 40-42; 20:1, 11-18

—Jesus was crucified with two other men at a place called Golgotha. (19:16-18)

—Jesus' body was placed in a tomb in a near-by garden. (19:41)

—Mary went to the tomb before dawn on the first day of the week. (20:1)

—Mary asked the angel in the tomb where the body of Jesus had been taken. (20:11-13)

—Mary turned around and did not recognize Jesus until He spoke her name. (20:14-16)

—Mary ran to tell the disciples that she had seen and spoken with Jesus. (20:17-18)

(**NOTE:** Use KJV Scripture for Adults; NRSV Scripture for Youth and Children)

I. Introduction

A. DEATH BY CRUCIFIXION

The Greek word translated "crucified" in John 19:16 comes from a verb meaning to stake or drive down stakes. A **stauros** is a pointed upright stake (Thayer). We call it a cross. It was used as a most cruel instrument of punishment, believed to have been invented by the Persians who first used this mode of execution. Borrowed by the Romans, it was used especially against slaves, robbers, insurrectionists, criminals, against those who committed piracy, treason, desertion in the face of the enemy, assassination, etc. Roman citizens were exempt. Jewish law did not ordain crucifixion. Blasphemers (Leviticus 24:23) and idolaters (Deuteronomy 17:5) were stoned, and then, as an additional penalty, some were hanged on a tree to show they were accursed. Deuteronomy 21:22-23 states: "And if a man have committed a sin worthy of death, and he be put to death, and thou hang him on a tree, his body shall not remain all night upon the tree, but thou shalt surely bury him that day (for he who is hanged is accursed by God)." Paul mentions this in Galatians 3:13.

The fact that Jesus Christ was hanged on a cross became a stumbling block to the Jews, for how could one accursed by God be their Messiah? From all accounts, death by crucifixion was a horrible way to die. The Romans started out first by scourging the victim. This was calculated to hasten impending death. Bearing the cross (or the upright beam only), the victim carried it to the place of execution. The condemned was then stripped of his clothing (John 19:23-24), and with his body fastened to the cross, large rusty spikes were driven through his hands and feet.

Then, he was left to linger, left to die from starvation, and insufferable thirst. Within two or three days, although longer for some victims, he was dead. Often the bodies were left on the cross to be devoured by vultures and beasts of prey.

The Jews, however, were allowed by the Romans to bury their dead on the day of crucifixion. Sometimes, it became necessary to hasten their demise. This would be accomplished by fire, hungry beasts, or breaking their bones with an iron mallet (John 19:31-33).

B. BIBLICAL BACKGROUND

In general, the order of events leading up to the crucifixion is as follows: Betrayed by Judas, our Lord was arrested and tried by the Jews, by the Sanhedrin. He was given an audience with Annas, father-in-law of Caiaphas the high priest. Annas sent Christ bound unto Caiaphas to a late night session. Then early in the morning, the sentence handed down by the Sanhedrin was ratified. Because the Roman government did not allow the Jews to execute capital punishment, it was necessary for them to have a Roman trial also. So the Lord was taken to Pilate. When Pilate discovered the Lord was a Galilean, he referred Him to Herod. Christ would not perform any miracles for Herod—in fact, would not even answer him— so Herod and his soldiers mistreated Christ and returned Him to Pilate. Once again before Pilate, our Lord was scourged, sentenced and delivered over to the soldiers. The men in the military mocked the Master, then took Him to be crucified. Here is where today's lesson begins.

II. Exposition and Application of the Scripture

A. THE LORD JESUS IS CRUCIFIED
(John 19:16-18)

Then delivered he him therefore unto them to be crucified. And they took Jesus, and led him away. And he bearing his cross went forth into a place called the place of a skull, which is called in the Hebrew Golgotha: Where they crucified him, and two other with him, on either side one, and Jesus in the midst.

The lesson begins with Pilate delivering the Lord Jesus unto the high priests to be crucified; and of course, the soldiers were to crucify Him for the Jews. All of Pilate's efforts to save Him had failed. He had sought to elicit pity from them by directing their attention to the pitiful condition of the Lord. However, the chief priests had announced their loyalty to Caesar by shouting, "We have no king but Caesar!" The people had screamed with murderous voices, "Crucify Him!"

And Pilate, afraid his job would be jeopardized if Rome ever got wind of a Jewish insurrection under his jurisdiction, succumbed to their wishes, and turned Christ over to the military. Evidently, the straw that broke Pilate's political back was the statement made by the Jews, "If you let this man go, you are not Caesar's friend; whosoever makes himself a king speaks against Caesar" (John 19:12). If such innuendo reached Caesar's ears, Pilate's career would be finished. Opinions differ about Pilate's motives here, but I find it difficult to believe Pilate turned the Lord over to be crucified because he wanted to please the Jews. I am inclined to believe that he despised the Jews, but got caught in a situation which threatened his political career. Pressured by the crowd, he went against his conscience.

Now the fact that John 19:17 states that the Lord bore His cross does not exclude the possibility He had help somewhere along the way. If John had said, "And carrying the cross for Himself all the way to Golgotha," then we would have reason to question the writer's accuracy. But no such statement is made. Our Lord was carrying the cross when He broke down under His burden. Gethsemane, betrayal, arrest, illegitimate court trial, sleeplessness, scourging, mockery, beating—all took their toll, and after the procession passed out of the city gate, the Lord fell beneath the load.

At this point, Simon of Cyrene was forced into service, and made to carry the cross to a place called **kranion.** Note the Greek word has given us the word, cranium. In Hebrew, the word is Golgotha; in Latin, the word is Calvary, or literally, place of a skull. More than likely, this was because the hill physically resembled a skull. Here our Lord was placed in the center of the two robbers, demonstrating to us that even in death, Christ is to have the place of central importance.

B. TWO WORDS FROM THE CROSS
(John 19:28-30)

After this, Jesus knowing that all things were now accomplished, that the scripture might be fulfilled, saith, I thirst. Now there was set a vessel full of vinegar: and they filled a sponge with vinegar, and put it upon hyssop, and put it to his mouth. When Jesus therefore had received the vinegar, he said, It is finished: and he bowed his head, and gave up the ghost.

Now, we find the Lamb of God actually nailed to the cross. Four of His last words have been uttered already. The fifth word, a statement of fact, is the briefest; it is recorded in John 19:28: "I thirst." The Greek is one word, **Dipso.** In English, a dipsomaniac is one with an abnormal, uncontrollable craving for alcoholic liquors. Centuries earlier, this thirst had been predicted by David in Psalms 69:21 and 22:15. Physical thirst is intended here, but we see also the cry of a soul that was being made sin. For sin causes dryness of spirit. And, He who knew no sin was made sin.

At this point, in an act of compassion, a vessel full of vinegar was set, and a sponge which was tied to the end of a rod with hyssop, having been soaked with the vinegar or sour wine, was pressed to His lips. And He drank. Earlier, when drugged wine was offered to Him, just before the Crucifixion, He refused (Matthew 27:34; Mark 15:23). He wanted to bear our sins in full awareness of what He was doing. It is suggested that this time He drank of an undrugged liquid in order to wet His parched throat, in order that He might speak with a loud voice, and say: "It is finished!"—it is fulfilled, accomplished (John 19:28), done, carried out, consummated, perfected, ended, completed.

This sixth word from the cross is one word in the Greek **(tetelestai);** literally, it has been finished (perfect tense), indicating what was started in the past still has present results. This was no lament of failure. This was no cry that the cookie had crumbled at Calvary! This was a shout of victory! And the words, He "gave up the ghost" point to a peaceful death. No one took His life; rather, He delivered His spirit to God the Father.

> *"Lifted up was He to die, 'It is finished' was His cry,*
> *Now in Heaven exalted high, Hallelujah, What a Savior!"* (Philip P. Bliss)

C. APPEARANCE TO MARY MAGDALENE
(John 20:11-18)

But Mary stood without at the sepulchre weeping: and as she wept, she stooped down, and looked into the sepulchre, And seeth two angels in white sitting, the one at the head, and the other at the feet, where the body of Jesus had lain. And they say unto her, Woman, why weepest thou? She saith unto them, Because they have taken away my Lord, and I know not where they have laid him. And when she had thus said, she turned herself back, and saw Jesus standing, and knew not that it was Jesus. Jesus saith unto here, Woman, why weepest thou? whom seekest thou? She, supposing him to be the gardener, saith unto him, Sir, if thou have borne him hence, tell me where thou hast laid him, and I will take him away. Jesus saith unto her, Mary. She turned herself, and saith unto him, Rabboni; which is to say, Master. Jesus saith unto her, Touch me not; for I am not yet ascended to my Father: but go to my brethren, and say unto them, I ascend unto my Father, and your Father; and to my God, and your God. Mary Magdalene came and told the disciples that she had seen the Lord, and that he had spoken these things unto her.

Mary (Mariam in Greek) Magdalene was deeply grieved. As if the death of the Lord Jesus had not been enough, now His body was missing also. The Jews were deeply concerned about what they deemed a correct burial, and did not lightly tolerate any disrespect paid to a corpse. She stood there, outside of the sepulchre, weeping, her unrestrained shedding of tears accompanied by loud sobbing. And while crying thus, she peeped into the sepulchre. She saw (for emphasis, present tense, "she sees," is used) two angels dressed in white, one sitting at the head, the other at the feet, of the place where the body of the Lord had lain.

"Woman"—a common way of addressing women; no harshness or disrespect is shown: John 2:4, 4:21, 8:10, 19:26)—"Why are you weeping?" Mary answered them, and as she turned around, perhaps aware that someone was behind her, there stood the Lord Jesus. But she did not know it was He. The Lord then proceeded to ask the same question as the angels, "Woman, why are you weeping?" adding, "Whom are you seeking?" Mary replied, mistaking Him for the gardener— and not really answering His questions—"Sir, if you have carried Him away, tell me where you have laid Him, and I will take Him away." What for? To complete the embalming. But how? What made her think she had the strength to remove His body?

Then the Lord called her by name, "Mary." How wonderful that must have sounded in her ears. She is the first human being to see the risen Lord. She turned herself, and said, "Rabboni" (my Master, or my Lord). Immediately, she fell at His feet and held Him as if never to let Him go. She had assumed He was here to stay, back for good as in the days prior to the crucifixion. Clinging to the old relationship, she wanted to keep Him there physically. How unfortunate is the King James Version, "Touch Me not" (John 20:17). This present tense command indicates He desired her to stop doing what she was doing. She had grabbed Him and was holding on for dear life. "Stop clinging to Me," is the command. Mary must come to realize that a new relationship, far greater, more glorious, was to be established. The experience of having Him with her permanently was not yet to be. Only when He finally ascended and sat down at the right hand of His Father—when the Holy Spirit had come to abide—then Mary would realize that He was with her permanently, indeed, in her, as her glorified Savior. Is it possible that the Holy Spirit now abiding in us makes the presence of Jesus Christ more real to us than His physical presence was to Mary? Have you discovered that it is better to be with Him now through the Holy Spirit, than it would have been with Him when He was on earth?

Finally, observe that Christ told Mary to go to His brethren, and inform them of His plans: "I am ascending unto My Father and your Father." Note, He did not say, "Our Father," God is Father, but in essentially different ways. He is the Father of Jesus Christ from all eternity by nature; He is our Father by adoption in a relationship which began when we were saved. The same is true of the words, "And to My God and your God." He does not say, "To our God." Because Jesus Christ is still a man, His human nature is still in subjection to God. But He tells the disciples, "Your God," because Christ is the Mediator between them and their God. In other words, the "My" for Christ is the basis for the "YOUR" for the disciples. Mary obeyed. What she did is a picture of what remains the task of the Church—tell others that Jesus Christ has risen from the dead!

III. Special Features

A. PRESERVING OUR HERITAGE

Unfortunately, in some church circles, it has been forgotten that every Sunday is celebration of the Resurrection of Jesus Christ. And well it should be celebrated, for "We serve a risen Savior!" The preachers in the early church were thrilled to herald Christ crucified, buried and risen. Now it is interesting to see that the crucifixion of Christ played a major part in the Negro Spirituals. To an enslaved people, getting up out of the grave was indeed Good News!

Some critics of Negro Spirituals disdain what they call the passivity and compensatory nature of the songs. But such characteristics do not lessen the value of waiting on the Lord, or emphasizing things to come (eschatology). Some Black slaves rejoiced in the fact that though "they crucified my Lord, and...The blood came twinklin' down...He bow'd His head an' died," but "He never said a mumbalin' word, not a word." They had this assurance: "Surely He died on Calvary." But He did not remain in the grave, for, "He rose, He rose, He rose from the dead...An' de Lord will bear my spirit home."

B. A CONCLUDING WORD

We began with Death by Crucifixion; we end the lesson with the Resurrection. The word for "resurrection" is a Greek word, **anastasis** from this is derived the beautiful name, Anastasia (rising again). Jesus Christ is the first fruits of the dead (1 Corinthians 15:20). All others who died and were restored to life, died again. So we speak of their restoration, not their resurrection. Only Christ presently has a glorified body or body of glory. God rewarded the women for their love and loyalty by allowing them to be the first and main witnesses to see the empty tomb. As best as we can determine, the events recorded occurred thus: Early Sunday morning, when it was still dark, Mary Magdalene, Mary the mother of James and Joses, Salome, and Joanna (and "other women") went together to the tomb at the same time. Mary Magdalene was so shocked at finding the stone of the tomb removed that she immediately ran off. The other women remained, and listened to the angel who appeared. By this time, Mary found Simon Peter and John, and told them of their discovery. The men ran ahead, found the tomb empty, and left to tell the other disciples. By now, Mary stood outside of the sepulchre weeping, and the Lord Jesus appeared unto her. In His second appearance, He met the other women. Third: probably, Simon Peter. Fourth: the two disciples from Emmaus. Fifth: the ten disciples (Thomas was absent). Sixth: He met the eleven disciples. On His seventh appearance, the seven disciples were fishing.

Eighth: He met all eleven, plus more than five hundred brethren. The ninth appearance is to James, our Lord's half-brother. Tenth: The Ascension. Eleventh: Saul (Paul) of Tarsus met Him on the road to Damascus. And twelfth, the apostle John saw Him on the isle of Patmos. What a marvelous record! We would add our names to the list of those who met Him in a still more wonderful way—through faith in His shed blood! No wonder we sing:

"I serve a risen Savior, He's in the world today;
I know that He is living, whatever men may say;
I see His hand of mercy, I hear His voice of cheer,
And just the time I need Him He's always near.
He lives, He lives, Christ Jesus lives today!

Jesus Appeared to His Disciples

Adult Topic—Believing Without Seeing

.....

Youth Topic—Believing Without Seeing
Children's Topic—Jesus Visits His Disciples

.....

Devotional Reading—Mark 9:14-24
Background Scripture—John 20:19-29
Print—John 20:19-29

• • • • • • • • • • • •

PRINTED SCRIPTURE

John 20:19-29 (KJV)

19 Then the same day at evening, being the first day of the week, when the doors were shut where the disciples were assembled for fear of the Jews, came Jesus and stood in the midst, and saith unto them, Peace be unto you.

20 And when he had so said, he shewed unto them his hands and his side. Then were the disciples glad, when they saw the Lord.

21 Then said Jesus to them again, Peace be unto you: as my Father hath sent me, even so send I you.

22 And when he had said this, he breathed on them, and saith unto them, Receive ye the Holy Ghost:

23 Whose soever sins ye remit, they are remitted unto them; and whose soever sins ye retain, they are retained.

24 But Thomas, one of the twelve, called Didymus, was not with them when Jesus came.

25 The other disciples therefore said unto him, We have seen the

John 20:19-29 (NRSV)

19 When it was evening on that day, the first day of the week, and the doors of the house where the disciples had met were locked for fear of the Jews, Jesus came and stood among them and said, "Peace be with you."

20 After he said this, he showed them his hands and his side. Then the disciples rejoiced when they saw the Lord:

21 Jesus said to them again, "Peace be with you. As the Father has sent me, so I send you."

22 When he had said this, he breathed on them and said to them, "Receive the Holy Spirit.

23 If you forgive the sins of any, they are forgiven them; if you retain the sins of any, they are retained."

24 But Thomas (who was called the Twin), one of the twelve, was not with them when Jesus came.

25 So the other disciples told him, "We have seen the Lord." But he said to them, "Unless I see the mark of

Lord. But he said unto them, Except I shall see in his hands the print of the nails, and put my finger into the print of the nails, and thrust my hand into his side, I will not believe.

26 And after eight days again his disciples were within, and Thomas with them: then came Jesus, the doors being shut, and stood in the midst, and said, Peace be unto you.

27 Then saith he to Thomas, Reach hither thy finger, and behold my hands; and reach hither thy hand, and thrust it into my side: and be not faithless, but believing.

28 And Thomas answered and said unto him, My Lord and my God.

29 Jesus saith unto him, Thomas, because thou hast seen me, thou hast believed: blessed are they that have not seen, and yet have believed.

the nails in his hands, and put my finger in the mark of the nails and my hand in his side, I will not believe."

26 A week later his disciples were again in the house, and Thomas was with them. Although the doors were shut, Jesus came and stood among them and said, "Peace be with you."

27 Then he said to Thomas, "Put your finger here and see my hands. Reach out your hand and put it in my side. Do not doubt but believe."

28 Thomas answered him, "My Lord and my God!"

29 Jesus said to him, "Have you believed because you have seen me? Blessed are those who have not seen and yet have come to believe."

KEY VERSE

Jesus saith unto him, Thomas, because thou hast seen me, thou hast believed: blessed are they that have not seen, and yet have believed.—John 20:29

OBJECTIVES

After reading this lesson, the student should be aware that:

1. The resurrected Savior was seen by His disciples;
2. His appearance helped dispel any doubts the disciples had; and,
3. His appearance prepared the disciples to be bold witnesses.

POINTS TO BE EMPHASIZED

Adult/Youth
Key Verse: John 20:29
Print: John 20:19-29

—While the fearful disciples were gathered in secret, Jesus appeared to them. (19)
—When Jesus showed the disciples His hands and His side they rejoiced. (20)

—Jesus gave the disciples His blessing of peace and sent them forth as God had sent Him. (21)

—Jesus gave the disciples the Holy Spirit and the power to forgive sins. (22-23)

—Thomas said he would not believe that Jesus was alive unless he saw and felt Him. (24-25)

—Later when Thomas saw Jesus' hands and side he believed. (26-29)

Children
Key Verse: John 20:29
Print—John 20:19-29

—Jesus went into the room where the disciples were meeting with the doors locked for fear of the Jews.

—The disciples rejoiced as they recognized Jesus by His nail-scarred hands.

—Thomas, who had not been with them, did not believe Jesus had visited them.

—A second time Jesus visited His disciples, He showed Thomas His scars and Thomas believed.

—Jesus said Thomas believed because there was proof as to who He was, but it is better to believe without seeing.

(NOTE: Use KJV Scripture for Adults; NRSV Scripture for Children and Youth)

TOPICAL OUTLINE OF THE LESSON

I. Introduction

    A. The First Great Commission Scripture
    B. Biblical Background

II. Exposition and Application of the Scripture

    A. First Appearance to the Disciples—Without Thomas (John 20:19-20)
    B. The Disciples are Commissioned (John 20:21-23)
    C. Thomas Refuses to Believe the Disciples (John 20:24-25)
    D. Second Appearance to the Disciples—With Thomas (John 20:26-29)

III. Special Features

    A. Preserving Our Heritage
    B. A Concluding Word

I. Introduction

A. THE FIRST GREAT COMMISSION SCRIPTURE

Usually when we talk about the Great Commission, we think only of Matthew 28:19-20. However, in addition to the Matthew Scripture, there are four other passages which constitute what is called the Great Commission. They are

Mark 16:15-16; Luke 24:46-47; John 20:21; and Acts 1:8. Although we believe the Gospel of John is the last of the gospels to be written, The Great Commission passage under study, John 20:21, was spoken before the Scriptures from the other gospels constituting the Great Commission. Furthermore, John 20:21 was spoken on the very day of resurrection.

It is indeed postresurrection time, and the disciples are huddled together in shut-door secrecy for fear of the Jewish leaders. Suddenly, Christ appeared in their midst, and said: "Peace be with you!" This was said in order to calm them, for "they were startled and frightened and thought they were seeing a spirit" (Luke 24:37). This peace was needed to quiet hearts, dispel alarm, take away fright. This peace was calculated to restore personal confidence.

The second "Peace to you" had a different purpose. This solemnly repeated greeting is called by Tasker the "peace of the pardoned sinner," a peace whereby disciples now become apostles. Westcott terms it the peace that prepares for work. Lenski states that it is the "basis for their new commission." Morris describes it as "a peace that is the fruit of Christ's death, burial, and resurrection" proved to them by showing in His hands, feet, and side the marks of His passion. Similarly, Stott says it is the "peace of conscience through His death, peace of mind through his resurrection." All in all, it is that peace required for witnessing. They are to be messengers of peace, men whose feet are shod with the preparation of the gospel of peace.

This briefest of the Great Commission Scriptures is couched in the words: "As My Father hath sent Me, even so send I you" (John 20:21). At this point, our Lord spoke to the ten disciples (for Judas was dead, and Thomas was absent). It is believed, however, that Christ spoke not only to the ten, but through them to all of the believers present at that time, and therefore by representation, the entire Church received these words. This means that the Lord Jesus speaks to every believer, and says: "So send I you!" Every Christian is a missionary. The Disciples saw Him and were sent forth; we were sent forth and shall see Him.

B. BIBLICAL BACKGROUND

The words "for fear of the Jews" (John 20:19) strike us as being an appropriate basis for a background study. We first encounter this phrase in John 7:13: "However, no man spoke openly of Him for fear of the Jews." Keep in mind that "the Jews" are the religious leaders of the nation—the Pharisees, Sadducees, et al. Those citizens who thought well of the Lord Jesus were afraid to make it known, lest they incur the wrath of the Sanhedrin and other Jewish authorities. And so only murmurs were heard; there was no open discussion concerning the Master.

In the story of the healing of the man born blind, the parents of the man would not volunteer any information concerning their son's healing, for they knew that the religious leaders had threatened to excommunicate anyone who supported the Lord (John 9:22; cf. John 12:42). We next read these words in John 19:38, where we are reminded that Joseph of Arimathea was a "disciple of Jesus, but secretly for fear of the Jews."

Finally, we see these same words in our Sunday school lesson. By now, the rumor that the tomb was empty had spread (Matthew 28:11). This would make the Jewish authorities all the more suspicious of any gathering of the disciples. It was for fear of the Jews that the disciples had secretly assembled themselves behind locked doors. Who knows what would have happened to them had the religious authorities discovered them? The threat to expel from the synagogue all who confessed Jesus as the Christ also included social ostracism, unemployment, family disowning, etc. Still later, after Pentecost, believers were persecuted, stoned (Stephen) by the Jews, and imprisoned and executed by the Romans. You see then the part played in today's lesson by the "fear of the Jews."

II. Exposition and Application of the Scripture

A. FIRST APPEARANCE TO THE DISCIPLES—WITHOUT THOMAS
(John 20:19-20)

Then same day at evening, being the first day of the week, when the doors were shut where the disciples were assembled for fear of the Jews, came Jesus and stood in the midst, and saith unto them, Peace be unto you. And when he had so said, he shewed unto them his hands and his side. Then were the disciples glad, when they saw the Lord.

It is believed that this is the fifth appearance of the resurrected Savior. Mark (16:14) calls the disciples the eleven, using that figure as a collective term, even as Paul used the collective term, the twelve (1 Corinthians 15:5; John 20:24), even though Judas was dead at the time. The fact is, ten of the disciples were present; Thomas was not there. Now it was the same day Christ had risen; it was evening, the first day of the week, Sunday. There they were, somewhere in the city of Jerusalem, in hiding.

Note the word "door" is plural, probably referring to the locked door of the house, and the locked door of the room in which they met. Despite such security, Christ came and stood in their midst—not a ghost, not a phantom, but a real, live, human being! His glorified body was not subject to the conditions which presently limit our natural, earthly bodies. His appearance was a miracle. He did not sneak in. He had not bribed the door keeper. He did not cloud their minds so they could not see Him. No, He was just there!

No motion is implied; we are not told He walked in. And the first thing He did was announce, "Peace be unto you." He then showed them the marks of His passion, the very marks whereby peace had been obtained. He showed them the price paid for the peace that was bought. This was also His way of convincing them He was not a phantom or ghost (Luke 24:37). In John, He showed them His hands and side (v. 20); John alone mentions His side (19:34). In Luke (24:39-40), Christ said: "See My hands and My feet, that it is I Myself..." Luke and John agree His hands were marked.

The hands and feet could either be tied or nailed to the cross; both methods were common. But it is evident the Lord's hands and feet were nailed (Psalm

22:16-18). "Then were the disciples glad, when they saw the Lord." Their fear was replaced by joy. He is always the source of our joy. And, we long for the day when we shall see Him, and be like Him, for we shall see Him as He is (1 John 3:2).

B. FIRST OF THE GREAT COMMISSION SCRIPTURES
(John 20:21-23)

Then said Jesus to them again, Peace be unto you: as my Father hath sent me, even so send I you. And when he had said this, he breathed on them, and saith unto them, Receive ye the Holy Ghost: Whose soever sins ye remit, they are remitted unto them; and whose soever sins ye retain, they are retained.

Here we have the first commission of what is called the Great Commission. Strong emphasis is put upon the fact that Christ is the Sent One—sent to speak the words of God, to perform the works of God, to judge the world by His miracles and His teaching, and to glorify the Father by perfect obedience to His will. Then, before returning at His ascension to His Father and God (John 20:17), it was necessary for the Sent One to send others. Here in John 20 is the first postresurrection appearance to the disciples as a group. Because it is His first appearance, it is necessary for Him to calm their troubled and frightened souls. The Prince of Peace desires that His representatives experience His peace as a prerequisite to being commissioned and sent out. So it is that God the Son, the Sent One of His Father, sends His disciples forth not only to do the works that He had performed, but "greater works than these."

In Genesis 2:7, the life of Adam is due to the breath of God. So, it is here in John 20:22 that the gift of spiritual life is imparted to the apostles. Here was a foretaste of a fuller outpouring manifested at Pentecost (Acts 2). Scofield calls it the spiritual preparation for their full endowment at Pentecost. A. C. Gaebelein says it is symbolical; Christ showed beforehand by these words that they would receive the Holy Spirit personally as the power and energy of His own risen life in them. We see that Christ conferred upon them the power of declaring through the preaching of the Gospel, in the power of the Holy Spirit, whose sins are forgiven, and whose sins are not forgiven. All genuine Christians are indwelt by the Holy Spirit, and have the privilege of presenting the Lord Jesus to unbelievers.

C. THOMAS REFUSES TO BELIEVE THE DISCIPLES
(John 20:24-25)

But Thomas, one of the twelve, called Didymus, was not with them when Jesus came. The other disciples therefore said unto him, We have seen the Lord. But he said unto them, Except I shall see in his hands the print of the nails, and put my finger into the print of the nails, and thrust my hand into his side, I will not believe.

The Hebrew word for Thomas, and the Greek word for Didymus mean Twin. But no mention is made of twin brother. For some reason, Thomas was not present when the Lord first appeared to the disciples. We are not told the reason for his absence. Perhaps he felt that such meetings with his peers were a waste of time, futile, inasmuch as the Lord Jesus had been slain. Perhaps he preferred to be alone in his grief over the Lord's death. At any rate, he was absent, and though the other disciples kept telling him (imperfect tense: "they kept saying to him", "they kept laboring to convince him") that they had seen the Lord, Thomas would not believe them. He was the pessimist of the group, always seeing the dark side of things (John 11:16). His blank incredulity was unreasonable. His mind was made up—closed up! Nothing would make him change his mind—except he personally had visual and tactual proof. Lenski thoroughly chastises Thomas for his attitude. Leon Morris is softer, suggesting that the Lord's death had so shocked Thomas that it was nigh impossible for Thomas to consider any change for the better. What is your opinion of Thomas? He certainly shows what Morris calls "a preoccupation with the wounds of" the Lord.

D. SECOND APPEARANCE TO THE DISCIPLES—WITH THOMAS
(John 20:26-29)

And after eight days again his disciples were within, and Thomas with them: then came Jesus, the doors being shut, and stood in the midst, and said, Peace be unto you. Then saith he to Thomas, Reach hither thy finger, and behold my hands; and reach hither thy hand, and thrust it into my side: and be not faithless, but believing. And Thomas answered and said unto him, My Lord and my God. Jesus saith unto him, Thomas, because thou hast seen me, thou hast believed: blessed are they that have not seen, and yet have believed.

A week later, the disciples are back in their secret meeting place. The doors are still locked, for the hostility of the Jews had not abated. This time, Thomas is present, having come, but still not convinced by the report of the other disciples. And once again, the Lord Jesus appeared. This is now the sixth postresurrection appearance of our Lord. He greeted them with peace and then proceeded to speak with Thomas. What He said to the disciple indicates that He knew every word Thomas had uttered. And, He knew then what was on Thomas' mind. Consequently, He commanded Thomas to do exactly what the doubting disciple declared was necessary in order for him to believe. Such knowledge on our Lord's part demonstrated Christ was alive at the time Thomas declared his lack of faith.

One of the problems encountered here is the question whether Thomas actually obeyed when the Lord told him, "Reach here your finger, and behold My hands; and reach here your hand, and thrust it into My side; and be not faithless, but believing" (John 20:27). I believe Thomas did as he was told. However, a number of scholars suggest Thomas did not touch the Lord. They claim that the sight of Christ was enough; just seeing Him did the job of removing doubts. It is said that there is nothing in the account to show that the disciple touched the Savior or took advantage of the proffered test.

The Lord Jesus demanded (in what Lenski calls peremptory imperatives), and Thomas did as he was told. A week earlier, you recall, the resurrected Savior had commanded the disciples to handle Him and they did so (Luke 24:39-40; 1 John 1:1). Morris puts too much weight on our Lord's reply, "Because you have seen Me, you have believed" (v. 29). Is not touching part of beholding? Thomas gave proof of his new-found faith with the words "My Lord and my God."

III. Special Features

A. PRESERVING OUR HERITAGE

One characteristic of a cult is its propensity to deny the Deity of Jesus Christ. This denial is also true of Judaism and Islam. The latter poses the greater threat to the Black Christian, partly because there are those who seek to convince us that Christianity is the White man's religion. However, on the cult scene, we find others vehemently rejecting the Deity of Jesus Christ. And in today's lesson described John 20:28 merely an excited exclamation by Thomas, as if in surprise he called out, "Oh, my God!" This is misinterpretation. This is absurd from a psychological point of view. Thomas had been convinced of the actual presence of One he deeply loved, and to have him blurt out in such an irrelevant cry is simply not natural. No such exclamations are found in use among the Jews! How it grieves our heart to see so many Black Americans deceived into denying the resurrected Savior is the God-Man. Thomas knew he was in the presence of Deity, and acknowledged it. "(Thou art) my Lord and my God!"

B. A CONCLUDING WORD

It is believed that the nailprints in His hands and feet will remain throughout eternity as reminders of the price paid at Calvary. Likewise, the wound inflicted in His side was retained by His resurrected, transformed, glorified body. Both Old and New Testaments prophetically and historically point out the resurrection body of our Lord retained its wounds (Psalm 22:16; Zechariah 12:10; John 20:25-29). John 20:29 is the key verse for our lesson. Our Lord pronounces a blessing on those who have believed sight unseen. Today, we see Him through the eyes of faith. We read and we believe. We hear and we believe (Romans 10:6-9, 17). We are blessed! And yet we yearn to see Him (1 John 3:2).

HOME DAILY BIBLE READINGS
Week of April 11, 1999
Jesus Appears to His Disciples

Apr. 5 M. John 20:19-23, Peace Be With You
Apr. 6 T. John 20:24-29, Unless I See
Apr. 7 W. Luke 24:13-27, On the Road to Emmaus
Apr. 8 T. Luke 24:28-35, Then Their Eyes Were Opened
Apr. 9 F. Luke 24:36-43, Touch Me and See
Apr. 10 S. Luke 24:44-52, He Opened Their Minds
Apr. 11 S. John 21:1-14, Jesus Showed Himself Again

Jesus, the Bread of Life

Unit III. Jesus Declared God's Message
Adult Topic—Bread That Lasts Forever

.....

Youth Topic—Multiplying Your Resources
Children's Topic—Jesus Fed the People

.....

Devotional Reading—Isaiah 55:1-11
Background Scripture—John 6:1-59
Print—John 6:11-12, 14, 26-27, 35-40, 47-51

· · · · · · · · · · · ·

PRINTED SCRIPTURE

John 6:11-12, 14, 26-27, 35-40, 47-51 (KJV)

11 And Jesus took the loaves; and when he had given thanks, he distributed to the disciples, and the disciples to them that were set down; and likewise of the fishes as much as they would.

12 When they were filled, he said unto his disciples, Gather up the fragments that remain, that nothing be lost.

.....

14 Then those men, when they had seen the miracle that Jesus did, said, This is of a truth that prophet that should come into the world.

.....

26 Jesus answered them and said, Verily, verily, I say unto you, Ye seek me, not because ye saw the miracles, but because ye did eat of the loaves, and were filled.

John 6:11-12, 14, 26-27, 35-40, 47-51 (NRSV)

11 Then Jesus took the loaves, and when he had given thanks, he distributed them to those who were seated; so also the fish, as much as they wanted.

12 When they were satisfied, he told his disciples, "Gather up the fragments left over, so that nothing may be lost."

.....

14 When the people saw the sign that he had done, they began to say, "This is indeed the prophet who is to come into the world."

.....

26 Jesus answered them, "Very truly, I tell you, you are looking for me, not because you saw signs, but because you ate your fill of the loaves.

27 Do not work for the food that

27 Labour not for the meat which perisheth, but for that meat which endureth unto everlasting life, which the Son of man shall give unto you: for him hath God the Father sealed.

.....

35 And Jesus said unto them, I am the bread of life: he that cometh to me shall never hunger; and he that believeth on me shall never thirst.

36 But I said unto you, That ye also have seen me, and believe not.

37 All that the Father giveth me shall come to me; and him that cometh to me I will in no wise cast out.

38 For I came down from heaven, not to do mine own will, but the will of him that sent me.

39 And this is the Father's will which hath sent me, that of all which he hath given me I should lose nothing, but should raise it up again at the last day.

40 And this is the will of him that sent me, that every one which seeth the Son, and believeth on him, may have everlasting life: and I will raise him up at the last day.

.....

47 Verily, verily, I say unto you, He that believeth on me hath everlasting life.

48 I am that bread of life.

49 Your fathers did eat manna in the wilderness, and are dead.

50 This is the bread which cometh down from heaven, that a man may eat thereof, and not die.

51 I am the living bread which came down from heaven: if any man eat of this bread, he shall live for ever: and the bread that I will give is my flesh, which I will give for the life of the world.

perishes, but for the food that endures for eternal life, which the Son of Man will give you. For it is on him that God the Father has set his seal."

.....

35 Jesus said to them, "I am the bread of life. Whoever comes to me will never be hungry, and whoever believes in me will never be thirsty.

36 But I said to you that you have seen me and yet do not believe.

37 Everything that the Father gives me will come to me, and anyone who comes to me I will never drive away;

38 for I have come down from heaven, not to do my own will, but the will of him who sent me.

39 And this is the will of him who sent me, that I should lose nothing of all that he has given me, but raise it up on the last day.

40 This is indeed the will of my Father, that all who see the Son and believe in him may have eternal life; and I will raise them up on the last day."

.....

47 "Very truly, I tell you, whoever believes has eternal life.

48 I am the bread of life.

49 Your ancestors ate the manna in the wilderness, and they died.

50 This is the bread that comes down from heaven, so that one may eat of it and not die.

51 I am the living bread that came down from heaven. Whoever eats of this bread will live forever; and the bread that I will give for the life of the world is my flesh."

I am the living bread which came down from heaven: if any man eat of this bread, he shall live for ever: and the bread that I will give is my flesh, which I will give for the life of the world.— John 6:51

OBJECTIVES

After reading this lesson, the student will better understand.

1. The spiritual significance of the miracle of the multiplied bread;
2. What it means to be called the Bread of Life;
3. The will of God the Father with respect to His Son; and,
4. The contrast of Manna with Christ.

POINTS TO BE EMPHASIZED

Adult/Youth
Key Verse: John 6:51
Print: John 6:11-12, 14, 26-27, 35-40, 47-51

—When Jesus miraculously fed 5,000 people, they identified Him as the expected prophet. (10-14)
—Jesus chided the people for believing in Him only because He had fed them with physical food and challenged them to seek spiritual food which endures forever. (26-27)
—Jesus described Himself as the bread of life which, if accepted, provided eternal life. (35-38)
—Jesus promised that those who believe on Him will have eternal life and be raised on the last day. (39-40)
—The ancestors who ate the manna died; but those who believe in Jesus, the living bread, will never die. (47-51)

Children
Key Verse: Luke 9:16-17
Print: John 6:1-15

—A large crowd followed Jesus because He healed the sick. (1-2)
—When He saw the people, Jesus asked Philip how they were going to feed them. (5)
—Philip told Him it would take six months wages to get enough food for everyone to have a little. (7)
—Andrew said there was a boy with five loaves and two fish, but that would not go far. (8)
—Jesus took the food, blessed it and directed the disciples to give it to the people. (11)
—Twelve baskets of food were left over after everybody was fed. (13)

(NOTE: Use KJV Scripture for Adults; NRSV Scripture for Youth and Children)

I. Introduction

A. THE DEFINITION OF MANNA

The Jews were not too far removed from Egypt when they began to murmur, and express their yearning for the flesh pots of that land. You will find the deliverance is described in Exodus chapter 14, and the murmuring is first recorded in Exodus chapter 16. Their complaints centered on food—they stated that Moses brought them out into the wilderness to kill them with hunger. Since they wanted meat, God sent them quails. But as for bread, He sent upon the ground a "small round thing, as small as the hoarfrost."

The Israelites asked one another, "What is it?" Transliteration of the two Hebrew words meaning "what is it" becomes manna. Moses told them: "This is the bread which the Lord has given you to eat." It became Israel's staple food for forty years; the Jews ate it (as well as other food) until they came to the borders of the land of Canaan (Exodus 16:35). It ceased abruptly when they entered Canaan.

Today's lesson presents "manna" and "bread from heaven" as typical of the Lord Jesus Christ Himself. Paul called "manna" spiritual food (1 Corinthians 10:3) To the overcomer in the church at Pergamum, the Lord promised to give to each the hidden manna (Revelation 2:17). Finally, note that "Bread" was often used to denote food in general, for bread was more generally used than any other article of diet. Since all life was depicted as depending upon the grain harvest—and the harvest in turn depended upon rain and sunshine— so bread, the bottom product of these Divine processes (Matthew 5:45), is seen as a special gift of God. "He sends the sunshine and the rain, He sends the harvest's golden grain." When the Lord Jesus called Himself the Bread of Life, He really appealed to the psychology behind the importance of bread.

B. BIBLICAL BACKGROUND

Here we find the Lord at the height of His Galilean ministry. However, it was the signs performed and not His teaching that attracted the people. A great crowd followed Him because it was attracted by His works of healing. This story of the feeding of the multitude is the only miracle recorded in all four Gospels. In the other accounts, the disciples would have sent the crowd away (Matthew 14:15; Mark 6:36; Luke 9:12), acting as if the Lord had forgotten to think of their needs. But the Lord sought to provide something for them to eat.

Why He turned to Philip we do not know. Perhaps Philip especially needed to learn a valuable lesson and have his faith tested (John 6:6)—or indeed, it was a test for all of the disciples! "Where shall we buy bread that these may eat?" inquired the Lord. Christ did not ask because He was perplexed. He knew, but Philip did not. Philip's answer is businesslike, calculated; he thinks only of buying. He answered: "Why just to give each one a little something to eat would require two hundred denarii." A denarius represented a day's pay for a common laborer. At this point, Andrew, the brother of Simon Peter, noticed a little lad with five barley loaves and two small fishes, but felt that even these would never suffice to feed such a crowd.

Philip (and the other disciples) did not see this episode as an opportunity to exercise faith in Christ; nor did they see the Lord's ability to meet the needs of the people. Christ had the people to recline, took the loaves, gave thanks, distributed the food to the disciples, and had them give the people as much as they wanted to eat. What a mighty God we serve!

II. Exposition and Application of the Scriptures

A. FEEDING OF THE FIVE THOUSAND
(John 6:11-12, 14)

And Jesus took the loaves; and when he had given thanks, he distributed to the disciples, and the disciples to them that were set down; and likewise of the fishes as much as they would. When they were filled, he said unto his disciples, Gather up the fragments that remain, that nothing be lost. Then those men, when they had seen the miracle that Jesus did, said, This is of a truth that prophet that should come into the world.

A little boy was invited to dinner by his buddy. At the table, he waited for someone to say grace, but no one did. He asked his friend's father about it, and he replied that they just did not bother to say grace in their house. At this the guest blurted out: "Why that's just like my dog, he just starts right to eating!" One wonders how many Christians fail to thank God for the food they eat? Here in preparation for feeding the approximately five thousand men, the Lord took the loaves of bread, and gave thanks.

"Make the men sit down" in verse 10 uses the noun **anthropos** for men. Anthropology is the study or science of man. But in the words, "so the men sat down, in number about five thousand," the word used for "men" is **andres,** which means males (the name Andrew means manly). This is why we say five thousand men plus women and children were fed.

What happened to the bread and fishes in the hands of our Lord we do not know. It was a miracle. To the antisupernaturalists we say, attempts to eliminate the miraculous here require more faith than we can muster. The truth is that the multitude had a substantial meal, not merely a scrap of food, but as much as they desired. Note the King James Version translates "fishes," and the Revised Standard Version, New International Version, and the New American Standard Bible render the word "fish." There is a distinction that we do not bother with in English. "Fish" refers to the same kind or species (two catfish, for example). "Fishes" points to different kinds or species (one catfish, one cod, for example).

Now once the people were filled, the Lord ordered the disciples to gather the fragments. Expositor's states: "Infinite resource does not justify waste." *Wycliffe Bible Commentary* says: "God's gifts are not to be wasted." MacDonald warns: "Don't squander what He has given us." America has been blessed with material goods, yet we must learn to conserve and use wisely what God has bestowed upon our nation.

The disciples did as they were told, and gathered some twelve baskets of fragments of the barley loaves, which remained over and above that which they had eaten. Then those who had seen the miracle exclaimed, "This is of a truth that prophet that should come into the world." Reference is to Deuteronomy 18:15, 18: "The Lord thy God will raise up unto thee a Prophet from the midst of thee...." The Jews looked for a particular prophet. Some believed it would be the Messiah Himself. Others believed he would be one of the old prophets raised from the dead, and returned to deliver Israel from the control of the Roman government.

B. FOOD THAT ABIDES FOREVER
(John 6:26-27)

Jesus answered them and said, Verily, verily, I say unto you, Ye seek me, not because ye saw the miracles, but because ye did eat of the loaves, and were filled. Labour not for the meat which perisheth, but for that meat which endureth unto everlasting life, which the Son of man shall give unto you: for him hath God the Father sealed.

When the people found the Lord Jesus on the other side of the sea, they inquired as to the time of His arrival. He did not answer their question directly, but in His reply rebuked their wrong spirit. "Verily, verily," is "amen, amen" in the Greek. Christ used this formula to draw attention to the importance of what He had to say. Thus, He spoke to the needs of their hearts. A faith that is based on seeing miracles does not please the Lord as does that faith which is based on believing what is heard (Romans 10:17).

Miracles are not needed to authenticate or verify the Word of God today. Unfortunately, some groups attempt to make God do now what He did centuries ago, not realizing that though He is the same God, He has different plans for different times, according to His will (Hebrews 2:4). You see why the Lord rebuked the motives of the sign-seekers. Interested only in the physical (their bellies), they missed the purpose of the signs, namely, to show them that Jesus was indeed the Christ. It is not wise, said our Lord, to make your supreme goal in life the satisfaction of the physical appetite, or as Paul put it, their "God is their appetite or belly" (Philippians 3:19).

Use of the present tense command forbids continuing an action that is already in progress: Stop working, do not continue working for the physical bread that perishes. Appropriate spiritual nourishment which Christ alone gives. Rather, busy yourselves to feed the soul with the word of God. Christ Himself is the Word, therefore He is the food. We should eat what He gives us (we should eat Him as it were), for He has the authority to give everlasting life. That authority is based upon the fact that the Father not only sent Him, but also sealed Him. God the Father confirmed Him as the One He sent to give this food. There is no higher authority. So that the miracles the people saw were God's stamp of approval, the Father's endorsement of the Son.

C. BREAD OF LIFE AND THE WILL OF GOD
(John 6:35-40)

And Jesus said unto them, I am the bread of life: he that cometh to me shall never hunger; and he that believeth on me shall never thirst. But I said unto you, That ye also have seen me, and believe not. All that the Father giveth me shall come to me; and him that cometh to me I will in no wise cast out. For I came down from heaven, not to do mine own will, but the will of him that sent me. And this is the Father's will which hath sent me, that of all which he hath given me I should lose nothing, but should raise it up again at the last day. And this is the will of him that sent me, that every one which seeth the Son, and believeth on him, may have everlasting life: and I will raise him up the last day.

Here our Lord played down the dependence upon physical bread and bodily eating. In one of the great "I AM" statements proclaiming the deity of Christ, our Lord made it clear that He is the Bread of Life who alone satisfies spiritual hunger. He not only has life in Himself, but is able to give life to others. However, one must come to Him, that is, believe on Him, and he or she will never hunger or thirst spiritually again. The Galileans had seen Him, yet had not believed in Him. By their unbelief they forfeited the gift of eternal life.

But the Lord was not discouraged by their unbelief, for they who are given to Him by God the Father shall indeed come to Him. Such faithful ones shall never be cast out or rejected by Christ. The double negative in Greek is emphatic: "he shall not not be outcast out" (John 6:37). In all of this salvation work (coming to Him, believing in Him), see the will of God the Father. For

Jesus Christ did not leave Heaven in order to do His own will, but the will of the Father who sent Him.

It was and is the will of God the Father and the delight of the Son that all given to Christ shall be kept, guarded, protected. It is the will of the Father that all who eat of the Bread of Life should be preserved. And "in that great gittin' up mornin" all the saved will surely fare well! The "last day" is that day when the Messiah comes and is fully vindicated. None given to Him are lost. Not now, not in the resurrection, not ever! Because it is the Father's will to preserve us, the believer has the guarantee of eternal life.

D. BREAD OF LIFE CONTRASTED WITH MANNA
(John 6:47-51)

Verily, verily, I say unto you, He that believeth on me hath everlasting life. I am that bread of life. Your fathers did eat manna in the wilderness, and are dead. This is the bread which cometh down from heaven, that a man may eat thereof, and not die. I am the living bread which came down from heaven: if any man eat of this bread, he shall live for ever: and the bread that I will give is my flesh, which I will give for the life of the world.

When the Jews demanded that the Lord Jesus give them a sign, like manna falling down out of the sky, the Lord set up a contrast to show the folly of their request. Once again the words "amen, amen" preface the announcement concerning the solemn way of life eternal (John 5:19; 6:32, 47). The manna given to the Jews helped maintain their physical life, but eventually they all died. The Bread from Heaven does not give physical life, for that is not its purpose. But it gives spiritual life, a life which physical death cannot touch.

Now we do not deny that the Christian who realizes his or her body is the temple of the Holy Spirit, and takes care not to pollute the temple with bad habits, may live "longer" on the average, or live "better" on the average, than unbelievers. Longevity and quality of life may well be ours. But we still die. What counts here is spiritual life—life abundant and life eternal! The manna that the Jews ate was a type (a prefiguring, a preshadowing) of Jesus Christ, giving life and strength to all who received and fed on it. The Bread from Heaven is Jesus Christ; He had to die in order to give His flesh for the life of the world.

Manna eaten, sustains for a while. Christ Jesus eaten, sustains forever.

III. Special Features

A. PRESERVING OUR HERITAGE

It may well be that a people who has suffered the ravages of Jim Crowism are especially susceptible to the offerings of a Fish and Loaves gospel. The Depression in the United States during the 1930's certainly gave the Father Divine movement tremendous impetus. When a minority lives within the midst of a materialistic majority society such as prevails today, it does not require much for that minority to take on the attitudes and values of the majority.

This may be but one aspect of the current emphasis on what is called the religious philosophy of "conceive it, believe it, achieve it." It is only natural (old-natured!) that last-hired, first-fired folks, poverty-level living people, should be gullible to the enticements of misguided religionists who claim believers should be neither sick nor poor. May Christians the world over fully realize that we are not to be like the people in this Sunday school lesson who followed the Lord primarily for what they could get out of Him. Let us not weary ourselves for that food which perishes!

B. A CONCLUDING WORD

John 6:51 is the Key Verse of the lesson. It teaches us that the Lord gives the bread which is His flesh for the life of the world. The giving of His flesh points to His death on the cross, where He shed His blood for you and me. He is the living bread. Just as the multiplied physical bread satisfied the hunger of the multitude, though only temporarily, those who eat the Lord's flesh and drink His blood (John 6:53-56) are permanently spiritually satisfied.

Such language seems strange to us today, but the "eating" and "drinking" are synonyms for believing. Such language has nothing to do with the Communion or Lord's Supper. Absorb Him into your life, even as you assimilate food, for He is spiritual food that perpetually nourishes the spiritual life. Augustine said: "Believe, and thou hast eaten." We see then that salvation is not by works or "doing the best we can," not by keeping the law, not by church membership, not by water baptism; not by obeying the Golden Rule, speaking in tongues, being "slain in the spirit," etc., but simply by believing in the Lord Jesus Christ, the Bread of Life.

HOME DAILY BIBLE READINGS
Week of April 18, 1999
Jesus, the Bread of Life

Apr. 12 M. John 6:1-15, There Is a Boy Here
Apr. 13 T. John 6:16-24, It Is I: Do Not Be Afraid
Apr. 14 W. John 6:25-40, Give Us This Bread Always
Apr. 15 T. John 6:41-51, I Am the Bread of Life
Apr. 16 F. John 6:52-59, This Bread Came Down From Heaven
Apr. 17 S. Nehemiah 9:6-15, Israel Was Given Bread From Heaven
Apr. 18 S. Psalm 78:17-29, Mortals Ate the Bread of Angels

Truth That Sets People Free

Adult Topic—How to Know the Truth

.....

Youth Topic—True Freedom
Children's Topic—Jesus Taught the People

.....

Devotional Reading—Psalm 51:1-9
Background Scripture—John 8:12-59
Print—John 8:12, 21-36

• • • • • • • • • • •

PRINTED SCRIPTURE

John 8:12, 21-36 (KJV)

12 Then spake Jesus again unto them, saying, I am the light of the world: he that followeth me shall not walk in darkness, but shall have the light of life.

.....

21 Then said Jesus again unto them, I go my way, and ye shall seek me, and shall die in your sins: whither I go, ye cannot come.

22 Then said the Jews, Will he kill himself? because he saith, Whither I go, ye cannot come.

23 And he said unto them, Ye are from beneath; I am from above: ye are of this world; I am not of this world.

24 I said therefore unto you, that ye shall die in your sins: for if ye believe not that I am he, ye shall die in your sins.

25 Then said they unto him, Who art thou? And Jesus saith unto them, Even the same that I said unto you from the beginning.

26 I have many things to say and

John 8:12, 21-36 (NRSV)

12 Again Jesus spoke to them, saying, "I am the light of the world. Whoever follows me will never walk in darkness but will have the light of life."

.....

21 Again he said to them, "I am going away, and you will search for me, but you will die in your sin. Where I am going, you cannot come."

22 Then the Jews said, "Is he going to kill himself? Is that what he means by saying, 'Where I am going, you cannot come'?"

23 He said to them, "You are from below, I am from above; you are of this world, I am not of this world.

24 I told you that you would die in your sins, for you will die in your sins unless you believe that I am he."

25 They said to him, "Who are you?" Jesus said to them, "Why do I speak to you at all?

26 I have much to say about you and much to condemn; but the one

to judge of you: but he that sent me is true; and I speak to the world those things which I have heard of him.

27 They understood not that he spake to them of the Father.

28 Then said Jesus unto them, When ye have lifted up the Son of man, then shall ye know that I am he, and that I do nothing of myself; but as my Father hath taught me, I speak these things.

29 And he that sent me is with me: the Father hath not left me alone; for I do always those things that please him.

30 As he spake these words, many believed on him.

31 Then said Jesus to those Jews which believed on him, if ye continue in my word, then are ye my disciples indeed;

32 And ye shall know the truth, and the truth shall make you free.

33 They answered him, We be Abraham's seed, and were never in bondage to any man: how sayest thou, Ye shall be made free?

34 Jesus answered them, Verily, verily, I say unto you, Whosoever committeth sin is the servant of sin.

35 And the servant abideth not in the house for ever: but the Son abideth ever.

36 If the Son therefore shall make you free, ye shall be free indeed.

who sent me is true, and I declare to the world what I have heard from him."

27 They did not understand that he was speaking to them about the Father.

28 So Jesus said, "When you have lifted up the Son of Man, then you will realize that I am he, and that I do nothing on my own, but I speak these things as the Father instructed me.

29 And the one who sent me is with me; he has not left me alone, for I always do what is pleasing to him."

30 As he was saying these things, many believed in him.

31 The Jesus said to the Jews who had believed in him, "If you continue in my word, you are truly my disciples;

32 and you will know the truth, and the truth will make you free."

33 They answered him, "We are descendants of Abraham and have never been slaves to anyone. What do you mean by saying, 'You will be made free'?"

34 Jesus answered them, "Very truly, I tell you, everyone who commits sin is a slave to sin.

35 The slave does not have a permanent place in the household; the son has a place there forever.

36 So if the Son makes you free, you will be free indeed."

KEY VERSE

Then said Jesus to those Jews which believed on him, if ye continue in my word, then are ye my disciples indeed; And ye shall know the truth, and the truth shall make you free.—John 8:31-32

OBJECTIVES

After reading this lesson, the student should be better informed about:

1. The meaning of the phrase "the Light of the World";
2. The danger of dying in one's sins;
3. The truth that sets men and women free; and,
4. Sin's enslavement.

POINTS TO BE EMPHASIZED

Adult/Youth/Children
Key Verse: John 8:31-32; John 8:29 (Children)
Print: John 8:12, 21-36

—Jesus identified Himself as the Light of the world and promised that those who follow Him would never be in darkness. (12)

—Because of their spiritual deadness certain people misunderstood the truth that Jesus spoke and would not be able to follow or find Jesus when He departed. (21-22)

—Jesus declared that His origin was from above while theirs was from below, and unless they accepted Him as Savior, they would die in their sins. (22-24)

—When answering the question regarding who He was, Jesus said He spoke for God, the Father, and He had much to condemn. (25-27)

—Many believed in the Son of Man when Jesus spoke of being lifted up and doing what is pleasing to God. (28-30)

—Jesus told the Jews that the truth of His word, rather than their ancestor Abraham, would make them free. (31-36)

(NOTE: Use KJV Scripture for Adults; NRSV Scripture for Youth and Children)

TOPICAL OUTLINE OF THE LESSON

I. Introduction

A. Jesus Christ and Light
B. Biblical Background

II. Exposition and Application of the Scripture

A. Jesus Christ the Light of the World (John 8:12)
B. Dying in One's Sin (John 8:21-24)
C. Who Jesus Christ Is (John 8:25-30)
D. The Slavery of Sin (John 8:31-36)

III. Special Features

A. Preserving Our Heritage
B. A Concluding Word

I. Introduction

A. JESUS CHRIST AND LIGHT

In last week's lesson, we saw the first "I AM" statement of our Lord—"I am the Bread of Life" (John 6:35). In today's lesson, we have the second "I AM" declaration—"I am the light of the world" (John 8:12). The Greek words **ego eimi** are emphatic; they assert, I and I alone! Falling from the lips of Christ, they constitute a very definite claim to Deity. Light refers to more than physical brightness, radiance, illumination or luminosity. There is the symbolic meaning of revelation, intelligence, knowledge, and awareness.

The Word in John 1:1 is also He who said in Genesis 1:3: "Let there be light," and there was light. As Light, Jesus Christ is God manifest in the flesh, for God is Light, and in Him is no darkness at all (1 John 1:5). He is the Creator, Source and Giver of Light. All the light men have, whether they walk in it or not, they owe to the Word made flesh, for Christ is the light that lights every man coming into the world (John 1:9).

As the predicted Messiah, He is "a light of the Gentiles" (Isaiah 42:6, 49:6). This truth was repeated by Simeon when he saw the child Jesus (Luke 2:32). At the Transfiguration scene, the Lord revealed in part that light which is essentially His. He also proved that He is the Light of the World by giving sight to the man born blind (John 9:5). It is no wonder then that we find this title used of Him three times: John 8:12, 9:5, 12:46—He is indeed the Light of the World!

B. BIBLICAL BACKGROUND

In today's lesson, we see a major or central issue regarding the conflict between the Lord Jesus and the religious leaders of His day (called by John, "the Jews"). It is interesting that from time to time, we read of Jewish leaders accusing the New Testament of being anti-Semitic. And John's use of the term, "the Jews," is often cited as an example of anti-Semitism. However, John himself was a Jew. And of course, the Lord Jesus Christ after the flesh was a Jew.

The issue is encouched in the question, "Who are You?" In John 8:25, the Pharisees kept saying (Imperfect tense) to Him, literally, "You—who are you?" Their tone is contemptuous; their words an explosive sneer, more like saying, "Who do you think you are!" Or as Plummer stated, the pronoun used is "scornfully emphatic!" How dare He tell them they shall die in their sins!

Using A. T. Robertson's *A Harmony of the Gospels,* I would arrange chronologically some of the verses I found dealing with this issue of the identity of Jesus Christ. (1) After the Lord told the paralytic that he was forgiven of his sins, the scribes and Pharisees began to reason, saying, "Who is this that speaketh blasphemy? Who can forgive sins but God alone?" (Luke 5:21). (2) In His last visit to Nazareth, after He taught them in their synagogue, men inquired, "Whence hath this man this wisdom, and these mighty works?" (Matthew 13:54). (3) After He spoke in the temple, the Jews marveled, saying, "How knoweth this man letters, having never learned?" (John 7:15).

(4) At the feast of the dedication at Jerusalem, the religious leaders surrounded our Lord, and said: "How long dost thou make us to doubt? If thou be the Christ, tell us plainly" (John 10:24). (5) Upon His entering Jerusalem all the city was moved, saying, "Who is this?" (Matthew 21:10). (6) Then when He came into the temple, the chief priests and the elders of the people came unto Him as He was teaching, and said, "By what authority doest thou these things? And who gave thee this authority?" (Matthew 21:23). (7) Finally, we see Him standing before the Sanhedrin and the question was asked, "Art thou the Christ? Tell us...Art thou, then, the Son of God?" (Luke 22:67, 70).

Keep in mind that one central conflict between the Lord and the Pharisees had to do with the origin of Christ. This is seen not only in John 8:25 in our lesson, but is repeated in John 8:53 when the Jews said, "Art thou greater than our father Abraham, which is dead? and the prophets are dead: whom makest thou thyself?" Perennially the question is: "Who are You?" Christ answers from His point of view and the words used indicate that He is God who became a Man.

II. Exposition and Application of the Scripture

A. JESUS CHRIST THE LIGHT OF THE WORLD
(John 8:12)

Then spake Jesus again unto them, saying, I am the light of the world: he that followeth me shall not walk in darkness, but shall have the light of life.

In addition to the information given in the Introduction, we add the following to further highlight the point. Scholars make mention of the fact that the lights connected with the ceremonies during the Feast of Tabernacles were not lit, and this darkness made it all the more fitting that Christ should declare He is the Light of the World, a light that can never be dimmed or extinguished. Note, He is the Light of the World-system **(kosmos);** He is not a parochial God with a restricted gospel. Christ is the source of the world's illumination. We Christians must kindle our torches at His bright flame, and then show to the world something of His light (Matthew 5:14). The light does us no good if not followed. Some men reject the light. Others claim to follow but are not whole-hearted disciples; they have no inner, spiritual attachment. To follow continuously is to believe and obey. To walk speaks of behavior, conduct. Thus to walk in darkness is to go astray, for darkness is a power which opposes light. The double negative is used for emphasis: "shall not walk." No one else can truthfully claim that to follow him causes permanent transformation. Christ is not only light, but a living light that gives life. He is the Light which is life.

B. DYING IN ONE'S SINS
(John 8:21-24)

Then said Jesus again unto them, I go my way, and ye shall seek me, and shall die in your sins: whither I go, ye cannot come. Then said the Jews, Will

he kill himself? because he saith, Whither I go, ye cannot come. And he said unto them, Ye are from beneath; I am from above: ye are of this world; I am not of this world. I said therefore unto you, that ye shall die in your sins: for if ye believe not that I am he, ye shall die in your sins.

The Pharisees are next informed that they will seek their Messiah when it is too late. Christ warned them that He will not be long with them. And unless they believe in Him, they will die unredeemed by Him. To die in one's sins is an Old Testament phrase. God warned in Ezekiel that the wicked "shall died in his iniquity" (Ezekiel 3:18; 18:18). To die, thus, is to die undelivered by the Messiah; it is to die in sin's bondage; it is to go to Hell. This is the inevitable consequence of persistent unbelief.

Because the Lord spoke of their being unable to find Him, the Jews thought He contemplated suicide. Actually, He predicted His death, burial, resurrection, and ascension. He then answered them by pointing out the deep differences between them (Isaiah 55:8-9). They were tied up with the world system; their origin was from below, from a different world. Because they lacked spiritual understanding and had failed to accept Him as their Messiah, they would indeed die in their sins. Only by attaching themselves to Christ could they avoid being identified with this world system, one ruled by its prince, Satan. Unless they come to believe that He is more than mere man, they can "never trust Him with that faith that is saving faith" (Morris, p. 447).

C. WHO JESUS CHRIST IS
(John 8:25-30)

Then said they unto him, Who art thou? And Jesus saith unto them, Even the same that I said unto you from the beginning. I have many things to say and to judge of you: but he that sent me is true; and I speak to the world those things which I have heard of him. They understood not that he spake to them of the Father. Then said Jesus unto them, When ye have lifted up the Son of man, then shall ye know that I am he, and that I do nothing of myself; but as my Father hath taught me, I speak these things. And he that sent me is with me: the Father hath not left me alone; for I do always those things that please him. As he spake these words, many believed on him.

We learned earlier (Biblical Background) the importance of the question broached in verse 25: "Who are you?" Christ had made it clear several times who He was, but the spiritual blindness of the Jewish leaders prevented them from accepting His truth. The Greek of verse 25 is a difficult passage. It has been variously rendered, "Why do I talk to you at all?" (RSV margin; NEB). Or, "What have I been saying to you from the beginning?" (NASB). However, I think the context is best suited by translating, "I am that which I speak," said Christ. What He revealed Himself to be, that is what He is. We agree with Lenski's rendering: "In general, that which I also am telling you" is the answer to the question, "Who are you?" Christ could have said more which would have added to their condemnation, but He held back. Because what He said is from God His Father, it is true.

However, the Jews cannot understand His allusion to His Father; and they will not until He is lifted up—crucified! Finally, He claimed again that He was the Sent One. By asserting He always does what pleases the Father, He implied a consciousness of sinlessness.

D. THE SLAVERY OF SIN
(John 8:31-36)

Then said Jesus to those Jews which believed on him, if ye continue in my word, then are ye my disciples indeed; And ye shall know the truth, and the truth shall make you free. They answered him, We be Abraham's seed, and were never in bondage to any man: how sayest thou, Ye shall be made free? Jesus answered them, Verily, verily, I say unto you, Whosoever committeth sin is the servant of sin. And the servant abideth not in the house for ever: but the Son abideth ever. If the Son therefore shall make you free, ye shall be free indeed.

True discipleship means staying in the Word of God; true disciples hold fast to that which they know. They do so not to be saved, but because they are saved. The Lord wanted these would-be disciples to know this. Whatever belief they had was shallow and superficial. Christ sought to deepen their faith, and move them to understand that the power of the truth to liberate men and women depends upon their continuing in His Word. The freedom spoken of is primarily emancipation from the slavery of sin. Resenting our Lord's remarks, the Pharisees responded: "If the truth you speak of is good only for slaves do not trouble us with it, for we are Abraham's seed! We were never in bondage to any man. So what do you mean, 'We shall be made free'?" Now one way of looking at their statement that they had never been in bondage is to interpret it to mean they had never lost their freedom of spirit. They had never accepted slavery.

If bondage means having been in captivity, then of course, they completely ignore history. For there were periods when the governments of Egypt, Assyria, Babylon, Persia, Greece, and at the time, Rome ruled over them. On the other hand, their very pride, blind arrogance, and hypocrisy indicate a kind of slavery.

The Jews did not realize this; they thought being a son of Abraham was sufficient for God's approval. Christ then pointed out to them the differences between the Son and a slave in the household of God. The slave has no rights, no security; he may be sold or transferred elsewhere at any moment. But as for the Son—He abides forever. He is "heir of all things" (Hebrews 1:2). And if the Son sets the slave free, the slave is free indeed!

III. Special Features

John 8:32 is a verse often used by various groups to cite the Black American's need for that which will liberate him from the shackles of Eurocentrism, segregation, exploitation, racism, lack of self-esteem, self-hatred, ignorance, etc. The biggest problem with the solutions offered is the definition of Truth. Taking a cue from Pilate, we would ask, "What is truth?" (John 18:38). John 14:6 answers: Jesus Christ, the Son of God, is the Truth. Therefore, we believe that "If the Son, therefore, shall make you free, ye shall be free indeed."

One of the central passions of the Negro Spiritual is this matter called FREEDOM. It is highly unlikely, however, that freedom from sin was meant by the creators of the Spirituals—unless, of course, they meant freedom from the sin of slavery! The slaves saw in the Exodus—the freeing of Israel from slavery in Egypt—their own hope of emancipation, and sang: "Go down, Moses 'Way down in Egypt land, Tell ole Pharaoh, To let my people go." From Daniel's survival in the lion's den came these words, "Didn't my Lord deliver Daniel, An' why not-a every man!" Freedom meant not being owned or controlled, treated as chattel, or property, restricted by unjust laws imposed by unjust men (Isaiah 10:1). Freedom included the right to exercise God-given talents.

B. A CONCLUDING WORD

There are at least two ways of looking at Jesus Christ as the Light of the World—Salvation and Sanctification. First, there is the matter of SALVATION. Through faith in the shed blood of Calvary—belief in His finished work on the cross—we are turned or removed from darkness to light (Acts 26:18). Since darkness is a picture of Hell (1 Samuel 2:9; Matthew 22:13), and Christ has paid the penalty of our sin so that we need not suffer Hell, we see why the Light of the World is our Savior. He brought us out of darkness into His marvelous light (1 Peter 2:9). And so we are grateful to God that the light of Salvation shined on us.

Second: Not only is this Light life, but it gives life in the midst of death; it gives light that dispels darkness. We consider this one phase of Sanctification which may be attributed to light, a walking in the light of which Christ said, "He who follows Me shall not walk in darkness" (John 8:12). Through Christ, we escape the pestilence that walks in darkness (Psalm 91:6). We are surrounded by the darkness of hatred (1 John 2:9, 11), opposed by the rulers of the darkness of this age, and tempted by the unfruitful works of darkness (Ephesians 6:12, 5:11).

HOME DAILY BIBLE READINGS
Week of April 25, 1999
Truth That Sets People Free

Apr. 19 M. John 8:12-20 I Am the Light of the World
Apr. 20 T. John 8:21-30 Many Believed in Him
Apr. 21 W. John 8:31-38 If You Continue in My Word
Apr. 22 T. John 8:39-47 Abraham's Children Do What Abraham Did
Apr. 23 F. John 8:48-59 Whoever Keeps My Word Will Never See Death
Apr. 24 S. Ephesians 5:1-14 Live As Children of Light
Apr. 25 S. Psalm 43:1-5 Let Your Light and Your Truth Lead Me

The Purpose of Jesus' Death

Adult Topic—Finding Life in Death

.....

Youth Topic—Giving One's All
Children's Topic—Jesus Praised by the People

.....

Devotional Reading—Romans 5:1-11
Background Scripture—John 12:20-50
Print— John 12:23b-28, 30-37, 42-43

• • • • • • • • • • • •

PRINTED SCRIPTURE

John 12:23b-28, 30-37, 42-43 (KJV)

23b The hour is come, that the Son of man should be glorified.

24 Verily, verily, I say unto you, Except a corn of wheat fall into the ground and die, it abideth alone: but if it die, it bringeth forth much fruit.

25 He that loveth his life shall lose it; and he that hateth his life in this world shall keep it unto life eternal.

26 If any man serve me, let him follow me; and where I am, there shall also my servant be: if any man serve me, him will my Father honour.

27 Now is my soul troubled; and what shall I say? Father, save me from this hour: but for this cause came I unto this hour.

28 Father, glorify thy name. Then came there a voice from heaven, saying, I have both glorified it, and will glorify it again.

.....

John 12:23b-28, 30-37, 42-43 (NRSV)

23b "The hour has come for the Son of Man to be glorified.

24 Very truly, I tell you, unless a grain of wheat falls into the earth and dies, it remains just a single grain; but if it dies, it bears much fruit.

25 Those who love their life lose it, and those who hate their life in this world will keep it for eternal life.

26 Whoever serves me must follow me, and where I am, there will my servant be also. Whoever serves me, the Father will honor.

27 Now my soul is troubled. And what should I say—'Father, save me from this hour?' No, it is for this reason that I have come to this hour.

28 Father, glorify your name." Then a voice came from heaven, "I have glorified it, and I will glorify it again."

.....

30 Jesus answered and said, This voice came not because of me, but for your sakes.

31 Now is the judgment of this world: now shall the prince of this world be cast out.

32 And I, if I be lifted up from the earth, will draw all men unto me.

33 This he said, signifying what death he should die.

34 The people answered him, We have heard out of the law that Christ abideth for ever: and how sayest thou, The Son of man must be lifted up? who is this Son of man?

35 Then Jesus said unto them, Yet a little while is the light with you. Walk while ye have the light, lest darkness come upon you: for he that walketh in darkness knoweth not whither he goeth.

36 While ye have light, believe in the light, that ye may be the children of light. These things spake Jesus, and departed, and did hide himself from them.

37 But though he had done so many miracles before them, yet they believed not on him.

.....

42 Nevertheless among the chief rulers also many believed on him; but because of the Pharisees they did not confess him, lest they should be put out of the synagogue:

43 For they loved the praise of men more than the praise of God.

30 Jesus answered, "This voice has come for your sake, not for mine.

31 Now is the judgment of this world; now the ruler of this world will be driven out.

32 And I, when I am lifted up from the earth, will draw all people to myself."

33 He said this to indicate the kind of death he was to die.

34 The crowd answered him, "We have heard from the law that the Messiah remains forever. How can you say that the Son of Man must be lifted up? Who is this Son of Man?"

35 Jesus said to them, "The light is with you for a little longer. Walk while you have the light, so that the darkness may not overtake you. If you walk in the darkness, you do not know where you are going.

36 While you have the light, believe in the light, so that you may become children of light." After Jesus had said this, he departed and hid from them.

37 Although he had performed so many signs in their presence, they did not believe in him.

....

42 Nevertheless many, even of the authorities, believed in him. But because of the Pharisees they did not confess it, for fear that they would be put out of the synagogue;

43 for they loved human glory more than the glory that comes from God.

KEY VERSE

And I, if I be lifted up from the earth, will draw all men unto me.—John 12:32

OBJECTIVES

After reading this lesson, the student should understand better:

1. Why the Lord Jesus died on the cross;
2. The spiritual battle with the forces of evil;
3. What the fear of man can do to one's relationship with God;
4. How obedience to God should become the first point in one's life; and
5. That the way in which suffering and trials are confronted, even death itself, is indicataive of one's faith (or lack thereof) in God.

POINTS TO BE EMPHASIZED

Adult/Youth
Key Verse: John 12:32
Print: John 12:23b-28, 30-37, 42-43

—Jesus knew that He must soon die in order to provide the opportunity for our salvation and He used the illustration of the grain of wheat to explain eternal life. (23-26)

—God's voice assured the people that Jesus had glorified God in His life and would do so again. (28-30)

—Jesus declared that His death and resurrection would end Satan's rule and make salvation available to all people. (31-33)

—The people questioned Jesus because they believed that when the Messiah came He would remain on earth forever. (34)

—Jesus challenged the people to believe in the light and become children of God, rather than continue to walk in darkness and be lost. (35-36)

—Many of the Jewish rulers believed that Jesus was the Christ, but were afraid to confess Him openly. (42-43)

Children
Key Verse: John 12:13
Print: John 12:12-19

—A great crowd had come to the city to attend the Jewish festival heard that that Jesus was coming to Jerusalem. (12)

—The people shouted praises as they went to meet Jesus. (13)

—Jesus fulfilled Scripture by riding into Jerusalem on a donkey. (14)

—The disciples later remembered that Jesus had fulfilled the Scripture. (16)

—The crowd gathered because Jesus had raised Lazarus. (17)

—The Pharisees saw the very large group of people who were shouting praises and said that the world was following Jesus. (19)

(NOTE: Use KJV Scripture for Adults; NRSV Scripture for Youth and Children)

I. Introduction

A. LIFE OUT OF DEATH

Here we deal with the exposition of John 12:24. Our study will help us greatly to understand better the purpose of the death of Jesus Christ. Recall that earlier, some Greeks were among those who had come up to worship. They went to Philip and expressed a desire to have an interview with the Lord. "Sir, we would (we wish, we desire) to see Jesus" (John 12:21). Philip told Andrew, then both of them went and told the Lord. Christ did not speak directly to the Greeks, but we assume they heard His words, perhaps conveyed to them by Andrew and Philip. The solemnity and importance of what He had to say is introduced by the words, "Verily, verily" (amen, amen).

In the approach of these Greeks, Christ saw a first fruit of the harvest to be reaped among all men (including Gentiles) through His dying. To receive a harvest of redeemed souls, He must first die. And so He answered their request indirectly with one of the great laws of harvest, for nature itself provided Him with an illustration of His own career. He would become a grain of wheat, fall into the ground, and die. If He did not die, He would abide alone. Seed will not produce anything until it falls into the ground and dies. The breaking open of the seed is likened to death's destruction. Paul brings this out in First Corinthians 15:36, when he states: "That which you sow is not made alive, except it die." A seed may remain dormant for a long period of time, but when conditions are just right, germination takes place. Changes occur, the seed coating is broken, a sprout comes forth and grows down into the soil to become a root.

Such is the development that the seed no longer looks anything like what it was originally, and in time, it becomes a plant and reproduces fruit and seeds.

You see why a seed is defined as the "specialized part of a plant that produces a new plant." And so we see the paradox—that which appears to be contradictory—which teaches the way to life is through death, the road to fruitfulness is through dying. It is through the death, burial, and resurrection of Jesus Christ that many are brought to life eternal.

"There is no gain but by a loss, You cannot save but by a cross; The corn of wheat to multiply must fall into the ground and die" (S. Zwemer).

B. BIBLICAL BACKGROUND

At this point in our lesson our Lord is in Jerusalem. John's account of Christ's entry into the holy city is purposely brief compared to the accounts given in the other Gospels. When the crowd heard He was coming to Jerusalem, they went forth to meet Him, and greeted Him with loud, enthusiastic shouts of Hosannas, branches of palm trees strewn before Him. All this had the effect of further stirring up the Pharisees. To their dismay, they expressed their "passionate hyperbole" (Lenski), "the whole world is gone after Him" (John 12:19). It is against this backdrop of murderous hate—and the pessimism of the Pharisees who felt all their efforts to contain or eliminate this Man called Jesus had ended in failure—that we find a contingent of Greek "God-fearers" expressing their desire to see the Lord. Their desire indicates in part that the time had come for Him to die for the whole world, both Jew and Gentile.

II. Exposition and Application of the Scripture

A. PLAN FOR HIS PASSION
(John 12:23b)

The hour is come, that the Son of man should be glorified.

The words of this verse are addressed to Andrew and Philip, two of our Lord's disciples, although reference is not to them alone. To them He answered: "The hour is come...." Earlier, we were told the time of His Passion had not come. Christ said to His unbelieving brothers: "My time is not yet come...for My time is not yet fully come" (John 7:6,8). We are later told in this same chapter that the religious leaders wanted to lay hands on Him, but dared not, "because His hour was not yet come" (John 7:30). And after He had spoken in the treasury, once again His enemies wanted to seize Him, but "no man laid hands on Him; for His hour was not yet come" (John 8:20).

All of these statements indicate that He was in charge. No man, no demon, no Devil forced His hand! The word rendered "hour" does not refer to sixty minutes of time, but rather to a general period of time. Indeed, reference here is to His death and to His resurrection. But everything is according to His schedule, not man's schedule. And note that whereas death is involved, it is not a matter of His defeat, but His triumph over the grave. He used the word "glorified" to describe His Passion! Other words are used elsewhere to describe His death. For example:

Luke 9:31 speaks of His decease (exodus) or departure; in John 10:18, He has authority to lay down His life; in Matthew 27:26, He is delivered to be crucified; John 19:30 speaks of His giving up the spirit. Surely, His death was different from that of any man—but imagine calling it an hour to be glorified!

B. THE LAW OF LIFE
(John 12:24-28)

Verily, verily, I say unto you, Except a corn of wheat fall into the ground and die, it abideth alone: but if it die, it bringeth forth much fruit. He that loveth his life shall lose it; and he that hateth his life in this world shall keep it unto life eternal. If any man serve me, let him follow me; and where I am, there shall also my servant be: if any man serve me, him will my Father honour. Now is my soul troubled; and what shall I say? Father, save me from this hour: but for this cause came I unto this hour. Father, glorify thy name. Then came there a voice from heaven, saying, I have both glorified it, and will glorify it again.

We next learn that life may be multiplied through death. At an hour or time set by the determinate counsel and foreknowledge of God, Christ will die and be buried. For further comments, see the Introduction, part A. Here then is our first paradox: Die to live. Out of death comes life. A second paradox is: Love life and lose it; hate it and keep it. Our Lord's attitude toward death is remarkable! Yet, what He has to say is for our benefit. Christians must also learn that the clinging to earthly life with a passion that suggests "when you're dead you're done" is unworthy of the believer. This is the paradox of life—love your life (soul) and lose it; hate it and protect or guard it. Hate is a strong expression, but it means put in last place. Love Christ so much that whatever else you love is hatred compared to what you have for the Lord. We are thus warned not to make food, clothing, houses, money, automobiles, pleasure the most important things in life. All such will perish! Our Lord's comments in John 12:25 are found in all the Gospels: Matthew 10:39; Mark 8:35; Luke 9:24.

A third paradox is seen in verse 26. The life of ministry is a life of honor. People with the "gimmes" are never happy. The more they get, the more they want. True living is slain by selfishness. Our Lord constantly taught the disciples the importance of the role of ministry, service, helping others. "What's in it for me?" is an attitude that enslaves, robs, demeans, causes the spirit and soul to wither, stultify and die. True greatness is never achieved by looking out for "Number One," unless of course Jesus Christ is Number One; and others constitute Number Two—and self is a distant Number Three. Acceptance of this teaching rewards the believer with honor from God the Father.

Now John 12:27 presents some difficulty of interpretation. If we have the Lord pleading with His Father to save Him from this hour (that is, keep Him out of it), then we find Him denying the very purpose for which He had come into the world. He was born to die. Yet there are scholars who say Christ's human spirit was so troubled at the prospect of facing such a cruel death that He expressed an all too natural desire to be saved from its horrors. Does such an interpretation imply disobedience or weakness on His part?

Another interpretation is that Christ prayed the Father would save Him "out of death" (Hebrews 5:7). This means He would suffer, but God the Father would pull Him out of the suffering. Leon Morris says we should see here "a hypothetical prayer at which Jesus looks, but which He refuses to pray." We can be sure that our Lord's will was for God the Father to glorify His own name. Speaking from Heaven, the Father publicly ratified the obedience of His Son. In Christ's earthly ministry, the name of the Father was exalted, and now as His death approaches, the Father's name will be glorified again.

C. THE DESCRIPTION OF DEATH
(John 12:30-37)

Jesus answered and said, This voice came not because of me, but for your sakes. Now is the judgment of this world: now shall the prince of this world be cast out. And I, if I be lifted up from the earth, will draw all men unto me. This he said, signifying what death he should die. The people answered him, We have heard out of the law that Christ abideth for ever: and how sayest thou, The Son of man must be lifted up? who is this Son of man? Then Jesus said unto them, Yet a little while is the light with you. Walk while ye have the light, lest darkness come upon you: for he that walketh in darkness knoweth not whither he goeth. While ye have light, believe in the light, that ye may be the children of light. These things spake Jesus, and departed, and did hide himself from them. But though he had done so many miracles before them, yet they believed not on him.

The people who stood nearby heard words, but did not understand their meaning. Some of them said it thundered; others claimed an angel spoke to Christ. The voice they heard was not because of Christ, but for the sake of the disciples and the entire multitude. Furthermore, its purpose was that they might recognize Christ as God. As for the world's judgment, this would soon be manifested by their rejection of the Lord of Glory and His subsequent death. By putting Him to death, they condemned themselves, showing what they thought of God's Son.

Satan is the ruler or leader of this present world-system; he is the god of this world-age (2 Corinthians 4:4), the prince of the power of the air (Ephesians 2:2). Note Satan's claim in the Temptation story is not disputed. He was not lying when he made his offer to the Lord Jesus (Matthew 4:8; Luke 4:6). Though he is the chief leader of evil spirits, and ruler in that atmospheric realm, here his defeat is predicted (John 16:11). For the Lord Jesus removed the sting of death and snatched victory out of the mouth of the grave (1 Corinthians 15:55), fulfilling the purpose of His coming (Hebrews 2:14).

See how God uses both wicked men and the Devil. By their rejection of Him, and the resultant crucifixion, the world system condemned itself. Satan was cast out, and the "Savior crucified is in fact the Savior glorified" (Alford). That which appears to men as defeat is actually that which draws men—Jews and Greeks

(Gentiles)—to Jesus Christ. And glory triumphs over ignominy and shame. Now when the people heard the mention of dying, they were puzzled, and responded that they had heard according to the Old Testament that the Messiah would live forever (Isaiah 9:7; Psalm 110:4; Daniel 7:14; Micah 4:7). If the Son of Man abides forever, what is this talk about being lifted up to die? How can this be? Without really answering their questions or offering further explanation, the Lord warned them to take advantage of the light while there was light (John 9:4). Darkness will soon fall and overcome them; and to attempt to walk in darkness is dangerous.

It is always best to take advantage of the light while it shines. Do not try to calculate how long it will last. Do not philosophize or seek logical proofs. Just believe! Step out into the light; let God's Word be what it is—a lamp unto your feet, a light unto your path (Psalm 119:105). Do this, for it is the will of God that we may be the sons (and daughters) of light—enlightened folks, walking circumspectly, not misled by the phonies of this wicked age. Having spoken these words, the Lord Jesus left, and hid Himself from them. And despite the many miracles He had performed before them, yet they believed not on Him.

D. FEAR AND FLATTERY
(John 12:42-43)

Nevertheless among the chief rulers also many believed on him; but because of the Pharisees they did not confess him, lest they should be put out of the synagogue: For they loved the praise of men more than the praise of God.

The exposition of the lesson closes with comments on some men who professed to believe on Christ, but failed to witness Him. "They did not confess Him." The word used is **homologeo,** which means literally, to say the same thing, agree with. It thus means to profess, declare openly, speak out freely—and this, of course, is exactly what these men refused to do. Many of the chief rulers were convinced that Jesus was the Christ. However, they dared not make known their convictions. One reason was their fear of excommunication. They knew that the fanatical Pharisees would not hesitate to throw them out of the synagogue. Recall that in John 9:22, 34 the man born blind was literally, physically thrown out as well. Excommunication from the synagogue, for whatever length of time, caused great hardship for that individual and his family.

Most commentators believe this unwillingness to confess Christ indicates there was no genuiness of faith to begin with. I agree, but would not include such men as Nicodemus, or Joseph of Arimathea among these fearful. For an additional condemnation is the fact that these leaders loved the praise of men more than the praise of God. Men who seek the honor of other men automatically prove themselves unworthy of the honor of God. We hear the Lord ask, "How can ye believe, who receive honor one of another, and seek not the honor that cometh from God only?" (John 5:44). So many times persons determine their worth by that which people think, rather than by that which God approves.

III. Special Features

A. PRESERVING OUR HERITAGE

One of the most popular hymns in our Black Churches is "Lift Him Up," number 198 in our *Baptist Standard Hymnal*. The Reverend Johnson Oatman, Jr., wrote:

"How to reach the masses, men of ev'ry birth? For an answer Jesus gave a key,
'And I , if I be lifted up from the earth, Will draw all men unto Me.'
Lift Him up, Lift Him up, Still He speaks from eternity,
'And I, if I be lifted up from the earth, will draw all men unto Me.' "

As you can see, the words come directly out of John 12:32. The verb rendered "lift up" **(upsoo)** means to raise high, exalt. Note that it is used twice in John 3:14. John interprets the lifting up as signifying death on the cross. There is also the interpretation which stresses the heavenly exaltation attained by the crucifixion. Thus, the "lifting up on earth is not to be separated from His exaltation into heaven."

It is this latter aspect of the meaning of the verb to "Lift up" that is emphasized in our churches. Thus, we are exhorted to lift Him up (not crucify Him) by trusting Him, and living as a Christian ought: "Let the world in you the Savior see, Then men will gladly follow Him who once taught, I'll draw all men unto Me.'"

B. A CONCLUDING WORD

Followers of the Lord Jesus Christ must always remember the purpose of His coming. He came (1) to die, (2) to destroy the Devil, (3) and to deliver all who would believe in Him (Hebrews 2:14, 15). We are to maintain that ready spirit, that willingness to prove the great paradoxes of the Christian faith, namely: (1) to find life in death. "We cannot live a Christian life until we have a Christian life to live" (Ironside). (2) True life is achieved only through sacrifice. The life of honor and true greatness is the life of ministry, the path of service to others.

HOME DAILY BIBLE READINGS
Week of May 2, 1999
The Purpose of Jesus' Death

Apr.	26	M.	John 12:20-26, We Wish to See Jesus
Apr.	27	T.	John 12:27-36b, For This Reason I Have Come
Apr.	28	W.	John 12:36c-43, Who Has Believed Our Message?
Apr.	29	T.	John 12:44-50, Whoever Believes in Me
Apr.	30	F.	Philippians 2:1-11, The Same Mind That Was in Christ Jesus
May	1	S.	Colossians 1:9-20, The Image of the Invisible God
May	2	S.	Colossians 2:1-15, Knowledge of God's Mystery

Jesus Taught About Servanthood

Unit IV. Jesus Prepared His Followers
Adult Topic—Living as Servants

.....

Youth Topic—Serving Others
Children's Topic—Jesus, Our Example

.....

Devotional Reading—Matthew 25:31-30
Background Scripture—John 13:1-35
Print—John 13:1-17

• • • • • • • • • • •

PRINTED SCRIPTURE

John 13:1-17 (KJV)

NOW before the feast of the passover, when Jesus knew that his hour was come that he should depart out of this world unto the Father, having loved his own which were in the world, he loved them unto the end.

2 And supper being ended, the devil having now put into the heart of Judas Iscariot, Simon's son, to betray him;

3 Jesus knowing that the Father had given all things into his hands, and that he was come from God, and went to God;

4 He riseth from supper, and laid aside his garments; and took a towel, and girded himself.

5 After that he poureth water into a bason, and began to wash the disciples' feet, and to wipe them with the towel wherewith he was girded.

6 Then cometh he to Simon Peter: and Peter saith unto him, Lord, dost thou wash my feet?

John 13:1-17 (NRSV)

NOW before the festival of the Passover, Jesus knew that his hour had come to depart from this world and go to the Father. Having loved his own who were in the world, he loved them to the end.

2 The devil had already put it into the heart of Judas son of Simon Iscariot to betray him. And during supper

3 Jesus, knowing that the Father had given all things into his hands, and that he had come from God and was going to God,

4 got up from the table, took off his outer robe, and tied a towel around himself.

5 Then he poured water into a basin and began to wash the disciples' feet and to wipe them with the towel that was tied around him.

6 He came to Simon Peter, who said to him, "Lord, are you going to wash my feet?"

7 Jesus answered and said unto him, What I do thou knowest not now; but thou shalt know hereafter.

8 Peter saith unto him, Thou shalt never wash my feet. Jesus answered him, If I wash thee not, thou hast no part with me.

9 Simon Peter saith unto him, Lord, not my feet only, but also my hands and my head.

10 Jesus saith to him, He that is washed needeth not save to wash his feet, but is clean every whit: and ye are clean, but not all.

11 For he knew who should betray him; therefore said he, Ye are not all clean.

12 So after he had washed their feet, and had taken his garments, and was set down again, he said unto them, Know ye what I have done to you?

13 Ye call me Master and Lord: and ye say well; for so I am.

14 If I then, your Lord and Master, have washed your feet; ye also ought wash one another's feet.

15 For I have given you an example, that ye should do as I have done to you.

16 Verily, verily, I say unto you, The servant is not greater than his lord; neither he that is sent greater than he that sent him.

17 If ye know these things, happy are ye if ye do them.

7 Jesus answered, "You do not know now what I am doing, but later you will understand."

8 Peter said to him, "You will never wash my feet." Jesus answered, "Unless I wash you, you have no share with me."

9 Simon Peter said to him, "Lord, not my feel only but also my hands and my head!"

10 Jesus said to him, "One who has bathed does not need to wash, except for the feet, but is entirely clean. And you are clean, though not all of you."

11 For he knew who was to betray him; for this reason he said, "Not all of you are clean."

12 After he had washed their feet, had put on this robe, and had returned to the table, he said to them, "Do you know what I have done to you?

13 You call me Teacher and Lord—and you are right, for that is what I am.

14 So if I, your Lord and Teacher, have washed your feet, you also ought to wash one another's feet.

15 For I have set you an example, that you also should do as I have done to you.

16 Very truly, I tell you, servants are not greater than their master, nor are messengers greater than the one who sent them.

17 If you know these things, you are blessed if you do them."

 KEY VERSE

Verily, verily, I say unto you, The servant is not greater than his lord; neither he that is sent greater than he that sent him.—John 13:16

OBJECTIVES

After reading this lesson, the student should have a better understanding of:

1. The true meaning of servanthood;
2. The need for cleansing in the life of the believer;
3. The blessing that comes from a life of service; and,
4. Our Lord as the Supreme example of servanthood and love.

POINTS TO BE EMPHASIZED

Adult/Youth/Children
Key Verse: John 13:16; John 13:15 (Children)
Print: John 13:1-17; John 13: 1, 3-15 (Children)

—As Jesus' death drew near, He gave His disciples an example of servanthood and love for them to follow. (1-5)
—Peter submitted to having his feet washed when Jesus explained that being His follower required cleansing by Him. (6-10)
—Jesus understood that being a servant would not win everyone. (11)
—Jesus encouraged His servants to follow His example of humble service to others. (12-16)
—Those who follow Jesus' model of service will be blessed. (17)

(NOTE: Use KJV Scripture for Adults; NRSV Scripture for Youth and Children)

TOPICAL OUTLINE OF THE LESSON

I. Introduction
A. The Devil and Judas Iscariot
B. Biblical Background

II. Exposition and Application of the Scripture
A. Knowledge of His Hour (John 13:1-3)
B. Washing the Disciples' Feet (John 13:4-11)
C. Purpose of Servanthood (John 13:12-16)
D. The Blessing of Doing What We Know (John 13:17)

III. Special Features
A. Preserving Our Heritage
B. A Concluding Word

I. Introduction

A. THE DEVIL AND JUDAS ISCARIOT

Judas Iscariot is one of the most tragic of Bible characters. At first glance, it may seem strange that mention should be made of him within the setting that emphasizes servanthood. Yet, the story of Judas shows how one is able to miss the blessings of being a servant because of the love of self. And we see that Judas was a thief from the beginning, for we learn from John 12:6 that he was pilfering (imperfect tense) from the money bag he maintained as treasurer of the Twelve.

We see that at the time of our lesson, the Devil had put into Judas' heart the plan to betray the Lord. Some scholars speculate that it was his disappointment with the Lord's failure to overthrow the Roman government that prompted the betrayal by this son of perdition (John 17:12). Overall, we see in Judas a selfish, greedy, ambitious man who allowed the cancer of avarice to weaken him spiritually until he perpetrated a most heinous deed.

When Satan was finished with Judas, he abandoned him—as he does all who become instruments in his hands—and Judas committed suicide. As we shall see in the Exposition, our Lord was aware of Judas' situation (vv. 2, 10, 11), and the fact that Judas also knew his cover had been lifted helped accelerate the events leading to betrayal.

B. BIBLICAL BACKGROUND

The Synoptic Gospels (Matthew 26:17-19; Mark 14:12-16; Luke 22:7-13) spend more time describing the events leading up to the last Passover and the washing of the Disciples' feet. According to tradition, the Passover celebration imitated the last meal in Egypt in preparation for leaving the land of oppression. It was eaten while Jehovah, passing over the houses of the Jews, slew the firstborn of the Egyptians (Exodus 12:12 ff; 13:2, 12). Time had come to eat the passover, and the disciples asked the Lord where should they prepare for it.

Christ sent forth two of the men into the city (Peter and John, Luke 22:8). He predicted they would meet a certain man bearing a pitcher of water, and they were to follow him. This man in turn would lead them to a house whose owner would be told, "The Master says, 'Where is the guest room, where I shall eat the passover with my disciples?'" And so it happened. They were shown a large upper room, furnished and prepared. And there they met as our lesson opens.

II. Exposition and Application of the Scripture

A. KNOWLEDGE OF HIS HOUR
(John 13:1-3)

NOW before the feast of the passover, when Jesus knew that his hour was come that he should depart out of this world unto the Father, having loved

his own which were in the world, he loved them unto the end. And supper being ended, the devil having now put into the heart of Judas Iscariot, Simon's son, to betray him; Jesus knowing that the Father had given all things into his hands, and that he was come from God, and went to God.

The Lord and the Twelve are at the feast of the passover. But John informs us of the fact that Christ knew ahead of time what was taking place. The predestined end was foreseen from the beginning. He knew that His hour was come. Many times He announced His time had not come. This meant that it was not yet time for Him to act. But as He drew closer to the cross, His time was more immediate. Now, He spoke of His time in terms of leaving the world and returning to God the Father. "It marks the decisive end of Jesus' ministry" (Morris). The hour had come for Him to depart. From the very beginning of the calling of the Twelve, He had loved them and that love would continue until the end. The end of what? Of His life in the flesh? (Alford); His earthly ministry? (MacDonald). There is the idea also that He exhibited His love for them unto the utmost or infinite degree; that He showed His love to the uttermost *(Pilgrim Bible),* in every possible way, and would continue to do so throughout eternity.

Earlier, the Devil (the Slandered) had put it into the heart of Judas to betray the Lord. Exactly when we are not told. The tense of the verb used shows Judas "harbored the thought for some time" (Lenski), before finally pulling it off. He had struck a bargain with the chief priests earlier. This is revealed in Matthew 26:14-15 where it is recorded Judas asked: "What will ye give me, and I will deliver Him unto You? And they bargained with him for thirty pieces of silver."

Some scholars (Leon Morris, for example) believe John 13:2 teaches that Satan conceived in his own heart that Judas should deliver the Lord. However, we will stick with the King James Version here, for we believe reference is to the heart of Judas. We see that the Lord Jesus knew what was going on. However, He chose not to expose Judas. It is suggested (Expositor's) that knowing the fiery temper of Simon Peter, James and John, if Judas had been unmasked earlier, he would have suffered a terrible fate at their hands. This section of the lesson closes with emphasis once again on who is in charge—Jesus Christ is! He is at the very threshold of Calvary. But the coming events must not be viewed as the secret plans of some diabolical, formidable foe. No. What is about to occur is known by the Savior as "coming from God" and "going to God." Our Lord is aware of His divine origin and of His sure return (ascension) to God the Father.

B. WASHING THE DISCIPLES' FEET
(John 13:4-11)

He riseth from supper, and laid aside his garments; and took a towel, and girded himself. After that he poureth water into a bason, and began to wash the disciples' feet, and to wipe them with the towel wherewith he was girded. Then cometh he to Simon Peter: and Peter saith unto him, Lord, dost thou wash my feet? Jesus answered and said unto him, What I do thou knowest not now; but thou shalt know hereafter. Peter saith unto him, Thou shalt never wash my feet. Jesus answered him, If I wash thee not, thou hast no

part with me. Simon Peter saith unto him, Lord, not my feet only, but also my hands and my head. Jesus saith to him, He that is washed needeth not save to wash his feet, but is clean every whit: and ye are clean, but not all. For he knew who should betray him; therefore said he, Ye are not all clean.

In the original language, the present tense is used: "He rises from supper, and lays aside His garments." This is called the historical present. It makes the picture more vivid; it places us there; it is as if we see the action taking place before us. It is mixed with the past tense, "and having taken up an apron or towel, He girded Himself about." Here His humbleness is seen in the performance of such menial service as washing feet. Imagine the Creator washing the feet of the creatures! And yet, as we shall see, the picture here of divine condescension is made all the more stark by the treachery and death ahead! Now, when the Lord approached Simon Peter, the apostle said in effect, "What are YOU doing?" The Greek is emphatic: "Lord, do You—You wash my feet?" Peter considered such a deed was unworthy of the Lord, and boldly spoke his mind. Christ informed the impetuous leader that he did not understand the spiritual significance of what was taking place. Spiritual enlightenment would come later.

Certainly, our Lord's statement is an encouragement to us, for now we see "in a mirror, darkly; but then, face to face"...now we know in part, but then shall we know even as also we are known (1 Corinthians 13:12). There are many Scriptures we do not understand; many events in life and in history that leave us puzzled; many mysteries that perplex us—but we shall understand it all better, by and by. Now Simon is not satisfied with this, and pulls back his feet (I suspect), saying, "You shall never wash my feet." The double negative is used again for stress; literally verse 8 reads: "Not shall you wash my feet ever-forever." Strong language! "In all eternity, never is Jesus to wash Peter's feet!" (Lenksi). Why did Simon so strongly object to submitting to the Lord's gracious ministry? Was it because he genuinely felt unworthy? Was he so proud he did not want to be dependent on anyone else? Was there a spiritual blindness which prevented him from seeing the incongruity or impropriety of a disciple not trusting his master or opposing him? Sometimes, we encounter people who are such great givers that they deny to others the same opportunity; they refuse to be on the receiving end. They thus prevent others from exercising their gifts and receiving a blessing. To Peter's refusal then, the Lord answered: "If I do not wash you, you have no part with Me." With this announcement, the Lord lifted the act of washing feet from mere menial service and gave it a spiritual significance. Looked at from the physical angle, we see the washing of feet as an act of hospitality. Since sandals were worn, it was easy for the traveler's feet to become dusty and tired. And so the courteous host would supply his guest with water and a slave would wash the feet of the weary traveler.

Bernard (ICC) points out the severity of our Lord's response. "To have part with" is to be a partner, to share. Note the Levites had no part in the inheritance of Israel (Deuteronomy 10:9; 12:12); Simon Magus had no part in the reception of the Holy Spirit (Acts 8:21); Christians have no part with unbelievers (2 Corinthians 6:15). Thus to not be a partner with Christ and His work of ministry was in essence to reject the principle taught concerning the dignity of ministry and servanthood.

"The question of security with respect to salvation is not involved in this doctrine" (Chafer). Upon hearing that he would not be a partner with his Lord, and that he would not have full fellowship with Him, Simon cried, "Lord, not my feet only, but also my hands and my head." In verse 10, the Lord used two different words for "wash." He said: "He that is bathed (louo, full bath, complete, used of the whole body) needeth not except to wash (nipto, partial, used of a part of the body: Thayer) his feet." Christ knew that Judas had not been born again, had never been saved. And He knew who was betraying Him. This is the reason He said, "Not all of you are clean" (bathed). Judas had not been cleansed inwardly.

C. PURPOSE OF SERVANTHOOD
(John 13:12-16)

So after he had washed their feet, and had taken his garments, and was set down again, he said unto them, Know ye what I have done to you? Ye call me Master and Lord: and ye say well; for so I am. If I then, your Lord and Master, have washed your feet; ye also ought wash one another's feet. For I have given you an example, that ye should do as I have done to you. Verily, verily, I say unto you, The servant is not greater than his lord; neither he that is sent greater than he that sent him.

The disciples needed to understand that what the Lord had done was an act of humility, devotion and love. In itself, humility is losing oneself in the service of others. So the emphasis is not so much on actually calling washing feet a sacrament or an ordinance. Note that Christ did not say, "Do what I did," but "I have given you an example that you should do as I have done to you." Thus, the foot washing was symbolic. We are to acquire the attitude expressed by the act! Imagine washing the feet of a man you know is at that very moment betraying you!

We are to be always willing to refresh and comfort other believers. The major point in the lesson then is the true dignity of service. And if the Master thus humbled Himself, how much more should His servants, His messengers! The God who became Man is seen as the Man who became a Servant! He who humbled Himself in Incarnation is seen humbled as a Servant.

D. THE BLESSING OF DOING WHAT WE KNOW
(John 13:17)

If ye know these things, happy are ye if ye do them.

Some of us know what to do as Christians, and we delight in our knowledge— but we don't do what we know. So it is that we may recognize our duty to manifest humility, but rarely put it into practice. There is a blessing in practicing a life of humility. The real value lies in doing what we know is right. Failure here is to have a head full of doctrine, and topple over because the feet are on the slippery road of "do-nothing"! "Has God commanded something? Then cast yourself of Him for help—and do it" (Nee).

III. Special Features

A. PRESERVING OUR HERITAGE

How prevalent is the practice of washing feet in our Black churches? In the mainstream Black Baptists and Methodist groups, only two ordinances are considered Scripturally required—Baptism and the Lord's Supper. However, in many smaller groups, especially those of the Pentecostal persuasion, foot washing is indeed observed, often in connection with the Communion service.

As best as we could determine from the *Handbook of Denominations in the U.S.,* (and assuming these are Black groups), here is the status of foot washing: Apostolic Overcoming Holy Church of God: worship includes foot washing. Seventh Day Adventists, with their high percentage of Black membership, foot washing is practiced as a preparatory service for Communion. Some Primitive Baptist groups also perform it.

Foot washing is practiced and recognized as an ordinance in our church because Christ, by his example, showed that humility characterized greatness in the Kingdom of God, and service, rendered to others gave evidence that humility, motivated by love, exists. These services are always held subsequent to the Lord's Supper. However, its regularity is left to the discretion of the pastor in charge.

B. A CONCLUDING WORD

Christians have been entirely cleansed once for all by the blood of Christ. We are citizens of heaven, made so by the washing of regeneration. However, in our daily walk, our feet are defiled. They can be cleansed by confession, for God is ever ready to forgive (1 John 1:9). In this way, we avoid breaking fellowship with our Lord. Living a clean life in a dirty age is indeed a challenge! Thank God for daily cleaning by the girded Servant who keeps the feet of His saints. Understand then that by stooping to wash their feet, Christ "turned a company of wrangling, angry, jealous men into a company of humbled and united disciples" (Expositor's).

HOME DAILY BIBLE READINGS
Week of May 9, 1999
Jesus Prepared His Followers

May 3   M.   John 13:1-11, He Began to Wash His Disciples' Feet
May 4   T.   John 13:12-20, Do You Know What I Have Done?
May 5   W.   John 13: 21-30, One of You Will Betray Me
May 6   T.   John 13:31-35, I Am With You Only A Little Longer
May 7   F.   Isaiah 42:1-9, Here is My Servant....
May 8   S.   Matthew 23:1-11, The Greatest Among You Will Be Your Servant
May 9   S.   1 Peter 2:18-25, Follow in Christ's Steps

Jesus, The True Vine

Adult Topic—Fruitful Christians

.....

Youth Topic—Love that Bears Fruit
Children's Topic—Jesus Taught About Love

.....

Devotional Reading—Job 23:1-12
Background Scripture—John 15:1-17
Print—John 15:1-17

• • • • • • • • • • • •

PRINTED SCRIPTURE

John 15:1-17 (KJV)

I AM the true vine, and my Father is the husbandman.

2 Every branch in me that beareth not fruit he taketh away: and every branch that beareth fruit, he purgeth it, that it may bring forth more fruit.

3 Now ye are clean through the word which I have spoken unto you.

4 Abide in me, and I in you. As the branch cannot bear fruit of itself, except it abide in the vine; no more can ye, except ye abide in me.

5 I am the vine, ye are the branches. He that abideth in me, and I in him, the same bringeth forth much fruit: for without me ye can do nothing.

6 If a man abide not in me, he is cast forth as a branch, and is withered; and men gather them, and cast them into the fire, and they are burned.

7 If ye abide in me, and my words abide in you, ye shall ask what ye will, and it shall be done unto you.

John 15:1-17 (NRSV)

"I AM the true vine, and my Father is the vinegrower.

2 He remove every branch in me that bears no fruit. Every branch that bears fruit he prunes to make it bear more fruit.

3 You have already been cleansed by the word that I have spoken to you.

4 Abide in me as I abide in you. Just as the branch cannot bear fruit by itself unless it abides in the vine, neither can you unless you abide in me.

5 I am the vine, you are the branches. Those who abide in me and I in them bear much fruit, because apart from me you can do nothing.

6 Whoever does not abide in me is thrown away like a branch and withers; such branches are gathered, thrown into the fire, and burned.

7 If you abide in me, and my words abide in you, ask for whatever

8 Herein is my Father glorified, that ye bear much fruit; so shall ye be my disciples.

9 As the Father hath loved me, so have I loved you: continue ye in my love.

10 If ye keep my commandments, ye shall abide in my love; even as I have kept my Father's commandments, and abide in his love.

11 These things have I spoken unto you, that my joy might remain in you, and that your joy might be full.

12 This is my commandment, That ye love one another, as I have loved you.

13 Greater love hath no man than this, that a man lay down his life for his friends.

14 Ye are my friends, if ye do whatsoever I command you.

15 Henceforth I call you not servants; for the servant knoweth not what his lord doeth: but I have called you friends; for all things that I have heard of my Father I have made known unto you.

16 Ye have not chosen me, but I have chosen you, and ordained you, that ye should go and bring forth fruit, and that your fruit should remain: that whatsoever ye shall ask of the Father in my name, he may give it you.

17 These things I command you, that ye love one another.

you wish, and it will be done for you.

8 My Father is glorified by this, that you bear much fruit and become my disciples.

9 As the Father has loved me, so I have loved you: abide in my love.

10 If you keep my commandments, you will abide in my love, just as I have kept my Father's commandments and abide in his love.

11 I have said these things to you so that my joy may be in you, and that your joy may be complete.

12 This is my commandment, that you love one another as I have loved you.

13 No one has greater love than this, to lay down one's life for one's friends.

14 You are my friends if you do what I command you.

15 I do not call you servants any longer, because the servant does not know what the master is doing; but I have called you friends, because I have made known to you everything that I have heard from my Father.

16 You did not choose me but I chose you. And I appointed you to go and bear fruit, fruit that will last, so that the Father will give you whatever you ask him in my name.

17 I am giving you these commands so that you may love one another."

KEY VERSE

I am the vine, ye are the branches. He that abideth in me, and I in him, the same bringeth forth much fruit: for without me ye can do nothing.—John 15:5

OBJECTIVES

After reading this lesson, the student should be informed about:

1. The symbolism of the Vine;
2. The doctrine of Eternal Security;
3. The difference between union and communion; and,
4. What it requires to live a fruitful life.

POINTS TO BE EMPHASIZED

Adult/Youth/Children
Key Verse: John 15:5; John 15:12 (Children)
Print: John 15:1-17; John 15:1-5, 7-12 (Children)

—Jesus described Himself as the true vine, God as the vinegrower, and His disciples as the branches. (1-3, 5)
—Christ's disciples can live fruitful lives that are pleasing to God only as they love and obey Christ. (4-5)
—Disciples who fail to obey Christ will not bear fruit and will be judged. (6)
—Jesus told His disciples if they kept His commandments their joy would be full and complete. (10-11)
—Jesus commanded His disciples to love one another joyfully as Jesus loved them, even to the point of laying down their lives for others. (12-13)
—Disciples are chosen by Christ to love and to serve one another. (16-17)

(NOTE: Use KJV Scripture for Adults; NRSV Scripture for Youth and Children)

TOPICAL OUTLINE OF THE LESSON

I. Introduction

A. The Loss of Salvation
B. Biblical Background

II. Exposition and Application of the Scripture

A The True Vine and the Vinedresser (John 15:1)
B. No Fruit, Fruit, More Fruit, Much Fruit (John 15:2-8)
C. Love and Obedience (John 15:9-14)
D. A New Closeness (John 15:15-17)

III. Special Features

A. Preserving Our Heritage
B. A Concluding Word

I. Introduction

A. THE LOSS OF SALVATION

John 15:1-6 is felt to be a very strong argument in favor of the possibility of losing salvation; and it is much used to support this belief held by many saints. However, as we shall see, this passage has to do with communion, not union. The Bible does not teach that we are saved so long as we bring forth fruit, and then lost when we fail to be productive. It is important to distinguish between salvation and service here. Use of the word "fruit" six times in the first eight verses indicates service is the thing dealt with.

Admittedly, strong language is used—purging, casting forth, withering, burning! But these refer to the methods God will use. Fruitlessness does not incur Hell or spiritual death. No loss of salvation is to be seen here. The burning is a judgment upon fruitlessness; it is not an abandonment to Hell. Remember: The branch is the potential of possible fruit-bearing, not the person. The believer is not the branch. Finally, keep in mind that the Bible does not contradict itself. Other Scriptures supporting eternal security teach that: (1) we were elected of God before the foundation of the world: Ephesians 1:4; Colossians 3:12; (2) there is no condemnation or separation: Romans 8:1, 38-39; (3) God saves to the uttermost and finishes what He starts: Hebrews 7:25; Philippians 1:6; (4) we cannot be plucked out of God's hands: John 10:28-29, (not by others, not by ourselves); (5) saved by grace, we cannot be lost by works: Ephesians 2:8-9 (6) We will never be cast out: John 6:37; (7) we are kept by the power of God: 1 Peter 1:5, and (8) sealed by the Holy Spirit: Ephesians 1:13-14.

B. BIBLICAL BACKGROUND

Israel is symbolized by three trees: the olive, the fig, and the vine. In the Old Testament, the VINE is a type or symbol of the nation Israel (it may also symbolize unregenerate man in general, Scofield). And in today's lesson, the Jewish nation is God's vineyard. However, it always pictures a degenerate Israel. The comparison always introduces a lament over her apostasy; or prophesies her quick destruction. For example: The vine of Jerusalem is destroyed by fire (Ezekiel 15:1-8); the once fruitful vine (Israel) is plucked up, cast down, and planted in the wilderness (Ezekiel 19:10-14). In Isaiah 5:1-7, we learn that Israel, the Lord's vineyard, brings forth wild grapes, an unpalatable bitter vintage, and shall be broken down, trampled, laid waste and made desolate. The prophet Jeremiah (2:21) laments that Israel, planted as a noble vine, has "turned into the degenerate plant of a strange vine" unto the Lord. Hosea (10.1) calls Israel "an empty vine," for even in the midst of her prosperity and luxury, judgment is coming! We see that throughout the Old Testament, Israel is pictured as a vine that is unfaithful and unfruitful. Throughout the Bible we can see how the use of that with which the people were familiar was used as a teaching tool to import spiritual knowledge.

II. Exposition and Application of the Scripture

A. THE TRUE VINE AND THE VINEDRESSER
(John 15:1)

I AM the true vine, and my Father is the husbandman.

We have seen that Israel is symbolized by the vine, but one that is degenerate, unfruitful, producing unpalatable, bitter or sour grapes. In Psalm 80:8-19, the psalmist pleads for the return of God's favor, for Israel, the vine brought out of Egypt has been blighted because of its selfishness and idolatry. The vine was broken down, plucked, wasted, devoured by wild beasts, burned with fire, cut down, and made to perish. Now in contrast, Jesus Christ is presented as the true vine, the new ideal of the spiritual Israel. Christ is a real vine, all that a vine should be spiritually speaking. The Lord supersedes Israel; He therefore represents Himself as the perfect fulfillment of what a vine should be and do. In other words, the Lord Jesus is the "fulfillment of God's purpose where Israel had failed" *(Eerdmans' Handbook to the Bible)*. Jesus Christ has taken the place of Israel in order to bear fruit for God the Father. And, Christ does so through believers.

God the Father is the Vinedresser. Georgos in Greek has given us the name, George (literally, earth-worker); he is a tiller of the soil, a farmer, a husbandman, here used of a vinedresser (Thayer). This means God the Father is both owner and caretaker, for He is the One who planted the vine in the earth.

B. NO FRUIT, FRUIT, MORE FRUIT, MUCH FRUIT
(John 15:2-8)

Every branch in me that beareth not fruit he taketh away: and every branch that beareth fruit, he purgeth it, that it may bring forth more fruit. Now ye are clean through the word which I have spoken unto you. Abide in me, and I in you. As the branch cannot bear fruit of itself, except it abide in the vine; no more can ye, except ye abide in me. I am the vine, ye are the branches. He that abideth in me, and I in him, the same bringeth forth much fruit: for without me ye can do nothing. If a man abide not in me, he is cast forth as a branch, and is withered; and men gather them, and cast them into the fire, and they are burned. If ye abide in me, and my words abide in you, ye shall ask what ye will, and it shall be done unto you. Herein is my Father glorified, that ye bear much fruit; so shall ye be my disciples.

First, our Lord deals with the "no-fruit" branch. Some people believe reference is to the false professor, one who pretends to be saved but really is not. Still others suggest we have here the believer who loses his salvation because he bears no fruit. Both of these ideas are not acceptable. A branch in Christ is a believer. Unbelievers are not in Christ. And as mentioned earlier, salvation is not determined by fruit-bearing. The "no-fruit" bearing Christian is one who is out of God's will. With the Father's chastening hand upon the self-willed believer, there is a "taking away." This involves a lifting up, thus making it easier for air and light to reach the vine. Or this lifting up may signify a removal of the life of the saint who is unfaithful. In short, physical death is one aspect of "lifting up." Next, the fruit-bearing branch is addressed. It is purged or cleansed, indicating the spiritual aspect of fruit-bearing. God uses trouble and suffering, heartache and pain to make our lives more fruitful.

Note that the cleaning agent is the Word of God. Because of the Word abiding in them, they are kept pure. The disciples (Judas had left) were already in a condition suitable for bearing fruit (John 13:10). In verse 4, we encounter the important word, abide. It means to remain, stay where you are. We abide in Christ by spending time in prayer, confessing and judging known sins, reading and obeying the Bible, being aware of our union with Christ, not allowing anything in our lives that would break fellowship with the Lord, or destroy our fellowship with other believers. Abiding indicates unbroken communion with Christ (Chafer).

We are in Him already. As Watchman Nee points out, Christ does not ask us to get ourselves into Him, so there is no taking ourselves out of Him. A sense of failure may lead us to feel we no longer abide, but we are to take God at His Word which assures us we are in Christ. The fruitful branch assimilates and is nourished by the sap of the vine. It is wholly dependent upon the tree; by its sap, it is quickened and made fruitful. In other words, life comes from the vine. And as a result, fruit comes from the branches.

Sometimes Christians forget this. We get to the point in life where we depend more upon our education, training, experience, expertise, long-time church membership, than upon the Lord Jesus Christ Himself, who said: "Without Me you can do nothing" (John 15:5). Verse 6 explains verse 2 in part, for we see the dreadful consequences of fruitlessness or failure to remain in Christ so far as service is concerned. Since the subject is fruit-bearing and not eternal life or salvation, we cannot interpret the rough language—casting forth, withering, casting into the fire, burning—as referring to salvation (1 Corinthians 3:15). Furthermore, we view the "not-abiding-in-Christ" man as a believer out of God's will. His prayerlessness and carnality have caused him to lose fellowship with Christ.

Fulfillment of the definitions given earlier for the word abiding leads to what we might call a successful prayer life. By abiding, we learn His will, we learn to think His thoughts, and in turn we can be sure our prayer requests are granted. In addition, the more fruit we bear (the much fruit), the more truly we become disciples who glorify God the Father. In short, "the Father is glorified both in the bearing of fruit and in their continuing to be disciples" (Morris).

C. LOVE AND OBEDIENCE
(John 15:9-14)

As the Father hath loved me, so have I loved you: continue ye in my love. If ye keep my commandments, ye shall abide in my love; even as I have kept my Father's commandments, and abide in his love. These things have I spoken unto you, that my joy might remain in you, and that your joy might be

full. This is my commandment, That ye love one another, as I have loved you. Greater love hath no man than this, that a man lay down his life for his friends. Ye are my friends, if ye do whatsoever I command you.

Imagine putting the Father's love for His Son on the same level as the Son's love for us! The exhortation is to abide in, to continue (same Greek word translated, abide) in our Lord's love. Obedience to our Lord's commandments is proof of abiding in His love, for if we truly love Him, we obey Him. Note the life of love produces joy; might we say, the life of obedience produces joy? Trust and obey, for there's no other way, to be happy in the Lord Jesus, but to trust and obey!

We are to keep all of His commandments, but Christ concentrates on the commandment for Christians to love one another, even as He loved us (verse 12). Christians loving other Christians is not an option; it is an order! Anticipation of His own death unveils the truth regarding His own devotion, the great love He has for us. In Romans 5:6-8, the apostle Paul said: "For when we were yet without strength, in due time Christ died for the ungodly...while we were yet sinners...." This does not contradict John 15:13, for Christ does not say that He laid down His life only for friends. The illustration of human love's willingness to sacrifice life for another is well taken. But what man does in this regard is no comparison with what the Son of God does. His sacrifice is unique! Finally, in this section of the lesson, we see that friendship with the Lord does not eliminate our need to be obedient to Him. Sometimes familiarity breeds contempt. We sing, "What a Friend We Have in Jesus," but must not allow that friendship to cause us to forget His Lordship.

D. A NEW CLOSENESS
(John 15:15-17)

Henceforth I call you not servants; for the servant knoweth not what his lord doeth: but I have called you friends; for all things that I have heard of my Father I have made known unto you. Ye have not chosen me, but I have chosen you, and ordained you, that ye should go and bring forth fruit, and that your fruit should remain: that whatsoever ye shall ask of the Father in my name, he may give it you. These things I command you, that ye love one another.

Note the progression concerning the Lord's relationship with the disciples. First, they are called servants. **Doulos** may also be rendered slave, bondman. Figuratively, a servant is one who gives himself up wholly to another (Thayer). Ordinarily, a servant is not taken into his master's confidence. Bond-slaves are expected to do what they are told; their work is clearly marked out. They obey without claiming to know the reason for the Master's actions. Second, they are called friends. **Philos** is a friend. Three times our Lord makes note of this friendship (verses 13-15). Because He admitted His disciples to His counsels, and withheld nothing from them, they are considered His friends. It does not mean they understood everything He told them, but the fact of the telling is important.

We show we are the Lord's friends by doing whatever He tells us to do. We obey Him, remembering that He speaks to us in confidence, revealing and sharing information with us—things He heard from God the Father. Third, they are called brothers (John 20:17). **Adelphos** means from the same womb. Here brother is used to designate common possessions, one Father and one inheritance; believers, as those who are destined to be exalted to the same heavenly glory which He enjoys (Romans 8:29).

The exposition closes with the repeated command to love one another. In the verses following (John 15:18-25), the word love appears to be replaced by the word hate. And we learn that Christians need to share their love with one another, for they certainly will not experience any love from the world.

III. Special Features

A. PRESERVING OUR HERITAGE

I want to expand comments on John 15:16, a verse that teaches us that God picks and places as He pleases, and makes productive as He wills. First, consider the fact that God PICKS. In recent days, we have heard much from Black theologians who ignore the sovereignty of God. We do not approve of what is called Eurocentrism, and we caution those who would consider themselves advocates of Afrocentrism. Bible Christians believe in Christocentrism. The God of the Bible is the Sovereign God, and is no respecter of faces or races. For Him, the issue is sin and not skin. Ordinarily, a man would pick out the teacher he liked best, the one he felt would do him the most good prestige-wise, the best in a chosen field, the one from whom he could best learn. But in this verse, the language is very strongly put: "You on your part did not choose Me, but on the contrary, just the opposite: I on My part chose you." Obviously, this eliminates all talk about "you take the first step, and God will take the second," or "God helps those who help themselves." The Bible teaches that there is none that seeks after God (Romans 3:11), no, not one. Rather, the Son of Man is come to seek and to save that which is lost. As it is for salvation, so it is for service. Christ reminds the disciples: You did not pick Me, I picked you! Black American Christians must be careful then not to "revise" history by attempting to make God choose that which is not supported by Holy Spirit led interpretation of the Scriptures.

Second, we learn that God PLACES. The verb translated ordained means to place, set, appoint, put. As used here, it is to appoint for one's use or to one's service. The God of the Bible is the One who "hath made of one blood all nations of men to dwell on all the face of the earth, and hath determined the times before appointed, and the bounds of their habitation" (Acts 17:26). He placed the planets in their orbits; the nations in their geographical locations; the races wherever they exist. And He has placed His servants where it has pleased Him that we should serve.

Third, it is God whose purpose in picking and placing is that we should be PRODUCTIVE. He desires that we bear fruit. First, there is the fruit of Christlikeness. Second, there is the fruit of successful service. Our incentive for such productivity is in no way dependent upon the color of our skin or who is Black in the Bible. To think otherwise is to deny God's sovereignty and to under-estimate the power of the Holy Spirit. So that those who ignore God's statement that in His Presence no flesh shall glory (1 Corinthians 1:29) will continue to flounder in the sea of humanism.

B. A CONCLUDING WORD

Abiding in Christ, maintaining an unbroken fellowship with Him, results in prayers that are effectual (verse 7); in fruit that is plentiful (verse 8); love that is eternal (verses 9-10); and joy that is celestial (v.11). Abiding in Christ has to do with service, not salvation. Abiding in Christ refers to communion, not to union. Abiding in Christ points to condition and not position. Abiding in Christ deals with fruit of the believer, and not the sinful wages of the unbeliever; for only the person whose sins have been cleansed by the blood of Jesus Christ abides in Him.

Within the condition of the human situation, all too often we come to believe that abiding in Christ is associated with life in the church or engaging in those activities and concerns that are clearly identified as works of the fellowship of believers. While we dare not fail to assemble ourselves together and to be en-riched by the community of believers, the proof of abiding in Christ is tested when we are at home with all of the problems associated with marriage and the rearing of children, when we enter the workplace and are faced with abrasive bosses and placed side-by-side with persons whose public behavior is completely obnoxious, when we face the difficulties of making ends meet and the financial pressures become over-bearing. All of these and more constitute that period in our lives that abiding in Christ must be demonstrated with a transcending and unfaltering faith.

The Christian life is not just "peaches and cream," but hills that are too high and valleys that are too low, coupled with the weary nights when the morning is a long time coming. These are experiences that develop Christian character and the person who is faithful to the end embodies that quality of life with which God is well pleased.

HOME DAILY BIBLE READINGS
Week of May 16, 1999
Jesus, The True Vine

May 10 M. John 15:1-11, I Am the True Vine
May 11 T. John 15:12-17, Love One Another As I have Loved You
May 12 W. Job 23:1-12, Oh, That I Might Find Him
May 13 T. Acts 9:10-19a, Saul, God's Messenger to the Gentiles
May 14 F. Romans 11:13-24, The Kindness and the Severity of God
May 15 S. Romans 11:25-36, By the Mercy Shown to You...
May 16 S. Mark 12:1-12, Finally He Sent His Beloved Son

The Spirit Empowers for Loving Obedience

Adult Topic—Help in Time of Need

.....

Youth Topic—New Leadership
Children's Topic—Jesus Made a Promise

.....

Devotional Reading—Hebrews 2:10-18
Background Scripture—John 14:15-31; 16:4b-15
Print—John 14:15-18, 24-26; 16:7-15

• • • • • • • • • • •

SCRIPTURE PRINT

John 14:15-18, 24-26; 16:7-15 (KJV)

15 If ye love me, keep my commandments.

16 And I will pray the Father, and he shall give you another Comforter, that he may abide with you for ever;

17 Even the Spirit of truth; whom the world cannot receive, because it seeth him not, neither knoweth him: but ye know him; for he dwelleth with you, and shall be in you.

18 I will not leave you comfortless: I will come to you.

.....

24 He that loveth me not keepeth not my sayings: and the word which ye hear is not mine, but the Father's which sent me.

25 These things have I spoken unto you, being yet present with you.

26 But the Comforter, which is the Holy Ghost, whom the Father

John 14:15-18, 24-26; 16:7-15 (NRSV)

15 "If you love me, you will keep my commandments.

16 And I will ask the Father, and he will give you another Advocate, to be with you forever.

17 This is the Spirit of truth, whom the world cannot receive, because it neither sees him nor knows him. You know him, because he abides with you, and he will be in you.

18 I will not leave you orphaned; I am coming to you."

.....

24 "Whoever does not love me does not keep my words; and the word that you hear is not mine, but is from the Father who sent me.

25 I have said these things to you while I am still with you.

26 But the Advocate, the Holy Spirit, whom the Father will send in my name, will teach you everything,

will send in my name, he shall teach you all things, and bring all things to your remembrance, whatsoever I have said unto you.

.....

7 Nevertheless I tell you the truth; it is expedient for you that I go away: for if I go not away, the Comforter will not come unto you; but if I depart, I will send him unto you.

8 And when he is come, he will reprove the world of sin, and of righteousness, and of judgment:

9 Of sin, because they believe not on me;

10 Of righteousness, because I go to my Father, and ye see me no more;

11 Of judgment, because the prince of this world is judged.

12 I have yet many things to say unto you, but ye cannot bear them now.

13 Howbeit when he, the Spirit of truth, is come, he will guide you into all truth: for he shall not speak of himself; but whatsoever he shall hear, that shall he speak: and he will shew you things to come.

14 He shall glorify me: for he shall receive of mine, and shall shew it unto you.

15 All things that the Father hath are mine: therefore said I, that he shall take of mine, and shall shew it unto you.

and remind you of all that I have said to you."

.....

7 "Nevertheless I tell you the truth: it is to your advantage that I go away, for if I do not go away, the Advocate will not come to you; but if I go, I will send him to you.

8 And when he comes, he will prove the world wrong about sin and righteousness and judgment:

9 about sin, because they do not believe in me;

10 about righteousness, because I am going to the Father and you will see me no longer;

11 about judgment, because the ruler of this world has been condemned.

12 I still have many things to say to you, but you cannot bear them now.

13 When the Spirit of truth comes, he will guide you into all the truth; for he will not speak on his own, but will speak whatever he hears, and he will declare to you the things that are to come.

14 He will glorify me, because he will take what is mine and declare it to you.

15 All that the Father has is mine. For this reason I said that he will take what is mine and declare it to you."

KEY VERSE

But the Comforter, which is the Holy Ghost, whom the Father will send in my name, he shall teach you all things, and bring all things to your remembrance, whatsoever I have said unto you.— John 14:26

OBJECTIVES

After reading this lesson, the student should be aware that:

1. The Holy Spirit is God;
2. The Holy Spirit has a threefold work toward the world;
3. The indwelling Holy Spirit of truth reveals truth to us; and,
4. The Holy Spirit strengthens and teaches all believers.

POINTS TO BE EMPHASIZED

Adult/Youth/Children

Key Verse: John 14:26

Print: John 14:15-18, 24-26; 16:7-15; John 14:15-21, 25-26 (Children)

—Jesus declared that those who love Him will obey Him. (14:15)

—Jesus promised that the Father would send the Holy Spirit to abide forever in His disciples, and to teach them all truth. (14:16-18)

—Jesus told His disciples that He must go away so that the Holy Spirit could come and prove that sin is unbelief in Jesus. (16:10)

—Jesus declared that the Spirit of Truth would glorify Jesus and guide His disciples into all truth (16:12-14)

(NOTE: Use KJV Scripture for Adults; NRSV Scripture for Youth and Children)

TOPICAL OUTLINE OF THE LESSON

I. Introduction

A. The Meaning of the Word Reprove, John 16:8

B. Biblical Background

II. Exposition and Application of the Scripture

A. The Holy Spirit Dwells Within (John 14:15-18)

B. The Holy Spirit Teaches All Things (John 14:24-26)

C. The Holy Spirit Convicts the World (John 16:7-11)

D. The Holy Spirit Glorifies Christ (John 16:12-15)

III. Special Features

A. Preserving Our Heritage

B. A Concluding Word

I. Introduction

A. THE MEANING OF THE WORD REPROVE, JOHN 16:8

We learn that the Comforter or Holy Spirit will reprove the world of sin, and of righteousness, and of judgment. Thus, the entire passage, John 16:7-11, hinges on the meaning of the word translated reprove. Alford states that his translation, reprove is far too weak, for the original word is more than outward rebuke. Moffatt's translation of the word as "convict...convincing" better expresses the double sense desired, for the Holy Spirit is one of convincing unto salvation while convicting unto condemnation.

Convict is favored by the New King James Version, New International, and the New American Standard Bible. Convince is used by the Living Bible, Revised Standard, and J. B. Phillips. Kittel states that the use of the Greek word **elegcho** in the New Testament means "to show someone his sin and to summon him to repentance." To blame, find fault with, reprove, convince in the sense of proof, to reveal, correct, bring to light or expose are definitions, but these are not the only meanings. To set right, to point away from sin to repentance are also good definitions.

The word implies educative discipline. You can see the difficulty scholars have had in defining or finding an exact English equivalent for this word. Keep in mind that in John 16:8 it is best to interpret **elegcho** to refer not only to an outward rebuke, but also reaching inwardly to the heart.

B. BIBLICAL BACKGROUND

A study of John 13:21-14:14 reveals several things which greatly saddened the disciples. First: there was the prediction of the betrayal of Christ. Second, there was the announcement that He was going away. As He had told the Jewish leaders earlier, so now He said to the disciples, "Where I go, ye cannot come." Third: there was the prediction of Simon Peter's denial. So you see why the apostles needed comforting.

Certainly, one thing that would help them would be their love for one another. Brotherhood that is practiced provides a support that enables believers to endure adversity. It seems that Simon Peter ignored what the Lord said about love, and in so doing opened the way for the Lord to foretell Simon's threefold denial.

At this point, the Lord reassured the disciples, for they were indeed quite disturbed. By continuing to believe in God the Father and also in Christ, they could stop letting their hearts be agitated, stirred up, troubled. Christ promised His personal return for them, and after further teaching concerning His relation with God the Father, and closing His teaching with the importance of prayer, we see the significant facts which preface today's lesson with the promise of the indwelling Holy Spirit. In spite of the effort of Jesus Christ to deepen the faith of the disciples, they could not bring themselves to understand that His death was within the plan of God for the redemption of the world and to reconcile humans unto Himself.

II. Exposition and Application of the Scripture

A. THE HOLY SPIRIT DWELLS WITHIN
(John 14:15-18)

If ye love me, keep my commandments. And I will pray the Father, and he shall give you another Comforter, that he may abide with you for ever; Even the Spirit of truth; whom the world cannot receive, because it seeth him not, neither knoweth him: but ye know him; for he dwelleth with you, and shall be in you. I will not leave you comfortless: I will come to you.

Once again, believers are exhorted to demonstrate their love for the Savior by their obedience to His commandments. William MacDonald warns Christians not to be browbeaten by those who would label us as legalists or puritanical because we seek to please Christ rather than please ourselves (*One Day at a Time,* p. 125). The Lord promised to pray to the Father, and the word rendered "pray" speaks of one making request of his equal. He will pray to the Father to send another Comforter.

Parakletos **(Paraclete)** is the word translated Comforter. Unfortunately, the word comfort today means ease, cheer, satisfy. In 1611, the word Comforter meant Strengthener (literally, "com" is with; "fort" is strength). Paraclete means One called alongside of (to help), one called to assist in a court of witness. This same word is used of Jesus Christ in 1 John 2:1, where it is rendered Advocate. The word another here means "like Me," another of the same kind. He would be of the same quality and character as the Lord. Furthermore, as the Lord Jesus is about to leave, the Holy Spirit will come to remain with them forever.

This same **Paraclete** is also called the Spirit of truth. Because His teaching is true and He glorifies Christ who is Truth (John 14:6), the world-system does not recognize Him or receive Him. Naturally, if the world did not recognize Jesus Christ as the Word it will not recognize the Holy Spirit as the Truth. Men claim to believe only in what they see, yet believe in the wind and in electricity. Because they cannot see the Holy Spirit, they do not believe He exists. The Holy Spirit is invisible, and cannot be perceived by a world whose vision is purely physical, nor can He be comprehended by human reason.

Note the Spirit abides with us, alongside of us, and in us. And the disciples have the assurance that the Lord will not leave them comfortless. This latter word is **orphanos** in the Greek; and it means bereaved, bereft (of a father, of parents; of those bereft of a teacher, guide, guardian—Thayer). In its primary meaning, it is rendered "fatherless" in James 1:27, but here in John it has the broader meaning of bereavement of any kind (ICC). You see the English word orphan derived from it. "I will not leave you orphans, friendless, without a Helper such as I have been to you." The promise, "I will come to you," speaks not of His future coming (as in verse 3), but in that coming which meets immediate need. Yea, what a Friend we have in Jesus—a very present help in "right now" trouble (Psalm 46:1)! Thank God we are not left alone in utter helplessness in this sin-sick world!

B. THE HOLY SPIRIT TEACHES ALL THINGS
(John 14:24-26)

He that loveth me not keepeth not my sayings: and the word which ye hear is not mine, but the Father's which sent me. These things have I spoken unto you, being yet present with you. But the Comforter, which is the Holy Ghost, whom the Father will send in my name, he shall teach you all things, and bring all things to your remembrance, whatsoever I have said unto you.

In verse 23, the truth is taught that "love Christ, keep His word." Now in verse 24, the negative side is taught: "love not Christ, keep not His word." Once again, the disciples are reminded of the close relationship between God the Father and His Son. For disobedience of Christ's Word means also the rejection of the Father's Word. We see again the truth in the statement, "I and My Father are One" (John 10:30). Refuse Christ and you refuse God the Father. Now they are advised that His speaking to them while abiding in the flesh would be replaced by a permanent spiritual abiding by the Holy Spirit.

The Comforter, that is, the Holy Spirit, whom the Father will send in the name of the Lord Jesus, will have the twofold responsibility of teaching and reminding. For one thing, He will teach the disciples all things—all things about the Christ and His Gospel. Indeed, the all things are limited by the needs and abilities of the disciples. While Christ taught them up to a certain point, the Holy Spirit would continue from there. The teaching process would not cease. But secondly, the Holy Spirit will bring all things to their remembrance. Those things the Lord had taught them would be remembered. We realize the fulfillment of this promise when we consider that the Gospels were written many years after the resurrection and ascension of our Lord! Here then is a reason for the completion of the canon of the New Testament!

C. THE HOLY SPIRIT CONVICTS THE WORLD
(John 16:7-11)

Nevertheless I tell you the truth; it is expedient for you that I go away: for if I go not away, the Comforter will not come unto you; but if I depart, I will send him unto you. And when he is come, he will reprove the world of sin, and of righteousness, and of judgment: Of sin, because they believe not on me; Of righteousness, because I go to my Father, and ye see me no more; Of judgment, because the prince of this world is judged.

Our Lord stated that is was expedient for Him to go away. The Latin root of this word means literally, to stick the foot out, to free the feet, thus to disengage, extricate or set right. That which is expedient is advantageous, profitable, advisable, that which is proper under the circumstances. The Greek word, **sumphero,** means to bear or bring together; the idea seems to be by putting things together a certain goal is achieved and is thus profitable, helpful. It is therefore for the good of the disciples that the Lord go away. Otherwise, the **Paraclete** will not come.

"But I am going away; and I will send Him. And when He is come He will execute a threefold judgment of the unbelieving world." We studied earlier the word translated reprove, and accepted the better rendering of convict the world-system of SIN. This means He will reveal to the unsaved the one sin of rejecting Jesus Christ. Men will either believe or receive what Jesus Christ did at Calvary, or reject Him. The very root or essence of sin is unbelief in Christ as the Son of God. Imagine calling Christ a sinner at the very moment their own sin led them to put Him to death!

Second: He will convict the world-system of RIGHTEOUSNESS. The world must know that man's attempt to make himself righteous in God's sight can only end in failure. True salvation is found only when men turn from all self-confidence and works, and place their confidence in Him who is the Righteousness of God. Unfortunately, men rejected the claims of Christ to be righteous. They found no real fault in Him, yet claimed that He had a demon, that He broke the Sabbath, kept bad company, etc. By raising Him from the dead, God the Father proved Christ is righteous. Christ's exaltation is proof of His righteousness.

Third: He will convict the world-system of JUDGMENT. Here attention is drawn to the cross. The defeat of the Devil on the cross, the victory over the grave is the guarantee of the final triumph over Satan, the prince of this world. "Judgment is the inevitable issue of the divine act of redemption" (A. J. Macleod, *New Bible Commentary*).

D. THE HOLY SPIRIT GLORIFIES CHRIST
(John 16:12-15)

I have yet many things to say unto you, but ye cannot bear them now. Howbeit when he, the Spirit of truth, is come, he will guide you into all truth: for he shall not speak of himself; but whatsoever he shall hear, that shall he speak: and he will shew you things to come. He shall glorify me: for he shall receive of mine, and shall shew it unto you. All things that the Father hath are mine: therefore said I, that he shall take of mine, and shall shew it unto you.

Having pointed out the ministry of the spirit with respect to the world-system, attention is now drawn to His ministry in the lives of believers. There is no contradiction here with the statement earlier (John 15:15) that He had made known to the disciples all things which He had heard of the Father. Naturally, those things which they could not at the time understand were withheld. And so He tells them that there are still many things which they cannot yet bear. But when the Spirit of Truth comes, He will guide them into all spiritual truth. God works with us where He finds us. We Christians must realize that we are always students; it takes time to learn the deep truths of the Scriptures.

The apostles are assured that the Holy Spirit would never speak independently of God the Father; "He will not speak on His own initiative" *(New American Standard Bible)*. The Holy Spirit's ministry is to glorify Jesus Christ. Holy Spirit led ministry exalts the Lord Jesus, not the speaker or preacher. We can use this principle to test all teaching and preaching. For sometimes men talk about

God but hardly mention the name of Jesus Christ. Such preaching is not of the Holy Spirit! Inasmuch as all of the attributes of God the Father also belong to God the Son, we can never exhaust speaking of His perfections, ministries, offices, love, grace, glory and fullness. The section closes (John 16:15) with what Alford calls a verse that "contains the plainest proof by inference of the orthodox doctrine of the Holy Trinity."

III. Special Features

A. PRESERVING OUR HERITAGE

The main thing that concerns us here is the deity and personality of the Holy Spirit. First, there is the unscriptural habit of calling the Holy Spirit "IT." Throughout the years I have observed members of our churches make the Holy Spirit a thing, an "it." While it is true that the Greek word for Spirit is neuter, it does not mean the Spirit Himself is neuter. He is a Person. The Person Jesus Christ said is another Comforter just like Him who would come; a Personal Being then takes the place of a Personal Being. We do not have an impersonal "it" taking the place of Jesus Christ. Furthermore, the Personality of the Holy Spirit is seen throughout the New Testament. He speaks, He is lied to, He teaches, guides into truth, convicts; He is grieved, quenched and hindered.

B. A CONCLUDING WORD

Without the Holy Spirit, we would be helpless, powerless, without truth, and without guidance. We would have no connection with God the Son or God the Father. What wonderful love that God should bestow upon us the Gift of the Holy Spirit, that is, the Holy Spirit Himself. By His encouragement, teaching and guidance, the disciples were empowered to experience a Christ more real to them than He had been before. They not only wrote of their experiences with the Lord while He was here on earth, but were led by the Spirit to write of things to come. Inasmuch as He has condescended to live in our bodies, to make them His temples, we rejoice in the assurance that He will never leave us. He abides forever. And His presence enables us to love the Lord Jesus and keep His Word.

HOME DAILY BIBLE READINGS
Week of May 23, 1999
The Spirit Empowers for Loving Obedience

May 17 M. John 14:15-24, If You Love Me, Keep My Commandments
May 18 T. John 14:25-31, The Holy Spirit Will Teach You
May 19 W. John 16:4b-15, When the Spirit of Truth Comes
May 20 T. 2 Corinthians 3:12-18, The Spirit of the Lord Brings Freedom
May 21 F. Galatians 4:1-7, No Longer a Slave But a Child
May 22 S. Ephesians 3:14-19, Strengthened With Power Through His Spirit
May 23 S. Romans 8:12-17, We Are Children of God

Jesus Prayed for His Disciples

Adult Topic—Interceding in Prayer

.....

Youth Topic—Prayer and You
Children's Topic—Jesus Prayed For His Friends

.....

Devotional Reading—Ephesians 6:10-20
Background Scripture—John 17
Print— John 17:1-5, 9, 11b, 15-24

● ● ● ● ● ● ● ● ● ● ● ●

PRINTED SCRIPTURE

John 17:1-5, 9, 11b, 15-24 (KJV)

THESE words spake Jesus, and lifted up his eyes to heaven, and said, Father, the hour is come; glorify thy Son, that thy Son also may glorify thee:

2 As thou hast given him power over all flesh, that he should give eternal life to as many as thou hast given him.

3 And this is life eternal, that they might know thee the only true God, and Jesus Christ, whom thou hast sent.

4 I have glorified thee on the earth: I have finished the work which thou gavest me to do.

5 And now, O Father, glorify thou me with thine own self with the glory which I had with thee before the world was.

.....

9 I pray for them: I pray not for the world, but for them which thou hast given me; for they are thine.

.....

11 Holy Father, keep through

John 17:1-5, 9, 11b, 15-24 (NRSV)

AFTER JESUS had spoken these words, he looked up to heaven and said, "Father, the hour has come; glorify your Son so that the Son may glorify you,

2 since you have given him authority over all people, to give eternal life to all whom you have given him.

3 And this is eternal life, that they may know you, the only true God, and Jesus Christ whom you have sent.

4 I glorified you on earth by finishing the work that you gave me to do.

5 So now, Father, glorify me in your own presence with the glory that I had in your presence before the world existed."

.....

9 "I am asking on their behalf; I am not asking on behalf of the world, but on behalf of those whom you gave me, because they are yours."

.....

11 "Holy Father, protect them in

thine own name those whom thou hast given me, that they may be one, as we are.

.....

15 I pray not that thou shouldest take them out of the world, but that thou shouldest keep them from the evil.

16 They are not of the world, even as I am not of the world.

17 Sanctify them through thy truth: thy word is truth.

18 As thou hast sent me into the world, even so have I also sent them into the world.

19 And for their sakes I sanctify myself, that they also might be sanctified through the truth.

20 Neither pray I for these alone, but for them also which shall believe on me through their word;

21 That they all may be one; as thou, Father, art in me, and I in thee, that they also may be one in us: that the world may believe that thou hast sent me.

22 And the glory which thou gavest me I have given them; that they may be one, even as we are one:

23 I in them and thou in me, that they may be made perfect in one; and that the world may know that thou hast sent me, and hast loved them, as thou hast loved me.

24 Father, I will that they also, whom thou hast given me, be with me where I am; that they may behold my glory, which thou hast given me: for thou lovedst me before the foundation of the world.

your name that you have given me, so that they may be one, as we are one."

.....

15 "I am not asking you to take them out of the world, but I ask you to protect them from the evil one.

16 They do not belong to the world, just as I do not belong to the world.

17 Sanctify them in the truth; your word is truth.

18 As you have sent me into the world, so I have sent them into the world.

19 And for their sakes I sanctify myself, so that they also may be sanctified in truth.

20 I ask not only on behalf of these, but also on behalf of those who will believe in me through their word,

21 that they may all be one. As you, Father, are in me and I am in you, may they also be in us, so that the world may believe that you have sent me.

22 The glory that you have given me I have given them, so that they may be one, as we are one,

23 I in them and you in me, that they may become completely one, so that the world may know that you have sent me and have loved them even as you have loved me.

24 Father, I desire that those also, whom you have given me, may be with me where I am, to see my glory, which you have given me because you loved me before the foundation of the world."

 **KEY VERSE** Holy Father, keep through thine own name those whom thou hast given me, that they may be one, as we are.—John 17:11

OBJECTIVES

After reading this lesson, the student should better understand that:

1. Intercession is an important aspect of prayer;
2. Eternal life is defined as "knowing" God;
3. Glorifying God is an essential phase of prayer; and,
4. Our God has "keeping" power.

POINTS TO BE EMPHASIZED

Adult/Youth/Children

Key Verse: John 17:11

Print: John 17:1-5, 9, 11b, 15-24; John 17:6-11 (Children)

—Having been given all authority, Jesus prayed that the Father would glorify Himself in the Son. (1-2)

—Jesus equated eternal life with a personal knowledge of the Father and the Son. (3-4)

—Jesus possessed glory in the presence of the Father before the world existed. (5)

—Jesus revealed the Father to His disciples and prayed for their protection in the world. (6-19)

—Jesus prayed for all persons who would believe through the testimony of the disciples. (20-24)

(NOTE: Use KJV Scripture for Adults; NRSV Scripture for Youth and Children)

TOPICAL OUTLINE OF THE LESSON

I. Introduction

A. What Does It Mean to Glorify?
B. Biblical Background

II. Exposition and Application of the Scripture

A. Glorifying God (John 17:1-5)
B. Prayer to Preserve (John 17:9, 11b)
C. The World and the Word (John 17:15-19)
D. A Perfect Oneness (John 17:20-24)

III. Special Features

A. Preserving Our Heritage
B. A Concluding Word

I. Introduction

A. WHAT DOES IT MEAN TO GLORIFY?

The noun glory and the verb glorify are found seven times in today's lesson on the intercessory prayer of our Lord. Originally, the word meant an opinion; when that opinion became a good one, then the idea of praise entered, and the old meaning of opinion disappeared. In time, the word **doxa** came to mean brilliance, effulgence, radiance, beauty, reflection, light, honor, fame, repute, majesty, splendor. Glory may consist in wealth, power, position, dignity, preeminence, esteem, exaltation, etc.

"In the New Testament, it denotes divine and heavenly radiance, the loftiness and majesty of God, and even the being of God and His world" (Kittel). God's glory is seen in His creation, in thunderstorms, the sun, moon and stars; various phenomena; cloud and smoke by day, shining of a flaming fire by night, etc. Kittel points out that God is intrinsically invisible, but when He reveals or declares Himself, we speak of His glory being manifested. Thus, to give God glory is to recognize the import of His deity; it is to acknowledge what is due to Him; His glory is His essential character, power and holiness.

In our lesson, Christ is glorified by the divine acceptance of His sacrifice by the Father. Note He requests: "Glorify Thy Son...glorify Thou Me with Thine own Self...I am glorified" (verse 1,5,10). And His reasons are: (1) that the Son may glorify the Father (2) Because the Son has glorified the Father on earth. The Father is to honor the Son with the glory the Son had before the world was, glory which the Father gave (verses 22, 24).

B. BIBLICAL BACKGROUND

Having just affirmed in chapter 16 that He has overcome the world, our Lord now looks forward to the cross. This longest of His recorded prayers marks the end of His earthly ministry. However, His work will go on through the efforts of the disciples, and later through those who are won to Christ. Note that this chapter is entitled, "The High Priestly Prayer." This is because it looks forward to our Lord's death on the cross as the consummation of His work as our High Priest. A priest is one who stands between man and God; he is man's representative before God. There is "one mediator between God and men, the man, Christ Jesus " (1 Timothy 2:5). Christ fulfilled the qualifications of a high priest listed in Hebrews 5:1-2. He offered Himself to God and carried His own blood into the heavenly sanctuary.

For many years, we heard of The Lord Prayer, the "Our Father which art in heaven" prayer in Matthew 6:9-13 (Luke 11:2-3). Originally intended as a model prayer for the disciples, many Christians use it as a prayer. And while the Lord is indeed its Author, the true "Lord's Prayer" is John 17. Lenski points out that our Lord spoke this prayer aloud before His disciples that they might hear Him talk to His Father and witness how He enters His passion as a victor, not a victim.

II. Exposition and Application of the Scripture

A. GLORIFYING GOD
(John 17:1-5)

THESE words spake Jesus, and lifted up his eyes to heaven, and said, Father, the hour is come; glorify thy Son, that thy Son also may glorify thee: As thou hast given him power over all flesh, that he should give eternal life to as many as thou hast given him. And this is life eternal, that they might know thee the only true God, and Jesus Christ, whom thou hast sent. I have glorified thee on the earth: I have finished the work which thou gavest me to do. And now, O Father, glorify thou me with thine own self with the glory which I had with thee before the world was.

The Greek word for "eye" is **ophthalmos,** from which we have derived the word ophthalmologist, or eye-doctor. Have you ever prayed with your eyes lifted up to heaven? Of course, our emphasis is not so much on body position as on heart condition. Note also the Lord called on God the Father **(pater)** some six times (verses 1, 5, 11, 21, 24, 25). His opening prayer states that the hour is come. The perfect tense, "has come," is used, giving His statement an air of finality (Morris). "Hour" is not defined, but it is something well known between Father and Son—a time for suffering and for glorification through death. Glory **(doxa),** of course, is honor, praise, exaltation, splendor, majesty, brilliance, radiance, opinion, power, light, etc.

Christ prayed that the Father would enable Him to do what He came to do, to accomplish the salvation for which He had come. By His death, resurrection and ascension, He would glorify the Father. By completing the act of redemption, glory will come to both Father and Son, for to glorify the Son is to glorify the Father, such is the close connection between the two. We learn that before time began, God the Father gave Jesus Christ authority over all flesh, and on the basis of what Christ did at Calvary, authority was granted to Him to give eternal life. But what is this "eternal life"?

Is it mere existence without end? According to verse three, it is knowing the only true God and Jesus Christ the Sent One. He or she who knows God has eternal life. This "knowing" is more than head knowledge; it is heart knowledge. It means to have an ever increasing intimate personal experience with the true God. One of the amazing things revealed in this prayer is the fact that Christians are gifts from God the Father to His Son. Note how often this is repeated: verses 2, 6 (twice), 9, 11, 12, 24. What a motley crew! (1 Corinthians 6:9-11).

Our Lord said that He had finished the work the Father gave Him to do. Yet, He spoke these words before Calvary. This use of the past tense is called anticipatory or proleptic. The thing is so certain that He can talk about it as already completed, perfected, accomplished. His entire earthly ministry is gathered up into one historical point. Finally, in verse 5, the last verse in this section in which Christ prayed for Himself, we see the very plain fact of the preexistence of God the Son in glory.

B. PRAYER TO PRESERVE
(John 17:9, 11b)

I pray for them: I pray not for the world, but for them which thou hast given me; for they are thine. Holy Father, keep through thine own name those whom thou hast given me, that they may be one, as we are.

The pronoun "I" is emphatic, as if to say, "I on My part am requesting." Christ shows great personal interest in the Eleven. He does not at this time pray for the world. This does not mean He felt the world was beyond redemption. It was simply His plan at this juncture to use His disciples to reach the world. Only here in John 17:11b do we find this wonderful title, Holy Father. It is a title of God the Father alone. Within that name, in all that it means, the disciples are to be kept, guarded against all unholiness while they are still in the world. The Father will do this through the Holy Spirit.

The God who works to save us from sin's penalty, also works to save us from sin's power, to keep us from worldliness; to protect us from the evil or Evil one, the Devil. God keeps us for Himself, and does so in His Name, His Word, the revelation of Himself. Note that the deepest sense of unity is found within the Name or revelation of God the Father. Our Lord's prayer is that we are guarded against all that would create disunity. The purpose of the keeping or guarding is that they may continually be one. John's Gospel is especially interested in unity (Kittel: John 11:52, 10:16, 30). True unity reflects the relationship between God the Father and His Son. Unity is based upon a basic abiding in Christ, and deals with the inner man, the unity of heart, spirit and will. Thank God for His keeping power. He keeps the feet of the saints from being taken; and keeps us from snares laid for us by evildoers, and from the strife of tongues. He keeps us as the apple of His eye; He keeps in perfect peace those whose minds are stayed on Him. That peace that passes all understanding keeps our hearts and minds through Christ Jesus. Yea, He who is able to keep that which we have committed unto Him against that day is the One who is able to keep us from falling, and to present us faultless before the presence of His glory with exceeding joy.

C. THE WORLD AND THE WORD
(John 17:15-19)

I pray not that thou shouldest take them out of the world, but that thou shouldest keep them from the evil. They are not of the world, even as I am not of the world. Sanctify them through thy truth: thy word is truth. As thou hast sent me into the world, even so have I also sent them into the world. And for their sakes I sanctify myself, that they also might be sanctified through the truth.

Since the disciples are not of the world, why leave them here? Why not take them out of the world, on to Heaven? We are to remain in but not of the world-system or world-age. Because all the hatred of the world directed against the disciples is inspired by Satan, Christ prayed for their protection from evil, or from the evil one, Satan. We see here also that asceticism and monasteries are not the answer. For a complete disassociation from evil, the Christian would have to "go out of the world" (1 Corinthians 5:10). The apostles would have to live in the world—the theater of their evangelical ministry—but they would need God's grace to keep them from its evil influences (ICC).

Our Lord spoke next of practical sanctification, the life of separation. Truth is to be the medium of their sanctification, for they are no strangers to the truth. The Christ they served is the Truth; and His Word is truth, composed entirely of truth, without any admixture of falsehood. Truth is the element in which this consecration or sanctification takes place. In this text, truth is the complete Christian revelation, all that God has revealed to man, all that He has spoken. And the knowledge of truth which He had imparted to them was to be expanded by the Holy Spirit.

The word translated to send is **apostello.** We have gotten the word "apostle" from it; and an apostle is one sent forth (with a commission). Thus, God the Father "apostled" His Son, and the Son "apostled" the disciples. What an honor bestowed here by Christ! He does not just leave them in the world, but sends them out into it. No wonder prayer was needed, for they were put on an "even so" level! It is as if Christ said: "I was sent, you are sent. I was sanctified, you are sanctified. I was commissioned, you are commissioned. I spoke truth, you speak truth. I performed miracles, you perform miracles. I taught, you teach; I preached, you preach. Love sent Me, love sends you. I had glory, you have glory." And so goes the "even so" (John 17:18).

D. A PERFECT ONENESS
(John 17:20-24)

Neither pray I for these alone, but for them also which shall believe on me through their word; That they all may be one; as thou, Father, art in me, and I in thee, that they also may be one in us: that the world may believe that thou hast sent me. And the glory which thou gavest me I have given them; that they may be one, even as we are one.

Here begins the section where the Lord prays for all future disciples or believers. In verses 1-5, He prayed for Himself; verses 6-19, He prayed for His disciples. And now in verses 20-26, He prayed for all believers throughout the entire age. Note that faith is essential. The Word preached must be believed. The Word is seen as the entire message which they preached, and which leads to faith in the finished work of Christ. Now the oneness of which Christ speaks is the opposite of that which the world emphasizes. Our oneness is internal, spiritual. Indeed, it resembles the essential oneness of the Godhead, the highest possible oneness in the world.

The unity that can be used of the Lord to persuade the world is not mere organization. Unity in its highest form is that relationship which exists between God the Father and God the Son. Men see this divine unity when they see Christians showing their love for other Christians. The purpose of this oneness is that the world-system might believe the Father sent the Son, to convince the world of their mission.

We believe that the glory of the Incarnate Word which Christ showed in His earthly ministry is the glory given the disciples (2 Corinthians 3:18). Morris calls this glory "the way of the cross...the path of lowly service culminating in the cross." It is this sharing of glory that resulted in spiritual unity. As the Holy Spirit proceeds to perfect us, mature us, the world will know the Father sent the Son whom He loved before the world began.

III. Special Features

A. PRESERVING OUR HERITAGE

We often talk about unity, Black togetherness. There are those who feel very strongly that if we were united as a people, we could achieve much, educate many, lift up our standards, live longer, etc. However, skin color is not a unifying force; neither is race. Sin is too deeply rooted for such matters as skin pigmentation, race, common adversity, etc. to unify men and women. On the other hand, there is a unity we have as Christians, and which we are to maintain (Ephesians 4:3). Without faith in the shed blood of the Lord Jesus, this oneness is impossible. It is a unity grounded in faith in Christ through the Word of God. No outside uniformity can produce this unity. If any group of Black Americans possesses the possibility of demonstrating true unity, it is that group which professes Christ as Lord and Savior, when will we let our potential become our practice?

B. A CONCLUDING WORD

The Lord prayed that believers may be made perfect, grown up, mature, fully developed in oneness. Three great unities are seen: that unity which exists among the Persons of the Godhead; that unity which is between the Godhead and the believer; and that unity among believers themselves. It was His desire that the world may know that the Father sent His Son, and that the Father loves the disciples (believers) even as He loves the Son, whom He loved before the very foundation of the world. The lesson closes with the Lord's expression of His desire that all given to Him by the Father may indeed be with Him.

HOME DAILY BIBLE READINGS
Week of May 30, 1999
Jesus Prayed for His Disciples

May	24	M.	John 17:1-5, This is Eternal Life
May	25	T.	John 17:6-10, I Have Made Your Name Known
May	26	W.	John 17:11-19, I Have Given Them Your Word
May	27	T.	John 17:20-26, That They All May Be One
May	28	F.	Luke 22:24-32, I Have Prayed for You
May	29	S.	Matthew 26:36-46, Could You Not Stay Awake With Me?
May	30	S.	Romans 8:31-39, Nothing Can Separate Us From God's Love

---

SUMMER QUARTER

June, July, August 1999

GENESIS: BEGINNINGS

General Introduction

Our lessons for this quarter are taken from the book of Genesis wherein the focus is on God's creation, God's relationship with the first human beings, and God's calling forth a people to live in covenantal relationship with Him.

The first session in Unit I, *"In the Beginning,"* deals with God's creation of the universe and His provision for the needs not only of humans, but all of His creatures. The last three lessons for the month concentrate on the topics of sin, judgment, and the opportunity for a new beginning within the context of God's grace.

Unit II, *"The Beginnings of a People,"* presents us with the opportunity to discuss God's call to Abram, God's promise to Abraham and Sarah, the test of Abraham's faith, and the reaffirmation of God's promises through the birth of Isaac and through the descendants of Jacob.

Unit III, *"A People Tested,"* discusses God's gracious presence with the people of Israel as they struggled with the problems of sin, conflicts and danger. The unit begins with Jacob's flight from his brother Esau, continues with Jacob's vision at Bethel, and concludes with the experiences of Joseph as the instrument of God in saving the brothers who sold him into slavery.

While the various lessons will deal mostly with the theological implications of the events concerned, the children will be able to grasp the meaning of the events as they are presented in story form.

The study of the "Beginnings" affords us the opportunity to come face to face with the spiritual understanding of our personal existence. There are those who will discuss the causal aspects of the creation and dare to place God in this cause-effect relationship. In a larger sense, we do not need to prove objectively that God created the world if such verification does not graphically alter the way in which we relate to Him. The point is that we as individuals accept by faith God as Creator and Sustainer and go forth to live lives consistent with that understanding. The fact is that when the writers of the book of Genesis (refer to a reputable Commentary dealing with the JEDP traditions) attempted to bring the history of Israel into focus, their compositions were basically confessions of faith relative to how they felt in the presence of God and whether or not the consciousness of God was consistent with their behavior. Humans, having been created in the image of God and housed in a perfect situation under perfect conditions, elected to affirm themselves rather than confirm the image and likeness of God through obedience, and the rest is history.

In any discussion of the creation, those who conceive of humans as emerging from a lower form of life experience difficulty in struggling to live on a moral and spiritual level which verifies that rise from the primeval ooze. On the other hand, those who embrace the faith that they were created by God dare to live "a little lower than the angels," rather than a little higher than the lower animals. The faith that God created the world and all that is in it is more than an argument, but a commitment; and we go forth to live lives consistent with that understanding.

God's Good Creation

Unit I. In the Beginning
Children's Unit—God Created All Things
Adult Topic—Accepting God's Provisions

.....

Youth Topic—Connected to Creation
Children's Topic—God Made the World

.....

Devotional Reading—Psalm 104:24-35
Background Scripture—Genesis 1:1—2:4a
Print—Genesis 1:1-2, 20-25, 29-31

SCRIPTURE PRINT

Genesis 1:1-2, 20-25, 29-31 (KJV)

IN the beginning God created the heaven and the earth.

2 And the earth was without form, and void; and darkness was upon the face of the deep. And the Spirit of God moved upon the face of the waters.

.....

20 And God said, Let the waters bring forth abundantly the moving creature that hath life, and fowl that may fly above the earth in the open firmament of heaven.

21 And God created great whales, and every living creature that moveth, which the waters brought forth abundantly, after their kind, and every winged fowl after his kind: and God saw that it was good.

22 And God blessed them, saying, Be fruitful, and multiply, and fill the waters in the seas, and let fowl multiply in the earth.

Genesis 1:1-2, 20-25, 29-31 (NRSV)

IN THE beginning when God created the heavens and the earth,

2 the earth was a formless void and darkness covered the face of the deep, while a wind from God swept over the face of the waters.

.....

20 And God said, "Let the waters bring forth swarms of living creatures, and let birds fly above the earth across the dome of the sky."

21 So God created the great sea monsters and every living creature that moves, of every kind, with which the waters swarm, and every winged bird of every kind. And God saw that it was good.

22 God blessed them, saying, "Be fruitful and multiply and fill the waters in the seas, and let birds multiply on the earth."

23 And there was evening and

23 And the evening and the morning were the fifth day.

24 And God said, Let the earth bring forth the living creature after his kind, cattle, and creeping thing, and beast of the earth after his kind: and it was so.

25 And God made the beast of the earth after his kind, and cattle after their kind, and every thing that creepeth upon the earth after his kind: and God saw that it was good.

.....

29 And God said, Behold, I have given you every herb bearing seed, which is upon the face of all the earth, and every tree, in the which is the fruit of a tree yielding seed; to you it shall be for meat.

30 And to every beast of the earth, and to every fowl of the air, and to every thing that creepeth upon the earth, wherein there is life, I have given every green herb for meat: and it was so.

31 And God saw every thing that he had made, and, behold, it was very good. And the evening and the morning were the sixth day.

there was morning, the fifth day.

24 And God said, "Let the earth bring forth living creatures of every kind: cattle and creeping things and wild animals of the earth of every kind." And it was so.

25 God made the wild animals of the earth of every kind, and the cattle of every kind, and everything that creeps upon the ground of every kind. And God saw that it was good.

.....

29 God said, "See, I have given you every plant yielding seed that is upon the face of all the earth, and every tree with seed in its fruit; you shall have them for food.

30 And to every beast of the earth, and to every bird of the air, and to everything that creeps on the earth, everything that has the breath of life, I have given every green plant for food." And it was so.

31 God saw everything that he had made, and indeed, it was very good. And there was evening and there was morning, the sixth day.

 **KEY VERSE** And God saw every thing that he had made, and behold, it was very good.—Genesis 1:31a

OBJECTIVES

After reading this lesson, the student should be better informed about:

1. The doctrine of Creation;
2. The fact that God is Creator;
3. The goodness of God's handiwork in creation; and,
4. God's providence.

Adult/Youth/Children
Key Verse: Genesis 1:31a
Print: Genesis 1:1-2, 20-25, 29-31

—God created heaven and earth from a formless void. (1-2)
—God created the world, blessed it, saying "Be fruitful and multiply." (20-25)
—God provided food to sustain all life. (29-30)
—God pronounced all creation good. (31)

(NOTE: Use KJV Scripture for Adults; NRSV Scripture for Youth and Children)

TOPICAL OUTLINE OF THE LESSON

I. Introduction

A. Creationism Versus Evolutionism
B. Biblical Background

II. Exposition and Application of the Scripture

A. In the Beginning God (Genesis 1:1-2)
B. The Fifth Day: Animal Life (Genesis 1:20-23)
C. The Sixth Day: Living Creatures (Genesis 1:24-25)
D. God's Assessment: Very Good! (Genesis 1:29-31)

III. Special Features

A. Preserving Our Heritage
B. A Concluding Word

I. Introduction

A. CREATIONISM VERSUS EVOLUTIONISM

Creationism is the doctrine that matter and all things were created, substantially as they now exist, by an omnipotent Creator, and not gradually evolved or developed *(Random House Dictionary)*. Thus, what Genesis chapter one teaches is accepted as true. Evolutionism is but a man-made theory, often taught as scientific fact, which holds that man accidentally evolved or sprung from some supposed original germ. We are not told from whence came this original germ. I should think that any system which is anti-God or anti-Bible is automatically evil—even that concept of evolution which calls itself "theistic." If the system is essentially wicked, what must be its influence in the lives of those who believe the system? And so I am perturbed not only by the dogmatic way in which the theory is taught as if it were fact, but also concerned with the moral effect the hypothesis of evolution has on its advocates.

Evolutionists are quick to call Creationism a religion. But the question of origins is in the final analysis a matter of faith, thus making evolutionism a religion also. Evolutionists would say that their concept "covers more ground than any of the others." We would respond, the Bible claims to cover all the ground. If there is a God—if the Bible is His Word—who would know better than He how things got started? Dr. Henry M. Morris and his colleagues suggest that "the study of science is seriously deficient unless a full and unbiased treatment of scientific creationism is included." Our continued exposition of the Scripture will help the student better understand our position favoring Creationism.

B. BIBLICAL BACKGROUND

We live in a world confused by the many philosophies and theories about the origin of the universe. The doctrine of creation is denied, and all kinds of ideas are postulated for the beginning of the universe. One of the great doctrines of the Bible is that of God the Creator. There are so many verses dealing with this matter that it is difficult to understand why we do not hear more preaching and teaching about God the Creator. Indeed, all of the "isms" invented by man are but vanity when seen in the light of the Scripture. Atheism, in its denial of the existence of God, is called foolishness by the Bible. For the atheist, there is no cause for anything, therefore there is no Creator.

Agnosticism, which claims we cannot know about God or His creation, does not want to be told that God says: "Here is the Bible! Take it, read it, and learn of God the Creator." Pantheism strives to make creation a part of God. Pantheists claim God and creation are one and the same thing. Pantheism teaches that God is everything and that everything is God. Thus, the Creator is confounded with what He has created.

Deism teaches that God is Creator, but He has no present relation to the world. God abandoned His creation when He completed it, and saw that everything "was very good." He remains indifferent to the world. The deist thus rejects the Bible, the revealed Word of God. But our Bible background is one which refutes all of these man-made speculations. "In the beginning God"—these four words alone wipe out every "ism" that denies the description of God the Creator as depicted in the Bible.

II. Exposition and Application of the Scripture

A. IN THE BEGINNING GOD
(Genesis 1:1-2)

IN the beginning God created the heaven and the earth. And the earth was without form, and void; and darkness was upon the face of the deep. And the spirit of God moved upon the face of the waters.

We do not know when this "beginning" was. We have no idea when the universe came into existence. Whenever it was, Christians have the assurance that it was not the result of blind chance. Whoever gave the "beginning" its beginning is the Mastermind behind it all. We believe that Person is God who "spoke, and it was done; He commanded, and it stood fast" (Psalm 33:9). Until God spoke, the universe did not exist. The word for God is Elohim, the first name of Deity in the Bible. Note that there is no attempt whatever in the Bible to prove the existence of God. He is, and always shall be. The Bible simply says, "Here He is!"

The "im" on Elohim is plural as it is in such Hebrew words as cherubim, seraphim, and yet, it is used with a singular verb. Theologians have suggested the use of the plural in this name for God signifies "plenitude of might" or exceptional dignity, unlimited greatness, intensity; it is sometimes called "plurality of majesty." L. S. Chafer states the name "portends the mystery of plurality in unity and unity in plurality." Elohim is derived from a root found in the Arabic language which means "to fear, to reverence." Thus, the meaning seems to be: "He who is in the highest degree to be reverenced" (New Bible Commentary). He is the God who by His very nature and works stirs up man's fears and awe.

The word translated "created" is **bara,** always used only of God, never of man. This Hebrew verb means to create out of nothing. Here is one major belief of Creationism, namely, God created **ex nihilo,** out of nothing. In other words, God did not need something in order to make something, for then we would be forced to ask, "Where did that something come from?" "Through faith, we understand that the worlds were framed by the word of God, so that things which are seen were not made of things which do appear" (Hebrew 11:3). "The creative act of God reflected in verse one, therefore, involved no preexisting material; a sovereign, all-powerful God created the heavens and the earth from nothing" (Thiessen). It is true that **bara** also means to cut down, divide, fashion. And keep in mind that other verbs meaning to make or form are also used with respect to the doctrine of creation.

There are several interpretations of verse two. Some scholars believe that when God first created the universe, He made it without form. They state that a great catastrophe occurred between verses one and two, suggesting perhaps that it was the fall of Lucifer who became the Devil. At any rate, there is the attempt to explain the earth being "without form, and void." According to Isaiah 45:18, the Lord did not create the earth waste and empty. Something happened to make it that way. A second idea is that the word rendered "was" should be translated "had become," —the earth had become waste and empty. The earth was not in the first place without form and void (Pilgrim Bible).

The Hebrew words **tohu wabohu** mean "without form, and void." The word **tohu** may mean waste in the sense of being not yet put into shape, rather than having been laid waste by some calamity (Leupold). And so, whether because of deliberate incompleteness in the original act of creation, or because catastrophe took place and ruined the original, we see that because God created the earth to be inhabited, the Holy Spirit brooded upon the face of the waters, and brought form out of that which had no form. The energizing Spirit of God moved and brought light where there had been darkness.

Two Persons of the Godhead are mentioned as taking part in creation—Elohim and the Holy Spirit. We recognize the Deity of the Holy Spirit here, for creation is an act of God. It must not be said that He was simply a force or instrument in the hands of Jehovah. He is God, the eternal Third Person of the Trinity (Hebrews 9:14)! The majority of the Scriptures dealing with creation refer to God the Father (Revelation 4:11). But the Holy Spirit's active involvement at creation is also mentioned (Job 33:4; 26:13; Psalm 33:6, 104:30; Isaiah 40:7). And of course, God the Son, the Lord Jesus Christ is described also as Creator (John 1:3; Colossians 1:16-17: Hebrews 1:2). Each member of the Godhead took part in creation. Here in Genesis 1:2, the Holy Spirit is seen as the Executor of the Divine purpose in creation.

Incidentally, no definite mention is made of the time when angels were created. Conservative scholars suggest they were created sometime before the creation of the heaven and the earth mentioned in Genesis 1:1. Recall that the angels (the sons of God) shouted for joy when the Lord laid the foundations of the earth (Job 38:4-7).

B. THE FIFTH DAY: ANIMAL LIFE
(Genesis 1:20-23)

And God said, Let the waters bring forth abundantly the moving creature that hath life, and fowl that may fly above the earth in the open firmament of heaven. And God created great whales, and every living creature that moveth, which the waters brought forth abundantly, after their kind, and every winged fowl after his kind: and God saw that it was good. And God blessed them, saying, Be fruitful, and multiply, and fill the waters in the seas, and let fowl multiply in the earth. And the evening and the morning were the fifth day.

God said literally: "Let the waters swarm with swarms of living creatures." So we are not to think of the waters themselves as producing the creatures. It was at God's command that the waters teemed with swimming creatures. The word "whales" is better translated "sea monsters" for this is what **tannim** in Hebrew means. This same Hebrew word is also rendered serpent or dragon (Deuteronomy 32:33) and dragon (Jeremiah 51:34). The word "fowl" or "bird" is literally, "flying things," and so may include insects as well. Such creatures further visibly demonstrate the power of the Creator.

The phrase "after their kind" or "after his kind" is one that emphasizes what Morrison calls reproductive integrity. It would appear that such language does not leave room for the theory of evolution. Indeed, the language reaches beyond just a single pair of each kind of the original and suggests that whole species, in something like their present multitude, were created (Kidner). Where "after their kind" is used, it deals with creatures whose reproductive systems are programmed in such a way that what is reproduced is of the same sort as that of the animal or plant.

C. THE SIXTH DAY: LIVING CREATURES
(Genesis 1:24-25)

And God said, Let the earth bring forth the living creature after his kind, cattle, and creeping thing, and beast of the earth after his kind: and it was so. And God made the beast of the earth after his kind, and cattle after their kind, and every thing that creepeth upon the earth after his kind: and God saw that it was good.

The phrase "every living creature" in verse 21 is repeated in verse 24, again showing that in this second act of creation, all animal life is included. "Creature" here is **nephesh** in the Hebrew, a word often rendered, "soul." It implies conscious life. Animals have souls, but not spirits. Plants do not have souls or spirits, so plants have no conscious life. But in the sense of having conscious life, animals are said also to have souls.

D. GOD'S ASSESSMENT: VERY GOOD
(Genesis 1:29-31)

And God said, Behold, I have given you every herb bearing seed, which is upon the face of all the earth, and every tree, in the which is the fruit of a tree yielding seed; to you it shall be for meat. And to every beast of the earth, and to every fowl of the air, and to every thing that creepeth upon the earth, wherein there is life, I have given every green herb for meat: and it was so. And God saw every thing that he had made, and, behold, it was very good. And the evening and the morning were the sixth day.

It appears that in man's dependence upon vegetation that all men at this time were herbivorous. Carnivores did not yet exist. Consideration of Genesis 9:2-3 supports this interpretation. It is only after the Flood that men are given authority to eat animal flesh. Proper interpretation of Genesis 9 provides no support for vegetarianism based on religious reasons. The lesson closes with the declaration of the benevolence of God. He looked at His handiwork and declared it to be very good. God cannot despise the work of His hands (Job 10:3).

Indeed, seven times (the number of perfection) in this first chapter we hear God's assessment of His creative acts—verses 4, 10, 12, 18, 21, 25, all state that what He saw, He considered good. And then in verse 31, the divine approval employs the superlative—and the whole is declared very good!

III. Special Features

A. PRESERVING OUR HERITAGE

The creation of man is not included in today's lesson, at lease not directly, for the lesson omits Genesis 1:26-28. However, verse 31 does cover the creation of man, and we hear the Lord's assessment: "And God saw everything that he had made, and behold, it was very good." Now the word **adam** means earthy, ruddy, reddish-brown. This means that Adam was not a White man. It is also a fact genetically that white may be gotten out of colored, but not colored out of white. In Acts 17:26, the apostle Paul states that God "has made of one blood all nations of men to dwell on all the face of the earth." The word "blood" is not in all manuscripts, so you may want to insert one "piece of clay," or just leave it, "has made of one." The "very good" of the "one" does not support the racial concepts of today which would make one race or skin color mentally, culturally, or morally superior to another group. Men should look at such factors as climate, diseases, earthquakes, wars, corruption, political upheavals, drought, pestilence, idolatry—the many things caused by sin—for reasons of differences between races. The search for genetic reasons upon which to base differences of intelligence among the races is underminded by our text from today's lesson. God in His infinite wisdom "has determined the times before appointed, and the bounds of their habitation" (Acts 17:26). Add to this the Scriptures which point out that the God of the Bible is no respecter of faces or races, and that in His presence no flesh shall glory (Romans 2:11; 1 Corinthians 1:29), and we have ample basis for exhorting Black American Christians to praise their Creator, and to never let any feelings of inferiority dismiss from our hearts and minds the plain teaching of God's Word. Previous conditions of slavery, present conditions of racism, and the many attempts to demean and denigrate should not be allowed to negatively affect the fact that we are Somebody in Christ. There are no such creatures as inferior human beings! When the God of the Bible created man, He looked, and saw that every thing He had made, behold, it was very good!

B. A CONCLUDING WORD

Three creative acts of God are seen in this first chapter of Genesis: (1) the heavens and the earth, verses 1-19; (2) animal life, verses 20-25; (3) human life, verses 26-31. From time to time, men have charged the Bible record with error. However, their hasty conclusions have been proven wrong, and they have had to withdraw their charges. From the very start our attention is drawn to God: "In the beginning God." It is therefore suggested that GOD FIRST should be our motto (MacDonald). We are better human beings only when we put Jesus Christ first. Seek first His kingdom is the command! (Matthew 6:33).

HOME DAILY BIBLE READINGS
Week of June 6, 1999
God's Creation

May	31 M.	Genesis 1:1-5 Day One of Creation
June	1 T.	Genesis 1:6-13 Days Two and Three of Creation
June	2 W.	Genesis 1:14-19 Day Four of Creation
June	3 T.	Genesis 1:20-23 Day Five of Creation
June	4 F.	Genesis 1:24-31 Day Six of Creation
June	5 S.	Genesis 2:1-4a Day Seven; God Finished Creation
June	6 S.	Psalm 104:24-35 O Lord, How Manifold Are Your Works!

God's Purpose for People

Adult Topic—Beginnings

.....

Youth Topic—Into a World of Choices
Children's Topic—God Gave People Responsibilities

.....

Devotional Reading—Ephesians 5:21-33
Background Scripture—Genesis 2:4-25
Print—Genesis 2:7-9, 15-25

● ● ● ● ● ● ● ● ● ● ●

SCRIPTURE PRINT

Genesis 2:7-9, 15-25 (KJV)

7 And the LORD God formed man of the dust of the ground, and breathed into his nostrils the breath of life; and man became a living soul.

8 And the LORD God planted a garden eastward in Eden; and there he put the man whom he had formed.

9 And out of the ground made the LORD God to grow every tree that is pleasant to the sight, and good for food; the tree of life also in the midst of the garden, and the tree of knowledge of good and evil.

.....

15 And the LORD God took the man, and put him into the garden of Eden to dress it and to keep it.

16 And the LORD God commanded the man, saying, Of every tree of the garden thou mayest freely eat:

17 But of the tree of the knowledge of good and evil, thou shalt not eat of it: for in the day that thou eatest thereof thou shalt surely die.

Genesis 2:7-9, 15-25 (NRSV)

7 then the LORD God formed man from the dust of the ground, and breathed into his nostrils the breath of life; and the man became a living being.

8 And the LORD God planted a garden in Eden, in the east; and there he put the man whom he had formed.

9 Out of the ground the LORD God made to grow every tree that is pleasant to the sight and good for food, the tree of life also in the midst of the garden, and the tree of the knowledge of good and evil.

.....

15 The LORD God took the man and put him in the garden of Eden to till it and keep it.

16 And the LORD God commanded the man, "You may freely eat of every tree of the garden;

17 but of the tree of the knowledge of good and evil you shall not eat, for in the day that you eat of it you shall die."

18 And the LORD God said, It is not good that the man should be alone; I will make him an help meet for him.

19 And out of the ground the LORD God formed every beast of the field, and every fowl of the air; and brought them unto Adam to see what he would call them: and whatsoever Adam called every living creature, that was the name thereof.

20 And Adam gave names to all cattle, and to the fowl of the air, and to every beast of the field; but for Adam there was not found an help meet for him.

21 And the LORD God caused a deep sleep to fall upon Adam, and he slept: and he took one of his ribs, and closed up the flesh instead thereof;

22 And the rib, which the LORD God had taken from man, made he a woman, and brought her unto the man.

23 And Adam said, This is now bone of my bones, and flesh of my flesh: she shall be called Woman, because she was taken out of Man.

24 Therefore shall a man leave his father and his mother, and shall cleave unto his wife: and they shall be one flesh.

25 And they were both naked, the man and his wife, and were not ashamed.

18 Then the LORD God said, "It is not good that the man should be alone; I will make him a helper as his partner."

19 So out of the ground the LORD God formed every animal of the field and every bird of the air, and brought them to the man to see what he would call them; and whatever the man called every living creature, that was its name.

20 The man gave names to all cattle, and to the birds of the air, and to every animal of the field; but for the man there was not found a helper as his partner.

21 So the LORD God caused a deep sleep to fall upon the man, and he slept; then he took one of his ribs and closed up its place with flesh.

22 And the rib that the LORD God had taken from the man he made into a woman and brought her to the man.

23 Then the man said, "This at last is bone of my bones and flesh of my flesh; this one shall be called Woman, for out of Man this one was taken."

24 Therefore a man leaves his father and his mother and clings to his wife, and they become one flesh.

25 And the man and his wife were both naked, and were not ashamed.

KEY VERSE

And the LORD God formed man of the dust of the ground, and breathed into his nostrils the breath of life; and man became a living soul.—Genesis 2:7

OBJECTIVES

After reading this lesson, the student will better understand:

1. The creation of man from the earth's dust;

2. The divine restrictions on man in the Garden of Eden;
3. The creation and naming of animals;
4. The creation of woman; and,
5. God's establishment of marriage.

POINTS TO BE EMPHASIZED

Adult/Youth/Children
Key Verse: Genesis 2:7
Print: Genesis 2:7-9, 15-25

—God made a living man from the dust of the earth. (7)
—God planted a garden in Eden that provided pleasure and nutrition. (8)
—God placed in the garden both the tree of life and the tree of knowledge of good and evil. (9)
—God gave humans responsibility and set limits on their behavior. (15-17)
—God created animals and man named them; but they did not fulfill man's deepest need for companionship. (18-20)
—God created man and woman to be partners with and companions to one another. (21-25)

(NOTE: Use KJV Scripture for Adults; NRSV Scripture for Youth and Children)

TOPICAL OUTLINE OF THE LESSON

I. Introduction

A. The Divine Nature of Marriage
B. Biblical Background

II. Exposition and Application Of the Scripture

A. Adam Created (Genesis 2:7)
B. A Garden Planted (Genesis 2:8-9, 15-17)
C. Eve Created (Genesis 2:18-22)
D. Marriage Instituted (Genesis 2:23-25)

III. Special Features

A. Preserving Our Heritage
B. A Concluding Word

I. Introduction

A. THE DIVINE NATURE OF MARRIAGE

Marriage is the will of God. This does not mean necessarily that all men and all women should be or shall be married. But marriage is a divine institution, and has as its purpose the perpetuation of the species, the joy of companionship and sex, and the fulfillment of God's plan for mankind on earth. The fact that God purposely made Eve for Adam (monogamy), and gave her to him, indicates that God Himself established marriage. This is why we call it Holy Matrimony. Unfortunately, these truths seem to be rapidly disappearing in our society. About half of all marriages in our country end in divorce. And often, even church ceremonies have lost their sacredness—the worldly music; the godless, alcohol-laced receptions; the extravagant cost of gowns, caterers, musicians, limousines, etc. Pastors have noted the desire of couples to write their own vows, often to eliminate the section dealing with the husband's rule (Genesis 3:16).

Note also that this relationship called marriage is between male and female. There is no such thing as same-sex marriage. Homosexuality is an abomination to God; the "one flesh" (Genesis 2:24) is only between a man and woman married to each other. With the husband "glued" (cleaving) to his wife, they are not to live with their parents. This is said three times in the Bible. First, by Moses in Genesis 2:24. Second, by the Lord Jesus in Matthew 19:5 (Mark 10:7). Third, by the apostle Paul in Ephesians 5:31. The verb translated "leave" in these New Testament Scriptures is a very strong one **(kataleipo),** meaning to abandon, leave helpless, forsake, desert, leave in the lurch. The verb rendered "leave" in Genesis 2:24 is **azab,** and it means to abandon, forsake in Hebrew. Evidently, the Lord does not want us to have parents and in-laws for crutches in our marriages. It is important for young married couples to tough things out on their own—depending, of course, on the guidance and direction of God and His Word.

B. BIBLICAL BACKGROUND

In the Bible, a covenant is a onesided (unilateral), God-initiated agreement between God and man. If its fulfillment depends upon man's faithfulness, it is conditional. And consequently, it may be broken, disrupted. If it cannot be broken by man, because it places no dependence on him, it is unconditional. It is God who says, "I will." The first covenant is the Edenic Covenant, and it is unconditional. It has to do with the life that Adam lived in the Garden of Eden before he disobeyed the Lord.

There are at least seven responsibilities listed for Adam based upon Genesis 1:26-30, and Genesis 2:15-17. They are: (1) Replenish: "Be fruitful, and multiply, and fill the earth; (2) Subdue the earth for man; (3) Rule: "have dominion over" the animals; (4) Eat: Maintain the garden, and eat of its fruits and vegetables. Note that the next three responsibilities are taken from the Scriptures in our lesson. (5) Work: "till and keep" the garden, Genesis 2:15; (6) Abstain: Do not eat of the tree of the knowledge of good and evil, Genesis 2:16-17; and (7) Death; the penalty for disobedience, Genesis 2:17. We see then that God made man responsible to populate the earth, subdue and rule over it, cultivate the Garden of Eden, and eat of all its produce except the fruit of the tree of the knowledge of good and evil. Disobedience of this sixth responsibility would bring death—immediate separation from God, and eventually physical death.

II. Exposition and Application of the Scripture

A. ADAM CREATED
(Genesis 2:7)

And the LORD God formed man of the dust of the ground, and breathed into his nostrils the breath of life; and man became a living soul.

Genesis 2:7 matches and completes Genesis 1:27 in the description of the making of man. Note the name LORD God. It is used for the first time in verse 4. In the first account of man's creation, Elohim is used (Genesis 1:27). Now in today's lesson, Jehovah-Elohim appears. The name Jehovah (or Yahweh) signifies a covenant relation with man. And, we learn that the different names of God are explained as indicating not a change in authorship, but in relationship. As Elohim, He is God the Creator. Add the name Jehovah, and He is also the Covenant God. Both His faithful mercy and His awe-inspiring power are seen in this compound name.

The Hebrew word **asah** means to form, make. God molded or shaped the man out of the dust of the ground. Remember, however, that the dust of the ground was created out of nothing, so that it is still proper to say God created man (Genesis 1:27, **bara**). Both earth and heaven can claim man. Man, Adam, was formed out of the ground, **adamah.** Thus Paul could say, "The first man is of the earth, earthy" (I Corinthians 15:47). As we noted in an earlier lesson, the word **adam** means red or ruddy, named after the red earth from which he was made, and therefore the skin color of the first man was not white!

Man's life came from God's very breath, thus making him a combination of dust and deity. He is both material and immaterial. Obviously, this account of the history of man's beginning in no way supports the theory of evolution. What God formed out of the dust of the ground was complete, lacking only the breath of God. What the Lord provided here removes the human being from other forms of life "as far as God is removed from His creation" (Chafer). For while animals also have the breath **(neshimah,** Genesis 7:22), and animals also have souls **(nephesh,** Genesis 1:24: "living creature"), they received them indirectly. Only man received his breath (spirit) and soul directly from God.

Three major inbreathings are recorded in the Bible: First, that by which man became a living soul, Genesis 2:7; Second, the resurrected Lord breathed on the disciples, imparting the Holy Spirit to them in preparation for their full endowment at Pentecost, John 20:22. Third, the Word of God is God-breathed, 2 Timothy 3:16. Today, the Holy Spirit lives in the bodies of all who believe in the Lord Jesus Christ. Finally, we see that man became a living soul. The word for soul here is **nephesh.** Some scholars teach that man must not be thought of as having a soul. However, man is a soul, and has a soul. Both things are true. Note the use of the word **nephesh** in 1 Kings 17:21-22. Through the intervention of the prophet Elijah and by the power of God, the soul of the widow's child came into him again, and he was brought to life. Animated by the Spirit of God, the lifeless clod of clay revived. How fearfully and wonderfully we are made (Psalm 139:14).

B. A GARDEN PLANTED

(Genesis 2:8-9, 15-17)

And the LORD God planted a garden eastward in Eden; and there he put the man whom he had formed. And out of the ground made the LORD God to grow every tree that is pleasant to the sight, and good for food; the tree of life also in the midst of the garden, and the tree of knowledge of good and evil. And the LORD God took the man, and put him into the garden of Eden to dress it and to keep it. And the LORD God commanded the man, saying, Of every tree of the garden thou mayest freely eat: But of the tree of the knowledge of good and evil, thou shalt not eat of it: for in the day that thou eatest thereof thou shalt surely die.

The Hebrew word **Eden** probably means "enchantment, pleasure, delight." As a place hedged about, it is the garden of delight. In the Greek translation of the Old Testament, called the Septuagint, it is called **Paradise,** a Persian name for just such a place of delight. What God caused to grow there is said to be pleasant to the eyes, and good for the stomach, for Eden was designed to be a beautiful home for Adam. We have here a real man, in a real garden with real trees that produce real fruit. it is an error to see the account here as merely symbolical. Two particular trees are singled out in order to provide the physical means of a spiritual test. God's purpose was to test Adam's loyalty and obedience to the divine will. First mentioned is the tree of life in the midst of the garden. It is named according to its relation to man, this is to say, its effect upon human life if the fruit of this tree is eaten. If after having disobeyed God, Adam had gotten hold of the fruit of the tree of life, he would have lived forever in his sinful condition, and ever approaching death. For the fruit of this tree conferred immortality.

The second tree mentioned is the tree of knowledge of good and evil. In itself, knowledge is not wrong. What is wrong is knowledge which seeks not to acknowledge God. Knowledge that ignores God is foolishness. Life is seen as obedience to the words, "thou mayest freely eat" and "thou shalt not eat." Obedience to God's Word is the issue here. Disobedience brings punishment—"dying, you shall die." When the Lord makes a law, He also establishes a penalty.

From the moment Adam ate of the tree, he became a dying creature. First of all, his spiritual relationship with God was disrupted. Separation took place immediately. In time, physical death was the inevitable result, and men have been dying ever since (Romans 5:12). Adam had been able not to sin, but upon disobeying God, he became a creature that was not able not to sin. Having inherited Adam's fallen nature, you and I came into this world unable not to sin.

Finally, on this section, we see that work is not a curse, but a blessing. We find that before Adam disobeyed God, he had work to do there in the Garden. Only after the Fall did the Lord curse the ground, making it more difficult to obtain a living from the ground (Genesis 3:17-19). He did not curse work. From the very beginning, Adam was given the task of dressing and keeping the Garden. The Hebrew word rendered to dress means to till, serve; the word translated to keep means to observe, take heed, watch. The basic idea of the root is "to exercise great care over" *(Theological Wordbook of the Old Testament).*

C. EVE CREATED
(Genesis 2:18-22)

And the LORD God said, It is not good that the man should be alone; I will make him an help meet for him. And out of the ground the LORD God formed every beast of the field, and every fowl of the air; and brought them unto Adam to see what he would call them: and whatsoever Adam called every living creature, that was the name thereof. And Adam gave names to all cattle, and to the fowl of the air, and to every beast of the field; but for Adam there was not found an help meet for him. And the LORD God caused a deep sleep to fall upon Adam and he slept: and he took one of his ribs, and closed up the flesh instead thereof; And the rib, which the LORD God had taken from man, made he a woman, and brought her unto the man.

Up to this point, the Lord saw His handiwork as good! Now for the first time we hear Him say, "It is not good..." Even with all of the animals present there, Adam was alone, incomplete. Literally, he needed a "helper like him." Animals and smaller wild animals were brought to Adam for him to name them. Each living creature was given a name that conformed with the type of life the animal lived. This served its purpose of causing Adam to realize his loneliness even more. Of course, there was not found among the animals "an help meet for him." God then caused Adam to fall into a deep sleep—"a divine anesthetic administered by the Great Physician" *(Parallel Bible Commentary),* and the Lord performed an operation on him. From Adam's rib, the LORD God made a woman, thereby establishing the unity of the race coming from one ancestor. Eve was not made out of the dust of the ground as was Adam. Nor is it said that God breathed into her nostrils. This would suggest that both her physical and immaterial natures were taken out of Adam.

D. MARRIAGE INSTITUTED
(Genesis 2:23-25)

And Adam said, This is now bone of my bones, and flesh of my flesh: she shall be called Woman, because she was taken out of Man. Therefore shall a man leave his father and his mother, and shall cleave unto his wife: and they shall be one flesh. And they were both naked, the man and his wife, and were not ashamed.

The intimacy of the relationship is seen in the statement: "This is now bone of my bones, and flesh of my flesh." This truest of kinship guarantees the woman's dignity; she is by no means made of inferior substance, but is literally a "helper like him," his very counterpart. Even the Hebrew words **ishshah** for Woman and ish for Man express in similarity of sound a kinship (Genesis 2:23). Marriage is seen as a holy appointment of God, for He "brought her unto the man," like a father of the bride. Celibacy is not then a higher or holier state. God established monogamy, and wherever it is violated in any society trouble results.

Finally, it is noted that Adam and Eve had no cause to feel shame. At this point neither had sinned, so that they were in complete harmony with God and with themselves.

III. Special Features

A. PRESERVING OUR HERITAGE

In recent days, Afrocentrists have joined with certain evolution-minded anthropologists, paleontologists, et al, who assert that the original Garden of Eden was in Africa, somewhere in present-day Tanzania. They thus deny the Mesopotamian basin is the "Cradle of Civilization." Afrocentrists claim that Africa "perhaps extended to the Tigris and Euphrates rivers," and that all this area was landlocked with the main continent.

The Bible does not support the Afrocentrists here. The history of the nations and tribes as portrayed in the Bible point to a common origin and ancestry, as located somewhere in the fertile crescent region, not Africa. According to the Scriptures, the Garden lay eastward, that is, east of Palestine, and was thus located in the region of Mesopotamia (literally, middle of the rivers). Eden lay then in the lower part of the Babylonian valley, somewhere in the land between the rivers Tigris and Euphrates. Beyond this, it is impossible to exactly locate the Garden. However, we need not violate the integrity of God's Word in an attempt to support the theories held by some Afrocentrists!!

B. A CONCLUDING WORD

Contrary to evolutionism, today's lesson argues for the immediate creation of man (Thiessen). Adam's body was made of the dust of the ground and inbreathed by God. Creationism thus gives man a position of dignity and responsibility totally absent from the theory of evolution. Eve was made directly by the Lord. God's purpose for mankind is seen best when we accept what the Bible teaches about man's creation. There is to be no mixing of animal flesh and human flesh (1 Corinthians 15:39). It is man made in the image of God who then fulfills God's purpose.

HOME DAILY BIBLE READING
Week of June 13, 1999
God's Purpose for People

June 7 M. Genesis 2:4b-14 The Lord God Planted A Garden...
June 8 T. Genesis 2:15-25 Therefore a Man ... Clings to His Wife
June 9 W. Ephesians 5:21-23 Husbands, Love Your Wives
June 10 T. Matthew 15:1-9 Honor Your Father and Your Mother
June 11 F. Matthew 19:16-22 Keep the Commandments
June 12 S. Mark 10:1-9 God Made Them Male and Female
June 13 S. 1 Corinthians 15:42-49 Perishable to Imperishable

Consequences of Sin

Adult Topic—Shattered Relationships

·····

Youth Topic—Shattered Relationships
Children's Topic—People Disobeyed God

·····

Devotional Reading—1 John 3:11-17
Background Scripture—Genesis 4
Print—Genesis 4:1-16

· · · · · · · · · · · ·

PRINTED SCRIPTURE

Genesis 4:1-16 (KJV)

AND Adam knew Eve his wife; and she conceived, and bare Cain, and said, I have gotten a man from the LORD.

2 And she again bare his brother Abel. And Abel was a keeper of sheep, but Cain was a tiller of the ground.

3 And in process of time it came to pass, that Cain brought of the fruit of the ground an offering unto the LORD.

4. And Abel, he also brought of the firstlings of his flock and of the fat thereof. And the LORD had respect unto Abel and to his offering:

5 But unto Cain and to his offering he had not respect. And Cain was very wroth, and his countenance fell.

6 And the LORD said unto Cain, Why art thou wroth? and why is thy countenance fallen?

7 If thou doest well, shalt thou not be accepted? And if thou doest not well, sin lieth at the door. And

Genesis 4:1-16 (NRSV)

NOW THE man knew his wife Eve, and she conceived and bore Cain, saying, "I have produced a man with the help of the LORD."

2 Next she bore his brother Abel. Now Abel was a keeper of sheep, and Cain a tiller of the ground.

3 In the course of time Cain brought to the LORD an offering of the fruit of the ground,

4 and Abel for his part brought of the firstlings of his flock, their fat portions. And the LORD had regard for Abel and his offering,

5 but for Cain and his offering he had no regard. So Cain was very angry, and his countenance fell.

6 The LORD said to Cain, "Why are you angry, and why has your countenance fallen?

7 If you do well, will you not be accepted? And if you do not do well, sin is lurking at the door; its desire is for you, but you must master it."

8 Cain said to his brother Abel, "Let us go out to the field." And when

unto thee shall be his desire, and thou shalt rule over him.

8 And Cain talked with Abel his brother: and it came to pass, when they were in the field, that Cain rose up against Abel his brother, and slew him.

9 And the LORD said unto Cain, Where is Abel thy brother? And he said, I know not: Am I my brother's keeper?

10 And he said, What hast thou done? The voice of thy brother's blood crieth unto me from the ground.

11 And now art thou cursed from the earth, which hath opened her mouth to receive thy brother's blood from thy hand;

12 When thou tillest the ground, it shall not henceforth yield unto thee her strength; a fugitive and a vagabond shalt thou be in the earth.

13 And Cain said unto the LORD, My punishment is greater than I can bear.

14 Behold, thou hast driven me out this day from the face of the earth; and from thy face shall I be hid; and I shall be a fugitive and a vagabond in the earth; and it shall come to pass, that every one that findeth me shall slay me.

15 And the LORD said unto him, Therefore whosoever slayeth Cain, vengeance shall be taken on him sevenfold. And the LORD set a mark upon Cain, lest any finding him should kill him.

16 And Cain went out from the presence of the LORD, and dwelt in the land of Nod, on the east of Eden.

they were in the field, Cain rose up against his brother Abel, and killed him.

9 Then the LORD said to Cain, "Where is your brother Abel?" He said, "I do not know; am I my brother's keeper?"

10 And the LORD said, "What have you done? Listen; your brother's blood is crying out to me from the ground!

11 And now you are cursed from the ground, which has opened its mouth to receive your brother's blood from your hand.

12 When you till the ground, it will no longer yield to you its strength; you will be a fugitive and a wanderer on the earth."

13 Cain said to the LORD, "My punishment is greater than I can bear!

14 Today you have driven me away from the soil, and I shall be hidden from your face; I shall be a fugitive and a wanderer on the earth, and anyone who meets me may kill me."

15 Then the LORD said to him, "Not so! Whoever kills Cain will suffer a sevenfold vengeance." And the LORD put a mark on Cain, so that no one who came upon him would kill him.

16 Then Cain went away from the presence of the LORD, and settled in the land of Nod, east of Eden.

If you do well, will you not be accepted? And if you do not do well, sin is lurking at the door; its desire is for you, but you must master it.--Genesis 4:7

After reading this lesson, the student should be aware that:

1. God determines how we are to worship Him;
2. The first murder was inspired by Satan;
3. The attitude of the worshiper is important;
4. We reap what we sow; and,
5. God is a merciful God.

POINTS TO BE EMPHASIZED

Adult/Youth/Children
Key Verse: Genesis 4:7
Print: Genesis 4:1-16

—Eve gave birth first to Cain and then to Abel. (1-2)
—Cain became angry when God accepted Abel's offering and not Cain's. (3-5)
—Cain killed Abel. (8)
—When God confronted Cain, he tried to hide from responsibility. (9-10)
—God punished Cain for his sin. (11-13)
—God banished Cain, but protected him from further violence. (14-16)

(NOTE: Use KJV Scripture for Adult; NRSV Scripture for Youth and Children)

TOPICAL OUTLINE OF THE LESSON

I. Introduction

A. Why Does God Ask Questions?
B. Biblical Background

II. Exposition and Application of the Scripture

A. Cain and Abel: Their Births (Genesis 4:1-2a)
B. Cain and Abel: Their Worship (Genesis 4:2b-7)
C. Abel's Murder (Genesis 4:8-10)
D. Cain's Punishment (Genesis 4:11-14)
E. God's Mercy (Genesis 4:15-16)

III. Special Features

A. Preserving Our Heritage
B. A Concluding Word

I. Introduction

A. WHY DOES GOD ASK QUESTIONS?

God directed four questions to Adam: "Where are you?...Who told you that you were naked?...Have you eaten of the tree, whereof I commanded you that you should not eat?...What is this that you have done?" (Genesis 3:9-13). In today's lesson, the Lord asked five questions, all of them directed to Cain: "Why are you angry? Why has your countenance fallen? If you do well, will you not be accepted?...Where is Abel your brother?...What have you done?" (Genesis 4:6-7, 9-10). One thing we can immediately dispose of is the idea that there is something God does not know. The God of the Bible is omniscient. But He often asked men questions in order to help men see the conditions of their own hearts. His questions are intended to pierce the heart of the hearer and lay bare his soul in some particular matter. Men are challenged by God's inquiries to reflect upon their actions. Divine interrogation gives men opportunity to confess, or ask for forgiveness. The question itself may be a rebuke, or an opening for the Lord Himself to reply and impart knowledge to the hearer. God's questions and man's answers constitute the thrust of today's lesson.

B. BIBLICAL BACKGROUND

When the Old Testament was translated into Greek, some of the Greek names were applied to the Hebrew Bible and remain until this day. We have Genesis, Exodus, Deuteronomy as examples. In Greek, Exodus means the way out; Deuteronomy means second giving of the law; and Genesis means beginning, inception, a coming into being, origin, creation. In chapter one, the story of Creation is told. The account is one of creationism, and in no way supports the theory of evolution. In six days, God completed His work, and declared His handiwork, "very good."

In chapter two, we learn more about the conditions of Adam and Eve, our first parents. Having created man on the sixth day, God then rested. More information is given concerning the creation of Eve, and the institution of marriage. What we learn about God's will for their lives helps us to better appreciate the events of the next chapter. For in chapter three, man is tested and flunks the test.

This is the purpose of each dispensation (plan, order, arrangement, system). God's examination finds men incapable of running their own lives without Him. Thus what takes place in this chapter is called the Fall. Satan's role is prominent. And we begin to see the ramifications of sin, the prediction of the coming of Christ (Genesis 3:15), and the expulsion of the first humans. This brings us to the Fourth Chapter where we see what happens when human beings begin to go out into the world, taking their sin natures with them! And yet, there is the promise of hope despite the curse of sin. Today's lesson, limited to the first 16 verses of Genesis chapter four, gives us an individual (Cain) instance of the early development of the now-sinful human race.

II. Exposition and Application of the Scripture

A. CAIN AND ABEL: THEIR BIRTHS
(Genesis 4:1-2a)

AND Adam knew Eve his wife; and she conceived, and bare Cain, and said,

I have gotten a man from the LORD. And she again bare his brother Abel.

To know a woman is a common euphemism for sexual union. The Sodomites demanded Lot to release his visitors to them that they "may know them" (Genesis 19:5). Mary said to the angel Gabriel, "How shall this be, seeing I know not a man?" (Luke 1:34). We still speak today of having "carnal knowledge." Incidentally, it is suggested that the sexual act was not part of life while Adam and Eve were in the Garden of Eden, but only after they were driven out did Adam know his wife (Keil and Delizsch). Eve's firstborn was named Cain, which means in Hebrew, acquisition. She had acquired a son by the help of Jehovah, and gratefully acknowledged divine enablement. Her next son was named Abel. The words "she again bore" constitute a phrase which does not support the idea that Abel was Cain's twin. Abel means that which ascends (vapor, vanity, a fleeting breath, nothingness). It is said she named him Abel because by this time she fully recognized that God's curse on creation made it subject to vanity (Romans 8:20).

B. CAIN AND ABEL: THEIR WORSHIP
(Genesis 4:2b-7)

And Abel was a keeper of sheep, but Cain was a tiller of the ground. And in process of time it came to pass, that Cain brought of the fruit of the ground an offering unto the LORD. And Abel, he also brought of the firstlings of his flock and of the fat thereof. And the LORD had respect unto Abel and to his offering: But unto Cain and to his offering he had not respect. And Cain was very wroth, and his countenance fell. And the LORD said unto Cain, Why art thou wroth? and why is thy countenance fallen? If thou doest well, shalt thou not be accepted? And if thou doest not well, sin lieth at the door. And unto thee shall be his desire, and thou shalt rule over him.

The brothers were led to pursue different occupations. Abel became a shepherd, a keeper of sheep and goats; Cain followed agriculture, farming, a tiller or cultivator of the soil. Each son assumed one aspect of what their father had done by himself. Their work was indeed honorable. Now do not overlook the words, "and in the process of time," literally, "at the end of the days." Consideration of this phrase helps answer some questions posed concerning the family of Adam and Eve. How much time passed between the birth of Cain and Abel and this incident regarding their worship is not known. We have reason to believe a considerable length of time elapsed (Keil and Delitzsch), and that Cain and Abel are grown men by now. That they had other brothers and sisters is brought out also in Genesis 5:4, where we learn that Adam "begot sons and daughters." We believe that "the process of time" makes room for the increase in the world's population.

On this particular day both Cain and Abel brought offerings to the Lord. The word for offering is **minchah,** and it speaks broadly of any type of gift man brings to God. However, we see that the Lord had respect unto Abel and to his offering, but had not respect to Cain and to his offering. Respect is the translation of a Hebrew word that means unto, look at, regard. Here in Genesis 4:4-5, it means "to look at with approval . . . to approve of" *(Theological Wordbook of the*

Old Testament). Keil and Delitzsch state that the look was "a visible sign of satisfaction," more than likely fire that consumed Abel's sacrifice.

The big question is why—why did God look with interest at the one and not the other? The answer is twofold; it lies both in the men themselves and in what they offered. Many conservative scholars believe that Adam taught his children how God wanted to be worshiped. He instructed them that the only acceptable approach of a sinner to God was by the blood of a substitute sacrifice. It is suggested that blood was shed when an animal was slain to provide coats of skin for Adam and Eve (Genesis 3:21). Cain brought fruit and vegetables, products of his own labor and toil, and thus represented a religious man who determined to worship God man's way. In his presumption, he denied the value of the blood sacrifice. But Abel did not ignore the blood atonement. He brought of the firstlings of his flock and of the fat thereof. He offered his best. Because the Bible mentions the names of Abel and Cain before making reference to their individual gifts, it is suggested that their attitudes influenced God to accept the one and reject the other. We would state that the very nature of their offerings reflected their inner beings, their "state of mind toward God." What Abel did was an act of faith (Hebrews 11:4); this must not be overlooked. Cain's sacrifice was pure formalism, going through the motions, evidently no real concern about his own sin. Note that what he brought was not even of his firstfruits.

Furthermore, his bad attitude is seen in his reactions to God's disapproval: (1) Rather than show sorrow, He was very angry, "burned up"; (2) His countenance fell in dejection, discontentment. Verse 7 is difficult to interpret. One idea is that God in mercy spoke to Cain and warned him: "Is it not so, if you do what is right, there is acceptance; and if you do not do what is right, then at the door there is sin, like a crouching wild animal, striving to attack you, but you should rule over it?" In this interpretation, the Lord warns Cain that sin will jump on him and destroy him, even as a beast would seize a man going out at the door. Worship correctly and be accepted!

Another interpretation informs us that the word "sin" means "sin offering." Thus Cain is given another chance to sacrifice properly. And he is assured that his younger brother would remain subordinate to him. This latter interpretation appears more acceptable, even though both ideas speak truths.

C. ABEL'S MURDER
(Genesis 4:8-10)

And Cain talked with Abel his brother: and it came to pass, when they were in the field, that Cain rose up against Abel his brother, and slew him. And the LORD said unto Cain, Where is Abel thy brother? And he said, I know not: Am I my brother's keeper? And he said, What hast thou done? The voice of thy brother's blood crieth unto me from the ground.

We read of no change, no repentance, no thanks for the warning or advice, no asking forgiveness for jealousy and hatred which culminated in murder! Is it any wonder that John states Cain was of the Wicked One (Satan), and he killed Abel because his own works were evil, and his brother's righteous? The word translated "slew" or "killed" is one used of killing an animal in sacrifice (1 John 3:12). Kenneth Wuest believes that Cain used a sharp stone or bone to slit Abel's throat. And now, one son is a murderer, the other a martyr. When God questioned Cain, "Where is Abel, your brother?", Cain's shameful, heartless, lying response was, "I don't know; am I my brother's keeper?" What defiance! The Hebrew word, **shamar,** translated "keeper," has the basic idea of meaning "to exercise great care over, to guard" *(Theological Wordbook of the Old Testament)*. Bloods (it is plural in the Hebrew, perhaps signifying the many drops shed) crying out signifies wrongs crying out to be righted (Luke 18:7-8; Revelation 6:9-10). "Innocent blood has no voice, it may be, that is discernible by human ears, but it has one that reaches God, as the cry of a wicked deed demanding vengeance" (Keil and Delitzsch). "The idea that blood exposed on the ground thus clamors for vengeance is persistently vivid in the Old Testament" (Skinner, ICC, Job 16:18; Isaiah 26:21).

D. CAIN'S PUNISHMENT
(Genesis 4:11-14)

And now art thou cursed from the earth, which hath opened her mouth to receive thy brother's blood from thy hand; When thou tillest the ground, it shall not henceforth yield unto thee her strength; a fugitive and a vagabond shalt thou be in the earth. And Cain said unto the LORD, My punishment is greater than I can bear. Behold, thou hast driven me out this day from the face of the earth; and from thy face shall I be hid; and I shall be a fugitive and a vagabond in the earth; and it shall come to pass, that every one that findeth me shall slay me.

There is a twofold result of Cain's evil deed and impenitence. First, the very ground from which Cain derived his livelihood would no longer yield productively for him; he would no longer be able to make a living as a farmer. Recall, the ground had been cursed earlier (Genesis 3:17). And now, the ground that soaked up the blood of Abel will do nothing for his brother, Cain. Second, Cain would become a vagabond, a fugitive, a wanderer throughout the earth. Apparently, Cain suffered no immediate pangs of conscience over having just committed fratricide. His concern was what he considered a harsh punishment. The killer was now afraid of being killed. His plea was that his punishment was too great. At least the word **(awon)** rendered "punishment" used by Cain means iniquity, guilt. Did he at last show acknowledgment of his sin to the Lord?

E. GOD'S MERCY
(Genesis 4:15-16)

And the LORD said unto him, Therefore whosoever slayeth Cain, vengeance shall be taken on him sevenfold. And the LORD set a mark upon Cain, lest any finding him should kill him. And Cain went out from the presence of the LORD, and dwelt in the land of Nod, on the east of Eden.

In mercy, God grants Cain special protection during his wanderings. Here we learn that the Lord put a curse on anyone who would take Cain's life. It is only later, in Genesis 9:6, that God provides for capital punishment for the murderer.

In addition, a protective mark was put on Cain. We do not know what the sign was, but it appears to have stopped anyone inclined to slay Cain.

How sad the words, "Cain went out from the presence of the Lord." We are reminded of Judas, who, having received the sop, went immediately out; and it was night (John 13:30). And Demas, who having loved this present world, left the apostle Paul (2 Timothy 4:10). **"Nod"** means wandering. It is the name of the region in which Cain lived his life of wandering.

III. Special Features

A. PRESERVING OUR HERITAGE

Black American Christians are warned not to fall into the trap of Cain. This is to say, beware of thinking we can worship God "any old kind of way." His desire is that we worship Him in spirit and in truth. We do not come into the world knowing how to worship the Lord. We must be taught. The basic principles of worship our foreparents learned are changed by the changing times. And yet in many of our churches, it seems that "anything goes." We have "Come as You Are" Sundays! Why some restaurants and business establishments have stricter clothing codes than some of our churches. We have come a long way, but where are we?

B. CONCLUDING WORD

The consequences of sin described in this chapter are frightening! There is first of all the attempt to worship God the way man wants to worship Him, and this evil is compounded by the denial of the blood sacrifice which points to Jesus Christ. Then when God accepts Abel's offering, Cain is angry because his sacrifice was not approved. He is then angry with God, and does not accept the opportunity to bring a sin offering (if our interpretation of verse 7 is correct). Moved by Satan, Cain allows his envy to grow into hatred, and then kills his own brother in a fit of jealousy. Surely, one sin leads to another. For when God inquires of Abel's whereabouts, Cain lies to the Lord, giving evidence of his lack of remorse. This lack of repentance is further observed when he complained of his punishment, but said nothing about the sinfulness of his sin. And so, he is punished.

HOME DAILY BIBLE READINGS
Week of June 20, 1999
Consequences of Sin

June 14	M.	Genesis 4:1-7 Sin is Lurking At The Door
June 15	T.	Genesis 4:8-16 Cain Murdered His Brother, Abel
June 16	W.	Genesis 4:17-26 The Birth of Enoch and Seth
June 17	T.	Isaiah 59:1-15 Iniquities Are Barriers Between You and God
June 18	F.	Proverbs 28:9-14 Forsaking Transgressions Will Obtain Mercy
June 19	S.	Matthew 5:21-26 But I Say to You
June 20	S.	Psalm 32:1-11 Happy Are Those Whose Transgression Is Forgiven

Judgment and New Beginning

Adult Topic—From Disaster to Hope

.....

Youth Topic—From Disaster to Hope
Children's Topic—God Made a Promise

.....

Devotional Reading—Deuteronomy 7:7-11
Background Scripture—Genesis 6:5—9:17
Print—Genesis 6:5-8; 7:1-4; 9:12-17

• • • • • • • • • • •

PRINTED SCRIPTURE

Genesis 6:5-8; 7:1-4; 9:12-17 (KJV)

5 And GOD saw that the wickedness of man was great in the earth, and that every imagination of the thoughts of his heart was only evil continually.

6 And it repented the LORD that he made man on the earth, and it grieved him at his heart.

7 And the LORD said, I will destroy man whom I have created from the face of the earth; both man, and beast, and the creeping thing, and the fowls of the air; for it repenteth me that I have made them.

8 But Noah found grace in the eyes of the LORD.

.....

AND the LORD said unto Noah, Come thou and all thy house into the ark; for thee have I seen righteous before me in this generation.

2 Of every clean beast thou shalt take to thee by sevens, the male and his female: and of beasts that are not clean by two, the male and his

Genesis 6:5-8; 7:1-4; 9:12-17 (NRSV)

5 The LORD saw that the wickedness of humankind was great in the earth, and that every inclination of the thoughts of their hearts was only evil continually.

6 And the LORD was sorry that he had made humankind on the earth, and it grieved him to his heart.

7 So the LORD said, "I will blot out from the earth the human beings I have created—people together with animals and creeping things and birds of the air, for I am sorry that I have made them."

8 But Noah found favor in the sight of the LORD.

....

THEN THE LORD said to Noah, "Go into the ark, you and all your household, for I have seen that you alone are righteous before me in this generation.

2 Take with you seven pairs of all clean animals, the male and its

female.

3 Of fowls also of the air by sevens, the male and the female; to keep seed alive upon the face of all the earth.

4 For yet seven days, and I will cause it to rain upon the earth forty days and forty nights; and every living substance that I have made will I destroy from off the face of the earth.

.....

12 And God said, This is the token of the covenant which I make between me and you and every living creature that is with you, for perpetual generations:

13 I do set my bow in the cloud, and it shall be for a token of a covenant between me and the earth.

14 And it shall come to pass, when I bring a cloud over the earth, that the bow shall be seen in the cloud:

15 And I will remember my covenant, which is between me and you and every living creature of all flesh; and the waters shall no more become a flood to destroy all flesh.

16 And the bow shall be in the cloud; and I will look upon it, that I may remember the everlasting covenant between God and every living creature of all flesh that is upon the earth.

17 And God said unto Noah, This is the token of the covenant, which I have established between me and all flesh that is upon the earth.

mate; and a pair of the animals that are not clean, the male and its mate;

3 and seven pairs of the birds of the the air also, male and female, to keep their kind alive on the face of all the earth.

4 For in seven days I will send rain on the earth for forty days and forty nights; and every living thing that I have made I will blot out from the face of the ground."

.....

12 God said, "This is the sign of the covenant that I make between me and you and every living creature that is with you, for all future generations:

13 I have set my bow in the clouds, and it shall be a sign of the covenant between me and the earth.

14 When I bring clouds over the earth and the bow is seen in the clouds,

15 I will remember my covenant that is between me and you and every living creature of all flesh; and the waters shall never again become a flood to destroy all flesh.

16 When the bow is in the clouds, I will see it and remember the everlasting covenant between God and every living creature of all flesh that is on the earth."

17 God said to Noah, "This is the sign of the covenant that I have established between me and all flesh that is on the earth."

KEY VERSE I will remember my covenant, which is between me and you and every living creature of all flesh; and the waters shall no more become a flood to destroy all flesh.—Genesis 9:15

OBJECTIVES

After reading this lesson, the student should have a better understanding of:
1. The effect of man's sin upon the heart of God;
2. The place of judgment in God's purpose for man;
3. The nature of the Flood;
4. The significance of the Rainbow; and,
5. The grace of God.

POINTS TO BE EMPHASIZED

Adult/Youth/Children
Key Verse: Genesis 9:15
Print: Genesis 6:5-8; 7:1-4; 9:12-17

—God was grieved with people's wickedness and regretted creating humans. (6:5-7)
—God decided to destroy human and animal life except for Noah and his family. (6:7-8)
—As God commanded, Noah built an ark and took his entire household and mating pairs of every living creature into the ark. (7:1-4)
—God covenanted with Noah and future generations that God would never again cause a flood to destroy all living creatures. (9:11-15)
—God gave the rainbow as a sign of that covenant. (9:16-17)

(NOTE: Use KJV Scripture for Adults; NRSV Scripture for Youth and Children)

TOPICAL OUTLINE OF THE LESSON

I. Introduction
   A. Man's Description of God
   B. Biblical Background

II. Exposition and Application of the Scripture
   A. God's Judgment Purpose (Genesis 6:5-7)
   B. God's Grace for Noah (Genesis 6:8)
   C. God's Judgment Flood (Genesis 7:1-4)
   D. God's Rainbow Promise (Genesis 9:12-17)

III. Special Features
   A. Preserving Our Heritage
   B. A Concluding Word

I. Introduction

A. MAN'S DESCRIPTION OF GOD

Our attention is drawn especially to Genesis 6:6: "And it repented the Lord that he had made man on the earth, and it grieved him at his heart." Note the two words, "repented," and "grieved." We have here what the theologians call words that are anthropomorphic and anthropopathic. You see the prefix, **anthropo.** This word means man. **Morphos** means form, shape. Together we have literally, "man-form." That which is anthropomorphic is man-formed. By it we mean we attribute human form or qualities to God. We see with our eyes; we know God sees, so we talk about the eyes of God. He also has hands (Ezra 7:6,9), a face (Numbers 6:25), fingers (Deuteronomy 9:10), back (Isaiah 38:17), etc.

The Hebrew word **(nacham)** for repent has a root which apparently contains the idea of "breathing deeply...drawing a deep breath" (Girdlestone), thus the physical display of deep feelings, usually sorrow, compassion, relief or comfort *(Theological Wordbook of the Old Testament)*. To say God repents means "he relents or changes his dealings with men according to His sovereign purposes." From our limited, earthly finite perspective, it only appears that God's purposes have changed. We must keep in mind that a change in human behavior brings about a change in divine judgment.

B. BIBLICAL BACKGROUND

A sovereign God has the right to judge that which He creates. Modern man seems not to accept this or appreciate it. Sin blinds us to sin's sinfulness and the fact that the wages of sin is death. The first judgment, of which little is known, is that of Lucifer who became Satan (Isaiah 14:12; Ezekiel 28:15), along with those angels who pledged him their allegiance. The second judgment is described in Genesis chapter 3, in what is called the Fall. Adam and Eve broke fellowship with God through disobedience and were expelled from the Garden. Prior to the Fall, Adam had both the ability to sin and the ability to not sin. As a result of the judgment upon sin, he lost the ability not to sin; he now has the inability not to sin.

A third judgment is seen in the punishment of Cain for murdering his brother, Abel. And now, today's lesson brings us to a fourth judgment—the Flood. Universal sin called for a universal flood, and only eight souls were saved. Man's wickedness is described as "great in the earth," and the inclination or his inner thoughts were evil all the time (Genesis 6:5). Christ described Noah's generation as one which was preoccupied with "eating and drinking, marrying and giving in marriage" (Matthew 24:37-38). By this description, our Lord emphasized how the people of Noah's day, though warned of the coming judgement, lived as if no such catastrophe would occur. And yet, we see the mercy and grace of God, for with such judgment God opens new doors, and we are given another chance. With judgment comes a new beginning.

II. Exposition and Application of the Scripture

A. GOD'S JUDGMENT PURPOSE
(Genesis 6:5-7)

And God saw that the wickedness of man was great in the earth, and that every imagination of the thoughts of his heart was only evil continually. And it repented the LORD that he had made man on the earth, and it grieved him at his heart. And the LORD said, I will destroy man whom I have created from the face of the earth; both man, and beast, and the creeping thing, and the fowls of the air; for it repenteth me that I have made them.

No evil escapes the notice of the all-seeing, all-knowing God of the Bible. The evil that He observes leaves Him no alternative but to react; His holy nature cannot do otherwise. In this brief span of time man inhabited the earth, that fallen nature inherited from fallen Adam ran "hog-wild." Sin gave man heart-trouble; man's diseased heart with its unlimited wicked designs or purposes pained the heart of God. Man's evil bent and deeds are highlighted and intensified by the words, "every...only...continually" (Genesis 6:5). We learn early that to claim there is some good in man is refuted by the Bible (Romans 7:18)

So grieved is God's heart at man's evil that He resolved to blot him out completely, "destroy" mankind—this is strong language. He was pained because His handiwork had been so ruined. This divine resolve from man's point of view makes it appear that God had changed His mind, and that now He was sorry He had made man. But God makes no mistakes. It is impossible for an omniscient God to regret His own actions. He does not change (Numbers 23:19); 1 Samuel 15:29; Zechariah 8:14). However, the language points to (again, from our point of view) a change in divine direction resulting from man's deeds. God cannot change His mind concerning wickedness. What looks like a change to us is God's holy reaction to our sin. As Chafer said: "God, though immutable, is not immobile." We repeat: The Lord's sorrow, in response to some change in man's conduct, does not indicate God changed His mind, but rather a different attitude on God's part in response. For want of a better term, God's readjustment to man's behavior is called by man an act of repentance.

B. GOD'S GRACE FOR NOAH
(Genesis 6:8)

But Noah found grace in the eyes of the LORD.

Here is the first time the word "grace" is found in the Bible, and we see love and mercy in action. This word for "grace" **(chen)** means favor, charm, etc. It signifies the condescending or unearned, undeserved, unmerited favor of a superior person to an inferior one—God to man. In mercy, rather than destroy man and beast, God would call out a remnant unto Himself. And so it was that Noah found grace in God's eyes. It is also said that Moses "found grace in the sight of the Lord" (Exodus 33:12). Noah was saved by grace. Out of all of the men on earth at that time, God showered His blessings down upon Noah. This was God's sovereign choice. Note the Lord's grace was not earned, but found. The threatened word of wrath of verse 7 becomes in verse 8 a reprieve for the human race. And God's grace to Noah became one cause of his being designated as righteous before God and his contemporaries. The divine choice was another step in God's purpose of redemption.

C. GOD'S JUDGMENT FLOOD
(Genesis 7:1-4)

AND the LORD said unto Noah, Come thou and all thy house into the ark; for thee have I seen righteous before me in this generation. Of every clean beast thou shalt take to thee by sevens, the male and his female: and of beasts that are not clean by two, the male and his female. Of fowls also of the air by sevens, the male and the female; to keep seed alive upon the face of all the earth. For yet seven days, and I will cause it to rain upon the earth forty days and forty nights and every living substance that I have made will I destroy from off the face of the earth.

The invitation to "come" is heard in the Bible for the first time. It will not be the last. In later history, God invited Moses to come up to Him into Mount Sinai (Exodus 24:12). In Isaiah, Jehovah invited Judah to come and reason together (1:18); and the unsaved were invited to come to the waters (55.1). "Come and see" was Christ's call to discipleship (John 1:39). To the first disciples came the call to service by Christ, who said, "Come after me, and I will make you become fishers of men" (Mark 1:17). "Come aside into a desert place, and rest a while" was His invitation to the apostles when they returned from their first preaching tour (Mark 6:31). The Lord Jesus invites all who labor and are heavy laden to come to Him and receive rest (Matthew 14:29). Finally, the Bible's last invitation: "And the Spirit and the bride say, Come. And let him that heareth say, Come. And let him that is athirst come" (Revelation 22:17). And so at the invitation of God, Noah's family entered the ark—saved by the righteousness of the head of the household—and yet there had to be on their part obedience to the divine call. God always desires to save whole families. We see this regarding the Philippian jailer, for he believed "in God with all his house" (Acts 16:34).

As for the animals taken into the ark, some are designated clean, others unclean; this distinction did not originate with Moses. "Sevens" means three pairs and an additional one (probably a male) for an offering of the animals designated as "clean." Thus "clean" means they were fit for sacrifice (Genesis 8:20), and later, after the Flood, to be eaten as food by humans.

We believe the flood was universal, not local. God promised to "rub out" the entire established order of things from off the face of the earth. His desire to "keep seed alive" makes sense only if the flood was indeed universal. A local flood would not need an ark as large as the one Noah built. Furthermore, Noah could have simply moved to a safer area. Rain for forty days and forty nights, plus water breaking forth from beneath the earth—all point to a universal flood. So that only eight souls were saved.

D. GOD'S RAINBOW PROMISE
(Genesis 9:12-17)

And God said, This is the token of the covenant which I make between me and you and every living creature that is with you, for perpetual generations: I do set my bow in the cloud, and it shall be for a token of a covenant between me and the earth. And it shall come to pass, when I bring a cloud over the earth, that the bow shall be seen in the cloud: And I will remember my covenant, which is between me and you and every living creature of all flesh; and the waters shall no more become a flood to destroy all flesh. And the bow shall be in the cloud; and I will look upon it, that I may remember the everlasting covenant between God and every living creature of all flesh that is upon the earth. And God said unto Noah, This is the token of the covenant, which I have established between me and all flesh that is upon the earth.

Here we learn that the rainbow was the guarantee God gave that He would never again flood the entire earth with a deluge of water. There are those who see the rainbow only as a natural phenomenon, one produced by the refraction of the rays of light from the drops of water which fall in a shower. But "the heavens declare the glory of God; and the firmament showeth His handiwork" (Psalm 19:1). Thus, the rainbow speaks of God's greatness, majesty and power. It was to be a constant reminder of Jehovah's sacred agreement that the earth would never again be devastated by a universal flood. More than likely, the rainbow existed already, though God could have created one that moment. God used this natural phenomenon as a sign or token, guaranteeing and giving assurance of His continued mercy and grace.

As the flood teaches us that a Holy God will not tolerate sin, but will certainly judge it, so the rainbow teaches us that He is a God of love, a God of the Second Chance. We are reminded that the rainbow arises from the conjunction of sun and storm, so here is a picture of mercy and judgment. Representing grace, the rainbow is set in the cloud, while the cloud represents judgment. He does not promise that a rainbow will be seen after every storm or in every cloud, but that when it is seen, God will remember His covenant. The rainbow speaks to us of the power, perfection, purpose and promises of God. We are assured that the Lord will fulfill every promise He has ever made. Indeed, for the one cleansed in the blood of Jesus Christ, rainbows are visible.

III. Special Features

A. PRESERVING OUR HERITAGE

Black American slaves were very sensitive to the world of nature, and this sensitivity is reflected in the spirituals. Of course, the sun took preeminence among the heavenly bodies, but mention is made also of the moon, stars, the sea, rivers (especially Jordan), clouds, thunder, lightning, etc. Now the rainbow was a great favorite. The Black poets borrowed from Noah's experience. Basically, Noah spoke of judgment; he symbolized deliverance, and example of the workings of faith and divine power. Because Noah found grace in the eyes of the Lord (Genesis 6:8), slaves saw him as the commander of the ark by virtue of his goodness. The best ark song, states Lovell, is "The Old Ark's A-Movering." Noah is mentioned in: "They Called Old Noah a Foolish Man."

Belief that God would eventually straighten things out gave the slaves great satisfaction, and helped them endure the evils of slavery. See then in the midst of the story of Noah and the ark a picture of Judgment Day. Our heritage demands that we not forget that "God's Going to Set This World on Fire" *(Spirituals Triumphant,* number 4, Sunday School Publishing Board). Indeed, thank God because of Christ there is no condemnation, and through Him, we shall escape "the fire nex' time." *(Black Song:* Lovell, pp. 247, 255, 259, 266, 379).

B. A CONCLUDING WORD

The lesson closes with Genesis 9:16-17. Here we are told that the rainbow will remind God of the everlasting covenant made between Him and Noah, along with every living creature. Animals share in man's doom and deliverance, thus indicating that all life is bound together (Romans 8:19-21). This is called the Noahic Covenant. It is unconditional, that is to say, it will be fulfilled regardless of what men may do. The initiative is with God; Noah is not represented as doing anything in the matter. He does not seek to establish the covenant, he does not decide what his covenant obligations are.

H. M. Morris suggests the covenant was made with Noah as a representative man rather than as an individual. The blessings of God freely bestowed upon His servants are not granted in return for services rendered. The following are the basic elements of the Noahic covenant: (1) There will be no more universal flood. The rainbow sign of God's promise is given; (2) Repopulate the earth. Man is responsible for protecting the sacredness of life which murder and suicide violate; (3) Human government established; (4) Men are no longer vegetarian or herbivorous only; (5) Prophetic declarations are made concerning Noah's sons: Ham, Japheth, and then Shem from whom Christ descended.

HOME DAILY BIBLE READING
Week of June 27, 1999
Judgment and New Beginning

June 21 M. Genesis 6:5-22 The Earth Was Corrupt In God's Sight
June 22 T. Genesis 7:1-16 You Alone Are Righteous Before Me
June 23 W. Genesis 7:17—8:5 God Remembered Noah
June 24 T. Genesis 8:6-22 The Waters Were Dried Up From the Earth
June 25 F. Genesis 9:1-7 God Blessed Noah and His Sons
June 26 S. Genesis 9:8-17 God Made A Covenant With Noah
June 27 S. Genesis 9:18-28 Noah Pronounces a Curse

God's Call To Abram

Unit II. The Beginnings of a People
Children's Unit—God Chose and Called a People—Part I
Adult Topic—Adventure in Faith

.....

Youth Topic—Adventure in Faith
Children's Topic—God Called Abraham

.....

Devotional Reading—Hebrews 11:8-12
Background Scripture—Genesis 11:27—12:9
Print—Genesis 11:31—12:9

● ● ● ● ● ● ● ● ● ○ ○ ○ ○

SCRIPTURE PRINT

Genesis 11:31—12:9 (KJV)

31 And Terah took Abram his son, and Lot the son of Haran his son's son, and Sarai his daughter in law, his son Abram's wife; and they went forth with them from Ur of the Chaldees, to go into the land of Canaan; and they came unto Haran, and dwelt there.

32 And the days of Terah were two hundred and five years: and Terah died in Haran.

.....

NOW the LORD had said unto Abram, Get thee out of thy country, and from thy kindred, and from thy father's house, unto a land that I will shew thee:

2 And I will make of thee a great nation, and I will bless thee, and make thy name great; and thou shalt be a blessing:

3 And I will bless them that bless thee, and curse him that curesth thee: and in thee shall all families

Genesis 11:31—12:9 (NRSV)

31 Terah took his son Abram and his grandson Lot son of Haran, and his daughter-in-law Sarai, his son Abram's wife, and they went out together from Ur of the Chaldeans to go into the land of Canaan; but when they came to Haran, they settled there.

32 The days of Terah were two hundred five years; and Terah died in Haran.

.....

NOW THE LORD said to Abram, "Go from your country and your kindred and your father's house to the land that I will show you.

2 I will make of you a great nation, and I will bless you, and make your name great, so that you will be a blessing.

3 I will bless those who bless you, and the one who curses you I will curse; and in you all the families of

of the earth be blessed.

4 So Abram departed, as the LORD had spoken unto him; and Lot went with him: and Abram was seventy and five years old when he departed out of Haran.

5 And Abram took Sarai his wife, and Lot his brother's son, and all their substance that they had gathered, and the souls that they had gotten in Haran; and they went forth to go into the land of Canaan; and into the land of Canaan they came.

6 And Abram passed through the land unto the place of Sichem, unto the plain of Moreh. And the Canaanite was then in the land.

7 And the LORD appeared unto Abram, and said, Unto thy seed will I give this land: and there builded he an altar unto the LORD, who appeared unto him.

8 And he removed from thence unto a mountain on the east of Bethel, and pitched his tent, having Bethel on the west, and Hai on the east: and there he builded an altar unto the LORD, and called upon the name of the LORD.

9 And Abram journeyed, going on still toward the south.

the earth shall be blessed."

4 So Abram went, as the LORD had told him; and Lot went with him. Abram was seventy-five years old when he departed from Haran.

5 Abram took his wife Sarai and his brother's son Lot, and all the possessions that they had gathered, and the persons whom they had acquired in Haran; and they set forth to go to the land of Canaan. When they had come to the land of Canaan,

6 Abram passed through the land to the place at Shechem, to the oak of Moreh. At that time the Canaanites were in the land.

7 Then the LORD appeared to Abram, and said, "To your offspring I will give this land." So he built there an altar to the LORD, who had appeared to him.

8 From there he moved on to the hill country on the east of Bethel, and pitched his tent, with Bethel on the west and Ai on the east; and there he built an altar to the LORD and invoked the name of the LORD.

9 And Abram journeyed on by stages toward the Negeb.

KEY VERSE

NOW the LORD had said unto Abram, Get thee out of thy country, and from thy kindred, and from thy father's house, unto a land that I will shew thee: And I will make of thee a great nation, and I will bless thee, and make thy name great; and thou shalt be a blessing.—Genesis 12:1-2

OBJECTIVES

After reading this lesson, the student should remember that:

1. Abram and his parents were called out of paganism;
2. By faith Abram left home not knowing where he was going;

3. God promised Abram he would become a great nation; and,
4. Abram honored God upon reaching Canaan.

POINTS TO BE EMPHASIZED

Adult/Youth/Children

Key Verse: Genesis 12:1-2

Print: Genesis 11:31—12:9; Genesis 12:1-9 (Children)

—Terah took his son Abram, daughter-in-law Sarai, and grandson Lot from Ur to the land of Haran. (11:31-32)

—God told Abram to leave his home and journey to an unknown land which God would show him. (12:1)

—God promised Abram that he would become a great nation; through Abram all people on the earth would be blessed. (12:2-3)

—Abram obeyed God and moved his wife, his nephew Lot, and his possessions to Canaan. (12:4-6)

—When Abram and his family reached Canaan, Abram built altars to honor God. (12:7-9)

(Note: Use KJV Scripture for Adults; NRSV Scripture for Youth and Children)

TOPICAL OUTLINE OF THE LESSON

I. Introduction

A. The Place of Abraham in Bible History

B. Biblical Background

II. Exposition and Application of the Scripture

A. Years Spent at Haran (Genesis 11:31-32)

B. God's Call and Promise (Genesis 12:1-3)

C. Abram's Obedience (Genesis 12:4-6)

D. Abram's Worship (Genesis 12:7-9)

III. Special Features

A. Preserving Our Heritage

B. A Concluding Word

I. Introduction

A. THE PLACE OF ABRAHAM IN BIBLE HISTORY

Abraham is one of the most important characters in the Bible. His name, whether Abram or Abraham, is mentioned in 27 Books of the Bible (16 Old Testament, 11 New Testament), and occurs over 300 times, with more than 70 of these found in the New Testament. He was the first of the men we commonly designate as Patriarchs. And as we shall see in future lessons, Abraham was the father of Isaac as well as of Ishmael, so that he is at once the forefather or progenitor of the Jews and Arabs. From information presently available to us, it is believed that Abraham lived in one of the most prosperous times in the history of Mesopotamia. We should then regard him as more than an ignorant, untutored shepherd. It was with pride that the Jews traced their origin to Abraham, and honored him as their father (John 8:39).

Paul held him up as an ideal example of true faith (Galatians 3:6). And we cannot forget that Abraham is called "the Friend of God" (James 2:23; 2 Chronicles 20:7; Isaiah 41:8). Keep in mind also the fact that God is often called, "the God of Abraham." In the New Testament, there is an astonishing wealth and variety of allusion to Abraham (ISBE). He truly played a significant role throughout the Scriptures, and our lives are enriched by the study of his life.

B. BIBLICAL BACKGROUND

One of the amazing things about the life of Abraham is the fact that he was called out of paganism! Archaeologists working in Mesopotamia have discovered that the city of Ur was dominated by a huge pagan temple dedicated to the Moon deity called **Nannar.** These shrines were called "ziggurats." They were terrace towers built for worship of pagan deities. It is believed the sign of the zodiac was on the top, indicating they practiced astrology, which was abomination to God (Deuteronomy 18:10).

Recall that the Tower of Babel (Genesis 11:4) was one of the biggest of these Babylonian "ziggurats." It was in the midst of such heathen surroundings that Abram suddenly heard the voice of God. Finally, on this matter, read Joshua 24:2, where it is said of Abraham's family that they served other gods.

II. Exposition and Application of the Scripture

A. YEARS SPENT AT HARAN
(Genesis 11:31-32)

And Terah took Abram his son, and Lot the son of Haran his son's son, and Sarai his daughter in law, his son Abram's wife; and they went forth with them from Ur of the Chaldees; and they came unto Haran, and dwelt there. And the days of Terah were two hundred and five years: and Terah died in Haran.

In verse 31, the family that went forth included Terah, his Son Abram and Abram's wife, Sarah; and Lot, Terah's grandson. Haran, the son of Terah and father of Lot had died. Genesis 11:28 states Haran died before his father Terah. This means "in the face of," so that we understand Terah was still alive when his son died. So these four (Terah, Abram, Sarai, Lot) left Ur of the Chaldees to go into the land of Canaan. It is believed that God called Terah, as well as Abram. Terah, as patriarchal head of the family, led the expedition to the city of Haran (named after Terah's son). However, when they arrived at Haran, Terah remained there. It is possible that he became involved again in the idolatry practiced there (Morris). Terah died in Haran at the age of two hundred and five years.

Genesis 11:31 is not to be seen as a command, but as a reference to the Lord's ultimate purpose for Abram. Because the first call came to him while in Ur of the Chaldees, according to Acts 7:2 and Genesis 15:7, the fact is that Abram did not know where the Lord wanted him to go. It was to a land that God would show him, so that at this point it was neither named nor described. Thus the stay in Haran was not a result of disobedience as suggested by some scholars.

The problem we have with the timing here is because Stephen's sermon in his account in Acts does not give facts in exact chronological order, but in the order in which they were narrated in Genesis. It is important to remember this as we further study the matter. In his account, Stephen seems to imply that Abraham did not leave Haran until his father, Terah, had died. We read: "Then came he out of the land of the Chaldeans, and dwelt in Haran; and from there, when his father was dead, he removed him into this land, in which ye now dwell" (Acts 7:4). Actually, Abram left Haran when his father was 145 years old.

Go over this carefully. Here are the definite facts taught in Genesis 11:26, 31-32, and 12:4. (1) Terah was 70 years old when Abram was born; (2) Abram left Haran when he was 75. This means that he left his father Terah when the father was 145 years old: (3) Terah lived to be 205 years old; (4) If Abram left Haran when his father was 145, this is to say, 70 plus 75, it means Terah spent another 60 years in Haran after Abram left. This would give us a total of 135 years spent in Haran by Terah.

But now in Acts 7, Stephen gives no ages. The words in Acts 7:4, taken literally, would mean Abram did not leave until Terah died at the age of 205. If you subtract Abram's age of 75 from the 205, you have Terah becoming Abram's father at the age of 130. This cannot be, since we are told Terah was only 70 when Abram was born. What then is the answer? Several hypotheses have been offered.

One: Accept the Samaritan text which makes Terah 145 at death, rather than 205. This is an unacceptable alteration made in the attempt to remove the apparent inconsistency. **Two:** Usually, the first named is the firstborn. But this second hypothesis does not consider the order of names in Genesis 11:26 as chronological. It makes Abram the youngest boy, suggesting Abram could have been born 60 years after the oldest boy, but states Abram is put first in the list because of his prominence. However, this idea is not acceptable either, considering the special miracle required to have Abram himself become a father at the age of 100 (Genesis 17:1, 17; Romans 4:17-21; Hebrews 11:11-12).

Three: Spiritualize the word "dead" in Acts 7:4. This is what H. C. Leupold and also H. M. Morris have done, teaching that Abram considered his father, Terah, "dead" spiritually because Terah supposedly relapsed into idolatry there at Haran. Lenski says this view is "without foundation." R. J. Knowling *(Expositor's Greek Testament)* also states there is "absolutely no justification in the context for making this refer to the spiritual death of Terah." **Four:** Here then is what I believe is the correct interpretation. Stephen followed the order presented in

Genesis. There you see mention is made of Terah's death before mention is made of Abram's leaving Haran. In other words, the fact in Genesis 11:32 is put before the fact in Genesis 12:4. And in his preaching, Stephen put the statements of Terah's death and Abram's leaving Haran in the same order. We see that Terah's death is anticipatory (Alford). And we have no solid basis for rejecting the inerrant Word of God.

B. GOD'S CALL AND PROMISE
(Genesis 12:1-3)

Now the LORD had said unto Abram, Get thee out of thy country, and from thy kindred, and from thy father's house unto a land that I will shew thee: And I will make of thee a great nation, and I will bless thee, and make thy name great; and thou shalt be a blessing: And I will bless them that bless thee, and curse him that curseth thee: and in thee shall all families of the earth be blessed.

First, note the Divine Call. The words "had said" indicate God spoke to Abram before he left Ur of the Chaldees. He was ordered to leave his country, relatives, and friends. Second, see the Divine Direction. He is told to head for a land that the Lord would show him. Third, see the Divine Promises. (1) God will make of Abram a great nation. This is more than in numbers, but includes greatness in every sense of the word; and it has to do primarily with Israel; (2) God will bless Abram, temporally and spiritually; (3) and make Abram's name great. He is to be made famous, the father of a multitude, a prince of God, a prophet, servant of God, friend of God, etc.

(4) Abram will be a blessing to others. (5) Then there are promises of blessings to the Gentiles; (6) and curses; (7) and finally, all families of the earth shall be blessed; this is fulfilled in Abraham's Seed, the Lord Jesus Christ. Only through Jesus Christ could this great blessing be achieved. In this promise then we see the Messiah, coming from the line of Abraham. Or as the writer in Hebrews 2:16 put it, "For verily he took not on him the nature of angels, but he took on him the seed of Abraham."

C. ABRAM'S OBEDIENCE
(Genesis 12:4-6)

So Abram departed, as the LORD had spoken unto him; and Lot went with him: and Abram was seventy and five years old when he departed out of Haran. And Abram took Sarai his wife, and Lot his brother's son, and all their substance that they had gathered, and the souls that they had gotten in Haran; and they went forth to go into the land of Canaan; and into the land of Canaan they came. And Abram passed through the land unto the place of Sichem, unto the plain of Moreh. And the Canaanite was then in the land.

We now see that what God commanded, Abram obeyed. He was seventy-five years old—a middle-aged man in those days—when he and his nephew, Lot, left the city of Haran. It was just as well they left, for there was no history recorded of all the days spent in that city. Abram took with him his wife, Sarai also, along with the goods and servants (souls: **nephesh)** he had gathered during his stay in Haran. God had blessed him materially, even as He had promised. And Abram left the city a wealthy man.

And so Abram and his entourage went forth and came into the land of Canaan. There Abram passed through the land unto the place of Shechem, one of the oldest cities in Palestine. They came unto the oak of Moreh. The word rendered "oak" is also translated **terebinth,** a tree of the cashew family, a source of crude turpentine. It was probably a well-known place used by religious teachers and their students. Note the mention of the fact that the "Canaanite was then in the land." This fact increases our awareness of the enormity of the promise made to Abram. To take over this territory would mean eliminating the present inhabitants. However, it appears that Abram's faith is not daunted by this apparent future difficulty.

D. ABRAM'S WORSHIP
(Genesis 12:7-9)

And the LORD appeared unto Abram, and said, Unto thy seed will I give this land: and there builded he an altar unto the LORD, who appeared unto him. And he removed from thence unto a mountain on the east of Bethel, and pitched his tent, having Bethel on the west, and Hai on the east: and there he builded an altar unto the LORD, and called upon the name of the LORD. And Abram journeyed, going on still toward the south.

With the words "the Lord appeared," we learn of that which is called a **theophany,** literally, a "God-appearing." Twice the same Hebrew word is translated "appeared" in verse seven. We have here the first mention of an actual appearance of God to man. It is a pre-incarnate appearance of the Lord Jesus Christ. Once again, God reassured Abram that his descendants will indeed possess Canaan. For the first time, it is announced that God will "give" the land of Palestine to His people Israel. This gift is unconditional.

Abram built an altar there to the Lord in thanksgiving. God's appearance had sanctified the ground, and now Abram built a place for worship there. The altar also had the effect of stressing the grace and undeserved mercy of the divine promise. **Bethel,** which means "House of God," was one of the sacred places of Canaan. An ancient city, it is mentioned more often than any other except Jerusalem. Abram pitched his tent between Bethel on the west, and Hai on the east. Once again, he erected an altar, proclaiming again his loyalty to the Lord. As he did at Shechem, so now at Bethel. By pitching his tent there, he let it be known publicly that he was taking permanent possession of the land. He then continued his journey. In verse nine, the word "journeyed" means to pull up stakes, pluck up tent pins. Thus Abram migrated in nomadic fashion to the **Negeb** or **Negev.** The transliterated Hebrew word means dry. Since the region was arid most of the year, and lay south of the larger part of Israel, the word came to mean south.

III. Special Features

A. PRESERVING OUR HERITAGE

Abram and his parents were pagans. And by the grace of God, Abram was called out of darkness into the light. The people at Ephesus were pagans—intelligent, but still heathen. In fact, Paul describes them as "without Christ, being aliens from the commonwealth of Israel, and strangers from the covenants of promise, having no hope, and without God in the world" (Ephesians 2;12). In the same manner, our foreparents on the Dark Continent were pagans. For all sinned and are falling short of God's glory. By the grace of God, slaves were brought here to America. Some heard the Gospel of Jesus Christ and were saved. For the Christ who died on Calvary is no respecter of faces or races.

But see in what happened to Abram a picture of what happened to our race. Abram was called out of idolatry by God. We were captured and enslaved out of idolatry. God appeared to Abram and guided him. We were introduced to Christ and many accepted His guidance. God blessed Abraham. He has also blessed us. Abraham became a blessing to others. America has been blessed by our Black presence—in the arts, athletics, religion, inventions, the fight for democracy, and as a pricking of the moral conscience of America.

B. A CONCLUDING WORD

All who have allowed their hatred to move them to anti-Semitism and persecution of the Jewish people have invariably suffered for it. God promised to curse them that curse Abram and his descendants. Men often misinterpret Matthew 25:40 because they fail to consider the word "brother" there. These "brethren" are Jews, and the entire passage has to do with the judgment of individual Gentiles and their treatment of the Jewish people during the Tribulation era. On the other hand, it will go well with those who bless Israel. One of the dire dangers of Blacks becoming anti-semitic is seen in Genesis 12:3. Anti-Semitism brings inevitable divine judgment. Haman found this out. Hitler also discovered the truth of God's Word concerning the Jewish people.

HOME DAILY BIBLE READING
Week of July 4, 1999
God's Call to Abram

June 28 M. Genesis 11:27-32 Abram and Lot Settle In Ur
June 29 T. Genesis 12:1-9 God Calls Abram
June 30 W. Acts 7:1-8 Stephen Recounts Abram's History
July 1 T. 1 Samuel 3:1-10 God Calls Samuel
July 2 F. Amos 7:10-15 God Calls Amos
July 3 S. Acts 9:1-9 God Calls Saul
July 4 S. Mark 1:16-20 Jesus Calls Disciples

A Promise Fulfilled

Adult Topic—Surprising Promises

.....

Youth Topic—Surprising Promises
Children's Topic—Isaac Was Born

.....

Devotional Reading—Deuteronomy 7:7-11
Background Scripture—Genesis 15:1—18:15; 21:1-7
Print—Genesis 15:1-6; 17:17-21; 21:1-2

• • • • • • • • • • •

PRINTED SCRIPTURE

Genesis 15:1-6; 17:17-21; 21:1-2 (KJV)

AFTER these things the word of the LORD came unto Abram in a vision, saying, Fear not, Abram: I am thy shield, and thy exceeding great reward.

2 And Abram said, Lord GOD, what wilt thou give me, seeing I go childless, and the steward of my house is this Eliezer of Damascus?

3 And Abram said, Behold, to me thou hast given no seed: and, lo, one born in my house is mine heir.

4 And, behold, the word of the LORD came unto him, saying, This shall not be thine heir; but he that shall come forth out of thine own bowels shall be thine heir.

5 And he brought him forth abroad, and said, Look now toward heaven, and tell the stars, if thou be able to number them: and he said unto him, So shall thy seed be.

6 And he believed in the LORD; and he counted it to him for righteousness.

Genesis 15:1-6; 17:17-21; 21:1-2 (NRSV)

AFTER these things the word of the LORD came to Abram in a vision, "Do not be afraid, Abram, I am your shield; your reward shall be very great."

2 But Abram said, "O Lord GOD, what will you give me, for I continue childless, and the heir of my house is Eliezer of Damascus?"

3 And Abram said, "You have given me no offspring, and so a slave born in my house is to be my heir."

4 But the word of the LORD came to him, "This man shall not be your heir; no one but your very own issue shall be your heir."

5 He brought him outside and said, "Look toward heaven and count the stars, if you are able to count them." Then he said to him, "So shall your descendants be."

6 And he believed the LORD; and the LORD reckoned it to him as righteousness.

.....

17 Then Abraham fell upon his face, and laughed, and said in his heart, Shall a child be born unto him that is an hundred years old? and shall Sarah, that is ninety years old, bear?

18 And Abraham said unto God, O that Ishmael might live before thee!

19 And God said, Sarah thy wife shall bear thee a son indeed; and thou shalt call his name Isaac: and I will establish my covenant with him for an everlasting covenant, and with his seed after him.

20 And as for Ishmael, I have heard thee: Behold, I have blessed him, and will make him fruitful, and will multiply him exceedingly; twelve princes shall he beget, and I will make him a great nation.

21 But my covenant will I establish with Isaac, which Sarah shall bear unto thee at this set time in the next year.

.....

AND the LORD visited Sarah as he had said, and the LORD did unto Sarah as he had spoken.

2 For Sarah conceived, and bare Abraham a son in his old age, at the set time of which God had spoken to him.

.....

17 Then Abraham fell on his face and laughed, and said to himself, "Can a child be born to a man who is a hundred years old? Can Sarah, who is ninety years old, bear a child?"

18 And Abraham said to God, "O that Ishmael might live in your sight!"

19 God said, "No, but your wife Sarah shall bear you a son, and you shall name him Isaac. I will establish my covenant with him as an everlasting covenant for his offspring after him.

20 As for Ishmael, I have heard you; I will bless him and make him fruitful and exceedingly numerous; he shall be the father of twelve princes, and I will make him a great nation.

21 But my covenant I will establish with Isaac, whom Sarah shall bear to you at this season next year."

.....

THE LORD dealt with Sarah as he had said, and the LORD did for Sarah as he had promised.

2 Sarah conceived and bore Abraham a son in his old age, at the time of which God had spoken to him.

KEY VERSE

And God said, Sarah thy wife shall bear thee a son indeed; and thou shalt call his name Isaac: and I will establish my covenant with him for an everlasting covenant, and with his seed after him.— Genesis 17:19

OBJECTIVE

After reading this lesson, the student should know more about:

1. The role of Abraham in God's plan;

2. The nature of God's promises;
3. Our proper response to divine promises; and,
4. The God of the Bible who fulfills His promises.

POINTS TO BE EMPHASIZED

Adult/Youth/Children
Key Verse: Genesis 17:19
Print: Genesis 15:1-6; 17:17-21; 21:1-2

— Abram questioned God's promise that he would become a great nation, for he was old and childless. (15:1-3)
—God assured Abram that he would have an heir and his descendants would be as numerous as the stars in the sky. (15:4-5)
—Abram laughed at God's promise because of his and Sarai's age and pleaded for Ishmael to receive God's covenant promises. (17:17-18)
—God declared that His covenant would be with the promised son, Isaac. (17:19-21)
—The promise was kept and Sarah bore a son whom they named Isaac. (21:17-21)

(NOTE: Use KJV Scripture for Adults; NRSV Scripture for Youth and Children)

TOPICAL OUTLINE OF THE LESSON

I. Introduction

  A. The Promises of God
  B. Biblical Background

II. Exposition and Application of the Scripture

  A. Promise: A Spiritual Seed (Genesis 15:1-6)
  B. Promises: Concerning Isaac and Ishmael (Genesis 17:17-21)
  C. Promise Fulfilled: Isaac Born (Genesis 21:1-2)

III. Special Features

  A. Preserving Our Heritage
  B. A Concluding Word

I. Introduction

A. THE PROMISES OF GOD

It is estimated that there are approximately 30,000 promises in the Scriptures, although the word "promise" is not always used in connection with those so designated. With such numbers, you can see why John Bunyan wrote: "The pathway of life is strewn so thickly with the promises of God that it is impossible to take one step without treading upon one of them."

Promises made by God are put into two categories: absolute and conditional. If absolute, they are fulfilled literally. If conditional, then their fulfillment depends upon the obedience or repentance of those involved in the promise. In the Old Testament, we find the following outstanding promises: (1) "The First Gospel" **(protevangelium),** the promise of the Messiah, Genesis 3:16; (2) Promise to never again curse the ground and flood the entire earth, Genesis 8:21; 9:11, 15; (3) Promise to make of Abraham a great nation in whom all families of the earth should be blessed, and to give the land of Canaan to him, and his seed, Genesis 12:2, 7.

Today's lesson involves this promise, and indeed is tied in with what is called the Dispensation of Promise; (4) the promise to David that his house would continue to sit on the throne, 2 Samuel 7:12, 13, 28. These and many more promises are found in the Old Testament. In the New Testament, promises are founded on Jesus Christ, and have their fulfillment in Him.

The apostle Paul argued that the promise Abram would be made "heir of the world" is not confined to Israel, but belongs to all who are children of Abraham by faith (Romans 4:13; Galatians 3:16, 29). God is true to His Word, faithful to Himself. Not a single one of the good and precious promises which the Lord made to Israel or to the Church has failed or will fail (Joshua 21:45; 2 Peter 1:4). His Word is truth.

B. BIBLICAL BACKGROUND

It is believed by some scholars that the words "after these things" in Genesis 15:1 refer directly to the events of chapter 14. Upon returning from the victory over the confederated kings (Genesis 14:1-17), and recapturing his nephew Lot, Abram received Melchizedek, king of Salem. Evidently strengthened by this fellowship with Melchizedek, Abram refused the spoils offered him by the king of Sodom. Perhaps later, Abram entertained fears and doubts about his uncompromising refusal of help, wondering if he thereby had made new enemies.

Would the defeated monarchs seek retaliation? There are those who maintain that the phrase "after these things" refers to the events of battle, meeting with Melchizedek, and refusing the offer of Bera, king of Sodom. Though he had refused the spoil or booty, the Lord would not allow Abram to be the loser. God would be his protection and his reward. Leupold does not believe Abram feared any such retribution from the defeated Eastern king, but that Abram feared remaining childless, and this fear of childlessness is the thing that caused Abram's restlessness and consternation. Skinner (ICC) suggests that while we presuppose a situation of anxiety on the part of Abram, we cannot with any certainty determine what caused Abram's fear. He calls "far-fetched and misleading" any attempts to establish a connection with the events of chapter 14. Keep in mind that the time gap between chapters 14 and 15 could be of such length as to make acceptable the idea that by now Abram's mind had returned to the fact that he was childless.

II. Exposition and Application of the Scripture

A. PROMISE: A SPIRITUAL SEED
(Genesis 15:1-6)

AFTER these things the word of the LORD came unto Abram in a vision, saying, Fear not, Abram: I am thy shield, and thy exceeding great reward. And Abram said, Lord God, what wilt thou give me, seeing I go childless, and the steward of my house is this Eliezer of Damascus? And Abram said, Behold, to me thou hast given no seed: and, lo, one born in my house is mine heir. And, behold, the word of the LORD came unto him, saying; This shall not be thine heir; but he that shall come forth out of thine own bowels shall be thine heir. And he brought him forth abroad, and said, Look now toward heaven, and tell the stars, if thou be able to number them: and he said unto him, So shall thy seed be. And he believed in the LORD; and he counted it to him for righteousness.

Whatever the cause for Abram's fear, which the Lord detected, God would also provide the cure. He came to Abram in a vision (Abram was awake, not asleep as in a dream), and commanded, "Fear not!" Why not? For at least three reasons. First, because God ordered it. Second, because He was Abram's shield. This meant He would protect him from all enemies. Third, because He was Abram's reward, an "exceedingly great" one at that! Thus God intervened with a vision at night to cheer His servant with words of comfort and promise.

But to the childless Abram, what good is wealth? Not even protection is enough. "Lord God, I have no children." As was the custom at the time, a servant could become the inheritor of the house. By law, Eliezer the Damascene would be the representative, "the son of the house," the heir of Abram. From Abram's point of view, to die childless and have one's name put out was a fate so terrible that not even God's assurance of fellowship and reward could bring joy. The words, "what wilt Thou give me" remind us that God first spoke to Abram in Genesis 12:2, and promised then: "I will make of thee a great nation...." This took place when Abram was seventy-five years old (Genesis 12:4). And in Genesis 13:16, the Lord again promised, "I will make thy seed as the dust of the earth...." Now, he is nearly eighty-five—and no children! And so the Lord let Abram know that it was not His plan to so use Eliezer. In Genesis 15:5, Abram's eyes were taken from the ground and directed to heaven. He of course could not count all the stars. The human eye is a remarkable instrument, capable of seeing perhaps some 6,000 stars on a clear night, and able to see a bright heavenly body some six trillion miles away. Beyond that, a telescope is needed, enabling men to see stars too numerous to count.

But to talk of billions of stars when at this point there was not even one child! Yet God said, "So shall thy seed be." With verse 6, we have one of the most important verses in the Bible. Abram took God at His Word. He believed God. He did not "stagger at the promise of God through unbelief, but was strong in faith, giving glory to God, and being fully persuaded that, what He had promised, He was able also to perform" (Romans 4:20-21). And God put righteousness (not works) to his credit. When Abram took God at His Word, He provided the means whereby righteousness might be attained. God put to Abram's credit the righteousness of Jesus Christ.

Abram acquired righteousness through his unconditional trust in the Lord. He had faith in God's promise and readily obeyed God's Word. Righteousness here is not an inherent moral characteristic; it is here a right relation to God. The apostle Paul quoted this Scripture twice: Romans 4:3; Galatians 3:6. James cited it also (James 2:23). In each quote, we find that Abraham is given as a type of all who are saved, and we are reminded that salvation is through faith, which is by grace, unto righteousness.

B. PROMISES: CONCERNING ISAAC AND ISHMAEL
(Genesis 17:17-21)

Then Abraham fell upon his face, and laughed, and said in his heart, Shall a child be born unto him that is an hundred years old? and shall Sarah, that is ninety years old, bear? And Abraham said unto God, O that Ishmael might live before thee! And God said, Sarah thy wife shall bear thee a son indeed; and thou shalt call his name Isaac: and I will establish my convenant with him for an everlasting covenant, and with his seed after him. And as for Ishmael, I have heard thee: Behold, I have blessed him, and will make him fruitful, and will multiply him exceedingly; twelve princes shall he beget, and I will make him a great nation. But my covenant will I establish with Isaac, which Sarah shall bear unto thee at this set time in the next year.

Now soon after the encounter recorded in Chapter 15, Abram's faith wavered, and he foolishly followed his wife's advice. Sarah, without child, and feeling it a disgrace and embarrassment not to have a child, suggested to her husband that he take Hagar (Egyptian slave girl) for a wife. Hagar became pregnant and gave birth to Ishmael. Sarah's attempt to "push God" failed. And once again, we find the Lord assuring Abraham that Sarah would indeed be a mother. Upon hearing that his wife would "be a mother of nations," and "kings of people shall be of her" (Genesis 17:17), Abraham laughed.

Both God and men laugh. However, God's laughter in Psalms 2:4, 37:13, and 59:8, describes His derision or scorn directed at the nations; His laughter is against the wicked. As for the laughter of men, it may be negative or positive. Negatively, there is that laughter which is a scorning, deriding, or mockery. Most of the Scriptures dealing with laughter have to do with this aspect (Job 12:4; 2 Chronicles 30:10; Nehemiah 2:19, etc.). In the New Testament, we read of those who laughed in scorn at the Lord Jesus (predicted, Psalm 22:7), when He stated the daughter of the synagogue ruler was "not dead, but sleeps" (Matthew 9:24). He became their laughing-stock, their butt of mockery. However, there is a lighter side of the laughter God gives, as seen in Job 8:21, and Psalm 126:2, where the Lord fills the mouths of the Israelites with laughter, singing and rejoicing. This aspect is also seen in the lives of Abraham and Sarah. In our lesson, in Genesis 17:17, Abraham fell upon his face, and laughed. Later, Sarah also laughed within herself, though in fear, she denied it (Genesis 18:12-15). The baby boy born to Abraham and Sarah in their old age was named Isaac ("he laughs"). This name has the same root as the word used to describe his parents' laughter, expressing not derision or scorn, but surprise, pleasure, gladness (ISBE).

Fourteen years had passed since the vision of Genesis 15:1; Abraham is an hundred years old, Sarah now ninety. Is it any wonder that Abraham's response to God's renewed promise moved him to laughter? Calvin said: "Not that he either ridiculed the promise of God or treated it as a fable, or rejected it altogether, but as often happens when things occur which are least expected, partly lifted up with joy, partly carried out of himself with wonder, he burst out into laughter." Delitzsch stated: "the promise was so immensely great, that he sank in adoration to the ground, and so immensely paradoxical, that he could not help laughing." Unlike Sarah's laughter in unbelief (Genesis 18:13), Abraham's response was in joyful wonder. There were no doubts or misgivings.

Abraham's love for Ishmael shows itself in the father's plea for additional blessing for Ishmael (whose name means, "May God hear."). His prayer implies anxiety that Ishmael may be excluded from the blessings of the covenant. God then described the fourfold blessing which would fall upon Ishmael: (1) He would be fruitful, prolific; (2) exceedingly great in numbers; (3) twelve princes would issue from his loins; and (4) Ishmael would become a great nation.

These blessings would not diminish God's relationship with Isaac. The convenant would be established with Isaac, the child of grace, not with Ishmael, the child of works. Then, having reassured Abraham's heart, the Lord once again promised that Sarah would bear a son. God even established the time—"at this set time in the next year."

C. PROMISE FULFILLED: ISAAC BORN
(Genesis 21:1-2)

AND the LORD visited Sarah as he had said, and the LORD did unto Sarah as he had spoken. For Sarah conceived, and bare Abraham a son in his old age, at the set time of which God had spoken to him.

As the Lord promised, He "visited" Sarah. The word rendered "visited" means to attend to, inspect. It points to "taking action to cause a considerable change in the circumstances of the subordinate, either for the better or for the worse" *(Theological Wordbook of the Old Testament)*. In Sarah's case, it was not to punish, but to bless; it was not in severity, but in mercy. Sarah conceived at the very time God had designated. He always comes on time!

When the Lord makes an appointment, He keeps it. There is no disappointment! He had said in Genesis 18:14: "At the time appointed I will return unto thee, according to the time of life, and Sarah shall have a son." Despite their ages—Abraham was one hundred, Sarah was ninety—God fulfilled the promise He had made some twenty-five years earlier (Genesis 12:4, 7). And so Isaac was born.

III. Special Features

A. PRESERVING OUR HERITAGE

With the influence of Islam growing among Black Americans, saints of color would do well to study again God's choice of Isaac and not Ishmael. Read again the promise the Lord made to Abraham concerning Ishmael (Genesis 17:20), as well as the promise He made to Hagar (Genesis 21:18). God had chosen Abraham to be the head of a special people, Israel, and limited the line after Abraham to Isaac, then to Jacob and his twelve sons.

Now Ishmael caused trouble later, and his descendants are still quarreling with the Jews. Ishmael is the forefather of the Arabs; and Isaac the progenitor of the Jews. Mohammed, the founder of Islam, came from the line of Ishmael. Today, there is still dispute over the ownership of the land. Present conflict is evidence of a deep-rooted hatred. Diplomats and statesmen (and women, Mrs. Albright) often indicate they are ignorant of the background of the problem or naive as to the root of the trouble. And worse, they have left out altogether any thought of Satan and his special hatred for Israel.

B. A CONCLUDING WORD

The Sunday school teacher has the wonderful opportunity of driving home the necessity of believing the Bible. Both teachers and students prosper with this belief in their hearts. And all who take God at His Word follow in the footsteps of Abraham, the man of faith. "The Lord had said unto Abram, Get thee out...So Abram departed, as the Lord had spoken unto him" (Genesis 12;1,4). "The word of the Lord came unto Abram," and God said, "So shall thy seed be" (Genesis 15:1, 6). Abram believed God. Here is the very heart of biblical Christianity—taking God at His Word. No man or woman, boy or girl can be declared righteous who does not in the simplicity of faith believe in the Lord. God promised the Seed through whom the world would be blessed. That Seed was Christ (Galatians 3:16). Thus Abram believed God and was justified. Recall, the Lord said: "Abraham rejoiced to see My day; and he saw it, and was glad" (John 8:56). God still justifies the sinner in the same way—we must put our trust in Jesus Christ the Savior.

HOME DAILY BIBLE READING
Week of July 11, 1999
A Promise Fulfilled

July	5	M.	Genesis 15:1-6, Your Very Own Issue Shall Be Your Heir
July	6	T.	Genesis 15:12-20, The Lord Made a Covenant With Abram
July	7	W.	Genesis 16:1-16, Hagar Bore Abram A Son
July	8	T.	Genesis 17:1-14, Your Name Shall Be Abraham
July	9	F.	Genesis 17:15-27, Sarah Shall Be Her Name
July	10	S.	Genesis 18:1-15, Sarah Laughed to Herself
July	11	S.	Genesis 18:1-7, Sarah...Bore Abraham a Son

A Test of Faith

Adult Topic—Giving All

.....

Youth Topic—Caught in the Middle
Children's Topic—Abraham's Faith Was Tested

.....

Devotional Reading—Daniel 3:16-26
Background Scripture—Genesis 22:1-19
Print—Genesis 22:1-2, 4-14

• • • • • • • • • • • •

PRINTED SCRIPTURE

Genesis 22:1-2, 4-14 (KJV)

AND it came to pass after these things, that God did tempt Abraham, and said unto him, Abraham: and he said, Behold, here I am.

2 And he said, Take now thy son, thine only son Isaac, whom thou lovest, and get thee into the land of Moriah; and offer him there for a burnt offering upon one of the mountains which I will tell thee of.

.....

4 Then on the third day Abraham lifted up his eyes, and saw the place afar off.

5 And Abraham said unto his young men, Abide ye here with the ass; and I and the lad will go yonder and worship, and come again to you.

6 And Abraham took the wood of the burnt offering, and laid it upon Isaac his son; and he took the fire in his hand, and a knife; and they went both of them together.

7 And Isaac spake unto Abraham his father, and said, My father: and he said, Here am I, my son. And he

Genesis 22:1-2, 4-14 (NRSV)

AFTER these things God tested Abraham. He said to him, "Abraham!" And he said, "Here I am."

2 He said, "Take your son, your only son Isaac, whom you love, and go to the land of Moriah, and offer him there as a burnt offering on one of the mountains that I shall show you."

.....

4 On the third day Abraham looked up and saw the place far away.

5 Then Abraham said to his young men, "Stay here with the donkey; the boy and I will go over there; we will worship, and then we will come back to you."

6 Abraham took the wood of the burnt offering and laid it on his son Isaac, and he himself carried the fire and the knife. So the two of them walked on together.

7 Isaac said to his father Abraham, "Father!" And he said,

said, Behold the fire and the wood: but where is the lamb for a burnt offering?

8 And Abraham said, My son, God will provide himself a lamb for a burnt offering: so they went both of them together.

9 And they came to the place which God had told him of; and Abraham built an altar there, and laid the wood in order, and bound Isaac his son, and laid him on the altar upon the wood.

10 And Abraham stretched forth his hand, and took the knife to slay his son.

11 And the angel of the LORD called unto him out of heaven, and said, Abraham, Abraham: and he said, Here am I.

12 And he said, Lay not thine hand upon the lad, neither do thou any thing unto him: for now I know that thou fearest God, seeing thou hast not withheld thy son, thine only son from me.

13 And Abraham lifted up his eyes, and looked, and behold behind him a ram caught in a thicket by his horns: and Abraham went and took the ram, and offered him up for a burnt offering in the stead of his son.

14 And Abraham called the name of that place Jehovah-jireh: as it is said to this day, In the mount of the LORD it shall be seen.

"Here I am, my son." He said, "The fire and the wood are here, but where is the lamb for a burnt offering?"

8 Abraham said, "God himself will provide the lamb for a burnt offering, my son." So the two of them walked on together.

9 When they came to the place that God had shown him, Abraham built an altar there and laid the wood in order. He bound his son Isaac, and laid him on the altar, on top of the wood.

10 Then Abraham reached out his hand and took the knife to kill his son.

11 But the angel of the LORD called to him from heaven, and said, "Abraham, Abraham!" And he said, "Here I am."

12 He said, "Do not lay your hand on the boy or do anything to him; for now I know that you fear God, since you have not withheld your son, your only son, from me."

13 And Abraham looked up and saw a ram, caught in a thicket by its horns. Abraham went and took the ram and offered it up as a burnt offering instead of his son.

14 So Abraham called that place "The LORD will provide"; as it is said to this day, "On the mount of the LORD it shall be provided."

KEY VERSE

And he said, Lay not thine hand upon the lad, neither do thou any thing unto him: for now I know that thou fearest God, seeing thou hast not withheld thy son, thine only son from me.—Genesis 22:12

OBJECTIVES

After reading this lesson, the student should be better informed about:

1. God's purposes in testing us,
2. What it means to fear God; and,
3. How Abraham and Isaac point to God and His Son.

POINTS TO BE EMPHASIZED

Adult/Youth/Children
Key Verse: Genesis 22:12; Genesis 22:8 (Children)
Print: Genesis 22:1-2, 4-14

—God tested Abraham by commanding him to sacrifice his son Isaac. (1-2)
—Abraham prepared to make the sacrifice, telling his son that God would provide the lamb. (4-8)
—Abraham built an altar, prepared the wood, bound his son, and laid him on the altar. (9)
—When Abraham reached out to kill Isaac, the angel of God called out to him to stop. (10-12a)
—After seeing that Abraham would have sacrificed his son Isaac, God knew Abraham feared and trusted God. (12b)

(NOTE: Use KJV Scripture for Adults; NRSV Scripture for Youth and Children)

TOPICAL OUTLINE OF THE LESSON

I. Introduction

   a. The Name Jehovah-Jireh
   b. Biblical Background

II. Exposition and Application of the Scripture

   A. God Commands (Genesis 22:1-2)
   B. Abraham Obeys (Genesis 22:4-6)
   C. Isaac Questions (Genesis 22:7-8)
   D. God Substitutes (Genesis 22:9-14)

III. Special Features

   A. Preserving Our Heritage
   A. A Concluding Word

I. Introduction

A. THE NAME JEHOVAH-JIREH

We have here one of the most interesting compound names of God. It is composed of the noun, **Jehovah,** and the verb **jireh.** Consider first the name,

Jehovah. Its original meaning and derivation is not known. However, in Exodus 3:14, the Lord said unto Moses, "I AM THAT I AM." Because of the words "I AM," it is believed by some scholars that the word Jehovah is connected with the verb "to be" or the verb, "to become." Jehovah (Yahweh) is said to be the personal proper name par excellence of the God of Israel (ISBE). He is thus the One who will be, the Coming One for that nation.

Now the verb jireh (from the Hebrew verb, **raah)** means to see; in Genesis 22:8, it means to see to it. In other words, it is to provide. This English word, provide, has Latin roots. The "pro" means before; the "vide" means to see. Because of our pre-vision, we make pro-vision (H. Dean). Combine the name Jehovah with the verb to see, and we get, "The Coming One Who Sees Ahead." He is the One who looks ahead and makes provision.

Now actually, strictly speaking, this name which occurs only once, and only here in Genesis 22:14, is the name of a place: "And Abraham called the name of that place Jehovah-jireh, as it is said to this day, In the mount of the Lord it shall be seen." But even as the Lord provided a substitute ram for sacrifice in that place, the deed done there became connected with the Doer. Christians recognize that compound names amplify our knowledge of God. We learn that He who condemns our sin also provides the substitute to take the place of the guilty sinner. Instead of Isaac being sacrificed, a ram was substituted. Instead of you and me suffering separation from God, Jesus Christ was substituted for us! Full provision was made at the cross of Christ. And the God of the Bible continues to care for our necessities. He answers our prayers and supplies our need.

B. BIBLICAL BACKGROUND

We though it would be helpful to talk about Human Sacrifice because in today's lesson, we find that God told Abraham to take his only son Isaac and offer him for a burnt offering. There are scholars who state that because of the moral difficulty this presents, the story of Genesis chapter 22 is not authentic. They reason that Abraham's concept of God was really that of some Philistine deity, for the Philistines believed in human sacrifices. And since human sacrifice is an abomination to the God of Israel, the story is not true. Others suggest that Abraham's readiness to offer up Isaac indicates that human sacrifice to Jehovah was an original custom in Israel, and that therefore the God of Israel was no other than Moloch, or possibly some other idol-god of similar character. However, such theories are pure speculation. Now what **is** true is that the God of the Bible hates the killing of human beings as sacrifices to Him or some man-made deity. And the story of Abraham and Isaac is proof that Jehovah takes no delight in the death of any man. He desires not to destroy life, but to save and sanctify it. A major point taught in today's lesson is that obedience is better than sacrifice. Repeatedly, the Jews were told that human sacrifice was an abomination (Deuteronomy 12:31). "And thou shalt not let any of thy seed pass through the fire to Molech..." (Leviticus 18:21).

Molech (Moloch, Milcom) was the name of the god to whom the Canaanites burned up their sons and daughters, and polluted the land with blood (Psalm 106:38). "The victims offered to the divinity were not burnt alive, but were killed as sacrifices, and then presented as burnt offerings" (ISBE). As God points out in Jeremiah 19:5, no such thing as the human sacrifice Judah offered to Baal ever came into the Lord's mind. Such a practice by Jerusalem was "harlotry" (Ezekiel 16:20). In summary, though human sacrifice was practiced in Abraham's day by surrounding heathen nations, it was never approved by the God of the Bible, never advocated, never even entered His mind!

II. Exposition and Application of the Scripture

A. GOD COMMANDS
(Genesis 22:1-2)

AND it came to pass after these things, that God did tempt Abraham, and said unto him, Abraham: and he said, Behold, here I am. And he said, Take now thy son, thine only son Isaac, whom thou lovest, and get thee into the land of Moriah; and offer him there for a burnt offering upon one of the mountains which I will tell thee of.

The chapter opens with the words, "And it came to pass after these things." What are "these things"? There were at least six great tests or crises in the spiritual life of Abraham up to this point. **First** was the "getting out" or separation from his own country, home, kindred and relatives (Genesis 12:1). The character of the land and the nature of the inhabitants heightened the challenge. A **Second** matter was the grievous famine in the land, causing Abraham to go to Egypt (Genesis 12:10). **Third** was separating from Lot, his nephew (Genesis 13:11). **Fourth** was surrendering his own plans for Ishmael, his son (by Hagar) (Genesis 17:20-21). **Fifth** was the delay in the birth of the heir promised by God. And **Sixth** was the offering up of Isaac, his son (by Sarah).

To understand rightly the significance of this traumatic incident in the life of Abraham in today's lesson, we must define the word "tempt," for in the King James Version we are told that God "did tempt Abraham." The Hebrew word **(nasah)** means to try, prove. Test is the best translation here. There is no connotation of committing evil. God never "tempted" anyone to do evil. Because men so often fail the test, the word tempt now connotes to solicit to evil, to seduce, to entice. James (1:13-14) makes it very clear that God tempts no man. However, He does test us. Note that Simon Peter speaks of the "trial of your faith" (1 Peter 1:6-7).

And so, while the Lord knew exactly what Abraham would do in this his "final examination," it had to be "proved" to Abraham and all others that he trusted absolutely in God's Word. While true that under trial, oppression, or testing, one may react unfavorably or flunk the test and do that which is evil, nevertheless the word testing does not automatically include the incitement to do evil. God tested Abraham's sincerity, loyalty, and faith. His purpose was to reveal Abraham's faith in a way no other test or crisis had done.

When God called Abraham by name, he responded, "Behold, here I am." The Lord then commanded him to take Isaac, and offer him up for a burnt offering. Note the two things that are said about Isaac: (1) He is Abraham's only son. This means Isaac was the dearest or most precious thing in the world to him. He was the son of a miraculous birth, unique; a son of old age. It also refers to him as the only son in the legal sense. Furthermore, as far as the fulfillment of God's promises were concerned, Isaac was indeed the "Only son." Ishmael would never enjoy the status with which Isaac was blessed. (2) He is the son whom Abraham loved. Here is the first occurrence of the word "love" in the Bible (Genesis 22:2). Reference is to a father's love for his son. And of course, we see a picture of God the Father's love for His Son, the Lord Jesus Christ. Earlier, we dealt briefly with the matter of human sacrifice. God does not tell Abraham to actually kill his son, but to "offer him there for a burnt offering." Yet there was no room for misunderstanding what God meant. For on principal, Jehovah strongly opposes such a wicked practice. God wanted Abraham to give "the spiritual sacrifice of his son" (Leupold). The testing demonstrated God's desire for complete surrender. Recall Hannah returning her son, Samuel, to the Lord (1 Samuel 1:28)—here now in a much more dramatic fashion is the surrendering of a beloved son to the Heavenly Father.

B. ABRAHAM OBEYS
(Genesis 22:4-6)

Then on the third day Abraham lifted up his eyes, and saw the place afar off. And Abraham said unto his young men, Abide ye here with the ass; and I and the lad will go yonder and worship, and come again to you. And Abraham took the wood of the burnt offering, and laid it upon Isaac his son; and he took the fire in his hand, and a knife; and they went both of them together.

On the third day of the trip, Abraham spied his destination, for God had ordered him to the land of Moriah, and to a specific mountain there in that range where Jerusalem is situated (2 Chronicles 3:1). To the young servants who had accompanied him and Isaac, Abraham ordered: "Stay here with the donkey; and I and the lad will go yonder and worship, and come again to you."

These words suggest Abraham believed they both would return. According to Hebrews 11:17-19, it appears that Abraham expected God to raise Isaac from the dead. This faith was all the more remarkable because up to this point in history, there was no record of any one being restored to life or resurrected. In humble submission to his father, Isaac perhaps now 18 to 20 years old, carried the fire wood upon his shoulders and went forth with his father to the place of sacrifice. It has been said that "the boy carries the heavier load, the father the more dangerous: knife and fire" (ICC).

C. ISAAC QUESTIONS
(Genesis 22:7-8)

And Isaac spake unto Abraham his father, and said, My father: and he said,

Here am I, my son. And he said, Behold the fire and the wood: but where is the lamb for a burnt offering? And Abraham said, My son, God will provide himself a lamb for a burnt offering: so they went both of them together.

At this point, Isaac, not in protest but in curiosity, inquired of his father, "We have fire and wood, but where is the lamb for a burnt offering?" We are not told what method was used to produce the fire. "Perhaps a lighted fagot or pan of embers" (Scofield). What went through Abraham's mind upon hearing this? Was his heart torn knowing what he had been commanded to do? Had each step toward the mount added agony to his soul? What would he answer? Hear then his response: "God will provide...." Such confidence is the high point of the chapter. Can you hear Abraham singing: "All you may need He will provide, God will take care of you; Nothing you ask will be denied, God will take care of you"? (D. D. Martin). Abraham's reply uses a common word for seeing with the eyes. However, here it has an extended or metaphorical meaning of "to provide." In English we say, "I'll see to it," or "I'll look out for it," meaning I will provide it. In essence Abraham said, "God is able to see to it in His own way." And we add, in His own good time. Abraham did not know at this point that his son would be spared death. But, he had faith to believe that whatever was necessary to do what God had commanded, God would supply. How, when, where, who? What counts is trusting God! It was this quiet assurance that led Abraham on to the assigned place.

D. GOD SUBSTITUTES
(Genesis 22:9-14)

And they came to the place which God had told him of; and Abraham built an altar there, and laid the wood in order, and bound Isaac his son, and laid him on the altar upon the wood. And Abraham stretched forth his hand, and took the knife to slay his son. And the angel of the LORD called unto him out of heaven, and said, Abraham, Abraham: and he said, Here am I. And he said, Lay not thine hand upon the lad, neither do thou any thing unto him: for now I know that thou fearest God, seeing thou hast not withheld thy son, thine only son from me. And Abraham lifted up his eyes, and looked, and behold behind him a ram caught in a thicket by his horns: and Abraham went and took the ram, and offered him up for a burnt offering in the stead of his son. And Abraham called the name of that place Jehovahjireh: as it is said to this day, In the mount of the LORD it shall be seen.

Abraham built an altar, laid the wood in place, bound Isaac, his son, and placed him on the altar on top of the wood. Then came another moment of faith— for Abraham stretched forth his hand, and took the knife to slay his son! This was no sham, no pretense on Abraham's part. Jehovah knew that Abraham intended following through—this was no pose! No play-acting! Had the Lord not intervened, Abraham would not have hesitated a second to perform his mission. But God did step in! The Abraham with the surrendered heart was made to stay the willing hand! Twice the Angel of the Lord called his name out of heaven: "Abraham, Abraham." This double call (along with "verily, verily") is often found in the Scriptures, and points to an urgency, a pay attention call! A stop whatever you're doing call!

"Now I know," said the Lord, "that you fear God." This does not mean that He did not know before. God is omniscient. But He knew now by experience because of the act of faith just demonstrated by a creature of time. And the true fear or reverence of God consists in total submission to His sovereign will. How wonderful Abraham must have felt upon seeing that God had provided a ram, caught in a nearby thicket by his horns. Instead of Isaac becoming a sacrifice then, the lamb provided by God was offered up for a burnt offering.

III. Special Features

A. PRESERVING OUR HERITAGE

The truth that God will provide has long been a foundation of what is called the "Black Church." Knowledge that the Lord does provide is one of the reasons why the words of the hymn, Amazing Grace, have gripped our hearts. We are indeed amazed when we realize that in spite of slavery, torture, cruelty, rape, and treated as chattel, our slave foreparents survived. It is because the God of the Bible saw to it. He responded in wonderful ways to the prayers of slaves who accepted the shed blood of Christ, and provided for us in spite of illiteracy, disenfranchisement, powerlessness, and despisement.

B. A CONCLUDING WORD

Abraham was sold out to God. He was God's man! Whatever the Lord said do, he was willing to do it! He would let nothing stand between him and the God he served. As someone has said, "God was Abraham's dearest treasure; God's will, his chief concern." What more severe test could God have imposed upon Abraham? What more excellent obedience could have been demonstrated? He instantly responded to the Lord's call. He never complained. Never protested. At first justified by faith (Genesis 15:6), now we find him justified or vindicated by works (Genesis 22:10).

HOME DAILY BIBLE READINGS
Week of July 18, 1999
A TEST OF FAITH

July 12 M. Genesis 22:1-8, Take Your Son, Your Only Son Isaac
July 13 T. Genesis 22:9-14, Abraham...Took the Knife to Kill His Son
July 14 W. Genesis 22:15-19, I Will Indeed Bless You
July 15 T. Daniel 3:16-26, We Will Not Serve Your Gods
July 16 F. Mark 14:32-42, Remove This Cup From Me
July 17 S. Hebrews 4:14—5:4, One Who in Every Respect Has Been Tested
July 18 S. 1 Corinthians 13:1-13, The Greatest of These Is Love

---

Deceit and Blessing

Adult Topic—Deceit and Blessing

.....

Youth Topic—Think Twice!
Children's Topic—A Blessing Was Lost

.....

Devotional Reading—Luke 16:1-19
Background Scripture—Genesis 25:19-34; 27:1-40
Print—Genesis 25:29-34; 27:30-37

• • • • • • • • • • • • •

PRINTED SCRIPTURE

Genesis 25:29-34; 27:30-37 (KJV)

29 And Jacob sod pottage: and Esau came from the field, and he was faint:

30 And Esau said to Jacob, Feed me, I pray thee, with that same red pottage; for I am faint: therefore was his name called Edom.

31 And Jacob said, Sell me this day thy birthright.

32 And Esau said, Behold, I am at the point to die: and what profit shall this birthright do to me?

33 And Jacob said, Swear to me this day; and he sware unto him: and he sold his birthright unto Jacob.

34 Then Jacob gave Esau bread and pottage of lentiles; and he did eat and drink, and rose up, and went his way: thus Esau despised his birthright.

.....

30 And it came to pass, as soon as Isaac had made an end of blessing Jacob, and Jacob was yet scarce gone out from the presence of Isaac his father, that Esau his brother

Genesis 25:29-34; 27:30-37 (NRSV)

29 Once when Jacob was cooking a stew, Esau came in from the field, and he was famished.

30 Esau said to Jacob, "Let me eat some of that red stuff, for I am famished!" (Therefore he was called Edom.)

31 Jacob said, "First sell me your birthright."

32 Esau said, "I am about to die; of what use is a birthright to me?"

33 Jacob said, "Swear to me first." So he swore to him, and sold his birthright to Jacob.

34 Then Jacob gave Esau bread and lentil stew, and he ate and drank, and rose and went his way. Thus Esau despised his birthright.

.....

30 As soon as Isaac had finished blessing Jacob, when Jacob had scarcely gone out from the presence of his father Isaac, his brother Esau came in from his hunting.

came in from his hunting.

31 And he also had made savoury meat, and brought it unto his father, and said unto his father, Let my father arise, and eat of his son's venison, that thy soul may bless me.

32 And Isaac his father said unto him, Who art thou? And he said, I am thy son, thy firstborn Esau.

33 And Isaac trembled very exceedingly, and said, Who? where is he that hath taken venison, and brought it me, and I have eaten of all before thou camest, and have blessed him? yea, and he shall be blessed.

34 And when Esau heard the words of his father, he cried with a great and exceeding bitter cry, and said unto his father, Bless me, even me also, O my father.

35 And he said, Thy brother came with subtilty, and hath taken away thy blessing.

36 And he said, Is not he rightly named Jacob? for he hath supplanted me these two times: he took away my birthright; and, behold, now he hath taken away my blessing. And he said, Hast thou not reserved a blessing for me?

37 And Isaac answered and said unto Esau, Behold, I have made him thy lord, and all his brethren have I given to him for servants; and with corn and wine have I sustained him: and what shall I do now unto thee, my son?

31 He also prepared savory food, and brought it to his father. And he said to his father, "Let my father sit up and eat of his son's game, so that you may bless me."

32 His father Isaac said to him, "Who are you?" He answered, "I am your firstborn son, Esau."

33 Then Isaac trembled violently, and said, "Who was it then that hunted game and brought it to me, and I ate it all before you came, and I have blessed him?—yes, and blessed he shall be!"

34 When Esau heard his father's words, he cried out with an exceedingly great and bitter cry, and said to his father, "Bless me, me also, father!"

35 But he said, "Your brother came deceitfully, and he has taken away your blessing."

36 Esau said, "Is he not rightly named Jacob? For he has supplanted me these two times. He took away my birthright; and look, now he has taken away my blessing." Then he said, "Have you not reserved a blessing for me?"

37 Isaac answered Esau, "I have already made him your lord, and I have given him all his brothers as servants, and with grain and wine I have sustained him. What then can I do for you, my son?"

KEY VERSE

And he said, Thy brother came with subtilty, and hath taken away thy blessing. And he said, Is not he rightly named Jacob? for he hath supplanted me these two times: he took away my birthright; and, behold, now he hath taken away my blessing. And he said, Hast thou not reserved a blessing for me?—Genesis 27:35-36

OBJECTIVES

After reading this lesson, the student should be thoroughly convinced that:

1. Spirituality is vastly more important than materiality;
2. Deceit is harmful even when believers practice it;
3. We live in an age of instant gratification;
4. Sometimes we reach the point of no return; and,
5. The grace of God is still able to prevail.

POINTS TO BE EMPHASIZED

Adult/Youth/Children
Key Verse: Genesis 27:35-36; Genesis 27:34 (Children)
Print: Genesis 25:29-34; 27:30-37

—Esau sold his birthright to Jacob for a meal. (29-34)
—Isaac gave Jacob the blessing of the firstborn son when Rebekah and Jacob tricked Isaac into thinking that Jacob was Esau. (1-29)
—After Isaac had blessed Jacob, and Jacob had departed, Esau came to receive the blessing. (30-32)
—Esau and Isaac were bitterly distressed when they discovered that Jacob had taken Esau's blessing. (33-35)
—Esau pleaded for his own blessing, but Isaac answered that it had been given to Jacob. (36-38)

(NOTE: Use KJV Scripture for Adults; NRSV Scripture for Youth and Children)

TOPICAL OUTLINE OF THE LESSON

I Introduction

A. The Point of No Return
A. Biblical Background

II. Exposition and Application of the Scripture

A. Esau Sells His Birthright to Jacob (Genesis 25:29-34)
B. Jacob Steals Esau's Blessing (Genesis 27:30-33)
C. Esau's Useless Remorse (Genesis 27:34-37)

III. Special Features

A. Preserving Our Heritage
B. A Concluding Word

I. Introduction

A. THE POINT OF NO RETURN

The emphasis on Esau's sad plight is not meant to absolve Jacob of his deceit and duplicity. But throughout the lesson, there prevails a sense of sadness, a sorrow felt for Esau, even though as Christians we recognize the hand of God in bringing about His Sovereign will in the life of Jacob, Esau's brother. Our attention is drawn to Hebrews 12:16-17 where what happened in Esau's life is used as a warning to professing Christians. One of the major points of the book of Hebrews is the fact that all who profess may not actually possess. The picture painted of Esau in this passage is strongly condemnatory.

The word for profane **(bebelos)** refers to that which is accessible, lawfully trodden upon (Thayer); it is a spot trodden and trampled on, lying open to the casual foot of every intruder or careless passer-by (Trench). It speaks of that which is unclean, unsanctified, unhallowed. Used of a person, it signifies one who is ungodly or godless, irreligious (Arndt & Gingrich). Such a man is far from God; his lack of holiness includes ethical deficiency. "Esau in Judaism is a type of the common mind which is unreceptive to God" (Kittel). He treats the sacred as if it were a common or secular thing (Lenski).

Esau's birthright or primogeniture was far from being common. It involved the headship of the family, great property rights, and the blessing of being in the bloodline of the Messiah. Esau traded all this away for one satisfaction of his appetite. Once this right was gone, it could not be recovered. The writer of the book of Hebrews used this story to warn those who professed Christ. In the midst of persecution, some who professed faith in the Lord Jesus were moved to give up their hope in Christ. All who finally relinquished their benefits in Christ committed an act which was irrevocable. As hard as Esau tried to get his father to change his mind, he could not get Isaac to undo what had occurred.

B. BIBLICAL BACKGROUND

Isaac was forty years old when he married Rebekah, but they had no children until Isaac was sixty years old. Even before the twins were born to Rebekah, she was informed by the Lord that two nations were in her womb; and it was predicted that the elder shall serve the younger. The apostle Paul mentioned this in Romans 9:11-12. As it happened, the firstborn boy was Esau, so named because he entered this world red all over like an hairy garment. Esau means hairy, **(hirsute.)** The other boy was named Jacob, which means supplanter, for even as Jacob emerged, he took hold on Esau's heel: "In the womb he took his brother by the heel" (Hosea 12:3: RSV).

You can see how the stage was set for future conflict: (1) Jacob's reaching-out entrance into the world: (2) the different dispositions and personalities of the twins; (3) the prediction made known to Rebekah concerning the boys; (4) the favoritism shown Esau by the father; (5) the love shown Jacob by the mother; (6) and then that inner quality for which the parents were not really responsible— the lack of faith on Esau's part, the faith demonstrated by Jacob (although his methods were wrong, his motives selfish, deeds reprehensible). Such are some of the characteristics of the two main persons in today's lesson. But the title, Deceit and Blessing, directs our attention primarily to Jacob.

II. Exposition and Application of the Scripture

A. ESAU SELLS HIS BIRTHRIGHT TO JACOB
(Genesis 25:29-34)

And Jacob sod pottage: and Esau came from the field, and he was faint: And Esau said to Jacob, Feed me, I pray thee, with that same red pottage; for I am faint: therefore was his name called Edom. And Jacob said, Sell me this day thy birthright. And Esau said, Behold, I am at the point to die: and what profit shall this birthright do to me? And Jacob said, Swear to me this day; and he sware unto him: and he sold his birthright unto Jacob. Then Jacob gave Esau bread and pottage of lentiles; and he did eat and drink, and rose up, and went his way: thus Esau despised his birthright.

The lesson begins with Jacob at home cooking, and Esau out on the field. As the King James Version puts it, Jacob sod pottage. "Sod" means boiled; it is the past tense of the verb to seethe. Here it is simply boiled food; intentionally indefinite, so that the specific description in verse 34 may be a surprise (ICC). Literally, Jacob "seethed a seething." At this point, Esau came in from the field, and he was faint (the Hebrew word means physically exhausted, wearied. "It can be occasioned by hunger and great exertion such as was the case with Esau" (TWOT). Esau both smelled and saw the pottage, and "asked with great passionate eagerness for some to eat" (Keil & Delitzsch). He said to Jacob, "Feed me! Let me swallow some of the red—that red there! For I am exhausted!" The spluttering language toned down by our various translations indicates that Esau could hardly control himself. He was so hungry that he pleaded, "Let me swallow; let me gulp down some of that red stuff there!" (Leupold)

Recall that we are told in Genesis 25:25 that when Esau was born, he came out of the womb red. Now in verse 30, we learn that his name was called Edom, which means red. And so the name Edom or Edomite was given to Esau based on his ruddiness, and on his desiring red pottage more than his birthright. Now Jacob's response seems so sudden you wonder how long he had planned for this very thing— "Sell me this day your birthright!" As mentioned before, in eastern countries, the birthright consisted in a double portion of the father's inheritance (Deuteronomy 21:17). This meant the oldest son would get twice as much as any other son. It included being the ruler over the entire family (Genesis 27:29), thus acting as priest, or spiritual leader. Women and children were not expected to have direct contact with God *(Pilgrim Bible)*. Then, a third blessing included being in the direct line of the Messiah promised by God.

Esau knew all of this, but still allowed his belly to be his god. Jacob also knew the significance of the birthright, but unlike Esau, he attached great value to it. We see Esau's disdain for spiritual blessings; we see his carnality as expressed by his preference for the material things of life. His attitude and values are heard in his reply: "Behold, I am at the point to die: and what profit shall this birthright do to me?" (Genesis 25:32).

Moved by his ravenous appetite, the feckless Esau was exaggerating when he claimed to be near death from hunger and exhaustion; but, his words show that immediate gratification was Esau's goal. Or, we could interpret his words to mean that he would someday die and at that point, the birthright would be worthless. Either way, Esau expressed his heart's thought: "I want what I want, and I want it now!" With these words (verse 32), he condemned himself. No wonder he is called immoral and profane by the writer in Hebrews 12:16. And so we see Jacob seized the opportunity to get hold of that which he had long coveted. Rather than trust God to work things out to fulfill the prophecy, Jacob devised his own means of getting things done.

"Swear to me this day!" demanded Jacob. The word translated "swear" means seven. It is first of all the number seven. Its symbolic usage indicates that ancients considered the sacred significance of the number seven. A prime example of this is the hallowing of the seventh day as the Sabbath day. We learn that the Hebrew verb "to swear" is identical with the number seven. Thus, the lexicon (Brown, Driver, Briggs) defines **shaba** as "to seven oneself, or bind oneself by seven things." "To swear in the Old Testament was to give one's sacred unbreakable word in testimony that the one swearing would faithfully perform some promised deed, or that he would faithfully refrain from some evil act" (TWOT). Esau responded by swearing unto Jacob, and thus sold his birthright unto his brother. The very fact that he made such an agreement shows he was not spiritually qualified to receive the birthright.

Upon completion of the deal, Jacob then fed Esau. Here we are told what kind of pottage Jacob had cooked. He gave Esau a savory dish of "bread and pottage of lentils." More than likely, these lentils were small, reddish beans used in soup and as a "pottage" with a reddish-brown color (ISBE). Well pleased with his bargain, the carnal Esau ate, drank, rose up, and went his way.

The section closed with the awful words: "Thus Esau despised his birthright." In the Old Testament, various Hebrew words translated "despise" mean: tread on, contempt or render contemptible, lightly esteem, loathe, reject. In the New Testament, various Greek words rendered "despise" mean: to put aside, dishonor, think down upon or think around, reckon for nothing, care little for. The Latin roots of the English word "despise" mean to look down at or upon. We might say Esau's despising of his birthright was despicable. The basic meaning of the Hebrew word **(bazah)** is "to accord little worth to something" (TWOT). Esau's very act of undervaluing his birthright implied contempt. For despising the birthright, Esau was condemned by God to insignificance.

B. JACOB STEALS ESAU'S BLESSING
(Genesis 27:30-33)

And it came to pass, as soon as Isaac had made an end of blessing Jacob, and Jacob was yet scarce gone out from the presence of Isaac his father, that Esau his brother came in from his hunting. And he also had made savoury meat, and brought it unto his father, and said unto his father, Let my father arise, and eat of his son's venison, that thy soul may bless me. And Isaac his father said unto him, Who art thou? And he said, I am thy son,

thy firstborn Esau. And Isaac trembled very exceedingly, and said, Who? where is he that hath taken venison, and brought it me, and I have eaten of all before thou camest, and have blessed him? yea, and he shall be blessed.

With the help of his mother, Rebekah, Jacob deceived his father Isaac and received the blessings of the firstborn, blessings which belonged to Esau. The story is one of lying, deception, trickery, conspiracy. Just as Esau had despised his birthright, suggesting that he was defrauded of that which he was incapable of appreciating, so here it comes to mind that Esau lost that which he was spiritually inadequate to appreciate.

This fact by no means makes Jacob angelic. What he did was immoral. Apparently, Jacob derived his inspiration from his mother, Rebekah. We believe that he first heard from her lips the prophecy that the older should serve the younger. She is the one who initiated and planned the deception (Genesis 27:5-17). Isaac was blind and feeble; he could not keep up with the scheming combination of a determined wife and an ambitious son. And of course, Esau was bogged down with material matters.

Having fooled his father, Jacob left. This next section of the printed lesson begins with Esau returning from hunting. As he entered, he narrowly missed an encounter with Jacob. One wonders what would have happened had they bumped into each other! Esau had made a delicious meal of venison, and brought it in for Isaac to enjoy. Isaac was surprised. "Who are you?" he asked. "I am your son, your firstborn Esau" was the reply. In a moment, Isaac knew what had occurred. He saw the hand of God involved in letting things fall out as they did. Once the blessing had been given, it could not be taken back. "Yea, and he shall be blessed." By its very nature, once spoken, such an oracle was irrevocable.

C. ESAU'S USELESS REMORSE
(Genesis 27:34-37)

And when Esau heard the words of his father, he cried with a great and exceeding bitter cry, and said unto his father, Bless me, even me also, O my father. And he said, Thy brother came with subtilty, and hath taken away thy blessing. And he said, Is not he rightly named Jacob? for he hath supplanted me these two times: he took away my birthright; and, behold, now he hath taken away my blessing. And he said, Hast thou not reserved a blessing for me? And Isaac answered and said unto Esau, Behold, I have made him thy lord, and all his brethren have I given to him for servants; and with corn and wine have I sustained him: and what shall I do now unto thee, my son?

When Esau heard his father's words, he cried with a great and exceedingly bitter cry, and pathetically pleaded with Isaac to bless him also. Isaac realized that he had been fighting God all along: he remembered his carnal preference of Esau. So he accepted defeat, and answered, "Your brother came with subtlety, and has taken away your blessing." The Hebrew word translated "subtlety" means deceit, and here describes the swindle perpetrated on Esau by Jacob. Deceitful speech is one of the most heinous offenses against God (TWOT). Esau then responded: "Is it because he was named Overreacher that he must always be overreaching me? Must he always dog my steps, be at my heels? Twice he has supplanted me and outwitted me!"

III. Special Features

A. PRESERVING OUR HERITAGE

Is it too late? Have we already sold our souls for a mess of pottage? Has materialism eaten out the soul of the Black American? If so, it is a sign of our success in becoming Americanized (integrated?), for the love of things, and the love of the dollar are indeed part of the American way of life. As Christians, we do not begrudge any one's success. God blesses—materially, physically, financially, etc.

He gives us richly all things to enjoy (1 Timothy 6: 17), but we are to control things, not have things control us. Spirituality is what counts in life, not materiality. Esau failed to realize this. Saints of color are cautioned: Do not become like Esau, "who for one morsel of food sold his birthright" (Hebrews 12:16-17). We are right now citizens of heaven! May we heed the exhortation to set our affections on things above, not on things on the earth (Colossians 3:2).

B. A CONCLUDING WORD

Earlier, Ishmael was excluded from the promised blessing; so now Esau is on the losing side. Their carnality or fleshliness was one cause. The frivolous way in which Esau sold his birthright for a bowl of soup shows his spiritual inadequacy. This by no means justifies the evil actions of Jacob (with the help of his mother). It is always amazing how God works things out, even to the point of using our evil deeds. His grace is indeed mysterious. He is able to make good come out of our bad. But, Christians are not to do evil in order that good may come out of it. We are not to sin in order that grace may abound (Romans 6:1). May we value the promises of God, and take Him at His Word, without attempting to "force God's hand."

HOME DAILY BIBLE READINGS
Week of July 25, 1999
Deceit and Blessing

July 19 M. Genesis 25:19-26, Jacob and Esau Are Born
July 20 T. Genesis 25:27-34, Jacob Buys Esau's Birthright
July 21 W. Genesis 27:1-17, Rebekah Schemes to Deceive Isaac
July 22 T. Genesis 27:18-29, Jacob Deceives Isaac
July 23 F. Genesis 27:30-40, Esau Sold His Blessing
July 24 S. Luke 16:1-9, Because He Had Acted Shrewdly
July 25 S. Psalm 24:1-6, Clean Hands and Pure Hearts

Jacob's Flight and Vision

Unit III. A People Tested
Children's Unit—God Chose and Called a People—Part II
Adult Topic—Running From Difficulty

.....

Youth Topic—Take Me to Your Leader
Children's Topic—Jacob Had a Dream

.....

Devotional Reading—Psalm 121:1-8
Background Scripture—Genesis 27:41—28:22
Print—Genesis 27:41; 28:10-16, 18-22

● ● ● ● ● ● ● ● ● ● ●

PRINTED SCRIPTURE

Genesis 27:41; 28:10-16, 18-22 (KJV)

41 And Esau hated Jacob because of the blessing wherewith his father blessed him: and Esau said in his heart, The days of mourning for my father are at hand; then will I slay my brother Jacob.

.....

10 And Jacob went out from Beersheba, and went toward Haran.

11 And he lighted upon a certain place, and tarried there all night, because the sun was set; and he took of the stones of that place, and put them for his pillows, and lay down in that place to sleep.

12 And he dreamed, and behold a ladder set up on the earth, and the top of it reached to heaven: and behold the angels of God ascending and descending on it.

13 And, behold, the LORD stood above it, and said, I am the LORD God of Abraham thy father, and the

Genesis 27:41; 28:10-16, 18-22 (NRSV)

41 Now Esau hated Jacob because of the blessing with which his father had blessed him, and Esau said to himself, "The days of mourning for my father are approaching; then I will kill my brother Jacob."

.....

10 Jacob left Beersheba and went toward Haran.

11 He came to a certain place and stayed there for the night, because the sun had set. Taking one of the stones of the place, he put it under his head and lay down in that place.

12 And he dreamed that there was a ladder set up on the earth, the top of it reaching to heaven; and the angels of God were ascending and descending on it.

13 And the LORD stood beside him and said, "I am the LORD, the God of Abraham your father and the

God of Isaac: the land whereon thou liest, to thee will I give it, and to thy seed;

14 And thy seed shall be as the dust of the earth, and thou shalt spread abroad to the west, and to the east, and to the north, and to the south: and in thee and in thy seed shall all the families of the earth be blessed.

15 And, behold, I am with thee, and will keep thee in all places whither thou goest, and will bring thee again into this land; for I will not leave thee, until I have done that which I have spoken to thee of.

16 And Jacob awaked out of his sleep, and he said, Surely the LORD is in this place; and I knew it not.

.....

18 And Jacob rose up early in the morning, and took the stone that he had put for his pillows, and set it up for a pillar, and poured oil upon the top of it.

19 And he called the name of that place Bethel: but the name of that city was called Luz at the first.

20 And Jacob vowed a vow, saying, If God will be with me, and will keep me in this way that I go, and will give me bread to eat, and raiment to put on,

21 So that I come again to my father's house in peace; then shall the LORD be my God:

22 And this stone, which I have set for a pillar, shall be God's house: and of all that thou shalt give me I will surely give the tenth unto thee.

God of Isaac; the land on which you lie I will give to you and to your offspring;

14 and your offspring shall be like the dust of the earth, and you shall spread abroad to the west and to the east and to the north and to the south; and all the families of the earth shall be blessed in you and in your offspring.

15 Know that I am with you and will keep you wherever you go, and will bring you back to this land; for I will not leave you until I have done what I have promised you."

16 Then Jacob woke from his sleep and said, "Surely the LORD is in this place— and I did not know it!"

.....

18 So Jacob rose early in the morning, and he took the stone that he had put under his head and set it up for a pillar and poured oil on the top of it.

19 He called that place Bethel; but the name of the city was Luz at the first.

20 Then Jacob made a vow, saying, "If God will be with me, and will keep me in this way that I go, and will give me bread to eat and clothing to wear,

21 so that I come again to my father's house in peace, then the LORD shall be my God,

22 and this stone, which I have set up for a pillar, shall be God's house; and of all that you give me I will surely give one tenth to you."

KEY VERSE

And, behold, I am with thee, and will keep thee in all places whither thou goest, and will bring thee again into this land; for I will not leave thee, until I have done that which I have spoken to thee of.— Genesis 28:15

OBJECTIVES

After reading this lesson, the student should be better informed about:

1. The determined nature of hatred;
2. One way that God revealed His will;
3. The scope of the Abrahamic Covenant; and,
4. Jacob's vow to tithe.

POINTS TO BE EMPHASIZED

Adult/Youth/Children
Key Verse: Genesis 28:15
Print: Genesis 27:41; 28:10-16, 18-22

—Esau, angry with his brother Jacob for having received his father's blessing, resolved to kill Jacob after Isaac died. (27:41)

—During his flight to Haran, Jacob dreamed of a ladder on which God's angels ascended and descended. (28:10-12)

—God spoke to Jacob during the dream, promising him God's presence, many descendants, and safe return to the land. (28:13-15)

—Jacob awoke from his dream filled with fear and awe and marked the place of his dream by anointing the stone he had used as a pillow. (28:16-19)

—Jacob vowed that if God would keep him safe and return him to his father's house, Jacob would give God one-tenth of his income. (28:20-22)

(NOTE: Use KJV Scripture for Adults; NRSV Scripture for Youth and Children)

TOPICAL OUTLINE OF THE LESSON

I. Introduction

A. The Significance of Tithing
B. Biblical Background

II. Exposition and Application of the Scripture

A. Esau's Hatred (Genesis 27:41)
B. Jacob's Dream (Genesis 28:10-12)
C. God's Promise (Genesis 28:13-15)
D. Jacob's Vow (Genesis 28:16, 18-22)

III. Special Features

A. Preserving Our Heritage
B. A Concluding Word

I. Introduction

A. THE SIGNIFICANCE OF TITHING

The first mention of giving a tithe occurs in Genesis 14:20 where it is recorded that Abram gave Melchizedek "tithes of all." This event is expanded in Hebrews 7:4: "Abraham, gave the tenth of the spoils." Interestingly, the word rendered "spoils" is literally, "the top of the heap." We would say that God does not want us to give Him what we scrape from the bottom of the barrel, but what is "the cream of the crop." The second mention of tithing is found in today's lesson, in Genesis 28:22, when Jacob vowed: "all that thou shalt give me I will surely give the tenth unto thee." Abram and Jacob together are examples of men who voluntarily tithed centuries before it became mandatory for Israel under Moses at Mount Sinai (Leviticus 27:30-32; Deuteronomy 14:22-29). Unfortunately, tithing became a fetish with the Pharisees (Matthew 23:23), and their legalism was spiritually devastating.

Tithing recognizes that God owns the whole thing; the tithe is a token that we are not the owners, but the owers. So we pay tithes to acknowledge divine ownership over the nine-tenths. If Old Testament Jews could tithe, with their limited knowledge of God, New Testament Christians, with their greater knowledge, should do no less. Unfortunately, some of our churches have made giving ten percent mandatory, either to become members or to hold office. This is legalism! Or, they have the Tithers to march around first! All of our giving should be voluntary, without show, and tied in with our appreciation for and love of the Lord who cleansed us in His blood.

B. BIBLICAL BACKGROUND

When Rebekah was told that her son Esau intended to kill his brother, Jacob, she called Jacob in and told him of Esau's plan. It would be only a matter of time when the father Isaac would die, so they thought, and then Esau could carry out the fratricide. Rebekah then entreated Jacob to obey her, and flee to Haran where her brother Laban live. "Stay with him a few days, until he cools off." A few days, as we later see turned out to be twenty years! Did Rebekah really think that Esau's hatred would dissipate so soon? That he would so easily forget what Jacob had done? Nonetheless, she quickly analyzed the situation and persuasively handled her husband and her favorite son.

"Go, and I will send for you later, for what sense is there in my losing both of you in one day?" Little did Rebekah know that she would never again on earth see Jacob! She had been instrumental in Jacob's deception of his father, Isaac (Genesis 27:5-17), and again, we see her plan for getting Jacob out of harm's way by sending him away, and giving as the motive for his journey her desire that Jacob marry from among her kindred. No mention is made of her death (except to tell us where she was buried, (Genesis 49:31), so we assume she died while Jacob was away living with Laban.

II. Exposition and Application of the Scripture

A. ESAU'S HATRED
(Genesis 27:41)

And Esau hated Jacob because of the blessing wherewith his father blessed him: and Esau said in his heart, The days of mourning for my father are at hand; then will I slay my brother Jacob.

By tracing the use of the verb to hate, we find examples of hatred throughout the Scriptures. Leah was hated (Genesis 29:31); Joseph's brothers hated him (Genesis 37:4). We find that Amnon hated Tamar; and in turn, Absalom hated Amnon (2 Samuel 13:15, 22). Ahab, king of Israel told Jehoshaphat, king of Judah, "I hate Micaiah," the prophet (1 Kings 22:8). And of course, the Lord Jesus Christ was hated, and believers are told: "If the world hate you, ye know that it hated me before it hated you" (John 15:18).

And now we see that Esau's crying and complaining turned into deep hatred for Jacob, so much so that he resolved in his heart to kill him once old man Isaac died. Which of the three characters was most to be pitied—Rebekah, Jacob or Esau? Match Esau's purpose of revenge with Rebekah's scheming with Jacob's deception, and see how their sins were beginning to take their toll. When would they learn that God is able to keep His promises without human scheming and deceit—or vengeance! The truth is, nobody in chapter 27 appears in a good light. Esau was willing to wait until Isaac died, for he did not want to cause his father any further grief.

Behind this willingness was his belief that his father would not live much longer. However, Isaac was one hundred and eighty years old when he died (Genesis 35:28). Now Isaac was forty when he married; sixty when the twins were born (Genesis 25:20,26). If Jacob was approximately seventy-seven at the time of our present story, it means that the father, Isaac, was one hundred and thirty-seven when Jacob left to go to his uncle, Laban. Isaac lived then some forty-three years more after Jacob left! "The days of mourning for my father are at hand" (approaching: RSV)—ha! so much then for hatred's plan for quick revenge!

B. JACOB'S DREAM
(Genesis 28:10-12)

And Jacob went out from Beersheba, and went toward Haran. And he lighted upon a certain place, and tarried there all night, because the sun was set; and he took of the stones of that place, and put them for his pillows, and lay down in that place to sleep. And he dreamed, and behold a ladder set up on the earth, and the top of it reached to heaven: and behold the angels of God ascending and descending on it.

And so Jacob obeyed his father and his mother, and went out from Beersheba (where Isaac was then living, Genesis 26:25) toward Haran. At a certain spot—seemingly accidental, but divinely chosen, when the sun had set, Jacob put down some stones for a pillow, and lay down to sleep. "He dreamed that there was a ladder set up on the earth, and the top of it reached to heaven; and behold, the angels of God were ascending and descending on it!" (RSV).

Note, the ascending is first. Ordinarily you would think of angels descending and ascending this ladder that extended from earth to heaven. The same thing is said in John 1:51, where the Lord speaks to Nathanael. It is thus implied that the angels were already on earth. They were present on earth, protecting the fearful, hook and crook of a man destined to be renamed Israel and to become the father of the twelve tribes of that nation. Keep in mind that the ladder was a picture of Jesus Christ, the Mediator, the Go-Between. It symbolized also communication with Heaven, divine uninterrupted fellowship. In addition Keil and Delitzsch suggest that the angels carry up to the Lord the wants of God's people, and bring down what they need, thus caring for God's people on earth.

C. GOD'S PROMISE
(Genesis 28:13-15)

And, behold, the LORD stood above it, and said, I am the LORD God of Abraham thy father, and the God of Isaac: the land whereon thou liest, to thee will I give it, and to thy seed; And thy seed shall be as the dust of the earth, and thou shalt spread abroad to the west, and to the east, and to the north, and to the south: and in thee and in thy seed shall all the families of the earth be blessed. And, behold, I am with thee, and will keep thee in all places whither thou goest, and will bring thee again into this land; for I will not leave thee, until I have done that which I have spoken to thee of.

Jehovah who identified Himself as the Lord God of Abraham, and the God of Isaac stood above that which God had promised to these two patriarchs. He now promised to Jacob. First, there is the vow that the Lord would give to Jacob and his descendants the land upon which he was lying. Second: There is the promise of a great number of descendants, as numerous as the dust of the earth. Third, his progeny will expand in every direction—west, east, north and to the south. Fourth: God predicted that all peoples on earth will be blessed through Jacob and his children. Fifth: The Lord assured Jacob that He would stay with him, watch over him wherever he went. Sixth: God would return him to this land. And Seventh, He would never abandon Jacob until He had done exactly what He promised to do.

Note the unconditional nature of these divine promises. "I will give...will keep...will bring...will not leave...." How God will accomplish all this is not our business to know. Our task is to take Him at His Word. What else could Jacob do! He couldn't change himself, nor had the Lord exhorted him to do so. The confidence expressed in this key verse (Genesis 28:15) is God's absolute confidence in Himself.

D JACOB'S VOW
(Genesis 28:16, 18-22)

And Jacob awaked out of his sleep, and he said, Surely the LORD is in this place; and I knew it not. And Jacob rose up early in the morning, and took

the stone that he had put for his pillows, and set it up for a pillar, and poured oil upon the top of it. And he called the name of that place Bethel: but the name of that city was called Luz at the first. And Jacob vowed a vow, saying, If God will be with me, and will keep me in this way that I go, and will give me bread to eat, and raiment to put on, So that I come again to my father's house in peace; then shall the LORD be my God: And this stone, which I have set for a pillar, shall be God's house: and of all that thou shalt give me I will surely give the tenth unto thee.

Visions are experienced by those who are awake; dreams by those who are asleep. Jacob awaked out of his sleep and realized that the Lord was there and Jacob had not known it. Remembering what he had dreamed, Jacob realized that the Lord was there in a special way. A merciful God had granted this revelation, and Jacob's immediate reaction was to tell of the impression made upon him. Perhaps for the first time in his life, Jacob was aware of God's presence right there at his side. It is interesting that the first thing Jacob thought of was not all of the promised physical or material blessing of the covenant, but the Person (Genesis 28:13) who spoke with him—the Lord God of Abraham and the God of Isaac. Early the next day, Jacob arose, and took the stone that he had put for his pillow and set it up for a pillar. This stone pillar was set up to indicate the holy spot where Jehovah revealed himself. So the stone was to be a memorial of the mercy manifested by God. The oil poured upon the top of the pillar was in keeping with the regular symbols of a memorial and consecration. Jacob then named the place Bethel, the house of God. Before this incident, the neighboring town was named Luz. And now because of Jacob's dream there, Bethel became one of the significant places in the Bible. In the vow that Jacob made, the word "if" is better rendered, "since." Otherwise it appears that Jacob sought to bargain with the Lord. He was not seeking to strike a bargain with God, as if to say, "Lord, if you will do that, then I will do this." No. Actually, Jacob accepted what the Lord promised, and in turn he makes a threefold vow: (1) Jehovah will be my God; (2) This stone shall be God's House; and (3) I will tithe all that I have. It is then in error to attempt to make Jacob a mercenary.

III. Special Features

A. PRESERVING OUR HERITAGE

Many different Old Testament characters are found in Black songs (Negro Spirituals): Moses and Daniel are two of the most popular. But also mentioned are Noah, Pharaoh, Joshua, Gideon, Samson, Delilah, David, Ezekiel, Jonah, the three Hebrew lads, et al. Our Sunday school lesson leads us to talk about Jacob.

He is seen in several different ways based upon our study of the Spiritual, "We Are Climbin' Jacob's Ladder." First of all (my order is arbitrary, not an order of importance), Jacob speaks of what is called FORTITUDE, a characteristic defined as "courage in facing pain, danger, or trouble" *(World Book Dictionary)*. In this Spiritual, it takes inner strength or fortitude for one to live the Christian life in a corrupt world. Thus the poet suggests to the sinner, "If you love my Jesus, why not serve Him?" What the listener thinks and feels thus becomes part of the song. Second, the Spiritual portrays Jacob as a SOLDIER fighting his way up to heaven. Climbing up to glory is an attractive journey, but it is a fighting operation. The Christian Jacobs on this earth understand that this vile world is no friend to grace, to help us onto God, and we are not carried to the skies on flowery beds of ease (Isaac Watts). Third, this Spiritual demonstrates the DETERMINA-TION of the singer to rise above his condition of servitude and "nobodiness." His mind is made up to climb up "round by round," even as is evident in the life of Jacob. For as the lesson shows from the Scripture, Jacob's beginning was one of trickery, deception, and supplanting. The poet is determined to go all the way, for he is heaven bound. Fourth, the poet used many objects as devices to accomplish his purpose of informing and transforming the hearer. He sang of such things as fountains, gates, wheels, robes, crowns, harps, chariots, horses, trains, etc. In the spiritual that points to our lesson, it is a ladder (Genesis 28:12). To the slave, climbing was an important matter.

B. A CONCLUDING WORD

We see in the life of Jacob the picture of a believer disciplined by the hand of God. When you look beyond his mixed motives and immoral methods, you see a man who took God at His Word and held on to spiritual values. He valued the things of God, and appreciated God's covenant with Abraham. In time, the Supplanter, Heel-Catcher, Overreacher matured—and Jacob became Israel. We observe in the life of Jacob a wonderful picture of the Grace of God. Finally, see in the life of Jacob also a picture of the nation (Israel) which descended from him. Because of sin and a lack of faith, a rejection of Jesus the Messiah, Israel has long sought to make it in this world on its own. Having been returned to their land some fifty years now, there still remains "the time of Jacob's trouble" (Jeremiah 30:7), another name for Tribulation. Only when the nation wrestles with God and accepts the Lord Jesus will it come to pass that "all Israel shall be saved" (Romans 11:26).

Jacob's Struggle at Peniel

Adult Topic—Facing Fear and Danger

.....

Youth Topic—Wrestling With the Future
Children's Topic—Jacob Returned Home

.....

Devotional Reading—Matthew 18:21-35
Background Scripture—Genesis 32:3—33:17
Print—Genesis 32:9-12, 24-30; 33:1-4

● ● ● ● ● ● ● ● ● ● ●

PRINTED SCRIPTURE

Genesis 32:9-11, 24-30; 33:1-4 (KJV)

9 And Jacob said, O God of my father Abraham, and God of my father Isaac, the LORD which saidst unto me, Return unto thy country, and to thy kindred, and I will deal well with thee:

10 I am not worthy of the least of all the mercies, and of all the truth, which thou hast shewed unto thy servant; for with my staff I passed over this Jordan; and now I am become two bands.

11 Deliver me, I pray thee, from the hand of my brother, from the hand of Esau: for I fear him, lest he will come and smite me, and the mother with the children.

.....

24 And Jacob was left alone; and there wrestled a man with him until the breaking of the day.

25 And when he saw that he prevailed not against him, he touched the hollow of his thigh; and the hollow of Jacob's thigh was out of joint, as he wrestled with him.

Genesis 32:9-11, 24-30; 33:1-4 (NRSV)

9 And Jacob said, "O God of my father Abraham and God of my father Isaac, O LORD who said to me, 'Return to your country and to your kindred, and I will do you good,'

10 I am not worthy of the least of all the steadfast love and all the faithfulness that you have shown to your servant, for with only my staff I crossed this Jordan; and now I have become two companies.

11 Deliver me, please, from the hand of my brother, from the hand of Esau, for I am afraid of him; he may come and kill us all, the mothers with the children.

12 Yet you have said, 'I will surely do you good, and make your offspring as the sand of the sea, which cannot be counted because of their number.'"

.....

24 Jacob was left alone; and a man wrestled with him until daybreak.

25 When the man saw that he did not prevail against Jacob, he struck

26 And he said, Let me go, for the day breaketh. And he said, I will not let thee go, except thou bless me.

27 And he said unto him, What is thy name? And he said, Jacob.

28 And he said, Thy name shall be called no more Jacob, but Israel: for as a prince hast thou power with God and with men, and hast prevailed.

29 And Jacob asked him, and said, Tell me, I pray thee, thy name. And he said, Wherefore is it that thou dost ask after my name? And he blessed him there.

30 And Jacob called the name of the place Peniel: for I have seen God face to face, and my life is preserved.

.....

AND Jacob lifted up his eyes, and looked, and, behold, Esau came, and with him four hundred men. And he divided the children unto Leah, and unto Rachel, and unto the two handmaids.

2 And he put the handmaids and their children foremost, and Leah and her children after, and Rachel and Joseph hindermost.

3 And he passed over before them, and bowed himself to the ground seven times, until he came near to his brother.

4 And Esau ran to meet him, and embraced him, and fell on his neck, and kissed him: and they wept.

him on the hip socket; and Jacob's hip was put out of joint as he wrestled with him.

25 Then he said, "Let me go, for the day is breaking." But Jacob said, "I will not let you go, unless you bless me."

27 So he said to him, "What is your name?" And he said, "Jacob."

28 Then the man said, "You shall no longer be called Jacob, but Israel, for you have striven with God and with humans, and have prevailed."

29 Then Jacob asked him, "Please tell me your name." But he said, "Why is it that you ask my name?" And there he blessed him.

30 So Jacob called the place Peniel, saying, "For I have seen God face to face, and yet my life is preserved."

.....

Now Jacob looked up and saw Esau coming, and four hundred men with him. So he divided the children among Leah and Rachel and the two maids.

2 He put the maids with their children in front, then Leah with her children, and Rachel and Joseph last of all.

3 He himself went on ahead of them, bowing himself to the ground seven times, until he came near his brother.

4 But Esau ran to meet him, and embraced him, and fell on his neck and kissed him, and they wept.

KEY VERSE

I am not worthy of the least of all the mercies, and of all the truth, which thou hast shewed unto thy servant; for with my staff I passed over this Jordan; and now I am become two bands.— Genesis 32:10

OBJECTIVES

After reading this lesson, the student will appreciate more of what it means to:

1. Give our fears over to the Lord;
2. Wrestle with God;
3. Have God change our names;
4. Be humbled by God; and,
5. Have God banish our fears.

POINTS TO BE EMPHASIZED

Adult/Youth
Key Verse: Genesis 32:10
Print: Genesis 32:9-11, 24-30; 33:1-4

—Jacob prayed to God for protection from Esau, whom Jacob feared would kill him. (32:9-11)
—Jacob wrestled all night with a mysterious stranger. (32:24)
—When it looked like neither would win, the stranger asked Jacob to let him go, but Jacob refused. (32:25-26)
—The stranger blessed Jacob and gave him a new name, Israel; then Jacob renamed the place Peniel because he had seen God face to face there. (32:27-32)
—The same day, a humbled and fearful Jacob met Esau and was surprised when Esau greeted him with an enthusiastic embrace. (33:1-4)

Children
Key Verse: Genesis 33:4
Print: Genesis 32:9, 11; 33:1-12

—Jacob prayed to God for protection from Esau, whom Jacob feared would kill him. (32:9)
—Jacob was concerned for the safety of his family. (32:10)
—Jacob divided his household in preparation to meet Esau. (33:1-2)
—Jacob offered gifts to his brother, Esau, to find favor with him. (33:8-11b)
—Esau accepted the gifts from Jacob. (33:11c)
—The same day, a humbled and fearful Jacob met Esau and was surprised when Esau greeted him with an enthusiastic embrace. (33:1-4)
—The members of Jacob's family showed respect for Esau. (33:5-7)
—Jacob offered his brother Esau many gifts that Esau refused to accept at first, but Jacob insisted that he take them. (33:8-12)

(NOTE: Use KJV Scripture for Adults; NRSV Scripture for Youth and Children)

I. Introduction

A. WRESTLING WITH GOD

The word "wrestle" occurs only once in the New Testament: "for we wrestle not against flesh and blood... (Ephesians 6:12). **Pale** is the Greek word, and it is seen in the English word, **palaestra,** "the place for wrestling," but which now means the "place for athletic exercises in general" (ISBE). As used in the general context of the figure of speech for the Christian's armor, it has the general sense of "Conflict" (Kittel). The believer's opponents in this battle are the Devil and demons.

In the Old Testament, we find two basic words for wrestling. One word is used in Genesis 30:8: And Rachel said, "With great wrestlings **(naphtulim)** have I wrestled **(pathal)** with my sister, and I have prevailed: and she called his name Naphtali." "Wrestlings," "wrestled," and "Naphtali" all come from the same verb, **pathal,** to twist. Because her maid, Bilhah, bore Jacob a second son, named Naphtali, Rachel's reproach was removed, for the offspring of her maid were considered Rachel's very own sons.

In Genesis 32:24-25, we twice read that Jacob "wrestled." The verb used is **abaq,** a Hebrew word suggesting the dust of the feet of one running away or fleeing, thus the idea of one who while wrestling, gets dusty from wallowing on the ground. Contrary to what some commentators teach, I see the wrestling as actual corporeal, physical wrestling. Allowing Jacob to wrestle with Him was God's way of answering Jacob's prayer for deliverance. It was necessary for God to deal with Jacob as an enemy; for the "Overreacher" needed to understand he was opposing God with all of his deceptions. Jacob "overcame God" by the power of faith and prayer, and not by the power of his flesh—for the Lord had put Jacob's carnal nature out of joint! Humbled in wrestling with the Lord, Jacob succeeded in possessing the covenant promise and the covenant blessing.

B. BIBLICAL BACKGROUND

Jacob's fear is described in Genesis 32:1-8. He had been ordered by the Lord to return home (Genesis 31:13). You would think that having the assurance of obeying the Lord would help eliminate fears. As he approached home, the messengers he had sent out on a peace mission returned and informed him that Esau was coming to meet him, accompanied by a band of some 400 men. This news filled Jacob with great fear that Esau would seek vengeance. In spite of God's revealing Himself to Jacob at both Bethel and Mahanaim (Genesis 31:13; 32:1), the returning brother was greatly alarmed. He then split his family into two groups, thinking that if Esau captured one group, the other would escape. His fears still dictated his strategy. Only later in life did Jacob learn rather than to trust his own understanding and scheming, to acknowledge the Lord and to lean on Him.

II. Exposition and Application of the Scripture

A. FEARFUL JACOB PRAYS FOR DELIVERANCE
(Genesis 32:9-11)

And Jacob said, O God of my father Abraham, and God of my father Isaac, the LORD which saidst unto me, Return unto thy country, and to thy kindred, and I will deal well with thee: I am not worthy of the least of all the mercies, and of all the truth, which thou hast shewed unto thy servant; for with my staff I passed over this Jordan; and now I am become two bands. Deliver me, I pray thee, from the hand of my brother, from the hand of Esau: for I fear him, lest he will come and smite me, and the mother with the children.

In this beautiful prayer, Jacob acknowledged that the God of his grandfather Abraham, and the God of his father Isaac, was also his God. He reminded the Lord that He was the One who commanded him to leave his own country and kindred (Genesis 31:3, 13), and make the journey to Canaan. God promised: "I will deal well with thee." Note Jacob's humility in this prayer, as he also acknowledged all of God's mercies and truth. He confesses his unworthiness to receive these expressions of the goodness of God. The word translated worthy **(qaton)** means little, small, insignificant, weak. "I have always been too little, and I am right now too insignificant to deserve all your expressions of 'steadfast love and all the faithfulness' (RSV) which You have shown to Your servant."

His concern for the safety of his family moved him to act first and pray later. Some Christians still do this; they make up their programs, then ask the Lord to bless what they have decided to do already. So he divided his family into two bands. His petition is sincere. "Deliver me, I pray thee...." This is the first time in the Bible we read these words for deliverance. Throughout the Bible, we find many more cries for deliverance falling from the lips of beleaguered believers. We especially hear such cries from the Psalms: DELIVER ME speedily from the sword, from the hand of and the will of my enemies, from all my transgressions, my blood-guiltiness, from the evil man, my persecutors, workers of iniquity, from lying, from oppressors, out of the mire, etc.

Thank God, He "knoweth how to deliver the godly out of temptation" (2 Peter 2:9). See in Jacob's plea his faith in Jehovah, as he literally throws himself upon the arm of the Lord. Too often, we depend upon deliverance from sources other than God. And so our prayer life is negatively affected. Jacob frankly admits he is afraid of Esau, and what his brother may do to Jacob's family and loved ones. "Deliver me from my brother Esau's hands (his power)! You promised to deal well with me. I take you at Your word. Deliver me!" By faith, Jacob knew that God's word never fails. In this classic model of Old Testament devotion, different aspects of prayer are seen: (1) invocation, verse 9; (2) thanksgiving, verse 10; (3) petition, verse 11; (4) appeal to God's faithfulness, verse 12. While the element of confession of sin, prominent in later prayers, is not strong here, there is confession of fear and unworthiness. And as Leupold points out, it is sin that makes us unworthy of God's kindnesses and acts of faithfulness.

B. TENACIOUS JACOB WRESTLES WITH GOD
(Genesis 32:24-26)

And Jacob was left alone; and there wrestled a man with him until the breaking of the day. And when he saw that he prevailed not against him, he touched the hollow of his thigh; and the hollow of Jacob's thigh was out of joint, as he wrestled with him. And he said, Let me go, for the day breaketh. And he said, I will not let thee go, except thou bless me.

We left Jacob in prayer. Now we find he has moved on toward the meeting with Esau. With his family, he passed over the ford, Jabbok, and sent them on ahead. "And Jacob was left alone." Luther said: "Every man holds that this text is one of the most obscure in the Old Testament." It is said there is no commentator who can explain Jacob's experience in such a way that he perfectly cleans up every difficulty in interpretation. Personally, I would take issue with the scholars who spiritualize the event.

Some claim the "wrestling" was simply agonizing prayer and crying, and describe it as a "real conflict of both mind and body, a work of the spirit with intense effort of the body" (Keil and Delitzsch). It was all this, but there is no reason why we should not take the wrestling literally. And, the resultant crippling of Jacob is taken physically also. How strange to read of a man like Jacob wrestling with God and God "losing" the match! This defeat does not impugn (oppose on attack as false or lacking integrity) God's omnipotence. God is Sovereign and does as He pleases.

Here, He was pleased to portray the power of prayer. Furthermore, remember God is the One who disabled Jacob. By a mere touch of the hollow of Jacob's thigh, the socket of his thigh was knocked out of joint. The renderings of wrenched (NIV), and sprained (Moffatt) are weak. Better put: Jacob's thigh was dislocated (NASB) or put out of joint (RSV). We believe that Jacob walked with a limp the rest of his life. Evidently, Jacob needed to be physically disabled in order to teach or warn him not to fall back on his old ways of using carnal, unspiritual methods and devices. Imagine God crying out to a frail, sinful man like Jacob—"Let Me go!" What grace! What condescension! What mercy, "for day is breaking," and it must not be that Jacob should see the face of God—that would bring death. Indeed, Jacob could not have endured seeing the face of the preincarnate Savior. Jacob knew what he was doing, as he persisted in prayer and in the desire to be blessed. He somehow recognized the divine nature of his antagonist. Jacob stood on God's promises and exercised true faith; his perseverance caused him to lose the physical battle, but to win a great spiritual victory. He held on to the angel (Hosea 12:4)—the Angel of Jehovah. Of course, God allowed Himself to be conquered. It was our Lord's desire, however, to purge Jacob of all of his self-sufficiency and fleshly striving.

C. CHANGED JACOB RECEIVES A NEW NAME
(Genesis 32:27-30)

And he said unto him, What is thy name? And he said, Jacob. And he said, Thy name shall be called no more Jacob, but Israel: for as a prince hast thou power with God and with men, and hast prevailed. And Jacob asked him, and said, Tell me, I pray thee, thy name. And he said, Wherefore is it that thou dost ask after my name? And he blessed him there. And Jacob called the name of the place Peniel: for I have seen God face to face, and my life is preserved.

Jacob refused to let go until the wrestler blessed him. His opponent asked, "What is your name?" The answer came, "Jacob." At that point, God changed his name from Jacob to Israel. The supplanter, overreacher, became literally, "he who strives with God; or God strives; or God rules." The change of name signified a change in life style, the entering of a new relation with God. When Abram and Sarai had their names changed, they were always called by their new names. God wanted to show that their new position was indeed a permanent one. They represented a divine destiny. However, both Jacob and Israel are interchangeably applied to the nation descended from Jacob, and represent a personal achievement (Leupold). Use of both names shows that (1) the spiritual state is determined by faith is Israel. Thus the covenant nation exists; and (2) the natural state is determined by flesh and blood, Jacob.

Jacob then said, "tell me, I pray thee, Thy name." The angel replied, "why do you ask after My name?" And without answering him further, He blessed Jacob there. To see the Angel of the Lord is to see God; to see Jesus Christ is to see God. But no man has seen God in His totality. That is impossible. First of all, He is everywhere present at the same time, and we are in but one place at one time. Second, He dwells in light which no man can approach (1 Timothy 6:16). We cannot even look at the sun with the naked eye at its brightest at noonday. So the truth remains: No man shall see Him and live (Exodus 33:20). No man has seen God at any time (John 1:18)—to these Scriptures we always add the words, "In His totality." He is the invisible God (Colossians 1:15).

Yet, the Bible records men stating they have seen God. Thiessen explains that when you see your face in the mirror, in a sense you see yourself. Yet in another sense, you do not literally see yourself. No man can see the very essence of God (Hebrews 1:3). What men have seen are the reflections of God's glory. Theophanies (God-appearances) are visible manifestations of God. What Jacob saw was only a dim vision of God, even though face to face. Then in mercy, for Jacob's own protection, the Lord withdrew at dawn and left Jacob alone at sunrise. Jacob called the place Peniel, which means, "the face of God."

D. HUMBLED JACOB IS FORGIVEN
(Genesis 33:1-4)

And Jacob lifted up his eyes, and looked, and, behold, Esau came, and with him four hundred men. And he divided the children unto Leah. and unto Rachel, and unto the two handmaids. And he put the handmaids and their children foremost, and Leah and her children after, and Rachel and Joseph hindermost. And he passed over before them, and bowed himself to the ground seven times, until he came near to his brother. And Esau ran to meet him, and embraced him, and fell on his neck, and kissed him: and they wept.

After this experience at Peniel, Jacob looked up and saw Esau coming, along with his four hundred men. Guilt and forgiveness approached each other, reminding us of the "Prodigal Son" (Luke 15:20-21). Time, by the grace of God, had rooted out the remaining malice in Esau's heart. God had also blessed Esau with great material possessions. Jacob still had some spiritual growing to do, but was well on his way. Evidently encouraged by the blessing obtained in the wrestling, Jacob divided up his family, and passed over before them to meet Esau. He humbled himself before his brother with a sevenfold bow. The salutation hints of a rather excessive obeisance, but we sense a sincere honoring of Esau by Jacob.

At the sight of his brother, Esau was carried away with emotion, and ran to him, embraced him, fell upon his neck and kissed him. They both wept. What a wonderful story of reconciliation after twenty long eventful years! God grant that we too can truthfully say, "What a wonderful change in my life has been wrought since Jesus came into my heart."

III. Special Features

A. PRESERVING OUR HERITAGE

When we think about this Special Feature entitled, "Preserving Our Heritage," we are perplexed as to whether to deal with Black American believers, Black American unbelievers, or just Black Americans. I fear the attempt to apply the Scriptures to both believers and unbelievers will get us into deep theological trouble. Take for example the matter of wrestling with God. Unbelievers do not wrestle with the Lord. So if we limit the wrestling to believers, we would suggest that in our days of adversity in White America, saints of color spent time in prayer, calling on the Lord to deliver them from the enemy (slavery, racism, Jim Crowism, etc.). We wrestled, God moved, and we were freed.

At least now our fear is that in the battle against the New Racism, we Black Christians have forsaken wrestling with God, and have joined forces with the unsaved. Consequently, we have a new champion—not Christ. We have new methods of achieving deliverance—not prayer or seeking God's will according to the Scriptures. Indeed, the new ways—which seem right to many of us—are ways that often leave Jesus Christ out!

For some, the new motto is: Seek ye first the POLITICAL kingdom, and all things will be added unto you. For others, HUMANISM is the answer! What would you add to this list? What are your thoughts concerning the spiritual significance of Jacob's wrestling to the Black American Christian? What is your response to the critic who would say, "Who wants to wrestle with God these days? We Blacks are already crippled for life."

B. A CONCLUDING WORD

"God delights in the faith of those who cling tenaciously to His promises and claim them in prevailing prayer" (Luke 18:1, 7: H. Morris). For many years, the Lord worked with and on Jacob. In order to be of use to God, Jacob needed to be honest, not a schemer; humble, not self-righteous; dependent upon God, not self-sufficient. To achieve this, the Lord crippled Jacob. What has it taken in your life to develop Christlikeness?

Lameness, sickness, loss of material possessions, heartbreak, imprisonment, etc.—whatever the crisis the Lord used to get us straightened out, we now rejoice. We now thank God for what He worked out in our lives. And we thank Him for altering our lifestyles—yea, the angels in heaven done changed our names!

It may be noted that the biblical concept of "Name" embodies the character and traits of the person. Changed names indicated a new thrust in personal destiny. Our name must be more than an external appendage to illusive conceptions of ourselves.

HOME DAILY BIBLE READINGS
Week of August 8, 1999
Jacob's Struggles At Peniel

Aug. 2 M. Genesis 32:3-8, Jacob Undertakes Reconciliation With Esau
Aug. 3 T. Genesis 32:9-21, Jacob Prepares Gifts for Esau
Aug. 4 W. Genesis 32:22-32, Jacob Wrestles With "A Man" At Jabbok
Aug. 5 T. Genesis 33:1-11, Esau and Jacob Are Reunited
Aug. 6 F. Genesis 33:12-17, Esau and Jacob Go Separate Ways
Aug. 7 S. Matthew 5:21-26, Jesus on Human Relations
Aug. 8 S. Matthew 18:21-35, Forgive Seventy-Seven Times!

Favored Son to Slave

Adult Topic—Family Difficulties

.....

Youth Topic—When Life Takes a Tumble
Children's Topic—Joseph Was a Favored Son

.....

Devotional Reading—1 Samuel 18:1-9
Background Scripture—Genesis 37:1-35
Print—Genesis 37:3-4, 17b-28

• • • • • • • • • • • •

PRINTED SCRIPTURE

Genesis 37:3-4, 37:17b-28

3 Now Israel loved Joseph more than all his children, because he was the son of his old age: and he made him a coat of many colours.

4 And when his brethren saw, that their father loved him more than all his brethren, they hated him, and could not speak peaceably unto him.

.....

17b for I heard them say, Let us go to Dothan. And Joseph went after his brethren, and found them in Dothan.

18 And when they saw him afar off, even before he came near unto them, they conspired against him to slay him.

19 And they said one to another, Behold, this dreamer cometh.

20 Come now therefore, and let us slay him, and cast him into some pit, and we will say, Some evil beast hath devoured him: and we shall see what will become of his dreams.

21 And Reuben heard it, and he delivered him out of their hands;

Genesis 37:3-4, 17b-28

3 Now Israel loved Joseph more than any other of his children, because he was the son of his old age; and he had made him a long robe with sleeves.

4 But when his brothers saw that their father loved him more than all his brothers, they hated him, and could not speak peaceably to him.

.....

17b "They have gone away, for I heard them say, 'Let us go to Dothan.'" So Joseph went after his brothers, and found them at Dothan.

18 They saw him from a distance, and before he came near to them, they conspired to kill him.

19 They said to one another, "Here comes this dreamer.

20 Come now, let us kill him and throw him into one of the pits; then we shall say that a wild animal has devoured him, and we shall see what will become of his dreams."

21 But when Reuben heard it,

and said, Let us not kill him.

22 And Reuben said unto them, Shed no blood, but cast him into this pit that is in the wilderness, and lay no hand upon him; that he might rid him out of their hands, to deliver him to his father again.

23 And it came to pass, when Joseph was come unto his brethren, that they stript Joseph out of his coat, his coat of many colours that was on him;

24 And they took him, and cast him into a pit: and the pit was empty, there was no water it in.

25 And they sat down to eat bread: and they lifted up their eyes and looked, and, behold, a company of Ishmeelites came from Gilead with their camels bearing spicery and balm and myrrh, going to carry it down to Egypt.

26 And Judah said unto his brethren, What profit is it if we slay our brother, and conceal his blood?

27 Come, and let us sell him to the Ishmeelites, and let not our hand be upon him; for he is our brother and our flesh. And his brethren were content.

28 Then there passed by Midianites merchantmen; and they drew and lifted up Joseph out of the pit, and sold Joseph to the Ishmeelites for twenty pieces of silver: and they brought Joseph into Egypt.

he delivered him out of their hands, saying, "Let us not take his life."

22 Reuben said to them, "Shed no blood; throw him into this pit here in the wilderness, but lay no hand on him"—that he might rescue him out of their hand and restore him to his father.

23 So when Joseph came to his brothers, they stripped him of his robe, the long robe with sleeves that he wore;

24 and they took him and threw him into a pit. The pit was empty; there was no water in it.

25 Then they sat down to eat; and looking up they saw a caravan of Ishmaelites coming from Gilead, with their camels carrying gum, balm, and resin, on their way to carry it down to Egypt.

26 Then Judah said to his brothers, "What profit is it if we kill our brother and conceal his blood?

27 Come, let us sell him to the Ishmaelites, and not lay our hands on him, for he is our brother, our own flesh." And his brothers agreed.

28 When some Midianite traders passed by, they drew Joseph up, lifting him out of the pit, and sold him to the Ishmaelites for twenty pieces of silver. And they took Joseph to Egypt.

KEY VERSE

Now Israel loved Joseph more than all his children, because he was the son of his old age: and he made him a coat of many colours.— Genesis 37:3

OBJECTIVES

After reading this lesson, the student should be better aware of:

1. The danger of parents showing partiality;
2. The sin of conspiracy;
3. The peril of going along with the crowd; and,
4. Man's inability to thwart the plan of God.

POINTS TO BE EMPHASIZED

Adult/Youth/Children
Key Verse: Genesis 37:3
Print: Genesis 37:3-4, 17b-28

—Israel loved Joseph more than his other children, and Joseph's brothers hated him. (3-4)
—Joseph's brothers conspired to kill him, (17b-20)
—One of the brothers, Reuben, persuaded the others not to kill Joseph, but to keep him prisoner in a pit instead. (21-24)
—When the brothers saw a band of traders coming, they sold Joseph into slavery for twenty pieces of silver. (25-28)

(NOTE: Use KJV Scripture for Adults; NRSV Scripture for Youth and Children)

TOPICAL OUTLINE OF THE LESSON

I. Introduction

A. The Lack of Brotherly Love
B. Biblical Background

II. Exposition and Application of the Scripture

A. Bad Family Relations (Genesis 37:3-4)
B. Conspiracy Against Joseph (Genesis 37:17b-20)
C. Joseph's Life Saved (Genesis 37:21-22)
D. Joseph Cast Into a Pit (Genesis 37:23-27)
E. Joseph Sold Into Slavery (Genesis 37:28)

III. Special Features

A. Preserving Our Heritage
B. A Concluding Word

I. Introduction

A. THE LACK OF BROTHERLY LOVE

The failure to exercise brotherhood comes to our attention very early in the Scriptures. "Am I my brother's keeper?" has become a well-known question, one asked by Cain who had just slain Abel his brother (Genesis 4:8-9). In an earlier lesson, we studied the hatred Esau had for Jacob (Genesis 27:41). Under the reign of king David, we found Amnon raped his half-sister, Tamar, and her brother, Absalom, caused Amnon's death (2 Samuel 13). And now in today's lesson, the brothers of Joseph hate him so much that, aside from Reuben, and possibly Judah, they are bent upon committing fratricide (Genesis 37:4, 5, 18).

These examples perfectly show the depth of the depravity of the human heart— to hate and kill one's own brother! Blood may be thicker than water, but men do not hesitate to let flow the internecine fluid of life. All Christians are brothers and sisters in Christ, and we are repeatedly admonished to love one another. In fact, such love is proof that we have been born again, proof that we have passed from death unto life (1 John 3:14).

God's Word informs us that it is God's desire that brethren dwell together in unity (Psalm 133:1). God's Word exhorts: "Let brotherly love continue" (Hebrews 13:1). "Love the brotherhood" (1 Peter 2:17; 2 Peter 1:7). He who does not love his brother abides in death. Christ commands that we love one another; in this way all men shall know that we are the disciples of Christ. Surely these Scriptures that speak of Christian brotherhood serve to convince us all the more of the heinousness of hatred among siblings, and the awfulness of fratricide.

B. BIBLICAL BACKGROUND

Seven men hold a position of prominence in the Book of Genesis. They are: Adam, Abel, Noah, Abraham, Isaac, Jacob, and Joseph. More space is given to the life of Joseph than to any of the others. His birth is recorded in Genesis 30:22-24. The one hundred and ten years that Joseph lived cover chapters 37 to 50. Many conservative scholars point out that Joseph was a type of Jesus Christ, even though the Bible does not actually label him as such. In Bible language, the word "type" refers to likeness. When a person resembles another in some essential feature, the two are called type and antitype (ISBE). In other words, a type is a shadow, a prefigure, a copy or pattern.

First, note that both Joseph and Christ were loved by their Father. Second, both rebuked the sins of their brothers. Someone has suggested, that this is the one flaw in Joseph's character—he was a tattletale. They cite what is said in Genesis 37:2: "...and Joseph brought unto his father their evil report." Third, both were hated by their brothers. Fourth, both were rejected by their brothers. Joseph's claims caused him to be labeled a "dreamer." Our Lord came unto His own, and they received Him not (John 1:11). Fifth, they were conspired against by their brothers and sold Joseph for twenty pieces of silver, our Lord for thirty pieces of silver (Genesis 37:28; Matthew 26:15). Sixth: Note their brothers' intention to kill them. And of course, the Lord Jesus was slain (Acts 2:23, 3:15). However, Joseph was slain only in intent and figure (Scofield).

Seventh, both were mistreated, unjustly punished. Joseph was falsely accused of attempted rape and put in jail (Genesis 39)—his feet shackled by iron fetters (Psalm 105:18). Christ was mocked, laughed at, ridiculed, lied on, traps set for Him, arrested, beaten, spat on, beard plucked, crucified. Eighth, both received a Gentile bride during the period of rejection: Joseph married Asenath (Genesis 41:45); Christ, the Church (Ephesians 5:25-32). Ninth, as the world was saved by the grain distributed in time of famine, so the Lord Jesus came to seek and to save that which was lost (Luke 19:10). Tenth, as Joseph revealed himself to his brothers, and reconciled them, so the Jews will eventually have their eyes opened, and recognize Jesus as the Christ (Messiah).

Eleventh, finally, there is the matter of exaltation. Joseph was lifted from a pit to Potiphar's place to prison to Pharaoh's palace. But his second place in command in Egypt pales into insignificance compared with the glory of the Lord Jesus who shall return to rule the world with a rod of iron! These then are some of the main points of likenesses when it is said Joseph is a type of Christ.

II. Exposition and Application of the Scripture

A. BAD FAMILY RELATIONS
(Genesis 37:3-4)

Now Israel loved Joseph more than all his children, because he was the son of his old age: and he made him a coat of many colours. And when his brethren saw that their father loved him more than all his brethren, they hated him, and could not speak peaceably unto him.

We have noted before the danger of parents expressing more love for one child than for another. We saw what happened in the case of Jacob and Esau: "And Isaac loved Esau...but Rebekah loved Jacob" (Genesis 25:28). Now we learn that Israel (Jacob) loved Joseph "more than all his children, because he was the son of his old age." And we might add, Joseph was the firstborn of Rachel, Jacob's favorite wife. It appears Jacob learned nothing from his own experience with respect to favoritism. The hatred produced in the lives of Jacob's sons will yield far greater heartbreak than that which occurred in Jacob's life.

This expression of partiality became one of the things that caused the brothers of Joseph to dislike him. The father even went so far as to make for Joseph "a coat of many colors"—a description taken from the Old Testament written in Greek (Septuagint). This was actually a tunic or a "long robe with sleeves" (RSV). It is literally, "a coat of extremities," one reaching down to the ankles, and with sleeves reaching to the wrists.

Usually, this upper coat had no sleeves, and reached only down to the knees. This gift was a sign of special honor and distinction, the kind of coat worn by children of nobility. It was a mark of the father's special affection. The Hebrew suggests "he made him a coat" is "he used to make him a coat." This means that when one coat wore out. Jacob would make another. Naturally, it stirred up jealous hatred in the hearts of the brothers. It is easy to see how the display of such favoritism could serve only to create trouble. "The coat was ostentatious and provocative" (Kidner). Add to this the fact that Joseph brought unto his father an evil (Genesis 37:2) report concerning the behavior of his brothers, and you have all the more reason why Joseph was not very popular with his older siblings.

See then this combination of events: (1) Joseph's reaction against the immoral conduct of his brothers, and his reporting it to their father; (2) the royal robe given Joseph, which set him apart from the rest. It is not certain exactly what was in Jacob's mind. Full rights of the firstborn had been given to Judah. Reuben, the firstborn forfeited his primogeniture when he committed incest, when he lay with Bilhah, his father's concubine: and Israel heard it (Genesis 35:22). On the other hand, the brothers may have inferred their father had chosen Joseph "to be the one through whom divine blessings would flow" (Wycliffe).

(3) Now add the matter of the dreams Joseph had which told of the brothers giving obeisance to Joseph. Their rebellion against the divine nature of what Joseph dreamed may have had a large part of play in their hatred, even though from their point of view, God had nothing to do with Joseph's dreams. You can readily understand why the brothers could not "salute" him, that is, speak peaceably (say shalom to him), offer him the usual greeting, "Peace be with you." Hatred prevented them.

B. CONSPIRACY AGAINST JOSEPH
(Genesis 37:17b-20)

For I heard them say, Let us go to Dothan. And Joseph went after his brethren, and found them in Dothan. And when they saw him afar off, even before he came near unto them, they conspired against him to slay him. And they said one to another, Behold, this dreamer cometh. Come now therefore, and let us slay him, and cast him into some pit, and we will say, Some evil beast hath devoured him: and we shall see what will become of his dreams.

On this occasion, Joseph searched for his brothers. He met a man who told him that he heard them mention going to Dothan. There Joseph found them. When they spied him at a distance coming their way, hatred gave birth to conspiracy (Hebrew verb, **nakal,** means to be crafty, deceitful, knavish); they deceitfully planned against him. Throughout the Scriptures, conspiracies are seen as wicked. Those involved—Korah against Moses, Absalom against David, Jezebel against Naboth, Haman against the Jews, Herod against the Baby Jesus, the Pharisees against the Lord Jesus—all faced the wrath of God.

"Here comes the Dreamer," they mocked; the Hebrew is literally, "Master (**baal:** lord) of dreams!" The decision was made to kill Joseph, and cast his body into a pit. What is called a pit here was a large hole in the ground with a narrow opening that had been used as an artificial cistern. Then, they would return home and tell their father that some wild animal had slain him, and devoured him. "Then we will see what shall become of his dreams!"

C. JOSEPH'S LIFE SAVED
(Genesis 37:21-22)

And Reuben heard it, and he delivered him out of their hands; and said, Let us not kill him. And Reuben said unto them, Shed no blood, but cast him into this pit that is in the wilderness, and lay no hand upon him; that he might rid him out of their hands, to deliver him to his father again.

Reuben, the oldest son of Jacob, then spoke up. He protested the idea of killing Joseph. He had in mind later returning to the pit, rescuing Joseph, and delivering him to their father. Even though Reuben's earlier infamous deed cost him the right of the firstborn, as the oldest son, he still felt an obligation to oppose the proposal to murder Joseph. And there appears to be no reason to doubt his sincerity even if his motive was to get back in favor with his father, Jacob. At any rate, Reuben was successful in dissuading them from their original plan. Had he been left in the pit, Joseph would have died eventually, and so with this in mind, the brothers agreed to do as Reuben suggested. But for the moment, Reuben had saved Joseph's life.

D. JOSEPH CAST INTO A PIT
(Genesis 37:23-27)

And it came to pass, when Joseph was come unto his brethren, that they stript Joseph out of his coat, his coat of many colours that was on him; And they took him, and cast him into a pit: and the pit was empty, there was no water in it. And they sat down to eat bread: and they lifted up their eyes and looked, and, behold, a company of Ishmeelites came from Gilead with their camels bearing spicery and balm and myrrh, going to carry it down to Egypt. And Judah said unto his brethren, What profit is it if we slay our brother, and conceal his blood? Come, and let us sell him to the Ishmeelites, and let not our hand be upon him; for he is our brother and our flesh. And his brethren were content.

When Joseph finally came near, the first thing his brothers did was to grab him and strip him of the coat he wore. The verb used means to strip off, as one would remove clothing or a soldier's armor, make naked. The context thus "may denote violent or judgmental action" (TWOT). And so Joseph was cast into the waterless cistern. Then look what the good brothers did—they sat down to eat! How callous, how cruel! One wonders if they threw a scrap or two to Joseph?

As God would have it, a company of Ishmaelites came from Gilead on their way down to Egypt. At this point, Judah said, "What profit is it if we slay our brother, and conceal his blood?" He suggested that instead, they sell Joseph to the Ishmaelites. Now Reuben was not present at this time, for he came back later only to discover the pit was empty (Genesis 37:29). Evidently, Judah also was not too keen on the idea of fratricide, and saw selling Joseph into slavery a better way of preventing those dreams from being fulfilled. At any rate, whatever their varying motives, the brothers agreed with Judah.

E. JOSEPH SOLD INTO SLAVERY
(Genesis 37:28)

Then there passed by Midianites merchantmen; and they drew and lifted up Joseph out of the pit, and sold Joseph to the Ishmeelites for twenty pieces of silver: and they brought Joseph into Egypt.

Note that three different names are given to the merchantmen: Ishmaelites, Midianties, and Medanites (literally: Genesis 37:36). These tribes were descendants from Abraham, and resembled one another very closely in their modes of life, their nomadic lifestyle. The terms are used interchangeably, so there is no error or contradiction involved; the band or caravan was composed of both Ishmaelites and Midianties. This aspect of the story ends with the information that Joseph was sold "for twenty pieces of silver."

Note the italicized word, pieces, put in by the translators. Coins were not invented until the seventh century B.C. The silver was weighed out and whatever was then the current price for slaves was paid. At a later date, Moses fixed twenty pieces of silver as the value of a boy between the ages of five and twenty (Leviticus 27:5); the average price of a slave was thirty shekels (Exodus 21:32). Of course, prices varied, depending upon the age, sex, health of the slaves. And so Joseph was taken to Egypt.

III. Special Features

A. PRESERVING OUR HERITAGE

The Bible is a book of truth. It does not sugar-coat sin. Human beings are portrayed as sinners terribly in need of a Savior, in need of a change. And the change that counts comes only through faith in the Lord Jesus Christ. This matter of human depravity is brought to our attention very vividly by today's lesson. It also brings to mind the fact—often resisted and denied by so many Black Americans—that Africans sold Africans into slavery. So, Black Africans were not only captured by European slave traders, but also captured and sold by Africans to the Whites. So much for Black Brotherhood!

Our study of the Bible opens our eyes to the cruelty within the human heart. The lust for power, prestige, position, money continues. And sin is not racially prejudiced, although racial prejudice is sin. This is why Black Baptists must never forget Biblical priorities! Sin is more important than skin. Without hearts that are right with God, we can never get right with each other. A bad vertical relationship (with God) can result only in a bad horizontal relationship (with man)—even with brothers.

B. A CONCLUDING WORD

In this moving story, the hand of God is seen in a remarkable way. Christians are encouraged by reading the life of Joseph. His surrendered approach strengthens us in the belief that our steps are ordered by the Lord. In the 13 chapters which depict the life of Joseph, God's calling throughout the 110 years Joseph lived is clear and unmistakable. There is never any hint of rebellion, complaint, fighting against circumstances, maltreatment, false accusation, incarceration, etc. Joseph left his life in the hands of God. Perhaps those dreams as a seventeen-year old lad so impressed his heart that he never doubted God's good hand was upon him. He believed God. Although it took thirteen more years before he could see more clearly the Lord's fulfilling of the dreams, Joseph never wavered.

Unfortunately, there are those today in our churches who do not realize that the call to service is not always one of peace. They would have us accept their Conceive-it, Believe-it, Achieve-it philosophy. These Seers of Success, these Prophets of Prosperity would by-pass the rejection, enslavement, false accusations, imprisonment experiences of life. However, when we take God at His Word, we realize that whatever evil occurs in our lives, God in Christ is able to make it work out to our good (Genesis 50:20; Romans 8:28).

HOME DAILY BIBLE READINGS
Week of August 15, 1998
Favored Son to Slave

Aug. 9 M. Genesis 37:1-11, Joseph, the Tattle-Tale and Dreamer
Aug. 10 T. Genesis 37:12-24, Joseph's Brothers Were Jealous of Him
Aug. 11 W. Genesis 37:25-28, Joseph Is Sold to Ishmaelites
Aug. 12 T. Genesis 37:29-36, Jacob Mourns Joseph's Imagined Death
Aug. 13 F. 1 Samuel 18:1-9, Saul is Jealous of David
Aug. 14 S. Matthew 20:1-16, The First Workers Are Jealous of the Last
Aug. 15 S. Luke 14:14-27, The Disciples Wonder Who is the Greatest

Opportunity to Serve

Adult Topic—Opportunities to Serve

.....

Youth Topic—Dreams Can Make a Difference
Children's Topic—Joseph Served Others

.....

Devotional Reading—John 6:1-13
Background Scripture—Genesis 39—41
Print: Genesis 41:14-16, 25-27, 34-40

• • • • • • • • • • •

SCRIPTURE PRINT

Genesis 41:14-16, 25-27, 34-40 (KJV)

14 Then Pharaoh sent and called Joseph, and they brought him hastily out of the dungeon: and he shaved himself, and changed his raiment, and came in unto Pharaoh.

15 And Pharaoh said unto Joseph, I have dreamed a dream, and there is none that can interpret it: and I have heard say of thee, that thou canst understand a dream to interpret it.

16 And Joseph answered Pharaoh, saying, It is not in me: God shall give Pharaoh an answer of peace.

.....

25 And Joseph said unto Pharaoh, The dream of Pharaoh is one: God hath shewed Pharaoh what he is about to do.

26 The seven good kine are seven years; and the seven good ears are seven years: the dream is one.

27 And the seven thin and ill favoured kine that came up after

Genesis 41:14-16, 25-27, 34-40 (NRSV)

14 Then Pharaoh sent for Joseph, and he was hurriedly brought out of the dungeon. When he had shaved himself and changed his clothes, he came in before Pharaoh.

15 And Pharaoh said to Joseph, "I have had a dream, and there is no one who can interpret it. I have heard it said of you that when you hear a dream you can interpret it."

16 Joseph answered Pharaoh, "It is not I; God will give Pharaoh a favorable answer."

.....

25 Then Joseph said to Pharaoh, "Pharaoh's dreams are one and the same; God has revealed to Pharaoh what he is about to do.

26 The seven good cows are seven years, and the seven good ears are seven years; the dreams are one.

27 The seven lean and ugly cows that came up after them are seven years, as are the seven empty ears

them are seven years; and the seven empty ears blasted with the east wind shall be seven years of famine.

.....

34 Let Pharaoh do this, and let him appoint officers over the land, and take up the fifth part of the land of Egypt in the seven plenteous years.

35 And let them gather all the food of those good years that come, and lay up corn under the hand of Pharaoh, and let them keep food in the cities.

36 And that food shall be for store to the land against the seven years of famine, which shall be in the land of Egypt; that the land perish not through the famine.

37 And the thing was good in the eyes of Pharaoh, and in the eyes of all his servants.

38 And Pharaoh said unto his servants, Can we find such a one as this is, a man in whom the Spirit of God is?

39 And Pharaoh said unto Joseph, Forasmuch as God hath shewed thee all this, there is none so discreet and wise as thou art:

40 Thou shalt be over my house, and according unto thy word shall all my people be ruled: only in the throne will I be greater than thou.

blighted by the east wind. They are seven years of famine.

.....

34 "Let Pharaoh proceed to appoint overseers over the land, and take one-fifth of the produce of the land of Egypt during the seven plenteous years.

35 Let them gather all the food of these good years that are coming, and lay up grain under the authority of Pharaoh for food in the cities, and let them keep it.

36 That food shall be a reserve for the land against the seven years of famine that are to befall the land of Egypt, so that the land may not perish through the famine."

37 The proposal pleased Pharaoh and all his servants.

38 Pharaoh said to his servants, "Can we find anyone else like this—one in whom is the spirit of God?"

39 So Pharaoh said to Joseph, "Since God has shown you all this, there is no one so discerning and wise as you.

40 You shall be over my house, and all my people shall order themselves as you command; only with regard to the throne will I be greater than you."

KEY VERSE

And Pharaoh said unto Joseph, Forasmuch as God hath shewed thee all this, there is none so discreet and wise as thou art: Thou shalt be over my house, and according unto thy word shall all my people be ruled: only in the throne will I be greater than thou.—Genesis 41:39-40

OBJECTIVES

After reading this lesson, the student will have knowledge of:

1. God's use of dreams;
2. The fear of famines;
3. Man's dependence upon God for food;
4. The fact that godly subjects are a blessing to rulers; and,
5. How personal discipline is essential to the dream.

POINTS TO BE EMPHASIZED

Adult/Youth/Children
Key Verse: Genesis 41:39-40
Print: Genesis 41:14-16, 25-27, 34-40

—When Pharaoh heard that there was a prisoner who could interpret dreams, he sent for Joseph and asked him to interpret his dream. (14-16)
—Joseph declared that God had used the dream to show Pharaoh that Egypt would have seven years of plenty followed by seven years of famine. (25-27)
—Joseph suggested to Pharaoh that the king save some of the crops from the years of plenty to carry the nation through the famine. (34-36)
—Pharaoh, impressed with Joseph's wisdom, appointed Joseph to be his second-in-command. (37-40)

(NOTE: Use KJV Scripture for Adults; NRSV Scripture for Youth and Children)

TOPICAL OUTLINE OF THE LESSON

I. Introduction
A. Dreams
B. Biblical Background

II. Exposition and Application of the Scripture
A. Pharaoh Interviews Joseph (Genesis 41:14-16)
B. Joseph Interprets Pharaoh's Dream (Genesis 41:25-27).
C. Joseph Recommends Procedure (Genesis 41:34-36)
D. Pharaoh Appoints Joseph (Genesis 14:37-40)

III. Special Features
A. Preserving Our Heritage
B. A Concluding Word

I. Introduction

A. DREAMS

Inasmuch as this lesson centers upon dreams and their interpretation, we shall spend extra time in our study of this phenomenon. Throughout man's history, dreams and their interpretations have been the occasion for investigation, speculation, and curiosity. Mystery, superstition, the desire to know the future, all have combined to move men to hold dreams in awe while yet seeking to fathom their meaning.

References to dreams and dreamers are found primarily in the Old Testament, with the books of Genesis and Daniel referring most often to them. Abimelech, Laban, Jacob, Joseph, the baker and the butler, the Pharaoh of Joseph's day, Solomon, Daniel, Nebuchadnezzar, and others in the Old Testament dreamed and their dreams were used by God. Indeed, God was the Source of their dreams. The New Testament has even less to say about dreams. What does occur in the New Testament is mostly found in Matthew's Gospel (1:20, 2:12, 13, 19, 22; 27:19), referring to Joseph, the magi, and Pilate's wife. These references are primarily warnings and announcements. In Acts 2:16-21, Peter mentions dreams, but quotes from Joel about an event still future.

And Jude 8 speaks of "filthy dreamers," a description in part of false teachers. So you see there is no mention of God revealing Himself in a dream to any Christian after the Resurrection of Christ. "The Bible, contrary to a notion perhaps too commonly held, attaches relatively little religious significance to dreams" (ISBE). Basically, then, we Christians of this present Church Age should not rely upon dreams! Christ nowhere referred to dreams, leading us to believe that He attached little if any importance to them.

God used them to write, to warn, to foretell. He used them to mold thoughts and guide actions. We cannot deny God has used dreams to communicate His will to men. But what about today? Today, we have the Holy Spirit living in our bodies, and we have the Bible. We are cautioned then not to attach too much importance to dreams today, but to depend upon the Bible and the Holy Spirit.

B. BIBLICAL BACKGROUND

Joseph suffered imprisonment because he refused to commit sexual immorality; he did what was right in the sight of God! In the very heat of the temptation, hear him say: "How then can I do this great wickedness, and sin against God?" (Genesis 39:9). You recall that Potiphar's wife falsely accused Joseph of attempting to seduce her. Actually, the opposite was true: she repeatedly sought to entice him—"day by day." And then one day, while her husband was away, she caught Joseph by the coat, and said, "Come to bed with me!" He resisted her advances, ran out of the house, and left his coat in her hand. She called her servants, lied to them, and then later when her husband came home, told him the same lie—that Joseph had sought to rape her. As a result, Joseph was put into prison.

All the time of his incarceration, Joseph was treated well. God took care of him, and gave him favor in the eyes of the warden. It came to pass that the king's baker and his butler (cupbearer) offended their king and were put in the same prison with Joseph. Some time later, both men dreamed the same night—and were saddened by their inability to interpret their dreams. They told their dreams to Joseph, and God enabled Joseph to interpret them. For the cupbearer, it was good news; within three days, he would be restored to his old position. For the chief baker, it was bad news; within three days, he would be hanged. And so it turned out, but the chief cupbearer forgot Joseph altogether.

Two years later, Pharaoh had a dream—in fact, two dreams—but hs magicians and wise men could not interpret them for him. At this point, the chief cupbearer remembered Joseph, told Pharaoh of the young imprisoned Hebrew who correctly interpreted his dream and that of the chief baker. Today's lesson begins at this juncture. And as the story unfolds, we continue to see the good hand of God in the life of Joseph.

II. Exposition and Application of the Scripture

A. PHARAOH INTERVIEWS JOSEPH
(Genesis 41:14-16)

Then Pharaoh sent and called Joseph, and they brought him hastily out of the dungeon: and he shaved himself, and changed his raiment, and came in unto Pharaoh. And Pharaoh said unto Joseph, I have dreamed a dream, and there is none that can interpret it: and I have heard say of thee, that thou canst understand a dream to interpret it. And Joseph answered Pharaoh, saying, It is not in me: God shall give Pharaoh an answer of peace.

Upon hearing from the chief butler of one who could correctly interpret dreams, the king immediately sent for Joseph, who was then quickly released from the dungeon. Joseph shaved his hair (ICC) and beard. Leupold speaks of a shaved head and body. And he changed his clothes, and went in before Pharaoh immaculately dressed. We are told that from the Egyptians' perspective, a prisoner with a beard signified degradation and slovenliness. Such a person would not be allowed in the presence of the king; those entering the royal presence must be meticulously clean.

Pharaoh then related to Joseph the reason he was summoned from prison; namely, he had dreamed a dream and no one could interpret it. "I understand," said the king, "that for you to hear a dream is to interpret it." "No, it's not my doing; it's quite apart from me," said Joseph. This corresponds with what he had replied earlier to the two imprisoned officers, when he sought to turn their attention to God, and away from himself; there he said, "Do not interpretations belong to God?" (Genesis 40:8). In this way, Joseph denied any infallible ability to interpret dreams. Then he said: "God will give Pharaoh an answer of peace." This means a favorable answer (RSV); the answer he desires (NIV); literally it is, God will answer the peace of Pharaoh (NASB marginal note); it is that which will be conducive to the well-being of Pharaoh.

B. JOSEPH INTERPRETS PHARAOH'S DREAM
(Genesis 41:25-27)

And Joseph said unto Pharaoh, The dream of Pharaoh is one: God hath shewed Pharaoh what he is about to do. The seven good kine are seven years; and the seven good ears are seven years: the dream is one. And the seven thin and ill favoured kine that came up after them are seven years; and the seven empty ears blasted with the east wind shall be seven years of famine.

Pharaoh related to Joseph that he dreamed of seven fat and sleek cows emerged from the Nile river, and grazed in the marsh grass. Then seven gaunt, skinny, sad looking cows came up, and ate up the first seven fat fleshed cows. But even as these bad cows ate up the good cows, the bad cows still looked bad! It didn't do them any good. The king then related how he awoke. But he dreamed again, and this time he saw seven full, good ears of grain growing on one stalk, and then seven withered ears sprouted up after the good ones, and swallowed them. This is the same thing Pharaoh had told his magicians, but they could not interpret the dream.

Joseph then informed the king that the two dreams were one and the same. Basically, Pharaoh had dreamed of seven years of tremendous prosperity followed by seven years of devastating famine; there would be seven years of plenty, followed by seven years of barrenness; seven years of fat followed by seven years of leanness. The whole land of Egypt would be affected during these fourteen years. And the fact that the Lord gave him the same dream twice meant it was a sure thing (Genesis 41:32). The number two is the number of witness; the matter was established by God; "verily, verily," it shall come to pass is the idea behind the repetition of the dream's thrust. Note the two-phase dream of Joseph earlier of the sheaves, and then of the heavenly host (Genesis 37:7, 9).

The common Hebrew word for famine in the Old Testament means "hunger." In the New Testament, the Greek word primarily means "failure," "want of food." Famine is an adversity not yet experienced by America. Yet one wonders how long God's grace and mercy will allow us to throw away daily tons of good food as garbage? In Bible days, famines were caused by lack of rain, hail storms, locusts plagues, other destructive insects, enemy soldiers besieging a city, pestilence. Keep in mind that at times God sent these things that caused famine, and He did so as punishment. Kidner states that what takes place here in Egypt at this time is not to be considered a divine act of judgment.

It is predicted by Christ that the end of the age will see an increase in the number and severity of famines in diverse places (Matthew 24:7). Revelation 6:5-6 predicts the time will come (during the Tribulation age) when a single meal will cost a day's wages! Accounts of citizens being reduced to cannibalism make for difficult reading. And yet, God predicted the time would come when famine would force the people of Israel to eat the flesh of their own children (Leviticus 26:29; Deuteronomy 28:53). It actually happened in the great famine in Samaria (2 Kings 6:28; see also Jeremiah 19:9; Lamentations 2:20, 4:10; and Ezekiel 5:10).

C. JOSEPH RECOMMENDS PROCEDURE
(Genesis 41:34-36)

Let Pharaoh do this, and let him appoint officers over the land, and take up the fifth part of the land of Egypt in the seven plenteous years. And let them gather all the food of those good years that come, and lay up corn under the hand of Pharaoh, and let them keep food in the cities. And that food shall be for store to the land against the seven years of famine, which shall be in the land of Egypt; that the land perish not through the famine.

It is one thing to announce what the future holds, and another thing to do something about that future. Pharaoh was pleased with Joseph's interpretation of his dreams, and believed the interpretation was correct in substance, certain and imminent. Joseph then advised Pharaoh to appoint officers over the country. Further, his plan included: (1) during the years of plenty, take twenty percent of the produce. Storing up the surplus would prevent wastage through careless supervision; (2) store up the grain; (3) Pharaoh would have complete control; (4) maintain the storage in the cities, and thus have it available during the seven years of famine.

D. PHARAOH APPOINTS JOSEPH
(Genesis 41:37-40)

And the thing was good in the eyes of Pharaoh, and in the eyes of all his servants. And Pharaoh said unto his servants, Can we find such a one as this is, a man in whom the Spirit of God is? And Pharaoh said unto Joseph, Forasmuch as God hath shewed thee all this, there is none so discreet and wise as thou art: Thou shalt be over my house, and according unto thy word shall all my people be ruled: only in the throne will I be greater than thou.

Both Pharaoh and all of his servants were delighted with the plan, recognizing that God was behind it. Then the king said to his servants, "Can we find such a man as this, in whom is the Spirit of God?" (RSV). Such a man—enabled by God to interpret dreams! Such a man—whose interpretation would be capable of supporting a fourteen year plan. Yes, the Spirit of Elohim was the Spirit of supernatural insight and wisdom, the very One who endowed Joseph with statesmanship and wisdom.

Such a man—who, in the midst of pagans who worshiped many gods, "was not embarrassed or hesitant" to repeatedly speak about the only true and living God (H. Morris). Pharaoh's use of the phrase "spirit of God" was one "colored by polytheism" (Kidner). Evidently, Joseph's statement concerning God (verse 16) accomplished its purpose. Whether Joseph thought of himself as a candidate for the position or not, the king's mind was made up.

He said to Joseph, "You shall be over my house, and according to your word shall all my people be ruled." The Hebrew word rendered "ruled" comes from a verb meaning to kiss: "on your mouth all my people will kiss" (TWOT). Of course, all the people could not kiss Joseph. But if they kissed any object received from him, this would be considered a sign of respect and submission. Thus, they would have "ordered themselves," that is, pay respect or homage and obedience to the commands of Joseph (TWOT).

Scholars are not sure of the title of Joseph's new office. Some see him merely as a chief steward, or food administrator, or an important officer with considerable authority. Others would entitle him grand vizier, or prime minister, or secretary of state. Whatever the title, he was in charge of all the land of Egypt (Genesis 41:41, 43, 44, 46, 55; 42:6; 45:8); and was subordinate only to Pharaoh: "only as regards the throne will I be greater than you," advised Pharaoh. God moved in mysterious ways to deliver Joseph from a dungeon and exalt him to second in command in all the land of Egypt.

III. Special Features

A. PRESERVING OUR HERITAGE

The question arose concerning Joseph's handling of the famine crisis: Did Joseph engage in the slave trade? Recall that as the famine grew, the people became desperate. At first, money was offered in exchange for grain. And the royal coffers grew tremendously as Joseph gathered up all the money and brought it into Pharaoh's house. When the money was depleted, Joseph said: "Give your livestock, and I will give you bread for your livestock." This was done, but when the year ended, and the land was even more exhausted, the people returned to Joseph and said: "There is nothing left in the sight of my lord but our bodies and our lands." And so the land became Pharaoh's (Genesis 47:16-20). At this juncture, critics of Joseph's economic policy claim that he was too harsh, and that he lacked sensitivity to the Egyptians' plight. The Egyptians became serfs—their property and bodies were owned by Pharaoh. Joseph's hard bargaining has been pointed to as enslavement of the Egyptians. Joseph is seen as having changed the fundamental law of the land in order to bring about a state of bondage which "substantially agrees with patriarchal and modern slavery." And Joseph's actions are said to prove him, as Pharaoh's counselor, to be a "friend of absolute slavery." Rather than censure Joseph's measures, or see proof of inhumanity, note that the people themselves suggested the plan to sell themselves and their land: "Buy us and our land for bread, and we and our land will be servants of Pharaoh" (v. 19). However, we do not have here any scheme of Joseph to enslave them. The plan emanated from the peasants, not from some sinister motives of Joseph.

Furthermore, Joseph's plan must be seen in its historical context. The Pharaoh was looked upon as a god, and was considered absolute ruler. Theoretically, all that the Egyptians owned belonged to the Pharaoh. In summary, it is not accurate to state that Joseph engaged in slave trade during the famine in Egypt and in Canaan.

B. A CONCLUDING WORD

Has the study of Joseph's life increased your admiration for him? One might assume that because of his doting father, Joseph would have turned out to be a soft, spoiled, selfish person. Instead, he proved to be a man of sterling character and wisdom. Undoubtedly, God used the adversities of life—sold into slavery by his brothers, falsely accused by Potiphar's wife, thrown into prison, forgotten—to help Joseph grow! We take note that up to this point in his life, Joseph: (1) never complained about the ignominy suffered at the hands of his brothers; (2) never rebelled against slavery; (3) maintained his moral integrity by resisting the enticements of Potiphar's wife; (4) showed humility in giving God the credit for interpreting dreams; and (5) demonstrated great wisdom in setting up a plan to handle the surplus food during the time of plenty, and the distribution thereof in the time of famine. Our hearts are encouraged by the life of Joseph.

While we are at a decided advantage to see the experiences of Jacob with his children in retrospect and to discern the hand of God in the encounters among and between the brothers, at the time of the occurrence itself, the purpose and plan of God is not made manifest. The emotions that characterized their behavior were real in and of themselves, and as such had no reference beyond the immediate day-to-day struggle on the part of Joseph to ingratiate himself to his father by reporting his brothers' misbehavior to their father. Standing in their shoes, the rejection of and dislike for Joseph on the part of his brothers served as a source of tension and threats against which they had to protect themselves.

Although it is not the spiritual thrust of the lesson itself, parents should be well advised to garner some words of wisdom from this experience of sibling rivalry that has its basis in the partiality shown on the part of parents. Within the concrete reality of the family situation, children are different, but each must be treated in such a way that personal dignity is affirmed. Jacob could have used tact in the way in which he dealt with the source of his knowledge of the misbehavior of the other boys, but his overt special treatment of Joseph did not add to the situation. In our day when delinquency and teenage crimes are on the rise, parents must examine themselves to ascertain whether they are part of the problem or participants in solutions and programs to allow siblings to "dwell together in unity" as this will undoubtedly have impact on how they relate to those outside the family, inclusive of the community and the world at large.

HOME DAILY BIBLE READINGS
Week of August 22, 1999
Opportunity to Serve

Aug. 16 M. Genesis 39:1-18, Joseph Resists Potiphar's Wife
Aug. 17 T. Genesis 39:19—40:8, Joseph is Imprisoned
Aug. 18 W. Genesis 40:9-23, Joseph Interprets Dreams of Fellow Prisoners
Aug. 19 T. Genesis 41:1-13, The King's Cupbearer Remembers Joseph
Aug. 20 F. Genesis 41:14-24, Pharaoh Relates His Dream
Aug. 21 S. Genesis 41:25-45, Joseph Interprets Pharaoh's Dream
Aug. 22 S. Genesis 41:46-57, Joseph is Restored to Pharaoh's Favor

Forgiven and Reunited

Adult Topic—Restoring Relationships

.....

Youth Topic—Restoring Relationships
Children's Topic—Joseph Forgave His Brothers

.....

Devotional Reading—Psalm 105:7-22
Background Scripture—Genesis 42—45
Print: Genesis 44:18-20, 33—45:7

PRINTED SCRIPTURE

Genesis 44:18-20, 33—45:7 (KJV)

18 Then Judah came near unto him, and said, Oh my lord, let thy servant, I pray thee, speak a word in my lord's ears, and let not thine anger burn against thy servant: for thou art even as Pharaoh.

19 My lord asked his servants, saying, Have ye a father, or a brother?

20 And we said unto my lord, We have a father, an old man, and a child of his old age, a little one; and his brother is dead, and he alone is left of his mother, and his father loveth him.

.....

33 Now therefore, I pray thee, let thy servant abide instead of the lad a bondman to my lord; and let the lad go up with his brethren.

34 For how shall I go up to my father, and the lad be not with me? lest peradventure I see the evil that shall come on my father.

.....

THEN Joseph could not refrain himself before all them that stood

Genesis 44:18-20, 33—45:7 (NRSV)

18 Then Judah stepped up to him and said, "O my lord, let your servant please speak a word in my lord's ears, and do not be angry with your servant; for you are like Pharaoh himself.

19 My lord asked his servants, saying, 'Have you a father or a brother?'

20 And we said to my lord, 'We have a father, an old man, and a young brother, the child of his old age. His brother is dead; he alone is left of his mother's children, and his father loves him.' "

.....

33 "Now therefore, please let your servant remain as a slave to my lord in place of the boy; and let the boy go back with his brothers.

34 For how can I go back to my father if the boy is not with me? I fear to see the suffering that would come upon my father."

.....

THEN Joseph could no longer control himself before all those who by him; and he cried, Cause every man to go out from me. And there stood no man with him, while Joseph made himself known unto his brethren.

2 And he wept aloud: and the Egyptians and the house of Pharaoh heard.

3 And Joseph said unto his brethren, I am Joseph; doth my father yet live? And his brethren could not answer him; for they were troubled at his presence.

4 And Joseph said unto his brethren, Come near to me, I pray you. And they came near. And he said I am Joseph your brother, whom ye sold into Egypt.

5 Now therefore be not grieved, nor angry with yourselves, that ye sold me hither: for God did send me before you to preserve life.

6 For these two years hath the famine been in the land: and yet there are five years, in the which there shall neither be earing nor harvest.

7 And God sent me before you to preserve you a posterity in the earth, and to save your lives by a great deliverance.

stood by him, and he cried out, "Send everyone away from me." So no one stayed with him when Joseph made himself known to his brothers.

2 And he wept so loudly that the Egyptians heard it, and the household of Pharaoh heard it.

3 Joseph said to his brothers, "I am Joseph. Is my father still alive?" But his brothers could not answer him, so dismayed were they at his presence.

4 Then Joseph said to his brothers, "Come closer to me." And they came closer. He said, "I am your brother, Joseph, whom you sold into Egypt.

5 And now do not be distressed, or angry with yourselves, because you sold me here; for God sent me before you to preserve life.

6 For the famine has been in the land these two years; and there are five more years in which there will be neither plowing nor harvest.

7 God sent me before you to preserve for you a remnant on earth, and to keep alive for you many survivors."

KEY VERSE

Now therefore be not grieved, nor angry with yourselves, that ye sold me hither: for God did send me before you to preserve life.—Genesis 45:5

OBJECTIVES

After reading this lesson, the student should appreciate more highly:

1. How Judah fulfilled his promise;
2. The nature of forgiveness;
3. The joy in the restoration of relationships; and,
4. The mysterious ways God accomplishes His purposes.

POINTS TO BE EMPHASIZED

Adult/Youth/Children
Key Verse: Genesis 45:5
Print: Genesis 44:18-20, 33—45:7

—When his brothers showed up in Egypt, they obtained an audience with Joseph without their realizing he was their brother. (44:18-20)
—When Joseph demanded that Benjamin stay in Egypt as a slave, another brother, Judah, offered himself as a substitute, for he did not want his father to suffer the loss of another favorite son. (44:33-34)
—Joseph revealed his identity to his brothers, asked about his father, and they were dismayed at his presence. (45:1-4)
—Joseph allayed his brothers' distress by assuring them that God sent him to Egypt to "preserve life." (45:5-7)

(NOTE: Use KJV Scripture for Adults; NRSV Scripture for Youth and Children)

TOPICAL OUTLINE OF THE LESSON

I. Introduction

A. Forgiveness
B. Biblical Background

II. Exposition and Application of the Scripture

A. Judah Informs Joseph (Genesis 44:18-20)
B. Judah Intercedes for Benjamin (Genesis 44:33-34)
C. Joseph Reveals Himself (Genesis 45:1-4)
D. Joseph Forgives His Brothers (Genesis 45:5a)
E. The Providence of God (Genesis 45:5b-7)

III. Special Features

A. Preserving Our Heritage
B. A Concluding Word

I. Introduction

A. FORGIVENESS

The word "forgiveness" does not literally occur in today's lesson, but the subject certainly plays a large part in the final chapters of Genesis dealing with Joseph and his brothers. In Genesis 50:17, we do find the word "forgive" twice: "Forgive...the trespass of thy brethren, and their sin...forgive the trespass of the servants of the God of thy father." These are the words Jacob commanded, before his death, that his sons speak to Joseph. Now in the Old Testament, three different Hebrew words are translated "forgive."

One word (kaphar) means to cover or shelter. When God covers sin, He disannuls it, treats it as non-existent (He casts it behind His back). This merciful disposition to shelter or cover the sinner is called forgiveness, and is connected with such doctrines as atonement and reconciliation. A second word (salach), which means to send away, or let go, is used only to denote the pardon God extends to the sinner; it is not used with respect to human beings forgiving other human beings. This brings us to the third Hebrew word (nasa), to lift up or away, carry, take. This is the verb used in Genesis 50:17, and so has reference to our lesson. It is used in the prayer of intercession by the messenger sent by Joseph's brothers. The idea is that sin can be forgiven and forgotten by God, because it is taken up and carried away. "Forgiveness was not a pagan virtue" (ISBE). This is made all the more obvious by the imprecatory (cursing) Psalms (i.e., 35, 79, 109). To forgive an offender was considered weak-spirited. In the case of Joseph's brothers, you can see that they were in an inferior position, one of submissiveness. They had no bargaining power whatsoever.

We accept the Beatitude which teaches: "Forgive, and ye shall be forgiven" (Luke 6:37). The verb used here **(apoluo)** means to loose away, undo, set free. We accept the admonition, "Be ye kind one to another, tenderhearted, forgiving one another, even as God in Christ, hath forgiven you" (Ephesians 4:32; Colossians 3:13). The verb used here **(charizomai)** means be gracious to or gratify, do a favor to, pardon. We rejoice in knowing that we have "redemption through His blood, even the forgiveness of sins" (Colossians 1:14; Ephesians 1:7). The verb used here **(aphiemi)** means to send away, let go. Thank God for forgiveness.

Finally, this too should be said. Sometimes, it is heard that we are to "forgive and forget." If by "forget" is meant wipe out from the memory, then we humans are asked to do the impossible, and to do that for which there is no scriptural support. The exhortation to "remember not" means not to hold accountable or judge and take revenge! It does not mean to erase from one's memory. When the Lord states that He will not remember our transgressions (Psalm 79:8; Jeremiah 31:34, Hebrews 8:12, 10:17, etc.), it is another way of saying He will not punish.

B. BIBLICAL BACKGROUND

A lot happened between our last lesson and today's lesson, between Genesis chapters 42:1 and 44:17. Joseph had become second in rank in Egypt. By now, the seven years of famine had caused the countries to come to Egypt to buy grain. Jacob too had heard there was food in Egypt, and sent ten of his sons there to purchase grain. Joseph tested them by accusing them of spying; he then kept Simeon as hostage, sending the others back home, requiring them to return with their youngest brother.

Finding their money in their sacks served to add to their fears. Because the famine persisted, it became necessary for the sons to return to Egypt. Jacob was unwilling to part with Benjamin, but the need of food overcame his reluctance. So this time, they took their youngest brother, Benjamin, with them. Judah then became surety (pledge, guarantee, bail) for Benjamin. He said to his father, Jacob: "You may hold me (personally: NIV) responsible for him" (NASB: Genesis 43:9).

And so the ten of them returned to Egypt to obtain grain, and to seek the release of Simeon. The lesson begins with all eleven brothers standing before Joseph, for Simeon had been brought out earlier (Genesis 43:23). Joseph entertained them and then sent them away. However, at Joseph's command, his steward of the house returned each brother's money to his sack, in addition to putting Joseph's silver cup into Benjamin's sack. Joseph had them followed and brought back. Their bags were searched, and the cup discovered. Joseph then threatened to make Benjamin his slave, but allowing the rest of them to return home in peace to their father. As we shall see, it was on this interview after this second trip to Egypt that Joseph could no longer control himself and keep secret his identity. As we read, we discover why the confrontation and reunion scene is considered one of the most dramatic in all literature (Morris).

II. Exposition and Application of the Scripture

A. JUDAH INFORMS JOSEPH
(Genesis 44:18-20)

Then Judah came near unto him, and said, Oh my lord, let thy servant, I pray thee, speak a word in my lord's ears, and let not thine anger burn against thy servant: for thou art even as Pharaoh. My lord asked his servants, saying, Have ye a father, or a brother? And we said unto my lord, We have a father, an old man, and a child of his old age, a little one; and his brother is dead, and he alone is left of his mother, and his father loveth him.

Of course, the brothers could not do as Joseph ordered; they could not allow Benjamin to remain. Judah led the way, and with his brothers approached Joseph and fell down to the ground before him. Judah—the same brother who years earlier coldly, ruthlessly suggested selling Joseph into slavery (Genesis 37:26-27)—now bowed, not knowing it was Joseph, to plead for the return of Benjamin. Back then, seemingly, Judah had no regard for breaking his father's heart. Now, he is concerned lest failure to return Benjamin "bring down the gray hairs of his father with sorrow to the grave." One of the highlights of the story is the spiritual growth of Judah. The deception and the heartlessness exhibited in chapter 37 immediately sour our opinion of Judah. But by the grace of God, a wonderful change is wrought. In chapter 43, we find him making himself surety for his youngest brother, Benjamin. And now in chapter 44, he pleads from the depths of his heart before Joseph, offering himself as a slave to take Benjamin's place. He who was willing to sell Joseph into slavery is now willing to become a slave for Joseph's brother! Progress is seen also with respect to Judah's regard for his father, Jacob. Callousness had become caring and sacrificial concern.

Speaking for himself and on behalf of his brothers, Judah rehearsed events leading up to their present dilemma (read verses 21-32). In what has been labeled as "one of the most skillful speeches in literature" (New Bible Commentary), in telling what happened, even though they were not guilty of stealing anything, Judah did not attempt to defend their actions. No excuses were made for their deeds; no denial was offered (see verse 16). The words "for thou art even as Pharaoh" remind us that when accused by an oriental despot, it is wise not to attempt to speak in self-defense.

B. JUDAH INTERCEDES FOR BENJAMIN
(Genesis 44:33-34)

Now therefore, I pray thee, let thy servant abide instead of the lad a bondman to my lord; and let the lad go up with his brethren. For how shall I go up to my father, and the lad be not with me? lest peradventure I see the evil that shall come on my father.

At last, we see the terrific change in Judah's heart. His plea, states W. W. White, is sustained, pathetic, simple and dramatic; it was, said another, the climax of God's dealing with Judah. Someone described Judah's words: "A more moving oration than oratory ever pronounced." Judah's speech is called "the finest specimen of dignified and persuasive eloquence in the Old Testament" (ICC). "One of the manliest, most straight-forward speeches ever delivered by any man" (Leupold). Luther describes Judah's prayer as what prayer ought to be, a perfect specimen of prayer.

Judah realized that he spoke with one in command in Egypt second only to Pharaoh. Joseph therefore had the authority to pardon or condemn. How moved Joseph was to hear how his aged father Jacob grieved upon hearing that if the youngest son was not brought to Egypt the next time, they were not to come at all! Even then, their presence was testimony to the severe struggle the father had in deciding to let them go. They needed food; Simeon would be released; Benjamin would be taken care of; and God would watch over the entire proceeding—these were the reasons Jacob acquiesced to let his sons return to Egypt.

C. JOSEPH REVEALS HIMSELF
(Genesis 45:1-4)

THEN Joseph could not refrain himself before all them that stood by him; and he cried, Cause every man to go out from me. And there stood no man with him, while Joseph made himself known unto his brethren. And he wept aloud: and the Egyptians and the house of Pharaoh heard. And Joseph said unto his brethren, I am Joseph; doth my father yet live? And his brethren could not answer him; for they were troubled at his presence. And Joseph said unto his brethren, Come near to me, I pray you. And they came near. And he said I am Joseph your brother, whom ye sold into Egypt.

Several things deeply moved Joseph: (1) The genuine love the brothers had for their father, and the desire not to break his heart by returning without Benjamin; (2) their expression of sincere love for Benjamin. Joseph sensed such devotion and tender affection and it drove straight through his own heart. (3) We might add that Joseph felt his brothers were truly repentant. They were not the old, cold envious bunch of twenty years ago. He was thoroughly convinced of their change. Joseph could no longer control (Hebrew: force himself) or restrain himself to pretend. His purpose had been served. All eleven brothers were there.

Jacob was at home but relatively well—so Joseph had been told (Genesis 43:27, 44:20). Joseph wisely dismissed the Egyptian servants. It was not an attempt to keep secret his relationship with his brothers; Pharaoh would soon know this. And when they were all gone, He made himself known to them. Imagine their shock upon hearing Joseph speak in their own language, let alone the shock of what he said—"I am Joseph! Does my father yet live?" His brothers could not answer him. Their tongues were temporarily glued to the roofs of their mouths. None of them uttered a word, no one answered him. They were terrified; the Hebrew word rendered "troubled" also means to hasten. This gives the idea of sudden terror, panic, alarm and astonishment (TWOT).

D. JOSEPH FORGIVES HIS BROTHERS
(Genesis 45:5a)

Now therefore be not grieved, nor angry with yourselves, that ye sold me hither:

"Now therefore be not grieved, nor angry with yourselves, that ye sold me here." This grief is said to be "sorrowful and angry distress of Joseph's brothers on recognizing him" (TWOT). How often Joseph must have thought of his unhappy experience of being sold into slavery by his own flesh and blood. Forgiveness comes, it seems, when you are able to look beyond all secondary causes and see God's good hand moving in your life. Awareness that God is in charge takes away feelings of rancor, and the desire for revenge. Whatever the Lord causes or allows to happen in the believer's life, it is calculated to enrich the saint, and make him or her more like the Lord Jesus Christ.

"You sold me, God sent me!" With these words, without bitterness or resentment, Joseph sought to remove all the blame for what they had done. It appears that all along Joseph tested his brothers in order to see what their attitudes were. Had they improved their relationship with their father? with each other? Did they remember the heart-broken Jacob when he looked upon Joseph's coat, torn and soaked in goat's blood? (Genesis 37:31). Were they sincere? Had they truly repented? In spite of Joseph's words of forgiveness, there persisted for many years among the brothers a fear, an uneasiness. This is seen even at the death of their father, when they expressed fear that Joseph "will certainly requite us (pay us back) all the evil which we did unto him" (Genesis 50:15).

E. THE PROVIDENCE OF GOD
(Genesis 45:5b-7)

For God did send me before you to preserve life. For these two years hath the famine been in the land: and yet there are five years, in the which there shall neither be earing nor harvest. And God sent me before you to preserve you a posterity in the earth, and to save your lives by a great deliverance.

Joseph was aware of the providence of God; he recognized the sovereignty of God. He acknowledged that the circumstances which caused him to be where and what he was—in Egypt, second in command—came about by the hand of

God who sent him ahead of his brothers. When his family came, God used Joseph to preserve them a posterity or remnant on earth, by delivering them from the danger of starving to death. At the time Joseph made known who he was, the seven years of plenty were over, and the land was now two years in famine. This left five more years when there would be neither plowing (earing is an Old English word for plowing) nor harvest. Because the brothers needed to know the main issue here was the will of God, Joseph attempted to explain God's plan and purpose. The brothers fitted in with God's ultimate purpose to preserve a nation called Israel, and eventually give Jesus Christ to the world.

III. Special Features

A. PRESERVING OUR HERITAGE

What Black American dares thank God for African slavery? Only the genuine Christian would be bold enough to say such a thing! Those who sold our foreparents into slavery certainly did not mean any good. They were greedy. Men will do anything for the love of money (1 Timothy 6:10). The millions of Black Americans who comprise the National Baptist Convention, U.S.A., Inc., grieve over the cruelty and murder of those slavery years. And yet, we recognize that God allowed our enslavement to happen. We are sobered by the fact that built on top of all that preceded, we stand as Christians, washed in the blood of the Lamb of God.

B. A CONCLUDING WORD

This entire story of Joseph and his brothers has been called a literary gem, a masterpiece of composition (W. W. White), "One of the sublime utterances of literature" (Wycliffe Bible Commentary). But it is far more than mere literature. It is the beginnings of the nation of Israel. It is a foreshadowing of the life of Jesus Christ. And practically speaking, it is an encouragement to us today. We have the joy of knowing that God is able through Christ to make all things—envy, hatred, desertion, enslavement, evil enticement and temptation, false accusation, imprisonment—work together for our good, for we love the Lord, and have been called according to His plan and purpose (Romans 8:28).

HOME DAILY BIBLE READINGS
Week of August 29, 1999
Forgiven and Reunited

Aug. 23 M. Genesis 42:1-17, Jacob Sends Ten Sons to Buy Grain
Aug. 24 T. Genesis 42:18-38, Joseph Conspires to See Benjamin
Aug. 25 W. Genesis 43:1-15, Jacob Agrees for Benjamin to Go to Egypt
Aug. 26 T. Genesis 43:16-34, Joseph Arranges a Meal for His Brothers
Aug. 27 F. Genesis 44:1-17, Benjamin Is Threatened With Slavery in Egypt
Aug. 28 S. Genesis 44:18-34, Judah Offers to Take Benjamin's Place
Aug. 29 S. Genesis 45:1-28, Joseph Reveals His Identity

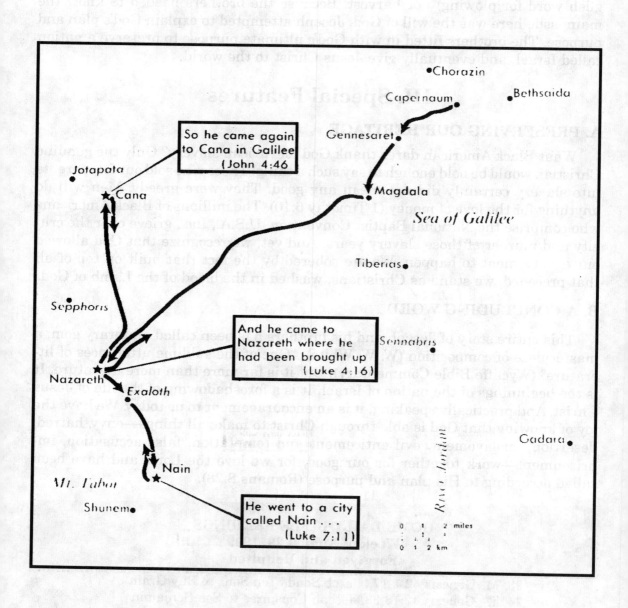

So he came again
to Cana in Galilee
(John 4:46

And he came to
Nazareth where he
had been brought up
(Luke 4:16)

He went to a city
called Nain . . .
(Luke 7:11)

Chorazin

Bethsaida

Capernaum

Gennesaret

Magdala

Sea of Galilee

Jotapata

Cana

Sepphoris

Tiberias

Sennabris

Nazareth

Exaloth

Gadara

Mt. Tabor

Nain

Shunem

River Jordan

0   1   2 miles

0   1   2 km

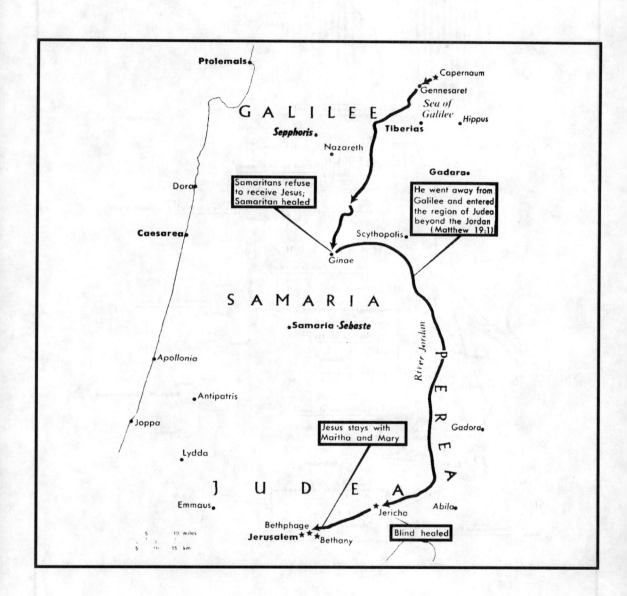

Ptolemais

Capernaum

Gennesaret

GALILEE

Sea of
Galilee

Sepphoris

Hippus

Tiberias

Nazareth

Gadara

Dora

Samaritans refuse
to receive Jesus;
Samaritan healed

He went away from
Galilee and entered
the region of Judea
beyond the Jordan
(Matthew 19:1)

Caesarea

Scythopolis

Ginae

SAMARIA

Samaria ·Sebaste

River Jordan

P
E
R
E
A

Apollonia

Antipatris

Joppa

Jesus stays with
Martha and Mary

Gadora

Lydda

J U D E A

Emmaus

Abila

Jericho

Bethphage

Blind healed

Jerusalem   Bethany

5   10 miles

5   10   15 km

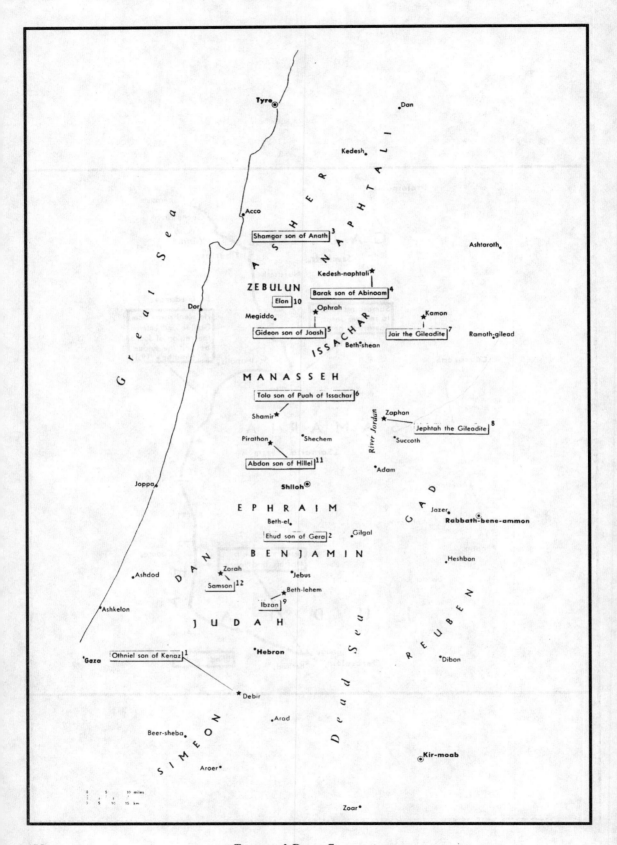

Tyre ◎

Dan •

Kedesh •

| Shamgar son of Anath | 3

Acco •

A S H E R

N A P H T A L I

Ashtaroth •

ZEBULUN

Kedesh-naphtali ★

| Barak son of Abinoam | 4

Elon | 10

Dor •

Ophrah ★

Kamon ★

Megiddo •

| Gideon son of Joash | 5

| Jair the Gileadite | 7

Ramoth-gilead •

Beth-shean •

I S S A C H A R

M A N A S S E H

| Tola son of Puah of Issachar | 6

Shamir ★

Zaphon •

River Jordan

Pirathon ★

Shechem •

| Jephtah the Gileadite | 8

Succoth •

| Abdon son of Hillel | 11

Adam •

Shiloh ◎

E P H R A I M

Beth-el •

Jazer •

Rabbath-bene-ammon

D A N

| Ehud son of Gera | 2

Gilgal •

B E N J A M I N

Heshbon •

Ashdod •

Zorah ★

Jebus •

| Samson | 12

Beth-lehem ★

| Ibzan | 9

Ashkelon •

J U D A H

G A D

R E U B E N

Gaza •

| Othniel son of Kenaz | 1

Hebron •

Dibon •

Debir ★

Arad •

Beer-sheba •

S I M E O N

Kir-moab ◎

Aroer •

0   5   10 miles
0 5 10 15 km

Zoar •

G r e a t   S e a

D e a d   S e a

Joppa •

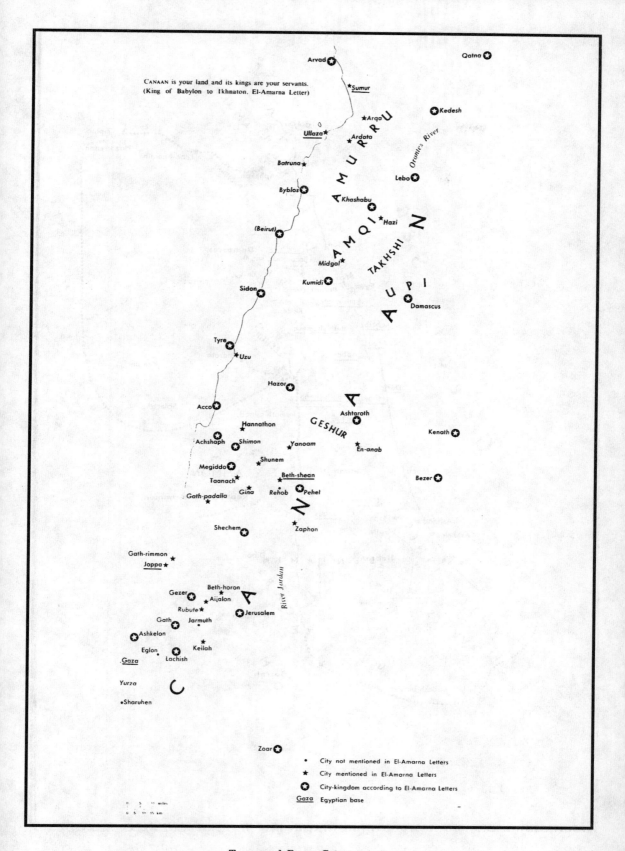

CANAAN is your land and its kings are your servants.
(King of Babylon to Ikhnaton, El-Amarna Letter)

Arvad

Qatna

Sumur

Arqa

Kedesh

Ullaza

AMURRU

Ardata

Batruna

Orontes River

Byblos

Khashabu

AMQI

Hazi

Lebo

(Beirut)

TAKHSHI

Midgal

Sidon

Kumidi

AUPI

Damascus

Tyre

Uzu

Hazor

Acco

Ashtaroth

GESHUR

Hannathon

Kenath

Achshaph   Shimon

Yanoam

En-anab

Megiddo   Shunem

Taanach   Beth-shean

Bezer

Gath-padalla   Gina   Rehob   Pehel

N

Shechem   Zaphon

Gath-rimmon

Joppa

River Jordan

Gezer   Beth-horon

Aijalon

A

Rubute   Jerusalem

Gath   Jarmuth

Ashkelon

Eglon   Keilah

Gaza   Lachish

Yurza

Sharuhen

C

Zoar

• City not mentioned in El-Amarna Letters

★ City mentioned in El-Amarna Letters

⊕ City-kingdom according to El-Amarna Letters

Gaza Egyptian base

0   5   10 miles
0   5   10 15 km

Townsend Press Commentary

453

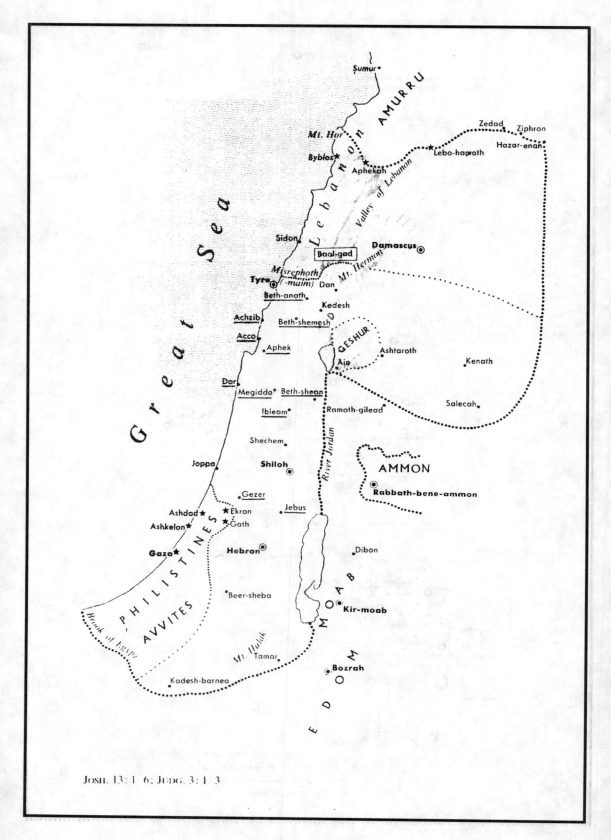

Great Sea

Şumur

Lebanon

AMURRU

Mt. Hor

Zedad   Ziphron

Byblos

Hazar-enan

Aphekah

Lebo-hamath

Valley of Lebanon

Sidon

Baal-gad

Damascus

Misrephoth
(-maim)

Mt. Hermon

Tyre

Dan

Beth-anath

Kedesh

Achzib

Beth-shemesh

Acco

GESHUR

Ashtaroth

Kenath

Aphek

Ain

Dor

Megiddo

Beth-shean

Ibleam

Ramoth-gilead

Salecah

Shechem

River Jordan

Joppa

Shiloh

AMMON

Gezer

Rabbath-bene-ammon

Ashdad   Ekron

Jebus

Ashkelon   Gath

Gaza

Hebron

Dibon

PHILISTINES

Beer-sheba

MOAB

AVVITES

Kir-moab

Brook of Egypt

Mt. Halak   Tamar

EDOM

Kadesh-barnea

Bozrah

Josh. 13: 1-6; Judg. 3: 1-3

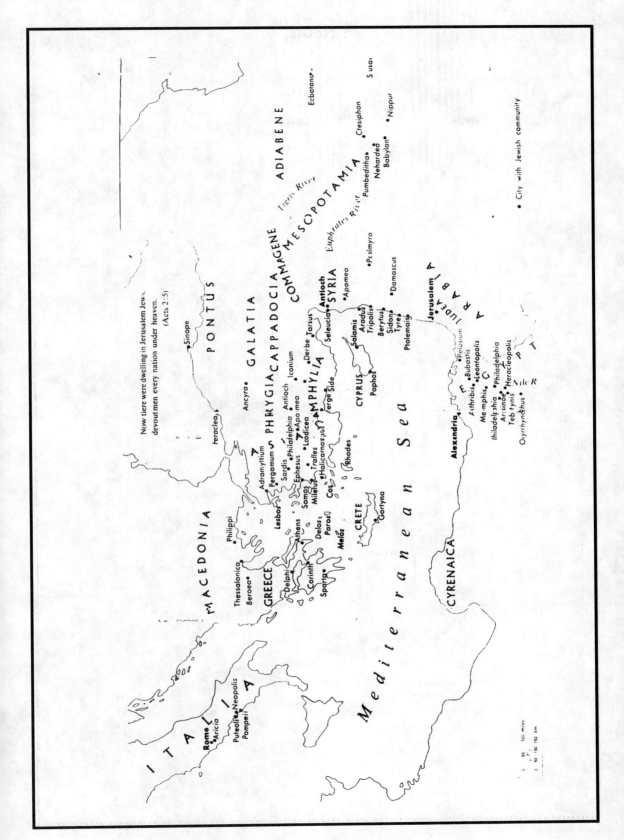

Now there were dwelling in Jerusalem Jews, devout men every nation under heaven.

(Acts 2:5)

• City with Jewish community

ITALIA
Rome •
Aricia •
Puteoli •
Neapolis •
Pompeii •

MACEDONIA
Philippi •
Thessalonica •
Beroea •

GREECE
Delphi •
Athens •
Corinth •
Sparta •

Delos •
Paros •
Melos •

CRETE
Gortyna •

PONTUS
Heraclea •
Sinope •

GALATIA
Ancyra •

PHRYGIA
Adramyttium •
Pergamum •
Sardis •
Philadelphia •
Ephesus •
Laodicea •
Samos •
Miletus •
Tralles •
Cos •
Halicarnassus •
Rhodes •

CAPPADOCIA
Antioch •
Apamea •
Iconium •
Derbe •
Tarsus •

COMMAGENE

PAMPHYLIA
Perge •
Side •

ADIABENE

MESOPOTAMIA
Tigris River
Euphrates River
Ecbatana •
Susa
Ctesiphon •
Pumbeditha •
Neharded •
Babylon •
Nippur •

SYRIA
Antioch •
Apamea •
Seleucia •
Palmyra •
Damascus •
Salamis •
Aradus •
Tripolis •
Berytus •
Sidon •
Tyre •
Ptolemais •

CYPRUS
Paphos •

ARABIA

JUDEA
Jerusalem •

EGYPT
Pelusium •
Alexandria •
Athribis •
Bubastis •
Leontopolis •
Memphis •
Philadelphia •
Arsinoe •
Heracleopolis •
Tebtynis •
Nile R.
Oxyrhynchus •

CYRENAICA

Mediterranean Sea

0   50   100 miles
0   50 100 150 km

Notes